Sexual Power

Sexual Power

Feminism and the Family in America

Carolyn Johnston

The University of Alabama Press
Tuscaloosa and London

Copyright © 1992
The University of Alabama Press
Tuscaloosa, Alabama 35487–0380
All rights reserved
Manufactured in the United States of America

∞

The paper on which this book is printed meets the minimum requirements
of American National Standard for Information Science-Permanence of
Paper for Printed Library Materials, ANSI Z39.48-1984.

Library of Congress Cataloging-in-Publication Data

Johnston, Carolyn, 1948–
Sexual power : feminism and the family in America / Carolyn Johnston.
p.cm.

Includes bibliograpical references and index.
ISBN 0-8173-0583-1 (alk. paper)
1. Feminism—United States—History.   2. Family—
United States—History.   I. Title.
HQ1410.J6   1992
305.42'0973—dc20   92-3421

British Library Cataloguing-in-Publication Data available

CONTENTS

Preface / vii

Acknowledgments / xv

1. The Colonial Window:
Good Wives and Witches (1607–1776) / 1

2. Republican Motherhood and the Angel in the House / 11

3. Feminism for the Sake of the Family and Community
(1800–1900) / 26

4. Power in the Bedroom and the Nursery
(1800–1900) / 50

5. The Sex Radicals:
Feminists against the Traditional Family / 73

6. The Suffrage Movement: Municipal Housekeeping
or Full Equality? (1848–1919) / 92

7. Exquisite Surrender? The New Feminists of the 1920s / 116

8. The Empowerment of Wives and Mothers:
Surviving the Great Depression / 144

9. The Paradox of Women's Power during World War II / 170

10. The Power of Mom: Domesticity, Motherhood,
and Sexuality in the 1950s / 201

11. Feminist Voices of the 1950s / 227

12. Miss America Good-bye:
The Modern Feminist Movement / 242

Conclusion and Prospect / 280

Appendix 1. A Portrait of Marriage in the 1930s / 299

Appendix 2. Black Women Oral History Project / 303

Appendix 3. The Feminist Movement in the 1970s:
A Chronology / 307

Notes / 311

Bibliographic Essay / 359

Bibliography / 369

Index / 393

PREFACE

One word more I should like to add, as I may not again speak or write on this subject. I should like to say to the men and women of the generations which will come after—"You will look back at us with astonishment! You will wonder at passionate struggles that accomplished so little: at the, to you, obvious paths to attain our ends which we did not take; at the intolerable evils before which it will seem to you we sat down passive; at the great truths staring us in the face, which we failed to see; at the truths we grasped at, but could never quite get our fingers round. You will marvel at the labour that ended in so little; but, what you will never know is how it was thinking of you and for you, that we struggled as we did and accomplished the little which we have done; that it was in the thought of your larger realisation and fuller life that we found consolation for the futilities of our own."

Olive Schreiner, 1911

Portholes of ships arriving in the New World from Europe, windows of rude huts first built by the colonists, lead windows brought from England for the homes of the prosperous, windows of southern plantation houses, windows of the slave quarters, oilcloth windows of sod houses on the frontier, urban slum windows, apartment windows, and windows of suburban houses—all of these are the actual windows through which women have looked out at the world. Windows are important in women's lives: protective windows in the maternity ward where the newborns can be seen, familiar kitchen windows where women have stood for hundreds of years washing dishes and looking out at the world, glittering department store windows promising material fulfillment, road-soiled car windows through which they have watched their husbands catching planes and trains, stained-glass windows of churches, small-paned school windows, grimy factory windows, and recently, windows of law schools, medical schools, and board rooms.

A window's shape, size, and quality of glass determine what one sees when looking out, and how one may be seen from the outside. Understanding American women's growing gender consciousness and its relationship to domestic and public power requires looking through the window of their political, legal, and economic status, as well as the changing cultural expectations of womanhood. These conditions have influenced women's attempts to achieve equality and autonomy and the ways in which they have seen the world and themselves.

My own experiences as a daughter, a student, a wife, an activist, a survivor of the sexual revolution, and a professor of women's history led me to explore the questions of this book: How have women's empowering experiences in the family shaped feminist consciousness and action? How have feminists confronted family issues? How have women exercised sexual power? How was it contained within the limits of patriarchal society at some times, while at other times it fueled the fires of feminist rebellion? How have race and class affected domestic politics and feminism?

My thesis is that historically, American women's contradictory experiences of empowerment and entrapment as wives and mothers led to the emergence of feminist consciousness and shaped feminist theory and demands. I demonstrate that many women's rights advocates, suffragists, and feminists from the 1840s through the 1980s had family issues—marriage, divorce, child care, housework, child custody—at the heart of their analysis of women's oppression, and they believed that reshaping the family to women's benefit would also benefit other family members and the larger society. Thus, feminists confronted family issues as a first priority in both the nineteenth and the twentieth centuries. This focus on family issues stemmed in part from feminists' growing awareness of their increased domestic power and also of its limitations because of their public powerlessness. Feminist profamily arguments differed from those of their opponents in their attempts to embrace the needs of women in a wide range of family types with different income levels and backgrounds.

My broad definition of feminism refers to an organized movement to eliminate social, economic, and political discrimination against women; feminist consciousness is an awareness that women as a group have been discriminated against on the basis of their sex, a willingness to fight male supremacy, and a belief in the possibility of a society in which men and women are equal. For the purposes of this book, I concentrate mainly on self-defined proponents of women's rights and women's emancipation. I contend that these women, who have been most often accused of being antifamily, are precisely the ones who have been profamily.

Throughout the book I am using the term "sexual power" to describe women's covert power within the family, which derives from their roles as wives, mothers, and homemakers. I am not arguing that covert, domestic power inevitably led all women, or even those women with the most domestic power, to become feminists. Rather I am exploring how feminists' domestic experiences and their awareness of the limits of domestic power led them to focus on family issues. Moreover, the growth of women's domestic power is not strictly linear, a story of progress from the colonial period to the present. It is contingent on numerous economic, social, and political factors and increases differentially in different periods for women depending on race and class.

Power in American society is generally associated with having money, status, and the ability to make decisions which affect or control the lives of many people. Until very recently, women's access to this kind of power has come through their fathers and husbands. Women have had less access to lucrative employment, prestige, and physical and economic security than men have. Furthermore, class and race have been major determinants of women's ability to exert power inside and outside families.

Excluded from most forms of public power until recently, women have primarily operated in the "love economy" of motherhood, housework, and voluntarism; although millions of women have been employed, they have still exercised power only covertly in their homes through emotional and sexual influence. Such covert sexual power relies on persuasion, manipulation, giving and withholding sex; it may be exerted in the nurturing of children and in making men dependent on women for daily needs of all kinds. Sexual power may be used to acquire material possessions, to influence family decisions, and generally to get one's way. Covert sexual power works only when it is unseen and undetected, like any subversiveness. When feminists of the 1960s and 1970s demanded public power, they also wanted overt power at home and were no longer content with the old covert tactics. This change caused havoc within relationships, since domestic politics functioned on men's belief that they were in control even when they were not. Many women began to realize the problematic nature of their sexual power in the face of violence, racism, economic dependence, and exploitation.

Though there are important racial and class differences within the pattern of women's traditional socialization in America, it has always emphasized the power of love, rather than a love of power. Women's self-worth was supposed to stem from being able to take care of others. Relationships were more important in this value system than personal autonomy or success. However, the traditional female values of nurturance, self-sacrifice, love of children, and emotional openness, although eulogized by men, have been considered less important for success than the male values of assertiveness, ambition, individualism, and self-reliance. Thus, women have faced a dilemma of trying to gain power in the public sphere while being defined primarily in terms of their relationships within the home.

When did women perceive that they faced this dilemma? If they were so oppressed, why did they not rebel en masse before the nineteenth century? How could women be so restricted legally, politically, sexually, and economically in the United States but take so long to come to a feminist consciousness? For many years, if women chafed within the confines of their separate sphere, they assumed that it was their fault, not the fault of a system of discrimination and disenfranchisement. From the crib, they learned appropriate female behaviors; from the pulpit they learned of Eve's sin and the divinely ordained roles of men and women. They read in popular literature that "liberation" was being rescued by a man—"falling in love." To challenge their fate meant challenging God, the church, the state, and the power of romantic love.

Faced with powerful contradictions between romantic ideals of the family and distressing realities, nineteenth-century feminists constructed profamily agendas, while at the same time they envisioned new forms of "family." The most important goal of feminism in the United States in both the nineteenth and twentieth centuries has been achieving a resolution of women's dilemma, which ultimately is a human dilemma—for both women and men: how does one marry or form other meaningful relationships, choose to have children, and still develop one's intellectual and creative abilities?

Because both aspects of this dilemma are important to women as well as to men, the feminist movements of the nineteenth and twentieth centuries generally succeeded when their aims were perceived as profamily and failed when they seemed to threaten the gender-structured family. The majority of feminists in both periods chose to focus on the alleviation of particular restraints on women in the short run, rather than sustaining a vision of full equality. However, by accepting and emphasizing sexual differences over sameness, nineteenth-century feminists inadvertently helped perpetuate their own subordination through protective labor legislation for women, sex-stereotyped jobs, and an emphasis on motherhood and domesticity as women's domain.

A renewed emphasis on sexual differences is apparent in the current retreat from sexual politics and egalitarianism into an emphasis on "women's ways of knowing," models of women's moral development which differ from men's, and a feminist theoretical preoccupation with emphasizing differences among women. While at some levels this strategy may be empowering for women by glorifying traditional female characteristics and contributing to a "female world of love and ritual," ultimately this position could be used to legitimize inequality in the law, the home, the corporation, and in other sectors of the work force.

In order to understand the recurring appeal of an ideology which emphasizes sexual differences and women's moral superiority, one must understand the development of women's covert sexual power within the home at a time when political and economic equality were and are denied. Thus, then and now, the domestic sphere and traditional female values seem a natural arena in which women can assert some measure of control over their lives and achieve self-esteem and dignity.

Much of the literature on feminism has focused on women's oppression and victimization, not on the power which women have historically exerted. My interpretation of American feminism differs from previous works because I argue that the gradual growth of feminist consciousness lies not simply in oppression or feelings of victimization but paradoxically in a growing sense of empowerment as wives and mothers. I trace how reproduction, sexuality, domesticity, and motherhood have been socially constructed. A purpose of this book is to examine how feminists and antifeminists have fought on the terrain of "family" issues and defined the meaning of "profamily."

This book is intended for general readers, students, and scholars. I am indebted to the work of many excellent scholars on whose work I am building. Since the early 1970s scholars have argued and refined a wide range of new interpretations of American women's lives. This book is synthetic in its focus on how domestic politics and feminism have been treated in the new scholarship about women of recent years. Despite the richness of the literature in the field, there has been a deficiency in interpretation giving enough credit to women's family and sexual experiences for the emergence of feminism and the construction of profamily agendas. Thus, my approach offers an opportunity to view the history of feminism and the family from a fresh perspective by drawing on existing scholarship as well as popular culture and numerous primary collections. Gender, race, class, and ethnicity affect the ways in which people perceive what constitutes a profamily stance. This book does not attempt to provide a comprehensive social history of American women of all races and classes, or simply a survey of American feminism. Much more needs to be known about the differing ways in which white middle-class women, African-American women, and working-class women developed a feminist consciousness, and how this was related to their domestic power. Therefore, I hope this study will inspire more exploration of the precise connections between women's domestic experiences and their development of feminist consciousness. What is clear is that family issues have been at the heart of the feminist movement's concerns since its emergence early in the nineteenth century.

Since much scholarly attention has focused on women's lives before the twentieth century, I deal primarily with the late nineteenth and twentieth centuries. However, in order to provide a context for the emergence of the women's rights movement, I present a brief overview of women's situation in America in the earlier periods, beginning in the first chapter with the paradoxical lives of colonial women. While the religious and social ideology of that era depicted women as clearly subordinate to men, they were empowered as wives and mothers and were indispensable to the colonial economy. Chapter 2 deals with the contradictory legacy of the American Revolution and the industrial revolution for women's empowerment and feminist consciousness. The third chapter focuses on the relationship of the domestic lives of the early advocates of women's rights to their feminist consciousness and on the centrality of family issues to their understanding of women's oppression. In chapter 4 I discuss the battle which raged in the nineteenth century over who would control female sexuality and how feminists supported family-related changes.

Chapter 5 concerns the most radical advocates for women's rights in the nineteenth and early twentieth centuries, including Frances Wright, Victoria Woodhull, Emma Goldman, and others who deplored the limits of women's sexual power within the domestic and public spheres, challenged the institution of marriage, and argued for women's free expression of sexuality and reproductive control. These radicals alienated many women from the women's rights movement, but they were part of an underground tradition advocating sexual freedom which eventually served as the foundation of the sexual liberation movement in the 1960s and 1970s.

Chapter 6 describes the material transformations which inspired feminist consciousness in the late nineteenth century and how the campaign for women's suffrage aimed to extend mother-love to the entire society. Chapter

7 explores feminists' attempts to achieve covert and overt power by combining marriage, motherhood, and careers in the 1920s. Chapters 8 and 9 deal with the dramatic consolidation of women's domestic power as a result of the Great Depression and World War II, as well as its limitations. Continuing in chronological fashion, chapter 10 explores the development of an exaggerated emphasis on domesticity in the 1950s and how this shaped the modern feminist movement. Chapter 11 explores the lives of some ambivalent feminists of the 1950s who protested the limits of domestic power.

Chapter 12 analyzes the radical and reformist wings of the contemporary feminist movement and discusses the ways in which women's empowering and oppressive experiences as wives and mothers have shaped the movement's agenda, theory, and accomplishments. In the Conclusion and Prospect I discuss the current feminist movement and new paradigms for the 1990s. While American women have faced discrimination and have been victimized, they have never been rendered powerless. This book is about the gradual emergence of women's power and feminist consciousness in the United States and the centrality of family issues to the ongoing feminist struggle.

ACKNOWLEDGMENTS

In the more than ten years which I have spent in writing this book, I have been constantly reminded that every book is a collaboration with other scholars, librarians, colleagues, students, friends, and institutions. While writing and research can be lonely at times, I have been very fortunate to be part of a beloved community.

I am grateful to my friends who took time from their own busy lives and scholarship to read drafts of this book, including Nancy Wood, Jewel Spears Brooker, Judith Green, Glenna Matthews, Nancy Hewitt, Steven Mintz, Wendy Kaminer, Hollis Lynch, Dudley DeGroot, and Bill Dickman. I thank them for their rigorous intellectual critiques and their cherished friendship. I am also greatly indebted to the responses of anonymous readers whose critiques strengthened the work enormously. Naturally any errors are my own responsibility.

Lloyd Chapin, the vice president for academic affairs of Eckerd College, offered his generous financial support in faculty development grants and his unflagging enthusiasm for the book. I am indebted to Eckerd College for two sabbaticals which were essential in completing this work. An early definition of sabbatical as a time of rest when the "land lies fallow and debts remain unpaid" pretty accurately describes the present institution. Any scholar on sabbatical leave knows the delirium of joy, waking up to the knowledge that one has a long stretch of time to think and write and that no committee meetings beckon. I also wish to thank Peter Armacost, president of Eckerd College, for his support.

Most scholars of women's history have had the extraordinary pleasure of working in the Schlesinger Library at Radcliffe College. I express my deepest appreciation to Barbara Haber, the curator of printed material at the Schlesinger

Library. She has read many drafts of this book and has offered me her insights, encouragement, expertise, and friendship for over a decade. I also want to thank Eva Moseley, the curator of manuscripts for the Schlesinger Library, who helped me navigate through the marvelous manuscript collections and saved me years of searching. I am very grateful to Patricia King, the director, and all her staff for their support. I never enter the Schlesinger Library without being filled with wonder and excitement. I also want to thank the librarians and staff of the Widener Library, the University of California Library at Berkeley, the Library of Congress, Smith College, and Eckerd College. David Henderson and Carol Parker of the Eckerd College Library cheerfully helped me secure literally hundreds of books on interlibrary loan without so much as a grumble.

My love of history began early. My seventh-grade teacher, Mrs. Gray, told me that I would be a historian. She was right. In high school, Miss Eugenia Rodgers taught me to love American history. On the first day of class, she said, "Today you begin a great adventure." That adventure extends to the present day. Warnie Finnell, Lillie Frank Fitzgerald, and Inez Clemmer taught me the meaning of inspired teaching. Wayne Flynt, my mentor in college, persuaded me to devote my life to history and the struggle for social justice because of his example. I want to also thank David Vess from Samford University, who taught me the joys and challenges of European history. Leon Litwack, Natalie Davis, Samuel Haber, Lawrence Levine, Henry May, Henry Nash Smith, and Martin Jay challenged me to achieve excellence. I am still trying. Their scholarship continues to inspire and amaze me.

I have benefited greatly from my students over the last sixteen years at the University of California at Berkeley, Colorado College, and Eckerd College. I want to thank Bruce Hawkins, Craig Weintraub, Tom Perdue, Gary Wolfe, Susan Chaffee, and Beth Zeeman. My students at Eckerd College have enlivened my scholarship and enriched my life. Among them are Susan Hyde, Chris McNary Payne, Kandee Altis, Jesus Subero, Xavier Landon, Masoud Laghai, John McNeilly, Mary Ann Marshall, Melissa Mackinnon, Jeff Thomas, Silvina Manrique, Judith Atkinson, Jason Hill, Mary Zimnick, Ginna Husting, Ginny Hawkins, Meredith Jordan, Nicholle DeMouy, Santiago Nunez, Eric Yaskot, Jenny Griffith, and Mark Tluszcz.

Beth Zeeman and Paul Stern generously housed me an entire summer in Somerville while I worked on the book. Hollis Lynch allowed me to write in a tropical paradise at his estate house in Tobago several summers. Bonnie Miller offered her artist's loft near South Station, Boston, while she was in

France, where I spent my last sabbatical. When I was at a loss to find a place in Boston, Chael Solari miraculously provided me with a home during the last stages of this book. For his generosity, wit, friendship, and encouragement, I offer my deepest thanks.

I also offer my heartfelt thanks to other friends for their support and the example of their own work: Patricia Pérez-Arce, Theresa Turner, Margaret Rigg, Mark Vickers, Jimmy Nolan, Mihai Spariosu, Mara Soudakoff, Kerry Buckley, Travis Absher, Richard Lee, Claud Sutcliffe, Joe Bearson, Greg Padgett, Molly and Bill Sterling, Valerie Kent, Shirley Davis, Richard Strilka, Bill Murrah, Jimmy Harper, Enrique Mallea, David Woods, Margaret Adam, Roger Donald, Ralph Brooker, and Brinda Mehta. I especially thank Mark Fishman, who helped decipher the mysteries of laser printing and inspired me by his own work.

A number of institutions and foundations have generously offered financial assistance along the way. I especially thank the Danforth Foundation and Woodrow Wilson Fellowship Program for supporting me in graduate school. I also thank the Ford Foundation Apprentice Scholars program for funding my research and that of my students Mark Tluszcz and Jenny Griffith. I express my appreciation to the Du Bois Institute at Harvard University, where I was a fellow in 1983–84 and 1989–90. Nathan Huggins and Randall Burkett, along with the fellows of the institute, especially Maryemma Graham and Catherine Clinton, were enormously supportive.

I am indebted to all those gifted scholars and activists whose work I acknowledge in this book. Without their diligent, insightful work, my own would be impossible. I am honored to be in the dialogue.

I am deeply appreciative to Malcolm MacDonald, the director of the University of Alabama Press, for his belief in this book, and to Craig Noll for his superb copyediting.

Finally, I offer my thanks to my parents, Alta and Eugene Johnston, for their loving support and infinite reservoir of faith in me. I also thank my sister, Nancy, who taught me the real meaning of "sisterhood." To my nieces, Jennifer and Patricia Smith, I dedicate this book. They are members of the vanguard of the next wave of feminism, and they are formidable.

1

THE COLONIAL WINDOW
Good Wives and Witches (1607–1776)

It may be said of a virtuous woman, that she is a religious woman; that {she} has bound herself to that God, whom she had by the sin and the fall of her first mother {Eve} departed from; she has a love which does not cast out the fear that is no fault, but confirm and settle her in that Fear of God; that all kind of Piety and Charity is prevailing in her disposition; that sobriety and Righteousness and Godliness are visible in her whole Behaviour; and, that she does Justice, loves Mercy, and walks Humbly with her God.

Cotton Mather, 1698

I am obnoxious to each carping tongue
Who says my hand a needle better fits,
A Poets pen all scorn I should thus wrong
For such despite they cast on Female wits:
If what I do prove well, it won't advance,
They'l say it's stoln, or else it was by chance.

Anne Bradstreet, 1643–69

Crowded into the hold of the *Mayflower*, the women aboard must have dreamed of starting over. From what were they fleeing? What kind of lives would they face in the New World? The first two hundred years of American women's lives were no golden age if one considers the harsh physical conditions, the high incidence of indentured servitude, slavery, their legal and political disenfranchisement, and the hazards of childbirth.

The lives of colonial white women present us with a paradox. On one hand, social and religious ideology depicted women as subordinate to men, yet the boundaries of women's and men's social and economic activities overlapped significantly. Although economic activity was structured around family enterprises and women's activities were clearly complementary and indispensable, women themselves were politically and legally invisible. On the other hand, they were active in politics—in demonstrations, informal lobbying, and petitioning. Women were viewed in Christian theology as the source of original sin, but in religious life, colonial women were actively engaged in church activities and were a focus of ministerial attention. They too might be "visible saints." Thus, colonial women were empowered within their roles as wives and mothers but were considered subordinate to men in all spheres of life.

The home was the center of production for men and women. Women worked in the house and sometimes in the field; they prepared food, butchered animals, tended gardens, made cloth and garments for family members, as well as candles, soap, and butter. Widows often took over their husbands' taverns, shops, or businesses. Some women became silversmiths, gunsmiths, upholsterers, jail keepers, lawyers, morticians, journalists, printers, nurses, and teachers. Sometimes women combined motherhood, marriage, and running mills, plantations, and shipyards.

Variation was a defining characteristic of colonial women's lives. They had diverse experiences depending on their race, class, geographic location, the local law, religion, and education. African-American women who were slaves in the South, white indentured female servants, and Native American women lived very different lives from those of white, prosperous women. However, they shared some common experiences. While living under radically different conditions, they married, had children, and performed domestic tasks.

Before 1660, women who lived in the Chesapeake colonies of Maryland and Virginia faced a very different environment from those in New England. Patriarchal ideals and practices were more implemented in New England for two reasons: the power of the Puritan church, and the development of more stable families. Whereas the Puritan church and the state were closely intertwined in New England, no comparable Anglican parish structure developed in the Chesapeake in the seventeenth century. Furthermore, during the first three-quarters of the seventeenth century, men outnumbered women in the Chesapeake, and the prevalence of diseases caused a high mortality rate for adults as well as children. More women in the Chesapeake married at younger ages, and they experienced widowhood more often. This may be why Maryland granted widows more legal independence than any other colony during the period.[1]

Most of the women who first migrated to the Chesapeake came as indentured servants who had very limited power, except to sell their labor. For passage to America and their maintenance and support during their service, they contracted to work for a certain number of years, often four or five. About one-third of colonial households had one indentured servant, and one-third of indentured servants were female. Perhaps as high as one-half of female colonists arrived in this status. Indentured servants were vulnerable to sexual abuse by their employers; one in five female servants wound up in court, pregnant before they finished their term of servitude. If the father did not buy out her term, she received two additional years for breach of contract, a fine, and a whipping. They were not permitted to marry while indentured, but once their contracts were satisfied, the vast majority of the women eventually married.[2]

Much more scholarly attention has focused on New England than on the Chesapeake, and therefore it is not possible to answer many of our questions about which area provided a better climate for women. Lois Green Carr and Lorena Walsh argue that if the ability to select marital partners and relative economic independence are the criteria, then Chesapeake women were better off than New England women. But given the higher incidence of teenage marriage, as well as the prevalence of disease and of illegitimacy, it is difficult to argue that the status of white Chesapeake women was higher than that of their New England counterparts. According to Mary Beth Norton, New England women seem to have enjoyed a preferable life-style if the criteria are better health, marital stability, a smaller age differential between husband and wife, and possibilities for religious expression. Drawing on the evidence of architectural remains, men's wills, and estate inventories, it seems that New England houses were better constructed and more spacious and contained more amenities like table linen; their domestic work spaces were more efficiently organized than those of southern counterparts.

Demographic disparities among the colonies began to disappear by the late 1700s. The founding of Pennsylvania, the Carolinas, and New York after 1660 introduced greater ethnic and religious diversity into the colonies. The sex ratio became more balanced, and mortality was reduced. With the introduction of slavery after 1660 and the gradual elimination of indentured servitude, Chesapeake families came to resemble families of New England more closely.[3]

African-American women suffered the worst oppression of all colonial women. They were kidnapped from their homes in what are now Nigeria and Angola; naked and crowded together in the dark hold of the slave ships, one-fifth of them died during the middle passage. Twice as many males as females were brought to the colonies. Some of the women were destined for the West Indies, others for the southern colonies. Once in Maryland and Virginia, they lived in slave quarters and worked in the fields or plantation houses. Tobacco and rice were the primary crops for the slave states in the seventeenth century. On plantations women performed the same field work as men and also became nurses, laundresses, and domestic workers. They were vulnerable to rape by their masters and their masters' sons. Frequently they had to face having their children sold away from them, thus making stable families very difficult. While marriage among slaves was considered illegal, except in New England, they did marry, and as recent scholarship has shown, they maintained stronger familial ties than formerly thought. Their status as property was the most defining aspect of their lives, shaping domesticity, marriage, and motherhood.[4]

By the end of the seventeenth century, there were 5,000 slaves in the colonies, with few of them in New England. Slave codes were drawn up in all the colonies by the 1660s. Extensive sexual freedom for slaves seems to have been permitted and accepted before marriage, and no stigma was attached to premarital pregnancy. Slave women had short life expectancies and low childbearing rates because of the unhealthy environment in the Chesapeake. As slavery grew phenomenally in the eighteenth century, sex ratios became more balanced, and women were able to find marital partners more easily and establish somewhat more stable families. Plantation records traced the lineage of slaves through their mothers.[5]

Colonial women in New England, the Chesapeake, Pennsylvania, New York, and the Carolinas experienced marriage and motherhood in radically different ways, depending on whether they were free, slave, or indentured. But their differences should not obscure the fact that they shared political and legal invisibility. Single "free" women were legally under the protection and control of their fathers, and married women surrendered their person and property to their husbands. A married woman was civilly nonexistent. As William Blackstone wrote in his widely used *Commentaries*, "By marriage, the husband and wife are one person in law; that is, the very being or legal existence of the woman is suspended during the marriage, or at least is incorporated and consolidated into that of the husband."[6] Nevertheless, colonial authorities were more lenient than English officials regarding free white women's property rights. For example, free colonial women were entitled to their personal clothing when they married, and a dowry was not required. Married women sometimes conducted businesses as agents of their husbands, or they might gain special dispensations by courts or legislatures to act as femes sole. Moreover, in some cases fathers arranged prenuptial property agreements in order to protect their daughters' inheritance. They also set up trusts and jointures for their daughters. If given a jointure, the woman received property at the time of her marriage, and she could use it upon the death of her husband.[7]

Two exceptional cases dramatized lapses in these general practices regarding free women's limited economic autonomy. Margaret and Mary Brent were granted manorial rights over thousands of acres in Maryland. Similarly, the widow Margaret Hardenbrook Philipse, who came over from Holland, converted her land resources in New Amsterdam into a merchant fortune and organized the first regular passages by ship across the Atlantic.[8] Most colonial women, however, derived their economic status exclusively from their fathers and husbands.

As in the economic sphere, free colonial women were expected to be subordinate within the domestic sphere, but also partners. A few of John Singleton Copley's paired portraits reflect the Puritan ideal of marriage— the husband and wife as sturdy mates and partners on the road to salvation. The man in one of these solemn couples wears a white wig and holds a ledger; his wife wears a ruffled cap and holds a Bible. As reflected in the legal code, a colonial wife owed her husband "reverent subjection." She typically bore seven or eight children, and the marriage was usually broken by one spouse's death before all the children were out of the home. Pregnancy meant walking through the "shadow of death." In Plymouth, for example, childbirth was likely to kill the mother in one out of thirty cases. One-fifth of the maternal deaths were caused by childbirth. Infant mortality was also extremely high. In seventeenth-century New England, one in ten babies died in healthy areas, and one in three in less healthy areas. Nonetheless, infant mortality in most places in the colonies was lower than in Europe.[9]

Childbirth in the colonial era presents us with a paradox. While childbirth was dangerous and reinforced cultural notions of female weakness, it also became an arena of female ritual and power. A woman had her child in the company of other women. Often she might give birth held in another woman's lap, or leaning against another as she squatted in the low "midwife's stool." Her baby's first milk would be from a lactating friend. A woman experiencing a very difficult delivery might have a drink of another mother's milk also, since this was considered a "sure remedy." Birth was surrounded by a sucession of female rituals. In addition to arousing the sympathy of husbands, who were excluded from the delivery room, childbirth's suffering might bind the mothers' children to them profoundly.

Ann Lake Cotton's experience was not unusual. She bore nine children in the twenty years between 1687 and 1707. She lost her first baby two months before the birth of her second. The next five survived infancy, but she lost three babies at or shortly after delivery. Dorothy Chadwick suffered an even worse fate. Ashley Bowen, a seaman from Marblehead, had dreamed about a woman whom he saw sitting on his sea chest. She had five moles on her right cheek and other distinguishing marks. Some weeks later he found the very woman he had dreamed about in a shoemaker's shop in Andover. He could hardly contain his joy upon finding the woman of his dreams, moles and all. She was already being courted, so he had to persist for another year in order to convince her to marry him. For him the story of troubles to be overcome ends there, but for Dorothy it was just the beginning. She had six children in the next twelve years, miscarried a seventh, grew ill, and died.[10]

Pregnancy often might carry with it a death sentence. Despite the fear of pregnancy, however, a colonial wife was expected to enjoy sex within marriage. The image of the Puritans as uptight prudes, which stems from the life-style revolution of the 1920s, simply was not true. They earned such a reputation through their severe punishments for sex outside of marriage. Premarital sexual activity was relatively rare; fewer than 10 percent of first children were born only eight and a half months after marriage. By the middle of the eighteenth century, the figure had increased to 40 percent.

Because of the power of Calvinist theology in New England, women were viewed as daughters of Eve, responsible for original sin, and therefore were considered especially lustful. In the colonies fornication brought equal penalties to men and women—public whipping or the pillory. Adultery was defined as fornication with a married woman and was punishable by death. This punishment was carried out a half dozen times within the colonies. If married men had affairs with single women, their offense was considered fornication. Thus, the double sexual standard prevailed.[11]

The Puritan husband was expected to be faithful and loving to his wife, to be a good provider, and to share equally in the childrearing. Both parents were expected to train their children in godliness. Parents attempted to instill in their children obedience to parental, church, and political authority, rather than emphasizing independent decision making. The father's word was law for the children as well as for the wife. The Calvinists viewed children as small adults and believed in infant depravity because of Eve's original sin. They referred to a baby as "it." Since the primary task of the Puritan parents was to break the child's will, the father played a prominent role in disciplining children. In contrast, Quakers believed in a more nurturant approach to childrearing.

A colonial woman's choice of a husband was the most important decision in her life, which her parents usually controlled. If her husband was a drunkard or abusive physically or psychologically, her life would be a living hell, since divorce was extremely difficult. Theoretically women could sue for divorce on the grounds of the husband's impotence, cruelty, abandonment, adultery, bigamy, or failure to provide. Seventy-six women petitioned for divorce or separation in New England in the seventeenth century. Divorce was easier to obtain in the Massachusetts Bay Colony than in England, but since only forty divorces were granted from 1639 to 1692, it is clear that the Puritan courts were very reluctant to separate wives and husbands. During this period, four times as many women as men brought divorce actions. Men were more free to abandon wives and children and begin new lives, without legal intervention.

At the same time, Massachusetts Bay and Plymouth passed the first laws against spousal abuse in the Western world. Church courts and civil courts enforced a criminal code which punished family violence in the New England colonies. Accusations of rape, incest, and family violence were relatively rare, but accusations of fornication were common. Between 1630 and 1699, at least 128 men were tried for spouse abuse. Punishments ranged from a fine to lashing, or public admonition. In contrast, 278 women were brought to court for heaping abuse on husbands. Their punishment, if found guilty, was fines or whipping also.[12]

Although spousal homicide and battering did occur, colonial men and women left more records of marital affection than of domestic brutality, conflict, and desertion. If a woman's husband resembled the husband of Anne Bradstreet, the famous American poet, she would be fortunate to have a marriage of love and mutuality. Bradstreet wrote of her husband, Simon:

> If ever two were one, then surely we.
> If ever man were lov'd by wife, then thee;

If ever wife was happy in a man,
Compare with me ye women if you can.[13]

No matter how satisfying the colonial woman's marriage, she was considered under her husband's authority. In their religious lives, however, they both were equally able to be "visible saints," recipients of salvation and members of the elect. While no one could ever be certain of salvation, various signs might reveal that one was saved. For example, if people were especially pious, performed good works, and were prosperous, God presumably had already smiled on them. In Pennsylvania in the seventeenth century women assumed an extremely important role in mediating family life, settling disputes, and determining discipline. While Puritan women had no similar formal role, around 1660 the number of female converts surpassed the number of male converts, and women gained more influence within churches where they formed a majority of members.[14]

While colonial married women were deprived of legal and political rights, their activities were valued because the social, religious, and economic spheres of men and women overlapped markedly. Since spinsterhood and bachelorhood were severely discouraged, women essentially had to marry. Unmarried adults were usually placed with a family and not allowed to live alone. Marriage and motherhood were women's destiny, and their feelings of entrapment and empowerment depended on their own expectations and personalities, as well as their husbands' characters.

If women stepped out of their prescribed roles, they were severely punished. Anne Hutchinson, who began to hold heretical religious views, held religious meetings with other women in Boston. She was so threatening to the Puritan hierarchy that she was banished to what later became Rhode Island. Similarly, Mary Dyer, a Quaker who believed that the inner light of godly wisdom resided in both women and men, was banished three times from the Massachusetts Bay Colony. Three times she returned, and finally, in order to silence her, the Puritan fathers hanged her. Thus, it is not surprising that women's proper sphere remained largely unchallenged except by religious heretics, Quakers, women who transgressed the morality of the community, and "witches."

The Salem witchcraft trials of 1692 revealed that women who transgressed sexual taboos or were economically threatening might be accused and sometimes executed. Witches were believed to fornicate with the devil, fly about on broomsticks at night, and even have the power to make the "male member" disappear. A total of 115 local people were accused of witchcraft, three-fourths of whom were women. Among those accused of being witches were a West Indian slave, Tituba, who was thought to practice black magic, Ann Hibbens of Boston, Anne Cole of Hartford, and Elizabeth Knight of Groton, Massachusetts. Ann Hibbens had been excommunicated for her successful and threatening economic dealings in Boston. Sarah Good, Sarah Osbourne, and Bridget Bishop had violated the community's sexual taboos by fornication or related sins. They all had experienced disputes with their neighbors over economic matters. Rebecca Nurse, who also was accused, was an honorable, aged wife and mother. However, she and her husband Francis were newly rich and were encroaching on the economic and social territory of the powerful Putnam family. Three of the most active accusers were Putnam girls. Clearly, unruly women and women who threatened the elites of the society feared being accused of witchcraft. Twenty convicted "witches" were put to death in a single year.[15]

John Demos has perceptively noted that witchcraft beliefs defined the boundaries of acceptable action and revealed ideals of behavior by identifying the opposite. He also claims that witchcraft accusations revealed tensions revolving around corporate control as opposed to individualism. The witch craze occurred in the 1690s at the time prosecutions for infanticide peaked and fornication prosecutions reached a new high. Female sexuality and maternal functions seemed preoccupations in these trials. Carol Karlsen observes that the witch trials reveal fears regarding female sexuality along with fears of social disorder. Female insubordination to men was alarming because it could lead to doubt about men's proper heirs.[16]

The Salem witch trials may also be seen in the context of the Puritans' attempts to encourage conformity by exercising a kind of religious terrorism amid challenges by other religious groups to their hegemony. The trials followed the Glorious Revolution in England, which saw the triumph of the Protestants over the Catholic King James II and his governor of New England, the Catholic Sir Edmund Andros. The Act of Toleration, rather than making Protestant control in the colonies stronger, actually made it less certain. The fact that women were the scapegoats revealed the superficial veneer of male beneficence and protection within the Puritan culture.

For a brief period the young women who accused the others of being witches held enormous power within the community. This kind of public power was indeed rare for women. Their lack of public influence stemmed in part from their lack of education. Since colonial women did not have access to education and most were illiterate, few records exist of their daily lives. Some letters, diaries, and autobiographies survived, but they do not reveal any widespread discontent with their status or revolt against their destiny of marriage and motherhood. In the seventeenth century, women's sexual power was limited because sex was tied to reproduction, childbirth was dangerous, and their role in parenting was circumscribed, since fathers controlled the transfer of property to children. However, stirrings of discontent began to surface during the American Revolution.

2

REPUBLICAN MOTHERHOOD AND
THE ANGEL IN THE HOUSE

*Is it upon mature consideration we adopt the idea, that nature is thus partial
in her distributions? Is it indeed a fact, that she hath yielded to one half of
the human species so unquestionable a mental superiority? I know that to both
sexes elevated understandings, and the reverse, are common. But, suffer me to
ask, in what the minds of females are so notoriously deficient, or unequal.*
　　　　　Judith Sargent Murray, "On the Equality of the Sexes," 1790

She loves with love that cannot tire;
And when, ah woe, she loves alone,
Through passionate duty love springs higher,
As grass grows taller round a stone.
　　　　　Coventry Patmore, *The Angel in the House,* 1897

The period surrounding the American Revolution bequeathed a contradictory legacy for women's empowerment. New ideals of womanhood and
marriage emerged. Yet the Revolution did little to alter the status of the
majority of American women. Nevertheless, the Revolutionary War forced
women to assume many of the responsibilities of their absent husbands and
inspired some women to demand equality. During the Revolution, patriotic
women joined in Stamp Act protest crowds in the 1760s protesting customs
merchants, boycotted British goods in the 1770s, and produced homespun
and goods for the military during the war years. On July 31, 1777, Abigail
Adams wrote to her husband, John, about an incident of women's direct
action. A group of women besieged the store of a merchant, demanding that
he stop selling coffee at exorbitant prices. When he refused, they seized him
by the neck and tossed him into a cart. Then they opened the warehouse, took
the coffee, and drove off. Throughout the war years, some women followed the

army as cooks and laundresses. Deborah Sampson even disguised herself as a man and fought for two and one half years with the revolutionary army, until she was discovered when being treated for the fever.

But the Revolution did not grant full citizenship to most American women, especially poor and African-American women. Northern states abolished slavery, and some voluntary emancipation occurred in the Upper South, creating a large, free black population. Some states revised their laws and practices to give widows more control over their inheritances. Many but not all states passed statutes legalizing divorce.

Scholarly debate has centered on the impact of the American Revolution on women's lives. Mary Beth Norton views it as an important turning point, while Linda Kerber stresses the absence of significant changes. It is beyond the scope of this chapter to explore this question in depth. For my purposes, the importance of the American Revolution lies in the way in which it inspired feminist consciousness among some women and generated a public debate over women's proper political role. Perhaps the most dramatic assertion by colonial women that they were entitled to a voice in public policy was the Edenton Proclamation. Fifty-one female North Carolinians declared in October 1774 their "sincere adherence" to the resolves of the provincial congress and proclaimed it their duty to "do everything as far as lies in our power" to support the "public good." Not only were these women asserting their right to acquiesce in political measures, but they were also assuming a duty to work for the common good. This was the first time female Americans formally claimed the responsibility of a public role for women.[1]

Since women's primary responsibility was believed to be to their families, they were generally thought to have no legitimate place in the political community. Consequently, their education was not considered important. Abigail Adams, Judith Sargent Murray, and Mercy Otis Warren, who were inspired by Enlightenment thought and the revolutionary ideology, deplored the denial of education to women and demanded that women share in the rewards of the Revolution. In 1779 Murray wrote two articles under the name of Constantia, demanding female education. They were published in 1790. Warren was a very effective propagandist and was the only major participant to write a history of the American Revolution.[2]

Abigail Adams, the wife of John Adams, wrote the following to her husband on March 31, 1776, asking him to "remember the ladies."

> I long to hear that you have declared an independancy—and by the way in
> the new Code of Laws which I suppose it will be necessary for you to make I

desire you would Remember the Ladies, and be more generous and favourable to them than your ancestors. Do not put such unlimited power in the hands of the Husbands. Remember all Men would be tyrants if they could. If perticuliar care and attention is not paid to the Laidies we are determined to foment a Rebelion, and will not hold ourselves bound by any Laws in which we have no voice, or Representation.[3]

Widespread rebellion by women would not occur for another seventy-two years. However, in an attempt to find an accommodation between female virtues and republican political aspirations, late eighteenth-century authors like Benjamin Rush argued that the Revolution had expanded the importance of women's domestic responsibilities. If the Republic was to flourish, women must educate their sons in civic virtues and admonish their husbands to be good citizens. This conception of "Republican Motherhood," as Linda Kerber has called it, endowed women's domestic function with political importance.

If the new political order required women to participate in the education of their sons, it logically followed that they had to become educated themselves. This line of thought opened up the possibility of arguments for women's education, a prerequisite for the development of feminist consciousness. In 1796 Charles Brockden Brown, America's first novelist, argued that differences between men and women were due totally to different educations. Despite fierce resistance, women's access to basic education improved dramatically in the early years of the Republic. Women's literacy increased; the literacy gap between men and women closed in parts of the new nation sometime between 1780 and 1850. In 1850 the first federal census which measured basic literacy revealed little difference between the ability of men and women in the Northeast to read and write. However, the literacy gap between the sexes during this era remained greater longer in the South than the North.[4]

In 1787 the Young Ladies Academy of Philadelphia was established, offering girls an education comparable to that which boys could obtain. In her salutatory oration on May 15, 1793, Priscilla Mason passionately argued for women's equal education. Just as many men had feared, once educated, women like Priscilla would no longer be content with subjection. She urged:

Our high and mighty Lords (thanks to their arbitrary constitutions) have denied us the means of knowledge, and then reproached us for the want of it. Being the stronger party, they early seized the sceptre and the sword; with these they gave laws to society; they denied women the advantage of a liberal education; forbid them to exercise their talents on those great occasions, which would serve to improve them. They doom'd the sex to servile or frivolous employments, on purpose to degrade their minds, that they themselves might hold unrivall'd, the power and pre-eminence they had usurped. Happily, a more liberal way of thinking begins to prevail. The sources of knowledge are gradually opening to our sex. Some have already availed themselves of the privilege so far, as to wipe off our reproach in some measure.[5]

Most American women of the eighteenth century did not have the privilege of education, but their literacy increased despite that handicap. The American Revolution set the stage for the emergence of the women's rights movement in the nineteenth century because of its ideology of equality and natural rights, including the right of revolution. It promised, but did not deliver on, its democratic ideals. Thus, the more educated women became, the more they began to demand their rights. Women's aspirations for self-fulfillment in marriage also increased. Parental control over courtship diminished, a development which allowed greater freedom in the choice of a spouse but which also contributed to higher rates of illegitimacy and abandonment. The ideal of a more egalitarian marriage emerged in the late eighteenth century, envisioning a democratic union whose chief aim was to promote individual happiness and serve the social order. The realities of family life naturally diverged from these ideals, and married women were still highly vulnerable to abusive or violent husbands. Recognition of these disparities would eventually fuel the fires of feminist rebellion.

In the colonial period hierarchical relations between husband and wife were perceived as necessary for maintaining order in the household, church, and state. Thus, rationales for women's subordination rested on biblical and social justifications, not on a belief in female incapacity. A logical consequence of the success of the American Revolution was the substitution of "natural" for social explanations of inequality. The presence of slavery and women's inequality might present ideological conflicts with republican ideals, but economic transformations reinforced them.

The growth of capitalist commerce and industry contributed to the emergence of a new sexual division of labor and an erosion of certain earlier legal rights. Although New Jersey granted women the right to vote two days after the Declaration of Independence, most states adopted the first explicit denials of women's right to vote during the 1790s. By the second or third decade of the nineteenth century, these developments gave rise to the notion of separate spheres for men and women. With the heightened association of women with piety, morality, purity, domesticity, and religion, free white women of property were elevated and isolated to the status of the angel in the house.

The Window of Cultural Expectations: The Power of "True Womanhood"

At the time when industrialization was causing radical transformations in American society, a new image of "true womanhood" emerged. In an increasingly competitive, ruthless, and materialistic world, white women of privilege were expected to preserve moral and religious values and to provide a haven to which men could return. Like the "Republican Mother," the angel in the house, or "true woman," was the custodian of civic virtue. For middle- and upper-class white women, the glorification of women's separate sphere led to enhanced covert, domestic power. For African-American and working-class women, however, the cult of true womanhood largely denied them the respectability ascribed to their middle-class sisters.

Regardless of the dominant notion that women should stay home, working-class women were forced to find employment outside of the home in order to help support their families. When northern industrialists needed female and male workers because of a labor shortage, they rationalized the employment of women by arguing that these operatives were single and that their employment would be temporary. When single women became teachers and nurses, the rationale was that they were still performing traditionally female, nurturant activities.[6]

As manufacturing developed and cities grew in the nineteenth century, the center of production was no longer in the home. Women's domestic labor consequently was devalued because it was unpaid. Industrialization at this point was creating rapid changes for only a small percentage of women in the United States. Some key actors in the first women's rights movement were part of this transformation, but probably as many were located in small towns and rural areas. Their response often included a recognition of what they saw as women's losses due to industrialization, especially the loss of their economic centrality to the family and thus, potentially, a loss of their power in the household.

An elaborate ideology of separate spheres for men and women developed as many men and some women went out to work for wages, while the majority of women stayed home to care for their children and keep house. Women's magazines, sermons, and the popular culture promoted what Barbara Welter has termed the "cult of True Womanhood," which formed a basis for sisterly relations and strong female bonding. Drawing on letters and diaries, Carroll Smith-Rosenberg describes the strength which nineteenth-century women drew from their relationships with other women within their separate sphere. Nancy Cott suggests that women as a separate group fostered a consciousness of women's own needs, identities, and restrictions and thus served as a preliminary stage in the emergence of feminism. Nancy Hewitt has challenged this interpretation by suggesting that Cott relied on a coincidence of timing and did not fully trace the cult of true womanhood leading to feminist consciousness. In analyzing the origins of the woman's rights movement in Rochester, New York, Hewitt contends that the women there who responded to Elizabeth Cady Stanton's call for collective action were Quakers, who had bypassed the ideology of separate spheres for most of their lives.[7]

While more research is needed to explain the specific links between the ideology of separate spheres and the emergence of feminist consciousness, we do know that prescriptive literature of the early nineteenth century extolled women's domestic sphere as an arena of power and that women's rights advocates perceived family issues as at the heart of their understanding of women's oppression. They argued for a larger sphere of women's influence on the basis of women's moral and nurturant powers, while they protested against the traditional restrictions of marriage.

Thus, not surprisingly, women as frequently as men were the architects in the construction of the so-called cult of true womanhood. Female writers wrote numerous domestic novels, Sarah Josepha Hale edited *Godey's Lady's Book*, the most popular women's magazine, and educated women like Catharine Beecher wrote treatises on the dignity of domesticity. Beecher advocated women's education and asserted that women are the equals of men. Although she glorified domesticity, she never married. She believed that women ought to exercise covert power but not be *perceived* as exercising it. She accepted women's political powerlessness but tried to gain status for women's paid vocations like teaching, nursing, and domestic service, since they resembled their *unpaid* work within the home. In *Mental and Moral Philosophy*, Beecher wrote: "Woman is to win everything by peace and love by making herself so respected, esteemed and loved, that to yield to her opinions and to gratify her wishes, will be the free-will offering of the heart."[8]

Along with her sister, Harriet Beecher Stowe, Catharine Beecher published their *Treatise on Domestic Economy* in 1841, as well as an enlarged version in 1869 called *American Woman's Home*. They presented a blueprint for colonizing the world in the name of Christian women. Rather than a retreat from the world, the home offered an economic alternative to the world by employing communitarian practices of village life. They relegated men to the periphery of the human sphere and made "women's" values of religion, motherhood, home, and family central to this millenarian vision.[9]

Thus, nineteenth-century women were not simply the dupes of a male conspiracy to relegate them to a separate sphere. Some women rightly understood that if they were excluded from the public sphere, they ought to claim moral superiority and to exert their influence covertly at home in order to have some power to affect the conditions of their lives. This approach, however, was fraught with hazards over the long term. Barbara Welter has pointed out that the cult of true womanhood contained the seeds of its own demise. While women's moral superiority would be used as a rationale for extending their sphere beyond the home, the view that women were significantly different from men could also be used to relegate them to a separate and unequal status in the law and in employment.[10]

From 1820 to 1860 this popularization of the cult of domesticity was a response to rapid social changes. Since women's limited social role was taken for granted by nearly everyone, no elaborate theoretical justification for the continued existence of inequality between the sexes was necessary. Instead, the literature of the period focused on the ways women could continue to exercise their traditional conserving function in the face of the destabilizing influence of the early industrial revolution. The fact that women's sphere and the nature of men's work were undergoing such dramatic changes in the Northeast led to a profusion of prescriptive literature telling women how they should view themselves and how they should behave. Women were expected to embody four cardinal virtues: piety, purity, submissiveness, and domesticity. A woman's power was supposed to reside in the home in her role as wife and mother. A proper woman was always charming, sacrificed herself daily for her family, and did not bother with politics or education. She found her fulfillment through serving others. The angel in the house was emotional rather than intellectual, spiritual rather than carnal. She was morally superior to men. Her influence was subtle but pervasive. One anonymous "friend of the fairer sex" wrote: "As the constantly-dripping water melts and perforates the hardest rock, so the influence of woman, constantly operating upon and influencing the mind of a man, eventually takes entire possession of those parts of his nature which are most susceptible of pure and high feelings."[11]

Presumably, if women failed to live up to the precepts of true womanhood, national disaster was inevitable. The writer of a discourse on "female influence" expressed the gravity of women's responsibility.

> Let her lay aside delicacy, and her influence over our sex is gone. On you, ladies, depends, in a most important degree, the destiny of our country. . . . Yours it is to decide, under God, whether we shall be a nation of refined and high minded Christians, or whether, rejecting the civilities of life, and throwing off the restraints of morality and piety, we shall become a fierce race of semi-barbarians, before whom neither order, nor honor, nor chastity can stand.[12]

The cult of true womanhood represented continuities and changes from previous ideals of womanhood. Colonial women and later "Republican Mothers" had also been expected to be chaste, pious, domestic, and submissive. However, because of religious revivals—the First Great Awakening in the 1740s, and the Second Great Awakening from 1800 to the 1830s—which stimulated emotional conversions and democratized salvation, women began to be viewed as naturally more religious than men and even morally superior because they dominated church membership in the early nineteenth century. This view of women marked a radical departure from the stern Calvinist emphasis on the particularly lusty nature of women, daughters of the temptress Eve. The conception of "Moral Motherhood" replaced "Republican Motherhood" as a way to harmonize domesticity and women's relationship to the public sphere. The cult of domesticity and moral motherhood may have been utilized by some men to subjugate women, but within the female sphere women developed their psychic and social resources and made use of the ideology for their own purposes.[13] At the same time, the idealization of domesticity kept many women from questioning their "proper sphere."

Material changes within an urban-industrial economy promoted the division of labor by gender. The fertility rate declined, since fewer children were needed than in an agricultural economy, and the smaller nuclear family began to lose its close contact with the community. Simultaneously, an increasingly egalitarian marriage replaced a more rigid, hierarchical marriage. Beginning in the late eighteenth century, the ideal marriage as portrayed in popular literature was a democratic union whose chief aim was to promote individual happiness and serve the social order.[14] The cult of domesticity both helped shape women's views of their own appropriate power and also justified the changes which had already occurred. The home became idealized as a sanctuary for men alienated by the capitalist society.

Because of the new industrialized presses, an unprecedented number of women began to read the same magazine—*Godey's Lady's Book*. On the eve of the Civil War, 150,000 middle- and upper-class women subscribed to this magazine. They read how to be ladies and enjoyed the domestic dramas and escapist stories set in medieval times in the style of Sir Walter Scott. They also found the words and music of new dances and directions for pronouncing French phrases or for drawing a rabbit. These readers were not troubled with stories about the ongoing decimation of Indians or the unpleasant subject of slavery.[15] "Ladies" were uninterested in politics, and unpleasant subjects might cause them to faint.

Nineteenth-century women also avidly read works by domestic novelists who emphasized the importance of chastity and piety and the importance of exerting a moral influence over men. But the novelists also dramatized the ambiguities of women's power: their passivity and dependence on men in marriage, combined with their manipulation of men in the home, within the context of their powerlessness in the public sphere. In this manner, they helped legitimize women's separate sphere. Simultaneously, they encouraged a consciousness of a collective female identity and were pragmatically feminist by encouraging women to extend female values to the public sphere.

Jane Tompkins has argued persuasively that since women were excluded from political and economic power, they had to have a way of defining themselves which gave them power and status. Therefore, domestic novelists made women's submission the basis on which to build a power structure of their own. Instead of openly rebelling against the culture's value system, they appropriated it for their own uses. Their novels represent an effort to reorganize culture from the women's point of view.[16]

American "ladies" wept over the trials of heroines in domestic novels like Susanna Haswell Rowson's *Charlotte Temple: A Tale of Truth*, first printed in the United States in 1794, which remained the overall best seller in the United States for over half a century. The tale is one of seduction, a simplistic retelling of Samuel Richardson's *Pamela*. Charlotte is the quintessential passive heroine. She is seduced by Montraville, a British soldier who betrays his promise of marriage and abandons Charlotte for a rich young woman. Charlotte's story ends with her penniless, alone and desolate, giving birth to her illegitimate daughter. She lingers only long enough to die in the arms of her father, who arrives too late to take her home. The moral is clear: young women must control their passions, distrust men, and remain with their parents until a proper marriage takes place. The cost of sexual passion is humiliation and death. Even an indifferent, inattentive husband is better than such a dreadful fate.

Nineteenth-century women were also reading Susan Warner's *Wide, Wide World*, published in 1850, which suddenly became the new overall best seller in the country, even surpassing *Charlotte Temple*. Warner's book is a blend of what one critic called "Home and Jesus." The heroine, Ellen Montgomery, is orphaned and goes to live with her grandmot' ·and aunt in the country. After many trials, Ellen ends up marrying a handsome, well-born clergyman and inherits a fortune. Susan Warner (the pen name of Elizabeth Wetherell) drew a large audience of women because she gave them the "sighs, tears, swooning, hysterics and expressions of heart-rending woe" at the same time as she described domesticity in loving detail. Warner lavishly describes pickling, baking, buttermaking and cooking.[17]

Warner presents an image of people dominated by external authorities who learn to transform their rebellious passion into humble conformity to others' wishes, thus conquering their own souls. In this fashion their powerlessness becomes a source of strength. Her in.plicit message is that the weak will eventually inherit the earth by exerting a moral force.[18]

Nineteenth-century women who read Warner's book could identify with the routine, ritual, and rhythm of their own domestic lives, and at the same time could escape from the harsher sides of marriage. This kind of domestic novel probably helped alleviate some of the frustrations and isolation of middle-class women and provided a sense of communal sympathy. Warner helped to justify the ideology of separate spheres by elevating, glorifying, and sentimentalizing the homemaker's role. A woman's daily cooking, washing, nursing, and baking were given dramatic significance, and her small trials assumed heroic proportion.

Explicit in the domestic novels, however, was an indictment of immoral, irresponsible men. Mrs. E. D. E. N. Southworth, Maria Cummins, Marion Harland, Augusta Jane Evans, Caroline Hentz, and T. S. Arthur portrayed wives in their novels as deserted by profligate or drunkard husbands, widowed, or suffering from insensitive and domineering men. These and other domestic novelists portrayed morally superior heroines who struggled to rescue men from their lust, alcohol, and the exploitative institution of slavery.[19]

Harriet Beecher Stowe was the most famous of the domestic novelists. In addition to writing *Uncle Tom's Cabin*, the first American novel to sell over a million copies, she wrote books and articles on how to achieve the good home. Her own experiences as a wife and mother of seven children both trapped and empowered her. Her husband, Calvin, a minister and professor, did not make enough money to support his family or to hire servants. Consequently, Stowe struggled to juggle her domestic and professional writing responsibilities. These experiences gave her the self-confidence to write about such a controversial topic as slavery because she believed strongly in the religious power of the home and the redemptive values of domesticity and love. She replied to a reader of *Uncle Tom's Cabin*: "I wrote what I did because as a woman, as a mother, I was oppressed and broken hearted with the sorrows and injustice I saw." Stowe believed that if women were empowered by more rights and opportunities, they would be better wives and mothers and would transform politics.[20]

Although domestic novelists like Stowe reinforced the ideal of the angel in the house and Christian sacrifice, they were also subtly subversive. As Helen Papashvily claimed in her study of domestic novelists: "Nonetheless the quiet women revolted, too, and waged their own devious, subtle, undeclared war against men—their manual of arms, their handbook of strategy was the sentimental domestic novel they read for half a century."[21]

The subversiveness of the domestic novelists lay in their criticism of men's treatment of women and in their portrayal of women's strength and resourcefulness in the midst of adversity. A number of the novelists also openly portrayed the tensions and conflicts within marriages. Nina Baym argues persuasively that the domestic novels represent a feminism that is moderate or limited or pragmatic. She believes that the point of this fiction has to do with how the heroine perceives herself. Thus, these novels are about women's psychology. The novels reveal that the way women perceive themselves is a libel on their own sex, a false self-perception that accounts for women's degraded and dependent position. They encourage feminine self-sufficiency and the extension of home values to the world.[22]

At the same time, domestic novelists also glorified martyrdom and reassured women that sacrificial love and suffering were redemptive. Loving sacrifice could bring more than a crown in heaven and personal redemption. The role of sacrificial mother could also bring tremendous power over husband and children by creating dependencies on her and by instilling a sense of obligation and guilt. The domestic novelists assumed that women were intrinsically strong, resourceful, and capable. With faith in God, women could overcome obstacles and even redeem the sinful men, by subterfuge if necessary. When forced by circumstances, some of the heroines managed to make their way in the world, too.

Depending on women's own experiences as wives and mothers, they received different messages from the domestic novels. Domestic novelists perpetuated a vision of female domestic power which was conservative in its emphasis on sexual differences and female moral superiority, conquering one's own soul and self-will, while at the same time offering a radical vision of Christian women in the home shaping the destiny of the nation. The "scribbling women" made money through their writing and frequently had to support their fathers and large families. Their own lives thus gave the lie to female helplessness.

Sophia Hawthorne and Elizabeth Peabody

Naturally women's experiences in the nineteenth century diverged from prescribed behavior, as they had in previous periods. Like the domestic novelists, Sophia Hawthorne and her sister Elizabeth Peabody were imbued with the ideals of true womanhood. In response they chose two different paths—one marriage, and the other a single, independent life. Sophia experienced marriage as empowering and became the angel in the house; her sister Elizabeth chose to remain single in order to pursue an intellectual life and professional career. For her, singlehood provided the straightest path to a feminist consciousness.

Sophia Peabody was an invalid, the victim of terrible headaches, until she met the dashing, handsome Nathaniel Hawthorne. He coaxed her into walks in the countryside and encouraged her to regain her health so that they could marry. Apparently they experienced a passionate, romantic courtship. Hawthorne wrote to her imagining that she was next to him in bed, "Dove, come to my bosom . . . . How many sweet words I should breathe into your ear in the quiet night—how many holy kisses would I press upon your lips." They postponed sexual intercourse until after marriage. After a three-year engagement, they married on April 3, 1843, when Sophia was thirty-three. Once married, they confirmed that sex was not simply a physical pleasure "but a spiritual joy" and "a wondrous instrument . . . for the purposes of the heart."[23]

Walking through Sophia and Nathaniel Hawthorne's first house, the Old Manse, is like entering the world of the Gothic novel. The gabled roof and dark corners suggest intrigue. Each had a work space. Sophia's studio for painting was on the first floor, directly below her husband's study. She seemed to have felt no repression in her marriage, although her mother had warned her that "men are domineering and inconsiderate, hurt you, and woman's only alternative to submission is ill-health." Sophia reassured her mother shortly after her marriage: "Do not fear that I shall be too subject to my Adam, my crown of Perfection. He loves power as little as any mortal I ever knew. . . . Our love is so wide and deep and equal that there could not be much of a difference of opinion between us on any moral point."

However, Hawthorne was no believer in the equality of men and women. He once wrote Sophia telling her how glad he was that she was an artist and not a writer, since art was not a self-revealing form of expression and writing was, as far as he was concerned. "I cannot enough thank God, that, with a higher and deeper intellect than other women, thou hast never—forgive the base idea!—never prostituted thyself to the public, as that woman [Grace Greenwood] has, and as a thousand others do. It does seem to deprive women of all delicacy." Although Sophia placed one of her paintings in a shop to be sold, since she was not a writer, she did not threaten her husband like the scores of domestic novelists who outsold him. In fact, she was exhilarated by the prospects of the satisfactions of marriage. On April 3, 1843, she wrote in her diary, "I could not be satisfied in feeling this mighty springing upwards and forwards unless I were in love. I am thankful that I first knew spring after I was married."

After writing these lines, she stood for a long while at the first two western windows of Nathaniel's study. Then she took her diamond ring and wrote in a small delicate script, "Man's accidents are God's purposes. Sophia A. Hawthorne 1843." Sophia's scrawled signature stands as a reminder of all the women of her class in the nineteenth century who waited by windows for their husbands to return. But her inscription was a romantic gesture, rather than a desperate one. She seemed to be fulfilled as a wife and mother. Sophia continued to paint until her first child, Una, was born on March 3, 1844. Afterward, she painted only lamp shades and fire screens in order to earn money when Nathaniel had difficulty supporting the family by his writing. Years later when she was in Rome, she lamented that she had not been able to study art there. She blamed her own lack of sufficient talent instead of marriage as the reason she abandoned her art. Her last words were, "I only wanted to live for you children, you know. I never wanted anything for myself except to be with your father." Sophia lived out the ideal of the angel in the house.

Sophia's sister, Elizabeth Peabody, chose a completely different path. She never married, and she was the first woman in Boston to open a bookshop. Her shop on West Street was the meeting place for intellectuals. Elizabeth also became a publisher of books, as well as the *Dial*, the main literary magazine of the transcendentalists. Margaret Fuller held her "Conversations" in Elizabeth's bookshop and drew scores of women to hear her speak of the women's needs for equal rights and intellectual companionship. Fuller told the women that they must retire within themselves and explore the ground-work of their own being. Her lecture series attracted women of the most prominent families of Boston, including names like Emerson, Peabody, Quincy, Lowell, Channing, Shaw, and Whiting. Fuller provided them with a striking example of a brilliant woman with public speaking ability and facility in defending her viewpoints. Elizabeth Peabody must have listened intently as Margaret Fuller spoke of the importance of women's developing self-reliance and self-respect. Inspired by female camaraderie, Elizabeth and these other women were experiencing that which in our own time would become known as consciousness-raising.

Margaret Fuller, Elizabeth Peabody, and Sarah Ripley were admitted to the intellectual circle of the transcendentalists (also composed of Ralph Waldo Emerson, Henry David Thoreau, William Ellery Channing, Bronson Alcott, George Ripley, and George Putnam) on an equal plane. They believed that "true womanhood" required education and reflection in order for women to develop self-reliance and therefore not "belong to anyone else."

Throughout her long life of ninety years, Elizabeth Peabody cultivated self-reliance. She worked along with Margaret Fuller and Bronson Alcott to found a progressive school in Boston, taught school for many years, and worked for the Sanitary Commission during the Civil War. She raised enough money to found a school for freed African-American children in Washington, D.C. Along with her sister, Mary, who married the famous educator Horace Mann, Elizabeth later founded the first public kindergarten in the United States. In addition, she wrote several books and crusaded for abolitionism, woman's suffrage, world peace, and the rights of Native Americans.

Having chosen "single blessedness," Elizabeth treasured her autonomy and independence and devoted herself to learning and service. Her sister Sophia, by contrast, was uninterested in crusades against injustice. She felt liberated from her ill health by marriage and cheerfully nurtured her husband's "genius." She was inhibited by marriage and motherhood from pursuing her artistic ambitions but seemed to be personally empowered by her relationship with the aspiring, if not very financially successful, writer. Their lives represent the dichotomy of the power of the angel in the house and her limitations.

American women's windows of experience from the colonial period to the Civil War were shaped by their absence of political, legal, and economic power. Social and religious ideology reminded women in the colonial period that they must be helpmates to men, in the revolutionary era that they must be Republican mothers, and in the early nineteenth century that they must be angels in the house. The ideal of the angel in the house excluded working-class and African-American women. At the same time, the widespread idealization of domesticity kept many middle-class women from questioning their assigned roles. Paradoxically women were both empowered and trapped by being relegated to a separate sphere from men. But faced with powerlessness in the public sphere and convinced of their moral superiority, middle-class white women made use of the cult of domesticity for their own purposes and began to consolidate their power within their separate sphere. A small group of women perceived glaring contradictions between prescriptive literature and their own experiences and began to question the condition of all women. The efforts of these women would change the shape of women's windows in the future. By the late antebellum period, many women came to regard the colonial window and the window of wifely domesticity as distorting lenses from the past.

3

FEMINISM FOR THE SAKE OF THE FAMILY AND COMMUNITY (1800–1900)

If the first woman God ever made was strong enough to turn the world upside down all alone, these women together ought to be able to get it right side up again! And now they are asking to do it, the men better let them.

Sojourner Truth, 1851

Our trouble is not our womanhood, but the artificial trammels of custom under false conditions. We are, as a sex, infinitely superior to men, and if we were free and developed, healthy in body and mind, as we should be under natural conditions, our motherhood would be our glory. That function gives women such wisdom and power as no male ever can possess. When women can support themselves, have their entry to all the trades and professions, with a house of their own over their heads and a bank account, they will own their bodies and be dictators in the social realm.

Elizabeth Cady Stanton, 1890

The activists for women's rights in the nineteenth century may have read *Godey's Lady's Book* and the same domestic novels as their neighbors, but they believed that women's moral superiority justified their working for women's equality inside and outside the home. Why did they challenge the prevailing restrictions on women? How did their own experiences in the family lead them to a feminist consciousness? How did their domestic experiences shape their feminist thought and action?[1]

Family issues—women's property rights, child custody, marriage, reproductive control, and divorce—were central to the early women's rights advocates' understanding of women's oppression. The Declaration of Sentiments passed in 1848 at Seneca Falls, New York, as well as the resolutions passed at other women's rights conventions, reflected the centrality of these concerns. Elizabeth Cady Stanton, along with many Quakers and Spiritualists, were the strongest advocates for marriage reform, both before and after the Civil War, when the women's rights movement as a whole narrowed its platform to concentrate on the vote. This emphasis on family issues stemmed from the supporters' own domestic experiences—empowering as well as restrictive—and from their outrage over the victimization of other women by abusive husbands. Aware of the precariousness of women's covert domestic power, many early activists for women's rights forged a feminist agenda designed to benefit women and their families. Elizabeth Cady Stanton, Susan B. Anthony, Lucy Stone, Antoinette Brown Blackwell, and other notable feminists who were dismayed by the slow progress of achieving public power sought to apply feminist principles in their own lives. They pursued two major alternative strategies: combining marriage, motherhood, and careers; or choosing single celibate lives dedicated to reform.

Many early advocates for women's rights came to a feminist consciousness as they perceived the disparities between their own experiences as wives and mothers and the cultural ideals of true womanhood. Some of them came to an awareness of their subordination when they were discriminated against in the abolitionist and temperance movements. In these movements they gained valuable political organizing experience through public speaking, lobbying, and petition campaigns. For others their feminist consciousness stemmed from their experiences as Quakers and Spiritualists. Women spoke in Quaker meetings, became ministers, held separate business meetings, and had equal educational opportunities.[2]

In 1840 Lucretia Mott, a Quaker minister, and Elizabeth Cady Stanton attended the World Anti-Slavery meeting in London with their husbands. Because the male abolitionists did not allow the female delegates to speak, Stanton and Mott vowed to hold a meeting to discuss the oppression of women when they returned.

But Stanton was a newlywed, and upon her return from England she dedicated herself to domesticity. She enjoyed the stimulating atmosphere of Boston and conversations with reformers and intellectuals. Servants relieved her of the most arduous housework, but her first three children, born in 1842, 1844, and 1845, consumed most of her time.

Only when her family moved from Boston to Seneca Falls in upstate New York did Stanton experience a feminist awakening, which stemmed as much from her frustrations as a wife and mother as from her indignation over discrimination against women in the antislavery movement. Suddenly she knew the anguish of the isolated housewife. Since she was unable to employ servants, she was forced to do her own housework and to care for her three rowdy boys without assistance. Even millionaires' houses of this era lacked indoor plumbing and central heating. Cooking was time consuming without any commercially canned foods or packaged cereals. Washing clothes was an arduous task, occupying one full day a week. Sewing all the family's clothes took long hours, since sewing machines were not available to home seam-stresses until after the Civil War. Daily housekeeping and child care thus were full-time jobs, leaving little time for any intellectual or creative life. Under these conditions, Stanton became extremely frustrated, then angry.

Stanton was not the first woman of her time to feel the pressures of domesticity, but she began to see that other women shared the same frustra-tions. She participated in what contemporary feminists would call a conscious-ness-raising group. On July 13, 1848, she visited her old friend Lucretia Mott. The two joined Mott's sister, Martha Coffin Wright, Jane Hunt, and Mary Ann McClintock around the tea table.[3] With the exception of Stanton, all the other women who gathered that day were dissident Hicksite Quakers who had recently left the Genessee Meeting because of resistance to political action by some of its members regarding antislavery and equality of women. Lucretia Mott had been advocating women's rights for the past forty years.[4] While tea parties have generally been considered frivolous social occasions where women gather to gossip, it was at this particular tea party that the women's revolt in the United States truly began, much as another "Tea Party," held seventy-four years earlier in Boston Harbor, heralded the beginning of the American Revolution. Over tea, the women poured out their discontent and outrage over women's inferior status. They decided to call a convention.

On a warm July morning in 1848, anticipating the beginning of their women's rights convention later that day, Elizabeth Cady Stanton awoke early with a sense of excitement and anxiety. The day before, she had argued with her husband, Henry, about the impending convention, and after some angry words, he had left town to avoid embarrassment. Henry disapproved of her brash actions; as an agent for the Anti-Slavery Society, he fervently believed that the issue of abolishing slavery should supersede all other concerns.

When the conveners issued the announcement of the women's rights convention in the newspapers, they did not know whether many would attend. However, whether from curiosity, boredom, or a sense of injustice, about three hundred people arrived at the convention that bright summer day in the small town of Seneca Falls. When these early women's rights pioneers arrived, the door of the Wesleyan chapel was locked, and Stanton's nephew had to be boosted through a window to open the door from inside.

Even before the meeting opened, a sense of expectation filled the chapel, where for a hundred years ministers had preached sermons on women's "divinely ordained subordination." Lucretia Mott's husband presided because none of the women felt confident enough to do so. A nervous but determined Elizabeth Cady Stanton read their Declaration of Sentiments to a mixed crowd of women and men.

> We hold these truths to be self-evident: that all men and women are created equal; that they are endowed by their Creator with certain inalienable rights: that among these are life, liberty and the pursuit of happiness. . . .
>
> The history of mankind is a history of repeated injuries and usurpations on the part of man toward woman, having in direct object the establishment of an absolute tyranny over her. To prove this, let facts be submitted to a candid world.[5]

Their Declaration of Sentiments was based on the Enlightenment philosophy of natural rights, Protestantism, and moral evolution. Modeled on the Declaration of Independence, it began with the same preamble, with the addition of women as self-evidently equal to men, and then presented a list of grievances which included four major areas: violations of natural rights, disabilities of married women, religious discrimination, and denials of opportunity for individual development.[6] It called for women's rights to their property, wages, and children and for their ability to make contracts, to sue and be sued, and to testify in courts of justice. Thus, from the beginning, family issues assumed a central place in the platform for women's equality.

Lively discussion on the deplorable condition of women followed the presentation of the Declaration of Sentiments. Finally, Stanton courageously called for the right of women to vote. Even Lucretia Mott thought this too bold an action, but the resolution carried by a small margin. As the convention ended, sixty-eight women and thirty-two men (a third of the people present) signed their names to the Declaration of Sentiments.[7]

Response to the Seneca Falls Convention was swift and almost wholly negative. Church leaders denounced the women's radical demands and "unfeminine" behavior. The *Philadelphia Public Ledger* and *Daily Transcript* wrote: "A woman is nobody. A wife is everything. A pretty girl is equal to ten thousand men, and a mother is, next to God, all powerful. . . . The ladies of

Philadelphia, therefore, under the influence of the most serious, sober second thoughts, are resolved to maintain their rights as Wives, Belles, Virgins and Mothers, and not as Women."[8] However, both Frederick Douglass's paper, the *North Star*, and William Lloyd Garrison's *Liberator* supported the women's demands. Horace Greeley wrote in the *New York Tribune*, "However unwise and mistaken the demand, it is but the assertion of a natural right and as such must be conceded." Nonetheless, the reformers were generally portrayed as sexless old maids and radical heretics. Stanton later wrote of the originators of the convention that they "were neither sour old maids, childless women, nor divorced wives, as the newspapers declared them to be."[9] Nearly all of the early feminists were married, and most of them had children.

Women in Rochester, New York, held a convention two weeks after the one at Seneca Falls, on August 2, 1848. The Rochester Convention generally resembled the one in Seneca Falls but differed in some important aspects. A woman presided over it, a call for the vote for women topped its agenda, and more emphasis was given to laboring women and women's economic independence. However, as with the Seneca Falls Convention, family issues were a top priority. The planning committee was composed of Amy Post (a former Hicksite Quaker), Sarah Hallowell, Sarah Fish (a former Presbyterian), Sarah Owen, and Rhoda DeGarmo. Whereas the Seneca Falls Convention was called to discuss the "social, civil, and religious condition and rights of women," the Rochester Convention was called to consider the "Rights of Women, Politically, Socially, Religiously, and Industrially."[10] Five "ultraist" women, as Nancy Hewitt has called them, had been present at the Seneca Falls Convention, including Amy Post and Catherine Fish Stebbins. They aided women who were abused, abandoned, or widowed. They also had more contact with African-Americans than the other groups of female reformers in Rochester. Their experiences with poor and victimized women strengthened their conviction that women must be economically independent and free from unequal marriages. These same women were among the organizers of the Rochester Convention.[11]

As did the Seneca Falls Convention, the Rochester Woman's Rights Convention considered resolutions regarding family issues. The leaders urged "women no longer to promise obedience in the marriage covenant" and to allow "the strongest *will* or superior intellect, whether man's or woman's to govern the household." They further urged them to claim equal authority not only within their own families but "on all subjects that interest the human family." They also denounced the husband's legal right to hire out his wife's labor and collect her wages.

Editorial response in the *Daily Democrat* of August 3, 1848, was critical of some of the "ridiculous propositions" of the Rochester Woman's Rights Convention, but it acknowledged the "practical good—the adoption of measures for the relief and amelioration of the condition of indigent, industrious, laboring females."

Two weeks after the Rochester Convention, Sarah C. Owen, Mrs. Roberts, Amy Post, and Mrs. Cavan, a tailor's wife, formed the Working Women's Protective Union. They wanted to form an alliance across class lines in order to achieve women's equality. The union aided Indians on the Cattaragus reservation as well as fugitive slaves, and they fought for women's property rights and against capital punishment.[12]

For some women, Spiritualism inspired them to make more radical demands. Spiritualism, which had its inception in 1848, was one source of a critique of the unequal institution of marriage in nineteenth-century America. With its explanation of the place of spirit manifestations, Spiritualism offered an alternative to Protestantism. Ann Braude has argued that Spiritualism became a (if not *the*) major vehicle for the spread of women's rights ideas in nineteenth-century America. As women's roles as mothers increasingly defined their social and religious identities, they were less willing to view those who died without a Christian conversion as damned. Spiritualist women argued for equal education, access to their property, economic independence, and freedom from unequal marriages. Prominent Spritualists included Anna Blackwell, eldest sibling of Elizabeth and Emily, Henry and Sam Blackwell, Harriet Beecher Stowe, Frances Willard, Isabella Beecher Hooker, William Lloyd Garrison, the Grimké sisters, Thomas and Mary Ann McClintock, Mary Livermore, Mary Wright Sewall, Paulina Wright Davis, Sojourner Truth, and Mary Todd Lincoln. Many dissident Quakers in upstate New York adopted Spiritualism and the fight for women's rights. Raps from "spirits" reportedly rocked the same table where Mott and Stanton wrote the Declaration of Sentiments and even a table in Stanton's house.

Many of the Spiritualist women had survived unhappy marriages that ended in divorce or desertion. They believed that the most serious obstacle to women's individual sovereignty was the institution of marriage. The critique of marriage was the major plank of the Spiritualist women's rights platform. Mediums denounced "the body and soul destroying marriage institution."

Spiritualists believed that true marriages could result only from spiritual attraction. Moreover, in their view, women's economic independence was a prerequisite for a true marriage.[13]

Regardless of whether their demands were radical or reformist, women's rights advocates focused their energies on holding conventions and political lobbying. After the Rochester Woman's Rights Convention other conventions were held in Worcester, Massachusetts, in 1850; Syracuse, New York, in 1852; New York City and Cleveland, Ohio, in 1853; Philadelphia in 1854; Cincinnati in 1855; and New York City in 1856 and 1860. Until after the Civil War, when a national organization was formed, agitation largely took place through speeches, writings, and lobbying of state legislatures. Achieving women's right to vote took another 72 years after the Seneca Falls Convention, 144 years after the signing of the Declaration of Independence. Charlotte Woodward was the only woman present at the Seneca Falls meeting to live long enough to vote in a presidential election.[14]

As during all revolutions, resistance to the women's rights movement was strong, sometimes subtle, but often fierce. Opponents of women's rights in the nineteenth century claimed that the enfranchisement of women would threaten the family, create discord, upset the divinely ordained separation of spheres, place an unbearable burden on women, and—horror of horrors— unsex them. The joys of motherhood, domesticity, and chivalry were intended to compensate women for their legal subordination. However, as Havelock Ellis once remarked, such chivalry was an ideal by which a woman was treated as a cross between an angel and an idiot.[15]

Ironically, the majority of white middle- and upper-class American women seemed to accept the role of the angel in the house. Shortly after the first women's rights convention, the *Ladies' Wreath* published a poem on the "rights" of the angel in the house, which may have expressed the beliefs of the majority of white middle- and upper-class American women.

> What are the Rights of Women?
> The right to love whom others scorn,
> The right to comfort and to mourn,
> The right to shed new joy on earth,
> The right to feel the soul's high worth. . . .
> Such women's rights, and God will bless
> And crown their champions with success.[16]

In contrast, while ministers, women's magazines, and novels exalted women's separate sphere, the early feminists believed that *in order* to be good wives and mothers, they must eliminate victimization in both the public and private spheres. They were "ladies" themselves and had internalized many of the values of true womanhood, but they felt bitterly the restrictions which marriage implied. They wanted to extend the beneficent influence of the angel in the house into the public sphere.

A feminist consciousness began to develop within a small group of women who began to recognize the disparity between romantic ideals of the family and the unsettling realities of women's oppression. Faced with legal discrimination against women in the public sphere, Elizabeth Cady Stanton and Susan B. Anthony chose different strategies to apply feminist principles in their own lives: Stanton chose marriage, motherhood, and a reform career, while Anthony chose singlehood and a life devoted to the struggle for women's rights. Other early advocates of women's rights attempted to create egalitarian marriages and at the same time to keep family issues at the center of the agenda of the women's movement.

Like other nineteenth-century feminists, Stanton internalized and fulfilled many of her society's expectations of women. She was married for forty-seven years and had seven children. However, she was unconventional in her enjoyment of sex and her refusal to choose between marriage and a public career. With her rosy cheeks, white curly hair, and plump figure, Stanton resembled Queen Victoria. In fact, Stanton was so plump that when she and Anthony went horseback riding in California, she wore out two mares and had to be carried by buckboard. Stanton fully valued her experiences as wife and mother and appreciated women's nurturant qualities, but she saw no reason why they should not also have the same freedoms which men enjoyed.

Stanton began to see her own frustrations as linked to the repressed condition of all women and fought against women's victimization inside and outside of the home. She felt keenly the restrictions of marriage and children on her physical mobility, time, concentration, and participation in the women's rights movement.[17] Stanton's strident criticism of the institution of marriage alienated some feminists who felt that an open assault on marriage might jeopardize support which they needed to secure the vote.

In contrast to Stanton, the tall, lean Susan B. Anthony looked to the unfriendly like a prudish, repressed school marm. She chose a celibate life and satisfied her needs for intimacy through her female network. Anthony's choice of "spinsterhood" was becoming more common in the nineteenth century, as the accompanying table shows.

Year of Birth	Percentage of women never marrying
1835–38	7.3
1845–49	8.0
1855–59	8.9
1865–75	11.0

Elizabeth Blackwell, the first woman doctor in the country, and Frances Willard, a crusader for temperance, were also spinsters by conscious choice.[18] Like Elizabeth Peabody before them, Anthony and the other spinsters who chose singlehood because they valued independence and personal autonomy more than marriage sometimes faced criticism, ridicule and sarcasm from detractors who saw their spinsterhood as a mark of failure as women.

Because Anthony was sensitive about the criticism of the uncommon path she had chosen, she was not as vocal as Stanton about marriage reforms, but she agreed with her in principle. When Anthony criticized the total control of husbands over their wives, women in Dayton "took up the cudgel" in defense of marriage.[19] Fearing this kind of opposition, Anthony was generally reticent in public on the issue of marriage and divorce. Privately, by the example of her own life, she rejected the institution as incompatible with her freedom. She playfully told Stanton that she could not imagine that "the man she loved, described in the Constitution as a white male, native-born, American citizen possessed of the right of self-government, eligible to the office of the President of the Great Republic, should unite his destinies in marriage with a political slave and pariah."[20] Anthony paid reverence to the "time-honored plan of making a home by the union of one man and one woman in marriage," but she acknowledged that vast numbers of women out of necessity or choice had to make homes for themselves, and they as well as married women were entitled to political and legal freedom.[21] Any time an activist for women's rights married, Anthony feared the loss of an ally, and she did not hesitate to make her strong feelings known—even to the point of irritation.

Anthony was quite influential in guiding the women's rights movement toward concentrating on suffrage guaranteed by a national constitutional amendment as the fundamental feminist goal, believing that other changes would follow. However, progress in attaining her goals was painstakingly slow. Anthony set out alone on Christmas Day of 1854 with fifty dollars which Wendell Phillips, a well-known abolitionist, had contributed. She sought names for petitions for married women's rights and for woman suffrage. She had enlisted sixty women in New York State to head the petition campaign. In six weeks she had 5,931 signatures for married women's rights, and 4,164 for woman suffrage. During one of New York's coldest winters, Anthony traveled by foot, train, and sleigh, carrying Stanton's tracts. Staying in unheated hotels and often completely exhausted, she managed to canvass fifty-four of New York's sixty counties by May. Anthony's perseverance eventually paid off. Five years later, in 1859, the New York legislators responded positively when Stanton spoke to the Judiciary Committee. They amended the existing Married Woman's Property Act to include child custody, property rights for widows, and control over earnings. However, they ignored the pleas for suffrage and easier divorce, changes which they feared would threaten the traditional family.[22]

Anthony prodded her friend to write and was exasperated when Stanton's family duties prevented her from greater participation in the cause. Once when she wanted Stanton to write a speech for an upcoming teacher's convention, Anthony wrote out of frustration: "I beg you, with one baby on your knee and another at your feet, and four boys whistling, buzzing, hallooing Ma Ma, set yourself about the work. . . . Such a body as I might be spared to rock cradles. But it is a crime for you and Lucy Stone and Antoinette Brown to be doing it."[23] Anthony frequently took care of Stanton's children and "stirred the pudding" while Stanton wrote.

Although Stanton felt constrained by her family's demands, she recognized that the family was the vehicle of many women's power and the source of their self-esteem. Her own success as a mother increased her self-confidence. To her friend Libby Miller, Stanton wrote of her tender feelings for her child, acknowledging the cost of her joy: "I have kissed and hugged [the baby] 'til she went to sleep. The joy a mother feels on seeing her baby after a short absence is a bliss no man's soul can ever know. There we have something that they have not! But we have purchased the ecstasy in deep sorrow and suffering."[24]

Stanton tried to achieve equality in her own marriage from the beginning. In Stanton's marriage ceremony the minister omitted the word "obey" from the service; Stanton also kept her own name and added her husband's.[25] Throughout the forty-seven years of marriage to Henry Stanton, Elizabeth Cady Stanton never enjoyed a particularly harmonious union. Henry was absent much of the time, and for many years the Stantons even had separate residences.

While many of her feminist contemporaries were afraid to attack the unequal institution of marriage, Stanton railed against its injustices, argued for easier divorce, and endorsed what she termed "self-sovereignty," the right of a woman to control her own person. This did not mean "free love," as espoused by Victoria Woodhull or later by Emma Goldman, but rather refusing sex when she wanted to. Stanton believed that the advancement of women in the public sphere was directly related to their position in the home. As a married woman, it was easier for Stanton than for Anthony to criticize the institution of marriage, since she was offering her critique from the inside. She expressed to Anthony the centrality of marriage reform to any other feminist gains.

> It is in vain to look for the elevation of woman, so long as she is degraded in marriage. I say it is a sin, an outrage on our holiest feelings to pretend that anything but deep, fervent love and sympathy constitutes marriage. The right idea of marriage is at the foundation of all reforms. . . . Man in his lust has regulated this whole question of sexual intercourse long enough. Let the mother of mankind whose prerogative it is to set bonds to his indulgence rouse up and give this whole question a thorough fearless examination. . . . I feel this whole question of woman's rights turns on the point of the marriage relation.[26]

In a similar vein, Paulina Wright Davis spoke passionately on the marriage question at the National Woman's Rights Convention in 1852 in Syracuse, New York. She insisted that "a true marriage was a union of soul and soul." She continued: "The true family is the central and supreme institution among human societies. All other organizations, whether of Church or State, depend upon it for their character and action. Its evils are the source of all evils; its good the fountain of all good. The correction of its abuses is the starting-point of all the reforms which the world needs."[27]

The pages of the *Revolution*, a periodical published by Stanton and Anthony, constantly reflected Stanton's passionate crusade to enhance the satisfaction of women in marriage. When she was chided in the Sunday *Times* for "neglecting her domestic duties" and encouraged to exalt her sex through an "example of domestic felicity," Stanton snapped:

> Ah! Sir, in recommending to our attention domestic economy you have assailed us in our stronghold. Here we are unsurpassed. We know—what not one woman in ten thousand does know—how to take care of a child, make

good bread, and keep a house clean. . . . Now let every man who wants his wife to know how to do likewise take *The Revolution* in which not only the ballot, but bread and babies will be discussed.[28]

Stanton first spoke out on the issue of marriage and sexuality in the 1850s while espousing temperance. Her letter to the Albany temperance meeting in 1852 was one of her first public demands for divorce reform.[29] Stanton was sympathetic to women suffering in abusive marriages, and she believed that their safety and autonomy were more important than keeping their families intact.

Evidently other women were beginning to come to the same conclusion as Stanton, because almost two-thirds of all divorces were granted to women in 1860, and the proportion began to rise.[30] However, regardless of the widespread evidence of many women's desire for easier divorce, legislative change was slow. As Elizabeth Pleck, a historian of family violence points out, the more radical the feminists' critique of the family underlying their specific legislative proposals, the lower was the chance of passing them.[31]

Throughout the pages of the proceedings of the woman's rights conventions are numerous stories of abuses of women in marriage, their having their children stolen from them, losing their wages and property, and suffering violence at the hands of their husbands. In 1860 and 1861 legislation was introduced to liberalize New York's restrictive divorce laws. This effort stimulated a debate over family issues at the 1860 National Woman's Rights Convention in New York City. Undeterred by successive failures to achieve easier divorce, Stanton introduced ten resolutions condemning current attitudes and laws on marriage and divorce at the tenth National Woman's Rights Convention.

After Stanton spoke for her resolutions, Antoinette Brown Blackwell then offered thirteen and spoke for them. Brown Blackwell believed that legal divorce should be possible under some few conditions, but moral divorce could never occur. She set forth quasi-religious views of what moral behavior in marriage should be.[32] She believed that marriage was an indissoluble union entailing lifelong moral obligations. She wanted to hold men to a more rigid responsibility in marriage for women's benefit.[33]

However, despite Antoinette's conservatism regarding easier divorce, she herself held radical views about egalitarian marriages. Her position must be seen within the context of her own experience as a wife and mother. She did not allow marriage and motherhood to deter her from her career, and she continued studying, writing, and preaching part-time, while caring for her children. In her essay "Social Progress" in *Studies in General Science*, published in 1869, Antoinette envisioned a society in which men and women would share both household tasks and paid employment. Later, in the November 8, 1873, edition of the *Woman's Journal*, she made her plan explicit.

> Wife and husband can be mutual helpers with admirable effect. Let her take his place in garden or field or workshop an hour or two daily, learning to breathe more strongly, and exercising a fresh set of muscles in soul and body. To him baby-tending and bread-making would be most humanizing in their influence, all parties gaining an assured benefit. . . . We need a general reconstruction in the division of labor. Let no women give all their time to household duties, but require nearly all women, and all men also, since they belong to the household, to bear some share of the common household burdens.

Not even Stanton had publicly suggested that men share child-care and domestic duties.

Later in life Antoinette happily admitted that her marriage had been a help, not a hindrance, to her public service because of her husband's "sustaining sympathy." She and Samuel Blackwell tried successfully to implement an egalitarian vision of marriage. This was possible in part because both of their lives were made easier by the presence of servants and governesses. Therefore, she and her husband had few domestic burdens to share. After Samuel's death, Antoinette wrote that he faithfully "redeemed" his promise to attend to home duties for almost fifty years.[34] It should be noted that, in general, for upper- and middle-class feminist couples, domestic egalitarianism involved relatively small sacrifices for the husbands.

In the earlier debate at the 1860 National Woman's Rights Convention, Ernestine Potowski Rose had described marriages very different from that of Antoinette Brown Blackwell: those in which "the husband holds the iron heel of legal oppression on the subjugate neck of the wife until every spark of womanhood is crushed out." She argued that a woman better met her obligations to her children through divorce than by keeping them in a home where "father and mother despise and hate each other, and still live together as husband and wife." She further contended that women must be financially independent and called for a divorce law which granted divorces because of personal cruelty, willful desertion for a year, or habitual intemperance.[35]

All three of these speakers—Stanton, Blackwell, and Rose—grounded their views in individualism. In opposition, Wendell Phillips criticized the speeches and moved that the text of them not appear in the journals of the convention. His motion was supported by Mrs. Abby Gibbons and William Lloyd Garrison. Phillips argued that only a distinct, relatively narrow movement had a chance to succeed. Susan B. Anthony entered the debate and supported Stanton's views. She told the convention: "Marriage has ever been a one-sided matter, resting most unequally upon the sexes. By it man gains all; woman loses all; tyrant law and lust reign supreme with him; meek submission and ready obedience alone befit it. Woman has never been consulted; her wish has never been taken into consideration as regards the terms of the marriage compact."[36]

The convention failed to vote on either Stanton's or Blackwell's resolutions, but Phillips's motion came to a vote and was rejected. This outcome is difficult to interpret, but it seems to indicate not only that opinion was divided on how to proceed on the controversial issue of divorce but also that the delegates considered family issues of importance and that the majority believed that their deliberations about them should be on the record.

When the divorce question was hotly debated in New York, Stanton, Rose, and Mott spoke at the capitol. Mott said "that she had not thought profoundly on this subject but it seemed to her no laws whatever on this relation would be better than such as bound pure, innocent women in bondage to dissipated, unprincipled men. With such various laws in the different States, and fugitives from the marriage bond fleeing from one to another would it not be better to place all the States on the same basis, and make our national laws homogeneous?" Mott made the most radical speech of the three, but covered hers with eulogies of good men and the sacredness of marriage.[37]

Stanton claimed that her awareness of the problem of abusive marriages stemmed from the sufferings of a friend of her girlhood. Her own discontent had come from the burdens of increased housework and child care. Her lack of power over her reproductive life increased her sense of subordination and contributed to the centrality of the birth control message in her feminist theory.[38]

Stanton continued her campaign for easier divorce by addressing the New York Senate Judiciary Committee in support of pending divorce legislation, but the slavery question drowned out other concerns. After the Civil War she returned to the questions concerning marriage.[39] In 1871 she gave a speech on marriage and motherhood in San Francisco and urged that a "woman must be at all times sovereign of her own body."[40] Stanton took pains to reassure an uncertain public that easier divorce and abolition of a double sexual standard would not, ultimately, destabilize society but would strengthen it.[41] She summarized her views in "Home Life" in 1875:

> When woman is man's equal the marriage relation cannot stand as it is to-day. But this change will not destroy it; as state constitutions and statute laws did not create conjugal and maternal love, they cannot annul them. . . . We shall have the family, that great conservator of national strength and morals after the present idea of man's headship is repudiated and woman set free.[42]

Through a marriage of equals both men and women would benefit. Stanton stated that because of the sacredness and responsibility of motherhood, women must be educated, have political rights, and be in control of their own destinies. At the founding convention of the National American Woman Suffrage Association in 1890, she again hammered away on the question of liberalized divorce.[43] Although Stanton pressed for radical changes, most of the early feminists did not challenge the institution of marriage itself, but they were concerned with other family issues like property rights and child custody.

Most nineteenth-century women apparently were content to exert their power covertly within the home or felt that they had few alternatives. Within the family sphere men's legal, traditional authority was vulnerable to psychological warfare and could be subverted by the men's affection or by their wives' clever manipulation. One nineteenth-century physician described this process succinctly: "Women are never stronger than when they arm themselves with their weakness."[44] Even Elizabeth Cady Stanton was not above resorting to feminine wiles and covert manipulation when other means failed. Once she urged a friend to buy a stove while her husband was away. When her friend looked frightened and asked her what she could do to assuage her angry husband when he returned, Stanton advised her to gaze out of the window with a faraway, sad look. She said that men could not resist beauty and tears.[45]

Ultimately, however, Stanton, Anthony, and the other early feminists were dissatisfied with manipulation and weakness as sources of power. They argued for openness between the sexes and a balance of power for men and women. In order to achieve this more balanced relationship, they promoted the study of physiological science and spoke frankly about the body itself. They believed that marital success and maintenance of the social order required that men become more like women by moderating their desires and behavior. They did not view mind and body as polarities and believed they must be integrated in a harmonious person and society. They agreed with Matilda Joslyn Gage that women must develop fully emotionally, intellectually, and physically in order to be healthy. Consequently, they believed that women must have control over their own bodies and restrain men's sexual demands.[46]

Stanton and Anthony were joined in these views by other feminists who objected strenuously to unrestrained passion and romantic love. They believed that in a sexually unequal society, romantic or sentimental love threatened women's interests. Both the *Revolution* and the *Woman's Journal*, edited by Lucy Stone and Henry Blackwell, warned of the hazards of romantic love. According to Laura Curtis Bullard, the editor of the *Revolution*: "Most of those who love are, or fancy themselves to be, in love with each other. Each imagines the other to possess those qualities which would make a life spent together delightful to both; and this expectation makes the disappointment when it comes, the harder to bear."[47] A writer in the *Woman's Journal* echoed the same sentiment: "Young persons who are so blinded by love that their judgment is rendered torpid . . . are soon and sadly undeceived by the experiences of married life; and such matches are most miserable."[48]

These early feminists believed that another source of misery in marriage stemmed from women's ignorance about their sexuality and men's excessive passion.[49] Lucinda Chandler, a moral reformer, argued in the *Revolution* that sexual equality would restore marital harmony: "Only the *equal* freedom of women and men in the marital relation will correct this disequilibrium. Only when there is no subordination or domination in marriage would each sex fulfill the offices and functions ordained to each *according* to the will or selfishness of one party."[50]

Romantic love and men's "excessive" sexual demands reinforced women's being defined primarily as sexual objects. An outward symbol of this objectification was the tyranny of fashion. If women continued to dress "fashionably," their corsets prevented circulation and caused headaches, pain, and general sluggishness, throwing their bodies completely out of balance.[51] Many of the early feminists believed that women's physical mobility was essential to mental freedom. However, like modern feminists, they were ambivalent about giving up "femininity" in exchange for partial equality. Stanton, Anthony, Elizabeth Smith Miller, and other daring feminists started wearing bloomers in the 1850s. These simple woolen skirts with pantaloons were a welcome relief from stays and corsets.[52]

Like their fellow feminists, Stanton and Anthony eventually discarded their bloomers because of the severe humiliation they faced. Crowds jeered at them, threw snowballs at them, and challenged their identity as women. The energy required to resist such humiliation was too great to justify the benefits of their protest again restrictive fashion, and they did not want to give credence to the argument that equality would "unsex women." Similarly, feminists in the 1960s and 1970s faced ridicule when they stopped wearing makeup, wearing high heels, and shaving their legs. Many feminists succumbed to the pressure of deeply held standards of femininity and feminine beauty. It is not surprising that some of the women's rights advocates of the 1870s were found at their conventions in "rich and elegant silks, trimmed with tasteful laces and cut in the latest fashion."[53]

Although they put away their bloomers, nineteenth-century feminists did not fully capitulate to fashion. They chose simplicity instead of ostentation, loosened their corsets, refused to lace themselves tightly, and wore loose-fitting clothing at home. No matter how radical their ideas were to their contemporaries, they believed themselves to be "ladies," and their true femininity was linked to being fully human, not birds of finery, romantic love objects, or sentimentalized mothers.

As we have seen, family issues, despite their controversial nature, remained a priority for the early women's rights movement. Stanton, Anthony, and the other women's rights activists had very limited success in achieving their long-range goals of legal, political, and economic equality for women. Their "private feminism," as opposed to their public feminism, may be seen in the choices they made within their own lives, choices they hoped would enhance their individual freedom and autonomy: Stanton's attempt to combine marriage, motherhood, and a career; and Anthony's single, celibate life.

Lucy Stone and Henry Blackwell, along with an entire network of other couples, pioneered in the creation of feminist marriages. Their experiences in egalitarian marriages shaped their feminist thought and action. They realized the possibilities of harmonizing individual ambitions and domesticity with lives of service. Yet, they still felt the constraints imposed upon them by a male-dominated power structure outside their homes and were outraged over the victimization of other women by violent or intemperate husbands.

Like Stanton, Lucy Stone combined feminist activism with marriage and a family, but she almost had a nervous breakdown when she decided to marry. When she had attended Oberlin College and first began to advocate women's rights, she steadfastly planned on never marrying because she did not want to relinquish her independence. Chances are Lucy Stone would have remained single had she not met an exceptional man, Henry B. Blackwell. In the fall of 1850 on her way from Illinois to the National Woman's Rights Convention in Massachusetts, Lucy Stone stopped by Cincinnati to cash a draft for the Anti-Slavery Society. She appealed to Blackwell for aid, since the draft was on the previous owner of his hardware store.[54]

Although Henry Blackwell did not see Lucy Stone again for three years, he was tremendously attracted to her, and he began to court her fervently. Their letters reveal the depth of anguish which nineteenth-century women could face as they approached marriage. Seven years her junior, Henry Blackwell came from an abolitionist family, and his sisters Elizabeth and Emily were doctors and advocates of women's rights. He implored Lucy to trust his love for her and his dedication to preserving her equality within marriage. Lucy was not easily persuaded, but he persisted for two years. In 1853 he wrote to her about his views on marriage.

> My idea of the relation involves no sacrifice of individuality but its perfec-
> tion—no limitation of the career of one, or both but its extension. I would
> not have my wife drudge, as Mrs. Weld has had to do in the house, while I
> found nothing on earth to do but dig ditches. I would not even consent that
> my wife should stay at home to rock the baby when she ought to be off ad-
> dressing a meeting, or organizing a Society. Perfect *equality* in this relation-
> ship (as in every other one where human beings are concerned) I would
> have—but it should be equality of Progress, of Development, not of Decay.

Blackwell also told her that he would remain a bachelor and adopt a dog as an object of affection unless together they could enhance both of their lives.[55]

Lucy grew to love Henry and believed the sincerity of his convictions about marriage, but she was terrified of "self-annihilation," which seemed the inevitable result of marriage for women. She suffered anxiety, terrible head-aches, and indecision. Henry reassured her that they would be mutual helpers and both of their lives richer by marrying, and Lucy wrote that she wanted the same.[56] Finally, Lucy Stone ambivalently and fearfully decided to marry, but she would keep her birth name. On May 1, 1855, Lucy and Henry used the occasion of their wedding to read a protest against the oppressiveness of the institution of marriage. Their protest reveals the oppressive legal condition of nineteenth-century women in marriage.

> While acknowledging our mutual affection by publicly assuming the rela-

tionship of husband and wife, yet in justice to ourselves and a great principle, we deem it a duty to declare that this act on our part implies no sanction of, nor promise of voluntary obedience to such of the present laws of marriage, as refuse to recognize the wife as an independent, rational being, while they confer upon the husband an injurious and unnatural superiority, investing him with legal powers which no honorable man would exercise, and which no man should possess.[57]

Lucy Stone's fears of annihilation were not realized, and she enjoyed a loving, companionate marriage based on equality until her death thirty-seven years later. Henry supported her activism and independence and gave the lie to her critics who expected marriage to "shut her up." Alice Stone Blackwell, their daughter, was born on September 14, 1857. Because of Lucy's fears about neglecting her child, she ceased her activism for ten years, then plunged in again with Henry as her fellow combatant. But even when she left the lecturing circuit, she and Henry published the *Woman's Journal*, the longest-lived women's rights paper.[58]

In the pages of the *Woman's Journal*, Stone and Blackwell published articles advocating the rights of married women to their property and children, and the necessity of divorce for those abused by their husbands. Stone believed in divorce on the grounds of drunkenness and also to end a loveless marriage. Beginning in 1876, she published incidences of "crimes against women." Because of her own experiences of empowerment in marriage, Stone was radical in her views against husbands who abused their wives. She advocated that every state erect whipping posts for wife beaters. She believed that only dread of pain and the disgrace of a public whipping would eliminate wife beating. Moreover, she supported legislation in 1879, 1883, and 1891 to protect a wife whose husband had been convicted of assaulting her. The legislation would have given the wife the right to a legal separation, child support payments, and child custody. The bills failed all three times.[59]

Lucy Stone wrote to her sister-in-law, Antoinette Brown Blackwell, expressing how strongly she believed that a wife must have a "right to herself."

It is clear to me that the question underlies this whole movement and all our little skirmishing for better laws, and the right to vote, will be swallowed up, in the real question, viz. has woman, as wife, a right to herself? It is very little to me, to have the right to vote, to own property & if I may not keep my body, and its uses, in my absolute right. Not one wife in a thousand can do that now, & so long as she suffers this bondage, all other rights will not help her to her true position.[60]

Perhaps Lucy Stone remained out of the public fight over marital reforms because she believed that too open a stand would alienate conservative constituents. Nonetheless, living out their feminist principles in their marriages, both couples—Lucy Stone and Henry Blackwell, and Antoinette Brown Blackwell and Samuel Blackwell—combined a fierce loyalty to the family and to women's equality.

A number of other couples in the nineteenth century also tried to resolve women's dilemma of combining work and love by applying feminist principles in their marriages. Lucretia and James Mott inspired the others. Lucretia Mott, a Quaker minister and mother of six children, formed the Women's Anti-Slavery Society and was a tireless crusader for women's rights. She "preached while bringing up the family, being in perfect amity with her husband who aided her in the care of the children."[61]

Lucretia's husband, James, was outwardly shy and reserved but warm and generous among his friends. He did everything to support Lucretia and accompanied her on her preaching and lecturing tours. Although a reformer himself, James did not seem threatened that his vibrant, energetic wife's reputation exceeded his own. Their granddaughter wrote that it was "impossible to contemplate the lives of these two" without realizing that "*his* life made *hers* a possibility." Lucretia was efficient and well organized. She explained that she was able to accomplish so much because she performed only necessary housekeeping duties; she did no fancy sewing or light reading, and she entertained simply. Many of the reformers who dined at the Motts' recalled that Lucretia would bring a cedar tub of hot water and a snowy cloth to the table after each meal. She would wash the silver and china without any interruption in her brilliant conversation.[62]

Angelina Grimké, another strong feminist, also attempted to have a marriage of true equals. Angelina, the daughter of a South Carolinian slaveholder, published *An Appeal to the Christian Women of the South* in 1836. She was notorious for speaking to audiences of men and women, at a time when it was considered improper for women to speak at all. She and her sister Sarah published *Letters on the Equality of the Sexes and the Condition of Women* in 1838.

On May 14, 1838, Angelina Grimké married Theodore Weld without the aid of a minister or magistrate. They stood before their friends and took each other's right hand. Theodore looked lovingly at his bride and said, "Angelina, I take you to be my lawful wedded wife, and promise to love, honor and cherish and in all things to recognize your equality with me." He "abjured all authority, all government, save the influence which love would give to them over each other as moral and immortal beings." Weld signed a statement giving up his legal rights to her person and property. Angelina promised to honor, prefer, and love him. Then they all knelt, and Theodore and Angelina prayed for God's blessing in marriage and in antislavery. Afterward, two ministers prayed, one black and the other white.

The first years of Angelina's marriage were filled with deep camaraderie and joy. In their middle thirties, Angelina and Theodore recaptured "the innocence and wonder of youthful love," which they integrated into their lives of passionate commitment to reform. They shared deep religious convictions and similar views on antislavery and women's rights. Yet despite the joys of her marriage, Angelina was also entrapped by it. The birth of three children, a miscarriage, and household chores left Angelina a cripple, in great pain from a prolapsed uterus and a hernia. Theodore's stress on self-denial, his fear of opening his private personal self to her, and Angelina's successive troubles with pregnancy caused Angelina to become very tense and to withdraw from public life. They both curtailed their public speaking careers but continued their antislavery agitation through writing and teaching. Angelina and Theodore saw their marriage as a witness to equality. They felt that they needed to redeem marriage from its perversions.

Although Theodore Weld sought to achieve egalitarianism in his marriage, he fell short of his ideal of supporting outspoken, strong women, especially in his relationship to Sarah Grimké. After a public speaking engagement at which Sarah spoke, Weld wrote to her that he had heard from some companions on a stagecoach that her manner of speaking was reported to be "monotonous and heavy" and that her delivery had weakened the power of the truth, rather than increasing it. He said that he was writing her in the spirit of brotherhood. This letter, however, made her doubt herself and the people whom she had trusted. After receiving Weld's letter, Sarah never spoke in public again. The woman who had written the first statement in the country of women's right to equality was vulnerable to Weld's challenge. Weld, who was considered a saint in the abolitionist crusade, did not earn such a title in the struggle for women's rights. But by 1850 the Weld-Grimké marriage had improved considerably.

After a dormant period of activism and the Civil War, the Grimké sisters and Theodore Weld plunged into the struggle for suffrage in the 1870s. Angelina and Theodore remained married until Angelina's death in 1879. Sarah lived with them all her life.[63]

Although Angelina Grimké, Lucy Stone, Lucretia Mott, and Antoinette Brown Blackwell faced difficulties in combining marriage, motherhood, and meaningful work outside the home, they had husbands who did as much as they could to empower them and who loved them as equals. Couples in the late twentieth century who are trying to create egalitarian marriages are still in the minority, but over a hundred years ago these male and female feminists pointed the way. In her study of the lives of fifty-one feminists in the nineteenth century, Blanche Glassman Hersh found that thirty-seven married and that twenty-eight of these had the full support of their husbands for their feminist activities. All but four of the women who married had children. Most of their husbands were urban, middle-class businessmen, editors, writers, teachers, lawyers, or reformers. A large minority were farmers and artisans. A large proportion of them grew up in a Quaker environment or gravitated toward more liberal denominations like Unitarianism and Universalism.[64]

The nineteenth-century feminist marriages were characterized by sharing of activities, decision making, and responsibilities. In addition to Lucy Stone and Henry Blackwell, Angelina and Theodore Weld, and Lucretia and James Mott, many other couples attempted to maintain marriages of equals. Among them were Abby Kelley and Stephen Symonds Foster, Harriet and William Robinson, Mary and Daniel Livermore, Elizabeth and Charles Miller, and Lydia Maria and David Lee Child. Their marriages allowed the women both personal emancipation and meaningful family lives.

Like James Mott, Stephen Symonds Foster was not threatened by his highly successful wife, Abby Kelley Foster. Since she was more in demand as a speaker than he was, Stephen stayed home, worked the farm, and took care of their daughter while Abby traveled extensively. Thomas Wentworth Higginson described them as "two of the very strongest individualities united in one absolutely independent and perfectly harmonious union."[65]

Harriet Robinson worked with her husband, William, on his antislavery newspaper in the 1850s. After the Civil War he helped her in her suffrage activities, and she edited a book of his writings. Similarly, Amelia Bloomer served as her husband's deputy when he was a postmaster and wrote articles for his newspaper. Later he helped her start her own journal, the *Lily*, and shared his newspaper facilities with her. They were married for fifty-four years and reared two adopted children.[66]

Mary A. Livermore and Daniel Livermore had a similar partnership. Mary contributed to Daniel's books and preached in his pulpit. He helped her with her lectures and collected her notes and letters for her autobiography. She was first coeditor and a reporter with him, and then with his help she started her own paper, the *Agitator*. With his help, she wrote *Woman Suffrage Defended*. In

1870 he gave up his paper and pastorate in Chicago to move to Boston so she could become editor of the *Woman's Journal*.[67]

Charles Dudley Miller, a lawyer from a prominent New York family, joined his wife, Elizabeth Smith Miller, in calling for the first national woman's rights convention. He supported her feminist endeavors, including her work for the *Revolution*. Perhaps most difficult of all for him, he accompanied Elizabeth in her bloomer outfit.[68] Similarly, David Lee Child and Lydia Maria Child, both abolitionists, had a "liberated marriage." Lydia Maria left home for long periods of time to edit the newspaper of the American Anti-Slavery Society. The fact that she later supported him with her writing did not seem to threaten him.[69]

These feminists did not reject domesticity but embraced both the public and private spheres. Like many couples of the late twentieth century who are pioneering in creating marriages of true equals, these nineteenth-century couples believed that in order for women and men to lead abundant lives, they had to share fully in both spheres. They did not always live up to their ideal, but they had a large enough network of people trying to do the same thing that they could be supportive of one another.

Nineteenth-century feminists were both empowered and angered by their experiences in marriage. Even the feminists with egalitarian marriages were angry over the abuses which other women suffered in marriage. Family issues were central to the early women's rights movement's analysis of women's oppression and were central to their demands for equality. Stanton, Wright, Rose, and Brown Blackwell along with many Quakers and Spiritualists were vigorous in their critique of oppressive marriages. The activists for women's rights in the nineteenth century did not see a split between their own individual goals and those of the family because they believed that the advancement of women would enhance their effectiveness in the family.

Because of the women's rights movement and economic and demographic changes in the country, by the end of the nineteenth century, women's position in marriage and the public sphere improved. Women gained more control over their own property, equal guardianship of their children, and entrance into some colleges and professions. Industrialization created employment opportunities for women. In the domestic sphere women began to expect more mutuality in marriage and to command more authority in the family. Parental control over marital choice declined, and divorce laws were liberalized, creating greater freedom for men and women. A simultaneous decline in fertility meant that women's lives were potentially less determined by their reproductive role. From 1800 to 1900 fertility of white women in the United States fell from an average of 7.04 children in 1800 to 3.56 in 1900.[70] Although no one can fully account for this decline, women began to have more control over the number of children they had, whether through birth control, abstinence, or abortion.

Although structural changes within the American economy and demographic shifts favored greater sexual equality, nineteenth-century women still did not have the vote, economic independence, or the benefits of full citizenship. Realizing that the achievement of women's equality in the culture would require many more years of struggle, nineteenth-century feminists like Elizabeth Cady Stanton, Susan B. Anthony, Lucy Stone, and Henry Blackwell, along with other feminist couples, developed their own strategies for achieving women's freedom in their personal lives. If both partners desired egalitarian marriages, the feminists were able to make their own domestic accommodation within an oppressive society.

4

POWER IN THE BEDROOM AND
THE NURSERY (1800–1900)

*The passions of men are much stronger and more easily inflamed {than those of
women}.*

Eliza Duffey, *What Women Should Know,* 1873

*Womanhood is the primal fact, wifehood and motherhood its incidents . . .
must the heyday of her existence be wholly devoted to the one animal function
of bearing children? Shall there be no limit to this but woman's capacity to endure the fearful strain on her life?*

Elizabeth Cady Stanton, undated

Although American women were excluded from most areas of public power
in the nineteenth century, they exerted their influence in the domestic sphere
covertly through their sexuality and through motherhood. Nineteenth-
century feminists were at their most radical in their call for women to assert
greater control over their personal lives, even though we might consider the
specific changes they advocated very conservative today. In the 1990s we tend
to think of feminist consciousness in terms of the breaking down of restrictions on women's autonomy; a century ago many feminists called instead for
restrictiveness and social purity in order to benefit women, the family, and the
community. They argued for women's right to say no to sex in order to gain
more autonomy. The widespread cultural expectations of female passionlessness
served as a means for many women to gain more control over their lives, or at
least some leverage. However, the consequence of passionlessness was denial
of feelings and an aggravation of preexisting race- and class-based barriers to
a more broad-based feminist solidarity. Passionlessness presumably did not
apply to African-American, immigrant, or working-class women.

At the same time, a struggle over the control of women's bodies emerged concerning the issue of abortion and the medical profession's control of childbirth and female sexuality, a fight which continues to the present day. As American women confronted the contradictions within a culture which defined them by their sex but denied that they had sexual feelings, they responded in a variety of ways. The majority did not rebel. But some women organized to "purify" society and purge it of intemperance and prostitution, which they believed corrupted sexual relations. Charlotte Perkins Gilman and her followers proposed more radical solutions to women's sexual subordination. Others attacked the sexual double standard and challenged the prevailing belief in female passionlessness in their more egalitarian, sexually expressive marriages.

Through the Bedroom Window

On a cloudy Saturday afternoon, J. Marion Sims, the famous father of American gynecology, knocked on the door of a young couple's house. In his doctor's bag he carried some ether, only recently discovered as an anesthetic. The young wife was afflicted with what Sims termed "vaginismus," a state of frigidity prohibiting intercourse. He "etherized" the wife and left her to her husband, who "cohabited with her with the greatest ease." Sometimes, he would visit the couple two or three times a week to promote "ethereal copulation."[1]

Not all American women in the nineteenth century had to be knocked out to have sex, but the prevailing prescriptive literature proclaimed that women were not sensual by nature and that sexual passivity was "normal" for them. Dr. William Acton, author of *The Functions and Disorders of the Reproductive Organs*, articulated this view: "The majority of women happily for them are not very much troubled with sexual feelings of any kind. What men are habitually, women are only exceptionally."[2]

This view of women as passionless reversed the widely held belief that women were highly sexed, even insatiable, which was prevalent in the United States until the 1790s. Previously women were believed to be less rational, and therefore their control over their passions was supposedly weaker than men's. In the colonial period Calvinists assumed that men and women were at least equally passionate, or that perhaps women were even more lusty than men. To the Puritans marriage was the proper outlet for sexual passion. However, as we have seen, the double standard prevailed in the colonies.

As Nancy Cott points out, the growth of the ideology of feminine passionlessness of women was tied to the spread of evangelical religion from the 1790s to the 1830s, which glorified women's spiritual and moral superiority. The Evangelicals stressed that passionlessness could be redemptive; women's moral superiority could be the agency of men's reform, and their passionlessness could restrain male sexual excess. By the middle of the nineteenth century, physicians and authors of advice literature also emphasized the virtue of female passionlessness. George Savile's *Lady's New Year's Gift* and John Gregory's *Father's Legacy to His Daughter* advised middle-class women that they were made for man's pleasure and service, but they also counseled women to use covert power—manipulation, restraint, affectation, and deception—to control men.[3]

Prescriptive literature emphasized that the goal of sex was procreation and that sexual pleasure for its own sake was a sin. However, Victorian marriage manuals stressed mutual orgasms as promoting conception. Did this mean women who wanted to avoid more children denied themselves pleasure? Did men expect sexual pleasure primarily from prostitutes who used birth control? Did women who enjoyed sex feel guilty?

Because of the reticence of nineteenth-century Americans about sexuality, the truth about their actual sexual practice is elusive. Few couples were bold enough to record their passion on paper. No Alfred Kinsey surveyed them, and no Masters and Johnson observed them. One cannot assume that prescriptive literature matched actual experience.

Through his analysis of a survey by Clelia Mosher, Carl Degler, a historian of the period, has argued provocatively (if with limited evidence) that the Victorian conception of women's sexuality was prescriptive, not descriptive of the practice even of middle-class women.[4] Mosher's survey is the only systematic study available on Victorian sexuality. Her study included a small sample of forty-five middle-class women. Thirty-five women testified that they felt desire for intercourse independent of their husband's interest, while nine said they never or rarely felt such desire. Mosher asked, "[Do] you always have a venereal orgasm?" to which five answered no, sixteen (35 percent) answered always or usually, and eighteen (40 percent) sometimes, not always, or no, but described certain instances. Because of the way the question was phrased, the answers were ambiguous; however, we can infer that three-quarters of the women experienced one or more orgasms sometime during their marriages. Twenty-five women answered that they had intercourse once a week or less, ten once or twice a week, nine more than twice a week, and one did not answer.[5]

Mosher's survey offers evidence for viewing the women as more reluctant than enthusiastic about sex because of their fear of pregnancy; however, it also reveals greater sexual activity and orgasmic delight than is generally assumed. Although the average rate of intercourse among the respondents was about once a week, the average preferred rate was about once a month. They generally believed their husbands needed sex more than they did, and they compromised on the frequency of intercourse because of their husband's needs.[6]

Peter Gay, a historian of Victorian sexuality, concurs with Degler's interpretation that our view of the Victorians as sexually repressed is highly exaggerated and that within marriage women enjoyed sexual relations and acknowledged that they had sexual feelings. Sex surveys conducted in the 1920s and 1930s also tend to challenge our stereotypes about Victorian sexuality.[7] But even if sexual practice diverged from prescriptive advice, women still faced a major contradiction between what they felt and what they were supposed to feel. Given women's fears about the hazards of childbirth and fear of venereal disease, it is not surprising that many of them may have seen the idea of passionlessness as a vehicle of control within their circumscribed roles. By downplaying their sexual, carnal nature and emphasizing their moral superiority, women could legitimately limit their family's size and gain more control over their reproductive lives. The cost of this enhanced control was that women had to deny their own sexuality.

Through the Nursery Window

As nineteenth-century white middle- and upper-class women gained some control over their reproductive lives, they also increased their influence as mothers. The maternal ideal, which became prevalent in the United States toward the end of the eighteenth century, helped to reinforce the cult of domesticity and the ideal of women's passionlessness. The maternal instinct in women was supposedly analogous to men's sex instinct.[8] Although the elevation of motherhood gave women more domestic power, the negative impact was that it led to more sexually differentiated roles and more rigid "separate spheres."

Paradoxically, at the same time women were relegated more influence in parenting, they were also told by "childrearing experts" that they needed special education to be good mothers. Mothers' receptivity to experts' childrearing advice resulted from the shift from an agrarian to an industrial society in which community ties were loosened, mobility increased, and the ties within the female community were broken. Frequently young mothers did not live close to relatives, who previously would have offered advice. In the second half of the nineteenth century many mothers respected a more scientific, psychological approach to childrearing because of the growing legitimacy of the social sciences.

G. Stanley Hall, whose influence was pervasive in the 1890s, emphasized the importance of educated motherhood. He urged that "we must first of all distinctly . . . educate primarily and chiefly for motherhood." Mothers, he believed, ought to respond appropriately to each new stage of a child's development. The idea of infant depravity had declined in the eighteenth century, and children began to be viewed as innocent, needing love and nurturing. Women, more than men, were seen as more suited for this sort of parenting. [9]

Whether experts urged moral or scientific motherhood, marriage and motherhood remained the primary goals of women's lives in the late nineteenth and early twentieth centuries. The glorification of motherhood may have reflected a nervousness about the falling birthrate in the United States. No scholarly agreement exists on why fertility declined in the nineteenth century. Economic interest encouraged some families to have fewer children. The growing scarcity of available land in certain areas may also have discouraged large families. The drop in fertility began with the northern middle class and ultimately extended to all groups in society at different times. Higher birthrates continued in the nineteenth century among immigrants and African-Americans, and in the South and rural areas. In general, but taking into account these regional and racial differences, large numbers of nineteenth-century couples turned to abortion and contraception to limit their families. Coitus interruptus was probably the most common means of birth control. The use of contraception led couples to think of sexual intercourse as separate from a reproductive act. As John D'Emilio and Estelle Freedman point out, sexuality was moving beyond marriage in several ways in the nineteenth century: in prostitution, in utopian communities, and in same-sex relationships. They argue that a shift was occurring in the nineteenth century from sexuality within the family in the context of reproduction to the realm of romantic and physical passion. Women and men became more self-conscious about sexuality as a personal choice and not just a reproductive responsibility. This change proceeded from industrialization and urbanization, which weakened the regulation of sexuality by a community. While the double standard of sexuality for men and women persisted, sexual desires became more associated with a romantic quest for emotional intimacy and even spiritual union, especially in the middle class.[10]

While the meaning of sexuality was changing for some couples, the mother's role in parenting was becoming more dominant, and the father's role diminishing. Childrearing literature spoke only to mothers, who were expected to transmit religious and moral values. The concept of fatherhood was largely absent in the journals and magazines of the period. Because men were physically absent from the home during the day, women assumed most of the childrearing responsibilities. The situation became so noticeable that Arthur Calhoun, a sociologist of the American family, remarked that "under the new order the homes come to be run for the women and children rather than for the man; he was a mere 'earning mechanism' by which they bought fine clothes and vacations."[11]

Other writers responded to men's neglect of home life. Timothy Dwight urged fathers to restore their dominance within the home, even at the expense of their business pursuits. He thought men should spend more time with their children. Rev. Winslow Hubbard also voiced his anxiety about the imbalance between men and women in the home. Joe Dubbert, an American historian, argues that at the turn of the century many American men viewed marriage as an institution dominated by women. He illustrates his point by analyzing the novels of Henry James. In his novels *The Portrait of a Lady* (1881) and *The Bostonians* (1886), James portrays marriage as a commitment defined primarily by the whims of the "new woman." Although this kind of literary statement does not mean that most American men shared Henry James's views, it confirms the sentiments of a number of contemporary commentators on marriage. The widely espoused belief in women's moral superiority implied that men were deficient. Popular magazines occasionally acknowledged men's failings. *Cosmopolitan* magazine reported that, on the basis of "thousands of letters" and "thousands of confessions," women thought men were actually weak. The feminists' assertion that women should exercise their moral influence to reform society implied that the male world was a failure.[12]

The Fight over the Control of Women's Bodies

Whereas white middle- and upper-class women gained more influence as mothers and some control over their reproductive lives through abstinence or birth control, a struggle was being waged over who would ultimately control their bodies. This fight focused on the right of abortion and on the medical profession's attempts to control childbirth and female sexuality. Before the nineteenth century there were no laws against abortions done in the first few months of pregnancy before quickening, or perceived movement of the fetus, which generally occurred late in the fourth month or early in the fifth month of pregnancy. According to James Mohr, before 1840 abortion was perceived in the United States as the act of the desperate, especially young woman who feared the opprobrium of society. After 1840 the social character of abortion seemed to change as evidence indicated that the married, native-born Protestant women of the middle or upper class constituted the highest proportion of those women having abortions.[13]

During the first half of the nineteenth century, many states passed laws against abortion, but women still sought abortions in large numbers from illegal abortionists. Increasingly, abortion began to be widely viewed as dangerous, illegal, and immoral. The medical profession led the antiabortion campaign in the second half of the century. Their response to the abortion "evil" stemmed in part from the general repressive public moralism, higher health standards (which made deaths from abortion less acceptable), and the physicians' attempts to consolidate their authority over unlicensed doctors and midwives.[14]

American male physicians began attending normal childbirths in the middle of the eighteenth century at the invitation of women. Urban and wealthier women believed that since physicians used drugs and instruments like forceps, they knew more than midwives. After 1847 physicians used powerful painkillers. In the late eighteenth century and throughout the nineteenth century, female attendants were also present, even when physicians attended home births. Until childbirth moved to hospitals, home births allowed women to choose attendants and retain more control over physicians' procedures. By 1940 still only 55 percent of American births occurred in hospitals. Class and financial ability largely determined women's childbirth experiences.[15]

As the medical profession became professionalized after the Civil War and gynecological surgery was more successful, doctors began to discredit midwives, who had previously delivered the majority of babies. Eventually they were so successful that by 1930 midwives had been almost eliminated. Delivery methods, performed by male doctors in hospitals in the 1920s and 1930s, placed women on rock-hard tables, legs spread-eagled in uncomfortable metal stirrups, arms pinned to their sides; drugs were given the moment they cried out. Natural childbirth was not encouraged, nor was the husband permitted to witness the birth, much less to comfort his wife during her "ordeal." For most women, childbirth was a time of agony, fear, and ignorance, when their lives were controlled by the male physicians who "delivered" them.

In addition to trying to eliminate midwives, doctors also battled against abortion. They tried to ascertain the number of abortions being performed. Although their statistics were highly unreliable, they estimated that as high as two million abortions were performed each year in the 1890s. Newspapers advertised "Portuguese Female Pills—not to be used during pregnancy, for they will cause miscarriage." Well-known abortionists practiced in major cities, and abortifacients were euphemistically advertised as promising "relief" for married ladies or to "regulate" menstrual periods.[16]

Abortion was an important option for women in the nineteenth century in the absence of reliable birth control methods, especially since doctors and the Roman Catholic church told women that the safe period was two weeks before the menstrual period, the very time a woman is most fertile. Many babies were "rhythm babies." Control of a woman's body was claimed by church, science, and law—all dominated by men who seemed little interested in what the American woman was feeling.

As a result of the success of the doctors' campaign and the social purity movement, women were caught in a double bind—to rid themselves through abortion of a child they did not want and thus risk disease, death, and social ostracism, or to become a baby machine at the mercy of doctors, husbands, and the opinions of a moralistic society. Thus trapped, most nineteenth-century women endured their fate, fearing to transgress the laws of church and state.

Nineteenth-century doctors believed that the psyche of the angel in the house was defined by her sexual organs. Therefore, gynecological surgery became a means to treat women's psychological disorders. Barker-Benfield reports that clitoridectomy was performed in the United States as a cure for female masturbation. Doctors railed that masturbation would lead to insanity, blindness, epilepsy, and even death. Clitoridectomies were performed from the 1860s until 1904. Female castration, or "normal ovariotomy," was first performed in the United States in 1872, widely done between 1880 and 1900, and continued into the first decade of the twentieth century.[17] This barbarous cure for masturbation and hysteria persisted because doctors believed that drastic measures were necessary.

By the end of the nineteenth century, the medical profession had established greater control over women's bodies by prohibiting abortion and by eliminating the widespread usage of midwives in childbirth. Feminists shared the doctors' opposition to abortion but still fought for women's right to control their own bodies.

The Feminist Response

In sharp contrast to the contemporary feminist movement's endorsement of abortion and birth control, the early women's rights advocates generally did not ally themselves with these causes. Henry C. Wright's *The Unwelcome Child* stated what became the most prevalent feminist position in the 1850s. Wright claimed that women alone had the right to determine when they would become pregnant and blamed the tremendous increase in the number of abortions in the country on selfishly sensual husbands. Elizabeth Cady Stanton agreed with Wright that abortion was the result of "the degradation of woman" in the nineteenth century, not of woman's rising consciousness or expanding opportunities outside the home. For Stanton and other feminists, the remedy was not legalized abortion open to all but "the education and enfranchisement of women," which would make abortion unnecessary because of the resulting egalitarian respect and elimination of sexual discrimination. Matilda Joslyn Gage contended "that this crime of 'child murder,' 'abortion,' 'infanticide' lies at the door of the male sex."[18]

In the 1850s and 1860s the medical profession began a systematic attack on permissive abortion practices. Carroll Smith-Rosenberg points out that this move stemmed from the complex interaction between long-term social and economic change and the wide-ranging effects such change had on the bourgeois birthrate, on relations between bourgeois women and men, on abortion practices, and on the needs of the medical profession. She claims that during the 1860s, 1870s, and 1880s, two conflicting mythic figures existed: the women writers' image of the lustful and uncontrollable husband, and the male writer's image of the unnatural, aborting wife. She believes that these both expressed bourgeois women's and men's disparate fears over social changes.[19]

In response to anxieties about the dangers which the family faced, many of the early advocates of the women's rights movement were involved in the social purity movement, which had first been organized to oppose the legalization of prostitution. Susan B. Anthony delivered a public address in Chicago in 1875 against the regulation of prostitution. She asserted that the "tap-root of the social evil was woman's dependence, woman's subjection." She believed that sex reform would not be achieved through the easy fix of regulating prostitution, but only as part of a thoroughgoing feminist transformation. Women must obtain equal education, equality in marriage, economic independence, and "all possible rights and powers to control the conditions and circumstances of their own and their children's lives." Stanton and Lucretia Mott also opposed regulation of prostitution.[20]

When the threat of regulation was not realized, social purity advocates began to campaign in the 1880s for prosecuting customers of prostitutes, as well as the prostitutes. The advocates of social purity also worked to reform prostitutes, censor pornography, stop abortion, and provide police matrons and sexually segregated prisons.[21]

Social purity advocates believed that women and children needed to be protected from alcohol, which inflamed the passions and caused men to go to prostitutes, who gave them syphilis, the scourge of the nineteenth century before any cure like penicillin. Venereal disease struck the kind of terror in the hearts of people that AIDS does in the 1990s. According to the advocates of moral purity, intemperance and prostitution meant the creation of a race of imbecilic, deformed, and infirm people. They believed that marriage had to be sanctified and that men must have higher moral values, or else venereal disease would taint future generations and endanger their wives. Therefore, women must be empowered politically to protect their homes from the hazards of industrial life, the saloon, and the brothel.[22]

Men's excessive drinking highlighted women's physical and economic vulnerability within the family. Temperance crusaders could focus on this vulnerability without openly challenging the family or attacking men personally. In addition, women opposed the saloon as a symbol of women's exclusion from men's lives. After work many men headed for the saloons, rather than their homes.[23]

The Women's Christian Temperance Union had 76,000 members by the turn of the century, becoming the largest American women's organization of the time or earlier. Frances Willard, the leader of the WCTU, was a strong feminist and helped move the organization toward support for suffrage.[24] Not all crusaders in the moral purity movement were feminists, but within the coalition was a very substantial women's rights contingent. Although disagreeement persisted over the issue of censorship and some members' endorsement of sex education, they agreed on the concept of voluntary motherhood. The feminists who favored voluntary motherhood were members of the suffrage movement, moral reform movements like temperance and social purity, church auxiliaries, and women's professional and service organizations. Even the free-love advocates, who disagreed over many issues with these other groups, also believed in voluntary motherhood.

The feminists argued that women ought to control their own bodies; they used the argument of a special motherly nature and sexual purity of women as a justification for increasing their status and freedom. They endorsed voluntary motherhood achieved through periodic or even permanent abstinence. Not all of them were against sexual activity within marriage without the intention of conceiving, but they invariably wanted to control male "sexual excess." The reformers wanted to minimize women's risks surrounding sex and childbirth and to discourage promiscuity.[25]

The crusade for purification of sexual mores was even more radical than the demand for education or the vote because the moral reformers invaded bordellos, befriended prostitutes, and publicly discussed rape, prostitution, and seduction. In trying to rescue prostitutes, the genteel lady reformers began to realize their common sexual, legal, and political oppression with working-class and lower-class women. Working-class women seemed most in need of uplift because their presumed greater sexual activity and their employment outside the home subverted strict notions of domesticity and the angel in the house. As Christine Stansell points out, sexuality was both a consequence of social autonomy and its metaphor. The factory girl's real sin was not premarital sex but her assertiveness with her fancy clothes and bold behavior. The possibilities for a life for working women outside the household were threatening to the traditional family.[26]

Like promiscuity and prostitution, alcoholism became a symbol for the endangerment of the home. The women's temperance crusade enabled women to gain a sense of strength in female collective action and to acquire leadership and organizational skills. An incident which occurred in Ohio in 1873 reflected the sense of empowerment which the moral crusaders experienced. Charles Van Pelt was a stubborn saloonkeeper who retaliated against the temperance women when they visited his saloon. He threw dirty water and beer on them. When they returned the next morning, he threatened them with a bloody ax. He was arrested, however, and afterward agreed to surrender publicly before the crusaders. Barrels of liquor were rolled out into the street and split open. Van Pelt repented, and even lectured on the temperance circuit for a short time.[27]

Both the moral reform groups and the women's rights advocates found women's passive social role intolerable, and they sought to assert female values in the "male" world. Members of both groups valued the experience of sisterhood and believed in female moral superiority.[28] But the women's rights advocates wanted not only to protect women from violent, abusive men who abandoned their families but also to eliminate the sources of women's victimization. Moreover, some feminists believed that women's acknowledgment of their own sexuality, not repression, would enhance their liberation.

Elizabeth Cady Stanton was open in her advocacy of both voluntary motherhood and the acknowledgment of female sexuality. She believed that women ought to enjoy their sexuality within marriage but also ought to have control over their own bodies. She believed that ignorance about their bodies, denial of pleasure, and loss of mutuality in marriage were the doleful consequences of denying women's sexual identities. Stanton attacked the ideas of passionlessness in her response to Walt Whitman's poem "There Is a Woman Waiting for Me": "He speaks as if the female must be forced to the creative act, apparently ignorant of the great natural fact that a healthy woman has as much passion as a man, that she needs nothing stronger than the law of attraction to draw her to the male."[29] On her lecture tours in 1871 Stanton held *women only* afternoon meetings in order to discuss "the gospel of fewer children & a healthy happy maternity." Stanton believed that if women would observe some simple health precautions, they could eliminate pain in childbirth.[30]

However radical Stanton was in her sexual ideology, she opposed birth control devices and abortion, though she sympathized with women who had abortions and believed that the abortion question exemplified women's victimization by laws made by men without their consent. She shared the view of other feminists in the nineteenth century that women ought to determine when and how often they wanted to get pregnant. Fearing that widespread legal birth control would give men more freedom to be irresponsible in their sexual behavior, she opted for the solution of voluntary motherhood.[31] Stanton wanted to limit men's sexual excess but not to deny women's sexuality.

Angela Heywood, a reformer for social purity, was more radical than Stanton in her attacks on men's unrestrained sexuality; she bitterly denounced men. Heywood deplored men's victimization of women: "Man so lost to himself and woman as to invoke legal *violence* in these sacred nearings, *should have solemn meeting with, and look serious at his own penis until he is able to be lord and master of it, rather than it should longer rule, lord and master, of him and of the victims he deflowers.*"[32] Although other feminists spoke more delicately, they basically agreed with Heywood's sentiment and fought to control male sexuality.

Charlotte Perkins Gilman, the major theoretician of the women's rights movement in the late nineteenth and early twentieth centuries, agreed with Heywood that men were oversexed. But she believed that women who were overly feminine were also "oversexed." She endorsed the principle of voluntary motherhood and believed that men ought to have higher moral standards, but she also believed that more fundamental changes were needed in order to liberate women. Whereas the crusaders for moral purity indicted women's physical and economic vulnerability within a male-dominated society, Gilman went further in analyzing the causes of women's subordination and offered solutions. Influenced heavily by the evolutionary theory of Lester Frank Ward and by socialism, she pressed for a radical reform of marriage and motherhood.

Gilman was a member of an old, distinguished New England family, the Beechers. Gilman was the great-granddaughter of Lyman Beecher, and the grandniece of Catharine Beecher, Harriet Beecher Stowe, Isabella Beecher Hooker, and Henry Ward Beecher.[33] She married Walter Stetson in 1884 and had a child in 1885. The restrictions of domesticity and child care plunged her into deep depression, relieved only when she was absent from her family.

Gilman fought her own private battle with attempts of the medical profession to control her sexuality and creativity. Like many women of the period, she sought help for her depression from Weir Mitchell, a famous physician of the time, who prescribed the "rest cure" and the water cure. Gilman was confined to bed, allowed no intellectual stimulation, and given cold baths. When Gilman underwent Mitchell's "cure," it drove her over the edge. Since her depression originally stemmed from her inability to express herself creatively, the enforced passivity and lack of intellectual activity were torturous. In Gilman's powerful, autobiographical story "The Yellow Wallpaper," the woman goes insane and begins to creep around the room, tearing the wallpaper off the wall in an attempt to free the "woman in the wallpaper."

Gilman divorced Stetson in 1894 after discovering that her spirits lifted considerably when she left him and her daughter for a stay in California. After years of writing and lecturing, she married Houghton Gilman in 1900. As revealed in their letters, they enjoyed a warm, satisfying relationship for thirty-four years. He supported her career and was a loving companion. But her relationship with her daughter, Katherine, was problematic. Katherine felt some bitterness toward her famous mother and felt abandoned. Katherine was very close to Grace Channing, her stepmother. Gilman and Grace Channing were very old friends, and when Gilman could not cope with being a single parent, she sent nine-year-old Katherine to live with Grace and her new husband, Walter Stetson, because she believed that Grace would be a better mother.

Not only was Charlotte considered notorious as a divorced woman, but she had "abandoned" her husband and child. [34] Ironically, Grace was also an aspiring writer and was highly intelligent, but she took the other fork in the path, stepped into Charlotte's place, and lived a traditional life as wife and mother. Both Grace Channing and Charlotte Perkins Gilman were forced to choose between career and motherhood.

Gilman did not believe that women ought to have to make such a choice. In 1906 she pointed out the injustice of forcing women to choose.

> We have so arranged life that a man may have a home and family, love, companionship, domesticity, and fatherhood, yet remain an active citizen of age and country. We have so arranged life, on the other hand, that a woman must "choose"; must either live alone, unloved, uncompanied, uncared for, homeless, childless, with her work in the world for sole consolation; or give up all world-service for the joys of love, motherhood, and domestic service. [35]

In *Women and Economics* (1898), Gilman attacked the patriarchal nature of marriage. She argued that to be free, women had to be economically independent. She called for new forms of domestic organization in the name of improved motherhood. Gilman wanted to replace the conventional home and conventional motherhood with a feminist model. Paid professional domestic workers would perform housework with efficiency, and collective kitchens and kitchenless apartments would free women from cooking. Professionals would provide child care in order to free women to work outside the home. [36]

Gilman protested the imprisonment of women in the home and the sharp segregation of the public world as men's province, and the home as exclusively women's. Some of the consequences of this division were inefficiency, waste, women's mental myopia, degradation of art, inferior mothering, narrowing of both men and women, and women's economic dependence. She did not attack the family unit as intrinsically oppressive to women but believed that housework and child care should be professionalized and made more scientific, benefiting all family members. [37] She argued:

> Is it not time that the home be freed from these industries so palpably out of place? That the care of the children become at last what it should be—the noblest and most valuable profession to the endless profit of our little ones and progress of the race? And that our homes [be] no longer greasy, dusty

workshops, but centres of rest and peace, no longer gorgeous places of entertainment that does not entertain, but quiet places of happiness.[38]

Gilman sought to replace women's "instinct, affection and duty" with "knowledge, practice, and business methods." Cooking, housekeeping, and child care would be done scientifically. Under this improved system, homes would be more beautiful, loving relationships more possible, and a "larger womanhood, a civilized womanhood" evolve. Gilman believed that "mother-love" was the source of all human affection but was limited by the traditional home. Because of the narrowing qualities of the private sphere for women, the home did not promote the courage needed to confront the problems of the society.[39] She believed that permanent, monogamous marriage was the highest stage of evolutionary development. While she believed that men and women were more similar than different, she acknowledged that they might make different contributions to society. In any case, both men and women must be able to be fully human.

Gilman tried to allay the fears of those who might think she was attacking motherhood. Her material feminism proposed to improve the environment for children, not by separating the mother and child, but by enabling women to be better mothers by eliminating the drudgery of housework, expanding their intellectual capacities, and giving them economic independence. By increasing the productive labor force by nearly one-half and cutting the cost of living by two-thirds, the home could be truly a place of "complete rest, comfort, peace, and invigoration." Gilman concluded her treatise on the home on a rhapsodic note.

So, living, really living in the world and loving it, the presence there of father, mother, and child will gradually bring out in it all the beauty and safety, the refreshment and strength we so vainly seek to ensure in our private home. The sense of duty, of reverence of love, honesty, transferred to the world we live in, will have its natural, its inevitable effect, and make that world our home at last.[40]

Earlier Stanton had occasionally run articles in the *Revolution* on cooperative housekeeping, and she had urged Anthony to include the topic on NAWSA's agenda in 1899, arguing that "woman's work can never be properly organized in the isolated home." At the time, few women agreed. When Gilman criticized the home as an isolated, domestic workplace where women worked without pay, a larger number of women endorsed her views.[41] Gilman's "material feminism" was based on utilizing technological improvements in order to professionalize housekeeping and child care, thus freeing women to be better wives and mothers and to gain economic independence. She was joined by Melusina Fay Peirce, Marie Stevens Howland, Victoria Woodhull, Mary Livermore, Ellen Swallow Richards, Mary Hinman Abel, Antoinette B. Blackwell, Mary Kenney O'Sullivan, Julia Ward Howe, Frances Willard, Henrietta Rodman, and Ethel Puffer Howes. Their ideas were preached for sixty years, but Americans did not rush to cooperative housekeeping in droves. Some community dining services were set up, and a few experimental cooperative ventures tried, but most Americans seemed intent on privatized family life.

Although kitchenless homes, professionalized domestic work, and child care seemed radical at the time, the material feminists maintained that women could become better wives and mothers if they were freed from drudgery. While social feminists sought to improve women's status in the home and to use their special nurturant powers and moral superiority to redeem society, the more radical material feminists proposed a strategy to accomplish these goals. They believed that their own fulfillment was tied to the fate of the family and sought to remove the restrictions of separate spheres. Like Gilman, they believed that women must become fully human: "It is our world, men and women, too. Not women alone and not men alone, it is our world. The pain and sickness, the disease, the vice, the crime, the shame of the world is our fault too. It is our fault because we are not fulfilling our place on earth as human beings. We are so busy being women."[42] Gilman contributed to the women's rights movement by analyzing the sources of women's subordination and recommending solutions to male supremacy. She believed that women would never be free until homemaking and motherhood were professionalized and they had economic independence and control of their bodies.

As we have seen, a debate raged over who would control female sexuality—the state, doctors, men, or women. By the 1880s, men controlled women's access to abortion. Feminists fought for women's right to control their reproductive lives through voluntary motherhood. How widespread the commitment was to voluntary motherhood would be difficult to document. One thing is clear—because of the decline in fertility, women's lives were less consumed by bearing and rearing children. Women's "superior" morality impelled them to enter the public sphere for their families' welfare. For some women, their increasing power in the domestic arena gave them the courage and anger to extend their sphere. The crusaders for moral purity fought against women's victimization in the home and struggled to eliminate alcohol and prostitution, which threatened their security.

For some women passionlessness became a vehicle of female power and feminist consciousness by encouraging female bonding. Passionlessness fostered a consciousness of women as a separate class, possessing superior moral qualities, who were defined as thinkers and workers, not just reproductive partners. However, passionlessness deprived women of enjoying their sexuality.

The ideology of passionlessness, like the cult of true womanhood, excluded African-American, working-class, and immigrant women, since they were stereotyped as more sensual by nature and as incapable of such self-restraint. The myth of the bad black woman had helped justify their rape by slaveowners and continued as part of the complex psychology of interracial sexuality. Southerners justified lynching of black men on the pretext of protection of white womanhood.[43]

Male control of female sexuality was one way to keep the white middle-class angel in the house. By the end of the nineteenth century, the medical profession had gained significant influence over childbirth, defining and managing female sexuality and controlling access to abortion. Feminists generally believed that voluntary motherhood was a key to women's autonomy. Faced with more legal, educational, and professional opportunities, some women chose a single, celibate life devoted to a profession and independence. Many working-class women, however, had to combine marriage, employment, and motherhood.

During Reconstruction African-Americans rushed to legalize and sanctify marriages, to locate missing family members, and to establish two-parent households. Demographic studies reveal that 70–90 percent of black families after the Civil War were two-parent families. Although female domesticity was part of the ideal of black family life, married African-American women were seven times as likely to work as white married women in the 1870s. By the end of Reconstruction, half of the black women over sixteen were in the paid labor force.[44] Black women in the 1890s were often leading the way in establishing marriages that deviated from the idealized Victorian model.

As African-Americans were struggling to establish stable families, some daring white middle- and upper-class couples were experimenting with unconventional marriages. Much more evidence exists about the sexual content of these couples' lives than about the lives of African-Americans.

Unconventional Marriages

The following portraits of four marriages represent nineteenth-century couples who attempted to work out satisfying relationships within the context of societal repression of sexuality and who became the forerunners of more egalitarian, sexually expressive marriages. The Cabots, Wards, Todds, and Londons departed from prescribed behaviors associated with marriage and courtship. Their unconventional relationships help to illustrate how women chose different paths to achieve autonomy and equality.

The Cabots of Boston embodied many nineteenth-century values but chose an unconventional kind of marriage. Ella Lyman and Richard Cabot met and fell in love in Boston in the 1890s. Their relationship was unlike most nineteenth-century marriages because of their wealth and advanced education. Their marriage marked a departure from societal expectations because they practiced the feminist principle of voluntary motherhood and sought to create a marriage of true equals. Like other nineteenth-century middle- and upper- class couples, however, the Cabots exchanged soulful letters exploring the dimensions of their feelings in the time before the invention of the telephone, which changed courtship irrevocably. Couples of their class expected mutuality, sympathy, and commonality in their relationships. They did not want emotional abandon, but rather the "appreciation of each other's character and the strong sympathy and similitude of thought and feeling."[45] In order to guard against the hazards of overidealization of one's mate, a danger inherent in romantic love, men and women sought candor in their relationships. Their letters reflected a preoccupation with exploring their deepest feelings and characters in order to be sure they loved each other for themselves. Both men and women were expected to exert self-control over their passions, but especially men.[46]

The Cabots shared many of these beliefs about relationships, but like the feminists of the early nineteenth century, they pioneered in the creation of a truly egalitarian marriage. Ella Lyman Cabot was an educator, author, and lecturer who lived from 1866 to 1934. She attended Radcliffe from 1889 to 1891 and took graduate courses at Harvard from 1897 to 1903. She subsequently taught ethics and applied psychology at private schools in Boston and at Pine Manor, Massachusetts, and wrote seven books on ethics and childhood education.[47] Ella's husband, Richard Clark Cabot, who lived from 1868 to 1939, was a physician and professor of medicine and social ethics at Harvard.

In an era when women felt that they had to choose between marriage and career, Ella refused to choose and sustained a rich career and a loving marriage. Their courtship extended over six years, during which they opened their hearts to one another. On October 24, 1889, Richard wrote to Ella: "You stand for many of the purposes and attainments I love best; you reveal possibilities I hardly dreamed of and make them ultimately possible for me too, you encourage only what is best in me."[48] Richard was deeply impressed by reading her diary, which she shared with him, and even years later he still referred to the impact which his reading of it had on him. She had written, "Above all things may we strive against the crime of indifference, beyond all things may we *care* intensely." Both of them were students of Josiah Royce, an American Hegelian. They "cared intensely" about philosophy and shared strong religious convictions.[49]

In addition to their long letters about philosophy and ethics, they discussed sexual roles and stereotypes. Once Richard wrote that he realized that women's education tended to leave courage undeveloped and that initiative in women was frowned on as unfeminine.[50] He respected Ella's intellectual gifts and encouraged her professional ambitions.

Nevertheless, when Richard proposed marriage, Ella was far from ready for such a change in her life. She was happy in her close relationship with her parents and enjoyed unrestrained gaiety with her friends. Consequently, she viewed marriage as inhibiting. She replied: "As yet I have not realized the meaning of marriage, and it is so sacred a tie that I must grow into the knowledge of it before I enter its presence. I am unworthy to share your life unless I can give myself to you with perfect oneness and I cannot now."[51] Despite Ella's reticence, Richard persisted, outlining how she could marry him and still maintain her independence.

> I mean marriage without children. You assume, as almost everybody does, that the earlier years of married life will of necessity be taken up in the care of children. You ignore the possibility, that *lies wholly in our own hands*, of not having children. I conceive that two people might find they could be better servants of God by living and working together in a house of their own and belonging specially to each, who yet found it expedient not to have any children. . . . If there are no children there is no need why the housekeeping should not be evenly divided between husband and wife, either of Pres[ident] Eliot's plan (the husband keeping house ½ the year and wife t'other), or dividing the daily work the whole year round.[52]

Although Richard proposed that they enter marriage and continue "absolutely equal," Ella was still unconvinced. Like Lucy Stone earlier, Ella was reluctant to trust such promises. She replied that she loved her life as it was, including her independence. She wrote, "My social atmosphere is so rich and yet free; I have in an unusual degree the maximum of doing what I want and the minimum of what bores me." She was less sure than Richard that men and women ought to marry resolving not to have children.[53]

Both Ella and Richard had other courtship possibilities. Another man had proposed to Ella, and Richard had greatly disappointed a woman who was in love with him. Finally, when Richard was going to go to Europe for a long time, Ella was compelled to decide once and for all. They were married on October 16, 1894.

The Cabots never had children, and they pursued their separate careers as planned. Their letters over their long marriage reflect the same devotion, appreciation, and loving for forty years, until the time of Ella's death. In 1929 Ella wrote to Richard:

> It is also your un-native nobly acquired patience that makes my love leap up like a fire revealing its deep glow with sudden joy. . . . Most of all though, it is still as it was since the beginning, when you are in the presence of eternal thoughts that I see you, and worship with you in the mountain peaks of music, of philosophy, of poetry, of consolation through faith, the heaven on earth, of deep and amazing love.[54]

Because of their determination not to have children, Ella and Richard Cabot were not typical of the nineteenth century, but their marriage reflected the feminist ideal of voluntary motherhood and an egalitarian marriage. The record does not reveal whether Richard stuck by his promise to do half of the housework, but he and Ella sustained a mutually rewarding partnership. Because Ella's culture idealized motherhood so much, she must have at times wondered whether she was giving up too much for her career. She did not believe that she could do justice to both a career and children, but she was immensely happy with the choices which she made.

Two other Victorian lovers had an unconventional relationship: Lester Ward and Lizzie Vought. Ward recorded their passionate romance in his journal from 1860 to 1870. When he met Lizzie in 1860, he fell madly in love with her, and within a month they were kissing and declaring their love for one another. By early the next year, the couple advanced to new levels of physical intimacy. Ward wrote, "The girl and I have had a very sweet time. I kissed her on her sweet breasts and took too many liberties with her sweet person and we are going to stop. It is a very fascinating practice and instills very sweet, tender and familial feelings in us, and consequently makes us happy."

A year after they had declared their love, they simply were unable to keep their resolution about stopping short of "sweet communion." Ward wrote on October 25, 1861, "Her mother was ill, but her sister had gone away and all was well. That evening and that night we experienced the joys of love and tasted the felicity which belongs to married life alone." They were married in August 1862, and Ward went to fight in the Civil War. According to Ward's diary, Lester and Lizzie enjoyed an extremely happy marriage. They were devoted to one another and continued to enjoy "entering Paradise" together. One would like to have Lizzie's view of the relationship in order to understand how she viewed intimacy before marriage, but she was silent on the question.[55]

After they were married and Lizzie became pregnant, they both felt that they could not afford a child at that time; parenthood would reduce the possibility of ever realizing their individual goals of self-improvement or their goals as a couple. Early in 1864, without her husband's knowledge, Lizzie aborted the child. The decision was the result of a preexisting understanding between the two of them. Ward was delighted that his wife was not having the child. In the summer of 1865, when he obtained a decent job in Washington, the couple did have a baby.[56]

Like the Wards, another couple enjoyed the joys of intimacy before marriage but seem to have stopped short of intercourse. After marriage, however, they defied conventional morality by having sexual affairs with others. Mabel Loomis grew up in Washington, D.C., during the Civil War, took romantic walks, and had numerous suitors. She wrote a journal of her erotic life which is singular in its explicitness and candor. Many middle-class women kept diaries in the nineteenth century, but few like Mabel recorded their sexual history. Mabel Loomis's diary charts her adolescent sexual awakening and her premarital sexual experimentation.[57]

After many flirtations, Mabel married David Peck Todd, a promising young astronomer. After their marriage on March 5, 1879, their sexual ardor only increased. Mabel wrote five months after they were married: "David is more passionately my lover than he ever was before our marriage, and I feel most deeply grateful to God for giving me in my husband a man whose fresh springs of deepest tenderness and love grow fuller & fuller every day, encompassing me with the sweetest life-fountains that a woman's life can ever know." Their daughter Millicent was conceived when Mabel tested her belief about fertility. Mabel believed that "the *only* fruitful time could be at the climax moment of my sensation—*that* once passed, I believed the womb could close and no fluid could reach the fruitful point." She was obviously wrong, and their coitus interruptus, which they normally practiced, was more reliable.[58]

The Todds had moved to Amherst in 1881. Shortly thereafter, Mabel began an affair with Austin Dickinson, Emily Dickinson's brother, lasting from the early 1880s until his death in April 1890. Their affair was scandal enough for the small town. Dickinson was also married, but because of his stature in the community, his neighbors ignored his infidelity. Austin came to Mabel's house in the evening, where upstairs, behind a locked door, they made love. David Todd and their daughter Millicent were fully aware of the affair, and David seemed to encourage it. He had begun to have affairs himself shortly after their marriage. The three went on trips together, and Austin and David were close friends. Mabel and David continued to have a close relationship, and for their own reasons sustained an "open marriage."[59]

Jack and Charmian London represented another kind of marriage in the early twentieth century. When Jack London met Charmian Kittredge, she was in her early thirties, unmarried, and making her living as a stenographer. She was experienced sexually and seemed to feel no guilt about it. They began a torrid affair while Jack London was still married, and later he left his wife and two children for her. London was looking for a mistress, but he was impressed by Charmian's openness and lack of inhibition. He wrote to her in 1903:

> This I do know, that I love you. My arms are about you. I kiss you on the lips, the free frank lips I know and love. I have been wondering why I love you, and I think, in a dim way, that I know. I love you for your beautiful body, and for your beautiful mind that goes with it. Had you been coy and fluttering, giving the lie to what you had always appeared to be by manifesting the slightest prudery or false fastidiousness, I really think I would have been utterly disgusted.[60]

Jack London and Charmian Kittredge were married in 1905. Charmian was perfect in her husband's eyes because she was androgynous. She was hearty, fenced, swam, rode horses, could sail a ship, and even boxed with him. Yet she retained many of the qualities of "true womanhood." She worshiped him, was submissive, typed all his manuscripts, and was totally devoted to him. She enjoyed sex tremendously, and she uninhibitedly recorded their lovemaking in her diaries, which she kept all of her life. They enjoyed an exciting, intimate marriage, sailed the South Pacific in their boat *The Snark*, and traveled all over the United States and the Caribbean. They played together, read together, and were genuine companions. But their marriage was not without tragedy; their daughter, Joy, died within a few days of her birth, and Jack London died at the early age of forty. Unlike Scott and Zelda Fitzgerald, whose relationship was so tortured, Jack and Charmian had a generally happy marriage and saw one another as genuine partners. One reason it worked so well was that Charmian was a "new woman," but she was traditional enough to "worship her man."[61]

Each of the four couples mentioned departed from the conventional stereotypes of Victorian sexuality and marriage. The Cabots had a truly egalitarian marriage based on developing their own careers; they practiced the feminist principle of voluntary motherhood and decided not to have children. The other couples engaged in premarital sexual experimentation, and in the Todds's case, in extramarital sexual encounters. These couples represented the stirrings within the country for a redefinition of marriage and women's roles within marriage and were pioneers of sexually expressive, egalitarian relationships. They continued in the tradition of the early feminists' attempts to create more freedom for women in marriage, but in the cases of the Wards, Todds, and Londons, they also sought sexual freedom. At the same time, a small group of radicals began to reject marriage as an institution and argued for free love.

5

THE SEX RADICALS
Feminists against the Traditional Family

No woman can call herself free who does not own and control her body. No woman can call herself free until she can choose consciously whether she will or will not be a mother.

Margaret Sanger, 1920

A true conception of the relation of the sexes will not admit of conqueror and conquered; it knows of but one great thing: to give of one's self boundlessly, in order to find one's self richer, deeper, better. That alone can fill the emptiness, and transform the tragedy of woman's emancipation into joy, limitless joy.

Emma Goldman, 1906

Certain topics were almost universally taboo in nineteenth-century America. Even husbands and their wives avoided discussing sex, homosexuality, prostitution, insanity, illegitimate children, birth control, and suicide. In a time when nudity was considered indecent, Hiram Powers's statue of a nude female titled *Greek Slave* caused an uproar. Some museums had a "ladies hour" when women could view the statue without the "blush-producing presence of men." An enterprising curator in Cincinnati put a calico blouse and flannel drawers on the statue to protect the viewer's modesty.[1]

Within this atmosphere of reserve, sex radicals like Frances Wright, Victoria Woodhull, Emma Goldman, Margaret Sanger, and the Greenwich Village radicals rejected the belief in female passionlessness and fought for women's control over their bodies and their sexuality. In contrast to most feminists, who saw marriage as a potential source of women's primary power and wanted men to live up to higher moral standards, the sex radicals represented a distinct minority. Because they believed that the institution of marriage trapped women economically and sexually, their views were considered dangerous to the mainstream feminists, who were afraid that the women's rights movement might come to be associated with encouraging sexual libertinism and thus be regarded as a threat to marriage and the family.

For some women like the Quakers, covert domestic power nurtured feminism. As we have seen, many advocates for women's rights throughout the nineteenth century focused on family issues because they were outraged over the victimization of women by intemperate, violent, and "overly sensual" men. In contrast, the sex radicals recognized that women fundamentally lacked power over crucial domestic sexual relations and therefore called for a radical feminist transformation of marriage and sexuality. Caught between opponents of women's rights who argued that the vote for women would destroy the family on one side, and the sex radicals on the other, moderate feminists may have been encouraged to take a more traditional, profamily stance. The radicals damaged the movement by alienating some prospective supporters; they made the reformers appear *less* radical, however, and thus made their views more acceptable.

To the moderates' chagrin, many of the radicals' ideas were assimilated by American society by the 1920s, when female sexuality was celebrated. Coming from diverse ethnic and class backgrounds and different time periods, the radicals were part of an underground tradition espousing free love, sexual liberation from marriage, and women's full sexual expression and reproductive control. Not only did they foreshadow developments of the 1920s and the sexual liberation movement of the 1960s and 1970s, but they also challenged the capitalist system. Despite the radicalism of these women, they too were unable to escape fully the specter of the angel in the house, and they had great difficulty resolving the central dilemma of their lives—combining love and achievement. But their advocacy of birth control, freer sexuality, and the removal of sexuality from the confines of marriage eventually became a kind of sexual orthodoxy years later.

The origins of free-love ideas lay in the utopian, communitarian movement of the early nineteenth century. Free-love advocates argued that women ought to be able to share their bodies with whomever they wished, without necessarily being married to that person. But they did not believe in indiscriminate, unemotional sexual relationships. Like Rousseau and other Enlightenment thinkers, they believed in the innate goodness of human beings and believed that institutions corrupted people. Applying these ideas to sexuality, they believed that repressive society caused people to develop obsessional sexual practices and that the natural state was that of self-regulating moderation. They had a romantic, idealized conception of the connection between love and sexuality and believed that traditional marriage tended to restrict one's natural desires.

Frances Wright, Victoria Woodhull, and Emma Goldman

Frances Wright was perhaps the first woman in the United States to espouse publicly the views of feminism and free love. Wright's picture appeared in the front of the first volume of *The History of Woman Suffrage*, written by Stanton, Anthony, and Matilda Joslyn Gage. Whether because of or despite her radical views, the authors regarded her as a foremother of the movement. In 1825 Wright became the first woman in the United States to oppose slavery publicly. Three years later, she was the first woman to speak in public before a large secular audience of men and women. She argued that women and men were equal and that women were entitled to equality in all areas of public life. Wright also attacked the wage slavery of the North and the hypocrisy of churches that ignored injustice around them, while sending missionaries overseas.[2]

A friend of Lafayette, Jefferson, and Robert Owen, Wright found few other friends in the United States when she came over from Scotland. Her views on slavery were progressive, and she was a proponent of free love and miscegenation. Wright spoke of sexual passion as the "strongest and . . . the noblest of the human passions" and "the source of the best joys of our existence." Influenced by Robert Owen's experiment at New Harmony, Indiana, Wright established Nashoba, a utopian community fifteen miles from Memphis, Tennessee, an inhospitable place for a social dreamer because of the conservative attitudes of the local population. Although she was an opponent of slavery, she purchased ten slaves and over two thousand acres. She hoped to have them purchase their freedom. Wright proclaimed that "as for the marriage laws, at Nashoba they would have no force." Miscegenation would be permitted as a means for solving the racial problem.[3]

Wright hoped to found a school and promote a loving, biracial community which would provide an alternative to the traditional home. She argued that the races were already mixing because of the rape of African-American women by white men, and "the only question is whether it shall proceed as it now does, viciously and degradingly, mingling hatred and fear with the ties of blood." Black and white children would be educated together at Nashoba, and the community would "leave the affections of future generations to the dictates of free choice."[4]

Wright opposed formal religion and private property. She extolled the values of the Enlightenment and believed in the power of rationality and education. In this respect, Wright shared many of the views of Mary Wollstonecraft, the well-known proponent of women's rights in the late eighteenth century. Wright believed that true affection between men and women could exist only when "power is annihilated on one side, fear and obedience on the other, and both restored to their birthright—equality."[5]

Nashoba was destined for failure because it was established in such a hostile environment and because Wright frequently left the colony for long periods when she suffered physical and emotional breakdowns. Finally she admitted defeat and freed her slaves in Haiti. After becoming pregnant, she married Phiquepal D'Arusmont and had a child, Frances Sylva, in December 1830 or January 1831. A second daughter was born on April 14, 1832, but died before she was three months old. Wright gave her first child the birth date of her second and always perpetuated the lie. Her daughter eventually rebelled against her mother's radical views and even opposed suffrage. Wright died on December 13, 1852, leaving a legacy of revolt against the most sacred institutions of the country. A small marker near the site of her radical colony succinctly reads: "To the South lay this plantation. Here, in 1827 [actually 1825], a Scottish spinster heiress named Frances Wright set up a colony whose aims were the enforcement of cooperative living and other advanced sociological experiments. It failed in 1830."[6]

Forty years later the ideas of free love were still considered highly subversive. Like Frances Wright, Victoria Woodhull, a ravishingly beautiful young woman, and her voluptuously plump sister, Tennessee Claflin, caused quite a furor because of their radical ideas and sexual practices. Woodhull came to the attention of the suffrage leaders when she was the first woman to address Congress on women's rights. She argued before the Judiciary Committee of the House of Representatives on January 11, 1871, that women had the right to vote under the Fourteenth Amendment. Elizabeth Cady Stanton and Susan B. Anthony were smitten with her charm, boldness, and strength of conviction. Although they personally disavowed free love, Victoria's personal charisma won them over.[7]

Woodhull summarized her views on free love in one of her bold speeches, on November 20, 1871.

> The law cannot compel two to love. . . . Two people are sexually united,
> married by nature, united by God. . . . Suppose after this marriage has con-

tinued an indefinite time, the unity between them departs, could they any more prevent it than they could prevent the love which came without their biddings? . . . All compelling laws of marriage are despotic, being remnants of the barbaric age in which they were originated, and utterly unfitted for an age . . . so enlightened in the general principles of freedom and equality, as is this. . . . Free love will be the religion of the future. Yes! I am a free lover. I have an inalienable constitutional right to love whom I may, to love as long or as short a period as I can, to change that love everyday if I please! . . .

So long as they [women] knew nothing but a blind and servile obedience . . . to the will and wish of men, they did not rebel; but the time has arrived . . . wherein they rebel, demanding freedom, freedom to hold their own lives and bodies from the demoralizing influence of sexual relations that are not founded in or maintained by love. And this rebellion will continue too, until love, unshackled shall be free to go forth, it shall be respected as holy, pure, and true. . . . Promiscuity in sexuality is simply the anarchical stage of development wherein the passions rule supreme. When spirituality comes in and rescues the real man or woman from the domain of the purely material, promiscuity is simply impossible . . . the very highest sexual unions are monogamic.[8]

Woodhull had married a drunkard when she was fourteen, and agonizing childbirth in poverty left her son, Byron, retarded. She also had a daughter, Zula Maud, by her first husband. With the help of Commodore Vanderbilt, she rose to the position of a Wall Street broker, living out the American dream of success. Not only did she shock people because of her financial position, but the daring and promiscuous Woodhull defied conventional morality by living with her second husband, Colonel James H. Blood, and her former husband, Canning Woodhull, who had become an invalid, at the same time. But despite the scandal surrounding Victoria, Stanton found her especially noble and thought that her "face, manners and conversation all indicate the triumph of the moral, intellectual and spiritual."[9] When the Suffrage Anniversary was celebrated in May 1871, the siren Woodhull appeared seated between Lucretia Mott and Elizabeth Cady Stanton. Woodhull's speech was electrifying. However, the more conservative suffragists like Lucy Stone, Mary Livermore, and Julia Ward Howe were simply aghast that the national association would apparently endorse Woodhull, and thereby her free-love doctrines.

Stanton and Anthony refused to forsake their flamboyant friend. On January 11, 1872, they stepped onto the stage of the National Woman Suffrage Association in Washington with Victoria Woodhull. When she spoke on the relationship of Spiritualism to political reform, even Anthony defended her, but she made it clear that the organization did not endorse temperance, labor reform, or Spiritualism. The association had planned to hold a convention at Steinway Hall in New York a few months later, on May 9 and 10, 1872. Woodhull issued a call in the *Woodhull and Claflin's Weekly* to form a Peoples' Party at the suffrage convention. When Anthony refused to convene jointly with Woodhull's group, Woodhull engaged Apollo Hall. The showdown came when the chinchilla-wrapped Woodhull glided onto the stage as the first evening session was about to adjourn and moved that they meet the next morning at Apollo Hall. Anthony refused to put the motion, declared Woodhull out of order, and adjourned the convention. Woodhull continued talking after Anthony had the lights turned out.[10] The friction between the radical young Woodhull and the staid but powerful Anthony had reached its peak.

When her powerful suffrage friends deserted her, Woodhull went public with the news of the affair between Henry Ward Beecher and Elizabeth Tilton, which Stanton had indiscreetly revealed to her on May 3, 1871. Woodhull published the account in the November 2, 1872, issue of her paper. She did not condemn Beecher but assailed a society which restricted natural instinct and enforced hypocrisy.[11] The scandal rocked the ranks of the suffrage movement, and Stanton defended Elizabeth Tilton as a victim.

However, the suffrage movement was already divided. Because of disagreement over the Fourteenth and Fifteenth amendments and personal conflicts, the women's rights movement split in 1869. Stanton and Anthony led the National Woman Suffrage Association, and Stone and Blackwell led the American Woman Suffrage Association. They would not unite until 1890, when the two suffrage organizations reunited to form the National American Woman Suffrage Association. The Beecher-Tilton affair exacerbated already-existing tensions between the two organizations. The AWSA generally believed in Beecher's innocence, and the NWSA assumed that he was guilty. Because of Beecher's enormous popularity and reputation, he weathered the storm, although not unscathed. Elizabeth and Benjamin Tilton were the personal casualties of the affair, as their lives were simply devastated by it. Benjamin Tilton considered suicide but reconsidered and became Woodhull's lover instead, creating an even more bizarre triangle. He eventually left the country for Europe.

Lucy Stone and Henry Blackwell viewed Woodhull's free-love doctrines as anathema. Their paper, the *Woman's Journal*, published homilies like "Let our homes be sacred, the marriage covenant inviolate, through the *mutual* tender faithfulness of husband and wife."[12] Henry Blackwell argued that when women were recognized as legal equals, free love would be suppressed, and "marriage become the immutable corner-stone of a redeemed and regenerate society."[13] Thereafter, the *Woman's Journal* published a few articles favoring companionate marriages and refuted the charge that suffrage would disrupt domestic harmony.

Victoria Woodhull spent time in jail for violating the Comstock Law against distributing obscene materials and fought endless legal battles. Finally, Woodhull found the cost of her radicalism too emotionally and financially debilitating. Rather than strengthening her commitment, imprisonment broke her resolve. Her opponents literally drove her out of the country. She moved to England with her sister and married an English millionaire, John Biddulph Martin. Even Victoria had her price. She recanted her free-love doctrines and espoused "purity" for the next fifty years. Victoria died a respectable ninety-year-old philanthropist in an old English manor. Victoria's sister, Tennessee, was similarly enterprising; she married an aging Sir Francis Cook and became "Lady Cook," exchanging her youthful radicalism for a fortune.

Because of their advocacy of sexual freedom, Frances Wright and Victoria Woodhull represented to most nineteenth-century feminists the "dastardly tyranny of licentiousness."[14] In contrast, most nineteenth-century advocates of women's rights wanted to increase women's power by extending their sphere and glorifying their nurturant role and moral superiority. They did not challenge the capitalist system or the nuclear family as Wright and Woodhull did. They believed that men must be held accountable to more moral behavior and women must be granted the vote, education, legal rights, and employment opportunities. Anthony and Stanton shared the assumption about female moral authority but rejected free-love doctrines. With the exception of self-proclaimed feminists, Spiritualists, and some Quakers, the second generation of suffragists of the late nineteenth and early twentieth centuries failed to emphasize controversial issues, fanatically battling for suffrage instead.

The genteel feminists found Emma Goldman even more threatening than Victoria Woodhull. Goldman was the most radical woman in America since Frances Wright and the most dangerous opponent of marriage in the United States at the turn of the century. Goldman even opposed suffrage as meaningless because she believed that the state itself must be destroyed. She proclaimed:

[Woman's] development, her freedom, her independence, must come from and through herself. First by asserting herself as a personality, and not as a sex commodity. Second by refusing the right to anyone over her body; by refusing to bear children unless she wants them; by refusing to be a servant to God, the State, society, the husband, the family, et cetera, by making her life simpler, but deeper and richer. That is by trying to learn the meaning and substance of life in all its complexities, by freeing herself from the fear of public opinion and public condemnation. Only that, and not the ballot, will set woman free, will make her a force hitherto unknown in the world, a force for real love, for peace, harmony: a force of divine fire, of life-giving; a creator of free men and women.[15]

She freely took lovers, felt no sexual guilt, and openly championed birth control and sexual freedom. She believed that sex was meant to be free of possession, a rich expression of love, and that marriage was legalized prostitution, the symbol of women's bondage. Frequently imprisoned and finally deported during the Red Scare, Emma Goldman never recanted her doctrine of free love or relented in denouncing marriage.[16]

Goldman believed that the majority who advocated women's emancipation were too narrow in their outlook "to permit the boundless love and ecstasy contained in the deep emotion of the true woman, sweetheart, mother, in freedom."[17] She saw that the problem was how to "be one's self and yet in oneness with others, to feel deeply with all human beings and still retain one's own characteristic qualities." Goldman's vision of liberation for a woman meant that she would be human in the truest sense, to fulfill her needs for assertion and creativity, as well as her love and motherly instincts. Women must realize that their freedom would reach as far as their power to achieve it and that inner regeneration was the first step. They must free themselves from the bondage of prejudices, customs, and tradition in order to begin the process of liberation.

According to Goldman, marriage and love had nothing in common because marriage was an economic arrangement which condemned women to lifelong parasitism and dependency. She felt that love could dwell only in an atmosphere of freedom and that marriage was antithetical to the development of women's imagination and social consciousness, an entrapment which promised protection and security at the cost of bondage.[18]

Goldman's dilemma was not like Stanton's—how to maintain an identity and remain married. Her struggle was to combine her passionate commitment to political and personal anarchism, and yet maintain a satisfying intimate relationship. Although she later denounced marriage as a form of prostitution, as a young woman she married Jacob Kershner, whom she divorced because he was impotent. Under family pressure, Emma remarried him but soon left him again for good. Although Goldman went on to have numerous lovers, she never married again. Johann Most, Alexander Berkman, and Ben Reitman were her most notable lovers, with Ed Brady, Arthur Swenson, and Frank Heiner in supporting erotic roles.

Goldman's devotion to the anarchist cause consumed her entire life. She shared her revolutionary zeal with Berkman, and together they planned to assassinate Henry Frick, a well-known capitalist. When the assassination attempt failed and Berkman was arrested, their relationship changed dramatically. Earlier Berkman had wanted her to settle down and discontinue her promiscuous relationships. After his release from prison, he was a broken man psychologically. Although they remained very close, their former intimate relationship had fallen victim to their long separation.

Johann Most, an older man, Emma's political mentor and lover, also wanted her to be more traditional. Although he loved her, he finally left her for another woman who wanted to have his children and to devote herself to him. Likewise, Ben Reitman, the grand passion of her life, also eventually married a conventional woman. Goldman met Reitman in 1908; he was a charismatic, handsome Chicago physician. For a decade Emma Goldman was consumed by her passion for him. She described her initial response to him in her autobiography: "I was caught in the torrent of an elemental passion I had never dreamed any man could rouse in me. I responded shamelessly to its primitive call, its naked beauty, its ecstatic joy."[19]

Candace Falk, author of *Love, Anarchy, and Emma Goldman*, uncovered hundreds of Goldman's and Reitman's letters in a guitar shop in Chicago. Goldman and Reitman were frequently away from one another, and they wrote steamy love letters, worked out their own erotic code letters and words, and barely skirted the laws banning "obscenity in the mails." Her "treasure box" longed for his "Willie," and she longed to have his face between her two joy Mountains—Mt. Blanc and Mt. Jura. She longed to suck the head of his "fountain of life." Both of them reveled in oral sex. She wrote, "I press you to my body close with my hot, burning legs. I embrace your precious head."[20] They may not have been the only couple to enjoy oral sex, but they seem to be almost the only ones to write about it.

Emma Goldman's torment was that after years of practicing free love, she no longer wanted anybody but Ben. Unfortunately, a lot of other women enjoyed his "Willie" too. Shortly before Labor Day 1908, Reitman wrote to her, confessing his numerous infidelities. He had lied to her from the beginning and had had sexual affairs with women even when he was on tour with her. He also confessed to embezzling money from *Mother Earth*, the anarchist magazine.

Goldman defended free love ideologically, but her jealousy tormented her. Her anarchist friends disliked Reitman and believed he was an opportunistic and vulgar hypocrite. Goldman's love was faltering, and the distance between her ideology and her experience widened. Goldman experienced the anguish of trying to live one's ideals personally and politically.

Like Woodhull, Goldman was misunderstood. She did not support promiscuity. Her idea of "free love" meant that one loved freely, expressing sexual passion without the constraints of marriage. For her sex was tied to love, tenderness, and respect for one another, but not exclusivity. When Reitman was able to satisfy her sexually more than her other lovers, she became possessive and jealous. However, she was even more tormented by Reitman's deceptiveness than his sexual infidelity. When Emma discovered that in every town she and Reitman had been on their tour, he had "romanced" women who came to hear her speak, she was devastated. He had lied to her constantly but asked her to forgive him and start again.[21] Whereas previously Goldman had no difficulty having other lovers, she found herself no longer responsive to the embraces of other men. She even thought of having a child with Reitman, although never very seriously.

After a decade of passion, periodic depression, and longing, Goldman's ties with Ben slackened. Ben met and married Anna Martindale and had a child with her. In contrast, Emma believed that a preoccupation with children led to mental and physical stagnation and that the family ultimately crushed the individual. Therefore, Ben's move toward conventional life and having a child deeply disturbed her. Marriage did not stop Ben's philandering, and he continued to make overtures to Emma. Ben's use of his sexual power over her seemed to compensate for her lack of respect for him politically and to retaliate in a way for her friends' rejection of him.

However painful her relationship with Reitman, Goldman never settled into a bourgeois family life or relented in her anarchist principles. Because of these principles and her advocacy of a freer sexuality, Goldman believed that marriage and motherhood inhibited a woman's creative, intellectual, and political expression. Intimacy was essential but did not have to be contained within the traditional nuclear family. She endured many disappointments in her romantic life, but she never recanted, even though her theories were sometimes at odds with her emotional longings.

The Greenwich Village Radicals

Like Frances Wright, Victoria Woodhull, and Emma Goldman, the Greenwich Village radicals challenged the expectations of true womanhood by calling for a freer expression of female sexuality and women's right to creative expression. Many of them were self-proclaimed feminists. Henrietta Rodman, Mabel Dodge Luhan, Floyd Dell, Neith Boyce, and Hutchins Hapgood migrated to Greenwich Village early in the twentieth century. They experimented with a more open sexuality, lived together before marriage, and enjoyed a bohemian existence. The young women wrote, painted, sculpted, or took jobs in the city and felt the exhilaration of personal freedom. They smoked in public, drank with the men, discussed their dreams and "complexes," and bobbed their hair. They were "flappers" before the term was coined. They had discovered Freud and found him liberating, rather than constricting as many late twentieth-century feminists have. They were lyrical or cultural feminists; although they supported suffrage, they wanted women to be able to express themselves fully—sexually as well as artistically.

Henrietta Rodman was a symbol of this new kind of feminism. She supported Charlotte Perkins Gilman's ideas and tried to live out her ideals. In April 1914 she organized the Feminist Alliance in New York City. She explained its goals: "Feminism is a movement which demands the removal of all social, political, economic, and other discriminations which are based on sex, and the award of all rights and duties in all fields on the basis of individual capacity alone."[22] Rodman wanted to improve the lives of middle-class, professional women who wanted a career, husband, and children. In the tradition of Gilman she proposed apartment houses with professionalized dining facilities, cleaning services, and Montessori schools, all conveniently available in the building.

Rodman bobbed her hair, smoked in public, wore sandals and smocks, and enjoyed an emancipated life. Rodman was born in New York City in 1878 and was educated at Columbia Teachers College. A married schoolteacher herself (though secretive about her marriage), she was influential in forcing the New York City Board of Education to allow married women to teach.[23] Rodman also worked in Margaret Sanger's birth control campaign and for the socialist candidate Morris Hillquit; like Jane Addams and Crystal Eastman, she was an active pacifist during World War I. After the war she organized a teachers' union. When she died at the early age of forty-five in 1923, her unconventional habits were becoming fashionable in the era of flappers.

In their fiction and their own lives, Susan Glaspell and Neith Boyce, who were also Greenwich Village radicals, addressed the conflicts of the "new woman," trying to achieve individual expression and yet fulfill traditional expectations. Glaspell's fictional heroines are deeply unhappy because they possess an insatiable desire for knowledge or self-expression and are thwarted by societal expectations of women. Some are romantic yearners who settle for premarital relationships and then marriage, but a number of them commit suicide. Glaspell captures the stirring of discontent of women who optimistically want to "have it all" but who feel cramped and smothered by conventional marriage. Neith Boyce's fictional heroines are less desperate and are generally portrayed as long-suffering and devoted to their husbands. But they too are deeply unhappy, managing stoically to persevere.

Both Glaspell and Boyce had feminist husbands, and they attempted to have liberated marriages. Boyce's husband, Hutchins Hapgood, assumed a large share of housework and care of their four children, in addition to his literary and reform activities. They had an "open marriage," and as Neith wrote to Mabel Dodge, "Both Hutch and I feel that we are free to love other people—but that nothing can break or even touch the deep, vital, passionate bond between *us* that exists now as it always has."[24]

Hapgood met Neith Boyce at the *Commercial Advertiser* when they both worked on that newspaper. In writing about Neith Boyce, Hapgood described his almost mystical attitude toward her. He said of their relationship: "Neith and I, like many another couple who on the whole were good fathers and mothers, were conscious of the latent feminism urging men to give up the ascendancy which women thought they had, and women to demand from men that which they didn't really want, namely so-called freedom from the ideal of monogamy."[25] Hapgood contrasted the differences in his generation's attitudes toward sex with those of the younger generation:

> The modern youth are neither so emphatic about the simplicities of sex, nor so spiritual in its further meaning. This is because the sexual act, to them, is more natural, so they are not obsessed as the Victorian was. . . .
>
> To us Victorians, sex did not need a skillful prolongation, nor the exploitation of one by the other, to his or her ultimate possibilities of sensation.

To us the merely animal act produced the spiritual emotion. To do that, it had to be very simple—a strong instinct, a simple satisfaction, and a lingering gratitude, due to a divine gift.[26]

Like Neith Boyce and Hutchins Hapgood and many earlier feminists, Susan Glaspell and her husband, George Cram Cook, viewed their marriage as a partnership of equals. Cook collaborated with her in writing a play, *Suppressed Desire*, which was a satire on Freudianism featuring a character resembling Henrietta Rodman. They had a mystical, romantic conception of love and tried to escape the perils of sexual jealousy.[27]

Edna St. Vincent Millay, a believer in sexual freedom and the ecstatic power of love, engendered a lot of jealousy herself with her love affairs. She won recognition for her poem "Renascence" when she was only twenty years old. After attending Barnard, then Vassar, in 1917 on her graduation she headed to Greenwich Village. Millay became a highly respected poet and an advocate for women's complete equality. She was highly sensitive to women's sexual, intellectual, and cultural restraints. Millay supported suffrage and believed that women must be free to express themselves creatively, to make passionate love to whomever they wished, and to escape the trap of conventional marriage.[28]

Mabel Dodge Luhan resembled Millay in her attitudes about sexual freedom, but she believed that women are dependent on men to realize their destinies. Luhan was sexually liberated; she married four times and had numerous affairs. Her central conflict was over her desire for autonomy and her intellectual and emotional dependence on men of genius to define her identity. Like Madame de Stael, Mabel was the consummate hostess. After eight years in Florence, she returned to New York and established the most famous salon in American history. Radicals, reformers, feminists, writers, and artists regularly came to her Fifth Avenue apartment to debate the issues of the day, from socialism to psychoanalysis.

Mabel sought to create a community for herself and to redeem herself through art, politics, love affairs, and psychoanalysis.[29] Luhan's affair with John Reed from 1913 to 1915 introduced her to political radicalism. She helped Reed organize the unsuccessful but ambitious Paterson Strike Pageant in New York, designed to aid the striking workers in Paterson, New Jersey. In 1912 only 2 percent of Americans controlled 60 percent of the personal wealth of the nation. One-third to one-half of Americans lived in poverty or close to subsistence. Along with the other Greenwich Village radicals, Luhan opposed this unequal distribution of wealth and railed against the sanctity of private property, conventional religion, the patriarchal family, and the sexual double standard. However, personally she enjoyed her considerable wealth, continued to marry, and could not harmonize her ideals and her life-style.[30]

At one of Dodge's soirees, Emma Goldman rose and blasted the Greenwich Village intellectuals for their "conservatism." She said that they were "a curse on the cause of workers," and she urged the workers who were present to act on their own and not to trust their fates to "college professors and lawyers who with the philanthropically inclined ladies only succeed in sentimentalizing the cause and making compromises which in time become real evils again."[31]

Mabel Dodge's idealistic pronouncements about the proletariat clashed with her own life-style in the same manner as her beliefs about sexual freedom. When she fell in love with John Reed, she experienced the same "conversion" to monogamy as Emma Goldman. Her various sexual adventures were purposeful, and she hoped for a deeper commitment. John Reed, however, resembled Ben Reitman, and he enjoyed numerous liaisons while still involved with Mabel. Reed's primary commitment was to Louise Bryant, whom he eventually married. Mabel wrote of her confusion and jealousy to Neith Boyce, who had a lot of practice in this matter.

> Reed & I love each other as much as any people can—that's why we torment each other so—but one of us has to give in on this. . . . Yet if I didn't *feel this* & feel this important it would be because I would have him as I would a whore—indifferent to what he did so long as he doesn't deprive me of himself. It *can't* be meant to be that way! . . . To him the sexual gesture has no importance, but infringing on his right to act freely has the first importance. Are we both right & both wrong—and how do such things end? Either way it kills love—it seems to me. This is so fundamental—is it what feminism is all about? . . . I know all women go thro this—but *must* they go on going thro it? Are we supposed to "make" men do things? Are men to change? Is monogamy better than polygamy?[32]

Mabel and her female friends experienced the tensions of trying to be "new women." Lois Palken Rudnick, her recent biographer, describes some contradictions which arose in Luhan because of this conflict: "Mabel projected the mental habits of the *fin de siècle femme fatale*, the hauteur of a Renaissance princess, the lust after status of the arriviste . . . the innocent coquetry of a Daisy Miller, and a cautious sense of marital propriety."[33] Luhan married four times because she had a desire for outward respectability and an emotional need to find a male genius. She did not trust her own intellectual or artistic abilities and was more comfortable playing the muse to men like Carl Van Vechten, Max Eastman, Floyd Dell, and D. H. Lawrence. But she did write her memoirs and a book on Taos.

Mabel's quest for self-fulfillment extended long after her affair with Reed ended. In 1918 she moved to Taos, New Mexico, and married a Pueblo Indian, Tony Lujan. For the rest of her life she promoted Taos as an artistic and spiritual center. She was a "new woman," with conditioning which extended back into the nineteenth century, and she lived with the realization that sexual liberation alone could not free her.[34]

The Greenwich Village radical women were not the only ones experimenting with an open sexuality. Joanne Meyerowitz points out in *Women Adrift* that between 1880 and 1930, large numbers of African-American and white women began to live apart from their families. They worked as garment workers, saleswomen, clerks, domestic service workers, teachers, nurses, and laundresses. These "women adrift," like the middle- and upper-class "new women," challenged Victorian sexual mores and the belief that all women needed the economic and moral protection of family life. The "new woman" fought for professional visibility and often espoused radical economic and social reforms. For the "women adrift," economic survival was primary, since their wages were generally extremely low. But like the "new women," when they expressed their sexuality openly, they challenged the belief in female "passionlessness" which was the basis of the claim of female moral superiority. For working-class women, sexual expression was tied both to sexual pleasure and also to a financial strategy to achieve security.

Some of these working women preceded the flapper in their dancing, flirting, wearing sexually revealing clothes, and engaging in premarital intercourse at least as early as bohemian communities. Of course, many women who sought romance and adventure found poverty, sexual exploitation, and loneliness. But cities also offered freedom from parental supervision, social networks, and perhaps a measure of self-assertion.[35]

Margaret Sanger

Early in her career Margaret Sanger shared many of the same beliefs of her Greenwich Village radical friends, but she began her birth control crusade because of her contact with poor and working-class women. She believed that women must be able to have control over their bodies and enjoy their sexuality. She dedicated her entire life to the single issue of birth control. Sanger, perhaps more than any other individual, deserves the credit for achieving public acceptance of birth control.

Sanger traces the beginning of her commitment to an incident involving Sadie Sachs. Sachs, a truck driver's wife, desperately sought contraceptive advice from her doctor, who callously told her to have her husband sleep on the roof. Living in poverty, with a number of children already, she could not face having another child. Like other desperate women who used catheters bought in the drug store or knitting needles to try to bring on an abortion, she contracted an infection and died while Margaret Sanger was attending her. The incident had a profound effect on Sanger, and she embarked on a campaign to eliminate such suffering. Margaret Sanger began her career as birth control advocate for the working class, but she later focused on middle- and upper-class women.

As a child, Sanger had seen her mother's health devastated by bearing eleven children. She believed that her mother's early death at the age of forty-nine of tuberculosis was brought on by the strain of bearing so many children. Margaret became a nurse, married William Sanger, and was pregnant within six months. Sanger eventually had two other children. Like Stanton, she became unhappy as a housewife. In order to improve her marriage, Sanger moved from Westchester County to Manhattan around 1910. She began working in the Lower East Side as a home nurse and became an activist for the Industrial Workers of the World, trying to organize textile workers. Along with Elizabeth Gurley Flynn, she organized the evacuation of children from Lawrence, Massachusetts, during an especially violent strike.

Sanger's conversion to feminism came through her own experience as a frustrated housewife, as well as her contact with Emma Goldman, lower-class women, and radical labor leaders. Sanger saw women's control over their own bodies as related to the demand for economic justice, and she dedicated her life to providing women of all classes with sex education, information on venereal disease, and birth control.

When Sanger experienced a sexual awakening, she began to have affairs, which her husband bitterly resented.[36] She believed in the "feminine" spirit, which was the source of women's moral superiority, and like other Greenwich Village radicals, believed romantically that the release of women's sexuality would have a beneficent effect on society.[37]

Because of the Comstock Law of 1873, Sanger's distribution of birth control literature and articles on venereal disease was deemed illegal. Her journal, the *Woman Rebel*, was declared unmailable. She had separated from her husband by 1914, and she went to Europe to do research on birth control methods. When she returned to the United States, she and her sister Ethel Byrne opened the Brownsville clinic in October 1916. Ten days later, the police shut it down and arrested them.

Once out of jail, Sanger began her crusade to establish doctor-staffed birth control clinics. Her chief opponent, Mary Ware Dennett, resisted the efforts of the medical profession to control access to birth control information, but lost. Not only did Sanger support the role of doctors, but she severed ties with her radical past, argued from eugenics, and sought funding from socialites and philanthropists, instead of socialists. In 1921 she organized the American Birth Control League, which later, in 1942, became the Planned Parenthood Federation of America. After divorcing her husband, she married the millionaire J. Noah Slee.

Sanger set up the Birth Control Clinical Research Bureau in New York City as well as the model for over three hundred birth control clinics established in the United States by 1938, staffed primarily by women doctors. She also fought for women's right to medical abortions. After losing some influence by the late 1930s, she played a major role in founding the International Planned Parenthood Federation in 1952.

Sanger was willing to abandon working-class women and her radical politics in order to achieve her objectives. The Red Scare of 1919–20 convinced her that her radical connections jeopardized her program, and she campaigned for birth control at any cost. As a result, the radical origins of the birth control movement were forgotten as birth control gained respectability and access became generally available. Sanger was even instrumental in the development of the birth control pill; she enlisted Katharine Dexter McCormick to support the work of Gregory Pincus, a biologist, who developed the pill, first sold in 1960.[38]

In her speeches advocating birth control, Sanger emphasized that birth control was a moral practice which spiritualized the sexual act.[39] Sanger's rhetoric may have been conservative, but her life contradicted it. Sanger continued to have sex outside of her second marriage and continued to live out the principles of free love. She was a consummate politician and pragmatist. Realizing that success depended on the funding from elites and the support of the medical profession, she moved away from radical socialism. Her advocacy of abortion and birth control were extremely radical demands in her lifetime because these practices had radical implications for traditional sex roles and certainly did not reinforce Victorian female passivity.

One must look to Sanger's own experience and actions as well as her rhetoric to discover the sources of her intentions. She believed that women and men were more different than similar, and her analysis had a material basis in her personal experience. Sanger feared that if women abandoned the argument for female uniqueness and superiority when full equality was not assured, they might lose a major dimension of their source of power.

Frances Wright, Victoria Woodhull, Emma Goldman, the Greenwich Village radicals, and Margaret Sanger were sex radicals in the nineteenth and early twentieth centuries. They all rejected capitalism and argued for sexual freedom and equality. Goldman alone of the four women opposed suffrage and believed that it was meaningless. But even these notorious women married and proclaimed the importance of traditionally female values. Although they challenged Victorian notions of female sexuality overtly, they still framed their arguments in terms of women's relationships within the Victorian family. Although the mainstream feminist movement was profamily and incorporated the cult of true womanhood into its rhetoric, aims, and agenda, these women's lives show that more radical voices were present.

The sex radicals tended to hurt the movement at the time, but many of their ideas later became pervasive in American society. Their lives illustrate an emerging radical feminist consciousness and a critique of women's lack of power over domestic and sexual concerns. In their own lives, they were both empowered and trapped by marriage when judged by Victorian standards. Stemming from the fact that American women were being defined primarily by their sexual and reproductive capacities, the issue of free love in the nineteenth and twentieth centuries became associated with the women's movement, to the horror of the majority of its advocates. Left unresolved was the question of whether women's sexual freedom liberates them or makes them more vulnerable to exploitation. The ideology of the angel in the house was so prevalent that radical women who challenged Victorian notions of female sexuality and capitalism itself found it enormously difficult to live out their principles, to combine love and achievement. It became quite obvious that when feminists challenged the family and traditional marriage, they ran up against fierce resistance and ostracism and became known as "whores of Babylon" and "devils in petticoats," instead of angels in the house.

The notorious women of the late nineteenth century were not alone in wanting to escape from binding roles. Harry Houdini, the magician who climbed out of locked boxes and defied death by hanging upside down and handcuffed above New York skyscrapers, captured the imagination of people who also dreamed of escape. Immigrants whom Jacob Riis photographed in New York ghettos wanted to escape poverty, black Americans wanted to escape from the tyranny of racism, and populists wanted release from the oppression of eastern bankers and industrialists. The middle class wanted to escape from the threats to their status posed by minorities and immigrants. Suffragists wanted to escape second-class citizenship. While some radical feminists challenged Victorian sexual mores and the traditional family and called for women's full emancipation, the majority of activists for women's rights attempted to claim political and economic power instead of sexual freedom.

6

THE SUFFRAGE MOVEMENT
Municipal Housekeeping or Full Equality?
(1848–1919)

To me feminism means that woman wants to develop her own womanhood. It means that she wants to push on to the finest, fullest, freest expression of herself. She wants to be an individual. . . . The freeing of the individuality of woman does not mean original sin; it means the finding of her own soul.

Rose Young, 1914

Public opinion in the future will regard men as quite essential to the home as are women; and women quite as essential to the world as men.

Winnifred Harper Cooley, 1913

No one thinks for a moment, or stops to think, that it's uncommon or unusual for women to go to the polls and vote. We don't even think of that. It's so common now. We don't think of the fight that was made for it. We just accept it. And that's the way with all these processes. To my mind, the whole process is a process of evolution.

Sylvie Thygeson, 104-year-old crusader
for suffrage and birth control, 1972

Armies of women attempted to seize more power in order to create a better world: to extend mother love to the society and assist families and children. Suffragists stood on soap boxes on every street corner, knocked at the doors of America, held conventions, lobbied legislators, and marched in suffrage parades with banners of orange and black, yellow and blue, purple and green and gold. The *Chicago Herald* reported a suffrage parade on a rainy day on June 7, 1916, when over five thousand women marched.

Over their heads surged a vast sea of umbrellas extending two miles down the street. Under their feet swirled rivulets of water. Wind tore at their clothes and rain drenched their faces. Unhesitatingly they marched in unbroken formation keeping perfect step. Never before in the history of Chicago, probably the world, has there been so impressive a demonstration of idealism, of consecration to a cause.

A delegate to the Republican convention came to the suffrage headquarters to say, "I watched it from a window where men stood eight and ten deep and many had tears in their eyes. They said, these women really mean it and we might as well make up our minds to it." When a man on the street called to a young girl in the procession, "You ought to be home with your mother," she exclaimed, "Mother is here, marching with me."[1]

The mothers, daughters, and a hundred or more men marching for women's suffrage that day were outraged that women did not have the vote in the United States. The 1916 parade marked a high point in the suffrage crusade, a movement which persisted for seventy-two years before fully achieving its goals. Many of the activists for women's rights were ready to die for the cause. They endured public and private ridicule and were victims of violence. When they were put in prison and went on hunger strikes, they had tubes shoved into their stomachs and were force-fed.

What explains the single-minded dedication of these feminists? How and why did they develop such a profound outrage over the condition of women? With their domestic power, what more did these women want? Why was the vote so important to them? How would suffrage affect the family? The mainstream feminist movement of the late nineteenth and early twentieth centuries was profamily in the sense that its participants fought for the vote in order to extend mother love to the society and in order to protect women and children from victimization. They also sought to increase women's autonomy through equal access to education and the professions, changes they believed would benefit other family members, as well as the community and the nation. However, by arguing from the basis of sexual differences, they inadvertently reinforced essentialist views of women's intrinsic nature, while the more radical wing of the movement pushed for full equality and emphasized sexual similarities.[2]

Suffragists had to confront the objection that suffrage would destroy marriage and the family. They shared a belief with the antisuffragists in the importance of the family, but mainstream suffragists believed that women needed the vote precisely *because* they were guardians of home and family— they needed the vote to protect the family and clean up society. They believed that within an urban industrial society, domestic, covert power was an insufficient foil against male political dominance. The most organized and best-financed antisuffragist group was the liquor industry. The members of that group knew how strongly women had supported temperance and prohibition, and they did not want to risk the consequences of women's voting. While most of the suffragists believed in women's moral superiority, they fundamentally disagreed with antisuffragists about women's proper sphere and capabilities. The antisuffragists believed in divinely ordained separate spheres, and some believed in women's physical and intellectual inferiority to men. They believed that women needed to be protected by men, and they were fully satisfied with the degree of covert power which they had.

Material Transformations and the Suffrage Movement

The gradual evolution of feminist consciousness was grounded in women's sense of empowerment as wives and mothers, as well as their feelings of victimization. Material transformations in the nineteenth and early twentieth centuries created a more congenial climate for feminism. The impact of the Civil War, industrialization, women's entrance into the labor force in larger numbers, and women's greater access to higher education all helped inspire feminist consciousness.

Before the Civil War, the women's rights movement remained small and decentralized, and it achieved few gains. Tremendous changes occurred in women's lives because of the Civil War, particularly in the South. As previously in the Revolutionary War, southern white women had to assume nontraditional roles, managing businesses, plantations, and households. As independence was forced upon them, they came to realize their strengths. Thousands of these women lost their husbands, lovers, and sons to the war. African-American women gained their freedom from slavery; they rushed to locate kin, to legalize marriages, and to try to establish stable families. Working-class women entered the labor force in greater numbers after the war. Men who returned from the war found that their wives had managed alone and had exercised an unusual amount of power within their restricted sphere of the home. John Andrew Rice, who formed his opinions about white southern women's power as a boy growing up in the South in the nineties, may have exaggerated their extent, but he identified significant war-related changes in sexual roles. He wrote: "In 1860 the South became a matriarchy. The men went away from home to other battlefields, leaving the women free to manage farm and plantation directly without their bungling hindrance;

when they returned, those who escaped heroic death . . . they found their surrogates in complete and competent charge and liking it."[3]

Because the South remained primarily agricultural much longer than the North, its history has been regionally distinctive. The white southern lady has been sentimentalized in novels, films, poetry, and the hearts of rebel men. The image of the southern belle at "Twelve Oaks"—flirting with her beaus, smelling of jasmine and magnolias—has lingered, along with traditional values about women's place on the pedestal, safely removed from sordid public life. However, behind the hoop skirt has been a clenched fist, and in order to understand why southern women came to a feminist consciousness later than women in other regions, one must look past the magnolias and mint juleps to the intimate sphere of domestic politics.

No one has captured the disparity between the ideal of the southern lady and the realities of her life so well as Anne Firor Scott. As Scott tells us, the true lady was a submissive wife "whose reason for being was to love, honor, obey and occasionally amuse her husband, bring up his children and manage his household." Physically weak, timid, modest and beautiful, the southern lady was graceful, "self-denying, and she was given to suffering in silence."[4]

Southern white women were supposed to resemble Ellen Glasgow's character in *Virginia*: "It was characteristic of her—and indeed of her generation—that she would have endured martyrdom in support of the consecrated doctrine of her inferiority to man."[5]

The extraordinary loss of life in the Civil War forced many southern women to abandon the "ideal" of dependence and gentility and compelled them either to enter the labor force or to manage alone. In the war over 622,000 men died from disease and wounds; 1,000,000 were killed or wounded. The North lost 364,511 men, and the South an estimated 258,000. The total financial cost of the Civil War probably surpassed $15 billion. The war also accelerated the process of national industrialization which was already underway.[6]

Economic conditions were changing, a situation which would create a more receptive climate for feminism nationally. Because the Civil War accelerated the process of industrialization in the United States, more employment opportunities were open to women as clerks, secretaries, mill workers, and members of service occupations. For example, in Virginia 5,000 women held manufacturing and mechanical jobs in 1870, and double that number did in 1890. In Mississippi during the same period the number of professional women increased from 700 to over 3,000.[7]

On the national level, in 1900 only 5 percent of all married women in the nation were employed outside the home. By 1910 this number had risen to 11 percent. In 1900 about 25 percent of all unmarried immigrant women worked, compared with 15 percent of all native-born women. In contrast, 43 percent of all African-American women were employed outside the home in 1900. Almost all of these employed African-American women were farm workers or domestics.

Although the barriers were still formidable, some African-American and white women began to enter the professions. Black women represented 3 percent of black lawyers in 1910 (compared with 0.5 percent for white women) and 13 percent of African-American doctors (compared with 6 percent for white women). Overall, female professionals composed 9.1 percent of the female labor force in 1910, and 11.9 percent in 1920.[8]

Greater access to higher education for women also inspired a feminist consciousness in the late nineteenth and early twentieth centuries. More women began to have aspirations beyond the home, realized their intellectual capabilities, and thus became more aware of the debilitating sexual discrimination which they faced. From 1870 to 1900 the number of women enrolled in institutions of higher learning multiplied almost eight times, from 11,000 to 85,000. Women constituted 21.0 percent of all students in colleges in 1870, 33.4 percent in 1880, 35.9 percent in 1890, 36.8 percent in 1900, 39.6 percent in 1910, and 47.3 percent in 1920.[9]

As Barbara Solomon points out, the first generation of female collegians (1860s to 1880s) knew they were pioneers enlarging the female sphere, but they still defined themselves as "true women" who were pure and pious, if not always domestic or obedient. The next generation of educated women (1890s to 1900s) were more spirited, expansive, and physically active, the "new women." The third generation of college women (1910s to 1920s) introduced a "new woman" who both foreshadowed the flapper and dedicated herself to Progressive causes.[10]

Female college graduates throughout these three generations confronted a choice between a career or marriage. Early female educators had attempted to reassure people that education would not spoil women for family duties and did not question the ideal of the angel in the house. But as the quality of the academic programs in women's colleges equaled that of men's and colleges became coeducational, many women viewed their education as preparation for vocations instead of for marriage. In 1910 only 12 percent of professional women married, as compared with 24 percent by 1930.[11]

The women's rights movement of the late nineteenth and early twentieth centuries enlisted its membership primarily from the ranks of these educated women, a large percentage of whom had entered professions as a kind of calling, forsaking marriage. While the overwhelming majority of women chose to be wives and mothers over following a career, college-educated women were more likely to be employed, remain unmarried, and either have no children, or fewer children than less-educated women.[12] While covert domestic power was not their primary experience or goal, the career women of this period who became advocates of women's rights still viewed family issues as primary to their reform agenda.

Americans were more highly educated at the turn of the century than in any previous period. Moreover, industrialization lightened domestic responsibilities by providing laundries, bakeries, ready-made clothing, and a variety of other services. Having smaller families relieved women from constant childbearing and childrearing. As a result, women of the middle and upper classes had more time to become involved in activities outside the home. They joined women's clubs, church groups, and reform organizations. Their increased intellectual awareness and experiences outside the home motivated many women to extend their influence to protect their families and to clean up the entire society.

Karen Blair, a historian of the women's club movement, notes that the literary club women who had been isolated and conditioned only to serve others increased their autonomy and education and found sisterhood in their clubs. They commanded respect for the "female" traits of morality and domesticity, and they enlarged their sphere. With the establishment of the General Federation of Women's Clubs in 1890, clubs began to shift their focus from cultural programs to "municipal housekeeping." By 1914 the GFW endorsed suffrage.[13]

As in the rest of the nation, southern black and white women discovered their public power, influence, and responsibilities through work in church organizations and voluntary associations. Their participation in voluntary associations increased dramatically after the Civil War. Women's missionary societies and the WCTU often gave southern women their first experiences of activism. In the last thirty years of the nineteenth century, women's organizations proliferated in the South, including literary societies, Browning and Shakespeare clubs, Daughters of the American Revolution, United Daughters of the Confederacy, self-help clubs, and mutual aid societies. As Anne Firor Scott points out, voluntary associations were vehicles utilized by women to circumvent overt legal and social barriers that prevented them from exercising political and social power.[14]

Women's voluntarism and their emerging feminist consciousness stemmed from material changes in their lives caused by industrialization. Many women slipped out of their tight corsets, began to ride bicycles, and challenged the image of the angel in the house. The "new woman" of the late nineteenth and early twentieth centuries challenged the cult of true womanhood while retaining many of the same qualities. This shift reflected the dramatic changes in women's lives in the nineteenth century: increased education, a relaxation of sexual mores, entrance into the labor force, greater legal equality, and entrance into the professions.

Through the Window of Popular Culture

Popular culture of the period began to portray the "new woman" and reflected stirrings of nascent feminism. By the 1890s a new image of womanhood, the "Gibson girl," appeared in popular magazines. A creation of Charles Dana Gibson, she became the symbol of the "new woman." With her hair piled atop her head, wearing a simple shirtwaist blouse and skirt, the Gibson girl was robust and athletic and possessed a hint of sensuality. In illustrations she was pictured playing tennis or golf or bicycling. She was assumed to be chaste, but a little rebellious, with a flash of mischief in her eyes. Her picture hung on living room walls and could be seen on ashtrays, teacups, saucers, spoons, tiles, wallpaper, and silk handkerchiefs. A hit song of 1906 was entitled, "Why Do They Call Me a Gibson Girl?" The Gibson girl's companion, the Gibson man, was distinguished, debonair, and chivalrous and always fell victim to his spirited companion's whims.[15]

The comics which proliferated in the early twentieth century portrayed both "new women" and traditional women. The comic strips "Lady Bountiful," "Phyllis," "Bringing Up Father" (with the characters Maggie and Nora), "Rosie's Beau," "Rosamond," "Ma," and "Sallie Snooks—Stenographer" depicted women as reformers, wives, working women, and mothers. Lady Bountiful, first portrayed as a kind of fairy godmother, later turned into a regular young woman whose good deeds boomeranged on her. Other female comic characters included fat, homely hausfraus; shrewish, social-climbing wives with rolling pins; glamorous, vacuous, dumb young women; a few spunky, adventuring young heroines; and a sexually harassed young stenographer.[16] In the comics, housewives cowed their husbands and chased them with rolling pins or simply quietly allowed their husbands to make fools of themselves. The theme of female dominance runs throughout early twentieth-century comic strips, reflecting the anxieties of men whose involvement and power in the family were diminishing. Although these comic-strip wives are often objects of derision, they are very dominant characters who represent the specter of female power at home.

The Gibson girl and female comic characters reflected the changes in women's aspirations and opportunities. They revealed both a hint of rebellion and the extent of women's domestic power, which was becoming formidable. By the early twentieth century, the stirrings of revolt had become a full-scale movement by women to claim overt political power.

The Suffrage Movement in the West

Women's entrance into colleges, the labor force, and the professions, accompanied by a decline in fertility and the westward migration, created a more congenial climate for feminism. The experiences of women in the West differed greatly from those of women in other regions. Because of the relatively low number of women there as well as their economic importance and effective agitation, western women won their political and legal rights more quickly than women in any other region. While the balance of power in the western families was with the men, frontier women often performed "men's work" as well as "women's work." They attempted to re-create their eastern domestic circles and routines. Women's position in western communities resembled that of colonial women; because there were relatively few women, they were allowed more independence. Widows assumed full responsibility for their families, and the qualities of fortitude, strength, and courage were essential. Submissive passivity could be dangerous, since both men and women were tested to their limits, simply to survive.

Thus, it is not surprising that the first victories for women's suffrage came in the West. In February 1870 a few of Utah's women voted in city and municipal elections, even before Wyoming women could exercise their right. Utah enacted woman suffrage at the time a struggle was going on over plural marriages. Congress revoked women's franchise in Utah at the time they forbade plural marriage in 1887 with the Edmunds-Tucker Act. However, women regained their franchise in 1896 when Utah became a state. Other western states granted women the vote in the late nineteenth century: Wyoming in 1870, Colorado in 1877, Nebraska in 1882, Oregon in 1884, Washington in 1889, and South Dakota in 1890. In addition, Michigan granted women suffrage in 1874.[17]

Because of low percentage of women, their proven competence, and the

West - needed enough wmn to form a state → attracted settlers

desires of those in the territories to attract enough settlers to become states and have congressional power, the western region was more progressive in granting women their rights than other sections of the country. Although western women may have sought to preserve gentility, circumstances forced them into nontraditional roles and made their presence in the West indispensable for the survival of the family.

The National Suffrage Movement

Although feminists made gains in the West after the war, they faced fierce resistance elsewhere. Historians of the period like Eleanor Flexner, Aileen Kraditor, William O'Neill, Ellen DuBois, as well as the suffragists themselves have told the heroic story of the battle to extend women's rightful sphere. Their accounts of the long struggle for women's franchise from 1848 to 1920 are both enspiriting and depressing. Carrie Chapman Catt, a suffrage leader of the early twentieth century, summarized the fight.

> To get the word male in effect out of the Constitution cost the women of the country fifty-two years of pauseless campaign thereafter. During that time they were forced to conduct fifty-six campaigns of referenda to male voters; 480 campaigns to urge Legislatures to submit suffrage amendments to voters; 47 campaigns to induce State constitutional conventions to write woman suffrage into State constitutions; 277 campaigns to get State Party conventions to include woman suffrage planks; 30 campaigns to get presidential party conventions to adopt woman suffrage planks in party platforms, and 19 campaigns with 19 successive Congresses.[18]

A young woman in high school today, reading a line in her history textbook simply stating "the Nineteenth Amendment granting women the vote passed in 1920," would never from those words imagine the ferocity of resistance to what she now takes for granted. One marvels at the energy expended to achieve what we now consider a natural right of women's citizenship, and one wonders what might have been accomplished if all that energy had been expended on other endeavors. To modern readers the obsessive concentration on suffrage may seem narrow or naive, but the vote symbolized more far-reaching goals. Mainstream suffragists and even self-proclaimed feminists viewed the vote as a profamily issue. Psychologically, the vote meant affirming women's right to reach out beyond the dependence of domesticity to achieve independence in the world, as well as elevating their status in the home. Pragmatically, the vote was the only issue at the time on which unity could be achieved by women across racial and class lines, and across political loyalties. Suffragists believed that they needed the vote in order to change other laws, to assist women and children, to equalize wages, to advance in professions, and to solve the problems of urban America—poverty, vice, and corruption.

After a brief surge in the 1890s, the suffrage movement fell into the doldrums by the end of the decade, and no new states granted woman suffrage from 1896 to 1910.[19] However, from 1910 to 1920, the movement gained new strength. The National American Woman Suffrage Association (NAWSA) had 13,000 members in 1893, 45,500 in 1907, and two million in 1917. Feminist activism rose from the low level of 3 major events in 1890 and 11 in 1900 to 64 in 1908 and 173 in 1915. From 1899 to 1908, Congress introduced 46 bills of special concern to women and passed 16. From 1908 to 1925, Congress introduced 208 such bills; 19 major pieces of legislation benefiting women were passed between 1917 and 1925.[20]

Carrie Chapman Catt was highly influential in rejuvenating the suffrage movement in the early years of the twentieth century. Catt emerged as a likely successor to Susan B. Anthony when the two groups of suffragists reunited in 1890 to form the NAWSA. Catt was a superb administrator and the epitome of the respectable matron. She believed that organization was the means to women's enfranchisement. Under Catt's leadership, the movement for suffrage became highly organized, concentrating on congressional action and state campaigns. She headed NAWSA from 1900 to 1904 and from 1915 to 1920.

Catt married Leo Chapman in 1885, two weeks after she met him, tossing aside a successful career as an educator. Her husband died about a year after their wedding. Six years later when she agreed to marry George Catt, she insisted that he sign a legal contract granting her two months in the fall and two months in the spring to devote to speaking and organizing for suffrage. Catt cheerfully agreed. After she became a widow again in 1905, she never remarried.[21]

Catt's feminism must be understood in the context of her Progressivism. She believed in a kind of communitarian feminism. Since her individualism was devoted to serving the larger good, freedom had meaning only if people served the community. She agreed with Herbert Croly, a Progressive writer, that an ideal democracy was composed of people who struggled together and cared about their mutual growth. Because she thought in terms of community rather than the individual woman, she approached the transformation of women's lives through politics and economics. Although she concentrated on achieving suffrage, she saw "winning the vote as an opening wedge." She did not believe that the vote was "a short cut to the millennium." However, she thought that it was a prerequisite for improving both women's status and the health of the society. Suffrage for women would improve the home, help fight vice and corruption in the society, and improve the possibilities for world peace and democracy. Catt also believed that the vote would give women dignity. She urged women to "rise up and refuse ever again to be slave, servant, dependent, or plaything."[22]

In contrast, the antisuffragists wanted to protect their "dependence." With ingratiating smiles they told their legislators, "Gentlemen, we trust you to take care of us and the government," and they opposed suffrage.[23] The antisuffragists believed that the female reformers were neglecting their husbands and children, and they were afraid that suffrage would lead to easy divorce and free love and would create too much stress for women. They wrote strident articles about the proper role of women as housewives and scoffed at the idea that women could do men's work. One writer scolded the women who "abandoned" their proper sphere:

> The home is our care. We may refuse children, and shrivel our souls and starve out that great love-force in a man which never expends itself save on his own child; we may turn home into one room of a boarding-house and live in public eating places, but homes and husbands and little children are going on in unbroken unity, and the women who see the most clearly are those who recognize that they are doing their full share of citizen work in building a home in which intelligently to keep safe men and children. The happiest husband of all is one whose wife thinks of him as her biggest child.[24]

Plagued with the charge by antisuffragists that the vote would break up the family by upsetting divinely ordained roles, the second generation of suffragists went on the offensive. Previously they had argued that women were entitled to the vote as a natural right and needed it in order to protect the family. Now, partially because of the growing strength of the Progressive movement nationally, the suffragists were more successful when they began to emphasize women's responsibility to reform society. They argued that women needed full citizenship in order to exert their moral influence in the public sphere.

While Carrie Chapman Catt saw women primarily as citizens, Jane Addams believed that women were first of all the guardians of home and family and that women's public action was a natural extension of the home in society. Although Addams never married, she was a champion of the family and municipal housekeeping. She articulated this ideology of feminist progressivism most fully in a pamphlet for NAWSA in which she wrote:

> Many women today are failing to discharge their duties to their own households properly simply because they do not perceive that as society grows more complicated it is necessary that woman shall extend her sense of responsibility to many things outside of her home if she would continue to preserve the home in its entirety. . . . A city is in many respects a great business corporation, but in other respects it is enlarged housekeeping. . . . If woman would fulfill her traditional responsibility to her own children; if she would educate and protect from danger factory children, children who must find their recreation on the street; if she would bring the cultural forces to bear upon our materialistic civilization; and if she would do it all with the dignity and directness fitting one who carries on her immemorial duties, then she must bring herself to the use of the ballot—that latest implement for self-government. May we not fairly say that American women need this implement in order to preserve the home?[25]

According to Addams, women had a duty to their families and to society to exert their moral influence. She did not question the sanctity of marriage or motherhood.

Alice Paul, one of the most militant of the suffragists, agreed with Addams that women ought to have the vote in order to exert their pacifist influence.

> I believe myself that women by nature are the great force for all these things that are constructive and up-building to a nation. . . . I think men contribute one thing and women another thing, that we're made that way. Women are certainly made as the peace-loving half of the world and the home-making half of the world, the temperate half of the world. The more power they have the better the world we are going to have.[26]

Anna Howard Shaw, the president of NAWSA from 1904 to 1915, agreed that the more power women had, the better the world would be. She extolled the virtues of motherhood and marriage but chose to remain single. Shaw once stated that people hurled at her the word "feminist," and she asked "and what does that mean? It is woman aspiring to be human, which is not a bad thing at all."[27] As a feminist, she believed marriage was "the holiest and divinest relation in life." Therefore, she believed marriage should be reformed into a higher and finer social institution by removing the word "obey" from the marriage ceremony and by achieving women's equality. When newspaper accounts misquoted her and tried to portray her as an enemy of marriage, she replied angrily to her friend Louisa Earle: "In fact my ideal of marriage is so high that anti-suffragists with their filthy, over-sex-developed minds cannot comprehend it."[28]

Shaw believed in the sanctity of motherhood but believed women should extend mother-love to the entire society. She wrote:

> We have heard that motherhood is a crown of glory, the greatest a woman can wear. We answer, No. Motherhood may or may not be a crown of glory; it may become a crown of shame. It requires that there shall be a something back of motherhood and in this something lies that which shall make it a crown of glory. The highest crown a woman can wear is womanhood—true, noble, strong, spiritual womanhood. . . . After this all things shall be to her a crown of glory, whether it be motherhood or spinsterhood. The mother-heart of woman that reaches out to the race and finds a wrong and rights it, finds a broken heart and heals it, finds a bruised life ready to be broken and sustains it—a woman instinct with mother-love, which is the expression of the Divine love, a woman who finding any wrong, any weakness, any pain, any sorrow, anywhere in the world, reaches out her hand to right the wrong, to heal the pain, to comfort the suffering—such a woman is God's woman.[29]

A close friend of Susan B. Anthony, Shaw was by Anthony's bedside when Anthony died in 1906. She wrote in her diary, "In the night she pressed my hand and laid hers in blessing on my head kissing me three times. . . . How shall we know how to carry on our work with her away?"[30] With Anthony's death, and Stanton's four years earlier, a new group of feminists continued the long fight for suffrage with single-minded devotion.

The importance of the South in the winning of women's suffrage helped make the national movement more conservative. Suffrage agitation in the South was slow to develop because of the association of suffrage with abolitionism. However, by the 1860s, southern women were vice presidents of the Equal Rights associations. Leaders of the southern suffrage movement were of such impeccable families that they could afford to be "radical" and at the same time "ladies"—charming, poised, beautiful, and intelligent. Four sisters—Mary, Anne, Sallie, and Laura Clay—and Madeline Breckinridge were suffrage leaders in Kentucky. In Mississippi, Belle Kearney worked for temperance and then suffrage. Nellie Nugent Somerville in Mississippi, Sue Shelton White and Elizabeth Avery Meriwether in Tennessee, Elizabeth Lyle Saxon in Louisiana, Pattie Jacobs in Alabama, and Mary Munford in Virginia were major leaders of the suffrage movement in the South. The number of suffrage groups in Alabama grew from two in 1910 to eighty-one by 1917. More and more newspapers in the South advocated suffrage after World War I.[31]

Historically, the South has been more resistant to feminism than any other region, largely as a result of southerners' support of evangelical religion, the strong kinship ties, a biracial caste system, and states' rights ideology. Only Tennessee, Kentucky, Texas, and Arkansas ratified the suffrage amendment; Virginia, Maryland, North Carolina, South Carolina, Georgia, Alabama, Louisiana, Florida, and Mississippi failed to do so.[32] More recently the majority of southern states remained intransigently opposed to the Equal Rights Amendment.

African-American Women and Suffrage

Largely because NAWSA wanted the support of the South, the organization's rhetoric was racist, and the white suffragists did not actively recruit African-American women. Although privately Anthony took a stand against racism, publicly she said nothing to alienate southerners. White suffragists even *appealed* to southern racism and nativism in order to get support for the Nineteenth Amendment.

Carrie Chapman Catt joined Anna Howard Shaw in endorsing votes for all—black, white, and immigrant—in an article in *Crisis* magazine in 1917. Just two years later, Catt used the 1910 census data to argue that the proportion of women to be enfranchised was higher among native-born groups than among immigrant groups. She further claimed that "white supremacy will be strengthened not weakened, by woman suffrage." However, Anna Howard Shaw wrote in her private correspondence that NAWSA should repudiate claims that woman suffrage would safeguard white supremacy throughout the South. She argued in her first NAWSA presidential address for universal human rights as a moral position. Catt's racist position, however, was the more dominant one in the organization.[33]

The national suffrage movement segregated its membership. Leaders often expressed blatantly racist views, and for fear of alienating southern support, kept silent as a whole on lynching and tacitly approved southern racism. Regardless of the racist nature of the suffrage movement as a whole, African-American women both fought racism within the movement and formed their own suffrage organizations. Unlike white women, they also had to launch a campaign to defend their virtue because of the widespread stereotype that black women were immoral. African-American women believed that woman suffrage would be beneficial to their families, would allow them to exert their moral influence to reform society, and would contribute to the empowerment of the race.

Maria W. Stewart was perhaps the first black woman in the United States to lecture in defense of women's rights. In the early 1830s, she called on black women to enter into all spheres: to develop their intellects and to be actively engaged in religion, education, business, and politics. She told an audience in Boston, "'Who shall go forward, and take off the reproach that is cast upon the people of color?' asked a voice from within: 'shall it be a woman?' And my heart made this reply—'If it is thy will, be it even so, Lord Jesus!'" The women Stewart spoke of approvingly early in her career—wives and mothers who exercised influence beyond the home—are replaced in her later work by examples of biblical and historical figures who wield genuine overt power and authority.[34]

In New Orleans, a committee of 500 African-American women organized with Mary J. Garrett as president. In 1878 they published a document demanding that black women be accorded every right and privilege guaranteed to their race by the Constitution and declaring that they would use every power in their hands to get these rights and privileges.[35]

Moreover, in spite of the white suffragists' racism, at least ninety prominent African-American women leaders supported suffrage, with two-thirds giving support during the decade before the passage of the amendment. African-American organizations that supported female suffrage included the National Federation of Afro-American Women, the National Association of Colored Women, Northeastern Federation of Colored Women's Clubs, and Delta Sigma Theta Sorority. Mary Ann Shadd Cary organized the Colored Women's Progressive Association in 1880. Strongly endorsing suffrage, Cary believed that the vote would empower women to help youth, enter more occupations, and agitate more effectively for "independence of thought and action." At least twenty African-American women's suffrage groups strongly endorsed woman suffrage.[36] The most prominent African-American suffragists were Sojourner Truth, Anna Julia Cooper, Nannie Helen Burroughs, Josephine St. Pierre Ruffin, Ida Wells Barnett, and Mary Church Terrell.

Josephine St. Pierre Ruffin, a suffragist since the 1880s, edited *Woman's Era*, an African-American woman's newspaper. She urged white suffragists to set aside their prejudices to allow African-American women to gain political equality. She believed that black women's clubs were organized not "for race work alone but for work along the lines that make for women's progress." Anna Julia Cooper also challenged racism within the woman suffrage movement. Her *A Voice from the South,* published in 1892, can be considered one of the original texts of the black feminist movement. Cooper was the one who first analyzed the fallacy of referring to the "black man" when speaking of black people and argued that just as white men cannot speak through the consciousness of black men, neither can black *men* fully and adequately reproduce the exact voice of the black *woman*.[37]

Cooper was one of three black women invited to address the World's Congress of Representative Women in 1893, and one of the few women to speak at the 1900 Pan African Congress Conference in London. She established the Colored Women's YWCA in 1905.[38]

Cooper was born in 1858, the child of a slave woman and a white master. She received a B.A. and an M.A. from Oberlin and taught in Washington, D.C. at the M Street High School. In 1925, at the age of sixty-seven, she received a Ph.D. in Latin from the University of Paris. She published two historical works in French. Cooper wrote the oft-quoted lines: "Only the BLACK WOMAN can say when and where I enter in the quiet undisputed dignity of my womanhood, without violence or special patronage, then and there the whole *Negro race enters with me.*" In her later life Cooper established Frelinghuysen University in Washington, D.C., an evening college for employed adults; she served as its president from 1929 to 1941. She died in 1964.[39]

Cooper believed in women's education, and she accepted the belief in women's moral superiority. She wrote, "The feminine factor can have its proper effect only through woman's development and education so that she may fitly stamp her force on the forces of her day." She believed the elevation of black women would raise the entire race. Cooper argued that it would be subversive of every human interest that the cry of one-half the human family be stifled. "Woman in stepping from the pedestal of statue-like inactivity in the domestic shrine, and daring to think and move and speak,—to undertake to help shape, mold, and direct the thought of her age, is merely completing the circle of the world's vision."[40]

Similarly, Nannie Helen Burroughs, founder of the National Training

School for Girls and secretary of the Woman's Auxiliary of the National Colored Baptist Convention, argued that black women needed the ballot because men did not value their virtue, and they needed protection. Furthermore, enfranchisement would aid education, help them in the work force, and contribute to race empowerment.[41]

Two other prominent African-American feminists battled against racism within the suffrage movement as they fought for women's equality. In 1913 NAWSA and the Congressional Union arranged a large suffrage march. Mary Church Terrell, a prominent African-American feminist and progressive, planned to lead the Delta Sigma Theta Sorority of Howard University, and Ida Wells-Barnett would lead Alpha Suffrage Club. Barnett was told that she could not march with the all-white Chicago contingency. Her group was to bring up the rear. However, in protest, Barnett waited with onlookers until the Chicago delegation passed by and then slipped into their lines. Terrell and Barnett were fighting for the enfranchisement of all women, including three million African-American women.[42] They also dedicated their lives to fighting against lynching.

Mary Church was born in Memphis and attended Oberlin. Her father was the South's first African-American millionaire. Both her parents were former slaves; her father was the son of his former master. When she was graduated from Oberlin in 1884, she became one of only three black women to have received college degrees. After graduation she traveled extensively in Europe, perfecting her French, German, and Italian. She returned to teach in M Street High School in Washington, D.C. There she married Robert Heberton Terrell, one of the first African-American graduates from Harvard. Since married women could not teach, she had to quit her teaching job. Even Terrell's wealth could not shield her from racism; three of her children died after only a few days, and Mary Terrell believed their deaths resulted from improper medical care in a poorly equipped, segregated hospital. She went to New York to have her daughter Phyllis.

Terrell became involved in community work as a member of the District of Columbia Board of Education and served three terms as the president of the National Association of Colored Women. She picketed the White House with the National Woman's Party on behalf of suffrage and was a member of the Women's International League for Peace and Freedom. She lobbied for progressive causes until her death at ninety.[43]

In her autobiography Terrell tells of her friendship with Susan B. Anthony, Alice Stone Blackwell, Henry Blackwell, Carrie Chapman Catt, and Harriot

Stanton Blatch. While she was fully aware of racism within the suffrage movement, she stated that "it was rare to find any of the original suffragists or their immediate families who were badly afflicted with race prejudice."[44]

Like Terrell, Ida Wells Barnett, an African-American journalist from Memphis, Tennessee, fought against racism and sexism. Barnett was the Rosa Parks of the 1880s. When a conductor asked her to leave the "white" section of a train bound for Woodstock from Memphis, she refused. Three conductors were needed to remove her, and she sank her teeth into the hand of one. She sued and won $500 in damages. Unfortunately, the case was later reversed. She dedicated her life to the enforcement of the Fifteenth Amendment, winning female suffrage, and opposing lynching.

Between 1882 and 1946, almost 5,000 people died by lynching. Lynching upheld white men's control over black and white women, and over black men. The presumed trade-off implicit in the southern code of chivalry was that the southern lady was obliged to obey the white man in exchange for protection from the black "rapist." Wells acknowledged that the primary rationale for lynching African-American men was the accusation of their rape of white women. Therefore, she defended the integrity of black manhood and the virtue of black womanhood. Because she challenged the very foundations of southern society, her presses were burned, and her life was threatened. As a result, she moved to the North. She formed the Alpha Suffrage Club in Chicago in 1914, and the Colored Women's Progressive Franchise Association in Washington, D.C.[45]

Barnett and Terrell joined other African-American women and white southern women in a campaign for better public schools, abolition of the convict lease system, abolition of child labor, better prison conditions, and protective legislation for women. Although the majority of southern white suffragists were racists, some did try to establish biracial alliances and work for social justice. In 1902 women's societies of the Southern Methodist church became the first groups of white southerners to criticize southern racial patterns openly. Later in 1930 Jesse Daniel Ames helped to bridge the racial barrier and established the Association of Southern Women for the Prevention of Lynching, an organization with 40,000 members at its peak.[46]

A consequence of the cult of the angel in the house, which emphasized women as nurturing mothers and gentle companions, was the exclusion of African-American and working-class women from the prerogatives of "womanhood." Not only were they considered aberrant for working outside the home, but they were also considered freely available sexually to upper-class males. Nevertheless, African-American suffragists shared a belief in female moral superiority and believed that woman suffrage would be beneficial to the family, would allow women to exert their moral influence to reform society, and would contribute to the empowerment of the race. Sojourner Truth, Stewart, Cooper, Burroughs, Ruffin, Barnett, and Terrell contributed greatly to the women's rights and civil rights struggles and steadfastly urged the white feminists to live up to their own ideals of democracy.

Working-Class Women and Suffrage

The national suffrage movement also failed to reach outside the middle and upper classes to respond to the needs of working women, except to advocate protective labor legislation. Members of NAWSA did not actively recruit them into the movement. Because of NAWSA's lack of interest in working-class women, Harriot Stanton Blatch, Elizabeth Cady Stanton's daughter, who had been active in England with militant suffragists, complained that NAWSA had ignored working women.[47] Blatch formed the Women's Political Union, patterned after the militant English Women's Social and Political Union led by Emmeline Pankhurst. The Women's Political Union was the first major attempt by an American suffrage organization to recruit working women. In 1910 the union sponsored the first of a number of suffrage parades in New York City.

Two other organizations, the National Consumers' League and the National Women's Trade Union League, were small but effective organizations which fought for working women. The NCL was established in 1899, incorporating other similar leagues which had been founded in the large cities. Florence Kelley was the guiding force of the NCL, which enlisted young women like Pauline and Josephine Goldmark and Frances Perkins. Members of the NCL and scores of other social feminists were aggressive in fighting for protective legislation for working women, a minimum wage, and the abolition of child labor.

The reform feminists favored labor legislation to regulate women's hours of employment and wages. They subscribed to traditional gender roles and therefore believed that, ideally, mothers should not have to work. Since many did, they believed that they and their children should be protected. The landmark court cases like *Muller v. Oregon* legitimized protective labor legislation for women, based on women's inferior physical capacity and childbearing capabilites. By embracing protectionism instead of equality, the reform feminists inadvertently helped to confine women in jobs traditionally defined as female, which were low paid with little possibility for advancement. Hours legislation especially hurt women who were printers and waitresses. Moreover, the legislation was ineffective in achieving pay equity and did nothing to assist professional women. In the long run, the legislation was actually harmful to women. But the widespread legislative successes in the short run illustrated the effectiveness of arguing on the basis of traditional sexual roles and for women's protection.[48]

Members of the National Women's Trade Union League, commonly referred to as WTUL, also generally supported protective labor legislation for women. The WTUL was founded in 1903 at an American Federation of Labor Convention by socialists, social workers, reformers, and a few trade unionists. Margaret Dreier Robins and her sister, Mary Dreier, joined Rose Schneiderman, Leonora O'Reilly, Helen Marot, and Pauline Newman as leaders of the organization. Members of the WTUL believed that their organization could transcend ethnic and class differences. In her book on Margaret Dreier Robins, Elizabeth Anne Payne describes the membership of the WTUL: "League women were immigrants' daughters who marched in suffrage parades, financiers' wives who bailed out strikers, broommakers who lobbied legislators, clubwomen who inspected sweatshops and lead factories, and laundresses and glove stitchers who looked to the women's movement as a natural ally in their industrial struggle."[49]

Robins was the head of the WTUL from 1907 through 1922. Like Jane Addams, she saw feminism not as a rejection of domesticity but as an extension of woman's role and power within the home into the public sphere. She accepted and celebrated separate but equal spheres for men and women. She encouraged women to "mother" the world. She believed that women were naturally social, generous, healing, and nurturing. Because she believed that the male character was essentially divisive, atomistic, short-sighted, and narcissistic, it was imperative that female values be infused into society. Robins poured a tremendous amount of her own money into the organization and resembled Alice Paul in her single-minded dedication and leadership style.[50]

The WTUL was the only feminist organization composed largely of working women or those who formerly worked. Members of WTUL sought to educate and organize both middle-class and working-class women to support the cause of women's labor. The WTUL led the garment strikes in 1910 and was supportive of the 1912 Lawrence strike. The organization experienced limited success because of the shortage of funds, the hostility or indifference of organized labor, and the difficulty of organizing women workers.[51] Working women were primarily unskilled workers, and the most influential labor union, the American Federation of Labor, did not organize unskilled workers. In 1900 only 3 percent of female factory workers were unionized; after the garment strikes in 1913, the number increased to 6 percent. The International Ladies' Garment Workers Union (ILGWU), an affiliate of the AFL, was the most successful women's union.[52]

The Radicals in the Suffrage Movement

As NAWSA became more conservative, a new wave of militancy grew within the movement when Alice Paul and Lucy Burns came to Washington in 1912, after spending time in England. Paul and Burns joined other militants like Mrs. Lawrence Lewis, Crystal Eastman, and Mary Beard. With NAWSA's initial support, they began agitating for a federal amendment. They staged a march the day before Woodrow Wilson was inaugurated, with 8,000 to 10,000 people marching. When the marchers were attacked by some of the crowd of 500,000, the secretary of war had to call out troops to quell the riot. A writer for the New York Times described the marchers' reactions: "Through all the confusion and turmoil the women paraders marched calmly, keeping a military formation as best they could. The bands played and hundreds of yellow banners fluttered in the wind."[53]

The militants finally broke with NAWSA and formed the Congressional Union in 1913, later renamed the National Woman's Party in 1916.[54] Winnifred Harper Cooley, a younger member of the NWP, summarized their demands besides the vote:

1. Abolition of all arbitrary handicaps calculated to prevent women's economic independence.
2. Opportunity for women to serve in all civic capacities.
3. Demand for single standard of morality.
4. Abolition of white slavery and prostitution.
5. The right to activity of expression and of creating social ideals quite unhampered by old superstitions.[55]

The radical suffragists also considered family issues a priority but opposed protectionism for women. They emphasized sexual similarities rather than differences. The clash between the NWP and mainstream suffrage movement may also be seen as differences between a more individualistic approach which focused on women's autonomy versus a communitarian approach which emphasized municipal housekeeping. The radicals adopted an agenda designed to achieve full equality for women.

Alice Paul characterized her position in the struggle for equality for women as a "feeling of loyalty to our own sex and an *enthusiasm* to have every degradation that was put upon our sex removed."[56] Paul believed that they must keep pressuring Woodrow Wilson, who was doing nothing to get the suffrage bill passed. The National Woman's Party's policy was holding the "party in power" responsible, regardless of the position of individual members.

When Wilson did nothing to push suffrage and followed the Democratic party's position that suffrage was a state issue, the militants took to the streets again. The militants picketed for three months in 1917 without major incidents. When the United States entered World War I in April of that year, passersby began to attack the picketers because they carried banners opposing the war, bearing the slogan "Democracy Should Begin at Home." The police began to arrest women in June 1917 for "obstructing traffic," and the women were sent to a workhouse prison for thirty days. In all, 218 women were arrested from twenty-six states, and 97 went to prison.

Ernestine Hara Kettler, one of those who went to prison, described her experience. She said that the women refused to work because they considered themselves political prisoners and would simply sit with their hands folded each day in the work room. She remembered that the food was one of the biggest problems. The food was rancid and had worms in it. She also described the violence which the women faced.

> The next group that came in was the one that went on a hunger strike, and they were brutally treated. They received very severe treatment. They were beaten and dragged across the patio from the superintendent's office to their cells. . . . Some women had broken ribs and were bleeding profusely and they weren't treated. Others had all kinds of lacerations.[57]

Officials of the prison shoved tubes into their stomachs and force-fed them. Alice Paul was one of those who experienced this degrading practice. Undaunted, the NWP picketed in Washington daily from January 1917 to July 1918.[58]

The day before a House vote on suffrage in January 1918, Wilson finally came out for woman's suffrage. The measure passed the House but failed to come up in the Senate because of political maneuvering. Wilson finally personally appealed to the Senate in October 1918 to pass it, but it failed by two votes. After a moratorium on demonstrations, the NWP began in January 1919 to burn the words of Woodrow Wilson in Lafayette Park, thereby keeping the cause vividly before the Congress and the public. Wilson began to exert his influence on the Democratic members of the Senate, and on June 4, 1919, the suffrage bill passed.

Carrie Chapman Catt had initially approved Alice Paul's idea of pushing for a federal amendment and of holding parades. However, when the militants started picketing and attacking Woodrow Wilson, Catt and most of the members of NAWSA were deeply offended and believed that the radicals were seriously damaging the cause. [59] Catt believed that suffragists ought to always be ladies and law-abiding citizens. In contrast, Paul believed that free women in control of their own lives ought to adopt unladylike tactics, even break the law if necessary in order to gain suffrage. Paul was very influenced by her time in England, when she worked with the British militant Emmeline Pankhurst.[60] Ultimately both the tactics of Catt's lobbyists and of the militants were necessary to secure the passage of the suffrage amendment. However, this split between Catt and Paul was deep and would continue after suffrage was won.

When Archduke Franz Ferdinand was assassinated, the suffrage movement was gaining tremendous momentum. As sweethearts said good-bye and men marched off to the war, women's lives changed dramatically. When large numbers of women entered nontraditional jobs during World War I, they did not question the fact that marriage and motherhood were their primary concerns. However, discrimination against women in the work force stimulated feminist campaigns to improve their wages and working conditions.

During World War I, 100,000 women entered the munitions factories, 5 percent of them working for the first time. Jobs like shipbuilding, woodworking, making machine guns and cartridges, and work in lumber yards had always been a male preserve. Now, however, women operated punch presses, drill presses, latches, milling machines, and metal machines. As grinders, welders, riveters, and crane operators, they were crucial to the war effort. According to the reports of 562 firms in 1919, over 58,000 women had been substituted for men, and 37,600 were in metal trades.[61] In the census of 1920, statistics revealed that over eight million women were employed in 437 different job classifications. Over 500,000 of the new women workers held clerical or similar positions, and another 450,000 entered the professions.[62] During World War I, millions of women performed their nurturant role as they made surgical dressings, replaced nurses in hospitals, fed national guardsmen on duty in their neighborhoods, knitted socks for the servicemen, and organized and planted Victory gardens.[63]

The impact of the Civil War and World War I, industrialization, the entrance of women into the labor force, and increased access to education and the professions created a more favorable climate for a feminist movement. In the period from 1860 to 1920, a national movement for women's rights galvanized, western women achieved suffrage, feminist Progressives gained protective labor legislation for women, and Greenwich Village radicals pioneered in sexual freedom for women. New opportunities for education and employment raised new questions about women's proper sphere and inspired a feminist consciousness. Birth control advocates helped make birth control available and more respectable, increasing women's control of their bodies.

When the feminists did not challenge the traditional family and argued that women needed the vote in order to protect their families and to improve the entire society, they found a large receptive audience. Since American women were increasingly empowered as wives and mothers, the profamily stance of the suffragists not only was pragmatically effective but stemmed from their own experiences with the limits of covert, domestic power. Regardless of how much leverage they might have as wives and mothers, they were still denied full citizenship and were vulnerable to marital violence, adverse property settlements, and economic dependence. However, by retreating from the battle for full equality and emphasizing sexual differences, they inadvertently helped reinforce their subordination in the long run. While the United States was fighting to "make the world safe for democracy," many women were fighting to create a democracy at home.

7

EXQUISITE SURRENDER?
The New Feminists of the 1920s

My mother brought me up to be a feminist. She also hoped I would be a Methodist and a good girl, but these were less important. So when I was very young I learned to be sorry for the downtrodden women. . . . I floated easily into suffragettism, feminism and other declarations of revolt. . . . I was sure there was a wonderful world ahead, full of intoxicating possibilities—from which I could only be excluded by man's viciousness, by man's tyranny.

The vote had always held a position of minor significance in the total credo of my feminism. Birth control was much more important, also the elimination of the family kitchen. I was convinced that in any just world the men would do the dishes. Most important of all to my growing creed was the right of women to work.

Thereafter I had only one religion, a sort of perverse feminism based on the convictions that women had all the children, men had all the fun, and men were pretty awful anyhow. I was still determined to have a career as much like a man as possible. And no babies. And no matrimony. . . . I had lived too long in a family of men who in times of distress remained pleasantly incapable of making a cup of coffee. I do not believe I could have married a southerner and if I had I am sure I would have murdered him the first time he asked for his slippers or the evening paper.

Lorine Pruette, 1927

On Armistice Day, November 11, 1918, an overjoyed American soldier jumped through a plate glass window in Paris out of sheer exuberance. While recovering in the hospital, his friends asked him why on earth he did it. He replied, "It seemed like the thing to do at the time." The same day in New York, eight hundred Barnard College women snake-danced in Morningside Heights. A young woman climbed the platform of "Liberty Hall" in Times

Square and sang the doxology to a reverently quiet crowd. Tons of ticker tape flooded the streets for returning veterans. A dummy of the Kaiser skidded down Wall Street as jubilant patriots wielded a firehose.[1]

An exuberant optimism swept the country, spilling over into one of the most controversial causes of the century—woman suffrage. The crest had been building for over twenty years. Only one more state was needed to grant women suffrage, and now the fate of the Nineteenth Amendment hung with the recalcitrant Tennessee House of Representatives, an unpredictable body that had passed laws outlawing the teaching of evolution and upholding school prayer. The night before the final vote Tennessean legislators were reeling through the halls of state dead drunk. Carrie Chapman Catt wrote that "in agony of soul suffragists went to bed in the early morning, but not to sleep."[2]

The next morning, on a hot, muggy August 18, 1919, twenty-four-year-old state congressman Harry Burn sat waiting for the Tennessee House of Representatives to vote on suffrage. Burn represented a rural district in eastern Tennessee opposed to suffrage. His mother was a dedicated supporter and had written him an urgent letter saying, "Don't forget to be a good boy and help Mrs. Catt put 'Rat' in Ratification."

The suffrage leaders were already in the gallery when the last legislator straggled in. When Seth Walker, the speaker of the house, called the body to order, the suffragists' hearts seemed to beat louder than his gavel. In a melodramatic attempt to rally the antisuffragists, Walker shouted, "The hour is come. The battle has been fought and won." He moved to table the issue, which tied 48-48. Walker demanded a second roll call, left his speaker's seat, and threw his arm around Banks Turner, a suffrage supporter. Walker whispered in Turner's ear. As Turner passed his call without a response, suffragists shivered, and a breathless silence filled the room. At the end of the roll call, Turner threw off the speaker's arm and shouted a defiant "no," to cheers and shouts.

Since the opposition's motion to table the suffrage bill tied, it meant that the measure itself had to come up for a vote. As Harry Burn's name was called, a hush fell over the hall. He voted "yes." A few minutes later Banks Turner also voted "yes." With a 49-47 vote, women had the suffrage, seventy-one years after the Seneca Falls Convention. When the governor signed the proclamation eight days later, on August 24 at 10:17 A.M., women's right to vote in the United States was official.

At the headquarters of NAWSA and at the NWP in Washington, D.C., phones rang, and women hugged each other, weeping tears of joy and fatigue. Although the fight for equality had really just begun, suffrage as a unifying force could no longer hold the feminist movement together. Carrie Chapman Catt recalled that in February 1920 at the last suffrage convention: "Women looked into each other's eyes and saw old, endearing memories of long, hard work leap to life. They were facing new things, new affiliations, separate ways, but the recognition of what the old things, the old supreme affiliations, the old way together, had done for them, singly and collectively, rested on them with a poignant inner compulsion."[3]

The woman's hour was striking; the suffragists pulled ribbons which were attached to the clapper of a bell in the middle of the convention hall, and the bell rang out.[4] While the suffragists celebrated their victory, many of the 26 million new voters were more concerned about the revolution in morals taking place than they were about their civic rights.

In a prophetic statement Anna Howard Shaw said:

> You younger women will have a harder task than ours. You will want equal-
> ity in business and it will be even harder to get than the vote for you will
> have to fight for it as individuals and that will not get you far. Women will
> not unite, since they will be in competition with each other. As soon as a
> woman has it for herself she will have entered the man's world and cease to
> fight as a woman for other women.[5]

Just as Shaw prophesied, feminism became individualistic in the 1920s after the vote was achieved. After suffrage was won, the national feminist movement split over the new celebration of female sexuality and the issue of protective labor legislation for women but continued its fight for political equality. As an organized movement, feminism did not have a large following because many people felt that the vote had solved the problems of inequality; a conservative political climate discouraged reform, and a new emphasis on female sexuality within egalitarian marriages promised greater fulfillment for women. Moreover, a movement for scientific housekeeping and scientific motherhood, as well as the reinforcement of women's "proper place" in popular culture, helped convince many American women that marriage was their destined vocation.

Although women did in fact enhance their position in egalitarian marriages and did begin to reclaim female sexuality as normal and natural, they were still excluded from most forms of overt public power. They exercised their influence covertly, primarily in the domestic sphere as mothers, wives, and consumers. In the absence of a large national feminist movement, individual feminists attempted to combine marriage, motherhood, and careers in their own lives. Even the women who viewed marriage as their vocation had high hopes for their daughters' greater freedom.

Farewell to Reform: The Politics of Reaction

Because of a conservative political climate, including the red-baiting of reformers and radicals, feminists were more reluctant to join a collective movement than earlier. The Ku Klux Klan gained immense support during the postratification years, boasting 4.5 million members in 1924. A year later, the Klan members marched in full regalia past the White House. Prohibition went into effect in 1920, ending more than half a century of agitation to control the production and sale of alcoholic beverages. Much of the prohibition movement's strength came from the rural, fundamentalist South and Midwest. Immigrants and Catholics in the urban centers were the strongest opponents of prohibition.

In the wake of the Russian Revolution, A. Mitchell Palmer, Woodrow Wilson's attorney general, began raids on suspected radicals. The Red Scare of 1919–20 resulted in over 6,000 arrests and over 500 deportations. Nicola Sacco and Bartolomeo Vanzetti were casualties of this hysteria. They were arrested for a murder in South Braintree, Massachusetts, and convicted on inconclusive evidence. Sacco and Vanzetti were electrocuted in 1927 without a fair trial. Many Americans believed that their only "crime" was being anarchists. In Dayton, Tennessee, John T. Scopes was tried for teaching the theory of evolution in his high school class. William Jennings Bryan, the famous populist orator and defender of the Bible, faced Scopes's brilliant defense lawyer, Clarence Darrow, in a dramatic trial. Traditional values, not just John Scopes, were on trial. Scopes was found guilty but was fined only $100. More important, the national ridicule of fundamentalism during the Scopes trial weakened efforts to enforce a particular value system legally.

Female Sexual Power

Within the context of a highly conservative political climate of the 1920s, young people rebelled against Victorian morality. Women's morals were changing, and the flapper replaced the Gibson girl. Previously, female passionlessness had been extolled; in the twenties female sexuality was celebrated. Symbolic of this shift, American women's skirts rose. In 1919 women wore their skirts six inches from the ground with black or tan stockings. Then skirts began to rise, somewhat startlingly at first. An enterprising commentator followed this trend and found that in 1919 the average distance of women's hems was 10 percent of the woman's height, or six or seven inches from the floor. By 1920 they had risen to 20 percent, retreated to 10 percent in 1923, rose to 15–20 percent in 1924, and by 1927 had exceeded 25 percent.[6]

Some women began to challenge Victorian notions of decency by wearing "daring" bathing suits. Before the First World War, women were arrested for smoking cigarettes in public, for using profanity, for driving automobiles without a man beside them, and for wearing shorts.[7] Policewomen on a Chicago beach in 1922 patrolled for decency, measuring swimsuits' armpits and necklines and arresting bathers in one-piece knitted suits with shoulder straps and short legs. When Olympic champion Ethelda Blubery took off her stockings before going for a swim in 1919, she was given a citation for "nude bathing."[8]

When Miss Washington, D.C., Margaret Gorman, strode across the stage as the first Miss America in Atlantic City in 1921, she wore an abbreviated Victorian bathing suit, which looked like a short dress but showed her bare knees. However modest she might seem to bikini-clad American women today, the audience gasped.[9] The demonstration against the pageant in 1968 protesting the portrayal of women as sex objects was a long way off. Most of the contestants in 1921 saw their participation as boldly liberated. Moreover, the suggestion that in 1984 Miss America would lose her crown for posing nude with another woman would have been simply unthinkable.

In the twenties, women also defied convention by dancing outrageous new dances. In 1911 Irving Berlin had written "Alexander's Ragtime Band," the waltz had suddenly faded in popularity, and new dance crazes swept in. Women danced the Fox Trot, the Horse Trot, the Grizzly Bear, and many others. One girl, according to a popular song of 1912, declared, "Mother said I shouldn't dare / To try and do the Grizzly Bear," but the girls nevertheless did try to do it, along with the "scandalous" Bunny Hug and Charleston.

As portrayed in popular culture, the flapper who danced these new dances was a daring young rebel who had a drink in one hand and a cigarette in the other. She wore short skirts and bobbed her hair. She was skinny, flat-chested, nervous, irreverent, and a vamp. The flapper's boyfriend wore a coonskin coat, bell-bottomed trousers, and a polka-dotted tie.

John Held, Jr., first immortalized the flapper in his illustrations for *Life* magazine. Earlier, Held's mother, an actress, had been Salt Lake City's first "Bloomer girl," shocking the town by wearing bloomers in public while riding a bicycle.[10] Many middle-class white youths, especially those in college, rebelled against their parents' values. Parents agonized when their children came in after all-night "petting parties" and believed that "freedom" was just another word for sin.[11]

Unlike feminists of the late nineteenth century, many rebellious young women in the 1920s viewed liberation as greater sexual and social freedom, not as building a career. Young college women planned on being able to support themselves after college but, unlike nineteenth-century women, did not enter college as one would a religious order, planning to forsake marriage. These young women differed greatly from many older feminists who believed that a woman's career was the most important thing in life. The ability to work, to create, and to support oneself was not as important as finding a husband to most of the younger women.[12]

In fact, women's greater sexual experimentation, especially in petting, which was becoming more acceptable, was in the context of impending marriage. Although sexual mores began to change, with more open discussion of sex and greater physical intimacy, young people accommodated their traditional upbringing by viewing such liberties as leading to the altar.[13] The process of the sexualization of love and the glorification of sex helped to recharge the momentum toward marriage.[14]

As we have seen, surveys on sexual behavior before Masters and Johnson were few and unscientific. They recorded vastly different estimates regarding the extent of premarital intercourse. The only consistent theme was that more American women were experiencing sexual activity before marriage than previously. G. V. Hamilton's survey of 1931 showed 61 percent of the women born in 1891 or later had premarital coital experience. Lewis Terman's study of 800 cases showed that 12 percent of the women married before 1912 were not virgins at the time, and the percentage rose to 32 percent in the years 1932–37.[15]

In the 1930s, when the impact of the changes in sexual mores could be seen dramatically, Dorothy Dunbar Bromley and Florence Britten found one-fourth of the undergraduate women and one-half of the men in their sample had experienced sexual intercourse. Similarly, in the thirties, Ernest W.

Burgess and Paul Wallin reported that 47 percent of the engaged women surveyed had had intercourse, three-fourths with only their future spouses. The researchers found that petting was acceptable for the unmarried young, and intercourse acceptable for those committed to marriage.[16]

In her book *The Lost Generation*, Maxine Davis captures the feeling of exhilaration of young people's cultural revolt in the twenties.

> I remember how my elders chilled in the very real fear as we in our salad days charlestoned down the Primrose Path, with debutante slouch and knee-length skirts. Our bobbed hair, cigarettes and hip flasks the very mark of Cain. They whitened when they read in the papers that we checked our stays at dances and debated the relative merits of free love and companionate marriage. We ourselves felt like a corps of Christopher Columbuses when we made the remarkable discovery that after a man and woman married, they still remained separate entities, something our naive parents never could have known. No, never! And we figured that it naturally followed that those separate entities should be allowed full freedom from each other. . . . now our vaunted freedom to live and love is ours only academically.
>
> . . . Still we of previous generations were not willing in our young years to accept life as we found it. Whether we wanted change in the conduct of our personal affairs or in the whole social structure, American youth has been inclined to take the bit in its teeth.[17]

Some Americans believed that jazz was responsible for the revolution in sexuality. To them, jazz epitomized licentiousness, indecent dancing, and savagery. In the *Ladies Home Journal*, John R. McMahon railed against jazz:

> Anyone who says the "youth of both sexes can mingle in close embrace"—with limbs intertwined and torso in contact—without suffering harm, lies. Add to this position the wriggling movement and sensuous stimulation the abominable jazz orchestra with its voodoo-born minors and its direct appeal to the sensory center, and if you can believe that youth is the same after this experience as before, then God help your child.[18]

A woman in Danville, Illinois, fought a lone battle against the "wicked age," going on a forty-eight-day fast to get her husband to quit smoking and join the church. It is not known whether she succeeded.[19]

The young people's cultural rebellion troubled many older feminists. Feminists of the nineteenth century had fought hard for women's "self-sovereignty," the right to control their own bodies and to refuse intercourse. Older feminists in the 1920s feared that greater sexual freedom might make women more vulnerable to exploitation and more widely regarded as sexual objects. For these reasons, they assessed the new morality not as liberating but as encouraging licentiousness. However, the flapper thought this notion terribly old-fashioned; to her, freedom meant the ability to say yes, not no. Dorothy Dunbar Bromley chastised the feminists of the 1920s by saying that they "rant about equality when they might better prove their ability." She claimed that the "new feminist is intensely self-conscious whereas the feminists were formerly sex-conscious." The focus on the joys of heterosexuality tended to weaken the ties among women, including women's identification with other women. No longer confined to a "separate sphere," many women lost the emotional support of an extended female network. Instead they anticipated greater fulfillment in egalitarian marriages.[20]

The Egalitarian Family

Gone was the ideal of a patriarchal marriage. The ideal marriage of the 1920s was a 50-50 partnership founded on frankness, tolerance, and an absence of dominance of either partner. One writer remarked, "The sturdy oak and the clinging vine in matrimony was once a delighting picture. Today it is rather sickening." Men were urged to win the respect of their wives and children.[21]

Women were promised emotional intimacy and sexual fulfillment with their husbands in the new egalitarian family of the 1920s. Not surprisingly, when 600 college female seniors were polled in 1919, they were divided on the question of whether they would attempt marriage, motherhood, and a professional or business career if they met the right man. The respondents were from colleges like Vassar, Mount Holyoke, Wellesley, Smith, and Bryn Mawr. Of those surveyed, 235 answered yes, while 302 said no. When asked, "Provided you could not have both marriage and a business and professional career, which would you sacrifice?" a resounding 522 answered that they would sacrifice career; only 51 would concede marriage, and 22 were undecided.[22]

Lorine Pruette's survey of 388 young women (median age of 16.5) similarly revealed women's enthusiasm for marriage, as well as their career aspirations. When asked whether they would choose careers or marriage, 61 percent (238) replied that they preferred careers and 149 (39 percent) home. If they could choose only one, marriage was the first choice of 212, versus 118 who would choose career. However, erasure was common on this question, revealing their ambivalence when forced to choose.[23]

In their study of young women's aspirations published in 1930, Phyllis Blanchard and Carlyn Manasses found that 82 percent of the 252 women surveyed preferred marriage, 13 percent preferred careers over marriage, 55 percent wanted marriage alone, and 38 percent wanted to combine marriage and a career. The respondents expected marriage to be the means for a fuller and richer life, an opportunity for sharing joys and sorrows with a companion. Of those surveyed, 92 percent wanted children, 7 percent had no desire for children, and 81 percent planned to use birth control.[24] Although college women were divided over combining marriage and career in the 1920s, they believed that a college education was compatible with motherhood.

As family relations became more democratized and rigid sexual roles began to break down, more emotional interaction was possible between husband and wife, and between parents and children. Smaller families of one to three children permitted more investment of time, money, and attention on each child, especially in the professional and business classes. These families could provide for advanced education for their children. The marriage rate rose between 1890 and 1920, as did the proportion of married people in the population. At the same time, age at marriage dropped: in 1890 the median age at marriage was 26.1 for men and 22.0 for women; by 1920 it was 24.6 for men and 21.3 for women.[25]

Women's higher expectations of fulfillment in marriage and their greater influence within the family, coupled with their new opportunities for education, stimulated individualistic demands. Willystine Goodsell, a commentator on the American family in the 1920s, urged that women try to reconcile their needs for personal growth and the interests of their families. She believed that the family ought to be genuinely egalitarian and that it should allow women self-realization. Goodsell believed that many women were forced to choose between love and children, and the free development of personality in congenial work. She argued for an ethic of individualism.

> Society unquestionably exacts from women so large a surrender of individuality after marriage as seriously to raise the ethical question whether such surrender, carried at times to the point of self-stultification, is either morally justifiable or socially serviceable. . . . In this age, the ancient principle of self-immolation always held before women is brought squarely into conflict

with a newer ethical conception that the highest duty of every individual is to develop all his talents for his own good as well as the benefit of humanity.[26]

Goodsell agreed that the "modern family" had undergone a transformation from a patriarchal form to a democratic one, an association of free individuals, united by love and mutual support, but she also wanted women to claim more power.[27] In their study of Middletown published in 1929, Robert and Helen Lynd corroborated Goodsell's assessment. Middletown adults regarded romance in marriage as essential, and they demanded more of life and marriage than their parents experienced.

When these higher expectations were not realized, more people divorced, especially since divorce was no longer so stigmatized.[28] Between 1870 and 1920 the number of divorces granted in the United States increased fifteenfold. In 1910 there were 8.8 divorces per 100 marriages. The figure rose to 13.4 divorces in 1920, and 16.5 in 1928, still a far cry from 1986, when half of all marriages ended in divorce.[29] Through an investigation of divorce records of Los Angeles and New Jersey, Elaine Tyler May found a reemphasis on traditional sexual role expectations. The 1920s divorce records showed an overwhelming concern with the husband's duty as provider and the wife's desire to be supported. Men's failure to fulfill this role often led to divorce court as swiftly as the women's failure to live up to the ideal of domesticity. Clearly women were using public, legal power to ensure their security within the family.[30]

Scientific Domesticity and Scientific Motherhood

In the 1920s the ideal of domesticity was changing dramatically. The preindustrial home was a manufacturing center where women performed an array of work requiring craftsmanship. By the end of the nineteenth century, the craft dimension of housework had virtually vanished. Beginning as early as the turn of the century, worried voices cried that domestic work was no longer respected. Were women becoming captains of a sinking ship? Glenna Matthews points out that in this period women were losing power to experts. Their power derived less from domesticity than from motherhood and emotional, sexual dimensions of marriage and their role as consumers. Women like Christine Frederick mounted a counteroffensive to the devaluation of housework and preached the ideal of "professional domesticity." She believed that a housewife was in reality a household engineer, who was simultaneously a manager and employee. She urged housewives to apply standards of efficiency and science to their tasks. Frederick thought that technology could actually dignify housekeeping as a full-time profession.[31]

Ellen Swallow Richards led domestic science into the scientific phase. She was trained as a chemist, but because she was a woman, she was not accepted by her profession—so she created one of her own. Richards believed that biochemistry would transform cooking into a precise laboratory exercise and that economics could revolutionize home budgeting and shopping. After the acceptance of the germ theory of disease, housewives felt a duty to protect their families by scrupulous cleaning and mounted a veritable sanitary crusade.[32] For some women, this conception of scientific housekeeping made the job of housewife more dignified and appealing.

Ultimately, however, the home economics movement failed to give status to domesticity. Nonetheless, a by-product of the crusade for "professional domesticity" was that it stimulated consumerism and was a boon to advertisers. By 1929, 80 percent of the family's needs were satisfied by purchases by women.[33] Advertisers spent millions trying to convince housewives to buy new labor-saving devices. Were housewives really "longing with all their hearts for smart, black taffeta dresses?" An ad for a Hamilton Beach carpet washer shows a woman on her knee beside it with her hands clasped as in prayer. Ads in the twenties tried to inspire guilt in women over children's scuffed shoes and the germs behind the bathroom sink, instead of lamenting the trials of servantless houses.[34] Housewives were told they could save at least three hours a day if they had technological servants. A toaster was only $4.00, a percolator $7.00, a kitchenette stovelette $15.00, and a fireless cooker $35.00. The biggest item was a full-size refrigerator for $470.00. A blue Monday of washing would be less blue with a washer with a wringer for $75.00. Hand electric irons and electric ironers could make the job less arduous. Dishwashers were also being sold. A vacuum cleaner was a "necessity." Advertisements portrayed domestic work as easy, fast, and efficient.[35]

Ironically, the image of ease and speed tended to devalue women's work because anybody with industry and the right appliances was supposed to do the tasks in no time. No craft was involved, and despite the efforts of Christine Frederick and Ellen Swallow Richards, techniques of efficiency were not applicable to the home where one worker performed such diversified tasks.

Whether women considered themselves "scientific" or not, the amount of housework which women did remained constant despite the invention of labor-saving devices. In 1924 women did about fifty-two hours a week of housework. In the twenties women devoted more time to shopping and caring for their children than in producing food and clothing. Industrialization had eliminated the work previously done by men and children, and also eliminated the drudgery of housework for women, but it did not reduce the amount of time demanded. By the 1960s, unemployed women spent fifty-five hours per week on housework, despite the much wider ownership of labor-reducing appliances and the availability of convenience foods.[36]

At the same time scientific housekeeping was espoused, more scientific approaches to motherhood also gained popularity. Within the "egalitarian family," women gained much more influence in parenting, a trend which began in the nineteenth century and became very apparent in the 1920s. Both husband and wife were no longer considered equally responsible for childrearing.[37] Robert and Helen Lynd discovered that the role Middletown's fathers played in childrearing was regarded as less important than that of the mother's. One business-class mother remarked, "My husband never pays any attention to the children."

Fathers still played an important part in the lives of their children, but the mother's role was central. Fathers were expected to be breadwinners and pals to their children. One frustrated father admitted, "I'm a rotten dad. If our children amount to anything, it's their mother who'll get all the credit. I'm so busy I don't see much of them and I don't know how to chum up to them when I do."[38]

Mothers and fathers in Middletown were bewildered by their children, who were being drawn away from home by their peer groups. Outside activities like athletics, dramatics, clubs, movies, and auto riding replaced "togetherness" in the family. A Middletown speaker at a Chautauqua lecture in the 1920s remarked, "We seem to be drifting away from fundamentals in our home life. The home was once a sacred institution where the family spent most of its time. Now it is a physical service station except for the old and infirm."[39]

Thus, with more responsibility for childrearing and more potential domestic power, women were also expected to rely on the advice of experts who advised anxious mothers on how to care for their children properly. In the midst of conflicting advice, women attended mothers's training classes and read manuals on childrearing. This proliferation of advice literature accentuated their feeling of anxiety and insecurity, since they were led to believe that their "mistakes" would damage their children permanently. Childrearing practices of the eighteenth century had focused on breaking the child's will. Because infant mortality was high, children were not the center of family life. By the 1920s the emphasis was on developing the child's intelligence, personality, and individuality. Along with the glorification of mothering came the warning in the 1920s of "smother love," of overmothering. John B. Watson warned them that mother love could be dangerous because it led to weak, dependent children with "crippled personalities" who were unable to make it in a competitive world of industrial capitalism. Watson proposed rigid feeding schedules, little or no affection, and training children to adjust to society's demands.[40]

Motherhood was no longer viewed as a natural, biological function, but as a complicated science. As childbirth moved increasingly into hospitals, women lost control over the birthing process. Some feminists in 1914 and 1915 had launched a national campaign for the use of the drug scopolamine. The drug made women in labor forget the pain, allowing them to awake from "twilight sleep" to find that they had delivered their babies. While these feminists were not successful in making scopolamine routinely available, they succeeded in making a painless childbirth more accepted than before. As Judith Leavitt points out in her book on the history of childbirth in the United States, women who gave birth in hospitals in the 1920s to the 1960s were so drugged that they did not experience one of their bodies' most powerful actions.

Just as women were expected to rely on physicians in "delivering" their babies, they also were obliged to keep up with the changing approaches to mothering. Watson's behavioristic approach slowly gave way to permissiveness. The dominant school of advice of the twentieth century was the reverse of Watson's recommendations. Mothers were urged to foster their children's individuality and to accommodate themselves to their children's needs.[41] The popularity of Freudianism in the United States lent legitimacy to the extremely important role of mothers in personality formation. As domestic work became more degraded, the cult of motherhood became more stridently proclaimed. Motherhood was seen as a profession demanding devotion, knowledge, and abundant patience.[42]

Because of women's increasing influence within the family, some writers in the 1920s expressed anxiety about the decline in patriarchal authority. Willard Waller, a sociologist at Barnard College, noted that the family had become a battleground of conflicting interests, each struggling for their share of the family income. The family's ties with the community seemed loosened, and high-pressure advertising stimulated greater and greater hunger for spending. Waller believed that the modern woman could not help but try to dominate her husband and "cannot help hating him if she succeeds." He pointed to the great decline in the authority of parents and the growing tendency of nonfamily agencies to assume much of the work of childrearing.[43]

Arthur Calhoun, a social historian of the family, joined Waller in expressing dismay over the changes within American families. He wrote in 1919 that the future of the family or home was "problematical." Likewise, Ernest R. Mowrer, a family sociologist, warned that the family seemed about to disintegrate. He pointed to the growing divorce rate and prevalence of desertion, as well as to the feminist demands for the "fullest development of individualism."[44]

While academic commentators warned that the family was endangered, other writers championed the changes and even proposed more radical alterations of marriage and motherhood. Floyd Dell optimistically celebrated the new egalitarianism in relationships and believed that when "patriarchalism was banished from the economy and home, people would live happy, unrepressed lives." He wrote, "Modernity re-establishes family life on the basis of romantic love."[45] Ellen Key, a Swedish feminist, championed free divorce, economic appreciation of domestic work, and motherhood. Key emphasized women's eroticism and sexual liberation and linked "motherliness" to heterosexual desire. She believed that women should be free to be unwed mothers, to form love relationships, and to end marriages if they were not sexually satisfied. However, she did not believe that women's fulfillment lay in competing with men politically and economically; rather, women would find happiness through their sex-specific destiny as wives, lovers, and mothers.[46]

Judge Ben B. Lindsey of Denver argued for "companionate marriages," dubbed "trial marriages" by some. Couples would marry, practice birth control, and have the right to divorce with mutual consent if no children had been born, and men would not generally have to pay alimony.[47] Suzanne LaFollette was even more radical than Key and Lindsey. She complained that marriage for men was a state, but a vocation for women. LaFollette argued for individual choice to rear children at home or in institutions. Her vision was that men would share in domestic labor, women would be economically independent, and illegitimacy would carry no societal stigma.[48]

Ethel Puffer Howes opened the Institute for the Coordination of Women's Interests at Smith College in 1925. She wanted to find ways for women to combine professional interests with motherhood. The institute opened a cooperative day-care center for the preschool children of employed mothers, a cooked-food service, and a school for "home assistants." She also tried to encourage careers for women which were conducive to part-time or home-based work. The institute lasted six years, but Smith eliminated it during the Great Depression. Perhaps Howes's experiment underscored the dilemma of educated women too boldly, or seemed irrelevant in a national economic emergency.[49]

"Sweet Surrender" in Popular Culture

While sociologists wrote about the disintegration of the family and radicals proposed alternatives to the traditional family, popular culture of the 1920s glorified marriage and motherhood as women's destiny. As we have seen, the new emphasis on sexual satisfaction for women in an egalitarian marriage, as well as the new emphasis on the challenges of scientific housekeeping and scientific motherhood, helped steer women into matrimony as their preferred vocation, convincing them that marriage would empower them, not entrap them in any way. The *Ladies Home Journal* continued to glorify romantic surrender and to depict marriage as a noble profession. One bold heroine, Sara, finally succumbs to her suitor's charms and says: "'Put 'em on, Dade,' she whispered. 'Put on the handcuffs.' He wheeled, shackling the slim wrists with his brown, hard fingers, and looked into the golden heady warmth of her eyes. Then he shackled his neck with her arms. . . . 'They tell me,' she laughed in exquisite surrender 'that marriage shackles bring [the] largest freedom. And I must have my freedom, you know!'"[50]

Another heroine, Emily March, is already married and also has a career. In the morning she and her husband each put on their hats and coats and go to work. They both do housework, and a cleaning woman comes twice a week. The "tragedy," however, is that Emily cannot cook, which is a source of great embarrassment to her in-laws. In a rash moment she invites all her relatives for Christmas dinner, which she plans to cook. Disaster is narrowly avoided, as two women from a local restaurant cook for her, directing her like an employee as they save the day. At the end of the story she has determined that she is going to learn to cook. Whatever else she may do, wifely duties must be attended to first.[51]

Working women in popular fiction of this period run the risk of castrating their husbands. Effie, one heroine, goes to work because her husband is an invalid. The marriage begins to deteriorate, and Effie even considers having an affair. Her husband, Walter, becomes extremely angry over her employment, and he finally explodes. Effie reassures him that she will quit her job and "give him back all she has taken from him." She promises to become a devoted, faithful wife again and to have his children. Walter remonstrates, "Dear, do you mean this truly? Won't you have to give up too much?" "Oh, Walter," she cries, "don't ask me questions like that. I've said what I'd do. Grab me and make me do it, before I change my mind." She ends up pregnant and satisfied, but still works two hours a day in her studio. When a friend asks her how she could endure giving up her highly successful job, Effie replies, "I'm not giving up my job, Vee. I've merely found a new and better one."[52]

Many of the heroines in popular fiction in women's magazines are working. Most of them, however, are dreaming of Prince Charming and hoping for a house and children. On the cover of the *Ladies Home Journal* of April 1922, a handsome prince is mounted on a noble steed, with a dewy-eyed damsel being carried away breathless by her beloved. On the back of the previous issue is an ad for Dutch Cleanser with a woman down on her knees scrubbing a bathtub. Was this the fate of princesses in the 1920s? No wonder housewives were nervous and harried. The laughing young girl could become the fatigued and disillusioned housewife unless she made the necessary adjustment and had a loving partnership.[53]

In order to make the marital partnership work, or to acquire some of those new technological domestic servants, women's wiles might still have to be used. Although frankness was good, a little manipulation never hurts—or so Corra Harris told her female readers of the *Ladies Home Journal*. "Your plain duty is to admire and flatter your husband. This may force you to warp your judgment, but do it." If a woman was an intellectual and smarter than her husband, she should be especially careful and realize that he was the one who brought home the bacon. "An idea now and then does very well." In most cases, Harris advised, a married woman should "entertain her husband with gossip, delivered amusingly with the proper histrionics."[54]

Although the women's magazines projected an image of domestic harmony in a technologized home, they also acknowledged that modern women expected to develop their personal powers within both the home and the public sphere. Articles featured women politicians, often shown with children if they had them, who told of their public activities. But they also emphasized that their loyalty to their families was their first priority. Accomplishments of the League of Women Voters and countless other women's organizations were recorded alongside an occasional article on women's rights.

Feminism in a Postsuffrage Era

The conservative political climate of the 1920s, as well as glorification of female sexuality and egalitarian marriages, shaped the nature of feminism during the period. Older feminists remained solidly committed to legal and political equality, while younger feminists were equally concerned with combining marriage and careers. To both groups feminism meant the freedom of a woman to decide her own destiny, free of traditional sex roles, free to exercise her individual conscience and judgment. It postulated that woman's worth stemmed from her common humanity, not from her relationships with other people.[55]

Although a "women's vote" failed to materialize after suffrage for women was granted, women continued to agitate for women's rights. They staged 321 events aimed to improve women's status between 1925 and 1929, and 493 in the 1930s, as compared with 26 events in 1968, 165 events in 1970, and 256 in 1975 during the height of the contemporary feminist movement.[56]

The most militant feminist party, the National Woman's Party, claimed 10,000 members in the 1920s, a drop from 35,000–60,000 in 1919–20. The NWP had become associated in the public mind with "sex antagonism" and an antimale stance, although this was a distortion of their views.[57] Alice Paul's leadership of the NWP was overpowering for some; she was charismatic and single-minded regarding women's rights. Under her leadership the party was tightly controlled from the top and was a single-issue party. Moreover, the party was considered opportunist and willing to accommodate racist sentiments.

At a commemorative conference at Seneca Falls in 1923, the NWP proposed the Equal Rights Amendment, which was introduced in Congress on December 10, 1923. (This same amendment failed to be ratified after fifty-nine years of struggle in 1982.) The Equal Rights Amendment failed to gain widespread support in the United States, and women's rights advocates bitterly disagreed about its advisability. Although the NWP more accurately analyzed women's situation than Catt's reformist wing, the radical tactics that accompanied their insight prevented them from gaining widespread support.[58] The NWP sought to eliminate protective legislation which treated women as "a class." The party wanted to join the concept of women's equality with the concept of women's sexual difference. Their challenge, therefore, was to achieve political solidarity among women, which required gender consciousness, all the while pushing for equality and endorsing the "human sex."[59]

The NWP continued to stage publicity events and to lobby presidents and members of Congress throughout the twenties. The party attracted such luminaries as Edna St. Vincent Millay, Georgia O'Keeffe, and Amelia Earhart. The clashes between the NWP and the NAWSA which had emerged during the suffrage campaign continued into the 1920s. The differences revolved around the temperaments, ideology, and tactics of the leadership. Catt's followers in the NAWSA had claimed two million women during the suffrage campaign. Aligned with the League of Women Voters and the Consumers' League, they believed that women needed protection, were different from men because of their mothering function, and owed their primary loyalty to the home. Their belief in intrinsic sexual differences allowed room for both moral superiority and economic subordination. The League of Women Voters, which the NAWSA became after suffrage was won, supported jury duty for women, funds to teach women how to care for babies, a merit system in the civil service, federal aid for vocational training, and a federal department of education. The league also supported minimum wage and hours legislation to protect female workers.

In contrast, the NWP members believed that male and female workers deserved equal protection. They were Victorian in their attitudes about women's moral superiority and generally negative in their view of "flapper morality." Paradoxically, they were also convinced that men and women shared more similarities than differences. They believed that women must be treated as human beings first and that their primary loyalties should be to themselves. Rheta Childe Dorr, a member of the NWP, described the "new woman" as "one who wanted to belong to the human race, not to the ladies aid society but to the human race."[60]

Belief in masculine and feminine uniqueness had been extremely noticeable in 1900, when a new generation of female scholars began to challenge these notions. Jessica Taft, Marion Talbott, Leta Hollingworth, Elsie Clews Parsons, and Helen Thompson conducted research which affirmed women's intellectual abilities and legitimized sexuality as a proper sphere of inquiry. Their conclusions presented a scientific challenge to the ideology of sexual difference, including women's claim to moral superiority. Consequently, these women, who were trained in the scientific skepticism of the university, rejected organized reform and adopted a highly individualistic feminist approach. They strongly endorsed the right of women to sexual expressiveness. Since they emphasized the similarities between the sexes, they regarded the feminism of their mothers' generation as strident and rejected "sexual antagonism." Their emphasis was on a desire for personal autonomy and self-fulfillment.[61] Although their research helped to encourage women's sense of intellectual competence and affirmed their sexuality, it also helped to erode the social ties which had held women together with a common purpose and tended to redefine the character of American feminism.

Dora Black, a member of the National Woman's Party, articulated a fundamental question which many feminists addressed inadequately: "Life isn't all earning your living. Unfortunately we fall in love and Feminism must take that into consideration."[62] NWP members advocated the views of Charlotte Perkins Gilman, who supported the professionalization of shopping, cooking, cleaning, and child care; they believed women need not choose between a career and a family. However, since they were solidly upper middle class themselves, they accepted most bourgeois values. They believed that Gilman's scheme would be sufficient for eliminating women's "double burden" of family and career.

The NWP members' distrust of men and ambivalence toward motherhood and homemaking were clear. In an article in the *Ladies Home Journal*, entitled "Women as Dictators," Mrs. O. H. P. Belmont stated, "Perhaps there is something very glorious about being a help mate, but if so it's time some man shared that glory." The NWP members generally supported easy divorce laws and the recognition of the wife's contributions to her marriage and family.[63] One NWP member, Doris Stevens, concluded that if housework was not professionalized and done by specialists, then wives should be paid. Housework debased the woman, socialized children to traditional gender roles, and provided the basis for low pay of women who were wage earners. Only 22 percent of the NWP's membership consisted of full-time homemakers.

The younger women in the NWP wanted to throw off the notion that they were antimale or that they believed in sex hostility. Jane Norman Smith remarked that "there must be good will and mutual understanding between the sexes. . . . I am not in the least bit anti-male." Despite such protestations, the term "feminism" in the 1920s carried a hint of sex antagonism and was threatening to men and most women. Women's competence and aspirations were also threatening. In addition to fighting for women's political and economic equality, the NWP feminists attacked the double standard of morality and opposed prostitution. They joined with the New York League of Women Voters to amend state laws to punish the customers as well as the prostitutes. Like the nineteenth-century feminists, they believed that men should be expected to come up to the moral and ethical standards of women.

Many NWP members, like Ruth Hale, were optimistic about reforming traditional marriage, viewing it as an experiment which was constantly being revised. Hale married, divorced, and subsequently "collaborated" with Heywood Broun. "The hope of the future . . . [is] in the husband and wife walking side by side, equals, partners, friends and lovers," proclaimed the party's paper, *Equal Rights*, in 1924. The majority of NWP members were married. Although single herself, Alma Lutz, a prominent member, stated her party's line: "There need be no choice between economic independence and babies. Both are possible and desirable."

However, NWP members were ambivalent toward motherhood. Whereas they believed that motherhood should be glorified, they believed that it necessitated a supreme sacrifice of women's creative and professional possibilities. They did not support the Sheppard-Towner Maternity Act because it singled out women as a special class for special protection. However, they did not want to abolish the act, but rather to reorient its thrust. They reached no consensus on whether mothers of young children should be employed, but a few suggested day-care facilities, or men's sharing child care.[64]

NWP members disagreed about alimony and birth control. Fundamentally they saw alimony as a payment for disabilities suffered by married women. Alimony would be obsolete only in a society of complete equality. While some supported birth control, other members feared that birth control would encourage licentiousness.

Carrie Chapman Catt had no such ambivalence about birth control: she totally opposed it. Catt responded to Margaret Sanger's appeal for her support of birth control with characteristic Victorian aplomb: "In my judgment you claim too much as a result of one thing. Most reformers do that. Your reform is too narrow to appeal to me and too sordid. It would give men control instead of urging men to emulate the moral virtues of women."[65]

While the League of Women Voters and the NWP differed on birth control and alimony, the issue of protectionism split the feminist movement of the 1920s more irrevocably. Between 1900 and 1920 a majority of states restricted the number of hours women could work. Ten states had an eight-hour limit for women's work day, twenty states had a nine-hour limit, and seventeen a ten-hour limit. Sixteen states outlawed night work (between 10:00 P.M. and 6:00 A.M.) in a number of occupations, and nine states had minimum-wage laws for women.[66] The feminists who believed strongly in "municipal housekeeping" had fought hard for these changes and opposed the Equal Rights Amendment because it would eliminate these protective laws and alimony. By mid-1922 the American Federation of Labor, the American Home Economics Association, Florence Kelley and the National Consumers' League, and Mary Anderson, the director of the Women's Bureau of the Department of Labor, all opposed the Equal Rights Amendment. Moreover, the NWP split with working-class activists who also supported protective legislation.[67]

The NWP strongly opposed protectionism, alienating many constituencies among American women. Alice Paul stated: "Personally, I do not believe in special labor legislation for women. It seems to me that protective labor legislation should be enacted for women and men alike in a trade or in a geographical district and not along sex lines. I think that enacting labor laws along sex lines is adding another handicap for women in the economic struggle."[68]

Feminists like Florence Kelley and Margaret Dreier Robins wanted to help families and working women by protecting them from long work days and night work. They also wanted to protect women as potential mothers. They based their case on physiological differences and were responding to dangerous and unhealthy conditions under which many worked. They sought short-term gains for women, while the NWP was more concerned about the long-term impact of sex-based legislation. As Deborah Rhode points out in her book *Justice and Gender*, the desirability of sex-based labor legislation depended on a complex series of trade-offs involving women's health, income, family responsibilities, and opportunities for advancement. The legislation affected women differently depending on class and race. Neither the social feminists nor the members of the NWP carefully examined the issue of which women would benefit, by how much, and at what cost? In the long run, the protective labor legislation tended to exclude women from higher-paying jobs, to limit opportunities for advancement in some cases, and to institutionalize sex-based wage differentials.

Unconvinced that sex-based legislation might eventually be used to discriminate against women, feminists like Carrie Chapman Catt wanted to use the women's vote to fulfill the promise of the long campaign—to bring women's special skills of housekeeping, nurturance, and compassion into the public sphere. Through agitation, the league and other organizations were able to pressure Congress to pass the Sheppard-Towner Bill in 1921, appropriating $1,480,000 for 1921–22 and $1,240,000 for the next five years ending on June 30, 1927. The money was to go for educational instruction in the health care of mothers and babies. They were able to get a two-year extension of the bill, but it expired on June 30, 1929.

At first politicians and political parties attempted to placate their new female constituency, but when no female bloc emerged, they largely ignored them. After 1925 the social feminists entered a period of frustration and defeat. Since they saw themselves as human first and women second, they fought primarily for social reform, without a special concentration on women's advancement. Along with the WTUL and National Consumers' League, the League of Women Voters had successfully pressed for higher standards in child welfare in individual states, and by 1924 twenty-nine states and the District of Columbia had children's code commissions. However, the Supreme Court struck down federal child labor laws in 1918 and 1922 and declared the minimum wage unconstitutional in 1923. In that year fifteen states had a minimum wage, but by 1930 only six did.[69]

The decade of the 1920s provided a foretaste of the New Deal for women in the political sphere. Until 1918 only Julia Lathrop held a major position in the federal government. By 1929 nearly 200 women were ranked as administrative and supervisory government workers. From 1913 to 1916, only 71 women received appointments to professional and scientific categories; from 1922 to 1925, however, 185 got such appointments.[70] Eleanor Roosevelt, Nellie Nugent Somerville in Mississippi, Sue Shelton White in Tennessee, Cornelia Bryce Pinchot, and Emma Guffy Miller in Pennsylvania, Ruth Hanna McCormick in Illinois, and Belle Moskowitz in New York had genuine access to political power, but they did not advance explicitly feminist agendas.[71]

Although some individual women gained more political power and collectively American women scored a few legislative victories, many feminists simply were exhausted after the long fight for suffrage and believed that women had to take advantage of the freedoms won and prove themselves as individuals. Lucy Burns, a militant comrade of Alice Paul's, quit her activism after the achievement of suffrage, saying: "Let them fight it now. I am not going to fight for these married women any more." And she did not.[72]

The New Feminists

In 1926 and 1927 the *Nation* published a rare portrait of feminists, which was reprinted by Elaine Showalter in *These Modern Women*. Seventeen women presented a composite view of the directions which feminism took in the decade. Their median age was forty. Only three of the respondents—Sue White, Victoria McAlmon, and Kate Gregg—had stayed single all their lives. These modern women differed from previous feminists in their insistence on the right to fulfillment in both public life and in relationships with men. They hoped to combine marriage, children, and a career. They "wanted it all" and felt keenly their own responsibility for working it out individually. Their lives reflected the exhilaration of those who succeeded as well as the frustration, resignation, and even bitterness of those who could not work it out. They also demonstrated a reliance on the new science and psychology.

Freda Kirchwey originated this project of interviewing feminists. She had bought and edited the *Nation*. When she married Evans Clark in 1916, she kept her own name, and when she became pregnant, she worked right up to the delivery day and returned to work shortly after the birth of her son.[73] Most of the *Nation*'s feminists led either independent married lives, were single, or had childless marriages. Overall, 23 percent of the female labor force in 1920 was married.

Inez Haynes Irwin, one of the feminists whom the *Nation* interviewed, spoke of her turn toward militance in the suffrage movement: "I became very impatient with the struggle waged on such scrupulously polite lines, and when the first militant in England threw the first brick, my heart flew with it."[74] Irwin, who was a journalist and novelist, wrote *The Story of the Woman's Party* and *Angels and Amazons: A Hundred Years of American Women*. She also worked as fiction editor for the *Masses*. She married Rufus H. Gillmore, a newspaper editor, whom she later divorced. In 1916 she married the journalist Will Irwin and enjoyed a satisfying marriage and career.[75]

Sue Shelton White represented the feminists who entered the political sphere. White had served as the southern leader of the National Woman's Party and was a lawyer and Democratic party politician. She chose to remain single and wrote: "Marriage is too much of a compromise; it lops off a woman's life as an individual. Yet the renunciation too is a lopping off. We choose between the frying-pan and the fire—both very uncomfortable."[76]

Kate L. Gregg earned a Ph.D. in English in 1916 and did not believe she could combine a career and marriage. She refused three proposals of marriage. Gregg seemed happy with her choice and remarked, "Perhaps the tranquil, peaceful, rich life I live is more of an argument than any words I shall ever say."[77]

Similarly, Phyllis Blanchard, a distinguished child psychologist, also chose a single life. She saw a necessity for balancing work, love, and marriage but was more optimistic than Gregg about the possibility of achieving this. Blanchard described her struggle: "Once or twice I was tempted to relinquish my profession for the ancient position of woman as wife, but the spirit of independence was too strong. I might play with the idea of submission to masculine authority, but at the first sign of any real or permanent enslavement I shrank away and clung to my liberty." She eventually married Walter Lacasse in 1925, and they settled in Philadelphia, where she began a long career with the Child Guidance Clinic. Her husband taught chemistry at the University of Pennsylvania.[78]

Cornelia Bryce Pinchot was boldly confident. Her wealth, position, and political influence allowed her the freedom to combine career and marriage. She described her view of the superwoman: "My feminism tells me that a woman can bear children, charm her lovers, boss a business, swim the Channel, stand at Armageddon and battle for the Lord—all in the days's work!"[79] When she was thirty-three, she married Gifford Pinchot, the Republican governor of Pennsylvania. Cornelia lost three times in a bid for a seat in the House of Representatives in the 1920s but was undaunted, remained vivacious, and campaigned tirelessly for her husband. Her wealth bought her the freedom to achieve that "harmony with cosmic forces" to which Blanchard claimed women were entitled.

Genevieve Taggard, Victoria McAlmon, and Crystal Eastman were socialists who envisioned revolutionary changes in the economic system as necessary for achieving sexual equality. Taggard was a poet, wrote for Max Eastman's *Liberator*, and contributed to the *New Masses*. She married twice, first Robert Wolf and then Kenneth Durant, the American director of the Soviet news agency Tass. She wrote that "marriage is the only profound human experience; all other human angles are its mere rehearsal. Like every one else I have wanted it. And yet having it, it is not all I want. . . . It is better to work hard than to be married hard."[80]

McAlmon was a teacher and was active in labor organizing. She ran unsuccessfully for Congress in Minneapolis in 1924, was fired from her teaching job because of her radicalism, and ended up a director of guidance and placement at Los Angeles City College.[81] In her essay in the *Nation* she sounded a note of disillusionment:

> I feel no need for more freedom, but I want a world in which the freedom I now have can be used. We women are free, but free for what? I move from disillusionment to fresh illusions. To be free makes life what it has always been, enticing. But my adventurous and questing mind were never so thwarted as it has been since I got my citizenship.

The industrial and political world is in the hands like mine today. Are we, while I live, going to get courage and wisdom to match our freedom? I am hopeful that we shall, but I suspect that I shall be disappointed as usual.[82]

In contrast, Crystal Eastman, a NWP member, lawyer, and activist, was determined to have both children and a career. Her first marriage, to Wallace Benedict, was unsuccessful, ending in divorce in 1915. Soon after the divorce she married Walter Fuller and went with him to live in England. She wrote with serenity:

I have lived according to the plan. I have had the "career" and the children and, except for an occasional hiatus due to illness or some other circum-stance . . . I have earned my own living. I have even made a certain name for myself. If I have not fulfilled the promise of my youth, either as a home-maker or a professional woman, I have never wavered in my feminist faith.[83]

Lorine Pruette had a very different view of the value of the feminist life from Crystal Eastman. She married and divorced twice, first Douglas Henry Fryer and then John Woodbridge Herring. The magical combination of work and marriage did not materialize, and she wrote in the spirit of F. Scott Fitgerald: "Thus, I have at a comparatively early age lost all my motivating faiths, faith in the righteous cause of women, faith in the recreating powers of science, faith in the ennobling possibilities of education. This is indeed a very sad state."[84]

In contrast, Lou Rogers, a political cartoonist, was ebullient and optimistic, and her sense of humor allowed her to survive rejection by New York editors and to build a satisfying career. She "plunged into the world" just as she had once plunged into a bottomless cove when she was a child. She "clambered up the springboard, and dived straight into the black water." Of all the women interviewed in the *Nation* series, she sparkled most with wit, self-confidence, and peace with herself. "I don't know exactly what people mean by disillusion-ment. I love to live and the longer I keep at it the greater capacity I have for living, and when I die, if it be so arranged that I lose my individual entity, I pray that I may become the lightning that snaps and crackles and whips through a thunder-storm."[85]

Running through all these essays is the struggle to achieve a balance between love and work, the exhilaration of the quest, the anguish of failure, and the myriad choices which feminists of the 1920s made. The feminist contributors believed that individuals had to struggle to apply feminist principles in their own lives and that profound changes in relationships between men and women could not be achieved by collective struggle alone.

Another view of the feminist goal of women's combining work and family emerges from the records of the Bureau of Vocational Information, an agency established to promote placement of college women in the 1920s. The bureau conducted numerous surveys of women in practically every field and specifically asked women lawyers about their careers and family life. By 1920 various states had admitted 1,586 women to the bar.[86] The lawyers whom the bureau questioned indicated a lack of feminist consciousness, as they had adopted an individualistic approach to reconciling their multiple roles. Paula Laddey of Newark wrote to Emma P. Hirth, the director: "Every woman has to solve her own problem whether she wants a career, or home. Personally I think the great majority of us want a home, but when fate has taken that, we throw ourselves into a career. That question is absolutely for individuals to solve."[87] Quite a number of the women stated that they had studied law to establish a closer companionship with their lawyer husbands.[88] Nora E. Dunn, an attorney in Elberton, Georgia, wrote that her career and family were in "perfect harmony": "I have never neglected my family for my profession but have always arranged so the two never conflict." She had two daughters and "the right kind of man."[89]

Others strongly repeated the conventional wisdom that woman's true sphere is in the home and that law and matrimony did not mix, although personally they seemed to be "mixing" them successfully.[90] One woman recommended "leaving it to God" to resolve the "seeming paradox between vocation and marriage." Another woman explained how she combined her career and family responsibilities; after four years of marriage she managed a home, looked after her own business affairs, and was at her office at least eight hours a day. She said it "takes energy, pluck, industry, application, and 'pep.'"[91]

Of the 300 women lawyers polled, most who responded espoused traditional views about the sanctity of home and motherhood. Except for the few unmarried and a few not practicing, they seemed to be effectively reconciling work and family responsibilities. Francis Kay Ballard, like many other women, adjusted to marriage by lowering her ambitions. She was first accepted by Harvard Law School in 1899, then was denied, when the faculty reversed its decision, so she went to the University of Pennsylvania Law School. After marriage she gave up her practice, had two sons, and worked at the Harvard Law library; eventually she became a librarian for a law firm.[92]

Almost all the women acknowledged the discrimination and resistance they faced, as well as the fatigue of two jobs if they were also homemakers. One woman, a graphologist, wrote that no solution to women's dual role would be found until the husbands helped with housework.[93] Regrettably, the members of the bureau failed to ask the same questions about work and family of working-class women. Whether they assumed that those other women worked sheerly out of economic necessity or not is unknown.

Three-fourths of American women did not work outside the home in the 1920s, but many of them realized increased autonomy within a marital partnership and the wider possibilities of what women could do and were doing. Although the majority of American women saw marriage as their vocation, increasing numbers of women entered the professions. In the 1920s, one out of seven doctorates was awarded to a woman; however, this number declined so that in 1956 only one of ten doctorates was awarded to a woman. Women's enrollment in college peaked in the 1920s; in the 1930s they held their highest percentage of total college faculty positions. There were 8,388 female physicians in 1930, as opposed to 9,015 in 1910, the decline beginning in the 1910s. The number of professional women reached a plateau in the 1920s and fell off in the thirties because of the economic depression.[94]

Because of articles in *Harper's, Scribner's*, and the *Forum* about professional women who had returned home, some assumed that women were disillusioned with their freedom and wanted their privileges back. But as Frank Stricker has pointed out, the women's decision to marry did not necessarily mean the rejection of a career, and the occupational statistics can be read in a more positive light. Women were subject to discrimination in employment, as well as the double burden of home and career associated with social conditioning for domesticity, but many also wanted to achieve, to stay intellectually alive, and to prepare for a career.[95]

Women in the 1920s were the first generation to vote. Psychologically this was a powerful symbol because it meant their opinions counted politically. If most American women were not feminists or flappers, an explosion of freedoms caused many stirrings. The "angel in the house" had become modernized. She was still domestic and supposed to be chaste and pious, but the flappers were no angels and certainly were not submissive. But even if some young women were naughty, they expected to settle down eventually into domesticity. American women had not abandoned all the old Victorian values, but many dreamed of having more freedom.

The daughters and granddaughters of American women in the 1920s would be the ones to realize more dreams and push the window of equality open still wider. World War I, technological changes, and new scientific approaches to housekeeping and motherhood opened new opportunities for women in employment and education and shaped their aspirations. At the same time, the American family moved away from a patriarchal form to a democratic, more egalitarian model. Because women were encouraged to satisfy themselves sexually, there was a relaxation of sexual mores, but their rebellion was still within the context of sexual experimentation which would lead to the altar. The emphasis on a companionate marriage weakened the bonds between women and undermined the possibility for a collective, feminist consciousness. While some women became more sexually liberated, they found that just as the vote did not bring them full equality, neither did freer sexuality.

No coherent national, collective feminist movement flourished in the 1920s. Internal divisions over the questions of female sexuality, protectionism, and the Equal Rights Amendment, the conservative political climate of the 1920s, and the success of achieving the vote left feminists in disarray. However, feminism became individualistic, and many feminists tried to combine marriage and career in their own lives. Women of the 1920s surveyed a different landscape than their mothers could have imagined, with more freedom than any previous generation of women. Little wonder that so many American women were confused and clung to traditional values or embraced only tentatively the new freedom. Just around the corner, however, was the Great Depression. Many dreams would be deferred, and hard times would demand the fortitude and courage of the pioneer women, not the gaiety of the flappers. As an American icon, Ma Joad, the strong matriarch in *The Grapes of Wrath*, would eclipse the flapper.

8

THE EMPOWERMENT OF WIVES AND MOTHERS
Surviving the Great Depression

Women in the thirties; when I think of them, I think they were courageous and achieving. And when they couldn't achieve themselves, they were anxious for their children to achieve. So many accomplishments started from the ambition of those mothers for their children. They made tremendous sacrifices.

Virginia Payne ("Ma Perkins"), in Jeane Westin,
Making Do: How Women Survived the '30's, 1976

There certainly was a change in our family and I can define it in just one word. I relinquished power in the family. Now I don't even try to boss. She controls all the money and I never have a penny in my pocket but that I have to ask her for it.

Mr. Adams, quoted in Mirra Komarovsky,
The Unemployed Man and His Family,
from interviews in 1935–36

As the famous crystal ball descended in Times Square on January 1, 1930, and Guy Lombardo played "Auld Lange Syne," most of the shivering crowd had little cause for celebration. After Black Thursday, October 24, 1929, depression settled on the country, in the pocketbook and on the mind. Two months after the stock market crashed, hundreds of businessmen had fallen or jumped to their deaths. Clerks in downtown hotels were asking guests whether they wished the room for sleeping or for jumping out of. At the Ritz, two men who had a joint account jumped hand-in-hand from a ledge on the eleventh floor.[1] In Kansas City, a man who couldn't get up the margin shot himself through the chest after exclaiming, "Tell the boys I can't pay."[2] All the breadlines joined together would have stretched from New York to Omaha. The mood of the nation was in direct contrast to the gaudy New Year's promise of Times Square.

Across the land, thousands of the unemployed were selling apples on street corners. Destitute, humiliated men left their families and walked the highways, sleeping in freight cars and packing crates, begging for handouts at America's back doors. Women went to work in ever-increasing numbers—as housemaids, cooks, laundresses. Others took to the streets as prostitutes. When women became breadwinners for the first time, they justified it with the belief that they were doing it for the family. For those who stayed at home, depression meant new emotional stress and near-starvation diets. For these women, it also meant putting children to bed early so they would not notice they had missed supper.

In the 1930s women shared the misery and destitution, but they also began to claim more overt power at home and in the public sphere. Through employment women gained overt power at home, especially in the homes of unemployed men who were unable to keep up their side of the marital partnership. Because of more widespread use of contraceptives, women gained more control of reproduction and their sexuality. Although no coherent national feminist movement flourished in the 1930s, through appointments in the New Deal, a network of women gained direct political influence. Moreover, through labor union activism, a significant number of women gained a sense of empowerment. As a result of their expanded role in the family and their experiences of outside employment, women gained more independence by glorifying and extending the traditionally female role, instead of challenging it. Changes within the family during the 1930s helped prepare the way for a full-scale demand for sexual equality in the 1960s because of the contradiction between women's empowerment and persisting discrimination against women in American society.

As tired revelers inched away from the damp chill of Times Square that New Year's Eve, they faced a bleak new year. The women were especially fearful. The Roaring Twenties had left an indelible imprint on the minds of American women, as those years of jazz and speakeasies quietly passed. The flapper, suddenly sobered by the economic realities of the time, no longer danced. Most likely, as a practical matter, she was learning how to use pork rind, bacon grease, bread scraps, and powdered milk as she tried to feed her family of four on five dollars a week. When she and 85 million other Americans spent twenty-five cents to escape to the movies each week, they wondered whether hard times would fade like the screen credits of a Valentino movie. Everybody hoped that Herbert Hoover was telling the truth when he said that the depression was nearly over and that men would soon be back to work.

The *New York World Telegram* described the birth of a baby in a shacktown located in a Brooklyn dump in March 1933. The ambulance came and took the woman to the hospital, while the father searched for baby clothes at the dump. At another dump in Chicago, twenty to thirty men and women waited as the garbage truck tipped and jumped to pick up whatever could be eaten before the clouds of flies descended.[3]

In sharp contrast, the affluent housewife with her red fingernails and stylish crepe de chine dress was probably thinking about buying a bird's-eye maple living room suite, a new gas range, or an electric vacuum cleaner. Wistfully, she might also have been thinking about the man she married, or the one who got away. After all, the message she got from the movies was not the same message she got from looking up and down her own street, where one out of four men was unemployed, and where one out of eighteen marriages was cracking apart. Her world was safe if she could bury herself in make-believe.

Greta Garbo, Jean Harlow, and Marlene Dietrich still filled the movie screen during the depression, but a new type of actress appeared. Bette Davis, Rosalind Russell, Katharine Hepburn, and Joan Crawford might submit to men in the movies and in the end prove that even for a tough, professional woman, marriage and sex were the most important things after all, but their characters possessed strength and intelligence rarely portrayed in female roles. Mae West was a hunter instead of the hunted; she enjoyed sex and laughed at it in a period when a morality code returned to Hollywood. She was independent, confident, witty, and tough, while at the same time glamorous and sexy. Walt Disney's Snow White sang "Some Day My Prince Will Come," but the reality of women's lives in the decade of the thirties contrasted sharply with the images projected of them on the screen.

Mae West might seduce men on the screen, but most American women could only fantasize such liberation. One woman recalled the prevalence of the sexual double standard: "I remember boys could be so cruel then and they could accuse a girl of liking it. Really. If a girl got the reputation of liking sex, she automatically had to be a nymphomaniac, because good girls didn't like it. We were only supposed to like everything that led up to it."[4]

Another survivor of the depression recalled attitudes regarding female sexuality in the thirties. "No woman thought of herself as sexy. If she did, she kept it a secret. She would have been considered a low-type person if she had ever admitted to any human being that she was sexy or that she had sexual feelings of any kind. If there were any sexy women around my part of the country [the Ozarks] at that time, I didn't know it." She continued, "No, the thing that held the women together was drudgery and their hatred of sex and having babies. I think that was their bond."[5]

On the screen, women learned that sex goddesses could be the object of violence. James Cagney began the trend in 1931 by hitting Mae Clark in the eye with a grapefruit in the movie *Public Enemy*. This practice became so common that one film critic wrote in 1938 that "today a star scarcely qualifies for the higher spheres unless she has been slugged by her leading man, rolled on the floor, kicked downstairs, cracked over the head with a frying pan, dumped into a pond, or butted by a goat."[6]

Best-sellers like *Gone with the Wind* combined sentimentality and nineteenth-century ideals of womanhood with images of strong women who knew how to survive tremendous adversity, even if it meant violation of the traditional code of femininity. Scarlett O'Hara's violent relationship with Rhett Butler was redeemed in the end because she had gained the strength through him to manage Tara alone. In the cinema and popular literature, women could vicariously be glamorous and sexy, add a career if they wanted, and still get married to the men they loved. At the same time, the violence against women reminded them of the cost of too much assertiveness.

One magazine article of the thirties described how to properly combine femininity and strength: "Your tennis champion by day will be adorable tonight with tulle and garlanded evening gown listening to some attentive youth whispering sweet nothings about her delicacy and charm. . . . The clear-eyed young goddess whose airplane defies an angry storm to wrest from it life and safety will tell you calmly how much she likes to cook and make her own clothes."[7]

Although women might dream about flying around the world like Amelia Earhart, they were reminded that failure to adjust to their domestic role brought tremendous hazards. As one doctor wrote: "The woman of today wants to be what she calls her own self as much as if she never married. This cannot be, even for those who successfully combine a career and domesticity. There ensues for the unadjusted woman a corroding dissatisfaction, an outward product of which is fatigue."[8]

The modern homemaker was expected to be efficient and more scientific than ever before because of all the new knowledge and gadgets available to her. She was a protector in the home and a consumer in the marketplace. This role meant staying aware of the times and being able to see that nothing threatened her family with disasters, an almost impossible responsibility accepted because of the insidious messages of movies and magazines.

In the popular fiction of the 1930s, women gave up careers for the men they loved. In one story, a newspaperman goes to New York to make his fortune and meets Francine, also a reporter. Francine loses her job because she dances with the Prince of Wales, instead of writing her story on him. "But as he watched her sewing in her apartment, her lovely face, flushed and happy over creamy lace and rosy ribbons, he knew more than ever that what he wanted for a wife was not a crack newspaperwoman, but simply this eternal female."[9]

Another female character is a very competent lawyer who falls in love with a man who asks her to marry him. "'No,' said Mary Jane, 'I'm wedded to my profession.' 'Then,' Tim replied, 'I'm stepping out to furnish it with grounds for divorce. You'll give up your profession and everything and marry me?' 'If I'm any judge,' Mary Jane said demurely, 'You'll be profession enough for any hard-working girl.'"[10]

A woman who picked up an issue of the *Saturday Evening Post* could read some stories about women aspiring to goals other than home and children. Many female characters were independent, aggressive, self-confident, and adventurous. The stories also revealed the obstacles women had to face because of their sex. But generally, women were portrayed as silly, childish, and irrational. A common female heroine of the magazine's fiction was a selfish, vain, beautiful manipulator who betrayed both men and women. Stories admonished women to avoid selfish ambition and not to ignore maternal responsibilities or damage their husbands' egos. Successful career women were portrayed as single or widowed. Aggressiveness was not seen in a context of achievement. Black and lower-class white women appeared only as servants in stories and advertisements.[11]

At the same time, however, the increased power of married women caused social anxiety. Married women in the comics of the 1930s were portrayed as taller and uglier than single women, and half were taller than their husbands. In the world of the funny papers, women acquire a thirst for power over their short, portly, bald husbands and dominate them. Blondie finally marries Dagwood and becomes the "perfect" wife. She is perceived as the boss of the house, and she controls the money, while at the same time she lavishes affection on her bungling husband and their adorable children.[12]

According to the movies, women's magazines, and comics, the female sphere was still unquestionably the home. If the angel in the house had to work outside the home, her job must not interfere with her family duties or lessen her femininity. She must be goddess, earth mother, and a study in charity and frugality. She was expected to use all the advice science had given her technologically and to maintain a home which was "economically sound, morally wholesome, mentally stimulating, artistically satisfactory, socially responsible, spiritually inspiring, founded upon mutual affection and respect."[13]

Such lofty ideals were physically and economically impossible for most American women. Although women during the thirties assumed their duties in a spirit of self-sacrifice, preservation of traditional roles within the family proved extremely difficult through the depression years. The American family began to assume new and varied forms as women demonstrated their strength and competence in multiple roles, from mothers to factory workers.

By the end of Franklin Roosevelt's first term, if in their own minds American women could not measure up to Mae West, the ultimate sex symbol, or Ma Joad, the strong matriarch in *The Grapes of Wrath*, they nevertheless exhibited extraordinary courage, perseverence, and resilience as they lived between two sharply delineated worlds. Duty and making do characterized their domestic lives, but another world was beginning to open as unprecedented numbers of women began working outside the home.

At the height of the depression, with one-fourth of the nation's workers unemployed, many women became breadwinners for the first time. Women had always worked, inside and out of the home, but generally female wage laborers had been single. In the thirties, married women worked outside the home in greater numbers than ever before, composing 35 percent of the female labor force by 1940, an increase over 29 percent in 1930, and 15 percent in 1900.[14] The total percentage of women in the labor force rose from 20 percent in 1920 to 25 percent in 1940, while the percentage of employed married women in the female labor force increased from 23 percent in 1920 to 36 percent in 1940. Although unemployment was very high, the number of women in the labor force increased more rapidly than in either of the previous decades.[15]

In 1930, of all the working women 29.7 percent were in domestic and personal service work, 18.9 percent in clerical jobs, 17.5 percent in manufacturing, 9.1 percent in trade, 14.5 percent in professional service, and 7.3 percent in agriculture. In 1930 one out of six female workers was African-American; 40 percent of all African-American women were employed outside the home, as opposed to 20 percent of all white women.[16] By 1940, for every ten female workers, three were in clerical or sales work, two were factory operatives, two were domestic workers, one was a professional (usually a nurse or teacher), and one was a service worker. Over half of the women were working more than fifty hours a week, and more than one-fifth worked over fifty-five hours. In addition to paid labor, according to studies, women also spent approximately sixty-one to sixty-three hours a week on housework, even with the new appliances.

Married women, especially, faced both discrimination in hiring and public resistance to their working. Discrimination in wages was pervasive, and figures from the Social Security Administration in 1937 revealed that women's average yearly pay was $525.00, compared with $1,027 for men. Even more bleak was the statistic that household workers in 1940 made $312.60 a year.[17] Twenty-six legislatures introduced bills banning employment of married women. School teachers who married were often fired, and at least six public opinion polls confirmed the hostility toward married women's working. One unemployed husband remarked, "I would rather starve than let my wife work."[18]

Even in the face of such vehement opposition, working women were less affected by unemployment than working men, principally because the administrative and clerical jobs were not eliminated to the same degree as those in production.[19] Consumer and service industries, where most women were employed, were also not as affected by the depression. Although women might be better off than men in finding work, about one out of five women normally employed was out of work at any point in the 1930s. Estimates ranged from 2.5 million unemployed women in 1931 to 4 million in 1933. Contrary to the myth that women worked for extra "pin money," 10 percent of the jobless women in 1930 headed households, and as high as 50 percent were responsible for dependents.[20]

Faced with the public hostility that she was taking a man's job, a working woman received about half the salary of a man, found a sex-stereotyped job, and if married, performed another full-time job at home. In spite of all the disadvantages of women's double burden, one cannot underestimate the impact on women of financial independence and of a growing belief in their ability to exert authority.

The Family and the Great Depression

According to popular wisdom, the depression brought families closer together. Kathryn Haskell, a seventy-four-year-old resident of Boone County, Missouri, confirms this romantic view: "My husband and I pulled together, literally, all our lives. We worked and struggled and we tried hard. We'd go out to cut white oak fence posts and I pulled my end of the cross-cut—a six foot cross-cut saw—and he pulled his. I always worked right with him except whenever I was pregnant."[21]

In many cases, the depression did bring families closer together as more recreational time was spent together. Divorce rates declined, and socializing outside the home decreased if travel was involved. Restaurants lost business, millions of telephones were taken out, and the mails became lighter because money was so scarce. Even marriage and motherhood were discouraged for single women. "Do you realize how many people in my generation are not married?" asks Elsa Ponselle. "I was going with a young commercial artist who lost his job. He had been so confident that it wouldn't happen to him, that it hit him like a ton of bricks. And he just disappeared."[22]

The mood was one of deferment—of material acquisitions, of children, of divorce, and of marriage. Women had little choice but to accept their situations, since they had few illusions about finding better husbands. They were in it for the duration. Some couples even managed to keep dancing: "Ray and I would get together at the kitchen table and we'd discuss our situation. Once in a while one of us would come up with some crackpot idea to make some money and that helped a little bit. And if the electricity wasn't turned off—which it was when we couldn't pay the bill—Ray would turn on the radio and we'd dance all over the house from the living room into the kitchen, down the hall and back again."[23]

Many families were drawn closer together, and yet probably just as many experienced bitterness and disillusionment. Desertions increased during the depression, and by 1932 over a million women and their children had been deserted. At least 5 percent of married people in 1930 were separated. One ingenious Manhattan couple imitated Claudette Colbert and Clark Gable in *It Happened One Night* (1934) and hung up a blanket in the middle of the room—less trouble than a divorce.[24]

"I just adored the ground my father walked on, but he ran off when I was ten, so it was just my mom and me from then on," Gena Hedger recalls. Another survivor of the thirties said that her father left when his restaurant folded because he refused to put in beer. Sometimes women themselves took to the road, as did one Radcliffe graduate named Ellen, whose mother tearfully took her out on the main highway north and pressed the family's last two dollars into her hand.[25]

Frustrations might also lead to increased violence within the family. In describing coal and steel communities in Pittsburgh, Lillian Cantor Dawson claimed that among the workers, it was the custom of the men to get drunk when things got too bad and to beat their wives. The wives could be heard screaming, yet many of them endured the abuse because they felt that their husbands were so miserable in their jobs that they deserved an outlet. [26]

Although many women suffered from violence and hardships, others tended to gain more power and influence within the family. Ironically, because of the women's socialization to expect their husbands to be dominant, their own increased "authority" did not necessarily enhance their self-esteem. While the depression intensified family intimacy in many instances, it often accentuated preexisting conflicts within families. Several sociological studies found that the depression caused role reversals in families and often weakened the authority of men in the family. Robert and Helen Lynd found in their study *Middletown in Transition* that while people's fundamental *values* about traditional sexual roles had not changed, they tended to sanction unprecedented *behaviors* like men's taking care of the house, and children's and women's working.[27]

Samuel Stouffer and Paul Lazarfeld's study of the family in the 1930s concluded that the tendency toward women's gaining more power in the family depended on the relative ability of the husband and wife to keep and find jobs.[28] Naturally, the responses of different families to the same pressures varied widely. Much depended on the nature of their particular social aspirations before the depression. Conflicts arising from the husband's unemployment depended on the amount of time he spent at home idle, as well as the percentage of unemployed in the same occupation.[29] Caroline Bird went further than Stouffer and Lazarfeld, claiming that her experience of the depression led her to believe that the balance of power in family life shifted in favor of women.

In a more empirical study than Bird's, Mirra Komarovsky investigated fifty-nine families on relief outside New York City. The parents were white, Protestant, between forty and forty-five years old, with two or three children. Komarovsky found that the depression altered sexual roles in the family and weakened men's power.[30] She defined the deterioration of the man's authority as a decline in the willingness of the family to accept his control, whether he succeeded in maintaining it through coercion or not. Using this definition, she found that unemployment clearly tended to lower the status of the husband in thirteen out of fifty-eight families. She found that even in families in which authority did not measurably shift, a considerable proportion of the men (twenty-two out of fifty-seven) exhibited a loss of emotional stability, break-down of morale, irritability, drinking, or unfaithfulness to their wives. In all of the families, the unemployed husband's authority depended largely on his own behavior and on predepression attitudes.[31]

However dramatic the shifts in marital power, unemployment chiefly brought to light the unsatisfactory domestic arrangements that existed in America prior to the depression. Some men experienced a deep frustration over their inability to perform their central duty of life, since employment was the touchstone of their masculinity. Mr. Baldwin became more thoughtful and kinder, and more helpful with the housework. But his wife's attitude remained antagonistic and accusatory. When he largely took over household duties, she said, "If you were employed you could hire a maid to do it."[32]

These changes in men's self-image seemed to affect their sexual activity. Although this kind of evidence is incomplete for all fifty-nine cases, Komarovsky recorded information on thirty-eight. Of these, sixteen indicated no change, and twenty-two cases revealed less frequent sexual relations. Four reported having no sex.[33]

In his study of fifty American families of the University of Michigan sociology students, *The Family Encounters the Depression*, Robert Cooley Angell found a shift in dominance of husband and wife but did not calculate it statistically. The ambiguity of these shifts may be seen in the Fleming family. Angell wrote, "The mother has assumed the true leadership of the family. She is merely a guiding hand, and in no way dominant." Some women openly asserted their dominance, while others led from behind more covertly and diplomatically. Because women had internalized the traditional role expecta-tions, even when they gained more bargaining power within marriage, they tried to minimize the effects on their husbands.[34] Although the shifts toward female dominance in the home were not the rule, clearly substantial changes were occurring.

In his work *Children of the Great Depression*, Glen Elder, Jr., argued that when the father's authority in the family derived mainly from cultural tradition, patriarchal attitudes, or affection among family members, it was most likely to survive economic failure. The shift of responsibilities which occurred in deprived households at all status levels in the Oakland sample created situations that favored wife dominance. Elder also noted that the lower the family standing before the depression and the lower the related economic status in 1933 versus 1929, the greater the likelihood of the mother's dominance as perceived by the children. He found in the middle-class families that the perception of the mother as more powerful than the father was highly related to the loss of family status during the depression. In both classes, he found an economically deprived father to be regarded less favorably by the children, and lower than the mother. This generalization did not apply to all or even most fathers who suffered economic losses, but the response was highly concentrated in the most deprived group of families.[35]

The lower the economic class, the greater the likelihood of the mother's assuming leadership. Because women's sphere expanded, particularly with outside employment, they became even more essential to the family than before. Elder noted that a typical characterization was that the mother consciously defined her labor for the family as an extreme sacrifice which could not be repaid by the children without damaging their independence and integrity. Therefore, mothers made every effort to avoid full reciprocation and to maintain the indebtedness of the children. These mothers' sacrifices generated personal power over the children through gratitude, guilt, and sense of obligation. Although Elder's sample was limited, his study reveals some of the psychological and social origins of the emphasis on home and family of the 1950s, as well as the impact of the mother-centered family of the depression.[36] More research is needed to determine the impact of the depression on African-American families.

Ruth Shonle Cavan and Katherine Howland Ranck confirmed the findings of other researchers that women's economic power increased their authority at home. In their study of 100 families in Chicago during the depression in 1934–35, they found that the common condition of the families was fear—of loss of status and of savings, of failure to have food and clothing, and of going on relief. A period of extreme disorganization in these families reached an end either through reorganization or disintegration.[37] The mother was the major wage earner in seven families and tended to assume dominance in other ways. Forty-one families demonstrated marital or general disorganization of a more or less severe type, and Cavan and Ranck discerned wife or child abuse in six families. In the hundred families, seven fathers died of illness, one committed suicide, one other father killed his wife and then himself, some children died, three mothers became mentally ill, several fathers and mothers suffered nervous breakdowns, and reactions of excessive worry and depression were prevalent.[38] Cavan and Ranck confirmed that the depression had caused severe disorganization in forty-one families and occasioned the reversal of roles of husbands and wives and parents and children in a significant number of families. Their conclusion was that crisis caused an exaggeration of previously existing family and personal habits.

When married women took jobs, their husbands frequently felt that they had failed to live up to their masculine responsibilities. Some husbands began to do more domestic work than they ever had before. In her study of 652 employed, married homemakers, Cecile Tipton LaFollette found that 73 percent of the husbands were assisting in household tasks and that only 127 of the women employed full-time maids regularly. Her study covered eighteen states and thirty-six cities. Husbands were sharing household tasks primarily in cases where the wives were contributing as much or more than the husband to the family's budget.[39]

Economic hardship caused tremendous strain in families, especially the poorest ones. Lilian Brandt's study of 900 social workers in New York City concluded that only the exceptional family did not experience serious domestic strain and deterioration of family harmony. She summarized the impact as follows:

> As a result of the economic conditions of the past two years . . . family affection has been sorely tried, conjugal and parental ties have been weakened, family groups have disintegrated, the source of income has shifted from the husband and father to the wife and children or to the public, paternal authority has lost force, home discipline has suffered, personality difficulties and family problems have been precipitated, and insecurity have increased.[40]

A story which appeared in the *Ladies Home Journal*, "Family Man," expresses an unemployed man's humiliation when his wife had to take a job. In this story, the wife has to lie about her marital status to get the job and also must endure the wrath of her husband who feels degraded when she asks him to do housework and to care for the children. He so resents this reversal of roles that he humbles himself with his former employer and finally gets his job back. At the end of the story, the husband decides to "liberate" his wife from her job and rushes down to her office with the children. He instructs them to run in and shout, "Mama."[41]

Role reversal proved painful in actual families, as well as in popular literature. In the Sieberg family, the father had never earned an adequate income, and as the husband's income decreased, the mother assumed more of the financial burden. She provided most of the income from her work as saleslady, while her husband maintained a tailor's shop. He also did most of the housework and wept over his wife's fatigue. Mrs. Roos had worked in a restaurant since 1924, when her husband was temporarily out of work because of an injury. When he lost his job in 1931, the financial burden fell on her, and the family received some money from the relief agency. Although Mr. Roos found it embarrassing to talk about it, he assumed the responsibility for housework as Mr. Sieberg had.

In the Lind family, a daughter supported the family of six for a year when her father lost his job. When she stopped working after marrying, the family went on relief. The most extreme reaction to a change in status occurred with Mr. Beczkowski. His wife and daughter viewed him as shiftless and profligate because he could no longer support the family. He chose suicide instead of enduring such humiliation.[42]

Another husband reacted more stoically when his wife and children began to lose respect for him: "It's only natural. When a father cannot support his family, supply them with clothing and good food, the children are bound to lose respect. . . . It's perfectly true that my word is not law around here as it once was." When his son Henry came in one evening as the family was almost finished eating dinner, Mr. Brady got up immediately and gave his place at the table to him, since there was no extra chair. Henry took the place as his entitlement, without thanking his father for it. Henry's wages of twelve dollars a week supported the whole family.[43]

Some unemployed men crept around the house trying to act as though they were not really there, making as few demands as possible, sexually and otherwise.[44] An unemployed husband lamented that "during the depression I lost something. Maybe you call it self-respect, but in losing it I also lost the respect of my children, and I am afraid I am losing my wife."[45] Mrs. Raparka, the wife of an unemployed man, assumed authority of her family when her husband failed to find work. She began to lose respect for him because she thought he was lazy. She asked him to scrub floors and to do the washing. But he refused to hang out the wash and be seen by the neighbors. Eventually, Mr. Raparka left to take a job as a farm worker for a few months. When he returned, his family had learned to manage without him. Feeling displaced, he left for New York and was not heard from again. Another unemployed husband explained the personal consequences of his economic plight, "Love flies out the window when the money goes."[46]

Many women, however, were understanding and supportive of their unemployed husbands. Aware of the shift in domestic power, they tried to make the husbands' dependence on them as painless as possible and showed great tact in their relationships with them. "I tried to cheer him up, and not ask whether he found a job each day," recalls another woman of the thirties. "I knew how badly he felt. But I knew he'd usually been at the pool hall all day." Cavan and Ranck emphasized that the wives' employment was in no way an attempt to usurp their husbands' role or compete with him but the assistance of a loyal helpmate. Thus they stopped working when the men found employment, or income increased.[47]

Although many men suffered from a crisis of confidence, even in the poorest families the wives outwardly deferred to their husbands in the 1930s. But women covertly wielded power. In one of the best studies of southern poor women, *Mothers of the South*, Margaret Jarman Hagood described an intriguing form of patriarchal organization among 254 tenant farmers' homes in the Carolina piedmont, Georgia, and Alabama.[48] The man was expected to carry the pocketbook. Women did all the housework and worked in the barn and the field. The men were not expected to help in the house. The bossiest wife seemed to believe herself subservient and did not complain about the division of labor. Seven-eighths of the women preferred field work to housework and were prouder of their prowess in the field and tobacco shed than in the kitchen.[49] One mother who said she preferred field work best, sighed and said, "But I gets mighty tired now—and there's never no rest."[50]

These women resembled the women of the nineteenth century who ran households without electricity and running water. A mother might have a cotton or tobacco patch from which she got money to buy her own and her children's clothes. This was the closest she came to any comparative economic independence or autonomy over any part of the farm income.[51]

However strongly patriarchy prevailed in form, it was not always practiced. Hagood found that in several families the wife was clearly the stronger personality and "bossed" her husband to some extent, but always within the form prescribed by tradition. Personality greatly affected actual practice. However, even if a wife was more dominant, there was no recognition of equality or awarding of nontraditional privileges.[52] Women might enjoy considerable power over a spouse in decision making without the traditional division of labor changing. It seemed to be easier and more likely for women to assume "masculine" duties than for men to assume "feminine" duties.

Given the crisis in masculinity among rich and poor, it is no wonder that men who felt threatened thrilled to the exploits of Dashiel Hammett's macho detective Sam Spade, who drank a lot and had sexual encounters with four or five exciting women without becoming emotionally involved. They could identify with Clark Gable as Rhett Butler, who told Scarlet O'Hara, "I don't give a damn." The depression triggered a severe masculinity-identity crisis. Sherwood Anderson's *Puzzled America* explored this sense of loss of manhood because of unemployment. Men tried desperately to recapture their old social values and struggled to justify their loss of prestige.[53]

By 1940 a writer for *Time* magazine wrote gloomily of marriage and family affection as "a grim panorama which gives the impression that Americans are an irritable, aggravated, dissatisfied people for whom marriage is an ordeal that only heroes and heroines can bear." In the 1930s Stewart Holbrook whined that the old he-man had been reduced to a check-writing eunuch after Theodore Roosevelt.[54]

A crisis over masculinity might result from destitution but could also be related to the shame of loss of status. The depression's impact on family life depended on the degree and extent of change in income as well as the state of the family before the crisis. In 1929 the top 0.1 percent of American families had aggregate incomes equal to the bottom 42 percent. There were 24,000 families who had a combined income as large as that shared by more than 11.5 million poor and lower-middle-class families. Of all American families, including unattached individuals, 71 percent had incomes under $2,500, 24,000 families earned over $100,000, and 513 families had incomes of over $1 million per year.[55]

As Americans battled against the catastrophes of drought, dustbowls, and hunger, they experienced the depression as a personal failure. The American dream of success in which they had placed their faith was put to its severest test. In most cases, as breadlines snaked across America and the destitute roamed the streets and fields in search of work, an increasing sense of failure prevailed. Yet, perhaps the dream was not flawed—it was only because they had not worked hard enough or saved enough or, as the preacher thundered from the pulpit, prayed hard enough. Few realized that women were asserting their authority more and more as unemployed men were prevented from keeping up their side of the partnership.

Depression settled on Americans like a big snow, blanketing everything to stillness. The corner shop was closed, as was the whole financial world. Money, like society's blood, just stopped circulating. One woman was brave in describing her experience: "We had to give up our home, which caused some worry, and our car is getting old. We used to get a new one every year. Our son will not get to go to college this year, but we try to concentrate on the things we do have. Things could be a lot worse."[56] Because of the Great Depression women's employment gained legitimacy privately, if not publicly, and women's consciousness about themselves and their ability to exert authority began to change. Women were forced to reconcile the needs of their families with their socialization into traditional female roles. Women gained more influence and power in the family by expanding and glorifying the female role, instead of challenging it.

As the decade dragged on and the New Deal offered hope to weary farmers trying to revive their drought-stricken land, the nation itself took heart. During the thirties, Shirley Temple tapped up and down movie staircases, and Little Orphan Annie, Dick Tracy, and Flash Gordon filled the comic papers. Will Rogers could make even President Roosevelt laugh. Still, the privileged flaunted their positions and seemed to taunt the less fortunate with their excesses. Brenda Frazier, a celebrated debutante, reportedly spent $60,000 on her coming-out party. Schools voted on the best-dressed girl.

Through the grimness, people cheered themselves by whistling "Happy Days Are Here Again" and by listening to "Amos and Andy" on the radio. They were absorbed by the kidnapping of the Lindberg baby, the disappearance of Amelia Earhart, sit-down strikes, Public Enemy John Dillinger, and the exploits of J. Edgar Hoover's G-men. To ease the pressure, the WPA provided jobs for eight million unemployed between 1935 and 1940, building and repairing airports, roads, schools, bridges, and railroad terminals. Colorful murals appeared on drab walls; a handful of photographers made an unprecedented record of life during the depression for the Farm Security Administration. Scores of seasoned writers turned out excellent state guidebooks, and newly revived actors and musicians trouped across the country, making America laugh again.

The country seemed to be waking up. In Chicago Frank Lloyd Wright unveiled the latest of his prairie school structures, Grant Wood unwittingly created a cliché with his *American Gothic*. The *New Yorker*, a magazine for "caviar sophisticates," passed its ten-year milestone. While such popular novelists as Erskine Caldwell and James T. Farrell were writing blockbusters about the "ill-housed, ill-clad, ill-nourished" present, America's comforting past was being revived by such new talents as Maxwell Anderson, Margaret Mitchell, and Kenneth Roberts. On Broadway, thousands flocked to see Clifford Odets's powerful new play *Waiting for Lefty*, Lillian Hellman's *Little Foxes*, and Marc Connelly's "divine comedy," *Green Pastures*.

The mood was almost light, yet the majority of Americans continued to survive on a shoestring, the wounds of the depression cutting into most of their everyday lives. Extravaganzas like Busby Berkeley's *Gold Diggers of 1933* offered a sharp contrast to most Americans, who were anything but "in the money." Most people were too preoccupied with making ends meet to become excited over the newsreels chronicling the rise of Adolf Hitler and Benito Mussolini, or to become concerned as civil war raged in Spain, Japan attacked China and conquered Manchuria, and Nazi Germany seized Austria and Czechoslovakia.

For most Americans, especially women, the thirties was a time of making do. One survivor of the depression in Tennessee sits on her porch and remembers:

> My life was less interrupted than my husband's. I canned food, saved every scrap of food, took in lodgers, and made clothes from feed sacks. The children looked to me for running the family. My husband would get so angry at times. One day he refused to do anything. He would go off into the woods and brood for hours. Finally, one day in 1938 I heard a shot and ran down into the field below our house to find him murdered and robbed. Everybody knew he carried some money with him, instead of always using the bank. They never found the men who did it. . . . That's what the Depression meant to me. I was more fortunate than most. Because everyone seemed poor, we didn't feel so poor, and at least we didn't starve.[57]

Claiming the Power of Birth Control

For some women, outside employment increased their sense of authority within the family, but the domestic role remained primary. Motherhood was paradoxically sentimentalized in popular fiction but also heartily discouraged for the single and recently married. Pregnancy was often seen as a disaster. A measure of women's increasing autonomy was the widespread use and acceptance of birth control during the depression. In the previous decade, the birth control movement assumed radical proportions and was often associated with socialism. Birth control stood not only for women's autonomy but for a revolutionizing of the society and power to the powerless. By the 1930s the movement became a liberal reform movement, embodying the "planned parenthood" focus, which was fully developed in the 1920s.[58]

Birth control was perceived as a means not to separate marriage and sexual practice but to strengthen women's positions within conventional marriages.[59] Middle- and upper-class families, frightened by declining incomes, practiced birth control and accepted it sexually and morally. Working-class women also seemed receptive to birth control. Birth control advocates sought to work through the New Deal welfare programs and stopped expressing explicitly the women's rights aspect of birth control. A few New Deal agencies began to fund birth control work surreptitiously in the late 1930s. Confidential memos in Margaret Sanger's files indicate that two projects under the Farm Security Administration funded nurses to educate the poor and migrant workers about birth control.[60] In 1930 only 40 medically directed birth control clinics existed in the United States. By 1936 there were 288 in over forty states.[61]

Although the birth rate fell and birth control became more respectable, people were still reticent about it, and many more were ignorant. A Montana woman remembers: "A woman didn't know any way to stop having babies; we had a flock of 'em before we knew how it happened. We didn't talk about such things among ourselves—not even women together—so if anybody had any information it was never passed along to me."[62] Knowledge of birth control among college women was also sketchy. Sexual mores had changed dramatically among young people in the 1920s, although the change had been well underway before then. By the 1930s, changes in sexual behavior had extended more broadly among the nation's youth. A report by Dorothy Dunbar Bromley and Florence Britten, *Youth and Sex*, a study of 1,364 college students in 1938, revealed new patterns of morals, though within definite limits. One-half of the male students and one-quarter of the female students had engaged in premarital sex.[63]

Older women often felt that they were caught between two worlds: the Victorian world of their mothers, and the more open, permissive world of their daughters. Frances Woodward Prentice described some of these feelings in an article in *Scribner's*:

I, who am 37 in this year of 1932, have fallen into a chronological air pocket. An air pocket inhabited by most of my female contemporaries. . . . In these days, when it is smart to claim significance, we feel peculiarly without point. We are trying breathlessly to straddle the tremendous gulf the war really did create; awkward Colossi, prevented from getting our feet firmly planted either Then or Now. . . . We were reared, educated and married for one sort of life, and precipitated, before we had a chance to get our bearings, into a totally different sort. . . .

We are not very successful at being naughty, anyway. Even our divorces are rather a bungle for the most part. Perhaps because we cannot take sex as lightly as the young, nor as calmly as the old.[64]

The depression created enormous conflicts for women of all ages. College women might dream of marriage and plan to work as a stopgap measure, taking careers less seriously than their predecessors in the 1920s, but the economic crisis made prospects for marriage bleak. Professional opportunities were also very limited. Married women might feel that motherhood was intended to be the greatest source of fulfillment, but having more children seemed like a disaster. Many felt that waiting and duty shaped their lives.

A New Deal for Women?

While most women were primarily concerned with survival, as we have seen, women began to enhance their power in the home, especially when they took paid employment. Their increase in power relative to men paradoxically reinforced certain "traditional" notions of women's sphere, but it also challenged them. The degree to which their domestic power enhanced women's self-esteem and autonomy depended on many factors: race, class, ethnicity, their earning power, personalities, their expectations about proper sex roles, and their husbands' reactions.

Through the more widespread use of contraceptives women gained more control over their reproductive lives. In addition to claiming more power in the intimate sphere of the family in the 1930s, some women found exhilarating possibilities in the public sphere of the New Deal administration. More women served in high administrative positions in the 1930s than ever before, a record unmatched until the 1960s. Among these were Julia Lathrop, Mary Anderson, Louise Stanley, Frances Perkins, Ellen Sullivan, Lucille Foster McMillan, Ruth Bryan Owen, Marion Glass Banister, Florence Jaffray Harriman, and Josephine Roche. While individual women gained more political power, they were not primarily concerned with advancing a specifically "feminist" agenda.

Although women made impressive strides in the New Deal, discrimination persisted. The CCC was limited to men, and women's camps at FERA and WPA were small in comparison. However, women made some progress, receiving maternity and pediatric grants.[65] The New Deal brought the government into people's lives in unprecedented ways, addressed women's needs, and gave a network of social feminists more access to political power.

Eleanor Roosevelt represents the quintessential feminist of the New Deal who believed in "municipal housekeeping." The president's wife was a central figure of the 1930s because she represented the realization of the nineteenth-century feminist ideal—extension of women's moral superiority and nurturant qualities to the public sphere. She was highly successful because she did not challenge the fundamental concepts of marriage and the family. Eleanor Roosevelt beamed a dual message for American women because of her fierce loyalty to her family and traditionalism on the one hand, and her active participation in affairs outside the home on the other. Eleanor Roosevelt's life presented a new vision of freedom for the average American woman. The First Lady justified venturing into the public sphere; in fact, she felt that the modern era demanded that she become involved in every aspect of the society in order to preserve the family. Although she became active in the public sphere, she was a model of Victorian womanhood. She remarked in an article for the *Ladies Home Journal*:

> For ten years I was just getting over having a baby or about to have one and so my occupations were considerably restricted. . . . I still lived under the compulsion of my early training; duty was perhaps the motivating force in my life, often excluding what might have been gay or pleasureable. I looked at everything from the point of view of what I ought to do, rarely from the standpoint of what I wanted to do.[66]

Eleanor Roosevelt was one of the greatest advocates of all the dispossessed in the twentieth century. She evolved from a timid, insecure woman who opposed suffrage in 1905, believing that it was a violation of women's proper role, to the first lady of the world, advocating the rights of all people. She had six children, helped to build and consolidate her husband's political career, worked in the settlement movement, as in every major movement for human rights of the century, and epitomized the importance of combining traditionally female values with public power and individual autonomy. In the 1940s she wrote: "You can never really live anyone else's life, not even your child's. The influence you exert is through your own life and what you've become yourself."[67]

During the 1930s Eleanor Roosevelt came into her own as a political figure and advocate of the poor and disfranchised. She toured the country, entering coal mines and slums, visiting relief projects and hospitals. Eleanor seemed to be everywhere. Her newspaper column, "My Day," and her lectures and radio shows reached millions. Through them, she conveyed to the American people her deep compassion for their suffering.

Eleanor Roosevelt was instrumental in getting Frances Perkins appointed as secretary of labor. She worked closely with Mary Dewson, a remarkable woman who headed up the Women's Division of the Democratic National Committee. Together they brought to Washington a dynamic network of women. Rexford Tugwell wrote of her powerful influence with Franklin Roosevelt. He remembered, "No one who ever saw Eleanor Roosevelt sit down facing her husband, and holding his eyes firmly, say to him 'Franklin, I think you should . . .' or, 'Franklin surely you will not' . . . will ever forget the experience."[68]

Eleanor Roosevelt continued her active career in politics and activism after Franklin Roosevelt's death. While remaining committed to women's rights, she was also committed to social justice for all. She believed that women's rights were essential to achieving human rights. She was more comfortable in her role as social critic and humanitarian than in public office. She declined a nomination for the Senate and a seat on the Democratic National Committee. Adlai Stevenson paid her tribute at her memorial service: "What other single human being has touched and transformed the existence of so many? . . . She walked in the slums . . . of the world, not on a tour of inspection . . . but as one who could not feel contentment when others were hungry."

Eleanor Roosevelt was the quintessential volunteer, working for the League of Women Voters, the Consumers' League, the Women's Trade Union League, the Democratic National Committee, and the American Association for the United Nations. She also wrote steadily for newspapers and magazines, earning as much as $90,000 a year, most of which she gave away. Truman appointed her U.S. representative to the United Nations, where she served until she resigned after Eisenhower was elected. In the hysterical anti-Communist period, Eleanor Roosevelt criticized McCarthy and argued against nuclear testing and capital punishment. Throughout her life, she fought for the rights of African-Americans, the poor, young people, farmers, and Native Americans.

Throughout her travels and journalistic career, Eleanor Roosevelt tried to promote women's rights and to speak to the concerns of American women. Despite her fame, impressive earnings, and national respect, she remained self-effacing. In the tradition of Jane Addams, she fought for human liberation. In 1954 she wrote: "The most rewarding activity for any woman, young or old, is to meet the needs of those nearest and dearest to her. She will not meet these adequately if she has no interests and occupations of her own." Her last speech to the Human Rights Commission of the United Nations in 1952 concerned the political rights of women. In the 1940s she shifted her position regarding the Equal Rights Amendment; she had opposed it because of protective labor legislation for women but came to believe that the amendment was needed. One of the reasons Eleanor shifted her position was that much of the protective legislation extended to women in the Progressive era had been extended to all workers, male and female, by the 1940s. In 1961 President John F. Kennedy appropriately appointed her as head of the Commission on the Status of Women.

Another outstanding woman of the 1930s who was extremely successful because she combined traditional values and humanitarian zeal was Mary McLeod Bethune, a close friend of Eleanor Roosevelt. Eleanor Roosevelt introduced Bethune, the most influential African-American woman of the 1930s, at one of her regular press conferences held exclusively for women reporters, a means of giving more status and prestige to women reporters.[69]

Mary McLeod Bethune was an educator, college president (1904–42), and administrator in the New Deal. Through Eleanor Roosevelt's influence, she was appointed to the National Youth Administration, whose task was to aid young people in finding employment during the depression and World War II. Bethune was the first member of her race to hold such a federal office. She also served as director of the Division of Negro Affairs. President Truman later appointed her to the Committee for National Defense during World War II; Bethune was also a consultant at the Conference to Draft a United Nations Charter. She was a founder and active member in the National Association of Colored Women and created the National Council of Negro Women in 1935. She also organized the Federal Council on Negro Affairs, popularly called "the Black Cabinet."

Bethune worked tirelessly to press for the New Deal's support of African-Americans and to support the emerging civil rights movement. She marched, picketed discriminatory businesses in Washington, D.C., and spoke regularly to the NAACP. FDR delivered on his promises to her when he appointed four African-American women to outstanding federal appointments.[70]

Beginning with $1.50, Bethune built a school on a garbage dump. She opened her school for girls in Daytona, Florida, in 1904. The school merged with Cookman Institute of Jacksonville, Florida, and became Bethune-Cookman College in 1929. Lucy Miller Mitchell, a friend and coworker, tells of Bethune's indomitable courage one night when the Ku Klux Klan marched on the school:

Mrs. Bethune stood out in the quadrangle with her arms folded, as the message came down to her that the Klan was coming. It was a bright moonlight night, and you could see the Spanish moss hanging from the trees. It must have made a perfect arch for the marchers, but it was an eerie scene. They must have been intimidated by the courage and presence which Mrs. Bethune exemplified, because they marched in one entrance around the quadrangle and out the other entrance.[71]

Bethune had married Albertus Bethune in 1898 and had one child, Albert McLeod Bethune, born in 1899. She separated from her husband shortly after her child was born because Albertus did not share her missionary zeal. She left to establish a mission school in Palatka, Florida. In spite of her own inability to balance marriage and a career, she firmly believed that African-American women had room in their lives to be wives, mothers, and career women. She thought African-American women should dedicate themselves to improving the condition of their race. Her success was largely due to her nonconfrontational style of cooperation and negotiation, which was similar to that of Booker T. Washington. Most African-American feminists and leaders were wives and mothers and struggled for rights of both their race and their sex. Bethune realized that no African-American woman could be free to claim her power until racism was eliminated. Bethune expressed her lifelong commitment: "For I am my mother's daughter, and the drums of Africa still beat in my heart. They will not let me rest while there is a single Negro boy or girl without a chance to prove his worth."[72]

Like Eleanor Roosevelt, Bethune did not challenge traditional sexual roles. Both women had critics, but they were enormously successful with their comprehensive program of social reform and their simultaneous support of marriage and motherhood.

The Power of the Union

While Mary McLeod Bethune focused her energies on elevation of the black race, other social feminists worked for peace and disarmament in the Women's International League for Peace and Freedom, for New Deal agencies, the League of Women Voters, and as union members.

Kate Pemberton explained the way in which working for labor unionism empowered women in the 1930s: "Because of my pop, I grew up with a feeling that it was great being a woman. We sure didn't call ourselves women's libbers, but there was a change in the late thirties especially among union women. We started considering ourselves capable of exerting authority." Women workers were difficult to organize because most of them were in unskilled jobs, and the AFL, the largest union, included only skilled workers. Moreover, married women with children had little time for union activities because of the double burden of job and family responsibilities. However, in times of severe crisis like the depression, some women became militant in the labor movement.

The 1936–37 sit-down strike at General Motors in Flint, Michigan, was one of the most dramatic pitched battles of labor in the thirties. Genora Johnson Dollinger describes an electrifying moment during the strike. The workers had laid down their tools and just remained in the plant, striking for the right to make every GM worker a member of the United Auto Workers; they brought auto production to a halt.

On the night of December 30, 1936, the temperature was below zero, and police battled strikers throughout the night, firing buckshot and tear gas into their pickets. Fourteen men were wounded, and Dollinger grabbed the megaphone of the sound car:

I'm talking to you women out there. You didn't know that mothers—(I meant myself)—are being fired on by police. The police are cowards enough to fire into the bellies of unarmed men. Aren't they also cowards enough to fire at mothers of little children? I'm asking you women out there behind the barricades to break through the police lines. Come down here and stand with your sons, your sweethearts, your husbands and help us win this fight.

Roused by her call, one woman started walking forward and slipped right out of her coat as the police tried to stop her. Other women followed her, and the police did not dare to fire into the backs of unarmed women. The UAW won the night. Dollinger organized the Women's Emergency Brigade, which confronted police and company thugs again, breaking out the windows of the factory when tear gas was hurled into it. The brigade was instrumental in winning the strike after four months. The red berets of the brigade did not care whether they were unfeminine in their militance. After the strike was over, the union leaders thanked the "ladies" for their heroic action, adding that the laundry was piling up at home and that the children badly needed tending.[73]

Some 800,000 women belonged to unions by 1939, an increase over the

250,000 members in 1929. Although men still controlled the hierarchies of the unions and unskilled workers were largely unorganized, significant changes for women in labor unions were occurring. The Women's Bureau estimated that one out of fifteen women belonged to the American Federation of Labor or the CIO. The National Labor Relations Act spurred unionization of men and women. In an unprecedented venture, the ILGWU even staged a musical—*Pins and Needles*. Garment workers made up the cast; the show grossed $1.5 million. Roosevelt invited them to do a command performance in the White House.[74]

On the surface of American life, women seemed to conform to the traditional images of femininity, but they began to change their attitudes about themselves. Women still bought corsets and entered beauty contests. Formerly bobbed hair grew into soft waves, and hemlines came down. Housework was less burdensome if one could afford the new electric mixers, vacuum cleaners, washing machines, and gas stoves. Between the recipes for cheap nutritious meals were advertisements for Mum deodorant (to "keep others from recoiling"), Ipana (to prevent the "tell-tale warning on your toothbrush"), and Hinds Honey and Almond Cream ("because he loves the touch of silken smooth hands"). The next pages of the magazines might carry articles stressing the strength, intelligence, and accomplishments of women.

By 1939 American women were beginning to see the disparity between their own lives and the images they had always had of themselves. When Hitler invaded Poland, Americans were swept by "swing" fever and danced to Benny Goodman, Glenn Miller, Count Basie, and Duke Ellington. Most Americans thought involvement in World War I had been a mistake and strongly favored staying out of another war. The effects of the depression had lessened somewhat, and the chaos in Europe seemed to resemble a Marx brothers movie, "over there."

Traditional female roles were generally reinforced by the depression. Paradoxically, the extension of the feminine sphere into the public arena also gave women more autonomy and authority, as individuals and in the family. At the same time, women still faced hostility toward their employment, as well as unequal pay and discrimination in the labor force. Because historians have often judged the progress of feminism by the degree to which traditional roles were challenged, they have distorted women's experience in the 1930s. They have failed to see the impact of the weakening of male authority during the depression years and have minimized the substantial sex role changes which did occur. While this power did not automatically benefit women, in subtle ways women's consciousness about themselves changed.

Some modern feminists have assumed that the fulfillment of women as individuals has usually been at odds with their role in the American family. However, the more these two aims have been integrated in the feminist movement, the more successful the movement has been. The depression helped prepare the way for the feminine mystique of the 1940s and 1950s by consolidating the traditional female role, but not for the reasons generally assumed. Because of the extension of power within the family and in the public sphere, women achieved tremendous pride as producers who were capable of nontraditional activities. They had more reproductive control and could choose to adhere to a less rigid sexual code. At the same time, women's aspirations were shaped by the values of duty and self-sacrifice, which ironically increased their power over husbands and children during the many trials experienced by depression-era families. Middle-class women of the 1930s did not dream of suburban houses or of having five children. Over coffee with neighbors, women did not discuss how they could find their creative selves through housework, nor did they confide that they might even be bored.

Suddenly, on December 7, 1941, the depression's mood of deferment and waiting was shattered by FDR's voice on the radio declaring that Pearl Harbor had been attacked. A very different group of partygoers gathered on New Year's eve after the "day of infamy." Many of the men would leave on the next train for war, perhaps never to return. More than the usual sadness seized the crowd.

9

THE PARADOX OF WOMEN'S POWER
DURING WORLD WAR II

There was one good thing came out of it in factories. For the first time in their lives they {women} worked outside the home. They realized they were capable of doing something more than cook a meal. I remember going to Sunday dinner. One of the older women invited me to. She and her sister at the dinner table were talking about the best way to keep their drill sharp in the factory. I never heard anything like this in my life. It was just marvelous. I was tickled.
Dellie Hahne, in Studs Terkel, *"The Good War,"* 1984

Bus depots and train stations were crowded with people the week after the bombing of Pearl Harbor. Freshly scrubbed young men in their brand new military uniforms looked very handsome, their nameplates and shoes shined. Their excitement disguised their nervousness. Many of the couples saying good-bye to one another had married after barely knowing each other; many had shared only one night together. Now they faced an uncertain future.

Tearfully, as the woman embraced her husband or lover, she thought, Will he be gone for years? Will he come back at all? Kissing her good-bye, the man wondered, will she be faithful? Is she already carrying my child? Margaret Mead sensitively described the plight of the war couples, noting that many faced "the experience of remaining romantically true over months and years to someone they hardly know at all, and the experience of giving everything at once, regardless of the future, to someone they hardly know at all."[1]

As the train pulled out and the soldiers leaned out of the windows, the lyrics of a popular song filled the station:

God bless America, land that I love,
Stand beside her and guide her
Through the night with the light from above.

After catching a final glance at their men through the train windows, the women returned home and began the long wait for their husbands, brothers, sons, and lovers, waiting for letters telling how they *were* some time ago. Florence Hollis, a social worker, remembers the plight of some of the war brides who went through periods of frustration, anger, and loss. She claims that they sometimes fell into states of hysterical grief and mourning; at other times, they bitterly blamed their husbands for being absent.[2] The war bride returned home by herself to spend time writing letters or cleaning her room. One service wife summed up her existence, "It's a lonesome life. You don't live, you just get along."[3]

The 50 million women in the United States responded differently to the wartime situation, depending on their level of income, marital status, race, geographic location, and stage in their life cycle.[4] Some believed that their patriotic duty was to stay at home and take care of their children, while others took war jobs out of necessity or patriotism, or in order to fight the intense loneliness.

Commentators like Karen Anderson, D'Ann Campbell, and Leila Rupp have cautioned against overemphasizing the impact of the Second World War on changing traditional attitudes about appropriate gender roles. They assert that wartime women experienced changes in work and family as temporary, rather than as deeper transformations. William Chafe and Alan Clive also claim that wartime women workers viewed their employment as temporary and believed that their primary role was still being wives and mothers. However, recent scholarship fails to acknowledge fully the war's impact on causing structural changes within the economy which later created a more receptive climate for feminism and dramatic social changes. Moreover, it fails to take into account adequately the differing responses to the war caused by race, class, and geographic location.

Like the Great Depression, the Second World War affected women's lives profoundly. The war was a major turning point for the history of women in the United States because it led to dramatic economic and social changes, making the liberation of women possible. Moreover, the experience of the war created a series of contradictions which led to a psychological awakening of women to their own power, an awareness of discrimination against them, and the emergence of feminist consciousness.

The Great Depression had increased women's domestic power, and the war greatly accelerated the process. Because of the disruption of family life during the war, both men and women longed to return to stability and security and a semblance of traditional roles. But women who had managed without their men, no matter how reluctantly and painfully, found it difficult to return to being submissive, dependent wives when their men returned.

The war experience created a reservoir of strength and resentment in women who had been socialized to be taken care of by a man but who ended up having to take care of themselves. Thrust into nontraditional roles, some women liked the new freedom; others resented it. As reflected in the popular culture of the period, women were excited by, as well as fearful and ambivalent toward, independence and achievement. Responsibility connotes power, although sometimes it may be more of a burden than a source of autonomy and self-esteem. But ultimately, the key to freedom was in reproductive control, sexual freedom, economic independence, education, and political and legal equality. The Second World War did more than any other single event in the history of the United States to lay the groundwork for radical changes in women's lives and consciousness.

The experience of World War II recast the dilemma of combining work and love. Women were urged to work *because* of their love of husbands, sons, and lovers, as well as their country. Outside work was no longer viewed as a threat to the family, but essential to its health. The entrance of large numbers of women into the labor force changed the lives of middle-class families by legitimizing two breadwinners. Women added another role, while retaining the traditional role.

Life on the Home Front

On the home front American women were free from bombing, devastation, and the dangers of combat. They learned new forms of fidelity—and sometimes infidelity. As Margaret Mead said, "They learned to live months on the memory of a few short days." In the absence of life-threatening hazards, women faced a thousand small irritations. They encountered housing shortages and other shortages which made routine chores more time-consuming and difficult. Sugar, coffee, fuel, oil, gasoline, butter, meats, cheese, canned foods, and finally shoes were rationed. Rich and poor alike endured rationing, since metal for asparagus tongs, beer mugs, spittoons, birdcages, cocktail shakers, hair curlers, corn poppers, and lobster forks was rationed along with the staples of life. Women also faced inadequate public transportation, and they were often sequestered at home.[5]

In order to help the war effort, Americans raised Victory gardens; by 1943, 20 million Victory gardens supplied one-third of all the country's fresh vegetables. Housewives saved tin cans, shortening, and other products for various salvage drives. They canned food at home as they had during the Great Depression. Others prepared "bundles for Britain" and bandages for the Red Cross.[6]

While doing housework, women listened to soap operas on the radio like "Vic and Sade" and to the new singing commercials. They also listened to "The Shadow," "Gangbusters," "Fibber McGee and Molly," and "The Jack Benny Show." They might see Irving Berlin's *This Is the Army* on the stage, or James Cagney in the movie *Yankee Doodle Dandy*.[7]

Consumer credit was virtually unknown, and entrepreneurs withheld products because they seemed to feel that life should not be easy on the homefront. Throwaway plates seemed wrong because a woman was supposed to wash dishes, and drive-in services would make everything too easy.

The GIs hoped their wives and lovers were not "going all the way" with anyone back home. They knew that "Casanovas" and "wolves" must be abundant. When the *Ladies Home Journal* sent questionnaires to soldiers, sailors, and marines inquiring about their ideal woman, the men replied that she was short, healthy, vital, and devoted to her home and children. They thought that her cooking ability was far more important to them than her intelligence or business ability. Her face was less important than her figure and disposition. She should play at least one outdoor sport and like to dance. She would not work outside the home, except in an emergency.[8]

If all American women did not fit the soldiers' image of their dream girl, most of them had their own visions of a dream boy. For some it was Clark Gable, and they shuddered when they heard he had passed his physical and was joining the army. Others were hysterical over a "nice, clean, skinny, practically voiceless kid with jug-handle ears and golf ball Adam's apple, named Frank Sinatra." Male and female teenagers went into "spasmodic imitations of sex convulsions in his presence."[9] Bing Crosby alone rivaled the "voice."

Americans who had listened to the big bands of Glenn Miller, Gene Krupa, and Tommy Dorsey now lined up to hear Ethel Merman sing Irving Berlin's "Annie Get Your Gun" and to see Cole Porter's spoof on Shakespeare, *Kiss Me Kate*. They laughed over the song on the radio "In Der Fuehrer's Face," which originated in a Donald Duck movie, and considered it naughty because "Bra-a-a-a-a-ack" was what you did in the Fuehrer's face. The word was the nearest one could come to spelling out the sound of breaking wind. Americans celebrated Christmas in 1942 and New Year's shortly after Guadalcanal had been won with a stubborn refusal to face the horrors of war.[10]

Women wore low-heeled shoes, ballerina slippers, and coats with a military cut. They wore shoulderpads, straight skirts, and evening wraps resembling Eisenhower jackets. A popular evening dress had a huge swooping air corps wing of gold lamé, curving across the bosom from one hip. Women often wore romper suits and slacks, enjoying more comfort, mobility, and convenience in their clothing because of the war. Young people wore sloppy-joe sweaters and flat-soled loafers. As William Manchester recalled, "The girls who would be women before the troopships came home would never again be so willowy." The average American woman weighed 120 pounds and was 5'5". She wore a shoulder-length pageboy or a curled bob.[11]

Corset manufacturers designed rubberless girdles, which meant whalebone in one model, and piano wire in another. The War Production Board ruled that girdles were necessary to women's health and could have priorities. Incidentally, girdles also inhibited the advances of would-be seducers. Since stockings were almost impossible to get, women painted on their seamlines, and some wore leg makeup.[12] But it would take more than consumer goods to sustain the women who were caught in the anguish of waiting.

The war gave many women and men greater economic security and lifted the nation out of the Great Depression. The world before the war was vastly different from the postwar society. In 1941 nearly nine million men were still unemployed, almost three million on WPA roles, and almost a third of all African-Americans were on relief. One out of seven Americans had a telephone, one in five a car; one-fourth of all homes lacked running water, and one-third had no flush toilets. Life expectancy was sixty-three. The average citizen left school after the eighth grade. [13] But just about everyone could read the comics.

Images of Female Power in Popular Culture

To escape from the strains of life on the homefront, 70 million Americans read the daily comic pages in the newspapers; Americans bought 12 million comic books each month.[14] In the 1940s female characters in the comics reflected a preoccupation with the war. Frequently they were sexy spies, nurses, or alluring camp followers. Wonder Woman appeared with her superhuman power and loads of sex appeal. The reporter Brenda Starr was always torn between her career and romantic interests. While the single women in the comics were trying to catch a man, having war adventures, or conquering evil as Wonder Woman was, the married characters were conquering their husbands. As in the tradition of the 1930s, married women were portrayed as very powerful in marriage, even dominant. Although they had to use covert power or manipulative feminine charms, they were definitely bosses at home, humoring bungling husbands and exercising their domestic power.[15]

Like the comics, the movies portrayed ambiguous images of female power. By 1946 some 60–100 million Americans went to the movies each week. During the war women composed the majority of film audiences. Female audiences flocked to see films portraying womanhood as strong, maternal, and sisterly. As Andrea S. Walsh observes in *Women's Film and Female Experience, 1940–1950*, female audiences favored films portraying women in central roles, "desiring yet distrusting and angry toward men, excited about as well as ambivalent toward and frightened of independence and autonomy." The popular women's films of the 1940s, including the maternal drama, the career woman comedy, and the film of suspicion and distrust, reveal a nascent feminism reflected by a wartime female consciousness.[16]

In contrast to the male-oriented films such as Westerns, crime dramas, and war movies, which focus on men's fear of intimacy and preoccupation with self-definition and male bonding, the "women's films" of the period from 1930 to 1950 were created mainly for a female audience. The films are generally shot indoors and convey the importance of human attachment and emotionality. The female stars generally play strong, sacrificial mothers, "wholesome girls," assertive career women, or threatened or insane wives.[17]

Of all the women's films, the maternal drama was the most popular with American women in the 1940s. On January 24, 1940, John Ford's film *Grapes of Wrath* opened with Jane Darwell as Ma Joad. Ma Joad, the strong matriarch who had been a symbol of female strength in the Great Depression, became an icon for the war years also. Although she clearly held the family together, she assumed power reluctantly, acting out of an emergency situation. If Pa had been capable of leadership, she would gladly have surrendered her position of authority. She exerted her power in the service of others.[18]

Although during the forties white actresses enjoyed more challenging roles as independent women, African-American actresses were still locked into stereotypical roles as domestics. Louise Beavers, Butterfly McQueen, and Hattie McDaniel played strong, compassionate domestics but were denied other roles.[19]

In many cases the film heroines of the 1940s, who survive perfectly well without men, still give up careers for the men they love. In *Together Again* (1944) Irene Dunne is a mayor who gives up her office to get married. Joan Crawford plays a neurotic woman obsessed with getting her daughter's love in *Mildred Pierce* (1945). The mother achieves financial success through sheer determination, first as a waitress, then as an owner of a restaurant. Both of her husbands are portrayed as unable to be successful breadwinners. Her daughter is a spoiled, egotistic woman who kills her stepfather. Although her mother tries to take the blame, the daughter ends up in jail at the end of the film. In an ambiguous ending, Crawford leaves with her first husband, leaving unanswered the question of whether the achieving female is ultimately dependent on a man. Nevertheless, Crawford does succeed on her own and achieves independence and wealth. Although she is vulnerable to romance, her ultimate trap is not dependence on a man but overmothering her daughter. A tension between female achievement and femininity is played out in many films of the period.

Other films of the 1940s portray women either as evil or as victims. Barbara Stanwyck plays both. In *Double Indemnity* (1944), she plots to kill her husband. Four years later, she played a bedridden victim in *Sorry Wrong Number* (1948). Ingrid Bergman plays the victim in *Gaslight* (1944) and in *Notorious* (1946).[20] These films portray women who are distrustful and suspicious of men, some of whom are trying to kill them. In a period when many women were hastily married to men whom they barely knew, they were attracted by these movies which dealt with their forbidden fears.

Another popular kind of women's film of the 1940s portrays a witty, successful, career woman. American women seemed to like films about individual women who were achieving, but they had rejected the 1936 film *A Woman Rebels,* about a nineteenth-century suffragist, starring Katharine Hepburn. Most American women of the war years did not have a collective feminist consciousness. But they enthusiastically went to see Katharine Hepburn in more subtly feminist films in the 1940s like *Woman of the Year* (1942) and *Adam's Rib* (1949). These films reveal the ambivalence which women felt toward achievement, assuming nontraditional roles, and domestic power.[21]

Thus, the films of the 1940s depicted women as strong, independent, and crucial to the war effort. As we have seen, actresses played matriarchs, career women, victims, war workers, and neurotics. Although marriage and motherhood were still portrayed as the sources of women's greatest happiness, achievement for women was depicted as fulfilling—as long as it did not threaten to replace love. Images of women's power were ambiguous in films; if women used their power for the good of their families, it was praised. If they used it for self-aggrandizement, they were condemned as selfish, deranged, and unhappy.

Empowerment through Paid Labor

The majority of American women who saw the films of the 1940s did not have glamorous careers to give up, because they were either housewives or they had "jobs." Women went into the labor force during the war in dramatic numbers. Because of the war emergency, the government had to mobilize women to work, despite deeply embedded cultural resistance to the idea of women's assuming men's place in the work force. Just as in World War I, but in much larger numbers, women replaced men in hundreds of job classifications previously closed to them. Women were spot and torch welders, hydraulic press operators, shell loaders, taxi drivers, football coaches, barbers, bus drivers, bellhops, crane operators, ferry command pilots, along with numerous other traditionally male posts. Lola Weixel expressed her enthusiasm when she began her job as a welder: "We were going to get in on the ground floor and be welders for ever and ever. It was almost an art, as well as a skill. It was a very beautiful kind of work. At the end of the day I always felt I had accomplished something. There was a product. There was something to be seen."[22]

Lyn Childs, who took a nontraditional job as a shipburner, described her motivation: "I took the job because, number one, I needed work; number two, I'd had bad experience in jobs before where I hadn't felt any pride in the kind of work I was doing; number three, there was a war on and the people were all enthused about helping out in every way they could."[23]

The sex-typing of jobs for women was justified by claims that women had greater manual dexterity than men, paid more attention to detail, were able to tolerate monotony better than men, and were physically weaker than men. In the auto industry, employers resisted hiring women until after the supply of male labor was completely exhausted. Even then, they did not incorporate women into men's jobs randomly. Instead, they established new patterns of occupational segregation for the duration, reconciling women's new economic situation with their traditional roles as wives and mothers.[24]

A cartoon of the period shows two working girls in front of a finishing school. One says, "I flunked in charm and social composure, but I passed in welding and riveting!" Another says, "That new foreman is simply divine—you've no idea how thrilling he is when he takes your hand in his, looks dreamily into your eyes and murmurs: 'Baby, you're the best little drill press operator in town!'"[25]

Propaganda appealed to women's patriotism and reassured them that they could remain feminine. One woman war worker who wrote a book about her experiences reassured her readers that she and her coworkers remained genteel. Nell Giles wrote: "I've always meant to tell you that the girls who work here use perfume through the day for a lift; that they work, if possible with a snapshot of someone they love before them, and that this man always wears a uniform; that they are modest in changing from dresses into smocks. Aren't these signs of gentility?"[26]

If women still had doubts about taking a war job, they were reminded that if they were "slackers," they might be responsible for some man's death. One recruiting advertisement of 1943 showed a grimy woman war worker who said, "Since I have found the place where I can serve my country best, I should feel as if there were blood on my hands—his blood—if there were no oil on my hands today."[27]

In order to mobilize the women for war work, the War Manpower Commission of the Office of War Information undertook a massive propaganda campaign. They used radio spots like the following:

> This is (name) speaking . . . speaking earnestly to the wives of (city). I'm a housewife, too . . . never worked outside my home until this year. Feeding my family and buying war bonds just didn't seem enough. So I got an 8-hour job, and managed to run my home besides. My husband's proud of me . . . and I've never been happier. I feel I'm *really* helping to make the war end sooner . . . and maybe saving the life of just one boy from home.[28]

Major magazines featured photographs of women in work clothes on their covers. Songs like "The Lady at Lockheed," "We're the Janes Who Make the Planes," and "Rosie the Riveter" glorified women workers. Dorothy Parker, a prominent journalist, remarked that it was "the day of the strong and sure; the day of the girl who comes marching down to cases like a soldier." Elizabeth Field described the entrance of a new, strong image of womanhood: "The Glamour Girl is practically interred along with the Gibson Girl and the

Flapper and the Boom Town Girl is here for the duration. And—after the war? Well, she's not worrying about that. She's got a job to do right now that's mighty important—and she's doing it!"[29]

In her book *Mobilizing Women for War,* Leila Rupp observes that the war propaganda emphasized that the woman worker, while performing nontraditional work, was still the same prewar woman who cooked, cleaned, and cared for her family. Patriotism was personalized. Women were expected to help the war effort in order to save the lives of loved ones and bring them home faster. The theme of the propaganda was that women were stepping out in the man's world temporarily, without forsaking their primary role. Moreover, they could still maintain their femininity. Thus, the propaganda did not challenge traditional assumptions about women's role in society. A newsreel called *Glamour Girls of '43* clearly delivered this message:

> Instead of cutting the lines of a dress, this woman cuts the pattern of aircraft parts. Instead of baking a cake, this woman is cooking gears to reduce the tension in the gears after use. . . . They are taking to welding as if the rod were a needle and the metal a length of cloth to be sewn. After a short apprenticeship, this woman can operate a drill press just as easily as a juice extractor in her own kitchen. And a lathe will hold no more terrors for her than an electric washing machine.[30]

A prominent billboard beamed the same message:

> What Job is mine on the Victory Line?
> If you've sewed on buttons, or made button holes on a machine, you can learn to do spot welding on airplane parts.
> If you've used an electric mixer in your kitchen, you can learn to run a drill press.
> If you've followed recipes exactly in making cakes, you can learn to load shells.[31]

The women's magazines perpetuated the same themes. An article in the *Woman's Home Companion* carried photographs of four women war workers dressed and made-up to be as beautiful as any women. The author announced that American women could learn how to put together tanks, weld, and rivet but also could look glamorous in overalls.

Women responded enthusiastically to the call to join the civilian industrial army. The proportion of women working increased from 25 to 36 percent, a rise greater than that of the previous four decades. The number of wives holding jobs doubled. The war sent 29,000 women into the Women's Land Army, helping to replace the farmers who had been shipped overseas. Women had access to skilled, higher-paying industrial jobs for the first time.[32] From April 1940 to August 1943, an additional 4.4 million women entered the labor force, 3 million more than formerly. Some 1.3 million were in agriculture, and the rest in manufacturing, clerical work, and the professions.

Female union membership more than tripled, increasing from 800,000 in 1939 to more than three million by 1945, with the most members in the CIO, chiefly in electrical, auto, and steel unions. Militant women helped win strikes during the Great Depression and participated in strikes during the war. In fact, there were more strikes during World War II than in the previous decade. The no-strike pledge notwithstanding, wildcat strikes continued throughout the 1940s. More women belonged to unions proportionately in 1950 than in 1980 (35 percent compared with 21 percent). The United Auto Workers membership was 28 percent female by the end of the war. But the double burden of outside employment and domestic responsibilities made participation in a union difficult for most women workers. The women who did join unions found overt sexism. Since male union members viewed women as temporary workers, they did not aggressively push women's issues like child care, and they retained separate seniority lists and separate job classifications for women and black men.[33]

The employed woman was likely to be married (56 percent), and one out of five had absent husbands. She was probably between the ages of twenty and forty-four. Nevertheless, a large number of older married women were also employed. Ten million women who had been working at the time of Pearl Harbor were still working in 1944.[34] Munitions production increased 225 percent during the first year of the war alone, and corporate profits increased from $6.4 to $10.8 billion. During World War II, 18 million women were in the labor force, 6 million for the first time. From 1940 to 1945 the percentage of women among all workers rose from 25 percent to 36 percent, which represented 28 percent to 37 percent of all women. The number of women in steel machinery, shipbuilding, aircraft, and auto factories rose from 230,000 in 1939 to 1.7 million in 1944, dropping to 580,000 in 1947. However, the majority of wives did not, at any one time, hold full-time jobs. Of the 28,510,000 wives whose husbands were at home in 1944, 76 percent were homemakers both then and at the time of Pearl Harbor.[35]

A profile of women in early 1944 reveals that 32.5 million married women and 2.7 million widowed or divorced women were running households. Their median age was forty-one; 10 percent were black, 8 percent had husbands in the service, 4 percent were separated from husbands or abandoned, and 88 percent had husbands at home throughout the war. Of the married women, 57 percent lived in cities, 21 percent on farms and one-fourth were employed full-time at any one time in 1944. One-third of the divorced or widowed women were employed during the same period. Overall, unemployment dropped from 17 percent in 1939 to 2 percent in 1942, where it stabilized for the duration of the war. Family income rose 48 percent.[36]

Women composed half of the workers in ordnance plants, 40 percent at the bomber plant at Willow Run, 12 percent in the shipyards, and 40 percent at aircraft assembly plants. Even when women proved their competence in their jobs, however, they received less pay than men did for the same work. Karen Anderson, who studied women war workers in Seattle, Baltimore, and Detroit, found that when women performed well in nontraditional jobs, bosses reassessed the nature of the jobs they were doing rather than the nature of women. They tried to change the jobs to fit traditional preconceptions of women.[37]

The hopes of prominent women's organizations that the female contribution to victory would lead to full equality were not realized. However, war work gave individual women a sense of independence and self-sufficiency. They could decide how to spend and how to save their own money, making them dependent on men more for love and devotion than for financial support or protection.[38]

This time of self-sufficiency and independence would be remembered later long after the war in the 1950s and 1960s. The women who came of age during World War II were not by accident the mothers of the women's liberationists of the 1970s. During the war most American women did not grasp the opportunities for liberation which the war offered. However, millions of married women found renewed self-worth. As one woman remarked, "I no longer stooge for my family. Everyone has to look after themselves. I am once again a person."[39] An author of a manual for female war workers, perhaps worried that they would become too independent, advised that the wife should "anticipate her soldier's desires when he came home on leave." She suggested, "Dress your prettiest, be your sweetest and gayest."[40]

Even if women tried to please their men, they were also learning to please themselves. The boost to the economy which the war brought meant that men and women enjoyed high wages during the war. By July 1946 the average wage in twenty-five manufacturing industries was $33.70 a week for women, and $50.78 for men. In 1941 the median income for the 32 million families in the United States was $2,000 a year. For 18 million families, however, the income was less than $2,000. For about 13 million—fully 40 percent of all American families—it was less than $900 a year; for 4 million, less than $312.[41]

War jobs sent 15–20 million people scrambling across the country in search of higher wages. The most crowded areas were Mobile County (Alabama), Hampton Roads (Virginia area), Norfolk, San Diego, Charleston (South Carolina), Portland, Vancouver, San Francisco, Puget Sound (Washington), Muskegon County (Michigan), and Detroit.[42] Cut off from relatives, many Americans led more privatized and anonymous lives. They were freer to break with tradition but were cut off from family ties and assistance as they created families of their own.

Coping with a war job and the needs of a family strained many women to the breaking point. Rationing made shopping very difficult for war workers, and few communities attempted to meet the needs of working mothers. Housing was almost impossible to secure, since only one million new housing units were built during the entire war. Between 20 and 40 percent of the two million workers and families who migrated to take war jobs were without adequate housing. Often they spent uncomfortable months without plumbing, heat, and running water. They occupied tents, chicken coops, and abandoned buildings until they found better accommodations. Then they might have to live with two or three other families in crowded quarters. Appliances which would have made domestic work easier disappeared from the stores. Food shortages compounded the families' difficulties.[43] But child care was perhaps the most serious problem.

In a propagandistic book designed to enlist women war workers, Laura Nelson Baker told of an enterprising woman who managed it all:

> What can the mothers who work in the factory do about their homes? Believe it or not, most of them take care of both jobs and do them well! One woman who works on the assembly line of an electrical-equipment plant has four children ranging from seven to fifteen, plus a husband who operates a gas station. Five separate times during the day she must have meals on the table ready to be eaten. . . . The family does its own work entirely, washing and ironing included. How does she manage? Chiefly, it is a matter of organization and co-operation of every member of the household.[44]

Not all the women war workers could manage two jobs. They sometimes had to miss work to get a ration card or to take care of a sick child. The absence of adequate child care for working mothers was so desperate that the government was forced to intervene in 1943. The government helped fund some child-care centers; as of February 1944, there were 66,000 children in federally supported facilities, a figure rising to 100,000 in the spring of 1945. The centers were often poorly run and poorly staffed, and many mothers felt guilty leaving their children there. The centers met less than 10 percent of the need. Government officials feared that if child-care centers were too convenient to defense plants, women might want to continue working after the war.[45]

The Lanham Act funds for day-care centers were awarded on a 50-50 basis, with communities contributing their share. Communities and industries did not provide child care extensively. The Thomas Bill, which would have increased child-care funding, was introduced to Congress in 1943. Opponents like the Catholic church triumphed, and although passing the Senate, the bill failed in the House. The United States did much less than England to enable working mothers both to contribute to the war effort and to have good child care. The presumption was that it was the individual woman's responsibility to give "primary" attention to her children, not the government's.[46]

The government offered cost-plus contracts to war factories in order to help defray the costs of community services for the workers. However, few employers took advantage of the offer. An exception was Kaiser Shipyards in Portland, Oregon, which operated a twenty-four-hour child-care center for working mothers on site. Kaiser also had an industrial credit union, carpooling networks, and a carry-out meal service. A tank plant in Peoria, Illinois, and a tent and uniform manufacturing shop in Cleveland, Ohio, also had child-care centers, but these services were rare throughout industry.[47]

Most mothers, employed or not, viewed child care as their major responsibility and thought that preservation of the American family was the purpose of the war. Few working mothers actually used day-care centers, either because they reacted against the "relief" image or because of the inconvenient locations, high weekly charges, and risks involved should the child become sick. Therefore, 90 percent of them made alternative arrangements, usually with family members.[48]

Mothers were bombarded with guilt from two contradictory sides. If they did not take a war job, they were slackers and lazy. If they did, they were deserting their children. Women who could not find adequate day care and were in unfamiliar towns with no relatives nearby were at a loss for support. The "latch-key" children (a term common in the 1930s for unsupervised children) often fended for themselves after school. The administrator of King County Welfare department in Seattle reported that some Boeing employees left their children asleep in locked cars in the parking lot while they worked. Other social welfare officials told of similar situations.[49] Juvenile delinquency increased, and the blame was placed squarely on the mothers.

Anna W. M. Wolf described a more subtle impact of absent fathers and working mothers on the children: "They felt it in the way young children feel things—not in any mysterious telepathic way, but quite specifically in her expression, her tone of voice, in the tension in her muscles as she bathed and dressed them."[50]

Older children were rushed into jobs and thus enjoyed more mobility, less parental control, and more independence. One woman who was young during the war summarized the loss of innocence she felt: "What I feel most about the war, it disrupted my family. That really chokes me up, makes me feel very sad that I lost that. On December 6, 1941, I was playing with paper dolls: Deanna Durbin, Sonja Henie. I had a Shirley Temple doll that I cherished. After Pearl Harbor, I never played with dolls again."[51]

Sometimes women war workers received pressure from their husbands to quit their jobs. Clovis Walker's husband urged her to quit her job at the Kaiser Shipyard in Richmond, California. He even hid her leather welder's apron and boots so that she could not report to work. Although she eventually quit, she resented her husband's attitude so much that when they visited his family in the East, she "just left him there."[52] Many men could not stand their wives' financial independence, even when they continued to perform their domestic responsibilities on top of their war jobs. Margaret White, who was a munitions worker, remembered accepting the double burden: "When your husband came home, you know, he propped his feet up and got a can of beer while you fixed dinner, or even if we weren't working the same shifts, you fixed dinner and left it where it would be convenient for him to get it."[53]

African-American Women during World War II

During the Second World War, African-American women also faced the double burden of employment and family responsibilities, made more difficult because of racist and sexist discrimination. However, the Second World War gave African-American women a chance to get out of domestic service in which they had traditionally been confined. Their employment in manufacturing increased from 50,000 in 1940 to 300,000 in 1944. In addition 100,000 African-American women found employment in white-collar jobs as secretaries, sales clerks, and switchboard operators. But they still lagged behind white women. Only one in thirty African-American women held white-collar jobs, compared with one in three of white women.[54]

Minority women constituted 10–19 percent of the female workers in large production centers like New York, Los Angeles, and Detroit. Between 1940 and 1944 the percentage of African-American female industrial workers rose from 6.5 percent to 18.0 percent of the work force. Their wages rose as much as 1,000 percent over prewar work. The number of skilled African-American workers and the number of African-Americans holding federal government jobs doubled during the war years. The number of African-American union members increased to 14 million in 1945, six times more than in 1940.

Mary McLeod Bethune led the National Council of Negro Women, a coalition of a hundred organizations. The council stressed racial solidarity, voter registration, and a "hold your job" appeal to women who had broken through racial barriers. The Illinois Association of Colored Women focused on defeating job restrictions and racial covenants in housing, in addition to the more usual USO activities. Racism extended even to the Red Cross, however, which segregated the blood of whites and African-Americans. [55]

But despite the greater opportunities for minorities in the war industries, many companies continued to refuse to hire black workers, even when they needed workers badly. President Truman did not order the integration of all the armed forces until 1948, following racial riots, hunger strikes, and the court-martial of fifty African-American sailors who refused to load ammunition ships in California after an explosion killed 342 men, the majority of whom were African-American. Some progress in achieving racial equality occurred because of the war. A. Philip Randolph, the leader of the Brotherhood of Sleeping Car Porters, met with other African-American leaders and called for mass public demonstrations and organization to secure war jobs and equal pay. The threat of 100,000 militant African-Americans marching on Washington, D.C. pressured President Roosevelt to issue Executive Order 8802, which outlawed discrimination in the defense industries because of race, creed, color, or national origin. FDR also created the Fair Employment Practices Commission. Although the executive order was not consistently enforced, it represented a significant improvement over having no legal recourse.[56]

Minority families made gains during the war. The labor force participation rates for the major ethnic and racial groups of women living in cities and small towns had begun to converge by 1950. African-American women were especially committed to paid employment. The income of African-American families more than doubled between 1939 and 1945.[57] With incomes still far below whites, African-American families had to try to live on $634 a year in southern cities, or $566 a year in the rural South. During the war a migration northward of a million African-Americans began. Racism persisted in the North and the South but was especially open and virulent in the South. Lynching of African-Americans continued throughout the war, even of men in their uniforms. Billie Holliday recalls the pervasive racism which she experienced in the South of the 1940s: "It got to the point where I hardly ever ate, slept, or went to the bathroom without having a major NAACP-type production." Lena Horne made a magnificent gesture of defiance in one of the first prisoner of war camps. The African-American guards had been seated in the back. Lena slowly stepped down from the stage, walked down the aisle, and with her back to the Germans, sang to her own people.[58]

Discrimination against African-American women continued unabated during the war. The availability of high-paying industrial jobs for women meant the equalization of income for many African-American and working-class white families. In many of these households, such jobs effectively eliminated the economic basis for women's dependence and subordination.

The Paradox of Female Independence

The Second World War created a gulf between the experiences of the soldiers and the women on the home front. The gulf would be difficult, if not impossible to bridge. The paradox of women's independence lay in the fact that it was thrust upon them and produced conflicting feelings of resentment, pride, and guilt. Dellie Hahne captured the feelings of many women who were caught between independence and a socialized dependence on men. She recalls:

> There was a letter column in which some woman wrote to her husband over-seas: "This is an exact picture of our dashboard. Do we need a quart of oil?" Showing how dependent we were upon our men. Those of us who read it said, This is pure and simple bullshit. 'Cause if you don't know if you need a quart of oil, drive the damn thing to the station and have the man show you and you'll learn if you need a quart of oil. But they still wanted women to be dependent, helpless.

I think a lot of women said, Screw that noise. 'Cause they had a taste of freedom, they had a taste of making their own money, a taste of spending their own money, making their own decisions. I think the beginning of the women's movement had its seeds right there in World War Two.[59]

Men on the war front worried about what was happening back home. Margaret Mead wrote that when asked about his thoughts when he approached Berlin, one soldier replied, "Well, mostly we've been wondering whether it's true that women are smoking pipes at home." Many men worried about whether the women were going to be so changed that they would not need them anymore. Mead captured the anxieties of men and women over their differing experiences of the war:

In wartime men and women get out of step and begin to wonder about each other. "What will he be like after all those years in the Army?" "What will she be like after all those years alone at home?" "Will he be harder on the children and want them to toe the line too hard? After all that's all he has seen for years." "Will she have learned to be so independent that she won't want to give up her job to make a home for me?" "Will he have got so used to having everything done for him, his clothes handed out, his meals set on the table, his allotment deducted, that he will hate having to sit down and plan how in the world we are going to pay the dentist's bill, or meet the payment on the house?" . . . "What's happened to his morals?" "What's happened to her morals?" "I do hope he won't have changed too much." "I hope she will look the same."[60]

Husbands wondered whether their wives were being unfaithful and whether they were getting used to living without them. Because of their war work, women learned more about their own strength and competence. They learned about unions, the value of money, and how to work in groups. They also felt that they were shortening the war, doing something to hasten the return of their husbands, sons, and lovers.

Peggy Terry, who took a war job, remembers:

The first work I had after the Depression was at a shell-loading plant in Viola, Kentucky. It was between Paducah and Mayfield. They were large shells: anti-aircraft, incendiaries, and tracers. We painted red on the tips of the tracers. My mother, my sister, and myself worked there. Each of us worked a different shift because we had little ones at home. We made the fabulous sum of thirty-two dollars a week. (Laughs) To us it was an absolute miracle. Before that, we made nothing.

You won't believe how incredibly ignorant I was. I knew vaguely that a war had started, but I had no idea what it meant.[61]

Women who had a taste of independence might long for the security of depending on a man, but they would find it difficult to be submissive again. Even during the war women received contradictory messages. They were urged to be physically strong, resourceful, and competent eight hours a day at work, but to remain weak, feminine, attractive, and dependent on men when they left their jobs.[62]

Margaret Wright, a munitions worker, recalls the irony of putting women in dangerous industrial jobs but not allowing them to be on the front lines: "Jobs were not safe. Women were 'too delicate' to go to war or do delicate things, but they would let us be blown up sifting gunpowder. Every last one of us who worked in that department was a woman, and it was very, very dangerous."[63]

Although not fighting at the front, women in the military challenged traditional notions of women's proper role. They composed 2 percent of the military personnel with 140,000 Wacs (Women's Army Corps), 1,000 Wasps (Women's Airforce Service Pilots), 100,000 Waves in the navy (Women Accepted for Voluntary Emergency Service), 23,000 Marine Corps Women's Reserve, 13,000 Coast Guard SPARs (the women's reserve of the Coast Guard), 60,000 in the Army Nurse Corps, and 14,000 navy nurses.[64] Lord and Taylor designed their uniforms to be as "feminine" as possible, and bras and girdles were standard equipment.[65] Their underwear was appropriately a khaki color. Although the number was relatively small, the presence of women in the military threatened many preconceptions about their abilities. For those military women, the experience was unforgettable. A former Wac who was a captain in Public Information recalls:

I had two tours of duty in Germany. . . . If it weren't for the war, I'd have probably stayed in Evansville as a newspaper woman. Maybe got a job in Indianapolis or Chicago. (Laughs) I wouldn't have traveled as extensively as I did. It really changed my life. A young woman my age never had an apartment away from her parents. My mother would have thought I was a fallen woman. This way, I could gloriously go off on my own and be on my own.[66]

Another former Wac, Carolyn Pratt, recalls the thrill of contributing to the war effort and of operating antiaircraft guns. Because of the war emergency she did not view her joining the service as a bold act, but simply as a patriotic duty. After the war she used the GI Bill to acquire her Ph.D. in psychology.

At peak strength, 271,600 women served in some branch of the military; a total of 350,000 women voluntarily entered the services at some point during the hostilities. The median age of Wacs was twenty-five. In 1943 approximately 70 percent of the Wacs were single, 15 percent married, 15 percent widowed, divorced, or separated. By 1945, half were single with no marriage planned for the near future but 16 percent were engaged. More than 4,000 African-American women were Wacs. Over 100 of them were officers. When Franklin Roosevelt ordered that African-American women be recruited, the Waves accepted only two black officers and seventy-two enlisted women, the SPARs took four, and the Marine Corps none.[67]

In 1943 a national underground smear campaign began, portraying all women soldiers as sexually promiscuous. American servicemen spread the rumors. Most servicemen responded to women in the military with amused condescension or open hostility, mostly the latter. Toward the end of the war, the government hired civilians to fill European posts for larger salaries than the Wacs made, thus contributing to a morale problem. Of the former Wacs, 29 percent of those polled wanted to be housewives, 40 percent wanted to work full-time, 8 percent wanted to go into business for themselves, and 8 percent wanted to go to school. Only 6 percent stayed in the service. Finally in 1948, Truman signed a bill giving women a regular place in the services and reserves.[68]

Along with the women who joined the military during the war, others joined the Red Cross. Accounts of their experiences tell of the empowering nature of their service and their excitement over the importance of their role. They also express the horror of seeing the face of war firsthand.[69]

Combat exposed the men to unspeakable horrors. Aside from the constant fear of death on the front lines, many soldiers faced the terror of their own savagery, as well as that of the enemy. Dreams of gallantry faded quickly when faced with the fear, death, and mutilation of war. Some of the women at home must have thought it better to be fighting than staring out windows, waiting for the postman to deliver a telegram saying that a husband, son, or lover had been killed. But both men and women dreamed of a house with a white picket fence in a quiet suburb, adorable children, and cheerful domesticity. However, the dream of domesticity seemed so far away. The question of fidelity was much closer.

Fidelity and Infidelity

A popular song of the time was "Is You or Is You Ain't My Baby?" The question haunted the minds of the soldiers and the women at home and seemed to intrude on their dreams of domestic bliss after the war. Much literature during the war condoned the "warrior's" infidelity as natural and inevitable but emphasized the importance of the wife's fidelity as crucial to postwar readjustment. A wife's infidelity was tantamount to sabotage. The double standard of sexuality was dramatically reinforced. Nevertheless, Kinsey's statistics showed an increase in extramarital relationships on the part of the young wives in the 1940s.[70]

Perhaps some women's sexual adventurousness stemmed from the strain of waiting or the more available birth control devices. By the early 1940s, women had more reproductive control over their lives because contraception had gained more respectability. Some 800 contraceptive clinics provided family planning services through public health programs. Among white, urban women surveyed in the late 1930s and early 1940s, 80 percent used contraceptives. In addition, medical experts estimated the number of illegal abortions at 300,000 to one million a year during the war, which was between 10 percent and 25 percent of births.[71]

If women lived near a military base, they could meet literally hundreds of men. The lonely men wanted companionship and sex. Pauline Kael recalls that soldiers would often try to make the girls feel guilty if they did not want to go to bed with them. If a soldier approached a girl on the street and she was not interested, he might say, "That's what we're fighting for; that's what we're giving our lives for."[72] The girls who danced at the USO and went out with soldiers a lot were called Victory girls. When they heard the song "Please Give Me Something to Remember You By," they knew which something their dates wanted.[73] Although there was more than a little premarital sexual activity during the war, the large number of hasty marriages resulted partially because many women wanted a ring in exchange for the "something." Judging from prewar trends, sociologists note that 1,118,000 more marriages took place between 1940 and 1943 than would have been expected. Because of the scarcity of men at home, many girls and women were even more preoccupied with getting and keeping a man than before the war.[74]

In 1940 there were 770,000 married women heading families with husbands absent. This number increased to 2,770,000 in 1945. The birthrate rose to 22 per 1,000 in 1943, the highest in two decades. Some enterprising women called Allotment Annies married more than one serviceman in order to receive their allotments.[75]

The Impact of World War II on Family Life

The overall effect on the family of the Second World War was disruption. As in the Great Depression, some families were strained to the breaking point. The response of a family to such a severe crisis was largely dependent on how unified it was before the war. Physical separation meant that a large number of couples had little or no experience with living in a daily, committed relationship. In order to cope with absence, they had to develop their own identities, friends, and interests, apart from their lives as a couple. They might write passionate, romantic letters to one another and speak of their dreams for life together after the war, but their respective, unique experiences created a chasm between them.

The war accelerated the rate of marriage, divorce, and births and reaffirmed the view that male activities were more important than those of females. The role of warrior was perceived as much more important than that of housewife. Whereas the Great Depression had threatened men's masculinity, the war reinforced it. Women might work in a factory, become professionals, join the military, or remain housewives, but Americans continued to believe that women's primary responsibility was to care for their husbands and children. As Paul McNutt, head of the War Manpower Commission, proclaimed, "The first responsibility of women with young children in war and peace is to give suitable care in their own homes to their own children."[76]

Americans accepted a redefinition of sexual roles during the war, but most of them viewed this as a temporary adjustment to the emergency. However, many women who had learned new skills and enjoyed relatively high wages wanted to continue working after the war ended. A poll of women in the United Auto Workers Union indicated that 85 percent of the women surveyed said they wanted to keep their jobs after the war.[77]

Although the attitudes of working women had changed, American public opinion remained essentially against married women's working. A survey of the American Institute of Public Opinion showed little change in Americans' attitudes toward working women since a 1937 poll. They still were opposed to married womens' working if they could be supported by their husbands.[78]

In 1943 a poll of the *Woman's Home Companion* showed that 75 percent of the magazine's readers responding reported that women should relinquish their war jobs after the war.[79] The same year, Marcelene Cox wrote in the *Ladies Home Journal*: "Many a woman will end her period of war work convinced that home after all, is the place where she can make her best conquest and secure her most beautiful rewards."[80] A year later, the *Ladies Home Journal* claimed that a national study revealed that most new women workers wanted to go home after the war. Nell Giles wrote, "If the American woman can find a man she wants to marry, who can support her, a job fades into insignificance beside the vital business of staying at home and raising a family—three children is the ideal number, she thinks."[81]

Two statements, one by Betty Allie, a State Workmen's Compensation official, and the other by Bill Jack, an industrialist, illustrate the way in which women were prepared psychologically to return home after the war. Allie remarked:

> Women are working only to win the war and will return to their home duties after the war is won. They will look on this period as an interlude, just as their men who have been called to service will consider military duties as an interlude. The women are like Cincinnatus, who left his plow to save Rome and then returned to his plow. Women will always be women.

Similarly, Bill Jack implored women workers:

> The coming of peace will work no unemployment hardship on you. You women have been employed because the armed forces called your husband, brothers or sons. . . . Each serviceman will get his job back when this war is won. And you women and girls will go home, back to being housewives and mothers again as you promised to do when you came to work for us. If all industry would adopt this simple policy, there would be no serious postwar unemployment.[82]

One poll in 1943 revealed that 75 percent of the young women surveyed preferred the housewife role, 6 percent preferred being single and having a successful career, and 19 percent wanted to combine marriage and career. Of the last group, only 20 percent would choose career over marriage.[83] Young women increasingly viewed marriage as a vehicle for independence and self-fulfillment, especially after the shift toward more egalitarian relationships in the 1920s and the increased emphasis on the woman's sexual fulfillment.

During the war, young adults increasingly found more freedom, more responsibility, and more autonomy than their parents had known. The development of a youth culture accelerated the transformation of the family structure from authoritarian to egalitarian. Parents consulted their children more and advised and suggested rather than commanded. The combination of an emergent youth culture and the unprecedented stresses faced by service families doubtless hastened transformations that shaped the main family forms in the 1950s and 1960s. Moreover, separation forced both husbands and wives to become more mature, independent, and self-reliant. Upon their return many husbands accepted the growing strength of their wives and were ready to share more decision making.[84]

The crisis of the war gave other couples a chance to dissolve marriages long dead. For others the war deepened their resolve to strengthen their relationships. More women married, married at younger ages, and had more children in the 1940s than in previous periods. Increases in both marriage and fertility were greatest among the best-educated, urban women, the ones with the most privileges and the most opportunities in life. Interviews during the 1940s and 1950s consistently indicated that women were acknowledged to have the major responsibility for raising children and maintaining the family budget. In blue-collar households of the 1950s employed wives exercised a little more power over decisions than full-time housewives.[85]

Most American women were not convinced of the need for sexual equality; effective large-scale organization to achieve their economic and political equality did not occur during the war years. Militant feminist groups like the National Woman's Party had the most far-reaching demands but enjoyed a very small following during the war. The largest, sedate women's clubs had modest aspirations. No women's caucuses sprang up in Congress or in the state legislatures.[86]

Postwar Adjustment

The searing experience of the war—involving concentration camps, the extermination of Jews, massive slaughter, and evil on a worldwide scale—was accompanied by a consciousness that men and women were capable of unthought of evils. On August 6, 1945, the United States dropped an atomic bomb on Hiroshima, killing 75,000 people and injuring 100,000. Three days later, another bomb was dropped on Nagasaki. On August 10 Tokyo sued for peace. On September 2, 1945, Japan officially surrendered.[87] Paul Gallico recalls some people's reaction to the dropping of the bomb.

> But the great majority of us trod softly that day and for many days thereafter thinking of the terrible and deadly force let loose in the world. We

went through the week of radio and news tension and jitters awaiting the news of the surrender of Japan and the return of peace to our sore and battered world.

When it came, the nation from its tiniest hamlets to its largest cities, broke loose in a wild two day celebration, one grand gargantuan bust to relieve strained nerves and emotions.

But thereafter most of us thought and talked again about that old world we had all known which was finished and done with because of what dropped on Hiroshima and Nagasaki, and what the new world and new era would be like.[88]

The war was over. The streets were full of people dancing, kissing, getting drunk; joy filled the country. The United States spent $245 billion on the Second World War, more than the combined budgets of the country from 1789 to 1940. The GNP had risen from $91 billion in 1939 to $215 billion in 1945. The Treasury Department estimated that Americans at home had saved $70 million; they were ready to spend.[89]

The returning veterans were greeted as heroes by their own people just as they had been by Europeans, with tears streaming down their faces as they saw the liberators. Estimates vary regarding the number of total casualties of World War II—dead, wounded, or crippled—from 45 to 55 million people, including 17–20 million Russians, 6 million Jews, 4.2 million Germans, 2.2 million Chinese, 1.4 million Japanese, and 291,000 Americans.[90]

As the soldiers streamed home, women were fired from their jobs in great numbers. Even the middle-class women who gladly returned home had a taste of independence which was never really lost. Home would never be the same again. As Margaret Mead predicted: "When the returning man looks his wife or sweetheart in the eye, between them will loom his years of danger and hardship which she cannot share or properly imagine, her flat empty years which she could not value because he was away, filled with comforts which he values highly because he missed them so keenly."[91]

Anticipating his return home, one navy doctor looked at himself in the mirror and saw that he had become bald and fat. When he wrote this to his wife, she replied, "You will find that three years have done quite a bit to me, too."[92] Husbands and wives had changed in thought and appearance. The movie *The Best Years of Our Lives* (1947) captures the dilemma of the returning veterans. Dana Andrews returns to his war bride, a shallow, fun-loving blonde. His wife had fallen in love with him as a dashing airman in uniform, and suddenly he is no longer gallant in civilian clothes. He has to take a lowly job in the store where he had been manager and is fired for defending another veteran. His wife soon leaves him when she realizes that she married "someone else." The man who returns does not fit her fantasies of him. The film also dramatizes the view of three male antagonists who believe that women must provide what the government and business did not, to repay them for sacrificing the best years of their lives.[93]

Adjustment was difficult for women too. Those who emerged from their wartime experiences with self-confidence found it quite difficult to be submissive and dependent again after they had managed alone. The husband was like a stranger to his children who had been born in his absence or were very young when he left. In one family, after the father returned, the first night home his little girl asked, "When is that man leaving so we can go to bed?" Suddenly, despite the joy of reunion, the man felt somehow superfluous, like an intruder in his own home. The wife might have to purchase marital harmony with her own individuality.

Some returning soldiers started drinking heavily or woke up in the middle of the night screaming with horrible nightmares. One wife tells of holding her husband for hours at night while he shook; she wondered whether he could ever forget. Then he began to slap her and the children around.[94] The return of the soldiers resulted in 600,000 divorces in 1946 alone, a record number. But there were 2.3 million marriages, also a record number. The divorce rate rose during the war from 8.8 percent per 1,000 in 1940 to 14.4 percent per 1,000 in 1945. By 1950 one-fourth of the marriages ended in divorce. In 1947 one out of every twenty-nine World War II veterans who had ever been married was divorced, as compared with one in sixty of the nonveterans.[95] The baby boom soon began, and hospitals were so crowded with pregnant women that they sometimes even went through labor in the halls.

Women had not drastically changed in their views of themselves as primarily wives and mothers. "Rosie the Riveter" stepped out of her overalls, still wearing her apron underneath.[96] But the Rosie who stepped out of her overalls and moved to the suburbs had changed in her view of her capabilities, her strength and ability to manage alone. Although propaganda prepared women to return home after the war, no amount of propaganda could keep women from realizing their own competence and independence or from developing different aspirations for their daughters. Rosie might prefer to stay at home, or she might be a working-class woman who would have to continue to work anyway, but at a lower-paying job. However, the stage was set for an awakening of women's consciousness. Most of the women who returned home were middle-class women who longed for stability, security, and a home as much as their husbands. They also saw it as a patriotic duty to bear "good citizens." As one woman put it, "We didn't retreat; we marched back to the home."

Charlcia Neuman, who worked for Vultee Aircraft from 1942 to 1945, expressed this same sentiment when she was interviewed by Sherna Gluck, a historian of women war workers.

> The idea was for the women to go back home. The women understood that. And the men had been promised their jobs when they came back. I was ready to go home. I was tired. I had looked forward to it because there were too many things that I wanted to do with my daughter. I knew that it would be coming and I didn't feel any letdown. The experience was interesting, but I couldn't have kept it up forever. It was too hard.[97]

Lola Weixel, a welder, had a very different interpretation of the "march homeward." She recalls: "I think they prepare women psychologically for whatever role the society wants at that particular time for them to play. After losing so many men, America wanted babies. And we wanted babies. That's o.k. But we gave up everything for that. We gave up everything." Another war worker recalls the messages she received from the postwar magazines. Suddenly articles told women how to cook dishes that took all day, whereas during the war they told women how to cook quickly and get on to work. Moreover, there were articles on the psychological development of one's children, a subject not mentioned during the war in the magazines.[98]

Robert LeKachman, a professor of economics at the City University of New York, recalls the postwar era.

> The boys came home, eager to make up for lost time. Newly married and Levittown selling homes for six or seven thousand dollars, four per cent mortgages, no down payment. A postwar boom that lasted until 1969. Eisenhower was the perfect symbol of the period. It was as though a massive dose of Sominex were administered to the whole population. There was now less concern for those beyond your immediate family.[99]

The postwar era was filled with lovemaking. William Manchester claimed that by comparing Kinsey's data and census data of the late 1940s, one finds that 55,311,617 married men were reaching 136,666,060 sexual climaxes a week, or one emission every 0.0048 seconds was occurring. Unfortunately he did not try to calculate the wives' orgasms too. A wife was getting pregnant once every seven seconds.

Manchester claims that the late 1940s were glorious times for young couples.

> To the young veterans and their brides the late 40s were exquisite years of easy laughter and lovers' vows, whose promises lingered like the fragrance of incense burning in little golden vessels on the altars of the heart. To be young and uncrippled was to be unbelievably lucky; to marry was to give of oneself, an exchange of gifts that multiplied in joy. It was a kind of fragile kaleidoscopic montage, held together by youthful passion of a million disjointed sounds, colors, scents, tastes, and snatches of quite ordinary Tin Pan alley music . . . of knowing what it was like to lie in bed chain-smoking in that last decade before they took the fun out of cigarettes.[100]

Young couples could buy a house with a government loan and purchase dishwashers, appliances, cars, and furniture which they had deferred buying for a long time. In fact, from 1946 to 1950 Americans bought 21.4 million automobiles, more than 20 million refrigerators, 5.5 million electric stoves, and 11.6 million television sets. More than a million new housing units were built in each postwar year to meet the housing shortage of the war. By the end of the decade a majority of families owned their own homes, with the number of owner-occupied houses increasing from 15.2 million in 1940 to 23.5 million in 1950. They were enraptured with capturing the American dream.[101]

After the spartan look of the wartime, women began to wear abundant skirts, pointed shoes, and falsies. Femininity was emphasized with "merry widows," which cinched in the waist to wasplike proportions and extended from bosom to thigh, almost as uncomfortable as the old corsets of another generation. Christian Dior was an architect of the new styles, and although many women resisted for a time, most of those who could afford the new styles threw their slacks and comfortable shoes into the back of the closet and jumped on the fashion bandwagon. They wanted to look like "women" again but ended up immobilized in pointed high heels and skirts which emphasized their "fragile" legs.

The new washing machines, dishwashers, and garbage disposals lightened domestic labor, but women still spent the same amount of time on housework as before, averaging 51–56 hours a week from the 1920s to the 1960s. Women simply developed higher standards, spent more time shopping and decorating, and spent more time with their children.[102]

Women began to rely on Dr. Spock's *Baby and Child Care* to help them to be good mothers. Spock's book, first published in 1946, urged mothers to enjoy their children, be more permissive, and promote their children's creativity and individuality. The generation of the 1960s testified to the success of such child-rearing practices.

The postwar era was not prosperous for all women; by 1950 women headed nearly 15 percent of all households, and one in ten children lived with their mothers only. Of all African-American families, 17.6 percent were headed by women, compared with 8.5 percent of white families. Unemployment rose from 1 million in 1945 to 2.3 million in 1946.[103]

White women voted more, but their actual political power declined when compared with the 1920s or the New Deal. Surveys showed women's voter participation increased from less than 50 percent in 1930 to 56 percent in 1948 and 62 percent in 1952. However, 87 percent of southern African-American women and 65 percent of African-American men had never voted by 1952.

The GI Bill produced dramatic changes in the social and cultural life of the nation. Although African-Americans were discriminated against in receiving GI Bill benefits (some received none at all), more African-Americans and working-class Americans, male and female, were able to attend colleges in greater numbers than previously. But for women, the gains were not impressive; in 1940 some 40 percent of college graduates were women (77,000), but in 1950, only one-third were women (104,000).[104]

The female labor force declined from 19,170,000 to 16,896,000. From 1945 to 1950 the percentage of all workers who were female fell from 36 percent to 29 percent, and the percentage of all women working fell from 37 percent to 32 percent.[105] Out of 18 million women, $3\frac{1}{4}$ million either voluntarily or involuntarily left the labor force in 1945. Although the number of women in the labor force in 1950 equaled that of the war years, the majority of women were locked into sex-stereotyped jobs, like Gladys Belcher. Belcher took extensive training as a welder but after the war she could get only kitchen work, which she did for the next seventeen years. She remembers:

> You have a lot of responsibility, especially a widow woman, a lone woman. My children had to be taken care of and I'd bought a little home. It had to be paid for. I had to get a job somewhere, somehow. I know that's what I was thinking about when I left there. I got a job in a restaurant working in the kitchen. Hot hard work. Heavy lifting. It was a lot harder than working in the shipyard and a lot less pay.[106]

By 1946, 80 percent of the wartime women workers were still employed, but only half of them occupied their wartime positions. The average weekly wage for women dropped from fifty to thirty-seven dollars. The trend toward women's employment in clerical work continued. By 1950 half of all female workers and two-thirds of white women workers were employed in that field. Although the number of women in the labor force rose after World War II, their occupational distribution resembled that before 1941. Drastic reductions occurred in the auto industry, where in 1943 women composed 25 percent of the labor force, but by March 1946, only 8 percent. The reduction occurred despite the protests of women auto workers. In 1944 a survey of female auto workers revealed that 85.5 percent wanted to keep their jobs in the industry. However, the management systematically fired the women, failed to honor seniority, and failed to inform the women of callbacks. When the Local 400 Women's Committee at the Ford Highland Park plant protested the firing of 103 women in April 1945, they failed to achieve their objective of preserving the seniority rights of those dismissed because of the intransigence of the management and lack of adequate support from their own union.[107]

Some feminists like Susan B. Anthony II, the niece of the great suffrage leader, argued for a comprehensive plan to enable women to work and to care for home and children. During the war, she lobbied for federal child care, health and recreation programs for war workers, and other home services. After the war, unions, feminists, and other women's organizations like the YWCA, the League of Women Voters, the WTUL, and the AAUW lobbied for a Full Employment Act (the Kilgore-Murray Bill) introduced in 1944 to broaden benefits and retrain workers. The bill was repeatedly defeated in the Congress.[108] The Equal Rights Amendment met the same fate. The amendment had received favorable reports by 1936 and 1937, but by 1940 it had received little attention from either house. In 1940 the Republican party and the Democratic party in 1944 adopted planks in their party platforms endorsing constitutional equality. The Judiciary Committee in both houses voted favorably in 1942, but the ERA failed to receive a majority vote in Congress.[109]

The ERA did not pass, but the seeds of revolt had been sown by the Great Depression and the Second World War. Although the war did not permanently alter sexual roles, women's participation in the labor force and in unions confronted them with many contradictions: they had not been paid wages equal to those of the men they replaced but yet were told constantly that they were absolutely essential to the war effort. They were expected to be strong and independent while the men were away but to return home eagerly after the war and be submissive again. Many women experienced a profound ambivalence. They knew their strengths and had demonstrated them openly. Suddenly they were again expected to resort to covert means of power. Since their accepted sphere had always been the home, they augmented their power there. Moreover, a second income became increasingly essential to maintain an acceptable or higher standard of living, at least within working-class households.

Women's growing covert power in the home and increased opportunities for a measure of economic independence were bound to clash eventually with their nostalgia for security and dependence. Americans had barely made the down payments on their new houses, settled into domesticity, and had their first child or two when the Soviet Union exploded its own atomic bomb, China became Communist, the Iron Curtain fell, and the Cold War began. The security they had longed for faded quickly, and just around the corner was the Korean War and Joe McCarthy.

10

THE POWER OF MOM
Domesticity, Motherhood,
and Sexuality in the 1950s

*The problem lay buried, unspoken, for many years in the minds of American
women. It was a strange stirring, a sense of dissatisfaction, a yearning that
women suffered in the middle of the twentieth century in the United States.
Each suburban wife struggled with it alone. As she made the bed, shopped for
groceries, matched slipcover materials, ate peanut butter sandwiches with her
children, chauffeured Cub Scouts and Brownies, lay beside her husband at
night—she was afraid to ask even of herself the silent question—"Is this
all?"*

Betty Friedan, *The Feminine Mystique*, 1963

*She {a black woman} has a harder time finding a mate, remains single more
often, bears more children, is in the labor market longer, has less education,
earns less, is widowed earlier, and carries a relatively heavier economic responsibility as a family head than her white sister.*

Pauli Murray (1964), in Gerda Lerner,
Black Women in White America, 1972

*I wouldn't go back to work now unless the wolf was banging the door down.
Oh, the luxury of an afternoon nap, reading the newspaper over a second cup of
coffee, dressing when and how I please, playing golf in the middle of the week,
cleaning like mad when an ambitious streak overtakes me, cutting out a new
dress for Lisa, or making a pie in the cool of the morning. But I think the ultimate luxury is knowing that there is absolutely no one to tell me what I must
do with my time. It is my decision. I can use it wisely or throw it away. I am
a free independent person and I love it!*

Letter to Betty Friedan, 1964

Dagwood Bumstead, the father in the comic strip "Blondie," is a caricature of the husband in the 1950s. However, underlying the humor is a portrayal of female domestic power. Dagwood is kind, dutiful, and well meaning. But he is a bungler, and he has completely given up any claim to authority.[1] Blondie is an efficient, sexy, shrewd boss. She keeps the family life running smoothly, while Dagwood is overwhelmed by neighbors, pets, door-to-door salesmen, and the vicissitudes of daily life at home.

Women's empowering and stifling experiences in the family in the 1950s helped lead to the emergence of feminist consciousness. In the 1950s American mothers became the dominant parents almost by default as their husbands became preoccupied with their jobs. Men who commuted to work from the suburbs were becoming largely absent fathers. American women consolidated their domestic power, which had been increasing since the nineteenth century. In exchange for security, marriage, and motherhood, many white middle-class women forfeited their own identities. Consequently, for many women their dominance in childrearing and their covert power over their husbands did not enhance their self-esteem. Moreover, as more and more married women with children entered the labor force, they faced glaring contradictions. The disparity between women's considerable, but contingent domestic power and relative powerlessness in the public sphere helped set the stage for a full-scale feminist revolt in the 1960s. The extreme emphasis on domesticity and motherhood as the only appropriate women's vocation and the many contradictions which women faced helped shape feminist thought and action in the 1960s profoundly.

African-American women's experiences as wives and mothers in the 1950s differed radically from white middle-class women's because of race and class; facing the double jeopardy of being black and female led many to develop racial and gender consciousness. African-American women had a long history of paid employment, marriage, and motherhood. They perceived that their main problem was not Friedan's "problem with no name" but racism.

Most white middle-class women in the 1950s viewed marriage and motherhood as a full-time profession; only 29.0 percent of American women were employed in 1950, and 34.5 percent in 1960. They measured female achievement by their effectiveness in running the household and rearing children, not by their accomplishments in the public sphere. After years of waiting for husbands to return from World War II, American women yearned for security, a happy home, and children. For many white middle-class women, their dreams came true.

The Social Context

In her excellent book *Homeward Bound: American Families in the Cold War Era*, Elaine Tyler May contends that the domestic ideology of containment and Cold War militance have risen and fallen together in recent decades. After World War II, a stable family life seemed essential for national security. Links were made between Communism and sexual depravity because sexual excess or perversion presumably would make individuals prey to Communist tactics. Such fears of sexual chaos tend to surface during times of rapid social change and crisis. May explains how the cold-war ideology and domestic containment reinforced each other.

> The modern family would, presumably, tame fears of atomic holocaust, and tame women as well. With their new jobs and recently acknowledged sexuality, emancipated women outside the home might unleash the very forces that would result in a collapse of the one institution that seemed to offer protection: the home. For women the rewards offered by marriage, compared to the limited opportunities in the public world, made the homemaker role an appealing choice.[2]

For most people, the 1950s conjure up a montage of hula hoops, 3-D movies, Davy Crockett coonskins, Kefauver hearings, Joe McCarthy, Patti Page, Pat Boone, Elvis Presley, and James Dean. Domesticity, respectability, religious faith, and security through compliance with the system were the dominant values of the 1950s.[3] Togetherness was almost a national obsession. The family gathered around the television if they could afford one. During every month of 1948 and 1949, more than 200,000 TV sets were sold. In January 1950, three million Americans owned TV sets. Another seven million sets were installed in that year alone. Americans spent more time watching television by 1956 than working for pay. By the end of the fifties, 86 percent of American families owned a TV; 98 percent did by 1967.[4]

The dream of financial security seemed to be coming true for many Americans. The number of homeowners rose dramatically, from a little over 9 million in 1950, to 32.8 million by 1960. The number of car registrations grew by over 21 million during the same decade. The population grew from 139.9 million in 1945 to 180.6 million by 1960. The baby boom began, and children fourteen or younger composed 31 percent (56 million) of the population in 1960, a jump from 24 percent (33.5 million) in 1945. The rural population shrank from 17.5 percent of the population in 1945 to 8.7 percent in 1960 (24.4 million to 15.6 million). Except for a brief recession in the early fifties, the economy boomed after World War II. Corporate receipts grew from $255 billion in 1945 to $849 billion in 1960.[5]

Popular culture of the 1950s is an indicator of dominant societal values. Beneath the simplistic, cheerful facade, films and television shows of the 1950s reflected anxiety over female dominance and manipulation at home and conveyed contradictory messages to women. Naturally, actual behavior diverged from prescriptive behavior, but popular culture was a window through which women viewed themselves.

"I Love Lucy," which had 34 million viewers by 1952, provides insight into women's domestic power in the period. In 1953, when Lucy had a baby during one episode, over two million more people watched the show than Eisenhower's inauguration the next day.[6] Lucy is not a working wife, but she is an aggressive oddball. She is alternately assertive and gentle. Her husband, Ricky, is not the tough guy; in fact, he is explosively emotional. Along with her neighbor Ethel, Lucy gets involved in one scheme after another. Both husbands and wives act in deceptive ways, and it seems that the marriages hold together because of dishonesty. Lucy is intelligent, strong, talented, and manipulates Ricky through either her wit or her tears. However, her power is covert, and even when she gets what she wants, she is constantly asking Ricky for forgiveness.[7]

Another popular television show of the 1950s, "The Adventures of Ozzie and Harriet," depicts an ideal family. Harriet is the "perfect mother." She makes cookies for her boys, and she is waiting for them when they come home from school. Her life revolves around her husband and children, and she is a happy homemaker. Harriet Nelson is always impeccably dressed while at home and always sympathetic. Ozzie resembles Dagwood in his ineptness, but he is benevolent, understanding, and "manageable." Their children's problems are not sex, drugs, or failure at school, but rather involve innocent flirtations, misunderstandings, and sibling squabbles. Even if the children defer to Dad, clearly Mom is in charge at home. But she wields her influence gently and tactfully.

American women by the millions watched soap operas, which were sexier versions of the domestic novel of the nineteenth century and the earlier radio soap operas. The stories dealt with adultery, divorce, illegitimacy, forgery, greed, incest, arson, murder, robbery, suicide, alcoholism, mental illness, bigamy, embezzlement, and accidental death. Robert Aaron, who supervised daytime programming for NBC, explained that the aim of the serial was constant reassurance that middle-class values were fine, that giving up a career for marriage was fine, and that life's little problems were the ones that really count.[8]

In television dramas of the 1950s, characters want to get along with others more than anything else. Yet for all the optimism in many shows, there is a shade of disillusion and a tinge of sadness. The living room is the favorite setting of these plays, and a family is the usual cast. The family is neither unusually happy nor constantly beleaguered with crisis. The father guides and administers the household but does not rule. Evil, which rarely visits these plays, is usually in the shape of a domineering wife or overly possessive mother. Although a comfortable income is assumed, the father's career is a shadowy presence in the background. Status is defined by a reasonably happy family life. Norman Podheretz describes a typical father in these productions.

> In his benign firmness, in his mature sobriety, in his sad, but determined sense of responsibility, in his unceasing efforts to keep the peace, we can detect the traces of the contemporary political climate. He reflects the feeling that the only safe oasis in a dangerous cold-war world is our own home, a home which, though it may once have been taken lightly, must now be preserved at all costs if the battle is not to be lost everywhere. And in the long series of plays which turn on a rediscovery of the father by the son, we find perhaps, the mark of a generation which has moved out of rebellion and skepticism into a patient and humble acquiescence; and we may here discover the role the new middle-class seems to have marked out for its own.[9]

American women eagerly read about the necessity for "togetherness" in their 1954 Easter issue of *McCall's*.[10] On the whole, stories and features in the *Ladies Home Journal, American, Good Housekeeping, Mademoiselle,* and *McCall's* dealt largely with manipulating the self in order to manipulate others. The manipulation was aimed generally at achieving affection. A typical story was Lorna Slocombe's "Let's Go Out Tonight" in *American* magazine. In contrast to the nineteenth-century wife, who tried to reform her husband, the heroine of this story settles for small tactical gains, achieved primarily by manipulation.[11]

Getting the husband to go out at night to see a movie could be a major victory. Movie attendance was cut to one-half its 1946 level by 1953, as 45 million fewer Americans were going to the movies each week. Television threatened the movie industry, forcing the closing of thousands of movie houses.[12]

The couple that did go out for that rare evening might see films which provided a cheerful message for women. Many of these films glorify domesticity and inequality and depict easy, optimistic conclusions to any problems. Gone were the films of the 1930s and 1940s about strong, witty, independent career women. Single women are usually portrayed as neurotic and lonely, if not self-destructive. Bette Davis in *All about Eve* (1950) and Gloria Swanson in *Sunset Boulevard* (1950) play single, lonely women whose lives are without real meaning. Joan Crawford continues to play the frustrated career woman. An exception to this negative portrayal of strong women is *African Queen* (1952), starring Katharine Hepburn and Humphrey Bogart. Hepburn plays an unhappy, middle-aged woman who finds fulfillment and redemption through Bogart, a strong, adventurous man. The film, however, also presents Katharine Hepburn (Rosie) as Bogart's equal partner. Although Hepburn verbally defers to Bogart, she conveys through her actions the image of a strong, adventurous woman who also gets her man.

Hepburn is unique in the 1950s. Replacing the strong heroines of the 1930s and 1940s and Ma Joad in the *Grapes of Wrath*, the quintessential screen ideal of the 1950s woman was a combination of Doris Day and Marilyn Monroe. Doris Day and June Allyson play the perfect candidates for marriage; they are perky, innocent, virginal, and gently manipulative. Marilyn Monroe plays the sexy, blond bombshell who is vulnerable, brainless, and childlike. Another blonde, Sandra Dee, plays the teasing teenager. Whichever movie an American woman saw, the overwhelming message was that fulfillment comes through marriage and children.[13]

Women's magazines, soap operas and other TV programs, and the movies thus reinforced the cultural expectations that women were destined for fulfillment through marriage and motherhood and that their influence, or "power," was appropriately exercised covertly. Failure to conform to these expectations brought unhappiness, isolation, and social ostracism.

The Paradox of Female Domestic Power

American women in the 1950s experienced a number of double binds. They were expected to find fulfillment as wives and mothers but not be too dominant at home. Moreover, women were discouraged from working outside the home but were criticized as economic parasites. Women's considerable power in the family contrasted sharply with their lack of public power, and they were vulnerable because of economic dependence and possible physical violence. These contradictions could produce extreme confusion and stress for American women and eventually led many of them to a feminist consciousness.

Betty Friedan's *The Feminine Mystique*, a rallying book of the modern feminist movement, describes the despair of many American housewives of the 1950s who had lost their identities by becoming full-time wives and mothers. The middle-class housewife's world was confined to "her own body and beauty, the charming of a man, the bearing of babies, and the physical care and serving of husband, children, and home."[14] Friedan summarizes her argument:

> It is my thesis that the core of the problem for women today is not sexual but a problem of identity—a stunting or evasion of growth that is perpetuated by the feminine mystique. It is my thesis that as the Victorian culture did not permit women to accept or gratify their basic sexual needs, our culture does not permit women to accept or gratify their basic need to grow and fulfill their potentialities as human beings, a need which is not solely defined by their sexual role.[15]

Friedan's analysis of women's retreat to the home rests on a societal conspiracy to seduce, cajole, and force women back into the home to become consummate consumers. She sees the major culprits as advertising executives who sold the image of the creative, happy homemaker; the educators who socialized women away from serious careers and into marriage; the Freudian analysts and Freudian popularizers who harped on penis-envy and chided women to adjust to their natural biological roles. She also attacks the functionalist social scientists like Margaret Mead, who emphasized the natural division of labor in the family between instrumental and expressive roles. Friedan accuses Mead of perpetuating a romantic view of motherhood.

Friedan paints a poignant picture of the casualties of substituting "togetherness" for equality for white middle-class women. She also explains how "housewifery expands to fill the time available." Technological change provided housewives with washing machines, dryers, vacuum cleaners, and numerous appliances in order to lighten the drudgery of housework. However, instead of doing less housework, women did more in the 1950s. Institutions and businesses performed most of the functions originally the responsibility of the mother. The housewife's role had been key to survival in the colonial period and into the twentieth century. However, her prestige began to fall as more and more professions developed to deal with the family's needs. Schools educated the children, doctors cared for their health, and businesses manufactured food and household goods. Despite the efforts of the home economics specialists to make homemaking a science, the denomination of *value* in American society became cash. Unpaid household labor was not counted by people as "real work." The American woman's major role, therefore, was to spend the family's income, bear and nurture children, and take care of her husband.

Whereas magazine articles during World War II told women how to cook quick, nutritious meals, in the fifties they urged them to produce gourmet creations which took all day to prepare. Later on in the same period, magazine articles urged wives to be "cholesterol conscious." Those gourmet meals which took a day or two to prepare were hazardous to the family after all, the hollandaise killing them slowly. Dr. Edward Newman assured women in *McCall's*, "A woman can be the dominating force in controlling the longevity of her husband."[16]

Although they were bombarded with propaganda about happy housewives, most middle-class women did not feel manipulated. They felt that they were choosing the best of all possible worlds. Instead of the feminist hope of the 1920s of combining marriage and careers, their hope was for affluence, sexual fulfillment, and a house full of children. Only when they achieved their dreams and lived within the confines of the feminine mystique did many of them feel trapped. When *Redbook* ran an article in September 1960 entitled "Why Young Mothers Feel Trapped" as an advertising stunt, the editors invited young mothers to write them detailing their problems. They were shocked when 24,000 replies arrived.[17]

Why did most white middle-class American women seem to accept cheerfully the feminine mystique? Both structural and psychological conditions prepared them for compliance. Many of the millions of women who had taken war jobs viewed their jobs as temporary and did not question their primary traditional role as wife and mother. Fears about recession and unemployment of the GIs had prompted a full-scale propaganda campaign to get women back into the homes even before the end of the war.

As we have seen, most of the women who were employed before the 1950s were in sex-stereotyped jobs and received 50–60 percent of the wages of their male coworkers. Combining motherhood and a job, much less a career, demanded almost herculean effort. No network of child-care centers offered assistance to women who might want to combine the two. Many women viewed homemaking as much more creative than working as a secretary, in a factory, or as a saleswoman. Women in nursing, teaching, or library science were willing to work before marriage, and they anticipated working after their children were older.

Options for women were circumscribed by the structural discrimination against women in the labor force. Advertising, television shows, novels, women's magazines, educators, and *husbands* reinforced the idea that a woman's fulfillment came through marriage and motherhood. Conditioning had firmly entrenched this notion, and deviance from this norm brought opprobrium. In an era devoted to conformity and adjustment, many women sought to emulate the Harriet Nelsons and Donna Reeds.

Women's complicity with their own subordination, however, could have negative personal consequences, especially for women who had career aspirations and hopes for an egalitarian marriage. Although the number of female college graduates fell in the 1950s, American women had been educated more than their roles demanded. If they were expected to be primarily wives and mothers, they would assert their dominance at home, and before long, wails could be heard across the country about domineering, castrating wives and mothers. As Friedan writes:

> To the great dismay of men, their wives suddenly became "experts," know-it-alls, whose unshakeable superiority at home, a domain they both occupied, was impossible to compete with, and very hard to live with. As Russell Lynes put it, wives began to treat their husbands as part-time servants—or the latest new appliance. With a snap course in home economics or marriage and the family under her belt and copies of Dr. Spock and Dr. Van de Velde side by side on the shelf; with all that time, energy, and intelligence directed on husband, children, and house, the young American wife—easily, inevitably, disastrously—began to dominate the family even more completely than her "mom."

Consequently, a *Redbook* article of 1962 describes the trapped feeling of young fathers. Their wives who quoted authorities on home management, childrearing, and married love had set up a tightly scheduled scheme of family living that left little room for the husband's authority. One young man said, "Since I've been married, I feel like I've lost all my guts. I don't feel like a man anymore. . . . I feel like something is bursting loose inside."[18] David Riesman, author of *The Lonely Crowd*, writes that one can go into many modern homes and find that the children hold the "strategic initiative," while the father is a marginal figure.[19] Mom was the dominant parental figure.

Betty Friedan states that women of the 1950s accepted a sense of martyred superiority. "At home, you *were* necessary, you were important, you were the boss, in fact—the mother—and the new feminine mystique gave it the rationale of a career." Consequently, if the daytime serials portrayed a strong husband and the wife was not the controlling one, the rating was inevitably low. The husband was acceptable only if he was manipulated by the good, kind, loving, all-wise wife.[20]

With the increase in female domestic power, it is not surprising that a campaign attacking "momism" began. Recruits during World War II had been given numerous psychological tests, and three million men were classified as emotionally unstable. Philip Wylie, author of *A Generation of Vipers* (1942), blamed overly protective mothers and passive or absent fathers for widespread emotional immaturity. He wrote that "our land subjectively mapped, would have more silver cords crisscrossing it than railroads and telephone wires. Mom is everywhere." Wylie states that the most needed verity is "Gentlemen, Mom is a jerk," and goes on to proclaim:

> The machine has deprived her of social usefulness; time has stripped away her biological possibilities and poured her hide full of liquid soap; and man has sealed his own soul beneath the clamorous cordillera by handing her the checkbook and going to work in the service of her caprices. . . .
>
> I give you mom. I give you the destroying mother. I give you her justice—from which we have never removed the eye bandage. I give you the angel—and point to the sword in her hand.[21]

Wylie even blames Mom for World War II. His misogynism knows no bounds. He claims that "in a thousand of her there is not sex appeal enough to budge a hermit ten paces off a rock ledge." His attack is primarily on materialism and consumerism, and Mom is the agent. In the rest of the book he attacks every other aspect of American society with verve. Although the advertisers and businessmen are also targets of his venomous wit, his attack on Mom is singularly vicious. Wylie's attack on female domestic power, while extreme, reflected the uneasiness which many men felt about women's increasing assertiveness in the home.

Perhaps it was inevitable that women who attempted to adjust to the "feminine mystique" would ultimately attempt to dominate their husbands and children. These same women might also begin to view their husbands as their only vehicle for status and mobility, driving them to be even more absorbed in their work. However, ultimately no amount of affluence could give them identities of their own. Covert power, no matter how effective, did not necessarily enhance their self-esteem. Increasingly, the contradiction between their considerable domestic power and lack of public power grew. Many of these white middle-class women "passed on to their daughters their own unspoken disappointment, self-denigration, and discontent."[22] Many of these daughters were destined to become vitriolic critics of the feminine mystique; many of their mothers would also seek escape.

Within feminist circles until the latter part of the 1980s, Friedan's analysis of the experiences of American women in the 1950s had been accepted and virtually unquestioned. However, her interpretation was flawed in several ways and influenced the modern feminist movement to overemphasize the male model of careerism. In the early 1960s Friedan urged that women develop a life plan, consider outside employment, and pursue a career. She viewed paid work as redemptive. Even before she wrote her book, however, women had been entering the labor force in large numbers. Friedan envisioned a society of middle-class professional husbands and wives, but realistically, even if women en masse aspired to professional careers, such a path was open to a very small minority of American women. Most working women had jobs, not careers. Employment alone could never redress the balance of power between men and women. Moreover, her analysis did not acknowledge the fact that working-class and African-American women were totally excluded from the possibility of full-time motherhood in the first place. Finally, Friedan's study was based on graduates of Smith College, a small, elite group of American women. For all the discontented, frustrated housewives, there existed as many women or more who did not question their role and seemed to accept it cheerfully.

Nevertheless, Friedan articulated the experiences of many American women, and thousands of them wrote to her in gratitude. These letters provide a window on the frustration and anguish of many middle-class women of the fifties and on some of the conditions which set the stage for the feminist revolt of the 1960s. A woman from Riverton, Wyoming, writes:

> I spent last night crying in my pillow, got up this morning, cooked Cream
> of Wheat with raisins, ironed three pairs of blue jeans, made certain my
> boys' faces were shining and clean before sending them off to Daily Vacation
> Bible School, fed the dog and the cat, mopped up the chocolate syrup that

the baby, the dog and the cat had enjoyed as a pre-breakfast snack, got into my handy station wagon and took my husband to the airport to catch a business-trip plane!! Now I should be tackling two bushels of ironing, after which I should vacuum up the dustballs that are drifting across the floors and pull down the equally numerous cobwebs which swing from the ceilings. . . . My silent scream as I stir the oatmeal, iron the blue jeans, and sell pop at the Little League baseball games is "Stop the World, I Want To Get On Before It's Too Late!" I love my family dearly and wouldn't trade them, or my life with them, for *anything*! But, as they go out each day to meet, and get involved in this great big wonderful world, I yearn to tag along![23]

A woman from Cleveland, Ohio, wrote that only laziness and an overdeveloped yearning to be protected and cared for could hold her back "from fully sprouting my wings."[24] Another woman wrote that those women who grew up and married before the Second World War were a peculiarly blessed generation because their mothers were determined to give them opportunities for development which they had missed. They wanted them to realize their talent and to marry and have children.[25]

A housewife from Fort Lee, New Jersey, wrote that she and her husband were sitting in Sardi's when an inebriated man leaned over and asked her husband, "What do you do?" Her husband replied, "I am an editor and freelance writer and an antique dealer." He was impressed, and then he asked her what she did. "I replied, I'm a housewife." He wrinkled his nose and said, "Is that all?" She concluded: "My friends realized that their day of gourmet cooking, overattentiveness to baby, and fastidiousness was rewarded with a backache, messy appearance, an overweight and bored husband and spoiled baby. They just didn't have *time* to be sexy and interesting."[26]

The letters to Friedan also reflected a loss of a sense of prestige and status as housewives because of technological advancements. They could not feel vitally important pushing the button of the washing machine. Some women poignantly wrote in the spirit of a woman from Great Neck, New York, "How could I have not understood all this myself?" But another wrote that women "held most of the power in the marriage due to male infantalism."[27]

Countless stories came in to Friedan of women who quit school to get married. Some of the women had given up career plans to marry and have children, but with remorse. "More than once," a woman from Oklahoma wrote, "have I cast aside a book or left a term paper in mid-stream to go and scrub a floor with all the grim remorse of a sixteenth century flagellanti."[28] A woman from South Carolina of genius IQ range wrote that she was a compulsive eater, prone to extreme depression. She was a domineering wife and mother; she loved her children "yet hated them, and had actually wished them dead."[29]

Rona Jaffe's survey of 1951 Radcliffe graduates for the *Ladies Homes Journal* in 1980 recorded the experiences of a number of Friedan's contemporaries who married what they wanted to be. One woman who was the wife of a college dean wrote, "If we wanted to be a lawyer or a doctor we married one. Many expected to find their identities through their husbands, and subsequently regarded their lives as failures." However, by 1980 they had become "articulate, intelligent, caring, strong, resilient individualists."[30] Remarking on the radical shift in women's choices since the 1950s, Gloria Steinem noted in the 1970s that American women were becoming the people they had hoped to marry.

The housewives who wrote Friedan described suicide attempts, nervous breakdowns, and tremendous despair. One wrote, "It has always disturbed me how one ceremony is supposed to dissolve a girl's brain."[31] In the same spirit, a writer from Massachusetts told of a southern woman with an IQ of 160 in South Carolina who gave her a seminar on "The Ways and Wiles of Southern Femininity." She taught her to wear baby blue, instead of navy, pink instead of red, and discard mind in favor of body. She said, "Honey, a fella cares more about what's in your sweater than what's in your head . . . so wear them, and talk less about world affairs."[32]

A twelve-year-old wrote Friedan that she had read her book and she agreed with it. So did her mother, who wanted to go back to work. But she could not find anyone to clean her large house. The daughter asked, "What do you think she should do?"[33] Clearly, the feminine mystique would hold few charms for that twelve-year-old.

Another woman writing to Friedan expressed her desperation as a housewife over losing her identity.

I did get what I wanted only it has an O. Henry twist. One day, several years ago, I crawled out of bed, looked at the split levels surrounding me, and I looked at myself and said, "this stinks. These people have no substance—and neither do I. I'm living in a vacuum, and there must be a way out or it's better to die." Yes, I took myself to a psychiatrist. It was a hard thing to face that I had literally "lit candles" for years to become a nonentity in a stupid, faceless society, known as suburbia. I threw away many talents for that. I mean I threw away the years that should have been devoted to de-

veloping my talents. I'm 40, and it's late, but it's not too late. I've committed myself to living as an individual again. I feel free and good.[34]

Whether most American women fit the profile of the desperate housewives
or not, one thing was certain: divorces declined in the 1950s. In 1867 there
were 0.3 divorces per 1,000 population; in 1914 there was 1.0 per 1,000
(100,000), in 1929, 1.7 per 1,000 (205,876), and in 1946 there were 4.3 per
1,000 (613,000). In 1950 the average was 2.6 divorces per 1,000 population,
and 2.2 per 1,000 in 1960. Marriages in 1950 averaged 11.1 per 1,000 and
8.5 in 1960.[35]

Not all the women who wrote Friedan thanked her for "changing their
lives." One told her she was "nuts"; she wrote, "I bet *you're* not happy at home
and I'll bet your children suffer because you don't know the joys of being a
real woman."[36]

Another "happy housewife" wrote, "I consider the job of housewife the
most feminine as well as the most important job there is; I am proud to view
the professional world only through the eyes and ears of my husband." In an
ominously prophetic letter from the vantage point of the 1990s, a working
woman wrote to Friedan, dispelling the myth of fulfillment in working
outside the home:

> The vast majority of working women don't have careers. We have jobs, just
> like men. We work for money to buy things that our families need. If we're
> lucky, we like our jobs, and find some satisfaction in doing them well, but it
> is hard to hold a commercial job, raise a family and keep a house. Most of us
> would be delighted to chuck the wage earning back in our husbands' lap
> and devote ourselves exclusively to homemaking and community projects.[37]

The Organization Man

Whether women suffered from the constraints of the feminine mystique or
aspired to it, their husbands were bombarded with an equally restricting
mystique. Like Willy Loman in Arthur Miller's *Death of a Salesman*, American men wanted above all to achieve social mobility and to be liked. They
were urged to adjust, conform, and above all achieve "maturity." The
"organization man mystique" was the male version of the feminine mystique.
Men's primary role was as breadwinner, and marriage and children allowed
them to accept responsibility with maturity. Novels of the period like *The*

Man in the Gray Flannel Suit and *Marjorie Morningstar* endorse maturity and domestication.

H. A. Overstreet's best-seller *The Mature Mind* even holds up maturity as an evolutionary achievement. Overstreet notes that the attitudes of mothers tend to be either "irritation or over-solicitude." The father has become "something between an absentee owner and a house guest." "The machine age has wrought changes of dubious import," he laments. "On the one hand, it has brought the mother too close to the children as a dominant psychological force. On the other hand, it has taken the father too far away from them."[38] Overstreet urges men to reclaim their rightful place at home as the mark of their maturity.

The man in the gray flannel suit accomplished his developmental tasks by his late twenties, married, and established himself in a white-collar job. Over the years, he would achieve mobility evidenced by larger offices and longer vacations. He would buy a house, find his social group with whom he shared martinis or highballs, and face the tribulations of suburban life. Unmarried men were considered homosexual or immature because they did not make commitments.

Beginning in the 1920s, American men experienced a decline in their view of themselves as rugged individualists and virile protectors. They were no longer evaluated on the basis of their ability to control life generally, but rather by their ability to *withstand* experiences and events that happened to them. As we have seen, the Great Depression exerted enormous strains on men's views of their masculinity when they failed as breadwinners. Essays, short stories, and sociological studies of the period attest to the fact that the mastery of the masculine component had become just an illusion. The Second World War bolstered men's traditional masculinity if they were in combat, but the majority were not. For those not engaged in fierce exploits, there was a sinking feeling that manning a desk was hardly being John Wayne or George Patton. Masculine toughness was not stylish in the corporation. Instead of brawn, mental and psychological prowess led to advancement.[39]

By the late 1940s and the 1950s, American men were occupying more white-collar jobs than blue-collar jobs, and the gray flannel suit was the uniform. William Whyte describes the ethos of these men in *Organization Man*. He has little doubt that the American dream of freedom, individual initiative, and success which had shaped manliness and masculine achievement is being seriously altered. Whyte claims that the new "social ethic" stresses the group as a source of creativity; belonging is more desirable than individualism in coping with complex modern society. The ethic employs science and scientific methodology as a way to achieve success, diminishing the importance of individual brawn and will.[40] David Riesman describes these middle-class men as "other-directed" in *The Lonely Crowd*. Earlier generations of Americans, he claims, were "inner-directed," internalizing adult authority. The "other-directed" man was a product of his peers: "In adult life he continues to respond to these peers, not only with overt conformity as do people in all times and places, but also in a deeper sense, in the very quality of his feeling. Yet, paradoxically, he remains a lonely member of the crowd because he never comes really close to the others or to himself."[41]

Eric Dingwall concludes that American women were suffering from having feminized men through covert tactics of influencing American society. But he blames the men equally for their own malaise and subjection. He charges that men do not understand or use their virile powers or know the meaning of love.[42]

Helen Hacker observed that many men of the fifties harbored resentment against women. Plays, novels, and films portrayed women as castrating Delilahs. She explained that this anxiety was a result of the new expectations about female sexuality. Previously virility was seen as a unilateral expression of male sexuality, but in the 1950s it was judged as an ability to evoke a full sexual response from women, a harrowing prospect for many men.[43] For inspiration some men bought condoms with a provocative nude picture of Marilyn Monroe reproduced on them in vivid color.[44]

Numerous commentators bewailed the plight of besieged men. David Cohn lamented that the American home was devoid of intimacy, mature affection, and friendship. The popular journals, novels, and movies depicted American men as harassed by women. Fathers were seen as basically incompetent when it came to children and family matters. J. Fisher hyperbolically wrote that never in history had society seen such a high proportion of "cowed and eunuchoid males." In 1957 Robert Mosken reported that authorities on human behavior concluded that women clearly dominated American males. The number of women owning securities had increased more than 35 percent between 1954 and 1958. Women owned $100 billion worth of stocks (60 percent of the individual shares of AT&T, 55 percent of DuPont, 54 percent of GE). *Fortune* credited women with making 60 percent of all consumer purchases, and a Gallup poll cited wives as participating in managing 71 percent of the funds of American households.[45]

Although some fathers might be seen pushing strollers and grocery shopping, Paul Landis challenged the notion that the men were doing significantly more domestic work. In 1953 he studied 543 households and examined eighteen tasks performed. Only three of those tasks (locking up at night, fixing broken things, and yardwork) even remotely approached 50 percent male participation. Most of the tasks (such as laundry, ironing, and cleaning) showed not even 10 percent male participation.[46] But to many men doing anything domestic was a dramatic shift. These men of the fifties did more domestic work than their fathers had, and less than their sons would do.

Men who chafed in the domestic harness railed against the women who seemed to be dominating them, drank to excess, had stealthy affairs, or made passes at their neighbors' wives. Others escaped into Mickey Spillane novels. If they felt impotent at home and at the office, for a few hours they could identify with Spillane's Mike Hammer, a 1950s Clint Eastwood, who had women whenever he wanted, slapped them around, and killed criminals and commies with a chilling absence of emotion.[47]

Along with detective novels, men also read westerns by Zane Grey, where there were no women at all and no white-collar employment. They watched "Gunsmoke" or "Bonanza," where Matt Dillon and Ben Cartwright did not have wives to worry about. They could escape into the world of the frontier, where masculinity was supreme, violence commonplace, and escape from domesticity was achieved by riding off into the sunset.

The women who suffered depression, boredom, and the anguish of losing their identities may have sat across from husbands who often had ulcers, died early of heart attacks, and did not find their jobs "fulfilling" either. As one survivor of the decade wrote, "Men have nothing to lose but their anguish." The man in the gray flannel suit could station himself in front of the television and tune out his wife and children, or he could retire into his study where "he was not to be disturbed." When Hugh Hefner's *Playboy* hit the stands in December 1953, he could lose himself in the fantasies of being a playboy attended by voluptuous "bunnies." The magazine was antimarriage and proconsumerism. The swinging single man with all the accoutrements of affluence and no dominating wife appealed to many men in gray flannel suits.[48]

In their splendid book *Intimate Matters: A History of Sexuality in America*, John D'Emilio and Estelle B. Freedman contend that entrepreneurs like Hefner presented a major challenge to the marriage-oriented ethic of sexual liberalism (sexual pleasure as crucial to personal happiness) by extending the logic of consumer capitalism to the realm of sex. Sex as a means of fulfillment and pleasure had replaced the nineteenth-century emphasis on the control of sexual impulses through self-management. They view Hefner's *Playboy* as an indicator of the coming sexual revolution, which gained momentum in the 1960s and encouraged sexuality outside of marriage.[49]

Sexual Power?

Although many of the "organization men" may not have felt very sexy, their wives were reading in popular magazines and books that they deserved to be orgasmic. In the 1950s American women were empowered by a greater emphasis on the naturalness of female sexual fulfillment. American housewives were becoming more interested in sex. Alfred Kinsey's *Sexual Behavior in the Human Female* caused quite an uproar when it hit the stands in 1953. Although it did not receive as much attention as the earlier report on male sexuality, it did cause a stir. Throughout the book Kinsey emphasized repeatedly that women have the same capacity for sexual expression as men do. He also established once and for all the primacy of clitoral eroticism. Kinsey further shocked people by refusing to label female homosexuality as perverse.

The reversal of nineteenth-century notions about female passionlessness to female sexual fulfillment had begun in the early twentieth century and gained much attention in the 1920s. Increasingly in the 1950s the female orgasm was becoming the standard of normality. Marriage manuals like that of Hannah and Abraham Stone focused on physiological advice and emphasized that male lust was healthy, and female inhibitions neurotic.

Although the emphasis on female sexuality as normal and natural implied that women were entitled to "sexual fulfillment," ironically, at the time the female orgasm was so highly prized, the dominance of Freudian ideology emphasized the "vaginal" orgasm as the premier act. Once again, women faced a double bind: their "sexual fulfillment" presumably depended on their submissiveness. Dr. Marie Robinson's *The Power of Sexual Surrender* sold a million copies. She extolled the ecstasy of orgasm, "a sensation of such beauty and intensity that I can hardly think of it without weeping." The women who could not achieve this ecstasy were described as immature, masculine, and abnormal. Robinson reduced female sexuality to passive compliance with the needs of her husband. She believed that women who reached orgasm via the clitoris were purely and simply frigid. She dismissed Victorians, suffragists, and flappers all as hopeless neurotics.[50]

Betty Friedan found that the housewives whom she interviewed were preoccupied with sexual fulfillment, or rather the lack of it. One thirty-eight-year-old mother of four told Friedan that sex was the only thing that made her "feel alive." But because her husband was disinterested and did not satisfy her, she was becoming contemptuous of him in bed. Other housewives who engaged in extramarital affairs found them equally unsatisfying. Friedan argues that sex had become a "strangely joyless national compulsion."[51]

The suburban wife, having just read *The Power of Sexual Surrender* or articles in women's magazines on how to improve her sex life, might wait anxiously for her husband to return from work, eager for intimacy, communication, and sex. But no amount of perfume or number of black negligees could make up for the housewife's craving for achievement if her only avenues were those of wife, lover, and mother. The beleaguered gray flannel man frequently might want to watch TV and then go to bed—to sleep.

As in the case with female sexuality, women in the 1950s faced both more and less control over reproduction. Practically women had more control of their reproductive lives with the wide dissemination of birth control information. In 1942 the Birth Control Federation changed its name to Planned Parenthood Federation of America, and its emphasis was on spacing children and planning family size. Margaret Sanger's original ties with radicalism were erased from consciousness, and the PPFA believed that sexual expression led to stability. Unlike their predecessors, they did not challenge social inequities in the family, sexual or class inequities of the medical system, or the imposition of a cultural pattern by the dominant majority. In the 1950s only 150 agencies in the entire country dispensed birth control information. By 1972 there were over 3,000.[52]

Although women had greater access to information about birth control and they could obtain contraceptives, the cultural pressure to have many children meant that they used birth control principally to space their children, not to limit family size significantly. The women of the 1950s produced 76,441,000 babies, the so-called baby boom (one-third of our present population). Americans of the fifties married earlier, had children more quickly—and more of them than before or since. Nevertheless, most illegal abortions were sought by married women who already had children. Estimates were that one million abortions were performed each year in the 1950s and that 5,000–10,000 women died each year due to avoidable complications of illegal abortions.[53]

Even with the high abortion rate, hospitals were crowded with women having babies in the 1950s. In her book *Brought to Bed: Childbearing in*

America, 1750–1950, Judith Walzer Leavitt claims that women lost their domestic power base and certain traditional controls when births took place in hospitals, rather than in homes. By 1940, approximately 55 percent of American women were delivering their babies in hospitals, and by 1950, the figure had risen to 88 percent. Since relatives and friends were excluded from hospital births, the female network was weakened. Childbirth had been exclusively under women's jurisdiction until well into the nineteenth century, and intervention by a male physician was still combined with a female presence until the first third of the twentieth century.[54]

As Richard and Dorothy Wertz document in their book *Lying-In: A History of Childbirth in America*, what had begun in the 1920s as a movement for greater safety, comfort, and efficiency for mothers and infants became an unpleasant and alienating experience for many women by the 1950s and 1960s. Women were cut off from husbands, friends, and relatives when they most needed their psychological support. The woman was given analgesics to reduce pain and scopolamine to erase the memory of pain. When ready to deliver, she was wheeled to the delivery room and placed on a table with stirrups. Her arms were strapped down, and her legs strapped high in the air, in the so-called lothotomy position. Labors and deliveries might be artificially slowed down or speeded up, depending on the "assembly line" needs and the convenience of doctors and staff.

Women gained in the increased safety of hospital births, especially with the introduction of antibiotics for infection. However, they often suffered psychologically because of the alienating atmosphere and feeling of being out of control of their bodies and lives. After the *Ladies Home Journal* printed a letter from a maternity nurse who urged investigation of "cruelty in maternity wards," hundreds of letters poured in from women recounting horror stories of their birth experiences in hospitals. Public homilies extolling motherhood as the highest duty and avenue of fulfillment for women clashed starkly with the actual birth experiences of women, especially poor and African-American women. This contradiction in women's lives set the stage for women's demands to regain control over their bodies and lives, including the birthing process.[55]

Empowerment and Discrimination in the Labor Force

Every account of the emergence of the modern feminist movement cites the entrance of women into the labor force as a crucial factor. What has been overlooked is the way in which employment enhanced women's self-esteem and bargaining power within the family and at the same time confronted them with a series of contradictions. Their growing dominance at home contrasted sharply with their disadvantaged status in the labor force.

American women continued to participate in the labor force in increasing numbers in order for their families to survive or to maintain middle-class status. The number of women over thirty-five in the work force jumped from 8.5 million in 1947 to almost 13 million in 1956. By 1960 the labor force included 24 million women. The participation of all women fourteen years and older in the labor force increased from 25.4 percent in 1940 to 29 percent in 1950 and 34.5 percent in 1960. The composition of female workers changed in the postwar period from mainly young and single to older and married workers. In 1950 only 12 percent of women with children under six were employed, compared with 19 percent in 1960. In 1955, 35 percent of the women who had children six years and older were employed.[56] At that time, women made up about 21 million out of a total labor force of 64 million.[57] In June 1978, the proportion of women sixteen and older in the labor force passed 50 percent for the first time in U.S. history.[58]

In the period from 1945 to 1975, 25 million women entered the labor force. According to previous trends, 10 million were expected to do so; nobody had expected the other 15 million to go to work. These women were largely the young "baby boomers."[59]

After World War II, the economy shifted from a largely manufacturing economy to a service economy. The decline in the birthrate during the depression had created a shortage of young single women. The rise in female college attendance and the trend toward early marriage also reduced the pool of eligible workers. Since the jobs in the service sector had to be filled, businesses recruited older women, often married women.[60]

Before Friedan urged women to work, millions had already taken that step. The percentage of working mothers with school-age children rose from 25 to 40 percent during the fifties. The number of men in the labor force increased 12 percent between 1947 and 1962, while the number of women rose 45 percent, and the number of married women working jumped 97 percent.[61] For the 40 percent of working mothers with children, their dilemma was not that of an isolated full-time housewife, but of juggling job, marriage, and children. Like the women of the 1930s, they had to be superwomen.

Many women were motivated to enter the labor force because they realized that they could contribute more to the family's economic stability by wage earning than by staying home and economizing, which they had done previously. The fact was brought out dramatically in the 1950s that the average woman had over forty years to live after her youngest child went to school. Women "helped out" their husbands by bringing in a little money. Most American women viewed their employment as supplemental. Moreover, by 1960 nearly 80 percent of employed women worked in female-stereotyped jobs. The bulk of the increase in the labor force participation in the 1950s occurred among women over forty-five, but the proportion of women with small children increased by one-third, and with children under six, by more than one-fourth. These women usually filled vacancies as stenographers, typists, nurses, teachers, and social workers.[62] By 1960, 90 percent of all women had worked outside the home at some point in their lives.[63]

Women's employment did not mean a radical alteration of traditional roles, but it did enable them to have more financial independence, enhancing their status in the family. By 1952, two million more women worked than in the peak years of World War II.[64] But women lost ground in professions overall. From 1930 to 1950 the educational aspirations of women actually fell: 43.7 percent of all college students were female in 1930, compared with 40.2 percent in 1940 and 30.3 percent in 1950.[65]

Data from the 1950s and 1960s reveal that wives' employment outside the home had little impact on traditional beliefs about women's role. Because their earnings rarely if ever equaled their husbands', women did not challenge their spouses' economic superiority. Most of the women who went to work viewed their jobs as extensions of their roles as wives and mothers.[66] However, women did realize their strength and competence in the public sphere. In time, many of these women would revolt against the discrimination which they found in the labor force.

African-American Women in the 1950s

African-American women's experiences as wives and mothers in the 1950s differed greatly from those of white middle-class women. African-American women did not suffer from the feminine mystique in the 1950s but rather from the double jeopardy of being black and female. Racism and poverty were the major obstacles for them, not a loss of identity. African-American women were expected to work, and at the same time be wives and mothers.

African-Americans shared some in the postwar prosperity, as their earnings in 1950 were four times the amount in 1940. Inequality still persisted, with most economic progress coming to African-Americans between 1942 and 1945. E. Franklin Frazier pointed out that in 1949 the median income of black families ($1,665) was only 51.5 percent of the median for white families ($3,232).[67]

By 1950, 68 percent of African-Americans still lived in the South, 28 percent in the North, and 4 percent in the West. Five years after the Second World War the earnings of southern African-American men averaged half those of southern white men, and their earnings declined to 46 percent by 1959. In 1950, one-third of all African-American wives were in the labor force, at a time when only one-fourth of all married women in the population were employed. By 1950, 60 percent of all African-American working women (as opposed to 16 percent of white working women) were in institutional and private household service jobs, and 40 percent of all employed white women had clerical or sales jobs as opposed to only 5 percent of black working women.[68]

African-American women headed 17.6 percent of all black households in 1950, as opposed to 8.5 percent female-headed white households. This figure rose to 28.3 percent in 1970 (10.9 percent for whites) and to 40.2 percent in 1980 (14.6 percent for whites). The number of women on welfare (Aid to Families with Dependent Children) rose from 3 million in 1960 to 11.4 million in 1975. Moreover, African-American women's fertility rate was 33 percent higher in 1950 than that of white women, and 25.3 percent of African-American wives were either separated, divorced, or widowed, compared with 10 percent of white women who had ever married.[69] African-American magazines like *Ebony* ran articles on working women who were wives and mothers as well as high achievers.[70]

Little wonder that many African-American women were unresponsive to the complaints of Betty Friedan. Instead of wanting to get out of the kitchen, many of them wanted a decent kitchen to come home to. Some of them may have viewed the "feminine mystique" with envy, rather than contempt. Their crucial economic and maternal role within the black family had enhanced their self-esteem, which led many black women in the 1960s to exclaim, "I've always been liberated." This statement is deeply ironic, given the double oppression which they have faced by being black and female. What they generally meant was that they have always worked outside the home and thus were already "liberated," or that they had been psychologically liberated by having self-esteem, especially as wives and mothers. Moreover, many African-American women were alienated from a predominantly white feminist movement.

The civil rights movement was an empowering experience for African-American women. The movement gained momentum in 1954 with *Brown v. Board of Education*, the Supreme Court case which ordered the desegregation of schools. African-American women were concerned with achieving civil rights, rather than exclusively women's rights. On Thursday, December 1, 1955, Rosa Parks boarded a bus in Montgomery, Alabama, and found a seat. When the bus filled up, the bus driver ordered her to give up her seat to a white man. She was tired and refused. When she was arrested at the next stop, the black community initiated a bus boycott in Montgomery. When asked in an oral history why she refused to give up her seat, Rosa Parks replied:

> I think it was because I was so involved with the attempt to bring about freedom from this kind of thing. I had seen so much within reach on the basis of the Whitney Young experience under the same situation that I felt that there was nothing else I could do to show that I was not pleased. . . . People have said that I was a great democrat, people say things like that, but I was not conscious of being. . . . I felt just resigned to give what I could to protest against the way I was being treated, and I felt that all of our meetings, trying to negotiate, bring about petitions before the authorities, that is the city officials, really hadn't done any good at all.

Parks was a former NAACP secretary, and she was supported by 80–90 percent of the African-American citizens. She used personal, familial, and community networks to mobilize politically. During the boycott, 42,000 people walked to work.[71] The Supreme Court, which had overturned the doctrine of separate but equal for schools and recreational facilities, now ruled that its decision applied to public transportation. The battle of Montgomery was won after 381 days.[72]

Throughout the 1950s, African-American women were the backbone of the civil rights movement, while African-American men were seen as the leaders in the media. Fannie Lou Hamer, Ella Baker, Septima Clark, and other well-known black women marched, sat-in, faced firehoses and the bared fangs of Bull Connor's dogs, and carried on a public and private struggle for dignity and social justice.[73]

In contrast to the courageous civil rights activists, if many Americans seemed withdrawn, cautious, unimaginative, and unadventurous, perhaps a more accurate description might be stunned. Having endured the Great Depression and a world war, suspecting internal Communist subversion, and experiencing depersonalization, Americans naturally sought refuge in domesticity.

Diversity characterized women's experiences in the 1950s as wives and mothers, experiences which both trapped them and empowered them. Race and class were extremely important in shaping their lives. The view of all women as unhappy and thwarted by domesticity is just as distorted as one which assumes that all women cheerfully accepted their roles. We do know, however, that American women became more dominant in the home in the fifties and exercised considerable covert power. The fifties were the seedbed of revolt of the 1960s, and the contradictory messages the women received spurred the development of feminist consciousness. They were encouraged to be educated but to stay at home, have babies, and find fulfillment as wives and mothers in a companionate marriage; at the same time, they were condemned for castrating their husbands and overmothering their children. They were "entitled" to sexual satisfaction in marriage, but their fulfillment supposedly depended on submission. They had greater access to birth control, but they were urged to have many children. Motherhood was glorified, but in hospital births they often experienced alienation and frustration. They were expected to take a job if financially necessary but not to let it affect their primary obligations as wife and mother.

In their employment, voluntarism, and community and organizational activities, many women were empowered, but they faced unequal wages and might be expected to defer to male authority. They gained more influence in parenting but were expected to inculcate traditional gender-role expectations in their children. They had more control over household consumerism but were deemed "economic parasites" by some commentators. Consumerism, the boom in the American economy, and rising expectations of what families considered essential to their life-styles sent millions of women into the labor force. There they discovered a deep disparity between their covert power at home and their relative powerlessness in the public sphere.

The majority of white American women in the 1950s did not perceive a forced choice between marriage and career. They viewed marriage and motherhood as a full-time profession. Female achievement was measured by women's effectiveness in running the household and rearing children, not by achievement in the public sphere. African-American women frequently were forced to combine employment, marriage, and motherhood. Covert domestic power without economic independence did not necessarily confer self-esteem or a sense of identity. However, women's increasing domestic power and the many contradictions between their own experiences and the social construction of motherhood, sexuality, and domesticity prepared the stage for the development of feminist consciousness and the wide-ranging demands of the women's liberation movement.

11

FEMINIST VOICES OF THE 1950s

For him she is sex—absolute sex, no less. She is defined and differentiated with reference to man and not he with reference to her; she is the incidental, the inessential as opposed to the essential. He is the Subject, he is the Absolute—she is the Other.

Simone de Beauvoir, The Second Sex, 1953

Like the girl who feared that she would make a successful career woman and would thereby jeopardize her future marriage, some girls appear to espouse the traditional role all the more passionately because they feel tempted by other goals.

Mirra Komarovsky, Women in the Modern World:
Their Education and Their Dilemmas, 1953

No collective feminist movement existed in the 1950s, but feminist consciousness was beginning to develop, and feminist writings appeared. The National Woman's Party continued to agitate tirelessly for women's rights. But antifeminism was widespread during the era and seemed to be cloaked with the authority of social science. Outspoken antifeminism of the 1950s reflected alarm about the possible threat to the traditional family by material transformations, the entrance of millions of women into the labor force, and their growing dominance at home. Women who had been bewitched by the feminine mystique and those who bore the multiple burden of housework, childrearing, and a job were possible prospects for rebellion and discontent. Feminism in the 1950s, however, generally found a hostile audience even among most of the professional, achieving women. The NWP and other women's organizations had lobbied for the Equal Rights Amendment during World War II. But instead of victory for women's rights after the war, feminists confronted a vicious antifeminist backlash. The ferocity of this antifeminism stemmed from fears about changes in sexual roles which had already occurred.

In 1947 Ferdinand Lundberg and Marynia Farnham published *Modern Woman: The Lost Sex*, a virulent attack on feminism. As Freudians, they deplored the feminists who "suffered from penis-envy," who sought to be like men, instead of adjusting to their natural, biological role as wives and mothers. This "feminist neuroticism" was presumably expressed in their ideology:

1. Women are identical with men (equal).
2. They should receive the same education as men.
3. They should be governed by the same moral standards.
4. They should have the same work opportunities.
5. They should have the same political rights.

Lundberg and Farnham believed that women who sought careers in traditionally male professions "denied their true natures, and were pitiable." They wrote that the clearest proof of one's femininity was to have a child.[1] The authors recommended that only a married woman with one child be allowed to teach school. Spinsters, often schoolteachers, would be encouraged to get married, or they would have to take other jobs. Bachelors should also be pressured to get married, and the tax system should reward married men. The authors urged fathers to derive status and prestige from fatherhood, as women did through motherhood.

Modern Woman was contradictory, reflecting an underlying agreement with later feminists that American housewives needed to be more productive. Lundberg and Farnham recommended part-time work, already done by a large number of women, as desirable for more married women. Therefore, full-time workers could work less time. Lundberg and Farnham recommended teaching, nursing, and medicine as possible appropriate areas for women to continue their nurturing outside the home. They did not explain how one could be a part-time doctor, however.

Lundberg and Farnham acknowledged that technology led to women's lack of function in the home, which "freed them for sleeveless idleness or to routinized menial tasks in business or industry." They wrote, "Neither can the perpetual window shopper, bridge player, and moviegoer make any valid claim to prestige. She may well be dismissed as a nonentity, for she is a nonentity." These antifeminists sounded very much like Friedan in her claim that housewives in the 1950s lost their identities.

Anticipating an increase in population if women took their advice about having many children, they offered a sinister, eugenic solution. If a population problem arose in the future, the "solution would probably lie in imposing public controls to prevent the breeding of certain strains."

Lundberg and Farnham acknowledged that a few women might also achieve distinction. They proclaimed, "A woman freed from 'household drudgery' who repairs to the laboratory and there discovers a cure for a baffling disease, or who makes some other cultural contribution may well have made a good ego bargain. But to few women is vouchsafed this distinction as to few men."

Modern Woman attacked feminism but at the same time recommended jobs for women. The authors even acknowledged the possibility of distinction for women of exceptional talent. But their central message was that American women ought to accept their natural, nurturant roles and celebrate domesticity, marriage, and motherhood. In order to accomplish their goals, they recommended federally subsidized psychoanalysis and cash subsidies for motherhood.[2]

While Farnham and Lundberg blasted feminism, some women's organizations began to disavow feminism also. The League of Women Voters, for example, even denied any particular concern with women's issues.[3] In 1951 the league withdrew from the International Alliance of Women because it was too feminist, and even left the Women's Joint Congressional Committee, a group against the Equal Rights Amendment. They left because they did not want to be affiliated solely with women's organizations, not because they supported the ERA. In fact, they dropped opposition to the ERA from its program because it did not seem important. Membership in the League of Women Voters increased by 44 percent from 1950 to 1958, extending over forty-eight states with 1,050 local leagues, composed of 128,000 members. The league was the training ground for many educated women during the fifties. Some members would go on to run for public offices in the 1970s and 1980s.[4]

Individual former feminists seemed to be defecting in the fifties. Doris E. Fleischman explained in the *American Mercury* why, after using her own name for twenty-five years, she had decided to use her husband's.

We were fervid idealists in those days, fighting usually for means rather than for ends. We feminists wanted our own personalities, wanted to throw off the ascendance of the male. What did we do about that? Not what you'd think. We grasped for a symbol—a name—instead of developing personalities of our own. We wore our Miss as a cosmetic, to conceal the underlying Mrs.

After recounting all the inconveniences and the embarrassments to herself and others over her maiden name, she admitted that she was tired of being Miss, and planned to take her husband's name. Lucy Stone would have been unsympathetic.[5]

The Survival of Feminism in the 1950s

Although some feminists were recanting and antifeminism was pervasive, feminism did not die in the 1950s, however faintly it may have flickered. Alice Paul and other members of the National Woman's Party saw to that. No large, collective, organized, focused feminist movement existed, but feminism survived through a loose network of organizations and individuals dedicated to improving the status of women. The conditions for the emergence of a mass women's movement, as described by Nancy E. McGlen and Karen O'Connor, were not present in the 1950s.

1. An organizational base or outside resources to facilitate its development are present;
2. Lines of communication exist among potential leaders;
3. A sense of collective oppression and a recognition of the need for a common solution develop within a sizeable group of women; and
4. A critical mobilizing event (or events) occurs.[6]

In the absence of these mobilizing factors, the NWP had become a small, elite organization. In the last years of the suffrage campaign, the NWP had 60,000 members. By 1945 the membership had dropped to 4,000, climbed back to 5,500 in 1953, and then dropped to 1,400 by 1965. Of these members, only 600–800 were active, dues-paying members during this period. Only women were able to join, a heretical condition in an era of militant heterosexuality. The members were primarily professional women, especially lawyers, some upper-class women, and a few workers. Membership was almost entirely white, although Mary Church Terrell belonged. In fact, some NWP members were conservative politically, racist, and anti-Semitic.

The NWP was committed to a single goal: legal equality. They worked relentlessly for the passage of the Equal Rights Amendment.[7] Many of the members had done so for over thirty years already. The Business and Professional Women's Club also worked for the ERA in the postwar period, launching "Operation Buttonhole" in 1953–54. The General Federation of Women's Clubs, the largest women's organization in the country, also supported the amendment, though not as vigorously as the BPW, which had 165,000 members by 1956.[8] In addition, the National Association of Colored Women, led by Mary Church Terrell, supported the ERA. Although this amendment was the major objective of the NWP, its members also worked to place women in policy-making roles and to promote the study of women's history.

Individual NWP members like Mary Beard concentrated on writing and teaching women's history. Beard's *Woman as a Force in History* focused on women as active participants in history and downplayed women's subjugation. Beard urged college presidents to promote the teaching of women's history and to acquire library materials on women. In 1949 she proposed a research institute as a resource for scholars of women's history and as a means to generate a revision of the curriculum to include scholarship on women.[9] Beard was highly influential with feminist scholars of the 1960s and 1970s.

In addition to fostering the study of women's history, the National Woman's Party played an important role for its members by creating a feminist group culture. The party emphasized the importance of suffrage history, provided an explicitly feminist identification and an intense commitment to the feminist cause, and provided the center of friendship and intimacy for members.

Nora Stanton Barney, Elizabeth Cady Stanton's granddaughter and daughter of Harriot Stanton Blatch, defined feminism in *Equal Rights*, the publication of the NWP: "A feminist is one who thinks women are primarily human beings with the same minds, ambitions, ability and skill, consciences, and power for evil and good, as men."[10]

Such a sentiment hardly sounds fanatical in the 1990s, but in the 1950s the NWP's pronouncements attracted few American housewives, who typically were tuned in more to soap operas on the television. Many of the NWP members were older women, often in their seventies and eighties. They often lived in couple relationships with other women or functioned in a world primarily of women. With such an intense national preoccupation with female sexual fulfillment, togetherness, heterosexual sexuality, and domesticity, these relationships struck most Americans as deviant. Close, intimate relationships among women, which were commonplace in the nineteenth and early twentieth centuries, were no longer so generally accepted, perhaps a casualty of Freud.

Internal conflicts within the NWP also served to weaken it. Alice Paul's leadership, considered dictatorial by some, had split the party in 1935, and in 1947 a lawsuit over the name and property resources of the party diverted their energies. The national chairwoman resigned in 1953 over the issue of expansion of membership.

Along with internal dissension within the women's rights movement, McCarthyism hampered feminist activism in the 1950s by creating an atmosphere of fear and distrust. As early as the 1920s, prominent female activists like Jane Addams and Carrie Chapman Catt were charged with being part of the "spiderweb" of Communist front organizations. Likewise, any form of activism in the 1950s was the target of Joe McCarthy. All of these factors strengthened the NWP's tendency to withdraw into themselves.[11] Although the NWP was insular, small, and virtually unknown to most Americans, the organization exerted its influence out of proportion to its size. The members kept alive the ERA and were influential in the establishment of the President's Commission on the Status of Women in 1961 and in including the basis of sex in Title VII of the Civil Rights Act of 1964.[12]

Feminism in the 1950s did not appeal to most educated, middle-class women because they did not feel they needed liberating. The majority of American women were not active in working for women's public power, assuming that covert, domestic power was the arena of their struggle. But as we have seen, African-Americans, male and female, did mobilize in the 1950s in great numbers to gain their equality.

As the civil rights movement gained more momentum in the 1950s, the women's rights movement, nationally represented by the National Woman's Party, responded. The party's members disagreed over the issue of integration of the organization, but segregation still prevailed. The NWP tried to make use of the civil rights successes and cooperate with the National Association of Colored Women. Many of the NWP's members, however, saw the civil rights movement and the women's rights movement as competitive.[13]

Lone Feminist Voices

Given the climate of complacency and conformity of the 1950s, it is remarkable that some women refused to believe in the feminine mystique. These lone feminist voices were like seeds buried underground, awaiting a more receptive hearing. Despite the virulent antifeminist backlash of the 1950s, strong voices were present, such as Eleanor Roosevelt and Alice Paul, whom we encountered in earlier chapters. Along with Simone de Beauvoir, Dorothy Thompson, Pearl Buck, Eve Merriam, and Margaret Mead, they argued that women should be free to express their intellect and creativity and to enjoy equality as human beings. With the exception of Simone de Beauvoir, who was the most radical of the group, they believed that women did not have to give up marriage and motherhood to achieve an authentic existence. Paul shared this belief, but she personally chose to remain single. They all objected to defining women by their biological capabilities. The lives of these women who endorsed women's rights represent the continuity within the American feminist movement from the 1940s through the 1960s.

Their lives also reveal tensions which would emerge in the modern feminist movement between the older and younger feminists. These women were superwomen who believed strongly that women needed to be self-reliant and to express their individuality. In their own lives, they found it difficult to combine achievement, marriage, and motherhood but regarded their dilemma as personal. Except for Paul, they did not fully acknowledge their indebtedness for their successes to former pioneer feminists, and they did not see themselves as a part of a broad movement for women's rights. Instead, they were trailblazers as achieving women in the public sphere. With the exceptions of de Beauvoir and Paul, they were uncomfortable with ideologies and theoretical explanations.

American women were aware of the achievements of notable women in the 1950s who might be empowering role models. They also had available feminist literature. But the majority of American women were too preoccupied with children or with trying to juggle jobs and family responsibilities to seek to claim their power collectively. Many of them would read the works of the following women later in the 1960s and develop an entirely different view of their own experiences in the 1950s.

Simone de Beauvoir

Simone de Beauvoir published her magnificent manifesto of feminism, *The Second Sex*, in France in 1949, and it was translated and published in the United States in 1953. De Beauvoir describes women's oppression within the framework of free will. She views women as living inauthentic lives because they are not the subject of their own lives. Her thesis is that women have been regarded as the Other. Therefore, women have been unable to achieve transcendence in the world by taking action; they have been in complicity in their subordination. She writes from a Marxist-existentialist position but criticizes any monistic explanation of women's condition including Marxism and Freudianism. She offers a feminist critique of religion, literature, psychology, and myth, and discusses every stage of a woman's life. She condemns the institution of marriage as stifling and exploitive of women. Her chapter on motherhood begins with a discussion of abortion, and she views pregnancy and motherhood not as empowering experiences but as oppressive. Her view is that women have been unable to achieve transcendence in the world by taking action, by creating; instead they have been tied to their reproductive roles and forced to remain in immanence. Consequently, women have been forced to live in bad faith and forsake freedom. The book still stands as the most important feminist manifesto of the twentieth century.

Reviewers of *The Second Sex* in France wrote rancorous reviews and accused her of everything from nymphomania to penis-envy. American reviewers were much more receptive, but wary of de Beauvoir's Marxist connections, they saw "red." The Cold War was at its peak; the Rosenbergs awaited execution at Sing Sing, and Joseph McCarthy was terrorizing the country in his search for Communists. One reviewer warned that the book should be read with "critical caution." *Saturday Review* published a long review entitled, "Six Experts Review *The Second Sex*." The experts included Karl Menninger, a psychiatrist; Philip Wylie, the author of *A Generation of Vipers*; Ashley Montagu, an educator; Phyllis McGinley; Margaret Mead, an anthropologist; and Olive Goldman, the U.S. representative to the UN Commission on the Status of Women. Menninger rehashed Freud and urged that the goals of individual women must be sacrificed to the greater end of the family and Civilization. Curiously, Philip Wylie, believed to be a vicious misogynist, called the book "one of the few great books of our era." However, he disagreed with her emphasis on material, economic, and social means for a solution, thus disassociating himself from any taint of Communism. Ashley Montagu claimed the book "ranks next to John Stuart Mill's *Subjection of Women*." Phyllis McGinley wrote, "Shame on me! What right have I to go about my humdrum tasks, wearing so cheerful a face? How can I traitorously sing as I add water to the frozen orange juice or put the slice of bread in the electric toaster?" Olive Goldman said that the fact that twenty-five years of suffrage had not given rise to an equal number of women politicans implied that something in *women* held them back.[14]

Margaret Mead was highly critical of de Beauvoir's chapter on motherhood. She wrote, "By denigrating maternity, she constructs a picture in which the only way a woman can be a full human being is to be as much like a man as possible." More recently, French feminists like Luce Irigaray, Hélène Cixous, and Julia Kristeva have also criticized de Beauvoir's dualistic thinking and privileging mind over body. However, within *The Second Sex*, one finds both social constructionist and essentialist lines of inquiry which stimulated the feminist conversation over whether nature or nurture determines women's experiences.

Most American women ignored *The Second Sex* when it was first published. It was long (over 600 pages in the edited American version) and highly philosophical. However, Betty Goldstein (later Friedan) read it, along with women scholars and educators.

Dorothy Thompson

After reading Simone de Beauvoir, Dorothy Thompson began to develop a feminist consciousness. The film *Woman of the Year* was supposedly about Dorothy Thompson, one of the most prominent women of the 1940s. Thompson called the film a "sickening travesty" and "thoroughly unconvincing."[15] It struck too close to home. Thompson did not belong to a collective feminist movement, and she would have been uncomfortable being labeled a feminist. She believed that women ought to be able to have professional careers, marriage, and children. She was a first-class journalist who wrote eight books, including *The New Russia* (1928), *I Saw Hitler* (1932), *Refugees: Anarchy or Organization?* (1938), *Political Guide* (1938), *Once upon a Christmas* (1939), *Let the Record Speak* (1939), *Listen, Hans!* (1942), and *The Courage to Be Happy* (1957). Her stormy marriage to Sinclair Lewis was front-page copy, and she combined a career, marriage, and motherhood.

Thompson wanted the rewards of achievement and of traditionally feminine values. Although she had a highly successful career, a famous husband, and a child, she had great difficulty in combining love and work. She was still vulnerable to the expectations of traditional femininity.[16]

After Thompson interviewed Hitler, she became one of his most vociferous critics and championed U.S. intervention from 1933 to 1941. After February 1936 her column "On the Record" in the *New York Herald Tribune* appeared in 170 newspapers. She also began to write for the *Ladies Home Journal* in 1937, and she became a radio commentator.

Thompson stated that her marriage came first, but her actions did not confirm such a priority. She frequently put her career before personal relationships. Yet, when the *New Yorker* was going to write a profile of her, she told Alexander Woolcott, a drama critic, what she wanted them to say.

> I wish someone would say that I am a hell of a good housekeeper, that the food by me is swell, that I am almost a perfect wife, and that I am still susceptible to the boys. In other words, I wish someone would present me as a female. I am tired of being told I have the brains of a man. What man? But leaving that aside, I haven't. . . . I stayed in Europe to be with another man; I left journalism to marry a third man. I re-entered it—in preference to other kinds of work—because I could write a column and stay home. That's heresy which the feminists wouldn't like, but it's a fact. Work with me has always been a by-product and a secondary interest; I'd throw the state of the nation into the ashcan for anyone I loved.[17]

Like the feminists of the 1920s, Thompson wanted professional success, but also the rewards of love and marriage. In the fall of 1939, she told her readers of *Ladies Home Journal*: "Society, at this moment, has a greater need of good mothers than it has of more private secretaries, laboratory assistants, short story writers, lawyers, social workers and motion picture stars. It is a better thing to produce a fine man than it is to produce a second-rate novel, and fine men begin by being fine children."[18]

The mobilization of women during World War II convinced Thompson that the shift in the roles of men and women would continue after the war. She wrote that women do not release their unique power for society because they "do not assert their *own* experience, affirm their *own* instinct, believe in their *own* wisdom, or struggle for their *own* values."[19]

Years later after reading Ashley Montagu and Simone de Beauvoir, she wrote in 1953, "But the woman who is talented and intellectually equipped for a demanding art or profession is, if she be fully feminine, torn between two functions. The feminist movement has never really faced up to this fact." She argued that factories and offices should provide nurseries and flexible office schedules. She concluded that the only group in society benefiting from the present system were the psychiatrists. Thompson continued to write about women's unfulfilled possibilities, but also on dieting (a lifelong obsession), geniuses she had known, childrearing, her delight in life's pleasures, and a faith in a divine, guiding presence.[20] She continued to write for the *Ladies Home Journal* until her death in 1961 of a heart attack. Through the example of her life, Dorothy Thompson represented a reluctant feminist. She was aware of the inequalities within the society, but she had been able to have a stunning career herself. In some ways she saw herself as exempt from discrimination, but she felt intensely the personal costs of her own success.

Pearl Buck

Pearl Buck seemingly was able both to achieve a brilliant career and to sustain a rewarding family life. Like Eleanor Roosevelt, Pearl Buck was an outstanding humanitarian. Her career demonstrates the truth that when feminists support domesticity, marriage, and motherhood, they succeed. Best known for her novel *The Good Earth*, which sold almost two million copies, she was a prolific writer, publishing from one to five books a year. Buck wrote over 100 books, countless articles, and scripts. In 1941 she wrote *Of Men and Women*, a feminist work in which she compares the situation of women in the United States and China. Chinese women who had been confined to the home became very powerful. They were able to understand the nature of men completely. Buck writes that: "they knew men's every weakness and used such weakness ruthlessly for their own ends, good or evil. Lacking other education, they devised cunning and wile and deviousness and charm, and they had men wholly in their power, confounding simple men by their wisdom and learned men by their childishness."[21]

In contrast to the Americans, the Chinese kept the women ignorant. Both to bind women's feet and to educate them would have been torture. In the United States they educated women and still sought to keep them in the narrow sphere of the home. Buck writes: "Of one thing I am sure, however, there will be no real content among American women unless they are made and kept more ignorant, or unless they are given equal opportunity with men to use what they have been taught. . . . And American men will not be really happy until their women are."[22]

Buck supported the ERA and was for letting women out of the home into the world and letting men into the home. Buck believed that women assumed the primary care of children and argued that American men saw less of their families than any other husbands and fathers in the world. She argued for nonsexist childrearing methods and urged men to participate more in raising their children. Buck wrote, "Men and women should own the world as a mutual possession. Let woman out of the home, let men into it, should be the aim of education." She did not assign absolute virtues or vices to either sex. Despite her feminist pronouncements, most Americans read her books about China, not about themselves.[23]

In her own life, Pearl Buck combined marriage and motherhood with her highly successful literary career. She married twice, first John Lossing Buck in 1917, with whom she had a daughter, who was retarded. After divorcing him, she married her publisher-editor, Richard Walsh, in 1935. She was the major wage earner for their family, which included six adopted and two foster children who came from different racial backgrounds. She worked tirelessly for international understanding and peace, for elimination of racism, and for the mentally retarded.[24] Buck urged women to get out of the home and into the labor force, which millions of American women did during World War II.

Eve Merriam

Eve Merriam's *After Nora Slammed the Door: American Women in the 1960s: The Unfinished Revolution* (1958) brilliantly describes the situation Friedan explains in *The Feminine Mystique*. Merriam's book did not raise the same stir as Friedan's later work because her audience was not yet so receptive. Her book describes how marriage and domesticity trapped women. Merriam claims that a dependent housewife cannot give of herself generously or receive with graciousness. Only a free person can give and receive without grudging and be responsive to lovemaking.[25]

According to Merriam, men of the 1950s tended to be passive and meeker than they once were. Many men had become compliant because they were most concerned with the safest income tax bracket and the most security. Their subservience and unquestioning loyalty were based on fear. Their wives felt guilty when they worked because they were "neglecting their homes and children." They also faced a double bind, feeling guilty when they did not work because they were not contributing to society.

In suburbia women became the sole parents with primary responsibility for the children, except for an occasional glimpse of the commuting father. Merriam states that the isolated and isolating nuclear family unit was thrown back on its own small resources. As she notes, it is a miserable state of affairs that puts women in such a position that they have to exult in their "huddled housepower." About middle-class women, Merriam notes, "In one way or another, I think we are all Xantippes, whether we live in the green-lawned suburbs or the gray pavemented cities. There is one now, terry-cloth turban tied around her pincurls, braking a station wagon into the parking lot. Shoving her husband up the steps of the commuting train, grimly turned home to her household batallion."[26]

Merriam's description of what Friedan later called "the problem with no name" reached a limited audience; however, she accurately analyzed the growing dissatisfaction of affluent housewives whose lives lacked meaning. As their children grew older and more and more of the mothers entered the labor force, they began to realize that they were not alone in their desperation.

Achieving women of the 1950s were reacting to ideological loyalties like Nazism, fascism, Communism, socialism, and anarchism. They did not want to label themselves as feminists. They believed that such ideological loyalties led to mass conformity and emphasized irrationalism. Moreover, they often believed that feminism emphasized the similarities of men and women and minimized the differences, especially the consequences of women's reproductive role. They had no doubt that they had equal intellects and deserved the same rights as men, but they believed themselves exceptional.

Margaret Mead

Margaret Mead believed that she was truly exceptional. Her life illustrates the feminist perspective, without any explicit ideological loyalties to feminism. She was an individualistic feminist who had every intention of having a career, husband, and children. Mead ended up having a smashingly successful career in anthropology, three husbands, a daughter, and innumerable intense friendships.

Betty Friedan accused Mead of perpetuating the feminine mystique. As a young student, Betty Goldstein (Friedan) met Mead and Gregory Bateson at a conference of topologists at Smith College (December 31, 1940–January 2, 1941).[27] If some people interpreted Mead's work as a justification for narrowing women's sphere, they greatly misunderstood the import of her work. Mead described the plasticity of human nature. She wrote of the Arapesh, where both men and women were "maternal" and feminine in personality and sexually passive. They were cooperative, unaggressive, and nurturant. The Mundugumor women and men were violent and aggressive and disparaged children. The Tchambuli women were dominant, managing partners, and the men were emotionally dependent.[28]

Margaret Mead's ambiguous feminism can be understood by her sense of herself as "not like other people." Her mother was a social scientist, and she was brought up in an intellectual atmosphere in which women were assumed to have the same intelligence and talents as men. She also saw her mother combining a life of scholarship with marriage and children and accepted this arrangement as normal. Friedan believed that Mead recognized "three classes of people: men, women whose lot it was to stay at home and bandage children's knees—and a very select company including Mead herself, to whom the rest of women do not apply."[29]

Marvin Harris, Mead's chairman at Columbia University, said that her intellectual position was clear: that wives, with very rare exceptions, should defer to husbands' careers. She did not ever argue for hiring more women in the department, although they were underrepresented. Her champion, Wilton Dillon, said that she clashed with feminists because of her strong notion of what a *lady* was. She greatly valued a traditional background, combined with doing caring things.

Once she turned down a presidency of a large university because she did not think the time was right for her to take it. She said that "women make poor administrators." However, she resented the fact that Columbia University kept her as an adjunct professor for so many years, and after she became famous, she declined a regular appointment when they offered it to her.[30]

Moreover, Mead claimed that classes of women were more exhilarating to teach than classes of men. She had intense, romantic, and sexual relationships with men and women. Ruth Benedict, her mentor and cherished friend, was her lover. A friend described Mead as spiritually homosexual, psychologically bisexual, and physically heterosexual.[31]

Mead wrote thirty-nine books (two edited and fifteen done with others), 1,397 other publications, produced forty-three records, tapes, and videotapes, and received twenty-eight honorary degrees and forty awards. She had a professional and romantic relationship with two men who became her husbands, Leo Fortune and Gregory Bateson. Her first husband, Luther Cressman, was a theology student who later switched into sociology.

Mead's daughter Catherine Bateson was born December 8, 1939. She describes her mother as deeply committed to motherhood but arranging all her physical care to be done by a nanny. Mead set up extended households for her daughter to live in while she spent sometimes years away from home. Mead's most painful divorce was that from Gregory Bateson, who left her. She had left her other husbands. After their divorce, Bateson and Mead remained friends and occasionally worked together. Bateson explained the breakup, "It was almost a principle of pure energy. I couldn't keep up, and she couldn't stop. She was like a tugboat. She could sit down and write three thousand words by eleven o'clock in the morning, and spend the rest of the day working at the museum."[32]

After World War II, Mead urged that men should participate more in the rearing of children, that the drudgery of household chores could be eliminated by technology, and that neighborhood collective units should help in rearing children. Social institutions had to change to accommodate women's aspirations.[33]

Mead's career reminds us of the impact of female scholars in developing feminist insights in a period when feminism as a national movement was unpopular. While it is beyond the scope of this chapter to discuss the issue in depth, it is important to note that much feminist ferment went into the social sciences, especially anthropology and sociology, in the period of the 1920s through the 1950s. New concepts of cultural diversity, relativism, and socialization were developed largely by women. These concepts would have relevance for new ways of thinking about traditional sexual roles.

As we have seen, even in a highly hostile climate for feminism, feminist voices were present, as well as empowering models of highly successful women. Eleanor Roosevelt, Alice Paul, Simone de Beauvoir, Dorothy Thompson, Pearl Buck, Eve Merriam, and Margaret Mead believed that women should be allowed to express all their talents in the public sphere and at the same time to enjoy marriage and motherhood. They believed that women's covert power within the family was inadequate. Simone de Beauvoir, alone of the feminists noted here, believed that marriage and motherhood trapped women in inauthentic existences. With the rebirth of feminism of the 1960s, most feminists followed the lead of achieving women like Roosevelt, Buck, Merriam, Thompson, and Mead, who combined marriage, motherhood, and personal achievement; only a minority responded to de Beauvoir's radical positions and Alice Paul's militancy.

12

MISS AMERICA GOOD-BYE
The Modern Feminist Movement

I predicted, starting our movement six years ago, that if society didn't restruc-
ture to permit women who have babies to move out of housewife drudgery into
the mainstream, the most spirited women would begin to repudiate marriage,
motherhood, children, even their own sexuality. Female chauvinism is a reac-
tion to the very denigration of women that our movement seeks to change.

Betty Friedan, *It Changed My Life*,
"Betty Friedan's Notebook," 1971–73

Goodbye, goodbye forever, counterfeit Left, counterfeit, male-dominated
cracked-glass-mirror reflection of the Amerikan nightmare. Women are the real
Left. We are rising powerful in our unclean bodies; bright glowing mad in our
inferior brains; wild hair flying, wild eyes staring, wild voices keening; un-
daunted by blood we who hemmorhage every twenty-eight days; laughing at
our own beauty we who have lost our sense of humor; mourning for all each
precious one of us might have been in this one living time-place had she not been
born a woman; stuffing fingers into our mouths to stop the screams of fear and
hate and pity for men we have loved and love still; tears in our eyes and
bitterness in our mouths for children we couldn't have, or couldn't not have, or
didn't want, or didn't want yet, or wanted and had in this place and this
time of horror. We are rising with a fury older and potentially greater than
any force in history, and this time we will be free or no one will survive.
Power to all the people or to none. *All the way down, this time.*

Robin Morgan, 1970

On September 7, 1968, Miss America contestants paraded in swimsuits
down the runway in Atlantic City. Outside, a group of feminists from New
York, New Jersey, Washington, D.C., and Florida protested the pageant's

objectification of women's bodies. They crowned a live sheep, auctioned off an effigy of "Miss America," and threw bras, girdles, curlers, and other beauty aids into a "freedom trashcan." As a tearful eighteen-year-old Judith Ann Ford, Miss Illinois, was crowned Miss America inside the hall, shouts rang out, "Down with Miss America!" "Freedom!" At that moment, a large white bedsheet floated down from the balcony bearing the inscription "Women's Liberation."[1] This media event was a culmination of years of feminist stirrings. The Miss America protest, a sit-in at the *Ladies Home Journal*, a hexing of the New York Stock Exchange by WITCH (Women's International Terrorist Coven from Hell) promoted a radical image of the feminist movement of the 1960s.

Radicalism within the feminist movement was largely a reaction to the extreme emphasis on women's domestic role in the 1950s, objectification of women as sex objects in the media, and blatant sexism in reform and radical movements of the sixties. The modern feminist movement continued to battle for political and legal power, but in a significant departure from the nineteenth-century movement, leaders demanded changes within the domestic sphere. Dissatisfied with wielding their power solely through their sexuality and motherhood, feminists sought overt power.

The vast majority of feminists of the period were profamily, liberal feminists, endorsing democratic principles and pushing for political, legal, economic, and social freedom for women. Historically, when American feminists have supported marriage and motherhood, they have eventually been successful. When they have challenged or condemned marriage and motherhood, they have failed to achieve their objectives and invited fierce resistance. This fact helps to explain the greater appeal of liberal feminism as opposed to radical feminism in the United States. Both the radical and reformist elements within the contemporary feminist movement have been in a dialectical tension, influencing one another and appealing to different constituencies.

Autonomy and women's self-esteem were at the heart of the resurgence of the feminist movement in the 1960s. Women's increasing dominance at home helped shape the theory, goals, strategies, and accomplishments of the movement. As we have seen, the family was the vehicle of women's power and entrapment. For many women, especially white middle-class women, covert power without public power led to a loss of self-esteem and to physical and economic vulnerability. The extreme emphasis on domesticity of the 1950s produced a backlash against it in the 1960s and generated a profound ambivalence among feminists over how to combine achievement, marriage, and motherhood. Liberal feminists wanted to reconstruct the family by empowering women as achievers and men as fathers. They wanted to improve women's status within marriage, and they argued for liberated motherhood. Radical feminists attacked marriage as an oppressive institution. To understand the contemporary feminist movement's stance toward the family, one must appreciate the differences in these two branches: the older reformist wing and the younger, radical women's liberationists. Both groups, however, sought to claim their power in the home and public sphere. Covert power was no longer sufficient.

The Social and Political Context

In the 1960s American women were better educated than ever before and remained single longer. In the 1950s young women had married at an earlier age. Almost three times as many women were enrolled in colleges in 1972 as in 1960 (3.5 million versus 1.2 million). In those twelve years the percentage of young women attending college more than doubled.[2]

After World War II, structural changes in the U.S. economy meant a larger number of American women were employed outside the home than ever before. Employment opportunities expanded most rapidly in clerical, sales, and service occupations, areas traditionally with a large number of women.[3] Since the pool of unmarried women was reduced in the 1950s, the tight postwar labor market encouraged a broader acceptance of married women in the labor force. From 1948 to 1960, the number of working mothers with school-age children increased 116 percent, while working mothers with preschool children increased 108 percent. By 1974, 37 percent of mothers with children under six were in the labor force.[4] Middle-income women entered the labor force faster than any other group in the population. But in 1966 women actually received a lower income relative to men than they did in 1939.[5]

Since women faced the problem of combining work and family within a society dominated by traditional assumptions about both, most middle-class women perceived more security in marriage than in the labor force. But by the early 1960s, one worker in three was a woman. In 1962 approximately three out of five women workers were married. In 1960 the average woman married at twenty and could expect to live to seventy-three. If she had her last child at thirty, by the age of thirty-five, she faced over half of her life ahead free of small children in the house.[6]

Through the Window of Popular Culture:
Homemakers, Genies, Witches, and Sex Symbols

Although large numbers of married women were working, popular magazines in the 1960s still portrayed women as happy homemakers. The typical heroine in women's magazines like the *Ladies Home Journal, Good Housekeeping,* and *McCall's* was a married woman with one or more children, and though she had been to college, her main occupation was housekeeping. Her goals were love oriented. In 1957 the magazine heroine's major problem was romantic; in 1967 she had a psychological problem. A married working woman, especially a career woman, was viewed as unwomanly and threatening.[7]

Fashion magazines continued to present an updated, sexier version of the feminine mystique, acknowledging that more women were employed. Television in the 1960s continued to perpetuate the same themes of happy domesticity but were becoming more sexually explicit. In contrast, "That Girl," with Marlo Thomas, and "The Mary Tyler Moore Show" depicted single career women who were in no hurry to get married.

The Barbie doll, one image of "true" womanhood in the 1960s, was glamorous and vacuous. Television shows like "Bewitched" (1964), starring Elizabeth Montgomery, and "I Dream of Jeannie," with Barbara Eden, reinforced the image of women as sexy playmates and adoring partners. Both female characters possessed superior, magical powers, an acknowledgment of women's increasing dominance at home. But these television heroines enlisted their supernatural powers in the service of their men. Helen Gurley Brown's *Sex and the Single Girl* (1962) advised women on how to enjoy love affairs without guilt. As editor of *Cosmopolitan,* Brown helped lend glamour to the sexual revolution.[8]

Films of the 1960s portrayed women variously, as sex objects, as viragos in *Who's Afraid of Virginia Woolf?* and as victims in *Alfie.* In most films of the 1960s, women played subordinate roles, were sexual playmates, or were simply absent. *Butch Cassidy and the Sundance Kid, Lawrence of Arabia,* and *Midnight Cowboy* focus on heroic males and male bonding. No strong career women starred in the movies of the 1960s. At the height of the sexual revolution, precipitated in part by the birth control pill, films like *I Am Curious Yellow, Blow-up,* and *Darling* reflected a new obsession with sexuality and promiscuity. Nudity became commonplace in films.

On Broadway in the early 1960s, *Camelot* and *The Man of La Mancha* captured the contemporary spirit of idealism in American society of the early

1960s. King Arthur and Don Quixote were symbols of the "impossible dream" of eliminating poverty, war, racism, and disease. When the young, dashing John F. Kennedy was elected president in 1960, a mood of optimism and social change captured the imaginations of many Americans. Kennedy turned Americans' gaze toward space and vowed to put a person on the moon before the end of the decade; he also inspired hope in people that they could make a difference and even "change the world."

The media exerted a powerful effect on the entire era of the sixties, particularly by televising the war in Vietnam and the somewhat less bloody but no less dramatic battle for civil rights in the South. Families saw sons killed on the six o'clock news. The whole world was watching when Bull Connor, the commissioner of police in Birmingham, turned the fire hoses on civil rights demonstrators and police dogs attacked women and children. The civil rights movement, which gathered momentum in the 1950s, grew in intensity, especially in the wake of the Supreme Court decision in *Brown v. Board of Education* in 1954. National guardsmen protected black school children as they integrated southern schools. Thousands marched, engaged in sit-ins, and demanded justice. Even before the civil rights movement climaxed in the march on Washington in 1963, another quiet revolution began.

The Resurgence of Feminism

The feminist movement of the 1960s drew on many sources, including the growing female anger over the inferior status of wage-earning women.[9] Women began to realize that regardless of their amount of power at home, they were still disadvantaged as workers in the public sphere. The feminist movement was also profoundly shaped by the civil rights movement, the sexual revolution, liberation movements abroad, the short-term economic boom generated by the war in Vietnam, and the entrance of large numbers of women into the labor force. Jo Freeman, a participant in and historian of the recent movement, points out that the emergence of the feminist movement in the 1960s arose within the context of preexisting communications networks, possessed a receptive network for the new ideas, and responded to the contradictions within women's lives. These contradictions stemmed from women's greater access to education and their work experience, and the contrasting persistence of discrimination in the public sphere.

As we have seen previously, from the 1920s to the 1960s, feminism as a collective struggle had reached a low point. Even when in 1922 and 1923 the

Supreme Court invalidated two of the major legislative gains, the minimum wage for women and abolition of child labor, women were not effectively mobilized. The surviving feminist organization, the National Woman's Party, remained small and elitist.[10]

From 1920 to 1960 only three women were elected to the Senate and only forty-four to the House of Representatives. Two women were appointed to cabinet positions during that forty-year period. By 1960 women constituted only 4 percent of the lawyers and judges, 6 percent of the doctors, and 1 percent of the architects.

Initially, the impetus for national action stemmed from the dramatic changes in women's lives and the persistence of discrimination against them. At the urging of Esther Peterson, in 1961 President Kennedy appointed the President's Commission on the Status of Women. As bridge figures from the 1950s to the 1960s, Margaret Mead and Eleanor Roosevelt appropriately served on the commission. Both were dedicated to the needs of families and women's equality. Mead writes in the commission's report *American Women*:

> Widening the choices for women beyond their doorstep does not imply neglect of their education for responsibilities in the home. Modern family life is demanding and most of the time and attention given to it comes from women. At various stages girls and women of all economic backgrounds should receive education in respect to physical and mental health, child care and development, and human relations within the family.[11]

Mead presents the basic assumptions of the commission; the first assumption is that anything peculiarly feminine is a handicap in the modern world. The second assumption is "that both males and females attain full biological humanity only through marriage and the presence of children in the home, whether they are born to a couple or are adopted by them." The third premise is that the right to work at a paid job is an intrinsic condition of human dignity.[12]

In the commission's report, Mead points out that more than half of all women between forty-five to fifty-four were in paid employment. Eight out of ten women were employed at some time during their lives. Yet women were earning only one in three B.A.'s and M.A.'s, and one in ten Ph.D.'s. Of the 68 million women fourteen years and over in the United States, 44 million were currently married and keeping house. Women's employment greatly enhanced the family's social status. The median family income of 46.3 million families was $5,737 in 1961; the 12 million dual-wage families had a median income of $8,154. The median income for 19 million women working full-time was $2,574 in 1961, which represented only 60 percent of the median wage for males.[13]

The commission recommended continuing education for women; child-care services; equality of opportunity in hiring, training, and promotion; equal pay; and equal benefits for widows. In addition, the members of the commission called for paid maternity leave and, in order to establish the principle of sexual equality in constitutional doctrine, asked for immediate ruling by the Supreme Court on the validity under the Fifth and Fifteenth amendments to the Constitution of laws and official practices discriminating against women. Notably, they did not push for the Equal Rights Amendment. Alice Paul and other members of the NWP feared that the commission would sidetrack the adoption of the ERA. While the majority of the commission's members opposed the ERA, their work ultimately helped trigger the resurgence of the feminist movement which endorsed the amendment.

The members of the commission recommended equal jury service in all states and urged women to seek elective and appointive offices at all levels of the government. Women were underrepresented in governmental positions. Only 2 out of 100 senators were female in the early 1960s, and only 11 women out of 435 representatives. Only two women had held cabinet rank in the government; six had served as ambassadors or ministers, none on the Supreme Court or Court of Appeals. One woman served as a judge on the U.S. Customs Court, and one on the U.S. Tax Court. Of the 7,700 seats in state legislatures, only 234 were held by women. Only 3.5 percent of the lawyers in the country were women.[14]

Many of the President's Commission's recommendations directly concerned the welfare of the family. Members of the commission called for adequate day care because of the desperate need of women and children for such services. Licensed day-care facilities were available for only 185,000 children, while three million mothers of children under six were working outside the home. Among families with children under six, 117,000 existed with only the father in the home, and nearly half a million had only the mother. A survey in 1958 revealed that 400,000 children under twelve had mothers who were employed full-time, with no provisions for their children's supervision.[15]

The commission's report, *American Women*, provided extensive documentation on discriminatory practices against women in government, education, and employment along with the recommendation that a cabinet officer be responsible for implementation of their program. Largely because the commission members took a conservative stance regarding the traditional family, their impact on national policy was dramatic. Their contributions have been underestimated by many commentators. The reformists had more impact on changing the law, while radical feminists had tremendous influence in changing national perceptions and many women's consciousness about themselves.

Stimulated by the report, governors appointed state commissions which met in 1966 for their Third Annual Conference of Commissions on the Status of Women. The revolutionary spark occurred when Martha Griffiths insisted that the Equal Employment Opportunity Commission, in charge of implementing the Civil Rights Act of 1964, refused to take seriously the problem of sexual discrimination. In the House of Representatives Griffiths denounced the agency for inaction a few days before the conference met.

A resolution regarding the EEOC met opposition among the conference participants, and before the end of the day twenty-eight women paid five dollars each to join the National Organization for Women (NOW), led by Betty Friedan. Catherine East of the Women's Bureau of the Labor Department cajoled Friedan into starting NOW. The formation of NOW marked the birth of the new feminist movement. Friedan had been a consultant for the commission, and her views were compatible with their reformist, profamily stance. In October 300 women and men gathered for an organizational meeting.[16] NOW officially came into existence on October 29, 1966. Thirty members were present at its birth in Washington, D.C., including Muriel Fox, Inka O'Hanrahan, Alice Rossi, Carl Degler, Marguerite Rawalt, Ollie Buller-Moore, Phineas Indutz, Gene Boyer, Catherine Conroy, Mary Eastwood, Dick Graham, and Caroline Davies.[17]

The NOW members wrote in their founding statement of purpose:

> It is no longer either necessary or possible for women to devote the greater part of their lives to child-rearing; yet childbearing and rearing which continues to be a most important part of most women's lives—still is used to justify barring women from equal professional and economic participation and advance. . . . We believe that a true partnership between the sexes demands a different concept of marriage, an equitable sharing of the responsibilities of home and children and of the economic burdens of their support.[18]

NOW's platform typifies the platform of liberal feminism, calling for the development of women as full human beings. It was strongly profamily. The members of NOW called for the passage of the Equal Rights Amendment, enforcement of antidiscrimination legislation by EEOC, safe and legal abortion, maternity leaves, welfare reform, job training for women, and equal credit practices for women.

Numerous women's organizations were founded in the 1970s. Early in 1973 approximately 75,000 people belonged to women's rights organizations, including NOW. The Women's Equality Action League (WEAL), a self-defined conservative group on the abortion issue, concentrated on other legal and economic problems of women. Dr. Elizabeth Boyer, an Ohio lawyer, was instrumental in founding it. On January 31, 1970, WEAL brought a class-action complaint against all colleges and universities holding federal contracts with the Department of Labor's Office of Contract Compliance. WEAL subsequently filed complaints against over 300 institutions.[19] The National Women's Political Caucus (NWPC) grew out of a meeting of 324 women on July 10–11, 1971, led by Bella Abzug, Gloria Steinem, Betty Friedan, and Shirley Chisholm. The NWPC, like WEAL, focuses on governmental and political action. Federally Employed Women was also established as an advocacy group for women in the government.[20]

Women's rights advocates of the 1970s were generally white, educated, middle-class women, usually in their forties and fifties, and likely to have professional training or work experience. They used traditional pressure-group tactics to achieve changes in laws and public policy to secure equal rights for women.[21] Few of these women sought a radical alteration of domestic roles, but their goals relating to abortion and child care marked a break with the former women's rights movement. Previously, the movement avoided confronting such controversial issues.

NOW hired its first poorly paid staff member, who worked for the organization out of her home. Three national offices were added in 1973, with between twelve and fifteen paid staff members in all. A legislative office operated in Washington, D.C., a public information office in New York, and an administrative office in Chicago. NOW staged a massive demonstration in August 1970 to commemorate the fiftieth anniversary of the Nineteenth Amendment. The three central demands were abortion on demand, twenty-four-hour child-care centers, and equal opportunity in employment and education. By 1980 NOW had 120,000 members, with 800 local chapters.[22]

Women's Liberation Branch

Differing greatly from the liberal feminist branch represented by NOW, the other major branch of the feminist movement consisted of younger, less highly educated women's liberationists. Both the older and younger groups of women became feminists mainly because their experiences led them to reject traditionalism and demand equal opportunity. Women born between 1946 and 1954 were in the first group of American women who were exposed to an alternative model of womanhood. While a college education enhanced a woman's status, these baby boom daughters realized that their educated mothers were frustrated with domesticity.[23] They believed in the American value of individualism and the American dream of mobility and freedom and rebelled when they realized that their gender prevented them from achieving their goals. Young people who had grown up under the shadow of the atomic bomb were impatient for social change; many believed passionately in social justice and their ability to change the world. This confidence was bolstered by the largeness of the baby boom cohort in college in the 1960s.

In contrast to the older, liberal feminist groups, which adopted a bureaucratic organizational model, the younger group embraced a collectivist model. Instead of hierarchical offices, a division of labor, and individualist achievement norms, the women's liberationists favored few rules, shared decision making, a minimal division of labor, and decentralization.[24]

The radical women's liberation movement grew out of women's reaction to sexism within the civil rights movement. In the 1960s most of the southern white women who participated in the early years of the civil rights movement came to it by way of the church. They perceived a glaring contradiction between Christian doctrine and racism in the South. For example, the Methodist Student Movement furnished many volunteers for the civil rights movement and published a radical magazine, *motive*.

Even before the advent of the feminist movement of the 1960s, the first women to link racial and sexual oppression were southern African-American and certain white women, from Sojourner Truth and the Grimké sisters in the nineteenth century to the reformers of the twentieth century. A number of southern women became active in the Women's Committee on Interracial Cooperation, and in the 1940s Virginia Durr in Alabama, Anne Braden in Louisville, Kentucky, and Lillian Smith and Paula Snelling in Georgia pioneered in linking sexual and racial repression in the South.[25]

A younger group of African-American and white women began to challenge sexism within the civil rights movement. White women, including Sandra "Casey" Cason, Dorothy Dawson, Jane Stembridge and Mary King, became prominent in the Student Non-Violent Coordinating Committee (SNCC). Cason married Tom Hayden, and Dorothy Dawson married Robb Burlage, a founder along with Hayden of Students for a Democratic Society

(SDS). The presence of white women in the organization eventually created tensions because of the incidence of sexual relationships between African-American men and white women. Because of sexism in SNCC, young African-American women, including Ruby Doris Smith Robinson, Donna Richards, and Diane Nash, held a half-serious, half-joking sit-in in 1964 in the SNCC office; they protested being relegated to typing and clerical work.[26]

Casey Hayden and Mary King, in collaboration with Mary Varela, wrote a position paper protesting sexism in SNCC in 1965. In the fall they sent a memo to a number of women in the peace and freedom movement. One month later, women who had read the memo staged an angry walkout from a national SDS conference in Champagne-Urbana, Illinois. Only a lone man from SNCC supported their action.[27]

Sexism in SDS also prompted reaction by women within the organization. Women held few leadership positions in SDS. Female membership on the executive committee ranged from 14 percent in 1961, 23 percent in 1962, 26 percent in 1963, down to 6 percent in 1964. No woman held a major national office until 1966, when Helen Garvey was named assistant national secretary, and 1968, when Jane Adams became the national secretary. In December 1965, older ERAP (Economic Research and Action Projects) women led a workshop.

Eastern male intellectuals dominated SDS and refused to take women's comments seriously. When a representative of the Women's Liberation workshop finished reading a statement at the 1967 convention, a man jumped up and proposed to separate analysis and resolution for purposes of debate and voting. When the chair ruled that the analysis was not subject to debate or a vote, the meeting erupted.[28]

At a similar meeting at the National Conference for New Politics in August 1967, Jo Freeman and Shulamith Firestone broke away from the women's caucus on the issue of the Vietnam War and drew up a resolution on women. Ironically, the group of men who were so committed to equality did not include women, and relegated them to domestic chores. A male delegate, William Pepper, pushed the women aside, patted Firestone on the head, and said, "Move on little girl; we have more important issues to talk about here than women's liberation." A week later, the women met in Chicago and drafted "To the Women on the Left."

With the assassinations of John F. Kennedy, Malcolm X, Martin Luther King, and Robert Kennedy, the idealism of the early 1960s was shattered. The student movement moved toward violence with the creation of the Weathermen; Black Power split the civil rights movement, and alienated many whites from the movement. In response to the divisiveness in the civil rights movement, the SDS focused its energies on opposition to the war in Vietnam. The motivation for a separate women's liberation movement grew, strengthened by incidents such as the following. In January 1969 Marilyn Salzman Webb spoke to an antiwar rally; members of the audience shouted, "Take her off the stage and fuck her."[29]

The radical wing of the women's liberation movement began to coalesce when over 200 women from thirty-seven states and Canada met in November 1968 in Chicago for the first women's liberation conference. Splits within the movement began to appear between the radical feminists and the Marxist feminists.[30] Smaller groups formed like the Redstockings of New York, including Ellen Willis and Shulamith Firestone. The Redstockings disrupted a public abortion hearing in New York and held their own proceedings.

Ti-Grace Atkinson, the president of the New York NOW chapter, left that liberal organization and helped to found the Feminists (October 17 movement), a radical feminist group. On September 23, 1969, the Feminists made clear their denunciation of marriage by picketing and distributing leaflets at the New York City Municipal Building Marriage License Bureau. Only a third of their members could be in formal or informal marital relationships.[31]

Ti-Grace Atkinson differentiates between a biologically determinist theory of sex class and one that recognizes the political and cultural determinants of biology. She contends that women's childbearing functions are not intrinsically oppressive, but to the extent that the political and cultural sex/gender systems utilize them to limit women to a specific sphere, reproductive functions oppress women. Her rhetoric regarding marriage was highly inflammatory. She called marriage "slavery," "unpaid labor," "legalized rape," and she denounced heterosexuality.[32] Because the Feminists passed numerous rules and criticized her for allowing the media to define her as the leader of their group, Atkinson left the group. The Feminists were the most antimale group in the movement. After Atkinson left, the Feminists voted to exclude all married women from membership. They created a ritual involving wine and marijuana as sacraments, chanted "Momma," and tore apart a papier-mâché man. Their interest in female mysticism, matriarchy, and female communities was based upon an essentialist view of women and prefigured cultural feminism.[33]

The major women's liberation groups met on November 21–23, 1969, in New York. Attending were some members of NOW, Boston Female Liberation, New Yorkers for Abortion Repeal, Redstockings, Stanton-Anthony Brigade, WITCH Resurrectus, Women's Liberation Club—Bronx High School of Science, Women Lawyers—Boston, and the Daughters of Bilitis. On the first evening of the conference, a young woman from Boston Female Liberation group mounted the platform. She took out a pair of scissors and, in a symbolic act, proceeded to cut her long flowing hair off to a close crop in protest of men's objectification of women as sexual objects.[34]

The radical feminist groups like Redstockings, The Feminists, New York Radical Feminists, and Cell 16 were deeply divided over critical questions. Fault lines developed over the politico-feminist split, lesbianism, whether to allow married members, who would speak, resentment over "media" stars, and other tactical and theoretical issues. Beverly Jones and Judith Brown, who were longtime workers in CORE (Congress of Racial Equality) and the Gainesville SDS, published a paper in June 1968 entitled, "To a Female Liberation Movement." The Florida paper was a frontal attack on the radical leftist politico position, and the earliest articulation of radical feminism. After Jones moved to Pennsylvania, Brown and Carol Giardina co-founded the first women's liberation group in the South, in Gainesville.[35]

Even the most radical feminists were in favor of liberated motherhood. In one of the workshops, "Early Childhood: Care and Education," women advocated more and better child-care facilities, equal partnership of men and women in marriage, and dealing realistically with the needs of children. In another workshop they discussed family structure and then examined "how women are forced into marriage, how this institution constitutes legal slavery, and the myth that marriage and family structure benefit women." They also discussed the economic function of the family units and how it helps maintain male supremacy.[36]

Differences in theory and strategy emerged during the congress, leading to the formation of new women's liberation groups. Reacting against the politico line of the Redstockings and the Feminists' rigidity of theory and structure, Anne Koedt and Shulamith Firestone formed New York Radical Feminists shortly after the congress.[37]

Although the women's liberation groups varied enormously concerning theory, strategy, and organization, radical and moderate feminists perceived the institution of marriage as it presently exists as legalizing women's subservient role. Rhetoric differed because moderate feminists described marriage as an unequal partnership and wished to restructure it, while radicals called it oppressive and wanted to abandon it.[38]

The women's liberation groups focused on the technique of consciousness-raising. By sharing experiences, women learned that "the personal is political." Problems which seemed unique to an individual came to be understood as socially rooted. They wanted to liberate themselves from ways of thinking which distorted and short-circuited their growth, keeping them subordinate to men.

Radical feminists believe that men dominate women in every area of life. Therefore, they assume that all relations between men and women are institutionalized power relations. Personal institutions like childrearing housework, love, sexual intercourse, and marriage reinforce male power; rape and prostitution are symptomatic of men's desire to dominate women. Many radical feminists tend to adopt a biologically determinist view and tend to disregard historical and cultural contexts. Therefore, they tend to emphasize female superiority, and yet simultaneously they overrate men's power. Radical feminists want women to regain control over their own bodies and eventually to build a female culture built on values of wholeness, trust, nurturance, sensuality, joy, and wildness.

At least four major varieties of feminism emerged in the 1960s: liberal feminism, radical feminism, socialist feminism, and Marxist feminism, each espousing different views of the traditional family. The feminist movement from 1963 to 1967 began with an egalitarian focus in an integrationist framework. Gloria Steinem, Betty Friedan, Caroline Bird, Helen Gurley Brown, and the members of NOW represented the liberal feminist paradigm. Elizabeth Janeway, Alice Rossi, Carolyn Heilbrun, and Cynthia Ozick believed in an androgynous paradigm. After 1967 a segment of the movement turned toward female militancy and female separatism. Their motto was "Sisterhood is powerful." Kate Millett, Germaine Greer, Shulamith Firestone, Ti-Grace Atkinson, Betsy Warrior, Dana Densmore, Abby Aldrich Rockefeller of Cell 16 of Boston, Mary Daly, and others offered a radical feminist paradigm.[39]

Radical Lesbianism

In 1970 lesbians staged the Lavender Menace Action, claiming the right to be public lesbians. Members of NOW felt that widespread homophobia within the country might cause many women to be alienated from the organization if lesbians were prominent. Finally, the majority of the members agreed that a movement for the liberation of all women would be hypocritical if it rejected women because of their sexual preference. Ultimately, because of the abortion issue and the acceptance of lesbianism within NOW, fragmentation occurred within the feminist movement. Only the campaign for the ERA gave cohesiveness to the national movement. Whereas 20,000 had marched in New York in 1970 on the anniversary of the vote, in 1972 only 5,100 marched. Radical lesbians and other radical feminists took over the march and tended to alienate suburban housewives, working women, welfare mothers, churchwomen, Junior Leaguers, and high school girls.[40]

Lesbianism, like the issue of free love in the nineteenth century, was a divisive issue within the feminist movement. The gay-straight split helped to fragment the feminist movement from 1970 to 1972. The conflict was especially bitter in Washington, D.C., where the lesbian-feminist group The Furies was formed. Betty Friedan reportedly led a campaign in 1970 to prevent lesbians from being elected or reelected to office in the New York chapter of NOW.[41] In the 1980s, when the feminist movement became embattled and slipped into the doldrums, lesbian feminists frequently remained the most active and committed, devoting themselves to assisting battered women, caring for rape victims, and fighting pornography.

Adrienne Rich and Mary Daly are major proponents of lesbian feminism. In much of her poetry and in her book *Of Woman Born: Motherhood as Experience and Institution,* Rich advocates the lesbian alternative as part of a continuum of female solidarity. She shares a belief in female superiority with the early feminists and advocates the need for a separate woman's culture and community in order to flourish within a patriarchal culture.

Mary Daly, a brilliant feminist theologian, also advocates lesbian separatism as the only means for female wholeness. In *Gyn/Ecology* Daly indicts patriarchal religions and patriarchal secular ideologies. She documents the connection between "dismemberment of the Goddess" in Christian doctrine and the ecological crisis and rape of the earth by patriarchy. She demonstrates a pattern of misogyny in Chinese footbinding, African genital mutilation, witch burnings, and American gynecology. Daly urges women to "spook, spark, and spin." Through the inner journey of achieving consciousness and the energy which comes from being woman-identified, Daly believes women can become truly creative, life-affirming people. Her focus is on personal transformation, rather than a political or economic revolution.

Rich and Daly emphasize the importance of personal transformation and do not directly address economic exploitation. Their work underscores a chief question of the feminist movement. Is the purpose of feminism to produce free and unfettered individuals, or to create a new form of community? Where is the emphasis to be placed? Is personal transformation or sociopolitical struggle the primary challenge?[42] Both Daly and Rich repudiate the patriarchal family and patriarchal religion as the most powerful institutions for maintaining women's subordination within the family.

Feminist Theology

A discussion of feminist theology is beyond the scope of this chapter, but because theology has been so powerful a rationale for women's domestic and public subordination, it is relevant to mention that in addition to the flourishing of a whole field of scholarship in feminist theology in the 1970s, organizations were also founded to challenge patriarchal religion and women's subordinate status within the churches. Stemming from feminist interpretations of the patriarchal nature of Christianity, the National Coalition of American Nuns was formed in July 1969. Numerous women's groups formed in the Protestant denominations to enhance women's power in the church, agitate for ordination, and develop a feminist theology.[43] The major objections to patriarchal religion were that God is viewed as male, that women's subordination to men is divinely ordained, that because of Eve, women by nature are evil or are "pure" like Mary. Many feminists also object strenuously to the view of women which Paul presents. The vigorous attempts within each denomination to advance the status of women distinguishes the contemporary movement from the first wave of feminism. Earlier, when Elizabeth Cady Stanton raised the same objections in her *Woman's Bible*, Susan B. Anthony was one of the very few feminists who was sympathetic. In contrast, the contemporary feminist movement has seen women's spirituality as key to women's claiming their own power.

Socialist Feminists

Another group within the radical branch of the feminist movement of the 1960s and 1970s was the Socialist Feminists. Drawing from the socialist tradition, some contemporary feminists emphasize the necessity of women's economic independence, control over the means of production, elimination of greed and competititon, and the creation of a caring community. Many of the socialist feminists favor developing communal alternatives to the nuclear family.[44]

Socialist feminists attempt to analyze abortion, sexuality, the bearing and rearing of children, and housework in political and economic terms. Moreover, they adopt a historical rather than universalistic and biologically determinis-tic manner. Juliet Mitchell, Jane Flax, Gayle Rubin, Nancy Chodorow, and Dorothy Dinnerstein are prominent socialist feminists. They claim that our inner lives, bodies, and behavior are structured by gender. This socialization process occurs when we are children and is reinforced throughout women's lives.

Socialist feminism connects masculine and feminine psychology with the sexual division of labor. Women are constituted essentially by their social relations. Socialist feminists seek the full actualization of women's human potential through free productive labor, free sexual expression, and bearing and rearing children freely.[45] Through a transformation of the economic foundation of society, work, sexuality, parenting, and childbearing must all be transformed.

Marxist Feminists

In contrast to Socialist Feminists, Marxist Feminists believe in the primacy of class struggle as the necessary precondition for the liberation of women and believe that Marxism can be revised to take feminism into account. Socialist Feminists share much of the same ideology but are much more critical of the sexist nature of Communist societies and the inadequacies of Marxist theory to explain women's condition. Marxist Feminists basically accept the Marx-Engels critique of society, which locates the family as the primary source of oppression and the first institution of private property and division of labor. Angela Davis, a charismatic African-American activist and philosopher, espouses Communism and feminism and believes in the necessity for radical revolution.

Radical feminists argue that the patriarchy (male-defined social institu-tions and value structure) is responsible for women's oppression, although most of them are also critical of capitalism. They oppose by-laws, elected officers, and central headquarters.[46]

Different feminist groups define the nuclear family as oppressive in various ways. Some feminists view the nuclear family as an economic institution, a cornerstone of capitalist ideology which shapes the values of competition, discipline, and possessiveness, as an institution which exploits women's unpaid labor and socializes children into their gender roles. Other feminists argue that the nuclear family discriminates against lesbians. Many feminists complain that it is emotionally and sexually repressive to men, women, and children.[47] Since challenges to marriage and motherhood were extremely threatening to most Americans, the liberal feminists gained a much larger following. They argued for egalitarian marriages, shared housework and parenting, and tolerance for family forms other than the traditional model.

Because of the radically antimale stance of a minority of radical feminists and antifamily rhetoric, many American women could not identify with the women's liberation movement. They viewed women's liberation as ultimately antifemale. Only about 15,000 women belonged to the most radical groups, but their influence was far greater than their numbers because of media attention. A Harris poll conducted in 1975, at the peak of the feminist movement, revealed that 63 percent of the women interviewed favored most changes designed to improve the status of women but quickly insisted that they were not "women libbers."[48] Some commentators argue that the radicals hurt the feminist movement and alienated many women with their strident antimale rhetoric, lesbianism, and militant tactics. However, if the radicals had not existed, the liberal feminists would have been viewed as the radicals, and the movement would never have gained such extensive media coverage. In contrast to the militants, the liberal feminists' demands seemed extremely reasonable.

Feminist Theory

Ideology is essential in any social movement as a means of explaining reality to potential participants. Women's experiences in the family of empowerment and entrapment during the 1950s significantly helped shaped the nature of the movement's theory. As we have seen, Betty Friedan's *The Feminine Mystique* provided the justification for liberal feminism; other more radical thinkers challenged the basic structure of the society. They condemned marriage as oppressive to women. Kate Millett argues in *Sexual Politics* that the family is patriarchy's chief institution. According to Millett, the major contribution of the family in patriarchy is the socialization of the children into patriarchal attitudes. In addition, the concept of romantic love affords a means of emotional manipulation of women. She calls for a sexual revolution that will eliminate all sexual inhibitions, abolish sex roles, guarantee complete independence of women, provide collective professionalization of child care, and abolish marriage.[49] Millett agrees with Simone de Beauvoir when she remarks: "In my opinion, as long as the family and the myth of the family and the myth of maternity and the maternal instinct are not destroyed, women will still be oppressed."[50]

Germaine Greer, another major spokeswoman for the recent feminist movement, indicts sexism in *The Female Eunuch*. According to Greer, women are figuratively castrated by the patriarchal system, unable to express themselves freely sexually or intellectually. She argues that if women simply adopt the masculine role, they are lost. Women must counterbalance the blindness of male aggressiveness with compassion, empathy, innocence, and sensuality.

Like Millett, Greer believes in women's free expression of sexuality. She freely admits that "the conventional moralist will find much that is reprehensible in the denial of the Holy Family, in the denigration of sacred motherhood, and the inference that women are not by nature monogamous." For Greer, the struggle must be joyous. Although her work is provocative and skillfully exposes the impact of patriarchal attitudes on women, she has no explicit political agenda except urging changes in consciousness and, at the end of the book, calling gratuitously for a socialist revolution.[51]

Shulamith Firestone was even more controversial than Greer. In *The Dialectic of Sex*, Firestone focuses on the oppressive dimensions of the family, marriage, and women's reproductive role. According to Firestone, the biological family is characterized by women's being at the mercy of their biology: menstruation, menopause, painful childbirth, nursing, and the care of infants. She believes that the natural reproductive differences between the sexes lead directly to the first division of labor, based on sex. Firestone advocates the elimination not just of male privilege but of sex distinction itself.[52]

Firestone believes that the power hierarchies in the biological family are intense and destructive to the individuals. Love itself is the pivot of women's oppression, as oppressive as childbearing. She argues that men cannot genuinely love and that women's clinging behavior stems from their objective social situation, which has not significantly changed historically. For her, pregnancy itself is barbaric. Her agenda for change includes freeing women from the tyranny of their reproductive biology, and the sharing of childbearing and childrearing roles by the society as a whole, men and women. In addition, women and children must enjoy full self-determination, including economic independence, sexual freedom, and total integration of women and children into all aspects of the larger society.[53]

Susan Brownmiller focuses on rape as the secret weapon of patriarchy in *Against Our Will*. Because of women's fear of rape they are kept subordinate to men through coercion. According to Brownmiller, biological differences between men and women are crucial determinants of social power. Brownmiller contends:

> Man's discovery that his genitalia could serve as a weapon to generate fear must rank as one of the most important discoveries of prehistoric times, along with the use of fire and the first crude stone axe. From prehistoric times to the present, I believe, rape has played a critical function. It is nothing more or less than a conscious process of intimidation by which *all men* keep *all women* in a state of fear.[54]

She goes on to claim that the mere threat of rape keeps all women's lives circumscribed by fear.

> A world without rapists would be a world in which women moved freely without fear of men. That *some* men rape provides a sufficient threat to keep all women in a constant state of intimidation, forever conscious of the knowledge that the biological tool must be held in awe for it may turn to weapon with sudden swiftness borne of harmful intent. Myrmidons to the cause of male dominance, police-blotter rapists have performed their duty well, so well in fact that the true meaning of their act has largely gone unnoticed. Rather than society's aberrants or "spoilers of purity," men who commit rape have served in effect as front-line masculine shock troops, terrorist guerillas in the longest sustained battle the world has ever known.[55]

Thus, Brownmiller argues that for women to truly claim their power, they must be free of the fear of rape.

Millett, de Beauvoir, Greer, and Firestone claimed that the nuclear family must be abolished if women's full humanity is to be achieved because the institution of the family is oppressive for women. In contrast, Gloria Steinem and Betty Friedan were advocates of androgyny and a redefinition of the family. Both Steinem and Friedan recognized one-parent families, two adults, childless families, extended-interest groups living together, single-sex groupings, and homosexual marriages as deserving legal and social legitimacy, alongside the traditional nuclear family. They believed that we must abandon the belief that motherhood is woman's primary vehicle for personal fulfillment.

In her writing and speeches, Gloria Steinem minimizes the differences between men and women. In her essay "Sisterhood" she writes:

> Women are human beings first, with minor differences from men that apply largely to the act of reproduction. We share the dreams, capabilities, and weaknesses of all human beings, but our occasional pregnancies and other visible differences have been used—even more pervasively, if less brutally, than racial differences have been used—to mark us for an elaborate division of labor that may once have been practical but has since become cruel and false.[56]

Betty Friedan endorses radical restructuring of the traditional family but makes conservative claims about her intentions. She summarizes her position in "An Open Letter to True Men":

> Only the extremists think women's liberation has to mean the end of marriage and the family, but it certainly will change marriage, the family, the way we raise children, even the architecture of the home, when we liberate ourselves and each other from the old sex role. I hope, and believe, women will *enjoy* being mothers when they stop living through and for their children, and feel better about themselves.[57]

According to Friedan, women must be able to have children and careers. They must be able to define their own identities and freely choose motherhood. For this reason, she strongly supports women's right to abortion. She argues, "I am saying that motherhood will only be a joyous and responsible human act when women are free to make, with full conscious choice and full human responsibility, the decision to become mothers."[58]

Friedan adopts the liberal values of independence, individualism, and equality of opportunity. She rejects the sex/class theory of women's oppression which Steinem accepts. Friedan claims that "it's a matter of simple justice and political right that women share political power, share as half the population in the decisions that affect their future and their lives, and contribute their own voice—which is not the same as man's voice—to the decisions of the whole society."[59] Friedan's feminism focuses on human rights, and her analysis is primarily psychological. She does not acknowledge that sexism affects women of different races and economic classes differently. She accepts the classic liberal interpretation of the autonomous self, without realizing that the way one responds to sexism is determined by race and class and therefore is not always a matter of individual choice. Friedan resembles women of the first generation of feminists in her belief that each individual has intrinsic value and that autonomy or self-fulfillment is a primary goal. The individual's dignity must be reflected in political institutions which do not violate her or his individuality.[60]

The central glaring contradiction within liberal feminism is that although women have gained access to the public domain, they have remained responsible for the private life of their family members. Moreover, liberal feminists who claim they want equality with men ignore the fact that men are not equal in the capitalist structure.[61]

In contrast to liberal feminism, radical feminism interprets women's oppression by men as a universal phenomenon, consistent throughout history. As Cellestine Ware points out, "Radical feminism is working for the eradication of domination and elitism in all human relationships. This would make self-determination the ultimate good and require the downfall of society as we know it today."[62]

In their study of the contemporary feminist movement, Myra Marx Ferree and Beth B. Hess point out that the ideological framework of both reformist and radical feminists is composed of three assumptions:

1. Women are a special category of people with certain common characteristics, whether biological or experiential, and either fixed or variable historically and culturally.
2. Only women ought to define what is feminine.
3. A recognition and dissatisfaction with living in a "man's world" where men define femininity and expectations of women.[63]

Both the liberal feminists and radical feminists agree on the primary goals of the movement: equal pay, access to the professions, reproductive freedom, and passage of the ERA. However, they differ in their views regarding sexuality, marriage, and motherhood. The liberal feminists want egalitarian marriages and shared parenting, while the radical feminists reject the institution of marriage, and some reject heterosexuality.

Feminism and Women of Color

Women of color were in both the liberal and radical branches of the feminist movement of the 1960s and 1970s. Because of the strong connections with the civil rights movement, members of the modern feminist movement were aware of the danger of racism within the movement and sought to recruit minority women. Radical feminists tended to treat women as a homogenized unity partially in reaction against the Left's dismissal of gender as less important than class. Reform feminists also tended to gloss over class and racial differences, which made many African-American and working-class women feel alienated from the feminist movement. Although large numbers of African-American women endorsed the goals of feminism, they did not join the organized feminist movement. Women of color have been prominent in NOW, including Pauli Murray, an African-American writer, attorney, and ordained Episcopal priest; Aileen Hernandez, an attorney and past president of NOW; and Florynce Kennedy, an attorney. Mary Berry, Shirley Chisholm, and Eleanor Holmes Norton were also prominent activists for women's rights during the period. Cellestine Ware helped found the New York Radical Feminists.

In 1973 African-American feminists formed Black Women Organized for Action in San Francisco; the National Black Feminist Organization in New York was established after a meeting of thirty women in New York and soon had 2,000 members in ten chapters. The National Council of Negro Women, headed by Dorothy Height, was an early supporter of the ERA. Other feminist organizations of black women are the National Alliance for Black Feminists and the National Association of Black Professional Women. African-American political lesbian groups such as the Combahee River Collective in New York formed in the early 1970s. In 1981 the National Coalition of 100 Black Women, led by Jewel Jackson McCable, had thirty chapters in twenty states. This national coalition focused on voter registration and political campaigns.[64]

When African-American women have perceived feminist goals as supportive of the family and the race in its entirety, they have embraced them. When they perceived the movement as antimale, antifamily, or racist, they have refused to identify with the movement or to participate. Even if the majority of black women did not actively participate, polls showed that they supported its aims even more than white women. A Virginia Slims poll conducted in 1972 by Lou Harris indicated that 67 percent of the black women were sympathetic to women's liberation groups, while only 35 percent of white women were willing to identify themselves as supportive. A Gallup poll in 1986 asked, "Do you consider yourself a feminist?" Of all the American women questioned 56 percent answered yes, while 4 percent answered that they were antifeminist. Of nonwhite women 64 percent considered themselves feminist.[65]

When racism within the feminist movement discouraged African-American women from participating, they formed separate feminist organizations. While white women were meeting in consciousness-raising groups trying to rediscover their own identities apart from their husbands and children, black women were worried about economic survival, educating their children, unemployment, and adequate child care. Another reason some black women were cool toward the feminist movement stemmed from their realization that white women shared class privilege with their husbands and careerist white women would need domestics and child care from someone; the someone was generally a woman of color. Yet another source of friction was the competition of black women with white women for black men. In addition, given the emergence of the Black Power movement in the 1960s, it is not surprising that many black feminists preferred all-black organizations.

From the nineteenth century to the most recent feminist wave, women's advancement in the United States has always been tied to the elevation of people of color. However, despite all the legislative changes promoting the rights of women and African-Americans and the radical changes in consciousness, the economic position of minorities in the 1970s and 1980s actually deteriorated. Legalized segregation has ended, but many African-American families are in desperate economic shape in the 1990s. The major shift in the African-American family since 1960 has been the increase in female-headed households. By 1980 one-half of all African-American children were living in homes without a father.[66] Single-headed female households increased dramatically in the period from 1950 to 1980. In 1950, 17.6 percent of African-American households were headed by a female, rising to 28.3 percent in 1970 and 40.2 percent in 1980.[67] This phenomenon must be taken into account in any discussion of black women's attitudes toward, and participation in, the feminist movement.

Most African-American women did not respond favorably to Friedan's manifesto of feminism because they viewed employment as a necessity, not a vehicle of liberation. They did not face the psychological effects of financial dependence and isolation in suburbia, but rather racism and sexism in the labor force. However, large numbers of African-American women supported the aims of feminism because they faced discrimination in employment and wages and often had to support single-parent households. Instead of praise for their perseverance and strength within the family in the face of adversity,

African-American women were labeled deviant for being "dominant." In his highly controversial book *The Moynihan Report: The Negro Family: The Case for National Action* (1965), Moynihan writes, "A fundamental fact of Negro family life is the often reversed roles of husband and wife." He claims that the black family is matriarchal.[68] Moynihan blames the "tightening tangle of pathology" within the black community on female-headed black households. Implicit in the matriarchy myth is the sexist assumption that patriarchy should be maintained at all costs and that women's subordination is necessary for the healthy achievement of manhood. Role sharing within black families has been a source of survival and stability. However, it is inaccurate to interpret equality between black men and women as female dominance.[69]

In response to denunciation of black "matriarchy," Eleanor Holmes Norton urges that the black family not attempt to imitate the white family's model.

> Black people who have been deprived of the ability to follow the pattern of American family life have a chance to start anew, to build a different kind of life where men and women are equal. Let's build an entirely new kind of family with the recognition that there may be two people who work, two people who are strong, and nobody has to be dependent. That's the only version of family life I consider viable for black people. Black family life will be a disaster if it copies white family life.[70]

Bell Hooks, writing in a similar vein, pointed out the necessity of black women's recognition of their strengths. She criticized the reformist approach to feminism. Both she and Angela Davis are revolutionary feminists, believing that capitalism must be destroyed. Hooks charged that much feminist thought reflects women's acceptance of the definition of femaleness put forth by the powerful. She believes that if the feminist movement stressed the powers women do exercise, while calling attention to sexist discrimination, exploitation, and oppression, it would have greater mass appeal. Women's obtaining power in the existing social structure might allow numbers of women to gain material privilege and more autonomy, but it will not end male domination as a system. "Sexism has never rendered women powerless. It has either suppressed their strength or exploited it. Recognition of that strength, that power, is a step women together can take towards liberation." Moreover, strength is not synonymous with dominance. Hooks argues that "had poor women set the agenda for feminist movement, they might have decided that class struggle would be a central feminist issue, that poor and privileged women would work to understand class structure and the way it pits women against one another."[71]

Regardless of the lack of responsiveness to their needs by the mainstream feminist movement, black women tend to affirm its aims. Willa Mae Hemmons studied eighty-two women in the early 1970s, forty-five black and thirty-seven white. They were contacted through clubs, schools, and various work agencies. She found no differences between black and white women's affinity for, or rejection of, female liberalism. Slightly more black women in the study endorsed the precepts of the women's movement than white women (47 percent to 46 percent). Black women committed to black liberation were also committed to women's liberation. Black women endorsed femininity more than white women did (two-thirds of the black women versus only two-fifths of the white). Black women were more unconcerned with giving up feminine behavior.[72]

African-American Feminist Leaders

African-American women were integral to the founding of the feminist movement. Pauli Murray's experiences illustrate the ways in which feminist consciousness developed among black women. Murray can be considered a mother of the contemporary feminist movement. She was one of the original founders of the National Organization for Women. While in law school at Howard University, she faced hostility over being a woman. When she excelled academically, she became more accepted and was even elected senior class president. She said that she entered law school preoccupied with the racial struggle and bent on becoming a civil rights attorney and graduated an "unabashed feminist as well."[73]

Murray responded to sexism within the civil rights movement and commented that on August 28, 1963, women were accorded little more than token recognition in the historic march on Washington. Not a single woman was invited to give a major speech or be part of the delegation to the White House. This was a deliberate move and was protested.[74] Ella Baker also commented in her writings on sexism within the civil rights movement. While women were the backbone of the movement, male leadership was always in the spotlight.

Murray was rejected for admission to graduate studies at the University of North Carolina because of her race. After she received a law degree in 1944 from Howard University, she received a fellowship and applied to Harvard Law School for admission to a a master's degree program. She was rejected by Harvard Law School because she was female. Murray was a close friend of Eleanor Roosevelt, but not even a letter from FDR succeeded in getting her admitted. Later she earned a master's degree from U.C. Berkeley, and she was a tutor in law at Yale, where she received her doctorate in 1965. When she found sexism in the church, she began to fight for women's rights and ordination. In 1977 she became one of the first women ordained in the Episcopal church. On February 13, 1976, in a little chapel where her grandmother Cornelia had been baptized more than a century earlier as one of "Five Servant Children belonging to Miss Mary Ruffin Smith," she read the gospel from an ornate lectern.[75]

Murray was a civil rights activist long before she was a feminist. She credits Caroline Ware with helping increase her awareness of parallels between racism and sexism.[76] Murray describes her coming to a feminist consciousness:

> It was about this time [1943] that my education in feminism took an important step forward. My discovery of the historical links between the struggles for the abolition of slavery and the rights of women gave me a new perspective that helped me balance the tensions created by the double burden of race and sex. Until now my haphazard awareness of discrimination because of gender had been submerged in an all-consuming preoccupation with racial injustice, and I tended to treat my first conscious exposure to sexism as an individual problem rather than shared with other women. . . . Nor did I fully grasp the significance of my Grandfather Fitzgerald's proud recollection that in his youth he once had the honor of sitting on the same platform with Susan B. Anthony.[77]

Murray saw no conflict between feminism and the goals of black liberation and believed that women's equality would also benefit the black family. In *Proud Shoes*, she wrote:

> Black women can neither postpone nor subordinate the fight against discrimination to the Black Revolution. . . . Because black women have an equal stake in women's liberation and black liberation they are key figures at the juncture of these two movements. . . . By asserting a leadership role in the growing feminist movement, the black woman can help to keep it allied to the objectives of black liberation while simultaneously advancing the interests of all women.

Murray died on July 1, 1985.[78]

Taking into account black women's differing needs and experiences and the perceived racism within the movement, it is not surprising that masses of black women did not join. Some black women were alienated by lesbianism within the movement, while black lesbians were affirmed by it. African-American women were integral to the formation of both wings of the feminist movement and served in powerful leadership roles. The same ideological divisions were represented among black feminists as among white feminists. Pauli Murray, Aileen Hernandez, and Eleanor Holmes Norton were liberal feminists; Flo Kennedy and Toni Cade Bambara were radical feminists; Audre Lorde, a radical lesbian feminist; Angela Davis, a Marxist feminist; Bell Hooks, a socialist feminist.

African-American women's experiences within the family and labor force led many to a feminist consciousness and to support feminist goals, perhaps even more than white women. Outspoken black feminists saw racism and sexism as parallel systems of oppression and regarded the elimination of sexism as beneficial to women, the black family, and their race as a whole. The devaluation of the homemaker and mother roles and the antimale, antifamily rhetoric angered many black women as they saw the black family in serious economic distress and despaired of the growing trend toward female-headed families within the black community. Instead of worrying about who would do the dishes, many black women were more concerned about economic survival and whether their children could be educated and have two parents at home. They already felt liberated to the extent that they were already out of the kitchen and in the work force. But most of them had jobs, not careers, and did not find them fulfilling. Their empowerment and sense of self-esteem flowed from their roles as wives and mothers and economic providers.

African-American women and other minority women, who had been in the labor force in greater numbers and longer than white women, felt keenly the need for equal pay. Therefore, while they faced the double discrimination based on race and gender, they did not share the loss of a sense of identity experienced by white middle-class women. But whether in jobs or careers, they faced difficulties juggling all their roles.

Although women of color often placed elimination of racism before sexism, a number of feminist organizations were formed in the Hispanic communities. In 1971 Chicana feminists in California opened a center for working women. The National Conference of Puerto Rican Women was founded in 1972, and the Mexican American Women's Association in 1974. The first American Indian Women's Conference met in New York City in 1975.[79] In addition, working women formed Working Women: A National Association of Office Workers (1979), Women Employed (Chicago), 9–5 (Boston), and Women Office Workers (New York).

In 1974 the Coalition of Labor Union Women was formed by 3,200 women from fifty-eight unions. They sought to organize women who were not in unions, increase women's role in union leadership, and support legislation benefiting women. Among professional women, seventy-five associations had women's caucuses in the early 1970s.[80]

Goals of the Feminist Movement: Equal Rights Amendment

Despite class, racial, and ideological differences and disagreements over the issues of lesbianism and abortion, the feminists of the 1960s and 1970s agreed on the passage of the Equal Rights Amendment. The campaign is part of a long fight by women to be considered equal citizens under the law. The struggle over the ERA represents continuity within the women's rights movement since 1923. The bill reads:

> Equality of rights under the law shall not be abridged by the United States or by any state on account of sex.
>
> The Congress shall have the power to enforce, by appropriate legislation, the provisions of this article.
>
> This amendment shall take effect two years after the date of ratification.

The Equal Rights Amendment passed the Senate on March 22, 1972, by a vote of 84 to 8, having passed the House of Representatives on August 10, 1970 (350 to 15) and again on October 12, 1971 (354 to 23).[81]

This amendment differs slightly from the original version of 1923, which read, "Men and women shall have equal rights throughout the United States and every place subject to its jurisdiction." The Senate held hearings before the Judiciary Committee in 1945, 1948, and 1956. During the first floor debate in 1946, the amendment failed 38–35. It passed the Senate in 1950 and 1953, with the Hayden rider assuring continuance of protective legislation. The House Judiciary Committee refused to hold hearings in the 1940s, 1950s, and 1960s.

In order to wrest the amendment from the Judiciary Committee of the House, Martha Griffiths took a surprise action by using the discharge petition on August 10, 1970. The amendment passed by a wide margin. The Senate then passed it in 1972.[82] Ratification seemed assured. In 1980 a Gallup poll revealed that 58 percent supported the ERA and 31 percent opposed it.[83]

Women would benefit in a symbolic way by the passage of the Equal Rights Amendment and would gain national sanction for ending sex discrimination. The legislative measures which had already passed were grounds for enforcement in the area of employment and equal pay, but these measures could be unenforced or revoked. Feminists believe that an amendment to the Constitution is essential for practical and psychological reasons.

A number of women opposed the Equal Rights Amendment because under it women could be drafted and would no longer be given preferential treatment in decisions regarding child custody and alimony. The ERA would also wipe out protective legislation for women.[84] The amendment, however, would give women the freedom to use any name they wish and to choose any domicile; it would obviate laws vesting management of community property in the husband alone and would prevent enforcement of sex-based definitions of marital functions. Therefore, women would not have a legal obligation to do housework or provide affection and sex unless men had the same duties. Moreover, men could not be assigned the duty to support the family financially simply because of his sex.[85] The amendment is based on the assumption that women should be treated as persons, as individuals, whose nature is the same as men's.

Because of NOW's vigorous campaign to ratify the ERA, its budget rose from $700,000 in 1977 to $8.5 million in 1982. Membership in NOW rose from 55,000 in 1979 to 210,000 in 1982. By the end of the campaign, more than 450 organizations, with a total membership of 50 million, had gone on record in support of the Equal Rights Amendment. Although almost unnoticed by the media, another, more militant group utilized direct action to hasten the passage of the amendment. On June 3, 1982, the Grassroots Group of Second-Class Citizens chained themselves to the railing before the Illinois Senate Chamber in a demonstration for passage of the ERA. They stayed four days and were finally carried out. They also conducted sit-ins in the governor's office and the floor of the House itself. They wrote in blood the names of ERA opponents on the marble floors of the capitol building in Illinois.

On August 26, 1980, twelve women chained themselves in front of the Republican National Committee headquarters in Washington; twenty-one women were arrested on November 17, 1980, for chaining themselves to the gates of the Mormon temple in Bellevue, Washington. In 1981 twenty women chained themselves to the White House fence, blocked the driveway, and were subsequently arrested for blocking the street. Women were arrested for climbing over the White House fence on February 15, 1982.[86] The militant action was so limited and so late that while their actions shocked people with their fervor, few if any legislators changed their minds as a result. The militants needed a larger network of support like the National Woman's Party had in the suffrage campaign in order to have a greater impact. Earlier when the NWP picketed the White House and members were arrested, there seemed to be no end to the number of demonstrators.

Even after an extension had been granted, the ERA failed to be ratified on June 30, 1982, falling three states short of ratification, after an extension had been granted. The amendment was defeated because many perceived it as anti-family. Although the defeat of the ERA was dispiriting, feminists have continued to work for changes in the rape laws, against wage discrimination, for better child care, and against spousal and child abuse and have worked to eliminate sex-role stereotyping in textbooks, the media, property laws, advertising, employment, divorce, and child-custody laws. They have fought against pornography, against sex-segregated employment, for reproductive control, and for the right to abortion.[87] While fragmentation may seem to characterize the current feminist movement, the decentralization is both a strength as well as a weakness. Florynce Kennedy once remarked to Gloria Steinem, "Unity in a movement situation is overrated. If you were the Establishment, which would you rather see coming in the door, five hundred mice or one lion?"[88]

The Fight for Legalized Abortion

The feminist movement's strong stand regarding abortion was perceived by some American women as antifamily. Like the early feminists in the nine-teenth century, modern feminists insisted on women's control over their own bodies and the reproductive process. Gloria Steinem, who publicly ac-knowledged that she had had an abortion, explains the anti-abortion argument:

> To them, abortion is constantly presented as the symbolic beginning of
> some horrifying future. It will destroy marriage and morality by removing
> childbearing as the only goal of sex and as God's will. It will limit the num-
> ber of future people like them, thus jeopardizing the future of a white ma-
> jority; it will endanger old or handicapped people by paving the way for eu-

thanasia; it will masculinize women by allowing them to choose an identity other than being vessels for other people's lives; and finally it will be the same as legalizing murder.[89]

Feminists won a major victory with the 1973 Supreme Court decision in *Roe v. Wade*, which made abortion legal in the first trimester. By 1979 the nation's reported abortion rate was 358 per 1,000 live births. The issue of abortion is so bitterly and passionately debated in the 1990s because abortion has become a symbolic battle over women's proper sphere. In 1982 the director of an abortion clinic and his wife were kidnapped, allegedly by people who opposed abortions. According to the reports of the National Abortion Federation, incidents of bombings and violence at abortion clinics escalated from 54 in 1983 to 173 in 1984 and 224 in 1985. Pro-lifers picket them daily.[90] They carry signs reading, "Ask about the Alternatives," "Abortion Exploits Women," "We Love You and Your Baby." One woman carries a small infant; graphic pictures of bloody fetuses are placed at the front of the parking lot, along with a table piled with models of fetuses at various stages. As women enter the clinic, they are harassed by the protesters, and from inside they can see them marching up and down the sidewalk. An excruciatingly difficult decision becomes even more anguished because of the atmosphere outside.

Feminists argue that childbearing is important, but not the determining thing in a woman's life. As more women acquire education equal to male contemporaries, they seek equal pay. But equal pay is contingent on equal work. In order to acquire equal work and refute the notion that they are working only for "pin money," women must challenge the assumption that their work is subordinated to their traditional, "primary" roles as wives and mothers. As Kristin Luker points out, "The recent debate on abortion is so passionate and hard-fought *because it is a referendum* on the place and meaning of motherhood." In her book *Abortion and the Politics of Motherhood*, Luker identifies pro-choice advocates as more educated than antiabortion advocates; they tend to have higher incomes and to be employed. Moreover, they have smaller families, are not religiously active, and are more likely to be unmarried or divorced than pro-lifers.[91]

Abortion is such a controversial issue because women are making the choice whether to become mothers, instead of accepting biological determinism. The locus of power then resides in the woman when she can decide to terminate a pregnancy, not in the state or with the father. Despite the storm of the right-to-lifers, who claim 11 million members, a *Life* magazine poll of November

1981 indicated 67 percent of those questioned felt that a woman who wanted an abortion ought to be able to obtain it legally; 90 percent felt that having an abortion could be "the right thing" for them.[92] In the 1990s women's rights are still being discussed in terms of what constitutes "profamily," with abortion as the most controversial question. Pro-choice advocates want to avoid women's entrapment by their reproductive system, and antiabortionists derive their power from the belief that women's primary role is maternal and domestic.

The Impact of the Feminist Movement

In addition to gaining reproductive control, the most dramatic changes for women are the legislative guarantees of equal rights. The accomplishments of the feminist movement are impressive. The three major legislative acts are the Equal Pay Act of 1963, Title VII of the 1964 Civil Rights Act, and Executive Order 11375. By 1972, 75 percent of NOW's 1968 Bill of Rights had been at least partially attained. The Educational Amendment Act became law on July 1, 1972, containing Title IX. The Revenue Act of 1971 entitled people with an $18,000 income to deduct child-care expenses up to $400 a month. The Comprehensive Health Manpower Training Act of 1971 and the Nurses Training Act of 1971 contained antidiscrimination provisions. The Ninety-second Congress also passed the Child Development Act, which Nixon vetoed. Abzug and Griffiths sponsored most of the more than twenty other bills of relevance to women during this session. Bill Brock sponsored the Equal Credit Opportunity Act, which passed.[93] A review of other major accomplishments and events of the feminist movement reveals astonishing changes over the last twenty years.[94]

In addition to the foregoing changes, women's studies as an academic discipline and scholarship on women in all fields are flourishing because of the feminist movement. This dimension of the women's rights movement represents continuity with Mary Beard's pioneering efforts in the 1930s and 1940s to legitimize the study of women's history. The first women's studies course was taught at Cornell in 1969. By December 1970 over 110 women's studies courses were in catalogs of American colleges and universities. By 1971 over 600 courses were being taught in 200 institutions. By 1982 innumerable courses and over 300 degree-granting programs existed in the field of women's studies.[95]

Women made impressive gains in graduate education in the 1970s. From 1970 to 1980, women went from 4 percent to 25 percent of business students, from 9 percent to 23 percent of medical students, and from 7 percent to 31 percent of law students. In the professions women made considerable gains also. From 1970 to 1979 the percentage of women lawyers rose from 4.7 percent to 12.4 percent; doctors from 8.9 percent to 11.0 percent. Women in state legislatures increased from 305 (3.5 percent of all officeholders) in 1969 to 991 (13 percent) in 1983. Women in local government increased from 4 percent of all officeholders in 1975 to 10 percent in 1981. In 1951 there were 10 women mayors, 244 in 1971, and 1,707 in 1981.[96] At the other end of the class structure, 55 percent of employed women in 1980 earned less than $150 a week, compared with only 22 percent of employed men. The percentage of women among the elderly poor increased from 60 percent in 1959 to 71 percent in 1982.[97]

The growing success of NOW is indicated by its rising fund-raising capacity. Its budget grew as follows:

1967	$6,888.38
1972	$99,505.93
1973	$293,499.00
1974	$430,000.00

The 1974 budget included $140,750 for the ratification of ERA and $34,900 for reproductive issues.[98]

By 1970 a media blitz on the feminist movement occurred, boosting membership in feminist groups. The *New York Times* increased its coverage of women dramatically in the late 1960s and early 1970s, carrying 168 items in 1966, 603 in 1970, and 1,814 in 1974. The items on legal and political aspects of women's rights and nontraditional roles increased from 27 percent in 1966 to 46 percent in 1970 and 56 percent in 1974.[99]

A hallmark of the growing strength of the feminist movement was the publication of *Ms.* magazine, the first major feminist publication, claiming 144,000 subscribers in 1972 and 196,000 in 1973. Gloria Steinem and Brenda Feigen Fasteau formed the Women's Action Alliance and brought out *Ms.* In 1972, 82 percent of *Ms.* subscribers said they did not belong to a movement group. That figure fell to 76.6 percent in 1973. As a group, the subscribers were generally highly educated, employed, but earning considerably less than their husbands.[100]

Congress considered 432 pieces of legislation on women's rights in the period from 1960 to 1966. Although Congress considered 884 bills concerning women's issues in all of the 1960s, they passed only 10. In the 1970s Congress passed 71 pieces of legislation concerned with women's rights and needs, 40 percent of *all* legislation aimed at women during the twentieth century.

The dramatic growth of the feminist movement is also seen in the number of events staged in the period from 1968 to 1975: 26 events in 1968, 165 in 1970, and 256 in 1975. The feminists sustained 116 events per year for the rest of the 1970s.[101]

Because of the strength of the feminist movement, films of the early 1970s began to portray strong female characters. Films like *The Turning Point*, *Julia*, and *An Unmarried Woman* depict women as independent, autonomous persons, with the strength of many 1930s characters. As if to compensate, at the same time films like *Pretty Baby*, *Blue Lagoon*, and *Tess* provided images of child-women as "innocent" as Lillian Gish earlier. *Kramer vs. Kramer*, a film of the 1970s, features a father who learns to take care of his son when his wife leaves to find herself. Changes in sexual roles were evident in the cinema.

In the 1980s *Tootsie* and *Victor-Victoria* dealt with the awareness which comes from impersonating the opposite sex. The rock music culture, which had been exceedingly sexist in the 1960s, moved toward androgyny in the 1980s, with stars like Boy George, Mick Jagger, David Bowie, and Prince, a radical departure from the 1960s.[102]

Antifeminism of the 1970s and 1980s

Not surprisingly, the drastic social changes resulting from structural changes in the economy, the war in Vietnam, the civil rights movement, and the feminist movement generated a fierce conservative backlash. Members of the New Right believe that feminists' advocacy of the ERA and women's reproductive rights is an attack on church and family. In order to understand the fierce backlash of the New Right against feminism, one must understand the tremendous impact of the movement in changing women's roles. Paul Weyrich, Richard Viguerie, Terry Dolan, Howard Phillips, and Phyllis Schlafly are major leaders of the New Right, representing the new religious right, the "profamily" right, and the political right.[103]

Women are the only oppressed group to organize against their own emancipation. Many women in the nineteenth and early twentieth centuries were against suffrage. Similarly, several contemporary antifeminist groups oppose the ERA and the entire feminist agenda. AWARE (Women against the Ratification of the ERA), FOE (Females Opposed to Equality), HOME (Happiness of Motherhood Eternal), WWWW (Women Who Want to Be Women), and the Eagle Forum are among the most vocal antifeminist organizations.[104] Phyllis Schlafly, who defined the issues and mobilized followers, was the single most important figure in defeating the ERA. Through her published reports, speeches, and extensive media coverage, Schlafly argued that the ERA would bring unisex toilets, allow homosexual marriages, permit unlimited abortion, send women into combat, and invalidate men's obligation to support their wives. With the divorce rate soaring, many women were afraid of the consequences of the ERA on their own futures. They believed that if divorced, they would be forced to go to work.

The basis of Schlafly's position is that what she calls the Positive Woman "understands that men and women are different, and that those very differences provide the key to her success as a person and fulfillment as a woman."[105] Schlafly favors equal employment, equal credit, and equal pay for women but believes that women must have the protection of marriage and privileges of femininity and that women should exercise covert power. She even recommends full- or part-time employment or community activities.

Schlafly launched the *Phyllis Schlafly Report* in 1967, which she published each month. In the 1970s the number of subscriptions grew from 3,000 to 35,000. She helped forge an unlikely coalition of Catholics, fundamentalist Protestants, and Orthodox Jews.[106] Schlafly calls feminists a "bunch of antifamily radicals and lesbians and elitists." She appeals to housewives who are tired of feeling guilty for staying home. Schlafly is charismatic, brilliant, and deeply religious. With her law degree, grass-roots organizing ability, and extensive conservative backing, she almost single-handedly defeated the ERA. She objects to the second section of the amendment, which gives the federal government enforcement powers. She also objects to the military conscription of women and the elimination of the preference toward women in alimony and child-custody cases and believes that women ought to be supported in marriage by men. She has been able to fan the fears of middle-aged housewives who are scared to death of divorce and of the threat of having to go to work. Schlafly writes: "Thus, if ERA is ratified, the aged and faithful mother, who has made her family her lifetime career, would have no legal right to be supported in her senior years. She would have to take any menial job she could get or go on welfare if her husband and children did not voluntarily choose to support her."[107] However, just as in the case of protective labor legislation, the defeat of the ERA can never guarantee women the security in marriage or preferential treatment in divorce which they seek.

On the night of ERA's failure, Schlafly held an "Over the Rainbow" celebration in Washington, D.C. She sent a congratulatory telegram to Ronald Reagan. Reagan was the first president in decades to oppose the amendment. In 1975 Schlafly had 50,000 members, while NOW had 108,000 paid members, and 135,000 when Reagan took office.

Schlafly opened an office in Washington in 1982 to work against sex education, against the nuclear freeze, and against feminists' campaign to eliminate sexism in school textbooks.[108] Leaders of the New Right are working to pass the Family Protection Act, to reestablish prayer in public schools, and to forbid federal funding for school textbooks that portray women in other than traditional roles. The FPA would also repeal federal laws against child and spouse abuse and would prevent sex-mixed sports.

In 1976 the Supreme Court upheld the Hyde Amendment, and *Harris v. McRae* in 1980 restricted federal financing of abortion under the Medicaid program. Consequently, Medicaid funding of abortion was lost in all but fourteen states and the District of Columbia. The Human Life Amendment has failed in each Congress since 1973, but the new bill declares it national policy that human life begins with conception and allows individual states to enact laws outlawing abortion.[109] A brilliant strategy of antiabortionists was claiming the tag "pro-life." Weyrich, Phillips, and Jerry Falwell helped to combine right-to-lifers, Catholics, Fundamentalists, and the Old Right. They capitalized on fears about poverty, drugs, unemployment, economic downward mobility, changing sexual roles, big government, and Communism. Many people felt a loss of control and wanted to return to the imagined "stable" world of the 1950s. Politicians like Ronald Reagan seized on simplistic formulas and tired truisms of the past.[110]

As we have seen, the feminist movement of the 1960s and 1970s was diverse, composed of liberal feminists, Marxist feminists, socialist feminists, radical feminists, and lesbian separatists. By far the largest group was the liberal one. In her book *Daring to Be Bad*, Alice Echols points out that after 1975 cultural feminism eclipsed radical feminism. The radical wing of the movement turned away from opposing male supremacy to creating a female counterculture where female values could be nurtured. Personal rather than social transformation became primary.[111] The ascendance of cultural feminism is reminiscent of the nineteenth-century feminist emphasis on extending mother-love to the entire society. Both envisioned a society guided by female concerns and values, including pacifism, cooperation, and nonviolence. They were basically both essentialist in their analysis of women's condition, and many in both eras created separate female communities. Both groups implied that women needed protection from victimization by men, the manifestations of which were domestic violence, rape, and pornography. The hazard of these approaches of protectionism or separatism is that they emphasized sexual differences. The same argument then frequently was used to keep women subordinate to men.

Radical feminists and cultural feminists were generally integrally involved in establishing rape crisis centers and wife abuse shelters, opening up lesbianism as an option for women, and changing language, style of dress, and makeup. *Roe v. Wade,* which was perhaps the most important judicial change for women, was a joint radical, liberal effort. The reform feminists recruited the largest numbers and achieved numerous goals. However, in concert with the radicals both were essential in transforming gender relations in the United States and effecting legislative changes.

When feminists embraced the family or family values, they were much more acceptable to the majority of American women, especially if the family was fairly traditional. When "family" referred to those headed by lesbians, prostitutes, or unmarried black teenagers, or when the families have been homeless, immigrant, Native American, African-American, or Hispanic, "profamily" arguments have been less successful. Although the rhetoric, tone, tactics, and leadership varied, all branches of the movement endorsed social, economic, political, sexual, and legal equality for women. Feminist consciousness grew out of different experiences which women had in families which trapped and victimized them and out of experiences which empowered them. Feminists of the 1960s and 1970s agreed that they would no longer define themselves primarily by their reproductive capacity and relationships to men but as autonomous individuals with public power.

CONCLUSION AND PROSPECT

In this book I have argued that American women's empowering and debilitating experiences within families led many to a feminist consciousness and shaped feminist agendas by making family issues central. Throughout the nineteenth and twentieth centuries, women's domestic power increased largely as a result of their greater access to education, the social impact of war, reduced fertility, entrance into the labor force, and industrialization. Coming from a position of strength, women entered the public sphere in order to clean up the society for the health of the family, protect women against male tyranny, and acquire full citizenship, employment, and equal wages. From the beginning of the women's rights movement, family issues such as voluntary motherhood, education to be good wives and mothers, and gaining the vote in order to protect the family were primary. Thus, from the perspective of the 1990s, their aims would be considered conservative.

Women's frustration within families, violence, abuse, and lack of acknowledgment also inspired women to organize for change. Their ambiguous experiences of both empowerment and entrapment shaped the development of feminist consciousness as well as feminist theory and action. Women's covert power in the family combined with economic dependence set up powerful contradictions and led feminists to construct profamily agendas. From the beginning, when the feminist movement's goals were perceived as profamily, they eventually succeeded; when they seemed to threaten the family, they failed.

Paradoxically, in the colonial period women had no political or legal rights if married, but they exerted influence in parenting and over the spiritual life of the family. They were also crucial to the family's economy, since the spheres of men and women overlapped considerably. Some women rebelled against their circumscribed role by becoming religious heretics or even "witches."

Around the time of the American Revolution, some women began to demand education and full citizenship. Although initially a small voice for women's equality, it would grow louder as the country began to industrialize and women were needed in the labor force. As we have seen, by the end of the nineteenth century white middle-class women who had acquired higher education were forced to choose between a career and marriage. African-American, immigrant, and working-class women frequently had no choice but to assume the multiple responsibilities of domesticity, motherhood, and paid employment.

American women began to assume more domestic influence throughout the nineteenth century as motherhood was glorified. However, domesticity began to be devalued in the twentieth century as technological innovations lightened the drudgery of housework. The turning points for women's covert domestic power were the Great Depression and World War II. Because of the economic emergency and then the exigencies of war, women had to assume more responsibility and dominance at home. Women's experiences were extremely diverse because of differences of race, class, ethnicity, and religion. However, they shared, if unequally, both the discrimination against women as a gender, as well as the positive economic opportunities which the war brought.

By the end of the Second World War, American women entered a period where ultradomesticity was glorified. One of the consequences was the baby boom, with over 76 million babies born. As we have seen, women assumed an exaggerated role in parenting at a time when more American women than ever before were highly educated. Their empowerment and entrapment within families set up contradictions in their lives which would help kindle the feminist movement of the 1960s and 1970s.

In the same sense that profamily issues shaped the nineteenth-century movement, a rejection of the overemphasis on domesticity helped shape the modern feminist movement. Nevertheless, the mainstream reformist element of the movement, which was the largest, retained a strong profamily focus, with child care, parental leave, reproductive freedom, and the Equal Rights Amendment as the top priorities. Although the radical feminists condemned the gender-structured family and redefined "profamily" issues, they made them central to their analysis and demands.

Just as critics of the early women's rights movement argued that it was disrupting the family, similar criticisms dogged the modern movement. Although clearly the more radical groups within the feminist movement opposed marriage itself, the more moderate feminists endorsed more egalitarian marriages, not unlike the "companionate marriages" of the 1920s or feminist marriages of the nineteenth century. In a departure from the earlier movement, modern feminists argued more stridently for women's *individual* rights. Like the radicals of the earlier movement, they wanted full citizenship as wives and mothers but wanted to be recognized as having individual identities.

Many women did not acknowledge their tremendous covert domestic influence even to themselves, and therefore it did not always serve the needs of their self-esteem, especially as the role of homemaker became socially devalued. While often highly effective, covert power is vulnerable to economic power and to physical violence. It is unacknowledged illegitimate power. Thus, it can eventually undermine one's dignity if it is the only vehicle of influence in interpersonal relations. Since feigned submissiveness is a prerequisite for exercising covert domestic power, women may actually come to believe in their own inferiority instead of simply acting the part.

Women's socially constructed value system, which focused on "the power of love" rather than love of power, clashed more and more with a national ethic of materialism, consumerism, and defining a person's success by the amount of money earned. Popular culture tended to reflect these changes in values and also the dramatic changes in women's lives. Paradoxically, in order to sell products, advertisers both created new images of women and reinforced traditional stereotypes. The images of true womanhood which helped shape women's aspirations have changed significantly from the early nineteenth century. The "angel in the house" gave way to the Gibson girl, the flapper, Rosie the Riveter, the feminine mystique, and then the superwoman mystique. However, the changes have been incremental, characterized more by adding roles than by eliminating the traditional expectations. The angel in the house of the nineteenth century was pious, pure, domestic, and submissive. In contrast, the superwoman of the 1970s freely acknowledged her sexuality and did not expect to be submissive to her husband. Although she had a career, she was still expected to fulfill her family responsibilities. She was more independent and individualistic, but still feminine. Ellen Goodman described her aptly:

> Supermom stayed home and when the kiddies came back from school she baked them cookies in the shape of pumpkins with raisin eyes and carrot noses. But now we have before us the ideal of Superwoman who prepares a well-balanced nutritious breakfast for her children, and her children eat it. She goes off to work where she makes $30,000 a year as an executive of a

law firm. She comes home and reads to her children, then serves dinner by candlelight to her husband.[1]

Just as being a "lady" in the nineteenth century was tied to class status, succeeding as a "superwoman" of the 1970s and 1980s depended on class status also. The superwoman needed wealth to secure her education and gain entrance into a profession, and wealth enough to hire other women to assume housekeeping and child-care duties. Those women who were not so fortunate simply had to add another role—a job—to their normal domestic responsibilities and try to cope with the double burden.

Films of the 1980s reflected this new challenge of trying to combine professional careers and marriage. However, they no longer portrayed strong female characters like Jane Fonda and Vanessa Redgrave, who starred in *Julia*, or Jill Clayburgh, who chose independence over Alan Bates in *An Unmarried Woman*. Married and unmarried women felt the pressure to be career women, lovers, and mothers, the new expectation which the film *Baby Boom* portrays. Diane Keaton, a high-powered Manhattan businesswoman, ends up opting for Sam Shepard, a baby, and life in Vermont, rather than life in the fast lane. The twist, however, is that she also starts her own new business in gourmet baby food, which is enormously lucrative.

In *Working Girl*, Melanie Griffith's Tess is the female Horatio Alger, who begins as a lowly secretary and, by luck and shrewdness, makes it to the top. Instead of wielding a Harvard M.B.A., she relies on sex appeal, the help of her lover, Harrison Ford, and intrinsic gutsiness. At the end of the movie, Tess achieves success and gets her man. A more traditional, nostalgic film is *Crossing Delancey*, in which Amy Irving plays Izzy, an independent woman who works in a bookstore in Manhattan. Her grandmother convinces her to marry Sam, a Lower East Side pickle seller. In contrast with Diane Keeton's and Melanie Griffith's characters, who end up "having it all," Amy Irving's character values a loving relationship over her independence.

More sinister portrayals of women occurred in the 1980s in the genre of violent films where women are sex objects who are raped, attacked with power tools, and slashed, the objects of intense hostility. While a far cry from the movie in which Cagney smashed the grapefruit in Mae Clark's face, these films also subliminally warn women of their vulnerability to male violence and the hazards of independence. What the cult of true womanhood of the nineteenth century has in common with the slasher movies is men's underlying fear of the power of women.

Advertisements in the 1980s began to feature yuppies, young urban professionals with BMW cars, and children with designer clothes and toys. Babies were suddenly featured, even in *Vogue* magazine. Presumably some members of the baby boom generation had finally reached a level of affluence needed to afford "having it all." The question arises whether American women as a whole are better off than they were twenty-five years ago?

Have American Women Come a Long Way?

American women have more educational and professional opportunities, more self-esteem and sense of empowerment, but economically only a small percentage of them are better off. The high rate of divorce and continuing discrimination in the labor force have made women more financially vulnerable than they were twenty-five years ago. Public policy has not addressed the needs of American families; women and children are therefore bearing the brunt of poverty.

The feminist movement was enormously successful in changing perceptions about gender and in changing people's lives. As we noted earlier, a 1971 Harris poll indicated that 40 percent of women favored the women's movement; 42 percent opposed it, and 18 percent were unsure. In contrast, a 1986 Gallup poll asked, "Do you consider yourself a feminist?" This time, 56 percent of American women answered yes, and only 4 percent said they were antifeminists. Of nonwhite women, 64 percent considered themselves feminists. Of the women with family incomes of $40,000, 55 percent saw themselves as feminists, as did 57 percent of those with family incomes of $20,000. A *Newsweek* poll in 1986 revealed that 71 percent of all women questioned believed that the movement has improved their lives and only 18 percent believed that it has not. In the age group between eighteen and twenty-nine, 88 percent of the women believed the women's movement had improved their lives.[2]

Americans' attitudes are also changing about family roles. Men in the 1990s may be as economically powerful in their families as their grandfathers were, but they no longer can take their authority for granted. They must prove their right to power or win power by virtue of their own skills and accomplishments in competition with their wives.[3] There is evidence that men are coming to an awareness of how sex roles restrict them also. At least seven national conferences of men's movement groups have met. One study in 1983 indicated that there were thirty local men's centers in 1981. The popularity of Robert Bly's *Iron John* and his "wild man" retreats are indicators that a significant number of American men are concerned about the damaging effects of traditional male socialization.[4] By 1970, one-third of the respondents in an opinion poll felt that men and women should share responsibility for small children; by 1980, 56 percent voiced this opinion. However, only 38 percent of the married couples said that the husband actually helped care for children; 64 percent supported efforts aimed at elevating women's status.[5]

Despite attitudinal changes regarding women's proper role, the reality of many women's lives is that they bear the multiple burden of domestic work, child care, and employment. Half of all mothers with preschool children worked in 1984, up from 12 percent in 1950 and 24 percent in 1970. According to the most recent Bureau of Labor statistics, 72 percent of women with children between the ages of six and seventeen are in the labor force, as well as 57 percent of women with children under age six and 53 percent of women with children under the age of three. Although women constitute more than 49 percent of the labor force, and 63 percent of all women were working in 1984, they still perform 80 percent of all work in the home, whether they work outside the house or not.[6] Studies reveal that American men's time doing housework has increased by only 6 percent in twenty years, despite the massive shifts of women into paid employment.[7] Rhetoric and practice still diverge. Out of a recent national sample of American adults, 63 percent reported that they preferred an equal marriage of shared responsibility with the husband and wife sharing the breadwinning and child-care functions.

While most men may need and appreciate their spouses' paychecks, they prefer that their working not interfere with their traditional duties. A 1965–66 study found that working women spent three hours a day doing housework, while their husbands spent only seventeen minutes. In the late 1970s men whose wives were employed spent ten more minutes a day doing housework than men who had wives who were full-time homemakers. The most helpful husbands logged just under eleven hours a week of housework. They tended to mow yards, play with children, take out the garbage, go to the supermarket, or shop for large household items. Generally they did not cook, clean, launder, or feed, bathe, or transport children. In research for her book *The Second Shift*, Arlie Hochschild studied fifty couples, ranging from working-class to upper-middle-class status, and found only 20 percent of them sharing household tasks and childrearing. Moreover, recent studies concluded that women spent fifteen fewer hours of leisure each week than their husbands. In other words, they work an extra month of twenty-four-hour days in a year compared with their spouses.[8]

Why do we not see a massive revolt by wives who are working the "second shift"? Three conditions help clarify this seemingly outrageous situation. In the first place, many women may feel ambivalent about abdicating control in the one area in which they have some power. Second, many women fear that insisting on sharing housework and child care will be perceived as a withdrawal of love. Finally, perhaps the most compelling reason why we are not witnessing a massive rebellion by working wives is that regardless of women's desires, they rarely have the economic power to back up their requests for sharing of domestic and child-care responsibilities. In most families female wage earners earn less than their spouses, and they are considered "junior partners."

Women in the professions have experienced the most dramatic gains in the last two decades. In 1972 women constituted 10.1 percent of physicians, 1.9 percent of dentists, and 4 percent of lawyers, compared with 1987 figures showing 17.6 percent of physicians, 4.4 percent of dentists, and 18 percent of lawyers. In addition, the percentages of women among all people receiving degrees in 1985 were 30.4 percent of M.D. degrees, 20.7 percent of dental degrees, and 38.5 percent of law degrees. Despite women's entrance in increasing numbers into the professions, women overall still do not receive equal pay within the United States. Only 10 percent of female workers earn more than $20,000. A quarter earn less than $10,000. Among working women, 45 percent are single, divorced, separated, or widowed. Women made 63 cents for every dollar earned by men in 1939, and 64 cents in 1985. In 1986 full-time women workers earned just under 69 cents for every dollar earned by full-time male workers. Only women in their early twenties came closer to parity with male salaries, earning 87.5 cents for every dollar earned by their male counterparts. Government statistics for 1989 revealed that women average 65 percent of men's income, with full-time working wives making 57 percent of men's income. Employed single mothers average $9,000 a year.

Since marriage has become so prone to divorce, women have lost the protection of financial security of the past, while failing to enhance their earning power as workers. In 1980 one out of two marriages ended in divorce. Sociologists now predict that soon two out of three marriages will end in divorce, twice as many as in 1966, and three times as many as 1950. Lenore

Weitzman states that a year after divorce the husband's standard of living has risen 42 percent, while that of the former wife and often her children has fallen 73 percent. In addition, fewer than 10 percent of former wives actually collect alimony payments; 60 percent of all divorced fathers contribute nothing to the financial support of their children. Approximately 4–15 million women are displaced homemakers in the United States. Moreover, female-headed households have risen by 72 percent since 1972; women now maintain 16.1 percent of all families, or one in six. In 1971 women headed 11.4 percent of all families. In 1983 children from households headed by single women accounted for almost a quarter of the entire population of children, and half of all poor children. Now 12 million children live in poverty, an increase of 3 million since 1968. The median wage for women who are full-time workers (year round) is $14,479.[9]

Women remain disadvantaged in the labor force because of the persistence of traditional attitudes regarding women's primary sphere; the difficulty of combining motherhood and employment without an enlightened, coherent national family policy; the absence of institutional and community support for parenting; and discrimination based on sex. Motherhood is a determining factor in a woman's earnings and job choices. June O'Neill of the Urban Institute reports that between the ages of 20 and 24, when most working women are childless, women earn 89 percent as much as men. The wage gap begins to widen during ages twenty-five to thirty-five, the main childbearing years. Women who have never married or borne children are the only ones to enjoy wage parity with men of comparable age, education, and experience. These women resemble the professional women in 1920, when only 12 percent of professional women were married. (Three-fourths of the women who earned Ph.D.'s in the half century before 1925 were unmarried. The reproductive rate of achieving women remained around zero.)

A study conducted in 1982 by Korn/Ferry International of 300 successful career women finds that 48 percent of the women were unmarried and 61 percent were childless. Similarly, of the 71 women in Harvard Law School's class of 1974, nearly half were childless after ten years.[10] By 1980 only 10 percent of women aged between forty and forty-five were childless. However, among women executives and high-level professionals, one-half were childless.

The biggest dilemma for professional women is reconciling motherhood and career. For other working women, the dilemma is financial survival, providing adequate child care, and having enough stamina to handle the double burden. Women's having children and being responsible for house-work prevents them from succeeding in their careers. As we have seen, even professional women work a "second shift" at home, unless they hire others to do it for them. Heidi Hartmann claims that men demand eight hours more service per week than they contribute. Aside from the physical and psycho-logical demands from working in the labor force and fulfilling the role of wife and mother, women are constrained by traditional assumptions about their primary function. Therefore, they are likely to take low-paying jobs in the pink-collar ghetto.

Some studies indicate that part of the wage differential between profes-sional men and women stems from differing aspirations. For example, female doctors often elect lower-paying specialties, and female M.B.A.'s often choose lower-paying jobs. Why they choose them, however, is not adequately ex-plored. Do they choose freely, or do they gravitate toward jobs which are less dominated by intransigent men or which are more compatible with family life?

Leaving aside women's choice of lower-paying jobs, the fact of sex dis-crimination persists. Mary Anne Devanna's study of ninety men and women who received M.B.A.'s from Columbia University between 1969 and 1972 reveals that although the men and women had the same aspirations and professional competence, the women were earning less ten years later.[11]

Instead of publicizing this sort of discrimination, it has become common-place to blame the feminist movement for disrupting the family and encour-aging women to adopt the male model of success. Sylvia Ann Hewlett argues in *A Lesser Life: The Myth of Women's Liberation in America* that American feminists of the 1960s and 1970s focused too much on women's cloning the male model of success and fighting for abstract equality. She compares the maternity-leave policies and child care of Western democracies and finds the United States appallingly backward.

Hewlett points out that 60 percent of working mothers have no right to maternity leave. In contrast, the advanced democracies of Europe have paid maternity leave, child allowances, subsidized day care, and free health services. In 117 countries women are guaranteed leave from employment for childbirth; the United States is the only industrialized country that lacks a statutory maternity leave.[12] Hewlett's comparison of the United States' situation with other European democracies fails to make clear that the salient difference is the socialist nature of those other countries.

A coherent national policy regarding children is essential. But mothers *and* fathers must be empowered. Yet, public policy lags far behind the changing realities of American families. In the Reagan administration such policy was nonexistent, and no bold initiatives have come thus far from the Bush administration. Although Ronald Reagan spoke of his commitment to the family, his policies reflected a callousness toward the needs of women and children. He considered child care as each family's responsibility. Three million more children have fallen into poverty since 1980, and 200,000 have lost their day-care subsidies.

The "traditional family" no longer is the norm. In fact, in the 1950s, only half of all American families consisted of a husband with a dependent wife and two or more children. Now a mere 5 percent of the population fits this model.[13] In American households, 60 percent of the adults live as married couples. In 1972, 33.7 percent of all couples had two breadwinners; in 1986, 54.5 percent of all couples had two. The percentage of women between twenty-five and fifty-four years old who work increased from 50 percent in 1971 to 66.6 percent in 1986.

Female inequality is a major threat to the welfare of American children. The assumption that mothers ought to care for their children, whether forced to work or not, has led to a Neanderthal approach to child care in the United States. A study in 1982 by the Department of Commerce revealed that children under five of working mothers were cared for in several ways: 40 percent in family homes (about half operated by nonrelatives); 23 percent by parents themselves through split shifts or other arrangements; 15 percent in group care, including nursery schools, preschools, and day-care centers (the percentage drops to 9.2 percent of the total if nursery schools and preschools are excluded); 11 percent by other relatives in the child's home; 6 percent by babysitters, housekeepers, and nannies; and 5 percent had no answer.

Because the United States has no comprehensive national child-care policy, only about 6 percent of the over 1.5 million family day-care homes, serving 6 million children up to the age of thirteen, are registered, licensed, and regulated. An attempt to coerce a return to traditional roles for women through job and wage discrimination and the absence of adequate day care has produced a national emergency for America's children. No wonder countless American women face inordinate pressures, guilt feelings, and frustrations in "doing it all."[14]

Even Orrin Hatch, one of the most conservative Republicans, has introduced a child-care bill. In a dramatic reversal, he now supports federal support for child care. The situation has reached such crisis proportions that even members of the radical right realize something must be done. Because of Pat Schroeder's and Christopher Dodd's more comprehensive bills, their opponents hope to seize the initiative on child care but so far have failed to provide adequate funding. In the nineteenth century, feminists gained legislation for easier divorce and against domestic violence through an alliance with conservative traditionalists; recently feminists against pornography have found themselves aligned with similar groups. A national emergency concerning child care exists and must be addressed immediately. As we have seen, the most far-reaching legislative changes for women have often been achieved when proponents have argued from a "profamily" position.

Feminists of the nineteenth and early twentieth centuries saw no contradiction between the elevation of women and the well-being of the family. Feminists of the recent movement had a more thorough analysis of sex roles and argued that families must be restructured. The vast majority of feminists embraced equal partnership in marriage, liberated motherhood, access of women to economic independence and meaningful work, which cannot by any stretch of the imagination be considered antifamily measures.

In *The Second Stage*, Betty Friedan addresses a central dilemma of the contemporary feminist movement: how women can achieve autonomy within the context of marriage and motherhood. However, her book is an inadequate analysis of the new directions for feminism in the 1990s because it focuses too narrowly on middle- and upper-class women. Friedan points out that the feminist movement has developed a "feminist mystique" which threatens to suppress women's needs for mothering children, nurturing relationships, and intimacy. She reiterates, however, that she never meant that for a woman to achieve personhood she had to repudiate marriage and motherhood. She argues for a redefinition of family which includes developing, strengthening, or recognizing new family forms. She is optimistic because while women are moving out of the home to enter the public sphere, men seem to be trying to disentangle themselves from the competitive rat race and turning more to the family for a new dimension of fulfillment. She contends that "virtually all women today share a basic core of commitment for the family and to their own equality within and beyond it, as long as family and equality are not seen to be in conflict."[15]

Friedan summarizes her approach as follows:

We are almost afraid to face the uncomfortable part of it because we don't want to risk going back to what we were before. We had begun to feel that to be liberated we had to be more independent than any human being can really be—completely independent of our men, our children. I think it is a relief now to realize that we can admit our need for love and home, that we can be soft as well as hard with our children and our husbands, that we can admit our dependence on them without giving up our identity. We have become independent enough to admit our need to be dependent, some of the time.[16]

Friedan's solution of flextime and her psychological approach resemble her approach to the "problem with no name" in her groundbreaking *The Feminine Mystique*. Her blind spot is not the family. She is a keenly astute political observer about pragmatic politics and the impact of rhetoric. However, she continues to adopt the liberal feminist, individual-centered ideology, which does not address the economic and structural changes necessary to assure women's psychological and financial security, meaningful work, and adequate resources for mothering.

Friedan's focus has always been in "changing ourselves." She agrees with Hewlett that simply adopting the masculine model cuts off part of women's personhood. However, the crucial issue is that the vast majority of American women have not even had the opportunity to "adopt the male model of success." They are still stuck in low-paying "female" jobs, while holding down the home front too. Just as earlier, many of them wished they "were oppressed by the feminine mystique," they now might equally wish they were "trapped by the male model of success."

Given the fact that women have still not made a dent in the struggle for equal pay or been able to receive assistance in housework or child care to a significant degree, one would imagine that the feminist movement would be thriving. However, on August 26, 1980, only 500 turned out to march for women's equality, as opposed to thousands in 1970.[17] The media seem more interested in reports on what is wrong with the movement than with feminist issues themselves. After the defeat of the ERA, the national movement received little media attention, and the term "postfeminism" became fashionable. The media seemed more interested in what the antiabortionists were doing than in feminist issues.

Suddenly a Supreme Court decision regarding abortion on July 3, 1989, sent shock waves throughout the society and framed the most passionate political issue of the next decade. The impending decision mobilized over 600,000 marchers the preceding April. In a Missouri case, *Webster v. Reproductive Health Services*, the Supreme Court undermined significantly women's constitutional right to abortion. In *Roe v. Wade* (1973), the Supreme Court declared that a woman's decision to have an abortion during the first trimester of pregnancy must be left to her and her doctor. It said that states may regulate abortion during the second trimester only to protect the woman's health, and may take steps to protect fetal life in the third trimester. State authority to regulate abortions after the first trimester was not made absolute, however. In the past decade, 1.5 million legal abortions have been performed each year. Before *Roe v. Wade* the mortality rate for illegal abortions performed outside of hospitals by people without medical training was an estimated 100 deaths per 1,000 abortions. When abortions were performed by medical practitioners in states where abortion was legal, only 3 deaths per 100,000 abortions occurred.[18]

In their recent decision, the Court stopped short of reversing *Roe v. Wade*. However, the justices restored Missouri abortion regulations. One requires doctors to determine, when possible, whether a fetus twenty weeks old is capable of survival outside the womb. Missouri may ban the use of tax money for encouraging or counseling women to have abortions not necessary to save life. Moreover, Missouri may ban public employees (doctors, nurses, health-care providers) from performing or assisting abortion not necessary to save life, and may ban use of public hospitals or other facilities for performing abortions not necessary to save life.

In his dissenting opinion, Harry A. Blackmun, author of *Roe v. Wade*, wrote, "For today, the women of this nation will retain the liberty to control their destinies. But the signs are evident and very ominous, and a chill wind blows."[19] How does one explain the dramatic mobilizing power of the recent decision for the feminist movement? Reproductive freedom is the cornerstone of women's ability to choose whether to be mothers or not. From this freedom also comes their ability to achieve education, political and economic power, as well as control over their sexuality. The abortion controversy is occurring within the wake of the sexual revolution of the 1960s and 1970s. Only one woman in five now waits until marriage to become sexually active, compared with almost one-half in 1960 who waited until marriage.

Abortion is a profamily issue. Poor women seek abortions because they cannot care for another child. Unwanted children are frequently resented, abused, and abandoned. Many are born to teenagers. Over one million teenagers become pregnant each year in the United States; almost half choose to have abortions. Teenage abortions account for one-fourth of all abortions performed in the United States. In 1987 families started by a birth to a teenager cost the federal government $19.27 billion in welfare payments,

Medicaid, and food stamps. Teenage mothers usually become locked in a cycle of poverty. Only one in fifty teenage mothers finishes college, as opposed to one in five among women who delay childbearing until their midtwenties.[20] The abortion issue will be at the top of the feminist agenda in the 1990s because of the tremendous impact a reversal or erosion of *Roe v. Wade* would have on all women's lives. On April 9, 1989, and again on April 5, 1992, many feminists who had been preoccupied with their own careers or jobs and struggling to juggle multiple roles suddenly stepped out to show their solidarity and assure the American public that the feminist movement was experiencing a resurgence, another wave.

The Next Wave: A Feminist Agenda for the 1990s

In order for a coherent national feminist movement to sustain momentum, women's rights organizations must form coalitions with the most aggrieved women: women working in pink- and blue-collar jobs, displaced homemakers, older women, union women, African-American and Hispanic women, and poor women. NOW must work closely with groups like the California Women's Economic Agenda Project, Women for Economic Justice in Massachusetts, and Women's Agenda in Pennsylvania, welfare rights activists, and African-American women's organizations.

The battle for entry into the professions has been won; however, professional women still need adequate child care and parental leave and still need to achieve financial parity with their male colleagues. These women will be receptive to feminism only when they personally experience discrimination. Likewise, another group of potential allies are young college women. They have a sense of entitlement, as the inheritors of the struggles of the 1960s and 1970s. Many of these young women assume the battle for equality has been substantially won and that they can combine marriage, motherhood, and career. Only when they encounter obstacles economically and psychically to achieving this objective will they be receptive to collective action.

Will the feminist movement be forced into a siege mentality and be perceived as a single-issue movement? Having to fight state-by-state to retain reproductive freedom resembles the approach required by the suffrage campaign, which consumed the energies of women for decades.

Members of the radical right pose as advocates for the family but in fact are antifamily. They advocate measures which adversely affect women and children (three-fourths of the nuclear family), as they are opposed to child care, birth control and sex education, abortion, and governmental support of mothers with dependent children. They would have the women and children (who bear 77 percent of the nation's poverty) solely responsible for their own economic well-being. That such policies could be construed as profamily is nothing less than Orwellian doublethink. Preservation of male domination of the family would not ensure that American families could thrive, especially given the structural changes within the economy and the necessity for women to be employed outside the home.

While many conservatives blame feminists for disrupting the natural order, they in turn support a nuclear arms buildup, engender anti-Communist hysteria, promote reckless disregard of the environment, and turn a callous shoulder to the poor and minorities. Lurking behind their political ideology is a millennial, religious impulse. Their agenda is based on the belief that the end of the world is near anyway, and therefore one's spiritual condition is more important than economic well-being or political justice. Advocates of the radical right seem unconcerned that most working women are locked into low-paying, dead-end jobs and must work for the welfare of their families.

Although the radical right is still a serious threat to feminist gains, even more dangerous threats are radical individualism and internal fragmentation. If women of the 1990s pursue their own personal objectives without staying connected to one another collectively, they will repeat the mistakes of women in the 1920s. Failing to take seriously the insight that "the personal is political," they will find their aspirations thwarted, and the superwoman mystique will become as oppressive as the feminine mystique was in the 1950s.

The current feminist movement faces new challenges as well as old struggles. A retreat from egalitarianism into what Wendy Kaminer calls "protectionist feminism" in A Fearful Freedom would ultimately reinforce women's subordination in the home and workplace. While it is extremely important to understand and appreciate differences among women, an overemphasis on difference will deflect attention from common grievances and the ways in which all women are discriminated against. The same debate which Alice Paul and Carrie Chapman Catt fought has reemerged—egalitarianism versus protectionism. Cultural feminism, which has the potential for focusing on personal rather than social transformation and the development of female counterinstitutions, may ultimately weaken women's drive for full equality. If feminists are to avoid the hazards of reinforcing sexually differentiated roles, they must find a way of valorizing traditionally female values as human values and not settle for short-term ameliorative measures in lieu of full equality. Feminist theory must expose the interlocking and parallel systems of oppression of racism and sexism.

In order to improve the status of women, a multifaceted agenda for social change is essential. The feminist movement's challenge is to reconcile the needs of women for achievement, financial independence, equal partnership in marriage and childrearing, reproductive control, education, mobility in professions and jobs, and payment for comparable worth. These objectives cannot be achieved simply through legislation alone. Because the traditional expectations about women's roles and the beliefs about the nature of men and women have been so deeply socialized, a complete restructuring of the economy, family, and education as well as a reinterpretation of theology and nonracist, nonsexist socialization of children must be achieved. Women must be relieved of the total responsibility for childrearing and housework, or women will remain disadvantaged economically. Only a comprehensive national family policy which guarantees high-quality child care, parental leave, family medical leave, and comparable-worth compensation will enable women and families to be liberated. In the 1990s the central challenge for feminists will be to maintain the gains which have been made, while under fierce attack by the New Right, and to establish common ground with the majority of American women who will marry, have children, and also work.

The ERA was reintroduced a week after it failed. NOW's strategy was to focus on state elections to oust opponents, before launching another nationwide campaign. Eleanor Smeal and Molly Yard urged another full-scale campaign for the ERA. In the summer of 1989 NOW also proposed a separate women's party at their annual convention in Cincinnati. For the feminist movement to get going again, more than a campaign for the ERA is necessary. Although the amendment is extremely important for establishing the principle of female equality once and for all, feminists must also fight to maintain reproductive freedom.

The feminist movement is beginning to regain national cohesiveness because of the threat of losing reproductive freedom. The movement now is composed of innumerable grass-roots struggles. In fact, its decentralization can be an advantage. As evidenced by a conference in Kenya in 1985, feminism is a global phenomenon. Whereas large differences exist regarding ideology and tactics, a great deal of unity exists regarding equal pay, child care, health care, rape, spousal and child abuse, and education. Feminism affirms the diversity of many forms of family association, acknowledging the changes which have already occurred in the nature of American families.

Along with the enormous freedoms which women enjoy come confusion and fear. As de Beauvoir urged, women must accept actively their freedom and responsibility. Without simply reversing roles with men, women must undergo personal transformation and at the same time transform American society. Today American women already have freedom only dreamed of in the nineteenth century. They are no longer expected to be angels in the house, but they are disadvantaged because of the economic vulnerability created by divorce, sex-segregated jobs and a national policy which has not recognized the realities of the new American "families" (not "family"). Another generation "will look back at us in astonishment," with a larger realization, it is to be hoped, and fuller lives. "All the way down, this time."

Appendixes

APPENDIX 1
A Portrait of Marriage in the 1930s

E. Lowell Kelly's longitudinal study of couples between 1935 and 1938 reveals couples of the 1930s who were attempting to create egalitarian marriages in the midst of economic crisis. Kelly's study provides a rare glimpse of women's aspirations in the 1930s, their courtship, and their experiences in marriage. Through personal contacts, newspapers, and other advertisements, Kelly recruited three hundred couples with a good deal of variation in social background. The participants were above average in intelligence and education and lived in Connecticut, an adjacent state, or in Indiana. They were white, generally between twenty and thirty years old. More than 35 percent of the participants' fathers were of working-class occupations. Kelly's follow-up study conducted during 1954–55 was successful in gathering information on about 75 percent of the original participants (see E. Lowell Kelly, "Consistency of the Adult Personality," *American Psychologist* 10 [1955]: 659–81). James Connolly, Kelly's former student, helped conduct the third study in 1979–80 and received responses from 370 (62 percent) of the original participants; 19 percent had died.

Kelly did annual follow-up questionnaires through 1941, when World War II intervened. By the time of the follow-up in 1954–55, 278 of the original engagements had resulted in marriage. Of the 278 marriages, 12 had been terminated by death, and 39 by divorce. In both the original study and the 1954–55 follow-up, the participants took a battery of tests including a personality test and filled out extensive questionnaires. Because of the wide range of questions concerning sexuality and marital satisfaction, the choice of partner, and childrearing, the Kelly study is a valuable source for understanding American families in the twentieth century.

Kelly's conclusions contradicted the data of Lewis M. Terman and Catherine Cox Miles, who found a shift toward more feminine scores for men and women after males demonstrated traditional traits of masculinity most strongly in high school and women in college. Kelly found small, but significant shifts in the masculine direction by both men and women by 1954–55.

Kelly's study is the most thorough exploration of couples marrying in the 1930s and yields insights into their expectations of marriage, sexual roles, sexuality, and parenting. Kelly first questioned the couples before they married, asking them why they chose each other and why they thought they would have a successful marriage. Overwhelmingly both men and women thought they were entering marriage with the idea of cooperation, love, and overcoming obstacles. As one young man put it, "We will help one another. We will always try to agree on everything. We will be true and love each other." They reported that they chose each other primarily for love and emphasized common social, educational, spiritual backgrounds, and interests. To these couples, marriage meant a "50-50" plan, an egalitarian partnership. Some openly declared their sexual attraction to the other as a significant factor. One participant's responses to these questions are worth quoting because he summarized the feelings of the others as well. When asked why he was marrying his partner, he replied:

1. Intellectually abler than any other woman I have met from a matrimonial standpoint.
2. Refreshingly independent; no clinging vine.
3. Plenty of initiative, and drive enough to spare.
4. Physically attractive as any woman I have known and decidedly more extroverted.
5. Passionate (and how) on occasion.
6. Best social background, education; ablest relatives.

To the question of why his marriage would be a success, he responded equally extensively:

1. We agree essentially in our views for any ideal marriage.
2. Intellectually and physically compatible.
3. More than usual amount of ability in arbitration.
4. Same professional interests and abilities.
5. Mutual love and respect for each other.
6. Respect for each others' parents, relatives, and friends.

The respondents claimed that their partners came closest to the "ideal" and that they "belonged together." One woman wrote, "In the first place, my fiancé came up to what I'd always had as an ideal. He enjoyed the same things as I did, had the same philosophy of life and those things combined with his unusual sympathy and understanding assured me that we were meant for each other."

Another woman who described herself and her partner as "very anxious to be the happiest people on earth," said she chose her future husband because of her sexual attraction to him and because he was versatile, an excellent dancer, thoughtful, attentive, generous, practical, ambitious, well liked by others, and intelligent.

Kelly's subjects held traditional values about role expectations; the women expected to find fulfillment as wives and mothers. However, a few women admitted that they wanted to dominate their mates, "which isn't good." Many of the women reported that their mothers had dominated the family and portrayed their mothers generally as totally dedicated to home and family and completely self-sacrificing. Those who worked outside the home, with a few exceptions of professional women, did not really want to. One replied, "Working denies me the privilege of being a good housewife and shall we say a patient mother, but I guess we will manage. We gals are never satisfied, or are we?"

The women seemed to accept the traditional role as satisfying and preferable to a career. "Marriage is my career," one woman wrote. "I chose it and now it is up to me to see that I do the job successfully—in spite of the stresses and strains of life." However, many of the women reported that they had given up promising careers or college for marriage. Their comments in 1954–55 about what they had sacrificed were not characterized by bitterness, but by a sense of having made a preferable choice, as well as the implication of lack of confidence that they would have been professionally successful.

Kelly's information concerning premarital sexual practice was scanty and impressionistic. Two contradictory themes emerged from responses of men and women regarding premarital sex. A number of women reported that premarital sexual practice generated guilt, frigidity, and lack of sexual adjustment in marriage. The other theme emerged mostly from men's comments that sexual experience before marriage had greatly facilitated sexual satisfaction in marriage. One woman remarked, "Only that I was afraid that some one might have learned that we had intercourse before marriage and I'd be disgraced—but this fear died after a few months." Not all the women felt this sort of guilt; one wrote cheerfully: "I think my marriage was affected by my sexual experiences—I enjoyed sex and was most anxious to be married and I'm sure my marriage has been happier because I had no fear or worry about sex in marriage."

This was a minority opinion, however, and more women than men were reticent on the issue of premarital sexual experience. When asked how much they valued sexual relations in marriage, the men and women expressed its importance generally within the top three rankings and indicated a responsiveness to the needs of their partners. They answered that it was important to have sex when their partners desired it more than when they desired it.

Kelly asked the couples to rate their marital satisfaction over the period of twenty years. If the marriages survived periods of discontent, a common pattern was of hills and valleys, with the marriage returning to relatively high levels of satisfaction. Overall, the worst time for the marriages centered on World War II and immediately afterward. At the time of Connolly's follow-up survey in 1979, most of the participants were very satisfied with their marriages, and more than 90 percent were "generally satisfied" with their present or most recent marriage. Slightly less (85 percent) declared that they would definitely or most likely marry the same person if they had their lives to live over. Kelly's study does not reveal the women's struggling to combine marriage and career. The women generally viewed marriage as their career. However, the couples had higher expectations about an egalitarian relationship and mutual sexual fulfillment than their predecessors. (See E. Lowell Kelly, "Personality, Marital Compatibility, and Married Life: A Twenty-Year Longitudinal Study, 1935–55," A431, Henry A. Murray Research Center, Radcliffe College. See M31, M147, Time 1; F43, F77, F198, F29, Marriage Report I., 258, F14, F83, Time 2. See also James Connolly, "Kelly Longitudinal Study Report to Participants," August 1980, 7, Henry A. Murray Research Center. This research used the Kelly Longitudinal Study 1935–55 data set [made accessible in 1979, including raw and machine-readable data files]. These data were collected by E. L. Kelly and are available through the archive of the Henry A. Murray Research Center of Radcliffe College, Cambridge, Massachusetts [producer and distributor].)

APPENDIX 2
Black Women Oral History Project

The testimonies of the following women, participants of the Black Women Oral History Project (BWOHP) conducted by the Schlesinger Library at Radcliffe College, reveal the diverse views which African-American women have held regarding feminism. Seventy-two oral histories were recorded, of which I had access to fifty-seven. Unfortunately not all of the women were asked specifically about their views of feminism in the form of a question such as, "What do you think about the women's movement or women's liberation?" Therefore in my rough calculations, I have noted the ones who strongly supported the movement, those who were ambivalent, and those who were strongly opposed to it. Of the fifty-seven transcripts which I read, eighteen were strongly in favor of the movement, two were in favor with reservations, three were definitely opposed, and thirty-four gave no indication either way and were not asked the question directly. In these cases I tried to discern from their other comments how they stood, but any conclusions here would be too speculative to be of value.

I make no scientific claims for the analysis of these oral histories. Likewise the seventy-two women of the project were selected by the project's advisory committee utilizing no scientific sampling techniques. Participants had professional careers in education, government, the arts, business, medicine, law, journalism, and social work. Others cared for their families and devoted their service to their communities, regions, and nation. All made significant contributions of varying kinds.

Many of the participants were born at the end of the nineteenth century, others early in the twentieth century, and the younger ones around 1916. The women in the project represented different geographic regions and classes, and their lives spanned the late nineteenth and twentieth centuries. Thus, they lived through dramatic changes in the cultural expectations of women and changes in status. Most of them were highly educated and were involved in numerous women's organizations, which would promote their awareness of the women's movement.

Christia Daniels Adair voiced the view that black women have always been liberated.

> I don't particularly care about women's lib because the Negro woman has always had to work.
>
> . . . Well. I never can remember the day when I wasn't liberated. I think there may be some category of women who haven't had an opportunity to serve, but Negro women have always been in a position to work and do things that they wanted to do. Now in this culture or in this generation, in this time, when they are aspiring for jobs that require better preparation, I just think if they just go on and prepare, that just like some of us took it upon ourselves to fight for votes, some others took it upon themselves to fight to have advanced education and got it, I think we can go on and do it too. I don't think anybody has to fall out about any of it.

(Oral history conducted by Dorothy R. Robinson, April 25, 1977, BWOHP, OH-31, 45, 12, 15.)

The African-American women who were interviewed frequently referred to their strong sense of identity. Most of them worked outside the home, although a few commented that their husbands did not want them to work. They seemed to be superwomen, juggling jobs or careers, husbands, and children; however, many of the professional women never married, including May Edward Chinn, a New York physician who practiced for fifty years. Eva B. Dykes joined Sadie T. M. Alexander and Georgiana Simpson in 1921 as the first black women to earn Ph.D.'s. Dykes was a professor at Howard University from 1924 and never married or had children.

Mary Thompson, a graduate of Tufts University Dental Schools, replied to the question "What do you think of women's liberation?" as follows: "We've always been liberated. Black women have always been liberated, haven't they? They've run most of their homes and all the rest of the stuff is for the birds." Thompson had two husbands, and no children. (Oral history conducted by Cheryl Gilkes, August 6–7, 1977, BWOHP, 130.)

As others did, Lucy Miller Mitchell, a specialist in early childhood education, openly declared herself a feminist: "Well, I heartily support it [the women's movement]. I guess you might label me a feminist if one can be a feminist at my age. I heartily support the aims and goals of today's thrust of the women's rights movement. I certainly support the Equal Rights Movement." (Oral history conducted by Cheryl Gilkes, June 17, 24, July 1, 6, 25, 1977, BWOHP, 74–75.)

Ann Tanneyhill accepted the consequences of the forked path and chose a career of activism over marriage. She worked with the Urban League. When asked about marriage, she replied, "I'm not saying I was never asked, but I just never had any interest in giving up what I considered a dedication and a commitment for marriage, because I did not believe that I could be married and do the things I wanted to do." (Oral history conducted by Cheryl Gilkes, April 11, 1978, BWOHP, 53–54.)

Audley Moore, a black nationalist, was openly hostile to the feminist movement. In her interview she emphasized the necessity of black women's supporting black men.

> The black woman has to share. She has to share in the full responsibility for the complete emancipation, the complete freedom of her people.
> Her role is to support, to understand first of all what has happened to her black men, that they have been singled out for destruction. . . . So tell me, what greater role the black woman has than to protect her black man, to build him up. . . . So she cannot afford to join those white women in their anti-male thing. She has no place in the white woman's movement.

(Oral history conducted by Cheryl Gilkes Townsend, June 6, 8, 1978, BWOHP, 61.)

In sharp contrast to Moore's views, those of Maida Springer Kemp were illustrative of many of the participants' attitudes. Kemp married twice and had one son, while working in the trade-union movement. She gave her views of the movement.

> The women's movement for me is like the trade union movement. There is a great deal of misunderstanding about what the women's movement is all about and when you have people writing about burning brassieres and doing [it], just talking about the ridiculous things that are done. . . . In any movement there are extremes, there are demagogues, and there are people who will use that movement in order to get some point of view which they have across. The women's movement has a fundamental basis which I think is correct for them to bring to the attention of the rest of this country, that they share in the woes and the success of this country, and there are women with a multitude of talents that ought to contribute to the national good. . . .

The early position of that, of NOW, the National Organization of Women for example, left the impression that those women were concerned only with middle-class values, and it had no relationship and bearing on other problems. It left the impression that they were the women who could talk about maids and checking accounts, and for a lot of the working women, the black women in the country, and the Chicano women, that, just turned them off. They weren't talking about the same thing. But they did not participate and have the sense of what the whole thing was about.

So, I am a supporter of the women's movement and in the same way that I think the labor movement is very often misunderstood, I think that the women's movement is misunderstood. As a matter of fact, you now have the head of the women's movement, a housewife.

Originally, the feeling was that the women's movement was anti-marriage, anti-family and anti the structure of what is considered the normal society. I don't think it was. I think in their anxiety to get a point of view across, some of their statements were erratic and did not make sense if you sat down to analyze what they were about.

Life is a combination of things: family, sharing, a personal relationship which does not rob you of your self-respect and your own identity; that's always important.

(Oral history conducted by Elizabeth Balanoff, January 4, 1977, BWOHP, 71, 100–101.)

APPENDIX 3
The Feminist Movement in the 1970s: A Chronology

The following information comes from Suzanne Levine, Harriet Lyons, and Gloria Steinem, *The Decade of Women: A Ms. History of the Seventies in Words and Pictures* (New York: G. P. Putnam's Sons, 1980), 6, 8, 10, 12, 16, 18, 20, 22, 24 (used by permission of *Ms.* magazine), and from Myra Marx Ferree and Beth B. Hess, *Controversy and Coalition* (Boston: Twayne, 1985), 95. These sources cite the following accomplishments and events of the feminist movement in the 1970s:

1970

Hawaii, Alaska, and New York become the first states to liberalize abortion laws.

The Senate holds the first ERA hearings since 1956. House subcommittee hearings on sex discrimination in education are the first in U.S. history.

New York City is the first major city to pass a bill banning sex discrimination in public accommodations after demonstrations at Biltmore Hotel men's bar and similar protests.

The first annual nationwide strike for equality celebrates the fiftieth anniversary of suffrage, as 50,000 people march down Fifth Avenue on August 26.

A sit-in at *Ladies Home Journal* by 100 women leads to supplement in August 1970 issue.

Congress to Unite Women meets in New York.

Lesbians stage Lavender Menace Action, asserting right to be public lesbians.

Feminist publications founded: *Ain't I a Woman?* (Iowa City, Iowa) and *It Ain't Me Babe* (Berkeley, Calif.).

1971

The University of Michigan is the first university to incorporate Affirmative Action Plan for hiring.

First females serve as Senate pages.

The National Women's Political Caucus organized.

Women's National Abortion Coalition formed.

Women's Action Alliance formed in New York by Gloria Steinem and Brenda Feigen Fasteau.

Congress passes the ERA; Hawaii is the first state to ratify.

The Equal Employment Opportunity Act of 1972 empowers EEOC to go to court with discrimination cases.

Title IX of Educational Amendments of 1972 passed, prohibiting sex discrimination in most federally assisted educational programs.

1973

Supreme Court legalizes abortion following successful arguments by Sarah Weddington and Marjorie Pitts Hames *(Doe v. Bolton* and *Roe v. Wade)*.

The Supreme Court also outlaws sex-segregated ads.

National Black Feminist Organization formed.

Benjamin Spock announces earlier sexist views on child care and revises his classic book. He writes in his new version of *Baby and Child Care,* "Both parents have an equal right to a career, if they want one, it seems to me, and an equal obligation to share in the care of their child, with or without the help of others."

Federal Home Loan Bank Board bars sex bias by savings and loan institutions.

NARAL, founded in 1969, changes name to National Abortion Rights Action League, whose objective is to preserve the 1973 Supreme Court decision.

1974

Passport Office allows use of "maiden" name.

Laura Cross, age eleven, wins National Soapbox Derby.

Kathryn Kirschbaum is denied BankAmericard unless she gets her husband's signature, even though she earns $15,000 a year as mayor of Davenport, Iowa.

The Supreme Court outlaws automatic exclusion of women from jury duty.

Time magazine breaks tradition in naming the "Man of the Year" by designating ten women for cover honors.

1976

Women are made eligible to become astronauts; the first women selected in 1978.

Sarah Caldwell is first woman to conduct the Metropolitan Opera after Beverly Sills refuses to sing unless Caldwell conducts.

Women are eligible for Rhodes Scholarships for the first time.

Women earn 57 cents for every dollar earned by men; of all full-time year-round workers, only 5 percent earn $15,000 or more.

1977

The Supreme Court rules that states and cities may bar use of public funds and public hospital facilities for elective, nontherapeutic abortions.

1978

Congress extends deadline for ERA ratification to June 30, 1982.

A Harris poll reports that support for the ERA is up to 55 percent, with 38 percent opposed, after a two-year period of erosion.

More women than men enter college for the first time in American history.

National Coalition against Domestic Violence is formed.

By 1978 over 300 shelters, hotlines, and groups were acting as advocates for victims of family violence.

1979

A Harris poll indicates that Americans favor efforts to strengthen and change women's status by 65 percent to 28 percent, up from 42 percent to 41 percent in 1970.

NOTES

1. The Colonial Window: Good Wives and Witches (1607–1776)

1. Mary Beth Norton, "The Evolution of White Women's Experience in Early America," *American Historical Review* 89 (June 1984): 597–602, 607.

2. Sara M. Evans, *Born for Liberty: A History of Women in America* (New York: Free Press, 1989), 26; Nancy Woloch, *Women and the American Experience* (New York: Alfred A. Knopf, 1984), 30.

3. Norton, "Evolution of White Women's Experience," 597–607; Lois Green Carr and Lorena S. Walsh, "The Planter's Wife: The Experience of White Women in Seventeenth-Century Maryland," *William and Mary Quarterly*, 3d ser., 34 (October 1977): 542–71.

4. Evans, *Born for Liberty*, 27; see also Allan Kulikoff, "The Origins of Afro-American Society in Tidewater Maryland and Virginia, 1700–1790," *William and Mary Quarterly*, 3d ser., 35 (1978): 226–59; Allan Kulikoff, "The Beginnings of the Afro-American Family in Maryland," in *The American Family in Social-Historical Perspective*, 2d ed., ed. Michael Gordon (New York: St. Martin's Press, 1978), 444–66. The works of Jacqueline Jones (*Labor of Love, Labor of Sorrow: Black Women, Work, and the Family from Slavery to the Present* [New York: Basic Books, 1985]), Deborah White (*Ar'n't I a Woman: Female Slaves in the Plantation South* [New York: W. W. Norton, 1985]), and Gloria L. Main (*Tobacco Colony: Life in Early Maryland, 1650–1720* [Princeton: Princeton University Press, 1982]) provide excellent accounts of African-American women during this period.

5. Woloch, *Women and the American Experience*, 78–79, 180–81.

6. Marylynn Salmon, "Equality or Submersion? Feme Covert Status in Early Pennsylvania," in *Women of American: A History*, ed. Carol Ruth Berkin and Mary Beth Norton (Boston: Houghton Mifflin, 1979), 94.

7. Marylynn Salmon, *Women and the Law of Property in Early America* (Chapel Hill: University of North Carolina Press, 1986); Stephanie Coontz, *The Social Origins of Private Life: A History of American Families, 1600–1900* (London: Verso, 1988), 94.

8. Mary Ryan, *Womanhood in America from Colonial Times to the Present* (New York: New Viewpoints, 1975), 22–23.

9. Ibid., 40, 57–58; Laurel Thatcher Ulrich, *Good Wives: Image and Reality in the Lives of Women in Northern New England, 1650–1750* (New York: Oxford University Press, 1982), 115; Robert V. Wells, "Women's Lives Transformed: Demographic and Family Patterns in America, 1600–1970," in *Women in America*, ed. Berkin and Norton, 27; Steven Mintz and Susan Kellogg, *Domestic Revolutions: A Social History of American Family Life* (New York: Free Press, 1988), 2; Coontz, *Social Origins of Private Life*, 82.

10. Ulrich, *Good Wives*, 129, 131, 145, 124–25.

11. Ryan, *Womanhood in America*, 53; Mintz and Kellogg, *Domestic Revolutions*, 19.

12. Elizabeth Pleck, *Domestic Tyranny: The Making of American Social Policy against Family Violence from Colonial Times to the Present* (New York: Oxford University Press, 1987), 20–21; Mintz and Kellogg, *Domestic Revolutions*, 10–12; Coontz, *Social Origins of Private Life*, 82, 94.

13. Ryan, *Womanhood in America*, 56.

14. Norton, "Evolution of White Women's Experience," 608–9.

15. Ryan, *Womanhood in America*, 72, 76–81; Woloch, *Women and the American Experience*, 45.

16. See John Demos, *Entertaining Satan* (New York: Oxford University Press, 1982); Carol F. Karlsen, *The Devil in the Shape of a Woman: Witchcraft in Colonial New England* (New York: W. W. Norton, 1987); and Paul Boyer and Stephen Nissenbaum, *Salem Possessed: The Social Origins of Witchcraft* (Cambridge: Harvard University Press, 1974).

2. Republican Motherhood and the Angel in the House

1. Mary Beth Norton, *Liberty's Daughters: The Revolutionary Experience of American Women, 1750–1800* (Boston: Little, Brown, 1980), 161; Norton cites the *Boston Evening Post*, February 12, 1770; "Ladies of the Association," *William and Mary Quarterly*, 1st ser., 8 (1899), 36; Peter Force, comp., *American Archives* (Washington, D.C.), 4th ser., 1 (1837): 891; Linda K. Kerber, *Women of the Republic: Intellect and Ideology in Revolutionary America* (New York: W. W. Norton, 1986; originally Chapel Hill: University of North Carolina Press, 1980), 41, 44; Nancy Woloch, *Women and the American Experience* (New York: Alfred A. Knopf, 1984), 80; L. H. Butterfield, Marc Friedlaender, and Mary-Jo Kline, eds., *The Book of Abigail and John: Selected Letters of the Adams Family, 1762–1784* (Cambridge: Harvard University Press, 1975), 184–85.

2. See Sara M. Evans, *Born for Liberty: A History of Women in America* (New York: Free Press, 1989), 43, 58. For more extensive background on colonial women, see Nancy F. Cott, "Eighteenth Century Family and Social Life Revealed in Massachu-

setts Divorce Records," in *A Heritage of Her Own: Toward a New Social History of American Women*, ed. Nancy F. Cott and Elizabeth H. Pleck (New York: Simon & Schuster, 1979), 107–61; Laurel Thatcher Ulrich, "Vertuous Women Found: New England Ministerial Literature, 1668–1735," in *A Heritage of Her Own*, ed. Cott and Pleck, 58–80; Lois Green Carr and Lorena Walsh, "The Planter's Wife: The Experience of White Women in Seventeenth-Century Maryland, *William and Mary Quarterly* 34 (1977): 542–71; John Demos, "Husbands and Wives," in *Our American Sisters: Women in American Life and Thought*, 4th ed., ed. Jean E. Friedman, William G. Shade, and Mary Jane Capozzoli (Lexington, Mass.: D. C. Heath, 1987), 9–22; and Estelle C. Jelinek, *The Tradition of Women's Autobiography: From Antiquity to the Present* (Boston: Twayne, 1986). The two major works on women and the American Revolution are Norton, *Liberty's Daughters*, and Kerber, *Women of the Republic*; see also Stephanie Coontz, *The Social Origins of Private Life: A History of American Families, 1600–1900* (London: Verso, 1988), 145, 147.

3. Alice S. Rossi, ed., *The Feminist Papers: From Adams to de Beauvoir* (New York: Bantam, 1973), 10–11.

4. Kerber, *Women of the Republic*, 159, 229, 11, 193; Coontz, *Social Origins of Private Life*, 148.

5. "From the Salutatory Oration, Delivered by Miss Priscilla Mason, May 15, 1793," in *Women of America: A History*, ed. Carol Ruth Berkin and Mary Beth Norton (Boston: Houghton Mifflin, 1979), 90.

6. Gerda Lerner, "The Lady and the Mill Girl: Changes in the Status of Women in the Age of Jackson, 1800–1840," in *A Heritage of Her Own*, ed. Cott and Pleck, 182–96; Coontz, *Social Origins of Private Life*, 99–100, 151–52, 155.

7. Nancy A. Hewitt, "Feminist Friends: Agrarian Quakers and the Emergence of Woman's Rights in America," *Feminist Studies* 12, no. 1 (Spring 1986): 27–49; see also Nancy F. Cott, *The Bonds of Womanhood: "Woman's Sphere" in New England, 1780–1835* (New Haven: Yale University Press, 1977), 197–201; Carroll Smith-Rosenberg, "The Female World of Love and Ritual: Relations between Women in Nineteenth-Century America," *Signs: Journal of Women in Culture and Society* 1 (1975): 1–29.

8. Jeanne Boydston, Mary Kelley, Anne Margolis, *The Limits of Sisterhood: The Beecher Sisters on Women's Rights and Women's Sphere* (Chapel Hill: University of North Carolina Press, 1988), 116, 120–21; for an excellent biography of Catharine Beecher, see Kathryn Kish Sklar, *Catharine Beecher: A Study of American Domesticity* (New Haven: Yale University Press, 1973).

9. Jane P. Tompkins, *Sensational Designs: The Cultural Work of American Fiction, 1790–1860* (New York: Oxford University Press, 1985), 143–45.

10. Barbara Welter, "The Cult of True Womanhood, 1820–1860," in *Dimity Convictions: The American Woman in the Nineteenth Century* (Athens: Ohio University Press, 1976), 21–41.

11. Mary Cable, *American Manners and Morals: A Picture of How We Behaved and Misbehaved* (New York: American Heritage, 1969), 105.

12. *Female Influence and the True Christian Mode of Its Exercise; a Discourse Delivered in the First Presbyterian Church in Newburyport, July 30, 1837* (Newburyport, 1837), 18, quoted in part in Welter, "Cult of True Womanhood," 26; Cable, *American Manners and Morals*, 104–5.

13. Cott, *Bonds of Womanhood*, 200.

14. Suzanne Lebsock, *The Free Women of Petersburg: Status and Culture in a Southern Town, 1784–1860* (New York: W. W. Norton, 1984), 17, 27–28, 32, 50–53, 233.

15. Cable, *American Manners and Morals*, 150.

16. Tompkins, *Sensational Designs*, 161, 124; see also Mary Kelley, *Private Woman, Public Stage: Literary Domesticity in Nineteenth-Century America* (New York: Oxford University Press, 1984), 308; Mary P. Ryan, *The Empire of the Mother: American Writing about Domesticity, 1830–1860* (New York: Haworth Press, 1982), 18.

17. Kathryn Weibel, *Mirror, Mirror: Images of Women Reflected in Popular Culture* (Garden City, N.Y.: Anchor Books, 1977), 12–14, 16–18; Helen Waite Papashvily, *All the Happy Endings: A Study of the Domestic Novel in America, the Women Who Wrote It, the Women Who Read It, in the Nineteenth Century* (Port Washington, N.Y.: Kennikat Press, 1972), 1–14, 29–30.

18. Tompkins, *Sensational Designs*, 165.

19. Papashvily, *All the Happy Endings*, 7, 63–95.

20. Ibid., 70–71; Glenna Matthews, *"Just a Housewife": The Rise and Fall of Domesticity in America* (New York: Oxford University Press, 1987), 30, 49–50. Matthews argues that Stowe's novel *Uncle Tom's Cabin* was so popular because of the widespread idealization of domesticity and the home in American culture. Her overall thesis is that this elevation of domesticity perished early in the twentieth century because of economic upheaval and evolutionary theory, only to be appropriated in the 1920s by technocrats and advertisers. See also Boydston, Kelley, and Margolis, *Limits of Sisterhood*, 53–54, 258, 260; Weibel, *Mirror, Mirror*, 22–23. See also Annegret S. Ogden, *The Great American Housewife: From Helpmate to Wage Earner, 1776–1986* (Westport, Conn.: Greenwood Press, 1986), 68; Jane P. Tompkins, "Sentimental Power in *Uncle Tom's Cabin* and the Politics of Literary History," in *The New Feminist Criticism: Essays on Women, Literature, and Theory*, ed. Elaine Showalter (New York: Pantheon, 1985), 83, 86, 91.

21. Papashvily, *All the Happy Endings*, 24.

22. Nina Baym, *Woman's Fiction: A Guide to Novels by and about Women in America, 1820–1870* (Ithaca: Cornell University Press, 1978), 18–19, 40.

23. For citations here and in the following paragraphs, see Louise Hall Tharp, *The Peabody Sisters of Salem* (Boston: Little, Brown, 1950), 4, 17, 39, 136, 149, 153, 157, 161–63, 181, 188–89, 198, 230–31, 269, 292, 317, 319–20, 324, 330–36. For the quotation from Hawthorne, see John D'Emilio and Estelle B. Freedman, *Intimate*

Matters: A History of Sexuality in America (New York: Harper & Row, 1988), 76, quoted from Peter Gay, *The Bourgeois Experience: Victoria to Freud;* vol. 1: *The Education of the Senses* (New York: Oxford University Press, 1984), 456–57.

3. Feminism for the Sake of the Family and Community (1800–1900)

1. In her splendid book *The Grounding of Modern Feminism* (New Haven: Yale University Press, 1987), 13–17, 4, Nancy F. Cott has pointed out that the term "feminism" did not come into wide usage in the United States until around 1913. The term seems to have been first used in the 1880s in France (*feminisme*) by Hubertine Auclert, the founder of the first woman suffrage society in France. Cott claims that the term began to be used in England in the 1890s, at first derogatorily. Like Gerda Lerner, she distinguishes between the nineteenth-century "woman movement," the suffrage and women's rights movements, and the modern feminist movement. As Cott observes, efforts to improve the status of women in the nineteenth century ranged from service and social action to campaigns for legal, political, and economic rights which were reformist to more radical attempts to achieve women's full emancipation and transform the social order. Cott's working definition of feminism contains three components: (1) a belief in what is usually referred to as sex equality but which might be more clearly expressed in the negative, as opposition to sex hierarchy; (2) a presupposition that women's condition is socially constructed, that is, historically shaped by human social usage rather than predestined by God or nature; (3) an assumption that women perceive themselves as a social grouping, not only as a biological sex. I accept Cott's definition as highly useful. Throughout this book, I consider both conservative and radical attempts to achieve women's equality as feminist, and also try to make the distinctions between self-proclaimed feminists, suffragists, advocates for women's rights, egalitarian feminists, protectionist feminists, reform feminists, and radical feminists. I am therefore attempting to distinguish the vast array of ideologies and strategies under the rubric of feminism. This kind of labeling is necessarily somewhat imprecise since it may seem to be static and not adequately describing women's changes in approach over time, or more complex positions. However, I have attempted to describe individual women's positions accurately.

2. Margaret Hope Bacon, *Mothers of Feminism: The Story of Quaker Women in America* (San Francisco: Harper & Row, 1986), 92–93; Elias Hicks challenged attempts to impose doctrinal orthodoxy and formed his own group of Friends. Hicksite groups of Quakers were strong in Ohio, Pennsylvania, New York, Maryland, Indiana, Illinois, and Canada. Lucretia Mott, Susan B. Anthony, Florence Kelley, and Alice Paul were dissident Quakers. Rural Hicksites continued to share responsibility on farms and in shops and were less influenced by the notion of separate spheres for men and women.

When Amy and Isaac Post were censured by Hicksites for participating in antislavery societies with non-Quakers, they formed the Congregational Friends at Waterloo. See also Ann Braude, *Radical Spirits: Spiritualism and Women's Rights in Nineteenth Century America* (Boston: Beacon, 1989), 58.

3. Elisabeth Griffith, *In Her Own Right: The Life of Elizabeth Cady Stanton* (New York: Oxford University Press, 1984), 51.

4. Bacon, *Mothers of Feminism*, 1, 92–94. Quaker women composed 30 percent of the pioneers of prison reform, 40 percent of women abolitionists, and 15 percent of the suffragists born before 1830.

5. Eleanor Flexner, *Century of Struggle: The Women's Rights Movement in the United States* (New York: Atheneum, 1974), 74–77.

6. Karlyn Kohrs Campbell, *Man Cannot Speak for Her: A Critical Study of Early Feminist Rhetoric*, vol. 1 (Westport, Conn.: Greenwood Press, 1989), 53, 57; Elizabeth Cady Stanton, Susan B. Anthony, and Matilda Joslyn Gage, eds., *History of Woman Suffrage*, 2 vols. (New York: Fowler & Wells, 1881–82; vol. 1 reprinted, Salem, N.H.: Ayer, 1985), 1:70–71, 73. The following grievances pertained to family issues: "He has made her if married, in the eye of the law civilly dead." "In the covenant of marriage, she is compelled to promise obedience to her husband, he becoming to all intents and purposes, her master—the law giving him power to deprive her of her liberty, and to administer chastisement." "He has so framed the laws of divorce, as to what shall be the proper causes, and in case of separation to whom the guardianship of the children shall be given as to be wholly regardless of the happiness of women— the law, in all cases, going upon a false supposition of the supremacy of man, and giving all power into his hands."

7. Flexner, *Century of Struggle*, 77; Campbell, *Man Cannot Speak for Her*, 50.

8. Griffith, *In Her Own Right*, 58; Stanton, Anthony, and Gage, *History of Woman Suffrage*, 1:804.

9. Griffith, *In Her Own Right*, 58, 51.

10. Braude, *Radical Spirits*, 57; Nancy A. Hewitt, *Women's Activism and Social Change: Rochester, New York, 1822–1872* (Ithaca: Cornell University Press, 1984), 132, 131; Stanton, Anthony, and Gage, *History of Woman Suffrage*, 1:75.

11. Hewitt, *Women's Activism*, 130, 238–40.

12. Ibid., 132, 134, 136.

13. Braude, *Radical Spirits*, 56–58, 27, 196, 117–18, 120–21, 127.

14. Flexner, *Century of Struggle*, 76–77.

15. Andrew Sinclair, *The Emancipation of the American Woman* (New York: Harper & Row, 1965), 119.

16. Mrs. E. Little, "What Are the Rights of Women?" *Ladies' Wreath* 2 (1848–49): 133, quoted in Barbara Welter, "The Cult of True Womanhood, 1820–1860," in *Dimity Convictions* (Athens: Ohio University Press, 1976), 40.

17. Lois W. Banner, "Elizabeth Cady Stanton: Early Marriage and Feminist Rebel-

lion," in *Women's America: Refocusing the Past*, ed. Linda K. Kerber and Jane DeHart Mathews (New York: Oxford University Press, 1987), 205. Stanton wrote to Anthony in 1858: "How rebellious it makes me feel when I see Henry going about where and how he pleases. He can walk at will through the whole wide world or shut himself up alone. As I contrast his freedom with my bondage I feel that, because of the false position of women I have been compelled to hold all my noblest aspirations in abeyance in order to be a wife, a mother, a nurse, a cook, a household drudge" (206).

18. Lee Virginia Chambers-Schiller, *Liberty, a Better Husband: Single Women in America: The Generations of 1780–1840* (New Haven: Yale University Press, 1984), 3.

19. Ellen Carol DuBois, *Feminism and Suffrage: The Emergence of an Independent Woman's Movement in America, 1848–1869* (Ithaca: Cornell University Press, 1978), 192.

20. Elizabeth Cady Stanton, *Eighty Years and More: Reminiscenses, 1815–1897* (New York: T. Fisher Unwin, 1898), 172.

21. Ellen Carol DuBois, ed., *Elizabeth Cady Stanton–Susan B. Anthony: Correspondence, Writings, Speeches* (New York: Schocken Books, 1981), 147.

22. Lois W. Banner, "Act One," *Wilson Quarterly*, Autumn 1986, 97.

23. DuBois, *Stanton–Anthony Correspondence*, 61–62; DuBois, *Feminism and Suffrage*, 28.

24. Griffith, *In Her Own Right*, 74, 93.

25. Stanton, *Eighty Years and More*, 72.

26. DuBois, *Stanton–Anthony Correspondence*, 55.

27. Stanton, Anthony, and Gage, *History of Woman Suffrage*, 1:534.

28. Elizabeth Cady Stanton, *Revolution*, January 22, 1868, 33, Schlesinger Library, Radcliffe College, Cambridge, Mass.; hereafter, SL.

29. Lois W. Banner, *Elizabeth Cady Stanton: A Radical for Woman's Rights* (Boston: Little, Brown, 1980), 61.

30. Chambers-Schiller, *Liberty, a Better Husband*, 194.

31. Elizabeth Pleck, *Domestic Tyranny: The Making of Social Policy against Family Violence from Colonial Times to the Present* (New York: Oxford University Press, 1987), 50. For accounts of domestic violence cited by early women's rights advocates, see Stanton, Anthony, and Gage, *History of Woman Suffrage*, 1:175–76, 88 (Emily Collins, wife beating), 562 (Clarina I. Nichols, children seized by sheriff).

32. Stanton, Anthony, and Gage, *History of Woman Suffrage*, 1:716–22, 724–35; Campbell, *Man Cannot Speak for Her*, 71, 74, 77.

33. Campbell, *Man Cannot Speak for Her*, 78; Leslie Wheeler, ed. *Loving Warriors: Selected Letters of Lucy Stone and Henry B. Blackwell, 1853–1893* (New York: Dial Press, 1981), 187.

34. Barbara Miller Solomon, *In the Company of Educated Women: A History of Women and Higher Education in America* (New Haven: Yale University Press, 1985), 37. See

also Blanche Glassman Hersh, "'A Partnership of Equals': Feminist Marriages in Nineteenth Century America," in *The American Man*, ed. Elizabeth H. Pleck and Joseph H. Pleck (Englewood Cliffs, N.J.: Prentice-Hall, 1980), 193–94. See also Antoinette Brown Blackwell, "The Relation of Woman's Work in the Household to the Work Outside," in *Papers and Letters Presented at the First Woman's Congress of the Association for the Advancement of Women . . . New York, October 1873* (New York: Mrs. William Ballard, 1874), 180; see *Woman's Journal*, November 8, 1873, quoted in Elizabeth Cazden, *Antoinette Brown Blackwell: A Biography* (Old Westbury, N.Y.: Feminist Press, 1983), 161–65.

35. Stanton, Anthony, and Gage, *History of Woman Suffrage*, 1: 731; Campbell, *Man Cannot Speak for Her*, 78.

36. Stanton, *Eighty Years and More*, 219; Campbell, *Man Cannot Speak for Her*, 80–81.

37. Campbell, *Man Cannot Speak for Her*, 79, 80–82; Stanton, Anthony, and Gage, *History of Woman Suffrage*, 1:425.

38. Stanton, Anthony, and Gage, *History of Woman Suffrage*, 1:718; Banner, "Elizabeth Cady Stanton," 207, 204.

39. DuBois, *Stanton–Anthony Correspondence*, 95.

40. Banner, *Elizabeth Cady Stanton*, 83.

41. DuBois, *Stanton–Anthony Correspondence*, 129. Abby Sage, an actress and writer, divorced her husband, Daniel McFarland, and became involved with Albert Richardson. McFarland shot Richardson in the offices of the *Tribune*. On his deathbed Richardson married Mrs. McFarland. However, the press vilified the divorced woman; McFarland was acquitted and granted custody of his son. See Griffith, *In Her Own Right*, 159–60.

42. DuBois, *Stanton–Anthony Correspondence*, 132–33.

43. Ibid., 137–38, 225.

44. Monlau y Roca, quoted in Peter Gay, *The Bourgeois Experience: Victoria to Freud*; vol. 1: *Education of the Senses* (New York: Oxford University Press, 1984), 430–31, 436. For articles on marriage and divorce see the following issues of *Revolution*: August 27, October 15, 22, 1868; April 8, 15, June 24, July 8, September 2, 23, December 16, 1869; February 10, March 3, 24, May 5, 19, July 7, August 18, September 22, December 1, 1870; March 16, 1871.

45. Margaret Forster, *The Grassroots of Active Feminism, 1839–1939* (London: Secker & Warburg, 1984), 235.

46. William Leach, *True and Perfect Union: The Feminist Reform of Sex and Society* (New York: Basic Books, 1980), 25, 21, 29, 27.

47. "What Justifies Marriage," *Revolution*, August 18, 1870, quoted in Leach, *True and Perfect Union*, 116.

48. Ibid.; see also "Happy Marriages," in *Woman's Journal*, February 18, 1871, quoted in Leach, *True and Perfect Union*, 116.

49. Leach, *True and Perfect Union*, 53.

50. Ibid., 92. See "An Appeal to Women," *Revolution*, September 7, 1871.

51. Leach, *True and Perfect Union*, 244, 246, 247–49.

52. Griffith, *In Her Own Right*, 72; see also Stanton, Anthony, and Gage, *History of Woman Suffrage*, where Stanton described the joy that she felt in her bloomers: "What a sense of liberty I felt, in running up and down stairs with my hands free to carry whatsoever I would, to trip through the rain or snow with no skirts to hold or brush, ready at any moment to climb a hill-top to see the sun go down, or the moon to rise, with no ruffles or trails to be limped by the dew, or soiled by the grass. What an emancipation from little petty vexatious trammels and annoyances every hour of the day. Yet such is the tyranny of custom that to escape constant observation, criticism, ridicule, persecution, mobs, one after another gladly went back to the old slavery and sacrificed freedom to repose. . . . Though the martyrdom proved too much for us who had so many other measures to press on the public conscience, yet no experiment is lost, however evanescent, that rouses thought to the injurious consequences of the present style of dress" (1: 470–71).

53. Leach, *True and Perfect Union*, 253.

54. Wheeler, *Loving Warriors*, 33–34.

55. Ibid., 45.

56. Ibid.; Lucy Stone to Henry B. Blackwell, April 8, 1855, 131.

57. Ibid., 135–36. Continuing, Lucy Stone and Henry Blackwell specified their grievances:

We protest especially against the laws which give to the husband:
1. The custody of the wife's person.
2. The exclusive control and guardianship of their children.
3. The sole ownership of her personal, and use of her real estate, unless previously settled upon, or placed in the hands of trustees, as in the case of minors, lunatics, and idiots.
4. The absolute right to the product of her industry.
5. Also against laws which give to the widower so much larger and more permanent an interest in the property of his deceased wife, than they give to the widow in that of her deceased husband.
6. Finally, against the whole system by which the "legal existence of the wife is suspended during marriage," so that in most States, she neither has a legal part in the choice of her residence, nor can she make a will, nor sue or be sued in her own name, nor inherit property.
We believe that personal independence and equal human rights can never be forfeited, except for crime; that marriage should be an equal and permanent partnership, and so recognized by law; that until it is so recognized, married partners should provide against radical injusticy of present laws, by every means in their power.
We believe that where domestic difficulties arise, no appeal should be made to

legal tribunals under existing laws, but that all difficulties should be submitted to the equitable adjustment of arbitrators mutually chosen.

Thus reverencing law, we enter our protest against rules and customs which are unworthy of the name, since they violate justice, the essence of all law.

58. Ibid., 173, 185.

59. Lucy Stone, July 11, 1885, January 29, 1876, *Woman's Journal*. See also Pleck, *Domestic Tyranny*, 102–3.

60. Wheeler, *Loving Warriors*, 186–87.

61. Solomon, *In the Company of Educated Women*, 37.

62. Hersh, "Partnership of Equals," 192.

63. Lawrence J. Friedman, *Gregarious Saints: Self and Community in American Abolitionism, 1830–1870* (Cambridge: Cambridge University Press, 1982), 146, 148; Judith Nies, *Seven Women: Portraits from the American Radical Tradition* (New York: Penguin, 1977), 27–30; Robert H. Abzug, *Passionate Liberator: Theodore Dwight Weld and the Dilemma of Reform* (New York: Oxford University Press, 1980), 199–200, 224–25, 245, 203, 209. Robert Dale Owen and Mary Robinson signed a statement affirming their equality when they married in 1832.

64. Hersh, "Partnership of Equals," 187–89; Hersh, *The Slavery of Sex: Feminist Abolitionists in America* (Urbana: University of Illinois Press, 1978), 234.

65. Hersh, "Partnership of Equals," 191.

66. Ibid., 197.

67. Ibid., 198–99.

68. Ibid., 193.

69. Ibid., 190–91; see also Friedman, *Gregarious Saints*, 145–46, 148. In his study of abolitionist couples Friedman challenges Hersh's view of the marriages which she studied. He argues that she equates the abolitionist husbands' sympathy of the extension of woman's sphere beyond the hearth to a desire for a partnership of equals. He believes that her view is too static and that marriages of some of them changed from troubled marriages to more loving ones, and some remained patriarchal. However, his interpretation does not really change the view of the aforementioned marriages as striving toward egalitarianism. His work does raise the important question of how to measure a partnership of equals.

70. For background, see Carl N. Degler, *At Odds: Women and the Family in America from the Revolution to the Present* (New York: Oxford University Press, 1980), 16, 36–38, 73, 181.

4. Power in the Bedroom and the Nursery (1800–1900)

1. G. J. Barker-Benfield, *The Horrors of the Half-Known Life: Male Attitudes toward Women and Sexuality in Nineteenth-Century America* (New York: Harper & Row, 1976), 113.

2. Barbara J. Berg, *The Remembered Gate: Origins of American Feminism: The Woman and the City, 1800–1860* (New York: Oxford University Press, 1978), 84.

3. Nancy F. Cott, "Passionlessness: An Interpretation of Victorian Sexual Ideology, 1790–1850," in *A Heritage of Her Own: Toward a New Social History of American Women*, ed. Nancy F. Cott and Elizabeth H. Pleck (New York: Simon & Schuster, 1979), 165–67.

4. Carl N. Degler, "What Ought to Be and What Was: Women's Sexuality in the Nineteenth Century," *American Historical Review* 79 (December 1974): 1479–90.

5. Carl N. Degler, *At Odds: Women and the Family in America from the Revolution to the Present* (New York: Oxford University Press, 1980), 262–63, 295.

6. Rosalind Rosenberg, *Beyond Separate Spheres: The Intellectual Roots of Modern Feminism* (New Haven: Yale University Press, 1982), 185; Degler, *At Odds*, 295.

7. Peter Gay, *The Bourgeois Experience: Victoria to Freud*; vol. 1: *Education of the Senses* (New York: Oxford University Press, 1984). See also Katherine Bement Davis, *Factors in the Sex Life of 2,200 Women* (New York: Harper & Brothers, 1939), 13, 232, 331–32; Rosenberg, *Beyond Separate Spheres,* 202. See also Robert Latou Dickinson and Lura Beam, *A Thousand Marriages: A Medical Study of Sex Adjustment* (Baltimore: Williams & Wilkins, 1931); Linda Gordon, *Woman's Body, Woman's Right: Birth Control in America* (New York: Penguin, 1977), 192–94. See also Lewis M. Terman, *Psychological Factors in Marital Happiness* (New York: McGraw-Hill, 1938); Gilbert Van Tassel Hamilton and Kenneth MacGowan, *What Is Wrong with Marriage* (New York: Albert & Charles Boni, 1919); Daniel Scott Smith and Michael S. Hindus, "Premarital Pregnancy in America, 1640–1966: An Overview and Interpretation," paper presented at the American Historical Association, New York City, December 1971; Gilbert Van Tassell Hamilton, *A Research in Marriage* (New York: Albert & Charles Boni, 1929); Daniel Scott Smith, "The Dating of the American Sexual Revolution," in *The Family in Social-Historical Perspective*, 2d ed., ed. Michael Gordon (New York: St. Martin's Press, 1978), 361–438; Carroll Smith-Rosenberg, "The Female World of Love and Ritual," *Signs* 1, no. 1 (September 1975): 1–29.

8. Joe L. Dubbert, *A Man's Place: Masculinity in Transition* (Englewood Cliffs, N.J.: Prentice-Hall, 1979), 17. In her book *The Cradle of the Middle Class: The Family in Oneida County, New York, 1790–1865* (New York: Cambridge University Press, 1981), Mary P. Ryan describes this transition in Oneida County, New York: "Put simply love had vanquished force and authority; the female had replaced the male in the social relations of childrearing by the 1840s" (189).

9. Sheila M. Rothman, *Woman's Proper Place: A History of Changing Ideals and Practices, 1870 to the Present* (New York: Basic Books, 1978), 98–99. See also Nancy Pottishman Weiss, "Mother the Invention of Necessity: Dr. Benjamin Spock's *Baby and Child Care*," *American Quarterly* 29 (Winter 1977): 519–46.

10. Gordon, *Woman's Body, Woman's Right*, 49; John D'Emilio and Estelle Freed-

man, *Intimate Matters: A History of Sexuality in America* (New York: Harper & Row, 1988), 58–59, 84, 134.

11. Dubbert, *Man's Place*, 103, 143; Peter Gabriel Filene, *Him/Herself: Sex Roles in Modern America* (New York: Harcourt Brace Jovanovich, 1974), 87.

12. Dubbert, *Man's Place,* 110, 83, 14, 21; Dubbert refers to the article by Ella Wheeler Wilcox, "Restlessness of the Modern Woman," *Cosmopolitan*, July 1901, 314–17.

13. Gordon, *Woman's Body, Woman's Right*, 52. See also James Mohr, "Abortion in America," in *Women's America*, 2d ed., ed. Linda K. Kerber and Jane De Hart-Mathews (New York: Oxford University Press, 1982), 190, 194.

14. Gordon, *Woman's Body, Woman's Right*, 53, 59–60.

15. Judith Walzer Leavitt, *Brought to Bed: Childbearing in America, 1750–1950* (New York: Oxford University Press, 1986), 4, 39–40, 198, 201, 203, 171.

16. Gordon, *Woman's Body, Woman's Right*, 53, 59.

17. Barker-Benfield, *Horrors of the Half-Known Life*, 120–21.

18. Mohr, "Abortion in America," 197.

19. Carroll Smith-Rosenberg, "The Abortion Movement and the A.M.A., 1850–1880," in *Disorderly Conduct: Visions of Gender in Victorian America* (New York: Alfred A. Knopf, 1985), 223, 242.

20. Mary P. Ryan, *Women in Public: Between Banners and Ballots, 1825–1880* (Baltimore: Johns Hopkins University Press, 1990), 123–24.

21. Gordon, *Woman's Body, Woman's Right*, 117.

22. Ibid., 116–20.

23. Barbara Leslie Epstein, *The Politics of Domesticity* (Middletown, Conn.: Wesleyan University Press, 1981), 103, 106.

24. Ibid., 115, 120–21.

25. Gordon, *Woman's Body, Woman's Right*, 96, 100, 103.

26. Christine Stansell, *City of Women: Sex and Class in New York, 1789–1860* (New York: Alfred A. Knopf, 1986), xii, 127.

27. Epstein, *Politics of Domesticity*, 131, 96–97.

28. Carrie Chapman Catt and Nettie Rogers Shuler, *Woman Suffrage and Politics: The Inner Story of the Suffrage Movement* (New York: Charles Scribners' Sons, 1923), 22; see also Stansell, *City of Women*, xiii, 127. Stansell argues that women as exemplars of virtue were especially fitted to attempt to uplift working-class women, whose sexual and social habits subverted strict ideas about female domesticity and purity. At the same time, the factory girl who engaged in premarital sex represented the possibilities of a life for women outside the household.

29. Gay, *Bourgeois Experience*, 119.

30. Richard W. Wertz and Dorothy C. Wertz, *Lying-In: A History of Childbirth in America* (New York: Free Press, 1977), 115; Gordon, *Woman's Body, Woman's Right*, 109.

31. Gordon, *Woman's Body, Woman's Right*, 108–9.

32. Ibid., 104.

33. Mary A. Hill, *Charlotte Perkins Gilman: The Making of a Radical Feminist, 1860–1896* (Philadelphia: Temple University Press, 1980), 5.

34. Ibid., 184, 110, 121–64; for an excellent new biography of Charlotte Perkins Gilman, see Ann J. Lane, *To "Herland" and Beyond: The Life and Work of Charlotte Perkins Gilman* (New York: Pantheon, 1990).

35. Charlotte Perkins Gilman, *Women and Economics*, ed. Carl N. Degler (New York: Harper & Row, 1966), xxviii.

36. Delores Hayden, *The Grand Domestic Revolution: A History of Feminist Designs for American Homes, Neighborhoods, and Cities* (Cambridge: MIT Press, 1981), 179, 184, 195.

37. Charlotte Perkins Gilman, *The Home: Its Work and Influence* (New York: McClure & Phillips, 1903), 117–23, 178–79, 138, 216–17.

38. Ibid., 122–23.

39. Ibid., 138, 157–58, 167, 170.

40. Ibid., 234, 289, 347.

41. Ibid., 3–4, 81, 92.

42. Charlotte Perkins Gilman, "Women and Vocation," undated lecture, Bureau of Vocational Information Records, Box 7, 29–40, SL.

43. Jacquelyn Dowd Hall, "'The Mind That Burns in Each Body': Women, Rape, and Racial Violence," in *Powers of Desire: The Politics of Sexuality*, ed. Ann Snitow, Christine Stansell, and Sharon Thompson (New York: Monthly Review Press, 1983), 328–49. For a more extensive discussion of lynching as means of social control, see Jacquelyn Dowd Hall, *Revolt against Chivalry: Jessie Daniel Ames and the Women's Campaign against Lynching* (New York: Columbia University Press, 1979).

44. Nancy Woloch, *Women and the American Experience* (New York: Alfred A. Knopf, 1984), 225, 227, 229; D'Emilio and Freedman, *Intimate Matters*, 46; see also Jacqueline Jones, *Labor of Love, Labor of Sorrow: Black Women, Work, and the Family from Slavery to the Present* (New York: Basic Books, 1985).

45. Ellen K. Rothman, *Hands and Hearts: A History of Courtship in America* (New York: Basic Books, 1984), 108.

46. Ibid., 109, 54.

47. Ella Lyman Cabot Collection, A-139, SL.

48. Ibid., Box 2.

49. Ella Lyman Cabot, Diary, January 10, 1891, ibid., Box 10F, 229v.

50. Richard Cabot to Ella Lyman, August 31, 1891, ibid., Box 2, folder 32.

51. Ella Lyman to Richard Cabot, August 17, 1892, ibid., folder 33.

52. Richard Cabot to Ella Lyman, June 11, 1893, ibid., folder 34.

53. Ella Lyman to Richard Cabot, June 12, 1893, ibid.

54. Ella Lyman Cabot to Richard Cabot, May 21, 1929, ibid., folder 41. The

Cabots may have had other reasons for not having children besides their dedication to their careers. Ella Cabot's health was precarious, and she seemingly was susceptible to pneumonia. Relatives of the Cabots recalled that Richard's medical judgment was that if Ella had a child, it might be fatal for her. Having no children of their own, they embraced a large company of other children. I am grateful to Richard Hocking, their godchild, for relating this medical information, and his permission to quote from the Cabot's Collection.

55. Gay, *Bourgeois Experience*, 127, 129, 130.

56. Mohr, "Abortion in America," 198.

57. Gay, *Bourgeois Experience*, 73.

58. Ibid., 81, 85.

59. Ibid., 94–95.

60. Carolyn Johnston, *Jack London: An American Radical?* (Westport, Conn.: Greenwood Press, 1984), 79.

61. For a full account of the relationship of Jack and Charmian London, see ibid.

5. The Sex Radicals: Feminists against the Traditional Family

1. Mary Cable, *American Manners and Morals* (New York: American Heritage, 1969), 156.

2. Celia Morris Eckhardt, *Fanny Wright: Rebel in America* (Cambridge: Harvard University Press, 1984), 282, 1. See also A. J. G. Perkins and Theresa Wolfson, *Frances Wright: Free Enquirer: The Study of a Temperament* (New York: Harper & Brothers, 1939).

3. Eckhardt, *Fanny Wright*, 2, 109, 123, 143, 156–57.

4. Ibid., 156–57.

5. Ibid., 173–74.

6. Ibid., 290, 295, 228, 235.

7. Emanie Sachs, *"The Terrible Siren": Victoria Woodhull* (New York: Harper & Brothers, 1928), 76.

8. Ibid., 132, 135–37.

9. Elisabeth Griffith, *In Her Own Right: The Life of Elizabeth Cady Stanton* (New York: Oxford University Press, 1984), 149. See also Ruth Barnes Moynihan, *Rebel for Rights: Abigail Scott Duniway* (New Haven: Yale University Press, 1983), 109.

10. Griffith, *In Her Own Right*, 151–52.

11. Ibid., 156–57. See also Sachs, *Terrible Siren*, 171–75.

12. L.A.F., "Our Homes," *Woman's Journal*, December 14, 1872, 394. For information on the split within the women's movement, see Eleanor Flexner, *Century of Struggle: The Women's Rights Movement in the United States* (New York: Atheneum, 1974), 142–55, 216. The bitter conflict over the Beecher-Tilton affair probably

explains why Wright was acknowledged as a foremother of the movement and Woodhull disinherited.

13. *Woman's Journal*, August 29, 1874, 310; "Equal Rights–Domestic Happiness," *Woman's Journal,* August 29, 1874, 278; see also October 31, 1874, 350; November 21, 1874, 374; December 26, 1874, 414–15; February 12, 1876, 56; June 24, 1876, 201; "The Wife Her Husband's Equal," *Woman's Journal*, March 14, 1874, 85.

14. Andrew Sinclair, *The Emancipation of the American Woman* (New York: Harper & Row, 1965), 37.

15. Candace Falk, *Love, Anarchy, and Emma Goldman* (New York: Holt, Rinehart & Winston, 1984), 125–26.

16. Alix Kates Shulman, ed., *Red Emma Speaks* (New York: Random House, 1972), 136–37, 159.

17. Ibid., 134–37, 142.

18. Ibid., 158, 164–65.

19. Emma Goldman, *Living My Life,* vol. 1 (New York: Dover, 1970), 420.

20. Falk, *Love, Anarchy, and Emma Goldman*, 78.

21. Ibid., 81.

22. June Sochen, *Movers and Shakers: American Women Thinkers and Activists, 1900–1970* (New York: Quadrangle, 1973), 36.

23. Ibid., 35.

24. Ibid., 75–79; on the "new woman," see also Carroll Smith-Rosenberg, "The New Woman as Androgyne: Social Disorder and Gender Crisis, 1870–1936," in *Disorderly Conduct*, (New York: Alfred A. Knopf, 1985), 245.

25. Hutchins Hapgood, *A Victorian in the Modern World* (Seattle: University of Washington Press, 1972; originally New York: Harcourt, Brace, 1939), 395.

26. Ibid., 587–88.

27. Sochen, *Movers and Shakers*, 80–81.

28. Sandra M. Gilbert and Susan Gubar, eds., *The Norton Anthology of Literature by Women* (New York: W. W. Norton, 1985), 1555, 1563.

29. Lois Palken Rudnick, *Mabel Dodge Luhan: New Woman, New World* (Albuquerque: University of New Mexico Press, 1984), 23, 29, 85–86.

30. Ibid., 60–61, 63, 86.

31. Ibid., 83.

32. Ibid., 96–97

33. Ibid., 48.

34. Lois Rudnick, "Mabel Dodge Luhan," in *Notable American Women: The Modern Period*, ed. Barbara Sicherman and Carol Hurd Green (Cambridge: Harvard University Press, 1980), 431–32. See also Judith Schwarz, *Radical Feminists of Heterodoxy: Greenwich Village 1912–1940* (Lebanon, N.H.: New Victoria, 1982), 1–2, 22–28, 30–31, 35–36. Mabel Dodge Luhan and the other Greenwich Village "new women" were members of the club Heterodoxy, founded by Marie Jenney Howe in 1912. This

luncheon club met every other week except in the summer and flourished until the 1940s. Composed of women of divergent political views, the criterion for membership was that a woman be of unorthodox views and interested in stimulating conversation and debate. The members were professional women of achievement and included authors, lawyers, journalists, stockbrokers, doctors, reformers, actresses, educators, scriptwriters, and labor agitators.

The membership included Crystal Eastman, Susan Glaspell, Henrietta Rodman, Rheta Childe Dorr, Florence Wooston Seabury, Ida Rauh, and Charlotte Perkins Gilman (socialists); Stella Coman Ballantine (anarchist, Emma Goldman's niece); Mary Logan Tucker (a strong military advocate and member of DAR), Fola LaFollette (daughter of Robert LaFollette, the famous Progressive), Elizabeth Gurley Flynn, and Rose Pastor Stokes (socialists and later Communists); and others who were pacifists, Democrats, and Republicans. Many of the members belonged to the NWP, including Doris Stevens, Inez Haynes Irwin, Harriot Stanton Blatch (Elizabeth Cady Stanton's daughter), Alison Turnbull Hopkins, and Paula Jacobi. Grace Nail Johnson was the only black member.

Members were heterosexual, lesbians, married women, never-married women, divorced women, and free-love advocates. Given the great differences in political views, sexual preference, and life-styles, the cohesiveness and longevity of the club are remarkable. But all the members shared a deep commitment to the advancement of women and the excitement of sisterhood. They believed that a woman's sphere was the entire world.

For an excellent study of Greenwich Village men and the new sexuality, see Ellen Kay Trimberger, "Feminism, Men, and Modern Love: Greenwich Village, 1900–1925," in *Powers of Desire: The Politics of Sexuality*, ed. Ann Snitow, Christine Stansell, and Sharon Thompson (New York: Monthly Review Press, 1983), 131–52.

35. Joanne J. Meyerowitz, *Women Adrift: Independent Wage Earners in Chicago, 1880–1930* (Chicago: University of Chicago Press, 1988), xix, xxii, 116, 125, 140–41; Smith-Rosenberg, "New Woman as Androgyne," 245, 252.

36. James Reed, "Margaret Sanger," in *Notable American Women,* ed. Sicherman and Green, 623–26.

37. Linda Gordon, *Woman's Body, Woman's Right: Birth Control in America* (New York: Penguin, 1977), 225.

38. Reed, "Margaret Sanger," 623–27.

39. Gordon, *Woman's Body, Woman's Right*, 224–25.

6. The Suffrage Movement: Municipal Housekeeping or Full Equality? (1848–1919)

1. Carrie Chapman Catt and Nettie Rogers Shuler, *Woman Suffrage and Politics:*

The Inner Story of the Suffrage Movement (New York: Charles Scribners' Sons, 1923), 251–52.

2. William O'Neill sought to give a name to women's reform activities regarding family, church, and household in his book *Everyone Was Brave: The Rise and Fall of Feminism in America* (Chicago: Quadrangle, 1969). Nancy Cott pointed out that his term "social feminism" collapsed important political, class, age, and tactical distinctions among women and obscured the rise of feminism as a self-named movement. Temma Kaplan used the term "female consciousness" among women in Barcelona, which reflects their shared sense of obligation to preserve and nourish life. I agree with Cott that "female consciousness" may be a useful term in understanding the history of black and working-class women's community lives and public actions, which has usually not been considered to be within the female equal rights tradition. In most instances I have avoided the term "social feminism" and have adopted instead "municipal housekeeping" in describing feminist attempts to extend mother-love to the society. See Nancy F. Cott, "What's in a Name? or Expanding the Vocabulary of Women's History," *Journal of American History* 76, no. 3 (December 1989): 815, 820, 826, 828.

3. Anne Firor Scott, *The Southern Lady: From Pedestal to Politics, 1830–1930* (Chicago: University of Chicago Press, 1970), 100; Catherine Clinton, *The Plantation Mistress: Women's World in the Old South* (New York: Pantheon, 1982), xv, 22. For excellent accounts of African-American women before and after the Civil War, see Elizabeth Fox-Genovese, *Within the Plantation Household: Black and White Women of the Old South* (Chapel Hill: University of North Carolina Press, 1988); Jacqueline Jones, *Labor of Love, Labor of Sorrow: Black Women, Work, and the Family from Slavery to the Present* (New York: Basic Books, 1985). For a fascinating article on southern women's growing disaffection with the Civil War, see Drew Gilpin Faust, "Altars of Sacrifice: Confederate Women and the Narratives of War," *Journal of American History* 76, no. 4 (March 1990): 1200–1228.

4. Scott, *Southern Lady*, 4.

5. Ellen Glasgow, *Virginia* (Garden City, N.Y.: Doubleday, 1913), 11, quoted in Scott, *Southern Lady*, 223.

6. Allen Nevins and Henry Steele Commager, *A Pocket History of the United States*, 5th ed. (New York: Washington Square Press, 1970), 219.

7. Scott, *Southern Lady*, 123.

8. Lois W. Banner, *Women in Modern America: A Brief History*, 2d ed. (New York: Harcourt Brace Jovanovich, 1984), 51, 65–66.

9. Barbara Miller Solomon, *In the Company of Educated Women: A History of Women and Higher Education in America* (New Haven: Yale University Press, 1985), 63, 58.

10. Ibid., 95. See also Sheila M. Rothman, *Woman's Proper Place: A History of Changing Ideals and Practices, 1870 to the Present* (New York: Basic Books, 1978), 106–7. The number of female college graduates rose from 1,378 in 1870 to 5,237 in 1900.

In 1900, some 85,000 women were enrolled in colleges; in 1920, a quarter of a million. In 1900, 17 percent of college graduates were female, as opposed to 40 percent in 1920.

11. Solomon, *In the Company of Educated Women*, 175.

12. Ibid., 118–19, 121–22.

13. Karen J. Blair, *The Clubwoman as Feminist: True Womanhood Redefined, 1868–1914* (New York: Holmes & Meier, 1980), 93, 119.

14. Scott, *Southern Lady*, 162–63; Scott, "The New Woman in the South," *South Atlantic Quarterly* 61 (Autumn 1962): 417–83, quoted in Anne Firor Scott, *Making the Invisible Woman Visible* (Urbana: University of Illinois Press, 1984), 214, 216, 253, 282.

15. Susan E. Meyer, *America's Great Illustrators* (New York: Harry N. Abrams, 1978), 217.

16. Maurice Horn, *Women in the Comics* (New York: Chelsea House, 1977), 15–45.

17. Eleanor Flexner, *Century of Struggle: The Women's Rights Movement in the United States* (New York: Atheneum, 1974), 159–63, 175; see also Lillian Schlissel, *Women's Diaries of the Westward Journey* (New York: Schocken, 1982), 10–16. See also Annegret S. Ogden, *The Great American Housewife: From Helpmate to Wage Earner, 1776–1986* (Westport, Conn.: Greenwood Press, 1986), 104–5. Although western women achieved suffrage before women in other parts of the United States, the West was no feminist paradise for them. Because the westward migration was the source of great hardships for women, their strength and competence were essential for survival. From 1840 to 1870 a quarter of a million Americans crossed the continent. In contrast to men, who wrote of hunting, fights, and battles with Indians, women who wrote diaries of their journey told of family concerns, deaths, illness, and accidents. When the women wrote of their decision to leave their homes and disrupt family life, their diaries expressed their anguish and fears. They did not speak of a sense of adventure. Most of the women went west because their fathers, husbands, and brothers had decided to go. They faced six to eight months of arduous travel, drenching rains, and scorching summers. Pregnancy could be a special nightmare for women on the journey. Women faced threats of epidemics, the deaths of children, constant moving from place to place, and the absence of physical comforts. Once homesteading, they were often quite isolated and longed for female companionship. For excellent accounts of two major western suffrage leaders, Esther Morris and Abigail Scott Duniway, see Flexner, *Century of Struggle*, 158–59, 160–63. See also Ruth Barnes Moynihan, *Rebel for Rights: Abigail Scott Duniway* (New Haven: Yale University Press, 1983), 84, 91, 88–89.

18. Catt and Shuler, *Woman Suffrage and Politics*, 107.

19. Sherna Gluck, ed., *From Parlor to Prison: Five American Suffragists Talk about Their Lives* (New York: Vintage Books, 1976), 7.

20. Ethel Klein, *Gender Politics: From Consciousness to Mass Politics* (Cambridge: Harvard University Press, 1984), 13–14.

21. Mary Gray Peck, *Carrie Chapman Catt: A Biography* (New York: H. W. Wilson, 1944), 120, 59–60, 144. Carrie Chapman Catt sought Emma Goldman out one day in Brooklyn and engaged her for a few hair treatments in order to hear of her theories. Catt spoke with Goldman about her principles of philosophical anarchism. We do not know how she liked her hairdo, but Catt thought that Goldman was doctrinaire and quite unrealistic.

22. Robert Booth Fowler, *Carrie Catt: Feminist Politician* (Boston: Northeastern University Press, 1986), 156, 161, 163, 71, 62–63, 92, 105.

23. Catt and Shuler, *Woman Suffrage and Politics*, 273.

24. Grace Duffield Goodwin, "Non-Militant Defenders of the Homes," 78, clipping without identification of date or periodical, Women's Rights Collection, SL.

25. Jane Addams, "Why Women Should Vote," pamphlet, National American Woman Suffrage Association, Women's Rights Collection, Folder 3, SL.

26. Alice Paul, "Conversations with Alice Paul: Woman Suffrage and the Equal Rights Amendment," an oral history conducted in 1972 and 1973 by Amelia R. Fry, Regional Oral History Office, Bancroft Library, University of California, Berkeley, 1976, 400, used by permission.

27. Anna Howard Shaw, "What the War Meant to Women," pamphlet A-68, Dillon Collection, folder 560, p. 17, SL.

28. Anna Howard Shaw to Louisa Earle, October 29, 1915, Dillon Collection, Box 23, folder 537.

29. Anna Howard Shaw, "Motherhood," Dillon Collection, Box 22, folder 482. See also Anna Howard Shaw, *The Story of a Pioneer* (New York: Harper & Brothers, 1915).

30. Anna Howard Shaw, Diary, March 11, 1906, Dillon Collection, Box 20A.

31. Paul E. Fuller, *Laura Clay and the Woman's Rights Movement* (Lexington: University Press of Kentucky, 1975); Scott, "Southern Women in the 1920s," *Journal of Southern History* 30 (August 1964): 298–318, quoted in Scott, *Making the Invisible Woman Visible*, 224. Recently much more scholarship has been done on southern suffragists. Wayne Flynt is currently completing a biography on Pattie Jacobs, a suffrage leader in Alabama.

32. Catt and Shuler, *Woman Suffrage and Politics*, 462.

33. Angela Y. Davis, *Women, Race, and Class* (New York: Random House, 1981), 110–13. See also W. E. B. DuBois, *Crisis* 4, (June 1912): 76–77; "Votes for All: A Symposium," *Crisis* 15 (November 1917): 19, cited in Barbara Hilkert Andolsen, *Daughters of Jefferson, Daughters of Bootblacks* (Macon, Ga.: Mercer University Press, 1986), 25–26, 40, 73; see also Elizabeth Cady Stanton, "Our Proper Attitude toward Immigrants," *American Woman's Journal,* March–April 1895, 91–92; Stanton, "The Sixteenth Amendment," *Revolution,* April 29, 1869, 266, and "Anniversary of the American Equal Rights Association," *Revolution,* May 13, 1869, 291 quoted in Andolsen, *Daughters of Jefferson, Daughters of Bootblacks,* 19, 31.

34. Marilyn Richardson, ed., *Maria W. Stewart: America's First Black Woman Political Writer* (Bloomington: Indiana University Press, 1987), 24, 70.

35. Jewel L. Prestage, "The Political Behavior of American Black Women," in *The Black Woman*, ed. LaFrances Rodgers Rose (Beverly Hills, Calif.: Sage Publications, 1980), 239.

36. Rosalyn Terborg-Penn, "Discontented Black Feminists," in *Decades of Discontent*, ed. Lois Scharf and Joan M. Jensen (Westport, Conn.: Greenwood Press, 1983), 261–62; Paula Giddings, *When and Where I Enter: The Impact of Black Women on Race and Sex in America* (Toronto: Bantam, 1984), 75.

37. Anna Julia Cooper, *A Voice from the South* (Xenia, Ohio: Aldine Printing House, 1892; reprinted New York: Oxford University Press, 1988), xiii; Giddings, *When and Where I Enter*, 83 (quotation by Ruffin).

38. Cooper, *Voice from the South*, xxvii.

39. Gerda Lerner, *Black Women in White America: A Documentary History* (New York: Vintage, 1973), 572; Cooper, *Voice from the South*, xxxiii, xxxix, xxix.

40. Cooper, *Voice from the South*, 56, 61, 74, 31, 121–22; Lerner, *Black Women in White America*, 572.

41. Paula Giddings, *In Search of Sisterhood: Delta Sigma Theta and the Challenge of the Black Sorority Movement* (New York: William Morrow, 1988), 56.

42. Giddings, *When and Where I Enter*, 127–28, 89–93; see also Terborg-Penn, "Discontented Black Feminists," 261–62, 89–93.

43. Barbara Sicherman and Carol Hurd Green, eds., *Notable American Women: The Modern Period* (Cambridge: Harvard University Press, 1980), 679–80; Giddings, *When and Where I Enter*, 18–20; Jones, *Labor of Love, Labor of Sorrow*, 194, 267.

44. Mary Church Terrell, *A Colored Woman in a White World* (Washington, D.C.: Ransdell Publishers, 1940), 145.

45. Marianna W. Davis, ed., *Contributions of Black Women to America*, vol. 2 (Columbia, S.C.: Denday Press, 1982), 189–90, 74–76; see also Jacquelyn Dowd Hall, "'The Mind That Burns in Each Body': Women, Rape, and Racial Violence," in *Powers of Desire: The Politics of Sexuality*, ed. Ann Snitow, Christine Stansell, and Sharon Thompson (New York: Monthly Review Press, 1983), 335.

46. Scott, *Southern Lady*, 196–98; Scott, *Making the Invisible Woman Visible*, 291; for an excellent analysis of the antilynching campaign by white southern women, especially Jessie Daniel Ames, see Jacquelyn Dowd Hall, *Revolt against Chivalry: Jessie Daniel Ames and the Women's Campaign against Lynching* (New York: Columbia University Press, 1979). In her article "The Mind That Burns in Each Body," 337, 334–45, Hall recounts that twenty-six white women from six southern states met on November 1, 1930, to form the association against lynching. Their aim was to break the tie between the tradition of chivalry and the practice of lynching. In 1931 Ames called a meeting of black and white women for a frank discussion of the split female image and double sexual standard. In 1972 Anne Braden, longtime activist in the civil rights movement, issued a pamphlet entitled *Open Letter to Southern White Women*. She urged white women "for their own liberation to refuse any longer to be used, and

to act in the tradition of Jessie Ames and the white women who fought in an earlier period to end lynching." Braden was afraid the antirape movement would find itself aligned inadvertently with racism.

47. Lois W. Banner, *Women in Modern America, A Brief History*, 1st ed. (New York: Harcourt Brace Jovanovich, 1974), 92, 122.

48. For excellent discussions of protective labor legislation, see Wendy Kaminer, *A Fearful Freedom: Women's Flight from Equality* (New York: Addison-Wesley, 1990), 61–77; Alice Kessler-Harris, *Out to Work: A History of Wage-Earning Women in the United States* (New York: Oxford University Press, 1982), 180–214.

49. Elizabeth Anne Payne, *Reform, Labor, and Feminism* (Urbana: University of Illinois Press, 1988), 4.

50. Ibid., 7, 118, 123, 125, 130, 138.

51. Banner, *Women in Modern America* (1984), 76–77.

52. Ibid., 71–72; O'Neill, *Everyone Was Brave*, 95–106, 114–16.

53. *New York Times*, March 4, 1913, quoted in Gluck, *From Parlor to Prison*, 19–20.

54. Flexner, *Century of Struggle*, 276–93.

55. Winnifred Harper Cooley, "The Younger Suffragists," *Harper's Weekly* 58 (September 27, 1913): 7–8, quoted in June Sochen, ed., *The New Feminism in Twentieth Century America* (Lexington, Mass.: D. C. Heath, 1971), 18–21.

56. Paul, "Conversations with Alice Paul," 29, 31, 197; see also Alice Paul, "Declaration of Principles of the National Woman's Party," November 11, 1922, Washington, D.C., Women's Rights Collection, Box 83, SL. In their Declaration of Principles they affirmed:

That the identity of the wife shall no longer be merged with that of the husband, but the wife shall retain her separate identity after marriage and be able to contract with her husband concerning that marriage relationship.

That a woman shall no longer be required by law or custom to assume the name of her husband upon marriage, but shall have the same right as a man to retain her own name after marriage.

That the wife shall no longer be considered as supported by the husband, but their mutual contribution to the family maintenance shall be recognized.

That the headship of the family shall no longer be in the husband alone, but shall be equally in the husband and wife.

That the husband shall no longer own his wife's services, but these shall belong to her alone as in the case of any free person.

That the husband shall no longer own his wife's earnings, but these shall belong to her alone.

That the husband shall no longer own or control his wife's property, but it shall belong to her and be controlled by her alone.

That the husband shall no longer control the joint property of his wife and himself, but the husband and wife shall have equal control of joint property.

That the husband shall no longer obtain divorce more easily than the wife, but the wife shall have the right to obtain divorce on the same grounds as the husband. That the husband shall no longer have a greater right to make contracts than the wife.

That women shall no longer be discriminated against in the economic world because of marriage, but shall have the same treatment in the economic world after marriage as have men.

That the father shall no longer have the paramount right to the care, custody, and control of the child to determine its education and religion, to the guardianship of its estate and to the control its services and earnings, but these rights shall be shared equally by the father and mother in the case of all children, whether born within or without the marriage ceremony.

That a double moral standard shall no longer exist, but the code shall obtain for both men and women.

57. Gluck, *From Parlor to Prison*, 247.

58. Klein, *Gender Politics*, 14–15; see also Sochen, *New Feminism in Twentieth Century America*, xv.

59. Catt and Shuler, *Suffrage and Politics*, 245.

60. Fowler, *Carrie Catt*, 150–51.

61. Grace Hutchins, *Women Who Work* (New York: International Publishers, 1934), 34; William Henry Chafe, *The American Woman: Her Changing Social, Economic, and Political Roles, 1920–1970* (New York: Oxford University Press, 1972), 51–52.

62. Chafe, *American Woman*, 49–50.

63. Peter Gabriel Filene, *Him/Herself: Sex Roles in Modern America* (New York: Harcourt Brace Jovanovich, 1974), 119.

7. Exquisite Surrender? The New Feminists of the 1920s

1. Frederick Lewis Allen, *Only Yesterday: An Informal History of the Nineteen Twenties* (New York: Harper & Row, 1931), 14–17.

2. Quotations here and in following paragraphs appear in Eleanor Flexner, *Century of Struggle: The Women's Rights Movement in the United States* (New York: Atheneum, 1974), 321–24.

3. Carrie Chapman Catt and Nettie Rogers Shuler, *Woman Suffrage and Politics: The Inner Story of the Suffrage Movement* (New York: Charles Scribners' Sons, 1923), 382.

4. Ibid., 383.

5. Emily Newell Blair, "Discouraged Feminists," *Outlook*, July 8, 1931, 158, 302.

6. Allen, *Only Yesterday*, 103–4.

7. Geoffrey Perrett, *America in the Twenties: A History* (New York: Simon & Schuster, 1982), 157.

8. Ellen Gerber, *The American Woman in Sport* (Reading, Mass.: Addison-Wesley, 1974), 10, 12, 14, 35.

9. Lois Banner, *American Beauty* (New York: Alfred A. Knopf, 1983), 268–69.

10. Susan E. Meyer, *America's Great Illustrators* (New York: Harry N. Abrams, 1978), 283, 285.

11. Ibid., 285–86.

12. Maxine Davis, *The Lost Generation: A Portrait of American Youth Today* (New York: Macmillan, 1936), 89.

13. Paula S. Fass, *The Damned and the Beautiful* (New York: Oxford University Press, 1977), 75, 260–62; Robert Cooley Angell, *The Campus: A Study of Contemporary Undergraduate Life in the American University* (New York: D. Appleton, 1928), 7.

14. For a perceptive analysis of courtship in the 1920s, see John Modell, "Dating Becomes the Way of American Youth," in *Essays on the Family and Historical Change*, ed. Leslie Moch and Gary D. Stark (College Station: Texas A & M University Press, 1983), 93, 102.

15. Gilbert Van Tassel Hamilton, *A Research in Marriage* (New York: Albert & Charles Boni, 1929); Lewis M. Terman, *Psychological Factors in Marital Happiness* (New York: McGraw-Hill, 1938).

16. Fass, *The Damned and the Beautiful*, 23, 275–76.

17. Davis, *Lost Generation*, 25–27.

18. John R. McMahon, "Unspeakable Jazz Must Go," *Ladies Home Journal*, December 1921, 116, quoted in Fass, *The Damned and the Beautiful*, 22; see also John R. McMahon, "Back to Prewar Morals: Toddling to the Pit by the Jazz Route—How New York Sets the Pace," *Ladies Home Journal*, November 1921, 106–8.

19. Paul Sann, *The Lawless Decade* (New York: Crown, 1962), 65.

20. Dorothy Dunbar Bromley, "Feminist—New Style," *Harper's*, October 1927, 552.

21. "Ideal Divorce Fodder," *Ladies Home Journal*, June 1927, 38. Grace Nies Fletcher, "Bringing Up Fathers," *Ladies Home Journal*, September 1927, 35, 199; Frederick F. Van de Water, "Confessions of a Dub Father," *Ladies Home Journal*, May 1925, 25, 97–98; E. Davenport, "When Father Helps with the Wash," *Ladies Home Journal*, June 1921, 83, 98; Josephine Baker, M.D., "Fathering and Mothering," *Ladies Home Journal*, March 1926, 46, 230, 232; Ruth Scott Miller, "Masterless Wives and Divorce," *Ladies Home Journal*, January 1925, 20.

22. Katherine Fullerton Gerould, "Cap-and-Gown Philosophers," *Delineators*, October 1919, Bureau of Vocational Information Records, Box 28, SL.

23. Lorine Pruette, *Women and Leisure: A Study of Social Waste* (New York: E. P. Dutton, 1924), 8, 46, 120, 124.

24. Phyllis Blanchard and Carlyn Manasses, *New Girls for Old* (New York: McCauley, 1930), 174–75, 179, 182.

25. Fass, *The Damned and the Beautiful*, 55, 59, 63, 65–66, 70, 72–73.

26. Willystine Goodsell, *Problems of the Family* (New York: Century, 1928), 269, 275–76.

27. Ibid., 387.

28. Robert S. Lynd and Helen Merrill Lynd, *Middletown: A Study in American Culture* (New York: Harcourt, Brace, 1929), 115, 128.

29. Allen, *Only Yesterday*, 115–16; see also Steven Mintz and Susan Kellogg, *Domestic Revolutions: A Social History of American Family Life* (New York: Free Press, 1988), 109.

30. Elaine Tyler May, *Great Expectations* (Chicago: University of Chicago Press, 1980), 125.

31. Christine Frederick, Bureau of Vocational Information Records, Box 1. For an excellent discussion of the ways in which the home economics movement denigrated women's domestic skills, see Glenna Matthews, *"Just a Housewife": The Rise and Fall Of Domesticty in America* (New York: Oxford University Press, 1987).

32. Barbara Ehrenreich and Deirdre English, *For Her Own Good: 150 Years of Experts' Advice to Women* (Garden City, N. Y.: Doubleday, Anchor Press, 1978), 128–29, 136–51.

33. Ibid., 192.

34. Joann Vanek, "Time Spent in Housework," *Scientific American*, November 1974, 116–21. See also Ruth Schwartz Cowan, "The 'Industrial Revolution' in the Home: Household Technology and Social Change in the Twentieth Century," *Technology and Culture* 17 (January 1976): 1–26.

35. John R. McMahon, "Making Housekeeping Automatic," *Ladies Home Journal*, September 1920, 3–4, 205.

36. Vanek, "Time Spent in Housework," 116–21; see also Ruth Schwartz Cowan, *More Work for Mother: The Ironies of Household Technology from the Open Hearth to the Microwave* (New York: Basic Books, 1983), 63–64.

37. Maxine L. Margolis, *Mothers and Such: Views of American Women and Why They Changed* (Berkeley: University of California Press, 1984), 12.

38. Lynd and Lynd, *Middletown*, 134, 148–49.

39. Ibid., 177–78.

40. Margolis, *Mothers and Such*, 20, 52–53. For an excellent analysis of John B. Watson's ideas, see Kerry W. Buckley, *Mechanical Man: John Broadus Watson and the Beginning of Behaviorism* (New York: Guilford Press, 1989).

41. Ehrenreich and English, *For Her Own Good*, 183–85, 177–79, 191, 212.

42. Barton W. Currie, "American Women of Today and Yesterday," *Ladies Home Journal*, April 1923, 34.

43. Willard Waller, *The Family: A Dynamic Interpretation* (New York: Cordon, 1938), 534, 433, 603.

44. Ernest R. Mowrer, *Family Disorganization* (Chicago: University of Chicago Press, 1927), 3, 18. For Calhoun's interpretation, see Arthur W. Calhoun, *A Social*

History of the American Family; vol. 3: *Since the Civil War* (New York: Barnes & Noble, 1960; originally pub. 1919).

45. Floyd Dell, *Love in the Machine Age: A Psychological Study of the Transition from Patriarchal Society* (New York: Farrar & Rinehart, 1930), 6–7, 403–4.

46. Ellen Key, *Love and Marriage* (New York: G. P. Putnam's Sons, 1911), 245, 289, 382. See also Nancy F. Cott, *The Grounding of Modern Feminism* (New Haven: Yale University Press, 1987), 46–49.

47. Judge Ben B. Lindsey and Wainwright Evans, *The Companionate Marriage* (New York: Boni & Liveright, 1927), v, 277, 179.

48. Suzanne LaFollette, *Concerning Women* (New York: Albert & Charles Boni, 1926), 63, 93–94, 108, 130–31, 195.

49. Cott, *Grounding of Modern Feminism*, 202–4.

50. Mae Foster Jay, "Marriage Is Like That," *Ladies Home Journal*, January 1927, 58.

51. Sophie Kerr, "All You Need Is a Cookbook," *Ladies Home Journal*, December 1928, 3–5, 76, 82.

52. Sophie Kerr, "Worldly Goods," *Ladies Home Journal*, March 1924, 35, 204, 213–14.

53. Abraham Meyerson, "The Nervous Housewife," *Ladies Home Journal*, November 1920, 26–27. See also S. Josephine Baker, M.D., "Marriage from the Side Lines," *Ladies Home Journal*, April 1926, 37.

54. Corra Harris, "On the Management of a Husband," *Ladies Home Journal*, 42, no. 3 (March 1925): 30.

55. Barbara J. Berg, *The Remembered Gate: Origins of American Feminism: The Woman and the City, 1800–1860* (New York: Oxford University Press, 1978), 5.

56. Ethel Klein, *Gender Politics: From Consciousness to Mass Politics* (Cambridge: Harvard University Press, 1984), 18, 22.

57. Nancy F. Cott, "Feminist Politics in the 1920s: The National Woman's Party," *Journal of American History* 71, no. 1 (June 1984): 55, 59.

58. William O'Neill, *The Woman Movement: Feminism in the United States and England* (Chicago: Quadrangle, 1971), 291.

59. Cott, "Feminist Politics in the 1920s," 68; Cott, *Grounding of Modern Feminism*, 50.

60. Rosalind Rosenberg, *Beyond Separate Spheres: The Intellectual Roots of Modern Feminism* (New Haven: Yale University Press, 1982), 54; see also Klein, *Gender Politics*, 16.

61. Rosenberg, *Beyond Separate Spheres*, 208–9.

62. Susan D. Becker, *Origins of the Equal Rights Amendment: American Feminism between the Wars* (Westport, Conn.: Greenwood Press, 1981), 250, 236–37, 235.

63. Ibid., 237.

64. Ibid., 238, 245–46, 248, 255, 258; see also Sheila M. Rothman, *Woman's Proper*

Place: A History of Changing Ideals and Practices, 1870 to the Present (New York: Basic Books, 1978), 157–58.

65. Rothman, *Woman's Proper Place*, 196.

66. Cott, "Feminist Politics in the 1920s," 50–51, 57.

67. Ibid., 60.

68. Ibid., 57.

69. J. Stanley Lemons, *The Woman Citizen: Social Feminism in the 1920s* (Urbana: University of Illinois Press, 1973), 145, 158, 181, 234, 238.

70. Ibid., 80.

71. Ibid., 111–12.

72. Alice Paul, "Conversations with Alice Paul: Woman Suffrage and the Equal Rights Amendment," an oral history conducted by Amelia R. Fry, Regional Oral History Office, Bancroft Library, University of California, Berkeley, 1976, 257.

73. Elaine Showalter, ed., *These Modern Women: Autobiographical Essays from the Twenties* (Old Westbury, N.Y.: Feminist Press, 1978), 3–6. © 1979 by Elaine Showalter, used by permission of the Feminist Press.

74. Ibid., 38.

75. Ibid., 33.

76. Ibid., 52.

77. Ibid., 73–75, 78.

78. Ibid., 108, 105.

79. Ibid., 126.

80. Ibid., 63–67.

81. Ibid., 109–10.

82. Ibid., 115.

83. Ibid., 87, 91.

84. Ibid., 68, 73.

85. Ibid., 101, 104.

86. Bureau of Vocational Information Records, originally Box 9, currently Bk-3, no. 138–51, microfilm, reel 6, July 14, 1920, SL.

87. Paula Laddey, April 15, 1920, Bureau of Vocational Information Records, reel 6.

88. Nina Wright Winston, Highland Park, Ill., Pauline B. Werner, Conn., April 20, 1920; Nora E. Dunn, Elberton, Ga., March 22, 1920; Elizabeth Knox Powell, Saskatchewan, April 19, 1920, ibid.

89. Nora Dunn, March 22, 1920, ibid.

90. Unsigned, April 6, 1920; March 7, 1920; April 19, 1920; March 1920, ibid.

91. March 3, 1920, ibid.

92. Francis Kay Ballard, March 8, 1920, ibid.

93. Louis Rice to Emma Hirth, November 17, 1924, Bureau of Vocational Information Records, Box 28.

94. Frank Stricker, "Cookbooks and Lawbooks: The Hidden History of Career Women in Twentieth Century America," *Journal of Social History* 10 (Fall 1976): 1–2.

95. Ibid., 8.

8. The Empowerment of Wives and Mothers: Surviving the Great Depression

1. John Kenneth Galbraith, *The Great Crash* (Boston: Houghton Mifflin, 1955), 128–32.

2. Caroline Bird, *The Invisible Scar* (New York: Van Rees Press, 1966), 8.

3. Grace Hutchins, *Women Who Work* (New York: International Publishers, 1934), 187–88.

4. Jeane Westin, *Making Do: How Women Survived the '30s* (Chicago: Follett, 1976), 107.

5. Ibid., 153–54.

6. Lois W. Banner, *Women in Modern America: A Brief History* (New York: Harcourt Brace Jovanovich, 1974), 200–201.

7. *Physical Culture,* May 1934, quoted in Judith Papachristou and Carol Wald, *Myth America: Picturing Women, 1865–1945* (New York: Pantheon, 1975), 58.

8. Abraham Myerson, M.D., "Remedies for the Housewife's Fatigue," *Ladies Home Journal,* March 1930, 115.

9. Sarah Addington, "Little Frog Big Puddle," *Ladies Home Journal,* April 1929, 12–13, 220, 223–25.

10. Clarence Budington Kelland, "Mary Jane—Lawyer," *Ladies Home Journal,* May, 1929, 7–8, 69.

11. Maureen Honey, "Images of Women in *The Saturday Evening Post,* 1931–1936," *Journal of Popular Culture* 10, no. 2 (Fall 1976): 352–58.

12. Maurice Horn, *Women in the Comics* (New York: Chelsea House, 1977), 3, 4, 92, 89, 130, 166.

13. Lita Bane, "New Values in Homemaking," *Ladies Home Journal,* October 1929, 37.

14. Susan Ware, *Holding Their Own: American Women in the 1930s* (Boston: Twayne, 1982), 29.

15. Valerie Kincade Oppenheimer, *The Female Labor Force in the United States: Demographic and Economic Factors Governing Its Growth and Changing Compositions* (Berkeley: University of California, Institute of International Studies, 1970), 1–24; see also Ruth Milkman's important article "Women's Work and the Economic Crisis: Some Lessons from the Great Depression," in *A Heritage of Her Own: Toward a New*

Social History of American Women, ed. Nancy F. Cott and Elizabeth H. Pleck (New York: Simon & Schuster, 1979), 507–41; Banner, *Women in Modern America,* 256.

16. Ware, *Holding Their Own,* 30, 25.

17. Ibid., 25, 27.

18. Mirra Komarovsky, *The Unemployed Man and His Family: The Effect of Unemployment on the Status of the Man in Fifty-Nine Families* (New York: Dryden Press, 1940), 61; see also Rosalyn Baxandall, Linda Gordon, and Susan Reverby, eds., *America's Working Women: A Documentary History, 1600 to the Present* (New York: Vintage, 1976), 245.

19. Alice Kessler-Harris, *Out to Work: A History of Wage-Earning Women in the United States* (New York: Oxford University Press, 1982), 260.

20. Ware, *Holding Their Own,* 32. See also Lorine Pruette, *Women Workers through the Depression: A Study of White Collar Employment Made by the American Woman's Association* (New York: Macmillan, 1934).

21. Westin, *Making Do,* 51.

22. Studs Terkel, *Hard Times: An Oral History of the Great Depression* (New York: Random House, 1970), 389.

23. Westin, *Making Do,* 82.

24. Ibid., ix; Robert S. McElvaine, *The Great Depression: America, 1929–1941* (New York: Times Books, 1984), 217; E. R. Groves, "Adaptations of Family Life," *American Journal of Sociology* 40 (May 1935): 772–79.

25. Westin, *Making Do,* 146, 141, 155.

26. Ibid., 183–84.

27. Robert S. Lynd and Helen Merrell Lynd, *Middletown in Transition: A Study in Cultural Conflicts* (New York: Harcourt, Brace, 1937), 176–78, 129–30, 167–68.

28. Samuel A. Stouffer and Paul F. Lazarsfeld, *Research Memorandum on the Family in the Depression,* Bulletin 29 (New York: Social Science Research Council, 1937), 36.

29. Ibid., 88–89.

30. Komarovsky, *Unemployed Man and His Family,* 1–6.

31. Ibid., 10, 23, 39, 56, 66, 68.

32. Ibid., 56, 72, 74.

33. Ibid., 130.

34. Robert Cooley Angell, *The Family Encounters the Depression* (New York: Charles Scribner's Sons, 1936), 83, 4–5, 8–9.

35. Glen H. Elder, Jr., *Children of the Great Depression: Social Change in Life Experience* (Chicago: University of Chicago Press, 1974), 88, 90, 95, 102.

36. Ibid., 65, 203, 88, 112, 210, 239. Richard A. Easterlin's research on the cohorts of the 1920s and 1930s emphasized the demographic effects of the relatively small size of these groups. They began married life coincident with postwar economic boom and had better job opportunities and economic advantages. He argues that because they grew up with scarcity during the depression, they developed a modest

taste for material goods. See Richard A. Easterlin, "What Will 1984 Be Like? Socioeconomic Implications of Recent Twists in the Age Structure," *Demography* 15 (November 1978): 397–432; Easterlin, *Birth and Fortune: The Impact of Numbers on Personal Welfare* (New York: Basic Books, 1980); Easterlin, *Population, Labor Force, and Long Swings in Economic Growth* (New York: Columbia University Press, 1968), 124; Andrew J. Cherlin, *Marriage, Divorce, Remarriage* (Cambridge: Harvard University Press, 1980).

37. Ruth Shonle Cavan and Katherine Howland Ranck, *The Family and the Depression: A Study of One Hundred Chicago Families* (Chicago: University of Chicago Press, 1938), ix, 6.

38. Ibid., 34, 37, 49, 59.

39. Cecille Tipton LaFollette, *A Study of the Problems of 652 Gainfully Employed Married Women Homemakers,* Contributions to Education, no. 619 (New York: Bureau of Publications, Teachers College, Columbia University, 1934), 87, 91.

40. Lilian Brandt, *An Impressionistic View of the Winter of 1930–31 in New York City* (New York: Welfare Council of New York City, 1932), 21.

41. Mona Williams, "Family Man," *Ladies Home Journal,* September 1939, 18–19, 42.

42. Cavan and Ranck, *Family and the Depression,* 60, 93–94.

43. Komarovsky, *Unemployed Man and His Family,* 97–101.

44. Bird, *Invisible Scar,* 50.

45. Komarovsky, *Unemployed Man and His Family,* 41.

46. Ibid., 56, 14, 46; see also E. Wight Bakke, *Citizens without Work: A Study of the Effect of Unemployment upon the Workers' Social Relations and Practices* (New Haven: Yale University Press, 1940), 133–40. Although all the investigations of the family during the depression give us a view of individual families and general response patterns, they suffer from methodological problems. Some interviewed only wives, others only the children, and often the samples were limited. However, the sheer number of the studies of families on relief, middle-class families, and working-class families does yield a fuller portrait of the American family than previously possible. The fact that so many scholars chose to focus on the family revealed the degree of national interest and anxiety about its fate during the depression. In order to answer many questions about changing sexual roles, we need to have reports of husbands, wives, and children within the same families. Ironically, because of the severe economic crisis, less money was available for research. Despite their limitations, the studies do reveal a shift toward more female power at home.

47. Cavan and Ranck, *Family and the Depression,* 83.

48. Margaret Jarman Hagood, *Mothers of the South: Portraiture of the White Tenant Farm Woman* (New York: W. W. Norton, 1977; originally Chapel Hill: University of North Carolina Press, 1939).

49. Ibid., 89, 92, 36.

50. Ibid., 91.

51. Ibid., 161.

52. Ibid., 164.

53. Joe L. Dubbert, *A Man's Place: Masculinity in Transition* (Englewood Cliffs, N.J.: Prentice-Hall, 1979), 209, 212; see also Lilian Symes, "The New Masculinism," *Harper's*, June 1930, 103.

54. Dubbert, *Man's Place*, 215, 213.

55. McElvaine, *Great Depression;* 38.

56. Winona L. Morgan, *The Family Meets the Depression: A Study of a Group of Highly Selected Families* (Minneapolis: University of Minnesota Press, 1939), 79; see also Hortense Calisher, *Herself* (New York: Dell, 1972), 14.

57. Conversation with Margaret Ross (author's grandmother), Cleveland, Tennessee, 1961.

58. Linda Gordon, *Woman's Body, Woman's Right: A Social History of Birth Control in America* (New York: Penguin, 1974), xvi.

59. Ibid., 115.

60. Ibid., 300, 310–17.

61. Sidney Ditzion, *Marriage, Morals, and Sex in America* (New York: Octagon Books, 1975), 386.

62. Westin, *Making Do,* 78.

63. Ware, *Holding Their Own,* 62–63.

64. Frances Woodward Prentice, "The Confused Generation," *Scribner's* 91 (January–June 1932): 50–52.

65. Ware, *Holding Their Own,* 89–90.

66. *Ladies Home Journal,* August 1937; Eleanor Roosevelt, "This Is My Story," *Ladies Home Journal,* July 1937, 29.

67. William H. Chafe, "Anna Eleanor Roosevelt," in *Notable American Women: The Modern Period,* ed. Barbara Sicherman and Carol Hurd Green (Cambridge: Harvard University Press, 1980), 601.

68. Quotations here and in following paragraphs are found in ibid., 597, 601; see also Eugenia Kaledin, *Mothers and More: American Women in the 1950s* (Boston: Twayne, 1984), 94–101.

69. Elaine M. Smith, "Mary McLeod Bethune," in *Notable American Women,* ed. Sicherman and Green, 76–80; see also Rosalyn Terborg-Penn, "Discontented Black Feminists," in *Decades of Discontent: The Women's Movement, 1920–1940,* ed. Lois Scharf and Joan M. Jensen (Westport, Conn.: Greenwood Press, 1983), 276; Gerda Lerner, *Black Women in White America: A Documentary History* (New York: Vintage, 1973), 134–35.

70. Smith, "Mary McLeod Bethune," 76–80.

71. Lucy Miller Mitchell, Black Women Oral History Project, conducted by Cheryl Gilkes, June 17, 24, July 1, 6, 25, 1977, OH-31, 13–14, SL.

72. Mary McLeod Bethune, "Faith That Moved a Dump Heap," *Who, the Magazine About People* 1, no. 3 (June 1941), quoted in Lerner, *Black Women in White America,* 143. See also Terborg-Penn, "Discontented Black Feminists," 274.

73. *With Babies and Banners* (New York: New Day Films, 1978), directed by Lorraine Gray; produced by Lorraine Gray with Anne Bohlen and Lyn Goldfarb; filmed in Flint, Michigan; edited by Mary Lampson and Melanie Maholick. This film was nominated for an Academy Award.

74. Ware, *Holding Their Own,* 40–44, 49.

9. The Paradox of Women's Power during World War II

1. Margaret Mead, "The Women in the War," in *While You Were Gone,* ed. Jack Goodman (New York: Simon & Schuster, 1946), 288.

2. Richard Lingeman, *Don't You Know There's a War On? The Home Front, 1941–1945* (New York: G. P. Putnam's Sons, 1970), 94.

3. Gulielma Fell Alsop and Mary F. McBride, *Arms and the Girl* (New York: Vanguard Press, 1943), 241.

4. D'Ann Campbell, *Women at War with America: Private Lives in a Patriotic Era* (Cambridge: Harvard University Press, 1984), 7–10.

5. Mead, "Women in the War," 286; Laurence Urdang, *The Timetables of American History* (New York: Simon & Schuster, 1981), 339; Paul Gallico, "What We Talked About," in *While You Were Gone,* ed. Goodman, 31; Karen Anderson, *Wartime Women: Sex Roles, Family Relations, and the Status of Women during World War II* (Westport, Conn.: Greenwood Press, 1981), 85–86.

6. William Manchester, *The Glory and the Dream: A Narrative History of America, 1932–1972* (New York: Bantam, 1974), 302–3; Anderson, *Wartime Women,* 86; Marjorie Longley, Louis Silverstein, and Samuel A. Tower, *America's Taste* (New York: Simon & Schuster, 1959), 272.

7. Manchester, *The Glory and the Dream,* 239; see also Urdang, *Timetables of American History,* 33.

8. Louis Paine Benjamin, "What Is Your Dream Girl Like?" *Ladies Home Journal* 59 (March 1942): 114, quoted in Leila J. Rupp, *Mobilizing Women for War: German and American Propaganda, 1939–1945* (Princeton: Princeton University Press, 1978), 151.

9. Gallico, "What We Talked About," 45; see also Manchester, *The Glory and the Dream,* 307–8.

10. Gallico, "What We Talked About," 35–37; see also Longley, Silverstein, and Tower, *America's Taste,* 273.

11. Manchester, *The Glory and the Dream,* 247, 305–6.

12. Lingeman, *Don't You Know There's a War On?* 121–23.

13. Manchester, *The Glory and the Dream*, 238–39.

14. Milton Caniff, "The Comics," in *While You Were Away,* ed. Goodman, 488–510.

15. Maurice Horn, *Women in the Comics* (New York: Chelsea House, 1977), 126, 129–30.

16. Andrea S. Walsh, *Women's Film and Female Experience, 1940–1950* (New York: Praeger Special Studies, 1984), 4.

17. Ibid., 4–5, 27–28, 37–38.

18. Ibid., 90–91; Bosley Crowther, "The Movies," in *While You Were Gone*, ed. Goodman, 513–15, 518.

19. Walsh, *Women's Film and Female Experience*, 28.

20. Ibid., 170, 183, 123–31.

21. Ibid., 144–47, 38. See also Susan M. Hartmann, *American Women in the 1940s: The Home Front and Beyond* (Boston: Twayne, 1982), 191–92.

22. Lingeman, *Don't You Know There's a War On?* 149, 152.

23. Miriam Frank, Marilyn Ziebarth, and Connie Fields, *The Life and Times of Rosie the Riveter* (Emeryville, Calif.: Clarity Educational Productions, 1982), 17.

24. Ruth Milkman, "Redefining 'Women's Work': The Sexual Division of Labor in the Auto Industry during World War II," *Feminist Studies* 8, no. 2 (Summer 1982): 337–39, 341.

25. Lingeman, *Don't You Know There's a War On?* 153.

26. Nell Giles, *Punch In, Susie* (New York: Harper & Brothers, 1942), 80.

27. Alan Clive, *State of War: Michigan in World War II* (Ann Arbor: University of Michigan Press, 1979), 188.

28. Rupp, *Mobilizing Women for War*, 141–42; see also *Behind the Lines: Gender and the Two World Wars*, ed. Margaret Randolph Higgonet, Jane Jenson, Sonya Michel, and Margaret Collins Weitz (New Haven: Yale University Press, 1987).

29. Rupp, *Mobilizing Women for War,* 146. Rupp quotes Dorothy Parker, "Are We Women or Are We Mice?" *Reader's Digest* 43 (July 1943): 72; Elizabeth Field, "Boom Town Girls," *Independent Woman* 21 (October 1942): 298.

30. Milkman, "Redefining 'Women's Work,'" 341.

31. Rosalyn Baxandall, Linda Gordon, and Susan Reverby, eds., *America's Working Women: A Documentary History 1600 to the Present* (New York: Vintage Books, 1976), 284.

32. Ibid., 280–81.

33. Frank, *Life and Times of Rosie the Riveter,* 34–35, 31, 33.

34. Lingeman, *Don't You Know There's a War On?* 148–49; see also Walsh, *Women's Film and Female Experience*, 54.

35. Campbell, *Women at War with America*, 72, 81–83; see also Lois W. Banner, *Women in Modern America: A Brief History* (New York: Harcourt Brace Jovanovich, 1974), 256–59. The number of women in professions rose slightly in some areas, but no dramatic increase occurred. Women composed 2.4 percent of the lawyers in 1940

and 3.5 percent in 1950, 4.6 percent of the doctors in 1940 and 6.1 percent in 1950. The percentage of college presidents and professors who were female fell from 27 percent in 1940 to 23 percent in 1950. Overall, the percentage of women in the professions fell from 13 percent in 1940 to 11 percent in 1950.

In 1944 and 1947, some 11 percent of the wives were working. At any one time during the war, 9 out of 10 mothers with children under six were not in the labor force. A striking statistic is that among women who were between fifteen and thirty-four in 1940, fully 85 percent worked at one time or another before 1960, and 56 percent had social security work experience by the end of 1942, before large-scale war employment of women began.

36. Campbell, *Women at War with America*, 167–68.

37. Anderson, *Wartime Women*, 83, 61.

38. Alsop, *Arms and the Girl*, 210.

39. Clive, *State of War*, 202–3.

40. Alsop, *Arms and the Girl*, 222–23.

41. Lingeman, *Don't You Know There's a War On?* 13–14, 156–57.

42. Ibid., 67–68.

43. Frank, *Life and Times of Rosie the Riveter*, 64–65.

44. Laura Nelson Baker, *Wanted: Women in War Industry: The Complete Guide to a War Factory Job* (New York: E. P. Dutton, 1943), 73.

45. Sheila Rothman, *Woman's Proper Place: A History of Changing Ideals and Practices, 1870 to the Present* (New York: Basic Books, 1978), 222–24.

46. Lingeman, *Don't You Know There's a War On?* 87.

47. Frank, *Life and Times of Rosie the Riveter*, 84; see also Lingeman, *Don't You Know There's a War On?* 111, 85.

48. Campbell, *Women at War with America*, 13–14.

49. Frank, *Life and Times of Rosie the Riveter*, 64, 83–84; Anderson, *Wartime Women*, 91.

50. Anna W. M. Wolf and Irma Simonton Black, "What's Happening to the Younger People?" in *While You Were Gone*, ed. Goodman, 67.

51. Studs Terkel, *"The Good War": An Oral History of World War Two* (New York: Pantheon, 1984), 8, 247.

52. Frank, *Life and Times of Rosie the Riveter*, 65–66.

53. Ibid., 68.

54. Campbell, *Women at War with America*, 218, 252; see also Baxandall, Gordon, and Reverby, *America's Working Women*, 284–87.

55. Campbell, *Women at War with America*, 69–70.

56. Baxandall, Gordon, and Reverby, *America's Working Women*, 284–85.

57. Frank, *Life and Times of Rosie the Riveter*, 17, 49, 51–54.

58. Lingeman, *Don't You Know There's a War On?* 165; Manchester, *The Glory and the Dream*, 243.

59. Dellie Hahne, in Terkel, *"Good War,"* 122.

60. Mead, "Women in the War," 274, 277–78.

61. Peggy Terry, oral history, in Terkel, *"Good War,"* 108.

62. Anderson, *Wartime Women*, 64.

63. Frank, *Life and Times of Rosie the Riveter*, 63.

64. Hartmann, *American Women in the 1940s*, 31–32.

65. Manchester, *The Glory and the Dream*, 274–75.

66. Evelyn Fraser, in Terkel, *"Good War,"* 125, 128.

67. Campbell, *Women at War with America*, 19–23.

68. Ibid., 37, 39, 45.

69. Frieda Wolff, in Terkel, *"Good War,"* 288–29.

70. Anderson, *Wartime Women*, 80; see also Walsh, *Women's Film and Female Experience*, 68.

71. Hartmann, *American Women in the 1940s*, 170, 172.

72. Pauline Kael, in Terkel, *"Good War,"* 124.

73. Manchester, *The Glory and the Dream*, 248.

74. Anderson, *Wartime Women*, 76–77.

75. Lingeman, *Don't You Know There's a War On?* 91–93.

76. Walsh, *Women's Film and Female Experience*, 62–63.

77. Frank, *Life and Times of Rosie the Riveter*, 19.

78. Rupp, *Mobilizing Women for War*, 177. Field agents of the Women's Bureau conducted a study of more than 13,000 women employed in several war-manufacturing areas: Springfield and Holyoke, Massachusetts; Baltimore; Erie County (the Buffalo area); Detroit and Willow Run, Michigan; Dayton and Springfield, Ohio; Kenosha, Wisconsin; Wichita, Kansas; Mobile, Alabama; Seattle and Tacoma, Washington and San Francisco and Oakland. See *Women Workers in Ten Production Areas and Their Postwar Employment Plans*, Women's Bureau Bulletin 209 (Washington, D.C., 1946).

79. Rupp, *Mobilizing Women for War*, 161; see "Give Back Their Jobs," *Woman's Home Companion* 70 (October 1943): 6–7.

80. Marcelene Cox, "Ask Any Woman," *Ladies Home Journal*, September 1943, 95.

81. Nell Giles, "What about the Women?" *Ladies Home Journal* 61 (June 1944): 22–23, quoted in Rupp, *Mobilizing Women for War*, 161.

82. Frank, *Life and Times of Rosie the Riveter*, 13, 94.

83. Campbell, *Women at War with America*, 225.

84. Ibid., 227–29, 212.

85. Clive, *State of War*, 202, 213; Campbell, *Women at War with America*, 225–26, 229–30.

86. Campbell, *Women at War with America*, 216–17.

87. Allan Nevins and Henry Steele Commager, *A Pocket History of the United States*, 5th ed. (New York: Washington Square Press, 1970), 467.

88. Gallico, "What We Talked About," 63.

89. Manchester, *The Glory and the Dream*, 290.

90. Leon Litwack et. al. *The United States: Becoming a World Power*, vol. 2 (Englewood Cliffs, N.J.: Prentice-Hall, 1982), 670; Mortimer Chambers et al., *The Western Experience*, 3d ed. (New York: Alfred A. Knopf, 1983), 1058.

91. Mead, "Women in the War," 289.

92. Lingeman, *Don't You Know There's a War On?* 97.

93. Brandon French, *On the Verge of Revolt: Women in American Films of the Fifties* (New York: Frederick Ungar, 1978), xix, xx.

94. Peggy Terry, in Terkel, *"Good War,"* 110–11.

95. Hartmann, *American Women in the 1940s*, 165; see also Walsh, *Women's Film and Female Experience*, 67.

96. Rupp, *Mobilizing Women for War*, 175.

97. Sherna Berger Gluck, *Rosie the Riveter Revisited: Women, the War, and Social Change* (Boston: Twayne, 1987), 169.

98. Frank, *Life and Times of Rosie the Riveter*, 94; see also Connie Fields, filmmaker, *Rosie the Riveter* (Emeryville, Calif.: Clarity Educational Productions, 1980), for Weixel's quotation.

99. Robert LeKachman, in Terkel, *Good War*, 68.

100. Manchester, *The Glory and the Dream*, 419, 429.

101. Hartmann, *American Women in the 1940s*, 8.

102. Ibid., 167–68, 203–4.

103. Ibid., 179, 7.

104. Ibid., 107.

105. Banner, *Women in Modern America*, 256.

106. Walsh, *Women's Film and Female Experience*, 78; see also Frank, *Life and Times of Rosie the Riveter*, 19, 21.

107. Nancy Gabin, "They Have Placed a Penalty on Womanhood: The Protest Actions of Women Auto Workers in Detroit-Area UAW Locals, 1945–1947," *Feminist Studies* 8, no. 2 (Summer 1982): 375–77, 382, 387; Frank, *Life and Times of Rosie the Riveter*, 19.

108. Frank, *Life and Times of Rosie the Riveter*, 20. See also Susan B. Anthony II, *Out of the Kitchen: Into the War* (New York: Stephen Daye, 1943), 9, 228.

109. Hartmann, *American Women in the 1940s*, 128, 130–31.

10. The Power of Mom: Domesticity, Motherhood, and Sexuality in the 1950s

1. Geoffrey Gorer, *The American People: A Study in National Character* (New York: W. W. Norton, 1964), 49. See also Russel Nye, *The Unembarrassed Muse: The Popular*

Arts in America (New York: Dial Press, 1970), 224–25. The issue of female domestic power in the 1950s has been virtually ignored in the scholarship of the period. Instead, women's victimization and entrapment have dominated the literature until recently. Betty Friedan's *The Feminine Mystique*, the influential book which helped mobilize women in the feminist revolt of the 1960s and 1970s, shaped the way historians viewed the period in women's history. To challenge her view of the housewives of the fifties as desperate, frustrated women seemed tantamount to questioning the rationale of the entire movement.

As feminist scholarship has matured, a number of books have questioned many of Friedan's assumptions and revealed great diversity in women's experiences in the 1950s, depending on their race and class. See, for example, Helen Lopata, *Occupation: Housewife;* Eugenia Kaledin, *Mothers and More;* and Sherna Gluck, *Rosie the Riveter Revisited: Women, the War, and Social Changes.* Glenna Matthews's *"Just a Housewife": The Rise and Fall of Domesticity in America* confirms, more than denies, Friedan's assessment of the period but presents a much more nuanced interpretation. Matthews argues that the devaluation of domesticity began long before the 1950s and traces the process historically. Two other books, *Survival in the Doldrums* by Leila Rupp and Verta Taylor and *Hearts of Men: American Dreams and the Flight from Commitment* by Barbara Ehrenreich, illuminate previously neglected areas of research about the 1950s. Clearly the 1950s are finally attracting scholarly attention.

2. Elaine Tyler May, *Homeward Bound: American Families in the Cold War Era* (New York: Basic Books, 1988), 10–11, 113, 225, 93–94, 97, 208; John D'Emilio and Estelle B. Freedman, *Intimate Matters: A History of Sexuality in America* (New York: Harper & Row, 1988), 292–95.

3. Douglas Miller and Marion Nowak, *The Fifties: The Way We Really Were* (Garden City, N.Y.: Doubleday, 1975, 1977), 7.

4. William Manchester, *The Glory and the Dream: A Narrative History of America, 1932–1972* (New York: Bantam, 1974), 584–85; Landon Y. Jones, *Great Expectations: America and the Baby Boom Generation* (New York: Coward, McCann & Geoghegan, 1980), 42.

5. Robert H. Bremner, "Families, Children, and the State," in *Reshaping America: Society and Institutions, 1945–1960*, ed. Robert H. Bremner and Gary W. Reichard (Columbus: Ohio State University Press, 1982), ix–x, 13.

6. Eugenia Kaledin, *Mothers and More: American Women in the 1950s* (Boston: Twayne, 1984), 27.

7. Miller and Nowak, *The Fifties*, 365–66.

8. Nye, *Unembarrassed Muse*, 413–14.

9. Norman Podheretz, *Doings and Undoings: The Fifties and After in American Writing* (New York: Farrar, Straus & Giroux, 1953), 272, 281–82.

10. Manchester, *The Glory and the Dream*, 692.

11. David Riesman, *The Lonely Crowd: A Study of Changing American Character* (New Haven: Yale University Press, 1950), 162, 203.

12. Jones, *Great Expectations*, 42.

13. Miller and Nowak, *The Fifties*, 328–29.

14. Betty Friedan, *The Feminine Mystique* (New York: Dell, 1974; originally New York: W. W. Norton, 1963), 31.

15. Ibid., 69.

16. Barbara Ehrenreich, *The Hearts of Men: American Dreams and the Flight from Commitment* (Garden City, N.Y.: Doubleday, Anchor Press, 1983), 85.

17. Friedan, *The Feminine Mystique*, 59.

18. Ibid., 246.

19. Jones, *Great Expectations*, 76.

20. Betty Friedan, *It Changed My Life: Writings on the Women's Movement* (New York: Random House, 1976), 15, 52.

21. Philip Wylie, *A Generation of Vipers* (New York: Faircut & Rinehart, 1942), 186, 189, 203; Steven Mintz and Susan Kellogg, *Domestic Revolutions* (New York: Basic Books, 1988), 164.

22. Friedan, *The Feminine Mystique*, 260, 314.

23. Letter to Betty Friedan from Riverton, Wyo., June 3, 1964, Betty Friedan Collection, Carton 19, folder 683, SL.

24. Letter to Friedan from Cleveland, Ohio, June 7, 1964, ibid.

25. Berkeley, July 30, 1964, ibid., folder 691.

26. Fort Lee, N.J., October 18, 1964, ibid., folder 693.

27. October 10, 1965, ibid., folder 698.

28. February 24, 1967, ibid.

29. March 9, 1964, ibid., folder 690.

30. Kaledin, *Mothers and More*, 43.

31. Letter to Friedan, Broadview, Ill., Betty Friedan Collection.

32. Hyde Park, Mass., February 9, 1964, ibid.

33. Upper Saddle River, N.Y., ibid.

34. South Carolina, March 9, 1964, ibid.

35. John Sirjamaki, *The American Family in the Twentieth Century* (Cambridge: Harvard University Press, 1969), 165. See also *Statistical Abstract of the United States*, Bureau of Census, U.S. Department of Commerce, 1983; *Historical Statistics of the United States: Colonial Times to 1970*, pt. 1, 1975.

36. Hickory, N.C., Betty Friedan Collection.

37. Glen Ridge, N.J., August 4, 1964, ibid.

38. H. A. Overstreet, *The Mature Mind* (London: Victor Gollanca, 1950; originally New York: W. W. Norton, 1949), 234–35.

39. Joe L. Dubbert, *A Man's Place: Masculinity in Transition* (Englewood Cliffs, N.J.: Prentice-Hall, 1979), 198, 208–9, 215, 245.

40. Ibid., 245.; see also Manchester, *The Glory and the Dream*, 578.

41. Riesman, *Lonely Crowd*, v.

42. Dubbert, *Man's Place*, 250.

43. Ibid., 251.

44. Manchester, *The Glory and the Dream*, 482.

45. Dubbert, *Man's Place*, 254–55.

46. Miller, *The Fifties*, 156.

47. Ehrenreich, *Hearts of Men*, 29, 41; Mickey Spillane, *One Lonely Night* (New York: E. P. Dutton, 1951), 165.

48. Ehrenreich, *Hearts of Men*, 42, 50.

49. D'Emilio and Freedman, *Intimate Matters*, 234, 302.

50. Mary P. Ryan, *Womanhood in America from Colonial Times to the Present* (New York: New Viewpoints, 1975), 272–73.

51. Friedan, *The Feminine Mystique*, 249–50.

52. Linda Gordon, *Woman's Body, Woman's Right*, 341–43; see also Kaledin, *Mothers and More*, 178.

53. Leo Kanowitz, *Women and the Law: The Unfinished Revolution* (Albuquerque: New Mexico, 1969), 26.

54. Judith Walzer Leavitt, *Brought to Bed: Childbearing in America, 1750–1950* (New York: Oxford University Press, 1986), 107, 171, 197, 205.

55. Richard W. Wertz and Dorothy C. Wertz, *Lying-In: A History of Childbirth in America* (New York: Free Press, 1977), 165, 170–71, 173; for letters to the *Ladies Home Journal*, see May 1958 issue (excerpts on 171–72).

56. Leila J. Rupp, "The Survival of American Feminism: The Women's Movement in the Postwar Period," in *Reshaping America*, ed. Bremner and Reichard, 36–37; see also Kaledin, *Mothers and More*, 64, 67.

57. Eric Goldman, *The Crucial Decade and After: America, 1945–1960* (New York: Vintage Books, 1956), 266.

58. Jones, *Great Expectations*, 165.

59. Ibid.

60. Ibid., 167–68.

61. Ibid., 168–69.

62. Sirjamaki, *American Family in the Twentieth Century*, 163; see also Kaledin, *Mothers and More,* 37.

63. Ryan, *Womanhood in America*, 327.

64. Nancy E. McGlen and Karen O'Connor, *The Struggle for Equality in the Nineteenth and Twentieth Centuries* (New York: Praeger, 1983), 323, 329.

65. Lois W. Banner, *Women in Modern America: A Brief History* (New York: Harcourt Brace Jovanovich, 1974), 257–59; Kaledin, *Mothers and More*, 54; Nancy Woloch, *Women and the American Experience* (New York: Alfred A. Knopf, 1984), 543. Women earned 15 percent of all Ph.D.s granted in 1920, but only 10 percent in the 1950s. They constituted 32 percent of college administrators and professors in 1930, 27 percent in 1940, 23 percent in 1950, and only 19 percent in 1960. The percentage of female doctors fluctuated from 4 percent in 1930 to 4.6 percent in 1940, 6.1 percent

in 1950, and 6.8 percent in 1960. (Medical schools openly admitted having quotas of 5 percent for female admissions; law schools had even lower quotas in the 1950s.) The percentage of female lawyers increased from 2.1 percent in 1930 to 2.4 percent in 1940 and 3.5 percent in both 1950 and 1960. The percentage of employed women who were professionals ranged from 14.2 percent in 1930 to 13 percent in 1940, 11 percent in 1950, and 13 percent in 1962.

66. Ryan, *Womanhood in America*, 327–29.

67. Giddings, *When and Where I Enter*, 256.

68. Jacqueline Jones, *Labor of Love, Labor of Sorrow: Black Women, Work, and the Family from Slavery to the Present* (New York: Basic Books, 1985), 260–61, 269.

69. Ibid., 234–35, 305–6.

70. Ibid., 269–71.

71. Kaledin, *Mothers and More*, 150; see also Manchester, *The Glory and the Dream*, 740–41; see also oral history conducted by Marcia McAdoo Greenlee with Rosa Parks, August 22, 23, 1978, transcript, p. 9, Black Women Oral History Project, SL.

72. Jones, *Labor of Love, Labor of Sorrow*, 279–80.

73. Ibid., 283–84.

11. Feminist Voices of the 1950s

1. June Sochen, *Movers and Shakers: American Women Thinkers and Activists, 1900–1970* (New York: Quadrangle, 1973), 198, 200. Sochen quotes Ferdinand Lundberg and Marynia Farnham, *Modern Woman: The Lost Sex* (New York: Harper & Brothers, 1947), 144.

2. Lundberg and Farnham, *Modern Woman*, 363–77.

3. Leila J. Rupp, "The Survival of American Feminism: The Women's Movement in the Postwar Period," in *Reshaping America: Society and Institutions, 1945–1960*, ed. Robert H. Bremner and Gary W. Reichard (Columbus: Ohio State University Press, 1982), 41–42.

4. Eugenia Kaledin, *Mothers and More: American Women in the 1950s* (Boston: Twayne, 1984), 33.

5. Doris E. Fleishman (Bernays), "Notes of a Retiring Feminist," *American Mercury* 68 (February 1949): 161–68.

6. Nancy E. McGlen and Karen O'Connor, *The Struggle for Equality in the Nineteenth and Twentieth Centuries* (New York: Praeger, 1983), 15.

7. Leila J. Rupp and Verta Taylor, *Survival in the Doldrums: The American Women's Rights Movement, 1945 to the 1960s* (New York: Oxford University Press, 1987), 26.

8. Rupp, "Survival of American Feminism," 44–45; Rupp and Taylor, *Survival in the Doldrums*, 45–47. Rupp and Taylor chronicle the preexisting and emergent women's movement organizations from 1945 to the 1960s. They include the

National Woman's Party, Business and Professional Women's Club, National Association of Women Lawyers, American Medical Woman's Association, and Pioneers (a group of women dedicated to winning recognition for pioneers of the suffrage movement) as core organizations. They cite the Connecticut Committee for the ERA, Massachusetts Committee for the ERA, Lucy Stone League, Women's Joint Legislative Committee, Industrial Women's League for Equality, and the St. Joan Society as emergent women's movement groups. They also include other women's movement organizations which were concerned with women's equality: General Federation of Women's Clubs, National Council of Women, American Association of University Women, National Association of Colored Women, a network of women active in the Republican and Democratic parties and women politicians, Zonta, Soroptimist, Altrusa, Federation of Women Shareholders (preexisting), and emergent organizations such as Women in World Affairs, Multi-Party Committee of Women, and Assembly of Women's Organizations for National Security. These peripheral organizations supported some of the goals of the core organizations and cooperated with them to achieve common goals, but without the same consistent level of involvement.

9. Rupp, "Survival of American Feminism," 45; see Rupp and Taylor, *Survival in the Doldrums*, 26, 70–76.

10. Rupp and Taylor, *Survival in the Doldrums*, 54.

11. Ibid., 139.

12. Ibid., 176–77; see also Rupp, "Survival of American Feminism," 55–56.

13. Rupp and Taylor, *Survival in the Doldrums*, 154.

14. Carol Ascher, *Simone de Beauvoir: A Life of Freedom* (Boston: Beacon, 1981), 123–27.

15. Marion K. Sanders, *Dorothy Thompson: A Legend in Her Time* (New York: Avon, 1974; originally Boston: Houghton Mifflin, 1973), 290.

16. Ibid., 1–39, 77, 85, 88–89, 94; Barbara Sicherman and Carol Hurd Green, eds. *Notable American Women: The Modern Period* (Cambridge: Harvard University Press, 1980), 683–86. Thompson was born in Lancaster, New York, in 1893. Her mother had five children and died of a bungled abortion. At college Thompson was in the Syracuse Equal Suffrage Club (1912) and continued to work for suffrage after graduation in the same territory covered by Elizabeth Cady Stanton and Lucretia Mott. After suffrage was won in New York, she moved to New York City in 1917 and to Austria in 1921. She married Sinclair Lewis on May 14, 1928. They were separated by 1937 and divorced in 1942. For additional information on Thompson's private life, see Sanders, *Dorothy Thompson*, 221, 183, 272–73, and Vincent Sheean, *Dorothy and Red* (Boston: Houghton Mifflin, 1963), 264.

17. Sanders, *Dorothy Thompson*, 242.

18. Sochen, *Movers and Shakers*, 185.

19. Ibid., 186.

20. Ibid., 188–89; Sanders, *Dorothy Thompson*, 340.

21. Pearl Buck, *Of Men and Women* (New York: John Day, 1941), 24–25.

22. Ibid., 75.

23. Ibid., 187, 184, 52–53; Sochen, *Movers and Shakers*, 177, 181–82.

24. R. Cohen, "Pearl Buck," in *Notable American Women*, ed. Sicherman and Green, 116–19.

25. Eve Merriam, *After Nora Slammed the Door: American Women in the 1960s—The Unfinished Revolution* (Cleveland: World Publishing, 1958), 33.

26. Ibid., 117, 137, 139, 165. Mirra Komarovsky, another feminist of the 1950s, resembled Merriam in her anticipation of Friedan's insights. In her book *Women in the Modern World: Their Education and Their Dilemma* (Boston: Little, Brown, 1953), Komarovsky avoids strident statements and steers a careful path. She does not disparage homemakers or career women. Her goal is to avoid linking the elevation of one with the degradation of the other. According to Komarovsky, some young husbands are caught between the demands of their occupations and the new ideal of a husband-companion. But she believes that it is possible for a wife to have a successful career if she has a cooperative husband. Like Pearl Buck, she urges that men take a more active part in the activities of the home and in childrearing (298, 164, 252).

27. Jane Howard, *Margaret Mead: A Life* (New York: Simon & Schuster, 1984), 225–26; see also Betty Friedan, *The Feminine Mystique* (New York: Dell, 1974; originally New York: W. W. Norton, 1963), 127.

28. Howard, *Margaret Mead*, 139–53, 162.

29. Ibid., 363.

30. Ibid., 365.

31. Ibid., 367.

32. Ibid., 253, 217, 244, 264–66.

33. Sochen, *Movers and Shakers*, 190–91.

12. Miss America Good-bye: The Modern Feminist Movement

1. Judith Hole and Ellen Levine, *Rebirth of Feminism* (New York: Quadrangle, 1971), 123; Marcia Cohen, *The Sisterhood: The True Story of the Women Who Changed the World* (New York: Simon & Schuster, 1988); Alice Echols, *Daring to Be Bad: Radical Feminism in America, 1967–1975* (Minneapolis: University of Minnesota Press, 1989), 93–94. Echols points out that Carol Hanish came up with the idea for protest in the summer of 1968 after watching Gunvar Nelson's experimental feminist film *Schmearguntz,* which contained footage of the Miss America Pageant. Robin Morgan did most of the planning for the Miss America Pageant protest. Alix Kates Shulman purchased sixteen tickets to get into the hall.

2. Paul C. Glick, *Some Recent Changes in American Families*, Current Population Reports Special Studies Series P–23, no. 52 (Washington, D.C.: Department of Commerce, Bureau of the Census, 1975), 3–5, 9, 13, 14, 21–52; an address given on October 25, 1974, published as "A Demographer Looks at American Families," *Journal of Marriage and the Family* 37, no. 1 (1975): 15–26.

3. Alice S. Rossi, "Women—Terms of Liberation, 1970," in *The American Sisterhood: Writings of the Feminist Movement from Colonial Times to the Present,* ed. Wendy Martin (New York: Harper and Row, 1972), 135.

4. Zillah R. Eisenstein, *The Radical Future of Liberal Feminism* (New York: Longman, 1981), 207.

5. Sara Evans, *Personal Politics: The Roots of Women's Liberation in the Civil Rights Movement & the New Left* (New York: Vintage, 1979), 8, 10.

6. Margaret Mead and Frances Balgley Kaplan, eds., *American Women and Other Publications of the Commission* (New York: Scribner's Sons, 1965; reprinted Washington, D.C.: Zenger Publishing, 1976), 21–24, 45–47.

7. Margaret B. Lefkovitz, "The Women's Magazine Short Story Heroine, 1957–1967," in *Toward a Sociology of Women,* ed. Constantia Safilios Rothschild (Lexington, Mass.: Xerox College Publishing, 1971), 37–39.

8. Katherine Fishburn, *Women in Popular Culture: A Reference Guide* (Westport, Conn.: Greenwood Press, 1982), 22.

9. Jane De Hart-Mathews, "The New Feminism and the Dynamics of Social Change," in *Women's America: Refocusing the Past*, 2d ed., ed. Linda Kerber and Jane De Hart-Mathews (New York: Oxford University Press, 1987), 443–45.

10. Ibid., 448–49; see also William Henry Chafe, *The American Woman: Her Changing Social, Economic, and Political Roles, 1920–1970* (New York: Oxford University Press, 1972), 29–30, 112; Jo Freeman, *The Politics of Women's Liberation: A Case Study of an Emerging Social Movement and Its Relation to the Policy Process* (New York: David McKay, 1975; reprinted New York: Longman, 1977), 35–37.

11. Mead and Kaplan, *American Women*, 32–33.

12. Ibid., 183–84.

13. Ibid., 21, 26–27, 35, 46, 88–89.

14. Ibid., 72–73, 210–13. After Johnson assumed the presidency after Kennedy's death, he appointed fifty-six women to posts by June 1964.

15. Ibid., 36–37.

16. De Hart-Mathews, "New Feminism and the Dynamics of Social Change," 447–49.

17. Betty Friedan, *It Changed My Life: Writings on the Women's Movement* (New York: Random House, 1976), 77, 83–84.

18. Freeman, *Politics of Women's Liberation*, 74.

19. Ibid., 152–53; see also Maren Lockwood Carden, *The New Feminist Movement* (New York: Russell Sage Foundation, 1974), 140.

20. De Hart-Mathews, "New Feminism and the Dynamics of Social Change, 449–50.

21. Evans, *Personal Politics*, 19; Freeman, *Politics of Women's Liberation*, 83–84.

22. Freeman, *Politics of Women's Liberation*, 82, 84, 97.

23. Ethel Klein, *Gender Politics: From Consciousness to Mass Politics* (Cambridge: Harvard University Press, 1984), 119.

24. Myra Marx Ferree and Beth B. Hess, *Controversy and Coalition: The New Feminist Movement* (Boston: Twayne, 1985), 49.

25. Evans, *Personal Politics*, 27–28.

26. Ibid., 30, 35, 53, 55, 74, 76, 81.

27. Ibid., 85, 97, 101.

28. Ibid., 112, 155, 190–91.

29. Ibid., 195–99, 224, 156. Heather Tobias, Vivan Leburg, Cathy Barrett, and Peggy Dobbins, young SDS women, formed WITCH in 1967.

30. Hole and Levine, *Rebirth of Feminism*, 126, 130.

31. Ibid., 136, 143, 144–46.

32. Ti-Grace Atkinson, *Amazon Odyssey* (New York: Links Books, 1974), 5–7; Steven Mintz and Susan Kellogg, *Domestic Revolutions: A Social History of American Family Life* (New York: Free Press, 1988), 207.

33. Echols, *Daring to Be Bad*, 181–83.

34. Hole and Levine, *Rebirth of Feminism*, 150–51; Leslie Tanner, ed., *Voices from Women's Liberation* (New York: Signet, 1970), 124–25.

35. Echols, *Daring to Be Bad*, 139, 63, 158. Meredith Tax and Linda Gordon helped found Bread and Roses, a socialist feminist group in Boston. Roxanne Dunbar formed Cell 16 in the summer of 1968 after moving to Boston from the West Coast. The group included Dana Densmore, Abby Rockefeller, Besty Warrior, Jeanne Lafferty, and Lisa Leghorn. Cell 16 became a cultural feminist group in 1970 with its valorization of female values, vilification of maleness, and belief in global sisterhood.

36. Tanner, *Voices from Women's Liberation*, 124–25.

37. Hole and Levine, *Rebirth of Feminism*, 150–52.

38. Ibid., 210–13.

39. Gayle Graham Yates, *What Women Want: The Ideas of the Movement* (Cambridge: Harvard University Press, 1975), 17–20.

40. Friedan, *It Changed My Life*, 252–53.

41. Echols, *Daring to Be Bad*, 219–20.

42. Adrienne Rich, *Of Woman Born: Motherhood as Experience and Institution* (New York: W. W. Norton, 1976); Mary Daly, *Gyn/Ecology: The Metaethics of Radical Feminism* (Boston: Beacon, 1978); see also Ferree and Hess, *Controversy and Coalition*, 41.

43. Freeman, *Politics of Women's Liberation,* 163.

44. Alison M. Jaggar, *Feminist Politics and Human Nature* (Sussex: Harvester Press, 1983), 124–31.

45. Ibid., 131.

46. Hole and Levine, *Rebirth of Feminism*, 108–9.

47. Ibid., 203, 239–42.

48. De Hart-Mathews, "New Feminism and the Dynamics of Social Change," 456; see also Maren Carden, *The New Feminist Movement* (New York: Russell Sage Foundation, 1974), 2.

49. Kate Millett, *Sexual Politics* (Garden City, N.Y.: Doubleday, 1970), 33, 35, 37, 62.

50. Friedan, *It Changed My Life*, 312.

51. Germaine Greer, *The Female Eunuch* (New York: Bantam, 1972; originally London: MacGibbon & Kee, 1970), 10–12, 118, 216–35.

52. Shulamith Firestone, *The Dialectic of Sex: The Case for Feminist Revolution* (New York: William Morrow, 1970), 8–9.

53. Ibid., 81, 142, 152, 226, 233–34, 236.

54. Susan Brownmiller, *Against Our Will: Men, Women, and Rape* (New York: Simon & Schuster, 1975), 14–15.

55. Ibid., 209.

56. Gloria Steinem, "Sisterhood," in *The First Ms. Reader*, ed. Francine Klagsbrun (New York: Warner Books, 1973), 5.

57. Friedan, *It Changed My Life*, 341.

58. Ibid., 125–26.

59. Ibid., 182.

60. Jaggar, *Feminist Politics and Human Nature*, 21, 33.

61. Eisenstein, *Radical Future of Liberal Feminism*, 188, 190–91, 231.

62. Cellestine Ware, *Woman Power: The Movement for Women's Liberation* (New York: Tower Publications, 1970), epigraph and 16.

63. Ferree and Hess, *Controversy and Coalition*, 27.

64. Paula Giddings, *When and Where I Enter: The Impact of Black Women on Race and Sex in America* (Toronto: Bantam, 1984), 344, 352; Echols, *Daring to Be Bad*, 101, 151.

65. Barbara Ehrenreich,"The Next Wave," *Ms.*, August 1987, 168, 216; see also Robert Staples, *The Black Woman in America: Sex, Marriage, and the Family* (Chicago: Nelson Hall, 1973), 187.

66. Jacqueline Jones, *Labor of Love, Labor of Sorrow: Black Women, Work, and Family from Slavery to the Present* (New York: Basic Books, 1985), 277.

67. Ibid., 305–6.

68. Giddings, *When and Where I Enter*, 324–25 (Moynihan quotation on 325); Jones, *Labor of Love, Labor of Sorrow*, 312.

69. Staples, *Black Woman in America*, 79.

70. Cellestine Ware, "The Black Family and Feminism: A Conversation with Eleanor Holmes Norton," in *First Ms. Reader*, ed. Klagsbrun, 41.

71. Bell Hooks, *Feminist Theory: From Margin to Center* (Boston: South End Press, 1984), 91–93, 90, 60–61.

72. Willa Mae Hemmons, "The Women's Liberation Movement: Understanding Black Women's Attitudes," in *The Black Woman,* ed. LaFrances Rodgers-Rose (Beverly Hills, Calif.: Sage Publications, 1980), 292, 296.

73. Pauli Murray, *Song in a Weary Throat: An American Pilgrimage* (New York: Harper & Row, 1987), 238; see also Murray, *Proud Shoes: The Story of an American Family* (New York: Harper & Row, 1956, 1978).

74. Pauli Murray, "The Negro Woman in the Quest for Equality," *The Acorn* (Lambda Mu Sorority, June 1964), quoted in Lerner, *Black Women in White America,* 596, 592.

75. Murray, *Song in a Weary Throat,* 239–41, 435.

76. Ibid., 198–99.

77. Ibid., 214–15.

78. Ibid., 436, 416.

79. Ferree and Hess, *Controversy and Coalition,* 84–86, 88.

80. Freeman, *Politics of Women's Liberation,* 163, 165–66.

81. Yates, *What Women Want,* 52.

82. Ibid., 54–55.

83. Pamela Johnston Conover and Virginia Gray, *Feminism and the New Right* (New York: Praeger, 1983), 8.

84. Yates, *What Women Want,* 57.

85. Susan Edmiston, "How to Write Your Own Marriage Contract," in *First Ms. Reader,* ed. Klagsbrun, 101.

86. Janet K. Boles, "The Equal Rights Movement as a Non-Zero-Sum Game," in *Rights of Passage: The Past and Future of the ERA,* ed. Joan Hoff-Wilson (Bloomington: Indiana University Press, 1986), 59; Elizabeth Pleck, "Failed Strategies, Renewed Hopes," in ibid., 118; Berenice Carroll, "Direct Action and Constitutional Rights: The Case of ERA," in ibid., 63–75.

87. Conover and Gray, *Feminism and the New Right,* 1, 54.

88. Gloria Steinem, "From the Opposite Shore," in *Outrageous Acts and Everyday Rebellions* (New York: Holt, Rinehart, & Winston, 1983), 355.

89. Steinem, "If Hitler Were Alive Whose Side Would He Be On?" in *Outrageous Acts and Everyday Rebellions,* 308.

90. Joseph M. Hawes and N. Ray Hiner, *American Childhood: A Research Guide and Historical Handbook* (Westport, Conn.: Greenwood Press, 1985), 626; Kristin Luker, *Abortion and the Politics of Motherhood* (Berkeley: University of California Press, 1984), 1.

91. Luker, *Abortion,* 118, 120, 193–96.

92. Connie Paige, *The Right to Lifers: Who They Are, How They Operate, Where They Get Their Money* (New York: Summit, 1983), 222.

93. Freeman, *Politics of Women's Liberation*, 171, 202–4.

94. See Suzanne Levine, Harriet Lyons, and Gloria Steinem, *The Decade of Women: A Ms. History of the Seventies in Words and Pictures* (New York: G. P. Putnam's Sons, 1980), 6, 8, 10, 12, 16, 18, 20, 22, 24; Ferree and Hess, *Controversy and Coalition*, 95. Appendix 3 contains a listing of these accomplishments and events of the feminist movement in the 1970s.

95. Ferree and Hess, *Controversy and Coalition*, 100.

96. Ibid., 144, 155; Klein, *Gender Politics*, 30–31; Lois Banner, *Women in Modern America* (New York: Harcourt Brace Jovanovich, 1984), 267.

97. Ferree and Hess, *Controversy and Coalition*, 144, 155.

98. Giddings, *When and Where I Enter*, 306.

99. Ferree and Hess, *Controversy and Coalition*, 75.

100. Freeman, *Politics of Women's Liberation*, 36, 154.

101. Klein, *Gender Politics*, 22.

102. A full discussion of women's literature which flourished in the 1970s is beyond the scope of this book. However, it must be acknowledged that the movement created a receptive climate for women writers and also empowered women to express their anger, joy, sorrow, and fantasies in fiction. Their work reached a large audience and perhaps helped American women come to a new consciousness of their power even more than did theoretical feminist works. Erica Jong's *Fear of Flying* shocked and delighted audiences because of her frank exploration of female sexuality. She views sex as a liberating, guilt-free adventure. She romanticizes the "zipless fuck"— sex with a total stranger. For Jong, feminism incorporated the sexual revolution: women's claiming their sexuality was a part of their liberation.

A large number of books, including Doris Lessings's *The Golden Notebook*, Margaret Atwood's *Surfacing*, Alix Kates Shulman's *Burning Questions* and *Memoirs of an Ex-Prom Queen*, and Marilyn French's *The Woman's Room,* explore the spiritual and social quests of women in a male-dominated society. These authors explore the internal and external obstacles to achieving wholeness. In *Woman on the Edge of Time,* Marge Piercy imagines a future, androgynous society, as Ursula Le Guin also explores in *The Left Hand of Darkness.*

African-American women authors came into national prominence in the 1970s and 1980s. Alice Walker's *The Color Purple*, Maya Angelou's *I Know Why the Caged Bird Sings*, Toni Morrison's *Tar Baby*, and Ntozake Shange's *For Colored Girls Only Who Have Considered Suicide When the Rainbow Is Enuf* capture the dignity, strength, and capacity for joy of black women who prevail. Zora Neale Hurston's and Gwendolyn Brooks's works were also widely read and praised.

103. Conover and Gray, *Feminism and the New Right*, 73, 75, 77.

104. Klein, *Gender Politics*, 27.

105. Phyllis Schlafly, *The Power of the Positive Woman* (New Rochelle, N.Y.: Arlington House, 1977), 11.

106. Carol Felsenthal, *The Sweetheart of the Silent Majority: The Biography of Phyllis Schlafly* (Garden City, N.Y.: Doubleday, 1981), 268–69, 277, 195.

107. Ibid., 289, 235–39. Schlafly, *Power of the Positive Woman*, 81.

108. Conover and Gray, *Feminism and the New Right*, 84–85, 87, 94, 205.

109. Ibid., 205–6, 6.

110. Paige, *The Right to Lifers*, 179.

111. Echols, *Daring to Be Bad*, 5.

Conclusion and Prospect

1. Ellen Goodman, in Jeanette Branin, "She Outlines the Realities for a Change," *San Diego Union*, June 29, 1977, quoted in Marjorie Hansen Shaevitz, *The Superwoman Syndrome* (New York: Warner Books, 1984), 2

2. Barbara Ehrenreich,"The Next Wave," *Ms.*, August 1987, 168, 216.

3. Eloise Salholtz, "Feminism's Identity Crisis," *Newsweek* 107 (March 31, 1986): 58–59; Robert O. Blood, Jr., and Donald M. Wolfe, *Husbands and Wives: The Dynamics of Married Living* (Glencoe, Ill.: Free Press, 1960), 29.

4. Myra Marx Ferree and Beth B. Hess, *Controversy and Coalition* (Boston: Twayne, 1985), 162; Robert Bly, *Iron John: A Book about Men* (Reading, Mass.: Addison-Wesley, 1990).

5 . Ethel Klein, *Gender Politics: From Consciousness to Mass Politics* (Cambridge: Harvard University Press, 1984), 92–93.

6. Sylvia Ann Hewlett, *A Lesser Life: The Myth of Women's Liberation in America* (New York: William Morrow, 1986), 112. See also Karen DeCrow, "Universal Child Care Is a NOW Priority," *Syracuse New Times*, January 18–25, 1989, reprinted in *National NOW Times*, April 1989, 5.

7. Hewlett, *Lesser Life*, 88–89; see also Steven Lagerfeld, "Measuring the Effects," *Wilson Quarterly*, Autumn 1986, 137.

8. John Scanzoni, *Sexual Bargaining: Power Politics in the American Marriage* (Chicago: University of Chicago Press, 1972, 1982), vii–viii; see also Arlie Hochschild, *The Second Shift: Working Parents and the Revolution at Home* (New York: Viking, 1989), 8, 271–73; Ruth Schwartz Cowan, *More Work for Mother: The Ironies of Household Technology from the Open Hearth to the Microwave* (New York: Basic Books, 1983), 200.

9. Hewlett, *A Lesser Life*, 51, 54, 60, 64, 66, 71, 109; see also Steven Mintz and Susan Kellogg, *Domestic Revolutions: A Social History of American Family Life* (New York: Free Press, 1988), 203, 242.

10. Lagerfeld, "Measuring the Effects," 132–33, 136.

11. Ibid., 133.

12. Hewlett, *A Lesser Life*, 96, 14–15.

13. Ibid., 85, 100, 129, 132, 135. In *Domestic Revolutions* Mintz and Kellogg claim that 15 percent of American families now fit the traditional model (203).

14. Deborah Fallows, *A Mother's Work* (Boston: Houghton Mifflin, 1985), 52–53.

15. Betty Friedan, *The Second Stage* (New York: Summit Books, 1981), 23, 26, 31–32, 47, 53, 133, 219.

16. Betty Friedan, *It Changed My Life: Writings on the Women's Movement* (New York: Random House, 1976), 250.

17. *National NOW Times*, April 1989, 1.

18. "Reshaping the Debate," ibid., 4.

19. *New York Times*, July 3, 1989, 1; *Cleveland Daily Banner*, July 23, 1989, 4–5; *Chattanooga Free Press*, July 3, 1989, 1.

20. *New York Times*, July 16, 1989, 1, 23; statistics by Center for Population Options; see also Mintz and Kellogg, *Domestic Revolutions*, 204.

BIBLIOGRAPHIC ESSAY

Since the 1960s scholars have developed a full range of new interpretations of American women's lives. The period before 1900 has received the fullest attention, but in recent years scholars have also focused on the twentieth century. As my bibliography indicates, I have examined both primary collections and an extensive range of secondary works in order to discover the ways in which American women's growing gender consciousness was rooted not simply in oppression but ironically in empowering domestic experiences. I have also attempted to discern the stance of the feminist movements of the nineteenth and twentieth centuries toward family issues.

For those interested in works most directly addressing domestic politics and feminism, the following works are illuminating. My own interpretation has benefited greatly from the insights of Nancy F. Cott, who wrote of the liberating as well as the oppressive nature of nineteenth-century separate spheres for men and women. See Cott, *The Bonds of Womanhood: "Woman's Sphere" in New England, 1780–1835* (New Haven: Yale University Press, 1977). Carroll Smith-Rosenberg has written imaginatively about the intimate relationships which developed during that period among women and the creation of a separate women's culture. See Smith-Rosenberg, *Disorderly Conduct: Visions of Gender in Victorian America* (New York: Alfred A. Knopf, 1985). Daniel Scott Smith and Kathryn Kish Sklar advanced our understanding of "domestic feminism" in the nineteenth century by pointing out that traditional gender roles could be empowering for some women. See Scott, "Family Limitation, Sexual Control, and Domestic Feminism in Victorian America," *Feminist Studies* 1 (Winter–Spring 1973): 40–57; Sklar, *Catharine Beecher: A Study in American Domesticity* (New York: W. W. Norton, 1973).

Limited attention has been paid to the relationship of feminism and the family. Only Carl N. Degler's ground-breaking work *At Odds: Women and the Family in America from the Revolution to the Present* (New York: Oxford University Press, 1980) attempted to integrate the history of women and the history of the family. He argued that the historic family has depended for its existence and character on women's subordination. While I agree that many of women's experiences within families have been oppressive, I argue that women's experiences as wives and mothers have also been empowering for some women and that contradictions in their experiences helped lead to feminist consciousness.

For an excellent survey of the history of American families, see Steven Mintz and Susan Kellogg, *Domestic Revolutions: A Social History of American Family Life* (New York: Free Press, 1988). Stephanie Coontz's *The Social Origins of Private Life: A History of American Families, 1600–1900* (London: Verso, 1988) is also a highly perceptive work.

For views on the relationship of contemporary feminism and the family, see Betty Friedan, *The Second Stage* (New York: Summit Books, 1981); Sylvia Hewlett, *A Lesser Life: The Myth of Women's Liberation in America* (New York: William Morrow, 1986); and Christopher Lasch, *Haven in a Heartless World: The Family Besieged* (New York: Basic Books, 1977).

Some illuminating texts in American women's history are Sara M. Evans, *Born for Liberty: A History of Women in America* (New York: Free Press, 1989); Nancy Woloch, *Women and the American Experience* (New York: Alfred A. Knopf, 1984); Lois Banner, *Women in Modern America: A Brief History*, 2d ed. (New York: Harcourt Brace Jovanovich, 1984). An older but helpful text is Mary Ryan's *Womanhood in America from Colonial Times to the Present* (New York: New Viewpoints, 1975). For other comprehensive works in women's history, see Barbara Ehrenreich and Deirdre English, *For Her Own Good: 150 Years of Experts' Advice to Women* (Garden City, N.Y.: Doubleday, Anchor Press, 1978); Peter Gabriel Filene, *Him/Herself: Sex Roles in Modern America* (New York: Harcourt Brace Jovanovich, 1974); and Maxine L. Morgolis, *Mothers and Such: Views of American Women and Why They Changed* (Berkeley: University of California Press, 1984). The best study of American domesticity is Glenna Matthews's *"Just a Housewife": The Rise and Fall of Domesticity in America* (New York: Oxford University Press, 1987).

For information on women's participation in the labor force, Alice Kessler-Harris's *Out to Work: A History of Wage-Earning Women in the United States* (New York: Oxford University Press, 1982) is indispensable. See also Rosalyn Baxandall, Linda Gordon, and Susan Reverby, eds., *America's Working Women: A Documentary History, 1699 to the Present* (New York: Vintage, 1976) for a fine collection of primary documents. In addition, see Barbara R. Bergman, *The Economic Emergence of Women* (New York: Basic Books, 1986), and Valerie Kincade Oppenheimer, *The Female Labor Force in the United States: Demographic and Economic Factors Governing Its Growth and Changing Composition* (Berkeley: University of California, Institute of International Studies, 1979); Susan Estabrook Kennedy, *If All We Did Was to Weep at Home: A History of White Working Women in America* (Bloomington: Indiana University Press, 1979); Ruth Milkman, *Women, Work, and Protest: A Century of U.S. Women's Labor History* (Boston: Routledge & Kegan Paul, 1985); and Elizabeth Anne Payne, *Reform, Labor, and Feminism* (Urbana: University of Illinois Press, 1988).

Views of women in popular culture and domestic fiction are richly explored in

Barbara Welter, *Dimity Convictions: The American Woman in the Nineteenth Century* (Athens: Ohio University Press, 1976); Kathryn Weibel, *Mirror, Mirror: Images of Women Reflected in Popular Culture* (Garden City, N.Y.: Anchor Books, 1977); Katherine Fishburn, *Women in Popular Culture: A Reference Guide* (Westport, Conn.: Greenwood Press, 1982); Jeanne Boydston, Mary Kelley, and Anne Morgolis, *The Limits of Sisterhood: The Beecher Sisters on Women's Rights and Woman's Sphere* (Chapel Hill: University of North Carolina Press, 1988); Jane P. Tompkins, *Sensational Designs: The Cultural Work of American Fiction, 1790–1860* (New York: Oxford University Press, 1985); Nina Baym, *Novels, Readers, and Reviewers: Responses to Fiction in Antebellum America* (Ithaca: Cornell University Press, 1984) and *Woman's Fiction: A Guide to Novels by and about Women in America, 1820–1871* (Ithaca: Cornell University Press, 1978); Maurice Horn, *Women in the Comics* (New York: Chelsea House, 1977); Susan E. Meyer, *America's Great Illustrators* (New York: Harry N. Abrams, 1978); Mary P. Ryan, *The Empire of the Mother: American Writing about Domesticity, 1830–1860* (New York: Haworth Press, 1982) and *Women in Public: Between Banners and Ballots, 1825–1880* (Baltimore: Johns Hopkins University Press, 1990); Andrea S. Walsh, *Women's Film and Female Experience, 1940–1950* (New York: Praeger Special Studies, 1984); June Sochen, *Enduring Values: Women in Popular Culture* (New York: Praeger, 1987); Lois Banner, *American Beauty* (New York: Alfred A. Knopf, 1983); Mary Kelley, *Private Woman, Public Stage: Literary Domesticity in Nineteenth-Century America* (New York: Oxford University Press, 1984); and Helen Waite Papashvily, *All the Happy Endings* (Port Washington, N.Y.: Kennikat Press, 1972).

The scholarship on African-American women and feminism is beginning to flourish, while much work still needs to be done. Two pioneering histories of African-American women are Paula Giddings, *When and Where I Enter: The Impact of Black Women on Race and Sex in America* (Toronto: Bantam, 1984), and Jacqueline Jones, *Labor of Love, Labor of Sorrow: Black Women, Work, and the Family from Slavery to the Present* (New York: Basic Books, 1985). Gerda Lerner's *Black Women in White America: A Documentary History* (New York: Vintage, 1973) is extremely valuable. See also Angela Y. Davis, *Women, Culture, and Politics* (New York: Random House, 1989) and, *Women, Race, and Class* (New York: Random House, 1981); Michelle Wallace, *Black Macho and the Myth of the Superwoman* (New York: Dial Press, 1979); Johnnetta B. Cole, ed., *All American Women: Lines That Divide, Ties that Bind* (New York: Free Press, 1986); Dorothy Sterling, ed., *We Are Your Sisters: Black Women in the Nineteenth Century* (New York: W. W. Norton, 1984).

The following works are also very insightful regarding the experience of African-American women: Deborah White, *Ar'n't I a Woman: Female Slaves in the Plantation South* (New York: W. W. Norton, 1985); Barbara Hilkert Andolsen, *Daughters of Jefferson, Daughters of Bootblacks: Racism and American Feminism* (Macon, Ga.: Mercer University Press, 1986); Darlene Clark Hine, "Rape and the Inner Lives of Black Women in the Middle West: Preliminary Thoughts on the Culture of Dissemblance,"

Signs 14 (4): 912–20; Bonnie Thorton Dill, "The Dialectics of Black Womanhood," *Signs* 4 (3): 543–55; La Frances Rodgers-Rose, ed., *The Black Woman* (Beverly Hills, Calif.: Sage, 1980); Rosalyn Terborg-Penn and Sharon Harley, eds., *The Afro-American Woman: Struggles and Images* (Port Washington, N.Y.: Kennikat Press, 1987); Toni Cade, ed., *The Black Woman: An Anthology* (New York: Signet, 1970); Gloria Joseph and Jill Lewis, *Common Differences* (Garden City, N.Y.: Anchor, 1981); Gloria T. Hull, Patricia Bell Scott, and Barbara Smith, eds., *But Some of Us Are Brave* (New York: Feminist Press, 1982). On African-American women and feminism, see especially the works by Bell Hooks, including *Ain't I a Woman: Black Women and Feminism* (Boston: South End Press, 1981), *Feminist Theory: From Margin to Center* (Boston: South End Press, 1984), and *Talking Back: Thinking Feminist, Thinking Black* (Boston: South End Press, 1989). Patricia Hill Collins's *Black Feminist Thought: Knowledge, Consciousness, and the Politics of Empowerment* (Boston: Unwin Hyman, 1990) is a ground-breaking work and contains an excellent bibliography of current work on African-American women and feminism. On the African-American family, see Herbert G. Gutman, *The Black Family in Slavery and Freedom, 1750–1925* (New York: Pantheon, 1976); Leon F. Litwack, *Been in the Storm So Long* (New York: Alfred A. Knopf, 1979); and Eugene Genovese, *Roll Jordan Roll* (New York: Pantheon, 1974).

Literature on the lives of colonial American women is lively. Laurel Thatcher Ulrich, *Good Wives: Image and Reality in the Lives of Women in Northern New England, 1650–1750* (New York: Oxford University Press, 1980) is an especially insightful book. The works of John Demos, Edmund Morgan, Marylynn Salmon, Lois Green Carr, Lorena Walsh, Gloria L. Main, Carol Karlsen, and Robert Middlekauf are also invaluable.

Elizabeth Pleck's *Domestic Tyranny: The Making of American Social Policy against Family Violence from Colonial Times to the Present* (New York: Oxford University Press, 1987) provides an insightful history of domestic violence and social policy. Linda Gordon also advances our understanding of domestic violence in *Heroes of Their Own Lives: The Politics and History of Family Violence* (New York: Penguin, 1988).

The scholarship on feminists' marriages is limited. Of interest are Blanche Glassman Hersh, *The Slavery of Sex: Feminist Abolitionists in America* (Urbana: University of Illinois Press, 1978), and Lawrence J. Friedman, *Gregarious Saints: Self and Community in American Abolitionism, 1830–1870* (Cambridge: Cambridge University Press, 1982).

In *Liberty's Daughters: The Revolutionary Experience, 1750–1800* (Boston: Little, Brown, 1980), Mary Beth Norton argues that the American Revolution had a dramatic impact on American women's lives. In contrast, Linda K. Kerber argues in *Women of the Republic: Intellect and Ideology in Revolutionary America* (Chapel Hill: University of North Carolina Press, 1980) that the impact of the American Revolution was minimal. She claims that the most significant effect was the development of the concept "Republican Motherhood," which helped to politicize women's mothering role.

Three ground-breaking studies of women during the late eighteenth and nineteenth centuries are Suzanne Lebsock, *Free Women of Petersburg: Status and Culture in a Southern Town, 1784–1860* (New York: W. W. Norton, 1984); Christine Stansell, *City of Women: Sex and Class in New York, 1789–1860* (New York: Alfred A. Knopf, 1986); and Joan M. Jensen, *Loosening the Bonds: Mid-Atlantic Farm Women, 1750–1850* (New Haven: Yale University Press, 1986). Joanne J. Meyerowitz's *Women Adrift: Independent Wage Earners in Chicago, 1880–1930* (Chicago: University of Chicago Press, 1988) is a perceptive analysis of single wage-earning women.

The most valuable sources on "sex radicals" are Celia Morris Eckhardt, *Fanny Wright: Rebel in America* (Cambridge: Harvard University Press, 1984); Candace Falk, *Love, Anarchy, and Emma Goldman* (New York: Holt, Rinehart & Winston, 1984); Alix Kates Shulman, ed., *Red Emma Speaks* (New York: Random House, 1972); June Sochen, *Movers and Shakers* (New York: Quadrangle, 1973); Lois Palken Rudnick, *Mabel Dodge Luhan: New Woman, New World* (Albuquerque: University of New Mexico Press, 1984); and Judith Schwarz, *Radical Feminists of Heterodoxy: Greenwich Village, 1912–1940* (Lebanon, N.H.: New Victoria Publishers, 1982).

The G. K. Hall series in American women's history, edited by Barbara Haber, is an extremely valuable contribution to the field. These books include Dorothy M. Brown, *American Women in the 1920s: Setting a Course* (Boston: Twayne, 1987); Susan Ware, *Holding Their Own: American Women in the 1930s* (Boston: Twayne, 1982); Susan M. Hartmann, *American Women in the 1940s: The Home Front and Beyond* (Boston: Twayne, 1982); Eugenia Kaledin, *Mothers and More: American Women in the 1950s* (Boston: Twayne, 1984); and Winifred D. Wandersee, *On the Move: American Women in the 1970s* (Boston: Twayne, 1988).

The scholarship on southern women is still not very extensive. Anne Firor Scott's work in this field is groundbreaking. See Scott, *The Southern Lady: From Pedestal to Politics, 1830–1930* (Chicago: University of Chicago Press, 1970) and *Making the Invisible Woman Visible* (Urbana: University of Illinois Press, 1984). Jacquelyn Dowd Hall's *Revolt against Chivalry: Jessie Daniel Ames and the Women's Campaign against Lynching* (New York: Columbia University Press, 1979) is a splendid book on Jessie Daniel Ames. See also Catherine Clinton's highly readable *Plantation Mistress: Woman's World in the Old South* (New York: Pantheon, 1982) and Elizabeth Fox-Genovese, *Within the Plantation Household: Black and White Women of the Old South* (Chapel Hill: University of North Carolina Press, 1988).

Important works on women's sexuality, childbearing, and courtship are Linda Gordon, *Woman's Body, Woman's Right: Birth Control in America* (New York: Penguin, 1977); G. J. Barker-Benfield, *The Horrors of the Half-Known Life: Male Attitudes toward Women and Sexuality in Nineteenth-Century America* (New York: Harper & Row, 1976);

Ann Snitow, Christine Stansell, and Sharon Thompson, eds., *The Politics of Sexuality* (New York: Monthly Review Press, 1983); Judith Walzer Leavitt, *Brought to Bed: Childbearing in America, 1750 to 1950* (New York: Oxford University Press, 1986); Richard W. Wertz and Dorothy C. Wertz, *Lying-In: A History of Childbirth in America* (New York: Free Press, 1977); Ellen Rothman, *Hands and Hearts: A History of Courtship in America* (New York: Basic Books, 1984); and Cynthia Eagle Russett, *Sexual Science: The Victorian Construction of Womanhood* (Cambridge: Harvard University Press, 1989). For a comprehensive history of American sexuality, see John D'Emilio and Estelle B. Freedman, *Intimate Matters: A History of Sexuality in America* (New York: Harper & Row, 1988).

For the standard interpretations of the early woman's rights movement and suffrage movement, see Eleanor Flexner, *Century of Struggle: The Women's Rights Movement in the United States* (New York: Atheneum, 1974); William O'Neill, *Everyone Was Brave* (Chicago: Quadrangle, 1969); Aileen Kraditor, *The Ideas of the Woman Suffrage Movement, 1890–1920* (New York: Columbia University Press, 1965); Ellen Carol DuBois, *Feminism and Suffrage: The Emergence of an Independent Women's Movement in America, 1848–1869* (Ithaca: Cornell University Press, 1978); Andrew Sinclair, *The Emancipation of the American Woman* (New York: Harper & Row, 1965); Elizabeth Cady Stanton, Susan B. Anthony, and Matilda Joslyn Gage, eds., *History of Woman Suffrage*, 6 vols. (New York: Fowler & Wells, 1881–86). See Inez Haynes Irwin's books for accounts of the Woman's Party by a participant: *The Story of the Woman's Party* (New York: Harcourt, Brace, 1921) and *Up Hill with Banners Flying* (Penobscot, Maine: Traversity Press, 1964); Sherna Gluck's *From Parlor to Prison: Five American Suffragists Talk about Their Lives* (New York: Vintage, 1976) is a wonderful collection of oral histories of participants in the suffrage movement. A valuable intellectual history of American feminism is Gayle Graham Yates's *What Women Want: The Ideas of the Movement* (Cambridge: Harvard University Press, 1975). For imaginative, original interpretations of women's rights activism, see Nancy Hewitt, *Women's Activism and Social Change: Rochester, New York, 1822–1872* (Ithaca: Cornell University Press, 1984); Mary P. Ryan, *Cradle of the Middle Class: The Family in Oneida County, New York, 1790–1865* (New York: Cambridge University Press, 1981); Margaret Hope Bacon, *Mothers of Feminism: The Story of Quaker Women in America* (San Francisco: Harper & Row, 1986); Ann Braude, *Radical Spirits: Spiritualism and Women's Rights in Nineteenth Century America* (Boston: Beacon, 1989); Margaret Forster, *The Grassroots of Active Feminism, 1839–1939* (London: Secker & Warburg, 1984); see also biographies of the leaders by Kathleen Barry (Susan B. Anthony), Elisabeth Griffith (Elizabeth Cady Stanton), Lois Banner (Elizabeth Cady Stanton), Margaret Forster (Lucretia Mott), Paul E. Fuller (Laura Clay), Ruth Barnes Moynihan (Abigail Scott Duniway), and Robert Booth Fowler (Carrie Chapman Catt).

William Leach's *True and Perfect Union: The Feminist Reform of Sex and Society* (New York: Basic Books, 1980) examines the public and private lives of women's rights advocates of the nineteenth century. Also notable are Barbara J. Berg, *The Remembered Gate: Origins of American Feminism: The Woman and the City, 1800–1860* (New York: Oxford University Press, 1978); Rosalind Rosenberg, *Beyond Separate Spheres: The Intellectual Roots of Modern Feminism* (New Haven: Yale University Press, 1982); and Sheila M. Rothman, *Woman's Proper Place: A History of Changing Ideals and Practices, 1870 to the Present* (New York: Basic Books, 1978). Ann J. Lane's book on Charlotte Perkins Gilman greatly advances our understanding of one of the most influential feminist thinkers. See Lane, *To "Herland" and Beyond: The Life and Work of Charlotte Perkins Gilman* (New York: Pantheon, 1990).

The following books are important contributions to our understanding of women's activism in the nineteenth century: Barbara Leslie Epstein, *The Politics of Domesticity* (Middletown, Conn.: Wesleyan University Press, 1981); David J. Pivar, *Purity Crusade: Sexual Morality and Social Control, 1868–1900* (Westport, Conn.: Greenwood Press, 1973); and Karen J. Blair, *The Clubwoman as Feminist: True Womanhood Redefined, 1868–1914* (New York: Holmes & Meier Publishers, 1980).

For relevant books on American women in the 1920s, see J. Stanley Lemons, *The Woman Citizen: Social Feminism in the 1920s* (Urbana: University of Illinois Press, 1973); Elaine Tyler May, *Great Expectations* (Chicago: University of Chicago Press, 1980); and Elaine Showalter, ed., *These Modern Women: Autobiographical Essays from the Twenties* (Old Westbury, N.Y.: Feminist Press, 1978).

Susan Ware's work on women in the 1930s is excellent. See her *Beyond Suffrage: Women in the New Deal* (Cambridge: Harvard University Press, 1981) and *Partner and I: Molly Dewson, Feminism, and New Deal Politics* (New Haven: Yale University Press, 1987). For varying interpretations of American women in the 1940s, see Leila J. Rupp, *Mobilizing Women for War: German and American Propaganda, 1939–1945* (Princeton: Princeton University Press, 1978); Alan Clive, *State of War: Michigan in World War II* (Ann Arbor: University of Michigan Press, 1979); and D'Ann Campbell, *Women at War with America: Private Lives in a Patriotic Era* (Cambridge: Harvard University Press, 1984); Sherna Berger Gluck, *Rosie the Riveter Revisited: Women, the War, and Social Change* (Boston: Twayne Publishers, 1987); Karen Anderson, *Wartime Women: Sex Roles, Family Relations, and the Status of Women during World War II* (Westport, Conn.: Greenwood Press, 1981); Miriam Frank, Marilyn Ziebarth, and Connie Fields, *The Life and Times of Rosie the Riveter* (Emeryville, Calif.: Clarity Educational Productions, 1982); and Ruth Milkman, *Gender at Work: The Dynamics of Job Segregation by Sex during World War II* (Urbana: University of Illinois Press, 1987).

Studies of American women in the 1950s are not numerous. See especially Betty Friedan, *The Feminine Mystique* (New York: Dell, 1974); Eve Merriam, *After Nora Slammed the Door: American Women in the 1960s—The Unfinished Revolution* (Cleveland: World Publishing, 1958); Glenna Matthews, *"Just a Housewife": The Rise and Fall of Domesticity in America* (New York: Oxford University Press, 1987); Helen Znaniecki Lopata, *Occupation: Housewife* (New York: Oxford University Press, 1971); Barbara

Ehrenreich, *Hearts of Men: American Dreams and the Flight from Commitment* (New York: Doubleday, Anchor Press, 1983); and Elaine Tyler May, *Homeward Bound: American Families in the Cold War Era* (New York: Basic Books, 1988).

On the feminist movement of the 1960s, the works by the participants are extremely important: Kate Millet, *Sexual Politics* (Garden City, N.Y.: Doubleday, 1970); Germaine Greer, *The Female Eunuch* (London: MacGibbon & Kee, 1970); Ti-Grace Atkinson, *Amazon Odyssey* (New York: Links Books, 1974); Gloria Steinem, *Outrageous Acts and Everyday Rebellions* (New York: Signet, 1986); Bell Hooks, *Feminist Theory: From Margin to Center* (Boston: South End Press, 1984); Pauli Murray, *Proud Shoes: The Story of an American Family* (New York: Harper & Row, 1956); and Robin Morgan, ed., *Sisterhood Is Powerful: An Anthology of Writings From the Women's Liberation Movement* (New York: Vintage, 1970). See also Myra Marx Ferree and Beth B. Hess, *Controversy and Coalition: The New Feminist Movement* (Boston: Twayne, 1985); Nancy E. McGlen and Karen O'Connor, *The Struggle for Equality in the Nineteenth and Twentieth Centuries* (New York: Praeger, 1983); Judith Hole and Ellen Levine, *Rebirth of Feminism* (New York: Quadrangle, 1971); Wendy Martin, ed., *The American Sisterhood: Writings of the Feminist Movement from Colonial Times to the Present* (New York: Harper & Row, 1972); Jo Freeman, *The Politics of Women's Liberation* (New York: Longman, 1977); Maren Lockwood Carden, *The New Feminist Movement* (New York: Russell Sage Foundation, 1974); and Sara Evans, *Personal Politics: The Roots of Women's Liberation in the Civil Rights Movement and the New Left* (New York: Vintage, 1979).

Two crucial contributions to the understanding of the contemporary feminist movement are Nancy F. Cott, *The Grounding of Modern Feminism* (New Haven: Yale University Press, 1987) and Leila J. Rupp and Verta Taylor, *Survival in the Doldrums: The American Women's Rights Movement, 1945 to the 1960s* (New York: Oxford University Press, 1987). In addition, see William Henry Chafe, *The American Woman: Her Changing Social, Economic, and Political Roles, 1920–1970* (New York: Oxford University Press, 1972), which was the ground-breaking work on American women in the twentieth century, and the revised edition, *The Paradox of Change: American Women in the Twentieth Century* (New York: Oxford University Press, 1991); Ethel Klein, *Gender Politics: From Consciousness to Mass Politics* (Cambridge: Harvard University Press, 1984); Joan Hoff-Wilson, ed., *Rights of Passage: The Past and Future of the ERA* (Bloomington: Indiana University Press, 1986); Susan M. Hartmann, *From Margin to Mainstream: American Women and Politics since 1960* (Philadelphia: Temple University Press, 1989); Susan D. Becker, *The Origins of the Equal Rights Amendment: American Feminism between the Wars* (Westport, Conn.: Greenwood Press, 1981); and Cynthia Harrison, *On Account of Sex: The Politics of Women's Issues, 1945–1968* (Berkeley: University of California Press, 1988). Alice Echols's *Daring to Be Bad: Radical Feminism in America, 1967–1975* (Minneapolis: University of Minnesota Press, 1989) contributes to our understanding of the history of radical feminism.

Kathleen Gerson's *Hard Choices: How Women Decide about Work, Career, and*

Motherhood (Berkeley: University of California Press, 1985) is a revealing study of women's conflicting work and family aspirations. Relevant discussions regarding feminism and family issues may be found in Jean Bethke Elshtain, *The Family in Political Thought* (Amherst: University of Massachusetts Press, 1982); Barrie Thorne and Marilyn Yalom, eds., *Rethinking the Family: Some Feminist Questions* (New York: Longman, 1982); Linda J. Nicholson, *Gender and History: The Limits of Social Theory in the Age of the Family* (New York: Columbia University Press, 1986); Susan Okin, *Justice, Gender, and the Family* (New York: Basic Books, 1989); Deborah L. Rhode, *Justice and Gender: Sex Discrimination and the Law* (Cambridge: Harvard University Press, 1989); Carol Gilligan, *In a Different Voice* (Cambridge: Harvard University Press, 1982); Wendy Kaminer, *A Fearful Freedom: Women's Flight from Equality* (New York: Addison-Wesley, 1990); and Cynthia Fuchs Epstein, *Deceptive Distinctions: Sex, Gender, and the Social Order* (New Haven: Yale University Press and Russell Sage Foundation, 1988). On childhood socialization of traditional sex roles, see Nancy Chodorow, *The Reproduction of Mothering: Psychoanalysis and the Sociology of Gender* (Berkeley: University of California Press, 1978), and Dorothy Dinnerstein, *The Mermaid and the Minotaur: Sexual Arrangements and Human Malaise* (New York: Harper & Row, 1976). Arlie Russell Hochschild's *The Second Shift* (New York: Viking, 1989) is a revealing study of how families are coping with both parents working and how women are working a second shift at home after their work days outside the home. Lenore J. Weitzman's *Divorce Revolution* (New York: Free Press, 1985) analyzes the impact of divorce on contemporary women.

The following works are valuable studies of housework and the implications for feminism of "women's work": Susan Strasser, *Never Done* (New York: Pantheon, 1982); Ruth Schwartz Cowan, *More Work for Mother: The Ironies of Household Technology from the Open Hearth to the Microwave* (New York: Basic Books, 1983); Delores Hayden, *The Grand Domestic Revolution: A History of Feminist Design for American Homes, Neighborhoods, and Cities* (Cambridge: MIT Press, 1981); and Delores Hayden, *Redesigning the American Dream: The Future of Housing, Work, and Family Life* (New York: W. W. Norton, 1984).

Alison M. Jaggar's works are indispensable on feminist theory. See Jaggar and Paula S. Rothenberg, eds., *Feminist Frameworks* (New York: McGraw-Hill, 1984), and Jaggar and Susan R. Bordo, eds., *Gender/Body/Knowledge: Feminist Reconstructions of Being and Knowing* (New Brunswick, N.J.: Rutgers University Press, 1989). Simone de Beauvoir's *The Second Sex* (New York: Alfred A. Knopf, 1953) is the original manifesto of twentieth-century feminism. Gerda Lerner's *The Creation of Patriarchy* (New York: Oxford University Press, 1986) is an ambitious and imaginative analysis of the origins of sexism. Nancy F. Cott, ed., *History of American Women* (London: Meckler, 1990) contains 490 outstanding articles from 141 journals and is an extraordinary contribution to the field.

From this brief survey we have seen the scholarship of the last thirty years on

American women has been impressive. In this essay, I have not attempted to mention all of the sources which I have considered, but rather highlight works which have some special relevance to the questions regarding feminism and the family, to which I am indebted. The bibliography which follows contains many additional valuable works. Despite the richness of the field, there has been a deficiency in the attention paid to feminism and family issues and to the relationship of domestic power to the emergence of feminist consciousness and achievements. My hope is that this book contributes to the conversation.

BIBLIOGRAPHY

Primary Collections

Henry A. Murray Research Center, Radcliffe College, Cambridge, Mass.

E. Lowell Kelley Longitudinal Study, "Personality, Marital Compatibility, and Married Life: A Twenty-Year Longitudinal Study, 1935–1955," A431

Arthur and Elizabeth Schlesinger Library, Radcliffe College

Jessie Abbott Collection
Alger Collection
Almy Collection
Black Women Oral History Project (transcripts published by Meckler [now K. G. Saur], Westport, Conn., 1990)
Bureau of Vocational Information Records
Ella Lyman Cabot Collection
Mary William Dewson Collection
Dillon Collection
Amelia Earhart Collection
Betty Friedan Collection
Charlotte Perkins Gilman Collection
Holt-Messer Collection
Alma Lutz Collection
Lorine Pruette Collection
Nellie Nugent Somerville Collection
Miriam Van Waters Collection
Marjorie White Collection
Women's Rights Collection

Sophia Smith Collection, Smith College, Northampton, Mass.

Mary Van Kleeck Collection

Newspapers, Magazines, Journals

Godey's Lady's Book. 1828–1838.
Ladies Home Journal. 1920–50.
Revolution. January 8, 1868–May 16, 1871
Woman's Journal. 1870–1915

Books and Articles

Abzug, Robert H. *Passionate Liberator: Theodore Dwight Weld and the Dilemma of Reform.* New York: Oxford University Press, 1980.

Adams, Willena C., ed. *Texas Cities and the Great Depression.* Austin, Tex.: Texas Memorial Museum, 1973.

Allen, Frederick Lewis. *Only Yesterday: An Informal History of the Nineteen Twenties.* New York: Harper & Row, 1931.

Alsop, Gulielma Fell, and Mary F. McBride. *Arms and the Girl.* New York: Vanguard, 1943.

Altbach, Edith Hoshino. *From Feminism to Liberation.* Cambridge, Mass.: Schenkman, 1971.

Anderson, Karen. *Wartime Women: Sex Roles, Family Relations, and the Status of Women during World War II.* Westport, Conn.: Greenwood Press, 1981.

Andolsen, Barbara Hilkert. *Daughters of Jefferson, Daughters of Bootblacks.* Macon, Ga.: Mercer University Press, 1986.

Angell, Robert Cooley. *The Campus: A Study of Contemporary Undergraduate Life in the American University.* New York: D. Appleton, 1928.

————. *The Family Encounters the Depression.* New York: Charles Scribner's Sons, 1936.

Aptheker, Bettina, *Tapestries of Life: Women's Work, Women's Consciousness, and the Meaning of Daily Experience.* Amherst: University of Massachusetts Press, 1989.

————. *Woman's Legacy: Essays on Race, Sex, and Class in American History.* Amherst: University of Massachusetts Press, 1982.

Ariés, Philippe. *Centuries of Childhood: A Social History of Family Life.* New York: Vintage, 1962.

Ascher, Carol. *Simone de Beauvoir: A Life of Freedom.* Boston: Beacon, 1981.

Atkins, Elizabeth. *Edna St. Vincent Millay and Her Times.* Chicago: University of Chicago Press, 1936.

Atkinson, Ti-Grace. *Amazon Odyssey.* New York: Links Books, 1974.

Bacon, Margaret Hope. *Mothers of Feminism: The Story of Quaker Women in America.* San Francisco: Harper & Row, 1986.

————. *Valiant Friend: The Life of Lucretia Mott.* New York: Walker, 1980.

Baker, Laura Nelson. *Wanted: Women in War Industry—the Complete Guide to a War Factory Job.* New York: E. P. Dutton, 1943.

Bakke, E. Wight. *Citizens without Work: A Study of the Effect of Unemployment upon the Workers' Social Relations and Practices.* New Haven: Yale University Press, 1940.

Banner, Lois, *American Beauty.* New York: Alfred A. Knopf, 1983.

————. *Elizabeth Cady Stanton: A Radical for Woman's Rights.* Boston: Little, Brown, 1980.

————. *Women in Modern America: A Brief History.* 2d ed. New York: Harcourt Brace Jovanovich, 1984. 1st ed., 1974.

Barbrook, Alec, and Christine Bolt. *Power and Protest in American Life.* New York: St. Martin's Press, 1980.

Bardwick, Judith M. *Women in Transition: How Feminism, Sexual Liberation, and the Search for Self-Fulfillment Have Altered Our Lives.* Brighton, Sussex: Harvester Press, 1980.

Baritz, Loren, ed. *The Culture of the Twenties.* Indianapolis: Bobbs Merrill, 1970.

Barker-Benfield, G. J. *The Horrors of the Half-Known Life: Male Attitudes toward Women and Sexuality in Nineteenth-Century America.* New York: Harper & Row, 1976.

Barnard, Hollinger F., ed. *Outside the Magic Circle: The Autobiography of Virginia Foster Durr.* Tuscaloosa: University of Alabama Press, 1985.

Barnouw, Erik. *A History of Broadcasting in the United States.* Vol. 1: *A Tower in Babel: To 1933*; vol. 2: *The Golden Web: 1933–1953.* New York: Oxford University Press, 1966–68.

Barry, Kathleen. *Susan B. Anthony: A Biography of a Singular Feminist.* New York: New York University Press, 1988.

Bateson, Mary Catherine. *With a Daughter's Eye.* New York: Washington Square Press, 1984.

Baxandall, Rosalyn, Linda Gordon, and Susan Reverby, eds. *America's Working Women: A Documentary History, 1600 to the Present.* New York: Vintage, 1976.

Baym, Nina. *Novels, Readers, and Reviewers: Responses to Fiction in Antebellum America.* Ithaca: Cornell University Press, 1984.

————. *Woman's Fiction: A Guide to Novels by and about Women in America, 1820–1870.* Ithaca: Cornell University Press, 1978.

Becker, Susan D. *The Origins of the Equal Rights Amendment: American Feminism between the Wars.* Westport, Conn.: Greenwood Press, 1981.

Belenky, Mary Field, Blythe McVicker Clinchy, Nancy Rule Goldberger, and Jill Mattuck Tarule. *Women's Ways of Knowing: The Development of Self, Voice, and Mind.* New York: Basic Books, 1986.

Berg, Barbara J. *The Remembered Gate: Origins of American Feminism: The Woman and the City, 1800–1860.* New York: Oxford University Press, 1978.

Bergman, Barbara R. *The Economic Emergence of Women.* New York: Basic Books, 1986.

Berkin, Carol Ruth, and Mary Beth Norton, eds. *Women of America: A History.* Boston: Houghton Mifflin, 1979.

Berry, Mary Frances, and John W. Blassingame. *Long Memory: The Black Experience in America.* New York: Oxford University Press, 1982.

Biller, Henry B. *Father, Child, and Sex Role.* Lexington, Mass.: D. C. Heath, 1971.

Bird, Caroline. *The Invisible Scar.* New York: Van Rees Press, 1966.

Blair, Karen J. *The Clubwoman as Feminist: True Womanhood Redefined, 1868–1914.* New York: Holmes & Meier, 1980.

Blanchard, Phyllis, and Carlyn Mannasses. *New Girls for Old.* New York: McCauley, 1937.

Blocker, Jack S., Jr. *"Give to the Winds Thy Fears": The Women's Temperance Crusade, 1873–1874.* Westport, Conn.: Greenwood Press, 1985.

Blood, Robert O., Jr., and Donald M. Wolfe. *Husbands and Wives: The Dynamics of Married Living.* Glencoe, Ill.: Free Press, 1960.

Bly, Robert. *Iron John: A Book about Men.* Reading, Mass: Addison-Wesley, 1990.

Boydston, Jeanne, Mary Kelley, and Anne Margolis. *The Limits of Sisterhood: The Beecher Sisters on Women's Rights and Woman's Sphere.* Chapel Hill: University of North Carolina Press, 1988.

Boyer, Paul, and Stephen Nissenbaum. *Salem Possessed: The Social Origins of Witchcraft.* Cambridge: Harvard University Press, 1974.

Brandt, Lilian. *An Impressionistic View of the Winter of 1930–31 in New York City.* New York: Welfare Council of New York City, 1932.

Braude, Ann. *Radical Spirits: Spiritualism and Women's Rights in Nineteenth Century America.* Boston: Beacon Press, 1989.

Bremner, Robert H., and Gary W. Reichard, eds. *Reshaping America: Society and Institutions, 1945–1960.* Columbus: Ohio University Press, 1982.

Brophy, Julia, and Carol Smart. *Women-in-Law: Explorations in Law, Family, and Sexuality.* London: Routledge & Kegan Paul, 1985.

Brown, Cynthia Stokes, ed. *Septima Clark and the Civil Rights Movement: Ready from Within.* Navarro, Calif.: Wild Trees Press, 1986.

Brown, Dorothy M. *American Women in the 1920s: Setting a Course.* Boston: Twayne, 1987.

Brownmiller, Susan. *Against Our Will: Men, Women, and Rape.* New York: Simon & Schuster, 1975.

Buck, Pearl. *Of Men and Women.* New York: John Day, 1941.

Buckley, Kerry W. *Mechanical Man: John Broadus Watson and the Beginning of Behaviorism.* New York: Guilford Press, 1989.

Butterfield, L. H., Marc Friedlaender, and Mary-Jo Kline, eds. *The Book of Abigail and John: Selected Letters of the Adams Family, 1762–1784.* Cambridge: Harvard University Press, 1975.

Cable, Mary. *American Manners and Morals: A Picture History of How We Behaved and Misbehaved.* New York: American Heritage, 1969.

Cade, Toni, ed. *The Black Woman: An Anthology.* New York: Signet, 1970.

Cain, Glen G. *Married Women in the Labor Force: An Economic Analysis.* Chicago: University of Chicago Press, 1966.

Calhoun, Arthur. *A Social History of the American Family.* Vol. 3: *Since the Civil War.* New York: Barnes & Noble, 1960. Originally pub. 1919.

Calisher, Hortense. *Herself.* New York: Dell, 1972.

Campbell, D'Ann. *Women at War with America: Private Lives in a Patriotic Era.* Cambridge: Harvard University Press, 1984.

Campbell, Karlyn Kohrs. *Man Cannot Speak for Her: A Critical Study of Early Feminist Rhetoric.* Vol. 1. Westport, Conn.: Greenwood Press, 1989.

Cantarow, Ellen, with Susan Gushie O'Malley and Shawn Hartman Strom. *Moving the Mountain: Women Working for Social Change.* Old Westbury, N.Y.: Feminist Press, 1980.

Caplow, Theodore. *Middletown Families: Fifty Years of Change and Continuity.* Minneapolis: University of Minnesota Press, 1982.

Carden, Maren Lockwood. *The New Feminist Movement.* New York: Russell Sage Foundation, 1974.

Carroll, Berenice A., ed. *Liberating Women's History: Theoretical and Critical Essays.* Urbana: University of Illinois Press, 1976.

Carson, Clayborne. *In Struggle: SNCC and the Black Awakening of the 1960s.* Cambridge: Harvard University Press, 1981.

Catt, Carrie Chapman, and Nettie Rogers Shuler. *Woman Suffrage and Politics: The Inner Story of the Suffrage Movement.* New York: Charles Scribner's Sons, 1923.

Cavan, Ruth Shonle, and Katherine Howland Ranck. *The Family and the Depression: A Study of One Hundred Chicago Families.* Chicago: University of Chicago Press, 1938.

Cazden, Elizabeth. *Antoinette Brown Blackwell: A Biography.* Old Westbury, N.Y.: Feminist Press, 1983.

Chafe, William Henry. *The American Woman: Her Changing Social, Economic, and Political Roles, 1920–1970.* New York: Oxford University Press, 1972.

————. *The Paradox of Change: American Women in the Twentieth Century.* New York: Oxford University Press, 1991.

Chambers-Schiller, Lee Virginia. *Liberty, a Better Husband: Single Women in America—the Generation of 1780–1840.* New Haven: Yale University Press, 1984.

Chayefsky, Paddy. *Television Plays*. New York: Simon & Schuster, 1955.

Chodorow, Nancy. *The Reproduction of Mothering: Psychoanalysis and the Sociology of Gender*. Berkeley: University of California Press, 1978.

Clark, Septima Poinsette, with Legette Blythe. *Echo in My Soul*. New York: E. P. Dutton, 1962.

Clinton, Catherine. *The Other Civil War: American Women in the Nineteenth Century*. New York: Hill & Wang, 1984.

———. *The Plantation Mistress: Woman's World in the Old South*. New York: Pantheon, 1982.

Clive, Alan. *State of War: Michigan in World War II*. Ann Arbor: University of Michigan Press, 1979.

Cohen, Marcia. *The Sisterhood: The True Story of the Women Who Changed the World*. New York: Simon & Schuster, 1988.

Cohn, David L. *The Good Old Days: A History of American Morals and Manners As Seen through the Sears Roebuck Catalogs*. New York: Simon & Schuster, 1940. Reprinted, New York: Arno Press, 1976.

Cole, Johnnetta B., ed. *All American Women: Lines That Divide, Ties That Bind*. New York: Free Press, 1986.

Collins, Patricia Hill. *Black Feminist Thought: Knowledge, Consciousness, and the Politics of Empowerment*. Boston: Unwin Hyman, 1990.

Cone, Fairfax M. *With All Its Faults: A Candid Account of Forty Years in Advertising*. Boston: Little, Brown, 1969.

Conover, Pamela, and Virginia Gray. *Feminism and the New Right*. New York: Praeger, 1983.

Conway, Jill K. *The Female Experience in Eighteenth and Nineteenth Century America: A Guide to the History of American Women*. New York: Garland Publishing, 1982.

Coontz, Stephanie. *The Social Origins of Private Life: A History of American Families, 1600–1900*. London: Verso, 1988.

Cooper, Anna Julia. *A Voice from the South*. Xenia, Ohio: Aldine Printing House, 1892. Reprinted New York: Oxford University Press, 1988.

Cott, Nancy F. *The Bonds of Womanhood: "Woman's Sphere" in New England, 1780–1835*. New Haven: Yale University Press, 1977.

———. *The Grounding of Modern Feminism*. New Haven: Yale University Press, 1987.

Cott, Nancy F., and Elizabeth H. Pleck, eds. *A Heritage of Her Own: Toward a New Social History of American Women*. New York: Simon & Schuster, 1979.

Cowan, Ruth Schwartz. *More Work for Mother: The Ironies of Household Technology from the Open Hearth to the Microwave*. New York: Basic Books, 1983.

Cromwell, Ronald E., and David H. Olson. *Power in Families*. Beverly Hills, Calif.: Sage Publications, 1979.

Daly, Mary. *Gyn/Ecology: The Metaethics of Radical Feminism*. Boston: Beacon Press, 1978.

Daniel, Rosemary. *Fatal Flowers*. New York: Holt, Rinehart & Winston, 1980.

Davis, Angela Y. *Women, Culture, and Politics*. New York: Random House, 1989.

————. *Women, Race, and Class*. New York: Random House, 1981.

Davis, Katherine Bement. *Factors in the Sex Life of 2,200 Women*. New York: Harper & Bros., 1939.

Davis, Marianna W., ed. *Contributions of Black Women in America*. Vol. 2. Columbia, S.C.: Denday Press, 1982.

Davis, Maxine. *The Lost Generation: A Portrait of American Youth Today*. New York: Macmillan, 1936.

De Beauvoir, Simone. *The Second Sex*. Translated by H. M. Parshley. New York: Alfred A. Knopf, 1953.

Deckard, Barbara Sinclair. *The Women's Movement: Political, Socioeconomic, and Psychological Issues*. New York: Harper & Row, 1975.

Decter, Midge. *The New Chastity and Other Arguments against Women's Liberation*. New York: Coward, McCann & Geoghegan, 1972.

Degler, Carl N. *At Odds: Women and the Family in America from the Revolution to the Present*. New York: Oxford University Press, 1980.

Dell, Floyd. *Love in the Machine Age: A Psychological Study of the Transition from Patriarchal Society*. New York: Farrar & Rinehart, 1930.

D'Emilio, John, and Estelle B. Freedman, *Intimate Matters: A History of Sexuality in America*. New York: Harper & Row, 1988.

Demos. John. *Entertaining Satan*. New York: Oxford University Press, 1982.

Diamond, Irene, and Lee Quinby, eds. *Feminism and Foucault: Reflections on Resistance*. Boston: Northeastern University Press, 1988.

Dickinson, Robert Latou, and Lura Beam. *A Thousand Marriages: A Medical Study of Sex Adjustment*. Baltimore: Williams & Wilkins, 1931.

Dickstein, Morris. *Gates of Eden: American Culture in the Sixties*. New York: Basic Books, 1977.

Dinnerstein, Dorothy. *The Mermaid and the Minotaur: Sexual Arrangements and Human Malaise*. New York: Harper & Row, 1976.

Ditzion, Sidney. *Marriage, Morals, and Sex in America*. New York: Octagon Books, 1975.

Donovan, Josephine. *Feminist Theory: The Intellectual Traditions of American Feminism*. New York: Frederick Ungar, 1985.

Dowdy, Andrew. *The Films of the Fifties*. New York: William Morrow, 1973.

Dowling, Colette. *The Cinderella Complex: Women's Hidden Fear of Independence*. New York: Summit Books, 1981.

Dreitzel, Peter. *Family, Marriage, and the Struggle of the Sexes*. New York: Macmillan, 1972.

Dubbert, Joe L. *A Man's Place: Masculinity in Transition*. Englewood Cliffs, N.J.: Prentice-Hall, 1979.

DuBois, Ellen Carol. *Feminism and Suffrage: The Emergence of an Independent Women's Movement in America, 1848–1869*. Ithaca: Cornell University Press, 1978.

————, ed. *Elizabeth Cady Stanton–Susan B. Anthony Correspondence, Writings, Speeches*. New York: Schocken, 1981.

Easterlin, Richard A. *Birth and Fortune: The Impact of Numbers on Personal Welfare*. New York: Basic Books, 1980.

————. *Population, Labor Force, and Long Swings in Economic Growth: The American Experience*. New York: Columbia University Press, 1968.

Eastman, Crystal. *On Women and Revolution*. New York: Oxford University Press, 1978.

Echols, Alice. *Daring to Be Bad: Radical Feminism in America, 1967–1975*. Minneapolis: University of Minnesota Press, 1989.

Eckhardt, Celia Morris. *Fanny Wright: Rebel in America*. Cambridge: Harvard University Press, 1984.

Ehrenreich, Barbara. *Hearts of Men: American Dreams and the Flight From Commitment*. Garden City, N.Y.: Doubleday, Anchor Press, 1983.

Ehrenreich, Barbara, and Deirdre English. *For Her Own Good: 150 Years of Experts' Advice to Women*. Garden City, N.Y.: Doubleday, Anchor Press, 1978.

Eisenstein, Hester. *Contemporary Feminist Thought*. Boston: G. K. Hall, 1983.

Eisenstein, Sarah. *Give Us Bread but Give Us Roses: Working Women's Consciousness in the United States, 1890 to the First World War*. London: Routledge & Kegan Paul, 1983.

Eisenstein, Zillah R. *Capitalist Patriarchy and the Case for Socialist Feminism*. New York: Monthly Review Press, 1979.

————. *The Radical Future of Liberal Feminism*. New York: Longman, 1981.

Elder, Glen H., Jr. *Children of the Great Depression: Social Change in Life Experience*. Chicago: University of Chicago Press, 1974.

Elshtain, Jean Bethke. *The Family in Political Thought*. Amherst: University of Masaachusetts Press, 1982.

Epstein, Barbara Leslie. *The Politics of Domesticity*. Middletown, Conn.: Wesleyan University Press, 1981.

Epstein, Cynthia Fuchs. *Deceptive Distinctions: Sex, Gender, and the Social Order*. New Haven: Yale University Press and Russell Sage Foundation, 1988.

Evans, Sara M. *Born for Liberty: A History of Women in America*. New York: Free Press, 1989.

————. *Personal Politics: The Roots of Women's Liberation in the Civil Rights Movement and the New Left*. New York: Vintage, 1979.

Ewen, Stuart. *Captains of Consciousness: Advertising and the Social Roots of the Consumer Culture*. New York: McGraw-Hill, 1976.

Falk, Candace. *Love, Anarchy, and Emma Goldman*. New York: Holt, Rinehart & Winston, 1984.

Fallows, Deborah. *A Mother's Work*. Boston: Houghton Mifflin, 1985.

Faludi, Susan. *Backlash: The Undeclared War Against American Women.* New York: Crown Publishers, 1991.

Fass, Paula S. *The Damned and the Beautiful.* New York: Oxford University Press, 1977.

Felsenthal, Carol. *The Sweetheart of the Silent Majority: The Biography of Phyllis Schlafly.* Garden City, N.Y.: Doubleday, 1981.

Ferree, Myra Marx, and Beth B. Hess. *Controversy and Coalition: The New Feminist Movement.* Boston: Twayne, 1985.

Ferriss, Abbott L. *Indicators of Change in the American Family.* New York: Russell Sage Foundation, 1970.

Filene, Peter Gabriel. *Him/Herself: Sex Roles in Modern America.* New York: Harcourt Brace Jovanovich, 1974.

Firestone, Shulamith. *The Dialectic of Sex: The Case for Feminist Revolution.* New York: William Morrow, 1970.

Fishburn, Katherine. *Women in Popular Culture: A Reference Guide.* Westport, Conn.: Greenwood Press, 1982.

Flexner, Eleanor. *Century of Struggle: The Women's Rights Movement in the United States.* Cambridge: Harvard University Press, 1959. Reprinted New York: Atheneum, 1974.

Flynt, Wayne. *Poor but Proud: Alabama's Poor Whites.* Tuscaloosa: University of Alabama Press, 1989.

Forster, Margaret. *The Grassroots of Active Feminism, 1839–1939.* London: Secker & Warburg, 1984.

Fowler, Robert Booth. *Carrie Catt: Feminist Politician.* Boston: Northeastern University Press, 1986.

Fox-Genovese, Elizabeth. *Within the Plantation Household: Black and White Women of the Old South.* Chapel Hill: University of North Carolina Press, 1988.

Frank, Miriam, Marilyn Ziebarth, and Connie Fields. *The Life and Times of Rosie the Riveter.* Emeryville, Calif.: Clarity Educational Productions, 1982.

Frazier, E. Franklin. *The Negro Family in the United States.* New York: Dryden Press, 1951.

Freeman, Jo. *The Politics of Women's Liberation: A Case Study of an Emerging Social Movement and Its Relation to the Policy Process.* New York: David McKay, 1975. Reprinted New York: Longman, 1977.

French, Brandon. *On the Verge of Revolt: Women in American Films of the Fifties.* New York: Frederick Ungar, 1978.

Friedan, Betty. *The Feminine Mystique.* New York: Dell, 1974. Originally New York: W. W. Norton, 1963.

———. "How to Get the Movement Going Again." *New York Times Magazine,* November 3, 1985.

———. *It Changed My Life: Writings on the Women's Movement.* New York: Random House, 1976.

———. *The Second Stage.* New York: Summit Books, 1981.

Friedman, Jean E., William G. Slade, and Mary Jane Capozzoli, eds. *Our American Sisters: Women in American Life and Thought*. 4th ed. Lexington, Mass.: D. C. Heath, 1982.

Friedman, Lawrence J. *Gregarious Saints: Self and Community in American Abolitionism, 1830–1870*. Cambridge: Cambridge University Press, 1982.

Fuller, Margaret. *Woman in the Nineteenth Century*. Boston: John P. Jewett, 1855.

Fuller, Paul E. *Laura Clay and the Woman's Rights Movement*. Lexington: University Press of Kentucky, 1975.

Galbraith, John Kenneth. *The Great Crash*. Boston: Houghton Mifflin, 1955.

Gallese, Liz Roman. *Women like Us*. New York: Signet, 1985.

Gans, Herbert J. *The Levittowners*. New York: Pantheon, 1967.

Garrow, David, ed. *The Montgomery Bus Boycott and the Women Who Started It: The Memoir of JoAnn Gibson Robinson*. Knoxville: University of Tennessee Press, 1987.

Gay, Peter. *The Bourgeois Experience, Victoria to Freud*. Vol. 1: *Education of the Senses*. New York: Oxford University Press, 1984.

Genovese, Eugene. *Roll, Jordan, Roll*. New York: Pantheon, 1974.

Gerber, Ellen. *The American Woman in Sport*. Reading, Mass.: Addison-Wesley, 1974.

Gerson, Kathleen. *Hard Choices: How Women Decide about Work, Career, and Motherhood*. Berkeley: University of California Press, 1985.

Giddings, Paula. *In Search of Sisterhood: Delta Sigma Theta and the Challenge of the Black Sorority Movement*. New York: William Morrow, 1988.

————. *When and Where I Enter: The Impact of Black Women on Race and Sex in America*. Toronto: Bantam Books, 1984.

Gilbert, Sandra M., and Susan Gubar, eds. *The Norton Anthology of Literature by Women*. New York: W. W. Norton, 1985.

Giles, Nell. *Punch in Susie*. New York: Harper & Brothers, 1942.

Gilligan, Carol. *In a Different Voice*. Cambridge: Harvard University Press, 1982.

Gilman, Charlotte Perkins. *The Home: Its Work and Influence*. New York: McClure & Phillips, 1903.

————. *Women and Economics*. Edited by Carl N. Degler. New York: Harper & Row, 1966.

Glick, Paul C. *Some Recent Changes in American Families*. Current Population Reports Special Studies Series P-23, no. 52. Washington, D.C.: Department of Commerce, Bureau of the Census, 1975.

Gluck, Sherna Berger. *Rosie the Riveter Revisited: Women, the War, and Social Change*. Boston: Twayne, 1987.

————. *From Parlor to Prison: Five American Suffragists Talk about Their Lives*. New York: Vintage, 1976.

Goldberg, Herb. *The New Male-Female Relationship*. New York: William Morrow, 1983.

Goldfarb, Lyn. *Separated and Unequal*. Silver Spring, Md.: Women's Work Project, 1976.

Goldman, Emma. *Living My Life: An Autobiography*. New York: Dover, 1970.

Goldman, Eric F. *The Crucial Decade and After: America: 1945–1960*. New York: Vintage, 1956, 1960.

Goode, William J. *World Revolution and Family Patterns*. New York: Free Press of Glenco, 1963.

Goodman, David. *A Parent's Guide to the Emotional Needs of Children*. New York: Hawthorn Books, 1959.

Goodman, Jack, ed. *While You Were Gone*. New York: Simon & Schuster, 1946.

Goodsell, Willystine. *Problems of the Family*. New York: Century, 1928.

Gordon, Linda. *Heroes of Their Own Lives: The Politics and History of Family Violence*. New York: Penguin, 1988.

———. *Woman's Body, Woman's Right: Birth Control in America*. New York: Penguin, 1977.

Gordon, Michael, ed. *The American Family in Social-Historical Perspective*. 2d ed. New York: St. Martin's Press, 1978.

Gorer, Geoffrey. *The American People: A Study in National Character*. New York: W. W. Norton, 1964.

Gouldner, Alvin W., ed. *Studies in Leadership and Democratic Action*. New York: Harper & Brothers, 1950.

Greer, Germaine. *The Female Eunuch*. New York: Bantam, 1972. Originally London: MacGibbon & Kee, 1970.

———. *Sex and Destiny: The Politics of Human Fertility*. New York: Harper & Row, 1984.

Griffith, Elisabeth. *In Her Own Right: The Life of Elizabeth Cady Stanton*. New York: Oxford University Press, 1984.

Gruenberg, Sidonie Matsner. *The Family in a World at War*. New York: Harper & Bros., 1942.

Gutman, Herbert G. *The Black Family in Slavery and Freedom, 1750–1925*. New York: Pantheon, 1976.

Haber, Barbara, ed. *The Women's Annual*. Boston: G. K. Hall, 1981.

———. *The Women's Annual; 1981: The Year in Review*. Boston: G. K. Hall, 1982.

———. *The Women's Annual, 1982–1983*. Boston: G. K. Hall, 1983.

Hagood, Margaret Jarman. *Mothers of the South: Portraiture of the White Tenant Farm Woman*. New York: W. W. Norton, 1977. Originally Chapel Hill: University of North Carolina Press, 1939.

Hall, Florence Howe. *Julia Ward Howe and the Woman Suffrage Movement*. Boston: Dana Estes, 1913.

Hall, Jacquelyn Dowd. *Revolt against Chivalry: Jessie Daniel Ames and the Women's Campaign against Lynching*. New York: Columbia University Press, 1979.

Hamilton, Gilbert Van Tassell. *A Research in Marriage*. New York: Albert & Charles Boni, 1929.

Hamilton, Gilbert Van Tassell and Kenneth MacGowan. *What Is Wrong with Marriage*. New York: Albert & Charles Boni, 1919.

Hapgood, Hutchins. *A Victorian in the Modern World*. Seattle: University of Washington Press, 1972. Originally New York: Harcourt, Brace, 1939.

Hareven, Tamara K. *Family and Kin in Urban Communities*. New York: New Viewpoints, 1977.

Harris, Barbara J. *Beyond Her Sphere: Women and the Professions in American History*. Westport, Conn.: Greenwood Press, 1978.

Harrison, Cynthia. *On Account of Sex: The Politics of Women's Issues, 1945–1968*. Berkeley: University of California Press, 1988.

Hartmann, Susan M. *American Women in the 1940s: The Home Front and Beyond*. Boston: Twayne, 1982.

———. *From Margin to Mainstream: American Women and Politics since 1960*. New York: Alfred A. Knopf, 1989.

Haskell, Molly. *From Reverence to Rape: The Treatment of Women in the Movies*. New York: Penguin, 1974.

Hawes, Elizabeth. *Anything but Love*. New York: Rinehart, 1948.

Hawes, Joseph M., and N. Ray Hiner. *American Childhood: A Research Guide and Historical Handbook*. Westport, Conn.: Greenwood Press, 1985.

Hayden, Delores. *The Grand Domestic Revolution: A History of Feminist Design for American Homes, Neighborhoods, and Cities*. Cambridge: MIT Press, 1981.

———. *Redesigning the American Dream: The Future of Housing, Work, and Family Life*. New York: W. W. Norton, 1984.

Henslin, James M. *Studies in the Sociology of Sex*. New York: Appleton-Century-Crofts, 1971.

Hersh, Blanche Glassman. *The Slavery of Sex: Feminist Abolitionists in America*. Urbana: University of Illinois Press, 1978.

Hewitt, Nancy A. *Women's Activism and Social Change: Rochester, New York, 1822–1872*. Ithaca: Cornell University Press, 1984.

Hewlett, Sylvia Ann. *A Lesser Life: The Myth of Women's Liberation in America*. New York: William Morrow, 1986.

Higgonet, Margaret Randolph, Jane Jenson, Sonya Michel, and Margaret Collins Weitz, eds. *Behind the Lines: Gender and the Two World Wars*. New Haven: Yale University Press, 1987.

Hill, Mary A. *Charlotte Perkins Gilman: The Making of a Radical Feminist, 1860–1896*. Philadelphia: Temple University Press, 1980.

Hirsch, Marianne, and Evelyn Fox Keller, eds. *Conflicts in Feminism*. New York: Routledge, 1990.

Hochschild, Arlie Russell. *The Managed Heart: Commercialization of Human Feeling*. Berkeley: University of California Press, 1983.

————. *The Second Shift: Working Parents and the Revolution at Home.* New York: Viking Press, 1989.

Hole, Judith, and Ellen Levine. *Rebirth of Feminism.* New York: Quadrangle, 1971.

Hoff-Wilson, Joan, ed. *Rights of Passage: The Past and Future of the ERA.* Bloomington: Indiana University Press, 1986.

Hooks, Bell. *Ain't I a Woman: Black Women and Feminism.* Boston: South End Press, 1981.

————. *Feminist Theory: From Margin to Center.* Boston: South End Press, 1984.

————. *Talking Back: Thinking Feminist, Thinking Black.* Boston: South End Press, 1989.

Horn, Maurice. *Women in the Comics.* New York: Chelsea House, 1977.

Horton, Myles, with Judith Kohl and Herbert Kohl. *The Long Haul: An Autobiography.* New York: Doubleday, 1990.

Howard, Jane. *Margaret Mead: A Life.* New York: Simon & Schuster, 1984.

Hull, Gloria T., Patricia Bell Scott, and Barbara Smith, eds. *But Some of Us Are Brave.* New York: Feminist Press, 1982.

Hutchins, Grace. *Women Who Work.* New York: International Publishers, 1934.

Irwin, Inez Haynes. *The Story of the Woman's Party.* New York: Harcourt, Brace, 1921.

————. *Up Hill with Banners Flying.* Penobscot, Maine: Traversity Press, 1964.

Jaggar, Alison M. *Feminist Politics and Human Nature.* Sussex: Harvester Press, 1983.

Jaggar, Alison M., and Susan R. Bordo, eds. *Gender/Body/Knowledge: Feminist Reconstructions of Being and Knowing.* New Brunswick, N.J.: Rutgers University Press, 1989.

Jaggar, Alison M., and Paula S. Rothenberg, eds. *Feminist Frameworks.* New York: McGraw-Hill, 1984.

Janeway, Elizabeth. *Man's World, Woman's Place.* New York: Dell, 1971.

————. *Powers of the Weak.* New York: Alfred A. Knopf, 1980.

Janiewski, Delores. *Sisterhood Denied: Race, Gender, and Class in a New South Community.* Philadelphia: Temple University Press, 1985.

Jardine, Alice, and Paul Smith, eds. *Men in Feminism.* New York: Methuen, 1987.

Jelinek, Estelle C. *The Tradition of Women's Autobiography: From Antiquity to the Present.* Boston: Twayne, 1986.

Jensen, Joan M. *Loosening the Bonds: Mid-Atlantic Farm Women, 1750–1850.* New Haven: Yale University Press, 1986.

Johnston, Carolyn. *Jack London: An American Radical?* Westport, Conn.: Greenwood Press, 1984.

Jones, Jacqueline. *Labor of Love, Labor of Sorrow: Black Women, Work, and the Family from Slavery to the Present.* New York: Basic Books, 1985.

Jones, Landon Y. *Great Expectations: America and the Baby Boom Generation.* New York: Coward, McCann & Geoghegan, 1980.

Joseph, Gloria I., and Jill Lewis. *Common Differences: Conflicts in Black and White Feminist Perspectives.* Boston: South End Press, 1981.

Kaledin, Eugenia. *Mothers and More: American Women in the 1950s.* Boston: Twayne, 1984.

Kaminer, Wendy. *A Fearful Freedom: Women's Flight from Equality.* New York: Addison-Wesley, 1990.

Kanowitz, Leo. *Women and the Law: The Unfinished Revolution.* Albuquerque: University of New Mexico Press, 1969.

Karlsen, Carol F. *The Devil in the Shape of a Woman: Witchcraft in Colonial New England.* New York: W. W. Norton, 1987.

Kay, Karyn, and Gerald Peary. *Women and the Cinema: A Critical Anthology.* New York: E. P. Dutton, 1977.

Kelley, Mary. *Private Woman, Public Stage: Literary Domesticity in Nineteenth-Century America.* New York: Oxford University Press, 1984.

Kelly, Joan. *Women, History, and Theory.* Chicago: University of Chicago Press, 1984.

Keniston, Kenneth, and the Carnegie Council on Children. *All Our Children: The American Family under Pressure.* New York: Harcourt Brace Jovanovich, 1977.

Kennedy, Susan Estabrook. *If All We Did Was to Weep at Home: A History of White Working-Women in America.* Bloomington: Indiana University Press, 1979.

Kerber, Linda K. *Women of the Republic: Intellect and Ideology in Revolutionary America.* New York: W. W. Norton, 1986. Originally Chapel Hill: University of North Carolina Press, 1980.

Kerber, Linda K., and Jane De Hart-Mathews, eds. *Women's America: Refocusing the Past.* New York: Oxford University Press, 1982.

Kessler-Harris, Alice. *Out to Work: A History of Wage-Earning Women in the United States.* New York: Oxford University Press, 1982.

Key, Ellen. *Love and Marriage.* New York: G. P. Putnam's Sons, 1911.

Klagsbrun, Francine, ed. *The First Ms. Reader.* New York: Warner Books, 1973.

Klein, Ethel. *Gender Politics: From Consciousness to Mass Politics.* Cambridge: Harvard University Press, 1984.

Kolkey, Jonathan Martin. *The New Right: 1960–1968, with Epilogue, 1969–1980.* New York: University Press of America, 1983.

Komarovsky, Mirra. *The Unemployed Man and His Family: The Effect of Unemployment upon the Status of the Man in Fifty-nine Families.* New York: Dryden Press, 1940.

———. *Women in the Modern World: Their Education and Their Dilemmas.* Boston: Little, Brown, 1953.

Korda, Michael. *Male Chauvinism! How It Works.* New York: Random House, 1972.

Kraditor, Aileen. *The Ideas of the Woman Suffrage Movement, 1890–1920.* New York: Columbia University Press, 1965.

Kurian, George, and Ratna Ghosh. *Women in the Family and the Economy.* Westport, Conn.: Greenwood Press, 1981.

Ladner, Joyce. *Tomorrow's Tomorrow.* New York: Anchor Books, 1971.

Lafollette, Cecile Tipton. *A Study of the Problems of 652 Gainfully Employed Married Women Homemakers.* Contributions to Education, no. 619. New York: Bureau of Publications, Teachers College, Columbia University, 1934.

LaFollette, Suzanne. *Concerning Women.* New York: Albert & Charles Boni, 1926.

Lagemann, Ellen Condliffe. *A Generation of Women: Education in the Lives of Progressive Reformers.* Cambridge: Harvard University Press, 1979.

Laird, Donald A. *The Psychology of Supervising the Working Woman.* New York: McGraw-Hill, 1942.

Lane, Ann J. *To "Herland" and Beyond: The Life and Work of Charlotte Perkins Gilman.* New York: Pantheon, 1990.

————, ed. *The Charlotte Perkins Gilman Reader.* New York: Pantheon, 1980.

Lasch, Christopher. *Haven in a Heartless World: The Family Besieged.* New York: Basic Books, 1977.

————, ed. *The Social Thought of Jane Addams.* New York: Irvington Publishers, 1982.

Leach, William. *True and Perfect Union: The Feminist Reform of Sex and Society.* New York: Basic Books, 1980.

Leavitt, Judith Walzer. *Brought to Bed: Childbearing in America, 1750 to 1950.* New York: Oxford University Press, 1986.

Lebsock, Suzanne. *Free Women of Petersburg: Status and Culture in a Southern Town, 1784–1860.* New York: W. W. Norton, 1984.

Lemons, J. Stanley. *The Woman Citizen: Social Feminism in the 1920s.* Urbana: University of Illinois Press, 1973.

Lerner, Gerda. *The Creation of Patriarchy.* New York: Oxford University Press, 1986.

————. *The Grimké Sisters from South Carolina: Pioneers for Women's Rights and Abolition.* Boston: Houghton Mifflin, 1967.

————. *The Majority Finds Its Past: Placing Women in History.* New York: Oxford University Press, 1979.

————, ed. *Black Women in White America: A Documentary History.* New York: Vintage, 1973.

Levine, David, Leslie Page Moch, Louise A. Tilly, John Modell, and Elizabeth Pleck, eds. *Essays on the Family and Historical Change.* College Station: Texas A & M University Press, 1983.

Levine, Suzanne, Harriet Lyons, and Gloria Steinem. *A Decade of Women: A Ms. History of the Seventies in Words and Pictures.* New York: G. P. Putnam's Sons, 1980.

Levy, David M., M.D. *Maternal Overprotection.* New York: W. W. Norton, 1966.

Lewis, Sinclair. *Cass Timberlane.* New York: Random House, 1945.

————. *Mainstreet.* New York: Harcourt, Brace, 1920.

Lifton, Robert Jay. *The Woman in America.* Boston: Houghton Mifflin, 1964.

Lindner, Robert. *Must You Conform?* New York: Rinehart, 1956.

Lindsey, Judge Ben B., and Wainwright Evans. *The Companionate Marriage.* New York: Boni & Liveright, 1927.

Lingeman, Richard. *Don't You Know There's a War On? The Home Front, 1941–1945.* New York: G. P. Putnam's Sons, 1970.

Litwack, Leon F. *Been in the Storm So Long.* New York: Alfred A. Knopf, 1979.

Litwack, Leon F., et al. *The United States: Becoming a World Power.* Vol. 2. Englewood Cliffs, N.J.: Prentice-Hall, 1982.

Longley, Marjorie, Louis Silverstein, and Samuel A. Tower. *America's Taste.* New York: Simon & Schuster, 1959.

Lopata, Helen Znaniecki. *Occupation: Housewife.* New York: Oxford University Press, 1971.

Luker, Kristin. *Abortion and the Politics of Motherhood.* Berkeley: University of California Press, 1984.

Lundberg, Ferdinand, and Marynia Farnham. *Modern Woman: The Lost Sex.* New York: Harper & Brothers, 1947.

Lutz, Alma. *With Love, Jane: Letters from American Women on the War Fronts.* New York: John Day, 1945.

Lynd, Robert S., and Helen Merrell Lynd. *Middletown: A Study in American Culture.* New York: Harcourt, Brace, 1929.

———. *Middletown in Transition: A Study in Cultural Conflicts.* New York: Harcourt, Brace, 1937.

McBroom, Patricia. *The Third Sex: The New Professional Woman.* New York: William Morrow, 1986.

McCarthy, Mary. *Memories of a Catholic Girlhood.* New York: Harcourt, Brace, 1946.

McDannell, Colleen. *The Christian Home in Victorian America, 1840–1900.* Bloomington: Indiana University Press, 1986.

McElvaine, Robert S. *The Great Depression: America, 1929–1941.* New York: Times Books, 1984.

———. *Down and Out in the Great Depression: Letters from the Forgotten Man.* Chapel Hill: University of North Carolina Press, 1983.

McGlen, Nancy E., and Karen O'Connor. *The Struggle for Equality in the Nineteenth and Twentieth Centuries.* New York: Praeger, 1983.

MacKinnon, Catharine A. *Feminism Unmodified: Discourses on Life and Law.* Cambridge: Harvard University Press, 1987.

McNally, Dennis. *Desolate Angel: Jack Kerouac, the Beat Generation, and America.* New York: Random House, 1979.

Main, Gloria L. *Tobacco Colony: Life in Early Maryland, 1650–1720.* Princeton: Princeton University Press, 1982.

Manchester, William. *The Glory and the Dream: A Narrative History of America, 1932–1972.* New York: Bantam, 1974. Originally Boston: Little, Brown, 1973.

Mannes, Marya. *More in Anger.* Philadelphia: J. B. Lippincott, 1958.

———. *Out of My Time.* New York: Doubleday, 1971.

Margolis, Maxine L. *Mothers and Such: Views of American Women and Why They Changed.* Berkeley: University of California Press, 1984.

Martin, Wendy, ed. *The American Sisterhood: Writings of the Feminist Movement from Colonial Times to the Present.* New York: Harper & Row, 1972.

Matthews, Glenna. *"Just a Housewife": The Rise and Fall of Domesticity in America.* New York: Oxford University Press, 1987.

May, Elaine Tyler. *Great Expectations.* Chicago: University of Chicago Press, 1980.

————. *Homeward Bound: American Families in the Cold War Era.* New York: Basic Books, 1988.

Mead, Margaret, and Frances Balgley Kaplan, eds. *American Women and Other Publications of the Commission.* U.S. President's Commission on the Status of Women. New York: Scribner's Sons, 1965. Reprinted Washington, D.C.: Zenger Publishing, 1976.

Mennel, Robert M. *Thorns and Thistles: Juvenile Delinquents in the United States, 1825–1940.* Hanover, N.H.: University Press of New England, 1973.

Merriam, Eve. *After Nora Slammed the Door: American Women in the 1960s—The Unfinished Revolution.* Cleveland: World Publishing, 1958.

Meyer, Susan E. *America's Great Illustrators.* New York: Harry N. Abrams, 1978.

Meyerowitz, Joanne J. *Women Adrift: Independent Wage Earners in Chicago, 1880–1930.* Chicago: University of Chicago Press, 1988.

Milkman, Ruth. *Gender at Work: The Dynamics of Job Segregation by Sex during World War II.* Urbana: University of Illinois Press, 1987.

————. *Women, Work, and Protest: A Century of U.S. Women's Labor History.* Boston: Routledge & Kegan Paul, 1985.

Miller, Douglas, and Marion Nowak. *The Fifties: The Way We Really Were.* Garden City, N.Y.: Doubleday, 1977. Originally 1975.

Miller, Jean Baker. *Toward a New Psychology of Women.* Boston: Beacon, 1976.

Millett, Kate. *Sexual Politics.* Garden City, N.Y.: Doubleday, 1970.

Mintz, Steven, and Susan Kellogg. *Domestic Revolutions: A Social History of American Family Life.* New York: Free Press, 1988.

Mitchell, Juliet, and Ann Oakley, eds. *What Is Feminism? A Re-examination.* New York: Pantheon, 1986.

Moch, Leslie Page, and Gary D. Stark, eds. *Essays on the Family and Historical Change.* College Station: Texas A & M University Press, 1983.

Moody, Anne. *Coming of Age in Mississippi: An Autobiography.* New York: Dell, 1968.

Morgan, Winona L. *The Family Meets the Depression: A Study of a Group of Highly Selected Families.* Minneapolis: University of Minnesota Press, 1939.

Mott, Frank Luther. *Golden Multitudes: The Story of Bestsellers in the United States.* New York: Macmillan, 1947.

Mowrer, Ernest R. *Family Disorganization*. Chicago: University of Chicago Press, 1927.

Moynihan, Ruth Barnes. *Rebel for Rights: Abigail Scott Duniway*. New Haven: Yale University Press, 1983.

Murray, Pauli. *Proud Shoes: The Story of an American Family*. New York: Harper & Row, 1956, 1978.

————. *Song in a Weary Throat: An American Pilgrimage*. New York: Harper & Row, 1987.

Myrdal, Alva, and Viola Klein. *Women's Two Roles: Home and Work*. London: Routledge & Kegan Paul, 1956. Reprinted Trowbridge: Redwood Press, 1970.

Nevins, Allen, and Henry Steele Commager. *Pocket History of the United States*. 5th ed. New York: Washington Square Press, 1970.

Nicholson, Linda J. *Gender and History: The Limits of Social Theory in the Age of the Family*. New York: Columbia University Press, 1986.

Nies, Judith. *Seven Women: Portraits from the American Radical Tradition*. New York: Penguin, 1977.

Norton, Mary Beth. *Liberty's Daughters: The Revolutionary Experience of American Women, 1750–1800*. Boston: Little, Brown, 1980.

Nye, Russel. *The Unembarrassed Muse*. New York: Dial Press, 1970.

Ogden, Annegret S. *The Great American Housewife: From Helpmate to Wage Earner, 1776–1986*. Westport, Conn.: Greenwood Press, 1986.

Okin, Susan Moller. *Justice, Gender, and the Family*. New York: Basic Books, 1989.

O'Neill, William. *Everyone Was Brave: The Rise and Fall of Feminism in America*. Chicago: Quadrangle, 1969.

————. *The Woman Movement: Feminism in the United States and England*. Chicago: Quadrangle, 1971.

Oppenheimer, Valerie Kincade. *The Female Labor Force in the United States: Demographic and Economic Factors Governing Its Growth and Changing Composition*. Berkeley: University of California, Institute of International Studies, 1970.

Overstreet, H. A. *The Mature Mind*. London: Victor Gollanca, 1950. Originally New York: W. W. Norton, 1949.

Paige, Connie. *The Right to Lifers: Who They Are, How They Operate, Where They Get Their Money*. New York: Summit, 1983.

Papachristou, Judith, and Carol Wald. *Myth America: Picturing Women, 1865–1945*. New York: Pantheon, 1975.

Papashvily, Helen Waite. *All the Happy Endings: A Study of the Domestic Novel in America, the Women Who Wrote It, the Women Who Read It, in the Nineteenth Century*. Port Washington, N.Y.: Kennikat Press, 1972.

Patmore, Coventry. *The Angel in the House*. London: George Bell & Son, 1897.

Payne, Elizabeth Anne. *Reform, Labor, and Feminism*. Urbana: University of Illinois Press, 1988.

Payne, Karen. *Between Ourselves: Letters between Mothers and Daughters, 1750–1982*. Boston: Houghton Mifflin, 1983.

Peck, Mary Gray. *Carrie Chapman Catt: A Biography*. New York: H. W. Wilson, 1944.

Pells, Richard H. *Radical Visions and American Dreams*. New York: Harper Torchbooks, 1973.

Perkins, A. J. G., and Theresa Wolfson. *Frances Wright: Free Enquirer: The Study of a Temperament*. New York: Harper & Brothers, 1939.

Perrett, Geoffrey. *America in the Twenties: A History*. New York: Simon & Schuster, 1982.

Pivar, David J. *Purity Crusade: Sexual Morality and Social Control, 1868–1900*. Westport, Conn.: Greenwood Press, 1973.

Pleck, Elizabeth H. *Domestic Tyranny: The Making of American Social Policy against Family Violence from Colonial Times to the Present*. New York: Oxford University Press, 1987.

Pleck, Elizabeth H., and Joseph H. Pleck, eds. *The American Man*. Englewood Cliffs, N.J.: Prentice-Hall, 1980.

Pleck, Joseph H. *The Myth of Masculinity*. Cambridge: MIT Press, 1981.

Podheretz, Norman. *Doings and Undoings: The Fifties and After in American Writing*. New York: Farrar, Strauss & Giroux, 1953.

Pogrebin, Letty Cotton. *Family Politics: Love and Power on an Intimate Frontier*. New York: McGraw-Hill, 1983.

Pruette, Lorine. *Women and Leisure: A Study of Social Waste*. New York: E. P. Dutton, 1924.

————. *Women Workers through the Depression: A Study of White Collar Employment Made by the American Woman's Association*. New York: Macmillan, 1934.

Rae, Andre. *Homemakers: The Forgotten Workers*. Chicago: University of Chicago Press, 1981.

Rhode, Deborah L. *Justice and Gender: Sex Discrimination and the Law*. Cambridge: Harvard University Press, 1989.

Rich, Adrienne. *Of Woman Born: Motherhood as Experience and Institution*. New York: W. W. Norton, 1976.

Richardson, Marilyn, ed. *Maria W. Stewart: America's First Black Woman Political Writer*. Bloomington: Indiana University Press, 1987.

Riegel, Robert E. *American Women: A Story of Social Change*. Rutherford, N.J.: Fairleigh Dickinson University Press, 1970.

Riesman, David. *The Lonely Crowd: A Study of Changing American Character*. New Haven: Yale University Press, 1950.

Rix, Sara, ed. *The American Woman 1987–88: A Report in Depth*. Women's Research and Education Institute in Washington, D. C. New York: W. W. Norton, 1987.

————. *The American Woman: A Status Report, 1988–89*. New York: W. W. Norton, 1988.

Rodgers-Rose, La Frances, ed. *The Black Woman*. Beverly Hills, Calif.: Sage Publications, 1980.

Roosevelt, Eleanor. *The Autobiography of Eleanor Roosevelt*. Boston: G. K. Hall, 1984.

Rose, Phyllis. *Jazz Cleopatra: Josephine Baker in Her Time*. New York: Doubleday, 1989.

Rosen, Marjorie. *Popcorn Venus: Women, Movies and the American Dream*. New York: Avon Books, 1973.

Rosenberg, Rosalind. *Beyond Separate Spheres: The Intellectual Roots of Modern Feminism*. New Haven: Yale University Press, 1982.

Rossi, Alice. *The Family*. New York: W. W. Norton, 1978.

————, ed. *The Feminist Papers: From Adams to de Beauvoir*. New York: Bantam, 1973.

Rothman, Ellen K. *Hands and Hearts: A History of Courtship in America*. New York: Basic Books, 1984.

Rothman, Sheila M. *Woman's Proper Place: A History of Changing Ideals and Practices, 1870 to the Present*. New York: Basic Books, 1978.

Rudnick, Lois Palken. *Mabel Dodge Luhan: New Woman, New World*. Albuquerque: University of New Mexico Press, 1984.

Rupp, Leila J. *Mobilizing Women for War: German and American Propaganda, 1939–1945*. Princeton: Princeton University Press, 1978.

Rupp, Leila J., and Verta Taylor. *Survival in the Doldrums: The American Women's Rights Movement, 1945 to the 1960s*. New York: Oxford University Press, 1987.

Russett, Cynthia Eagle. *Sexual Science: The Victorian Construction of Womanhood*. Cambridge: Harvard University Press, 1989.

Ryan, Mary P. *The Cradle of the Middle Class: The Family in Oneida County, New York, 1790–1865*. New York: Cambridge University Press, 1981.

————. *The Empire of the Mother: American Writing about Domesticity, 1830–1860*. New York: Haworth Press, 1982.

————. *Womanhood in America from Colonial Times to the Present*. New York: New Viewpoints, 1975.

————. *Women in Public: Between Banners and Ballots, 1825–1880*. Baltimore: Johns Hopkins University Press, 1990.

Sachs, Emanie. *"The Terrible Siren": Victoria Woodhull*. New York: Harper & Brothers, 1928.

Safilios-Rothschild, Constantina, ed. *Toward a Sociology of Women*. Lexington, Mass.: Xerox College Publishing, 1972.

Salmon, Marylynn. *Women and the Law of Property in Early America*. Chapel Hill: University of North Carolina Press, 1986.

Salper, Roberta. *Female Liberation*. New York: Alfred A. Knopf, 1972.

Sanders, Marion K. *Dorothy Thompson: A Legend in Her Time*. New York: Avon, 1974. Originally Boston: Houghton Mifflin, 1973.

Sann, Paul. *The Lawless Decade*. New York: Crown, 1962.

Scanzoni, John. *Sexual Bargaining: Power Politics in the American Marriage*. Englewood Cliffs, N.J.: Prentice-Hall, 1972, 1982.

Scharf, Lois. *To Work and to Wed: Female Employment, Feminism, and the Great Depression*. Westport, Conn.: Greenwood Press, 1980.

Scharf, Lois, and Joan M. Jensen, eds. *Decades of Discontent: The Women's Movement, 1920–1940*. Westport, Conn.: Greenwood Press, 1983.

Schlafly, Phyllis. *The Power of the Positive Woman*. New Rochelle, N.Y.: Arlington House, 1977.

Schlissel, Lillian. *Women's Diaries of the Westward Journey*. New York: Schocken, 1982.

Schramm, Sarah Slavin. *Plow Women Rather Than Reapers: An Intellectual History of Feminism in the United States*. Metuchen, N.J.: Scarecrow Press, 1979.

Schwarz, Judith. *Radical Feminists of Heterodoxy: Greenwich Village, 1912–1940*. Lebanon, N.H.: New Victoria, 1982.

Scott, Anne Firor. *Making the Invisible Woman Visible*. Urbana: University of Illinois Press, 1984.

————. *The Southern Lady: From Pedestal to Politics, 1830–1930*. Chicago: University of Chicago Press, 1970.

Scott, Anne Firor, and Andrew M. Scott. *One Half the People: The Fight for Woman Suffrage*. Philadelphia: J. B. Lippincott, 1975.

Segal, Lynne. *Is the Future Female? Troubled Thoughts on Contemporary Feminism*. London: Virago Press, 1987.

Shaevitz, Marjorie Hansen. *The Superwoman Syndrome*. New York: Warner Books, 1984.

Shannon, David A. *The Great Depression*. Englewood Cliffs, N.J.: Prentice-Hall, 1960.

Shapiro, Laura. *Perfection Salad: Women and Cooking at the Turn of the Century*. New York: Farrar, Straus & Giroux, 1986.

Shaw, Anna Howard. *The Story of a Pioneer*. New York: Harper & Brothers, 1915.

Sheean, Vincent. *Dorothy and Red*. Boston: Houghton Mifflin, 1963.

————. *The Indigo Burning: A Memoir of Edna St. Vincent Millay*. New York: Harper & Brothers, 1951.

Shorter, Edward. *The Making of the Modern Family*. New York: Basic Books, 1975.

Showalter, Elaine, ed. *The New Feminist Criticism: Essays on Women, Literature, and Theory*. New York: Pantheon, 1985.

————. *These Modern Women: Autobiographical Essays from the Twenties*. Old Westbury, N.Y.: Feminist Press, 1978.

Shulman, Alix Kates, ed. *Red Emma Speaks*. New York: Random House, 1972.

Sicherman, Barbara, and Carol Hurd Green, eds. *Notable American Women: The Modern Period*. Cambridge: Harvard University Press, 1980.

Simpson, Jeffrey. *The American Family: A History in Photographs*. New York: Viking, 1976.

Sinclair, Andrew. *The Better Half: The Emancipation of the American Woman*. New York: Harper & Row, 1965.

Sirjamaki, John. *The American Family in the Twentieth Century*. Cambridge: Harvard University Press, 1969.

Sklar, Kathryn Kish. *Catharine Beecher: A Study in American Domesticity*. New Haven: Yale University Press, 1973.

Smith, Daniel Blake. *Inside the Great House: Planter Family Life in Eighteenth Century Chesapeake Society*. Ithaca: Cornell University Press, 1980.

Smith-Rosenberg, Carroll. *Disorderly Conduct: Visions of Gender in Victorian America*. New York: Alfred A. Knopf, 1985.

Snitow, Ann, Christine Stansell, and Sharon Thompson, eds. *Powers of Desire: The Politics of Sexuality*. New York: Monthly Review Press, 1983.

Sochen, June. *Enduring Values: Women in Popular Culture*. New York: Praeger, 1987.

—————. *Movers and Shakers: American Women Thinkers and Activists, 1900–1970*. New York: Quadrangle, 1973.

—————, ed. *The New Feminism in Twentieth Century America*. Lexington, Mass.: D. C. Heath, 1971.

Solomon, Barbara Miller. *In the Company of Educated Women: A History of Women and Higher Education in America*. New Haven: Yale University Press, 1985.

Spelman, Elizabeth V. *Inessential Woman: Problems of Exclusion in Feminist Thought*. Boston: Beacon, 1988.

Spender, Dale. *Feminist Thinkers: Three Centuries of Key Women Thinkers*. New York: Pantheon, 1983.

Spock, Benjamin. *Baby and Child Care*. New York: Hawthorn/Dutton, 1976.

Spruill, Julia Cherry. *Women's Life and Work in the Southern Colonies*. New York: W. W. Norton, 1972.

Stansell, Christine. *City of Women: Sex and Class in New York, 1789–1860*. New York: Alfred A. Knopf, 1986.

Stanton, Elizabeth Cady. *Eighty Years and More: Reminiscences, 1815–1897*. New York: T. Fisher Unwin, 1898.

Stanton, Elizabeth Cady, Susan B. Anthony, and Matilda Joslyn Gage, eds. *History of Woman Suffrage*. 6 vols. New York: Fowler & Wells, 1881–86. Vol. 1 reprinted, Salem, N.H.: Ayer, 1985.

Staples, Robert. *The Black Woman in America: Sex, Marriage, and the Family*. Chicago: Nelson-Hall, 1973.

Steinem, Gloria. *Outrageous Acts and Everyday Rebellions*. New York: Holt, Rinehart & Winston, 1983. Reprinted New York: Signet, 1986.

—————. *Revolution from Within: A Book of Self-Esteem*. Boston: Little, Brown, 1991.

Sterling, Dorothy, ed. *We Are Your Sisters: Black Women in the Nineteenth Century*. New York: W. W. Norton, 1984.

Sternsher, Bernard. *Hitting Home: The Great Depression in Town and Country*. Chicago: Quadrangle, 1970.

Stimpson, Catharine. *Women and the "Equal Rights" Amendment: Senate Subcommittee Hearings on the Constitutional Amendment, Ninety-first Congress.* New York: R. R. Bowker, 1972.

Stimpson, Catharine, and Ethel Spector Person. *Women, Sex, and Sexuality.* Chicago: University of Chicago Press, 1980.

Stone, Lawrence. *The Family, Sex, and Marriage in England, 1500–1800.* New York: Harper & Row, 1977.

Stouffer, Samuel A., and Paul F. Lazarsfeld. *Research Memorandum on the Family in the Depression.* Bulletin 29. New York: Social Science Research Council, 1937.

Strasser, Susan. *Never Done.* New York: Pantheon, 1982.

Susman, Warren. *Culture and Commitment, 1929–1945.* New York: George Braziller, 1973.

Tanner, Leslie B., ed. *Voices from Women's Liberation.* New York: New American Library, Signet, 1970.

Terborg-Penn, Rosalyn, and Sharon Harley, eds. *The Afro-American Woman: Struggles and Images.* Port Washington, N.Y.: Kennikat Press, 1987.

Terkel, Studs. *"The Good War": An Oral History of World War Two.* New York: Pantheon, 1984.

———. *Hard Times: An Oral History of the Great Depression.* New York: Random House, 1970.

Terman, Lewis M. *Psychological Factors in Marital Happiness.* New York: McGraw Hill, 1938.

Terrell, Mary Church. *A Colored Woman in a White World.* Washington, D.C.: Ransdell, 1940.

Tharp, Louise Hall. *The Peabody Sisters of Salem.* Boston: Little, Brown, 1950.

Thom, Mary, ed. *Letters to Ms.: 1972–1987.* New York: Henry Holt, 1987.

Thorne, Barrie, and Marilyn Yalom, eds. *Rethinking the Family: Some Feminist Questions.* New York: Longman, 1982.

Tompkins, Jane P. *Sensational Designs: The Cultural Work of American Fiction, 1790–1860.* New York: Oxford University Press, 1985.

Ulrich, Laurel Thatcher. *Good Wives: Image and Reality in the Lives of Women in Northern New England, 1650–1750.* New York: Oxford University Press, 1982.

———. *A Midwife's Tale: The Life of Martha Ballard Based on Her Diary, 1785–1812.* New York: Vintage, 1991.

Urdang, Laurence. *The Timetables of American History.* New York: Simon & Schuster, 1981.

Vorse, Mary Heaton. *A Footnote to Folly: Reminiscences of Mary Heaton Vorse.* New York: Farrar & Rinehart, 1935. Reprinted New York: Arno Press, 1980.

Walker, Alice. *In Search of Our Mothers' Gardens.* New York: Harcourt Brace Jovanovich, 1983.

Wallace, Michele. *Black Macho and the Myth of the Superwoman.* New York: Dial Press, 1979.

Waller, Willard. *The Family: A Dynamic Interpretation.* New York: Cordon, 1938.

Walsh, Andrea S. *Women's Film and Female Experience, 1940–1950.* New York: Praeger Special Studies, 1984.

Wandersee, Winifred D. *On the Move: American Women in the 1970s.* Boston: Twayne, 1988.

Ware, Cellestine. *Woman Power: The Movement for Women's Liberation.* New York: Tower Publications, 1970.

Ware, Susan. *Beyond Suffrage: Women in the New Deal.* Cambridge: Harvard University Press, 1981.

———. *Holding Their Own: American Women in the 1930s.* Boston: Twayne, 1982.

———. *Partner and I: Molly Dewson, Feminism, and New Deal Politics.* New Haven: Yale University Press, 1987.

Weibel, Kathryn. *Mirror, Mirror: Images of Women Reflected in Popular Culture.* Garden City, N.Y.: Anchor Books, 1977.

Weitzman, Lenore J. *The Divorce Revolution.* New York: Free Press, 1985.

Welter, Barbara. *Dimity Convictions: The American Woman in the Nineteenth Century.* Athens: Ohio University Press, 1976.

Wertz, Richard W., and Dorothy C. Wertz. *Lying-In: A History of Childbirth in America.* New York: Free Press, 1977.

Westin, Jeane. *Making Do: How Women Survived the '30s.* Chicago: Follett, 1976.

Wexler, Alice. *Emma Goldman in America.* Boston: Beacon, 1984.

Wheeler, Leslie, ed. *Loving Warriors: Selected Letters of Lucy Stone and Henry B. Blackwell, 1853–1893.* New York: Dial Press, 1981.

White, Deborah. *Ar'n't I a Woman: Female Slaves in the Plantation South.* New York: W. W. Norton, 1985.

White, Lynn. *Educating Our Daughters.* New York: Harper & Brothers, 1950.

Woloch, Nancy. *Women and the American Experience.* New York: Alfred A. Knopf, 1984.

Wylie, Philip. *A Generation of Vipers.* New York: Faircut & Rinehart, 1942.

Yankelovich, Daniel. *New Rules: Searching for Self-Fulfillment in a World Turned Upside Down.* New York: Random House, 1981.

Yates, Gayle Graham. *What Women Want: The Ideas of the Movement.* Cambridge: Harvard University Press, 1975.

Zaretsky, Eli. *Capitalism, the Family, and Personal Life.* New York: Perennial Library, 1986. Originally published as a series of articles in *Socialist Revolution*, nos. 13–15 (January–June 1973).

INDEX

Aaron, Robert, 204

AAUW. *See* American Association of University Women

Abel, Mary Hinman, 65

Abortion, 51, 54, 56, 59, 250; opposed by physicians, 57–58; opposed by early women's rights leaders, 58, 61; supported by Margaret Sanger, 89; in the 1950s, 219; the fight to legalize, 272–74; restricted federal financing of, 278; and modern feminist movement, 291–93. *See also* National Organization for Women; *Roe v. Wade*; *Webster v. Reproductive Health Services*

Abortion and the Politics of Motherhood, 273

Abuse of wife, 7, 37, 44; during the depression, 151–52

Abzug, Bella, 250, 274

Acton, William, 51

Adair, Christia Daniels, 304

Adams, Abigail, 11, 12

Adams, President John, 11, 12

Adam's Rib, 176

Addams, Jane, 84, 103, 111, 164, 232

"Adventures of Ozzie and Harriet, The," 204

AFL. *See* American Federation of Labor

African-American families: after the Civil War, 66; in the labor force, 66; discrimination against in the GI Bill, 198

African-American women: in colonial times, 3–4; bypassed by the "cult of true womanhood," 15, 25; birth rates among, 54; stereotyped as sensual, 66; living apart from their families, 87; in the professions, 96; support the suffrage movement, 106–10; gain appointments during the New Deal, 165; as actresses, 175; during WWII, 184–86; in the military, 189; in the 1950s, 202, 222–26; in the civil rights movement, 224, 251–52; and feminism in the 1960s and 1970s, 263–70; in oral history project, 303–6

African Queen, The, 206

After Nora Slammed the Door: American Women in the 1960s—The Unfinished Revolution, 238

Against Our Will, 261

Agitator, 47

Aid to Families with Dependent Children, 223

Ain't I a Woman? 307

Alaska: liberalizes abortion laws, 307

Alcott, Bronson, 24

Alexander, Sadie T. M., 304

"Alexander's Ragtime Band," 120

Alfie, 245

All about Eve, 206

Allie, Betty, 192

Allyson, June, 206

Alpha Suffrage Club, 108–9
Altrusa (women's movement organization), 350 (n. 8)
American, 205
American Association of University Women, 199, 350 (n. 8)
American Birth Control League, 89. *See also* Sanger, Margaret; Planned Parenthood Federation of America
American Federation of Labor, 111–12, 136, 167–68
American Gothic, 159
American Home Economics Association, 136
American Indian Women's Conference, 269
American Medical Woman's Association, 350 (n. 8)
American Mercury, 229
American Revolution: impact on women, 11–15, 281; effect on nineteenth-century women's rights movement, 14
American Woman, 247, 248
American Woman Suffrage Association, 78. *See also* National American Woman Suffrage Association
American Women's Home, 17
Ames, Jesse Daniel, 109
"Amos and Andy," 159
Anderson, Karen, 171, 181
Anderson, Mary, 136, 162
Anderson, Maxwell, 159
Anderson, Sherwood, 157
Andrews, Dana, 194
Andros, Sir Edmond, 9
"Angel in the House," 15–25, 32, 60, 282; and the sex radicals, 74, 90; challenged by the "new woman," 98, and exclusion of African-American women, 109; modernized, 142
Angell, Robert Cooley, 153
Angelou, Maya, 356 (n. 102)
Angels and Amazons: A Hundred Years of American Women, 138
"Annie Get Your Gun," 173

Anthony, Susan B., 27, 104, 105, 108, 257, 268; compared with Stanton, 33–35; on "weakness" of women, 40–41; on prostitution, 58–59; and Victoria Woodhull, 76–78
Anthony, Susan B., II, 199
Antifeminism, 227–28, 276–78. *See also* Feminism
Anti-Slavery Society, 28
Appeal to the Christian Women of the South, An, 45
Army Nurse Corps, 188
Arthur, T. S., 20
Assembly of Women's Organizations for National Security, 350 (n. 8)
Association of Southern Women for the Prevention of Lynching, 109
Atkinson, Ti-Grace, 253, 255
Atwood, Margaret, 356 (n. 102)
Auclert, Hubertine, 315 (n. 1)
Awakening, First and Second Great, 18
AWARE. *See* Women against the Ratification of the ERA

Baby and Child Care, 198, 308
Baby Boom, 283
Baby boom. *See* Birth rate
Baker, Ella, 224, 267
Baker, Laura Nelson, 182
Balanoff, Elizabeth, 306
Ballantine, Stella Coman, 326 (n. 34)
Ballard, Francis Kay, 141
Bambara, Toni Cade, 269
Banister, Marion Glass, 162
Barbie doll, 245
Barker-Benfield, G. J., 57
Barnett, Ida Wells, 107, 109–10
Barney, Nora Stanton, 231
Basie, Count, 168
Bates, Alan, 283
Bateson, Catherine, 240
Bateson, Gregory, 239–41
Baym, Nina, 21
Beard, Mary, 112, 231, 274

Beavers, Louise, 175
Beecher, Catharine, 16, 62
Beecher, Henry Ward, 62, 78
Beecher, Lyman, 62
Beecher-Tilton affair, 78, 324 (n. 12)
Belcher, Gladys, 198
Belmont, Mrs. O. H. P., 134
Benedict, Ruth, 240
Benedict, Wallace, 140
Bergman, Ingrid, 176
Berkley, Busby, 159
Berlin, Irving, 120, 173
Berry, Mary Frances, 264
Best Years of Our Lives, The, 194
Bethune, Albert McLeod, 166
Bethune, Albertus, 166
Bethune, Mary McLeod, 165–66, 185
Bethune-Cookman College: from merger
    with Mary McLeod Bethune's school for
    girls, 165. *See also* Cookman Institute
"Bewitched," 245
Bird, Caroline, 152, 255
Birmingham, Ala.: and civil rights
    movement, 246
Birth Control Clinical Research Bureau
    (New York City), 89
Birth Control Federation, 219. *See also*
    Planned Parenthood Federation of
    America; International Planned
    Parenthood Federation
Birth rate: falls in nineteenth century, 48–
    49, 54, 65; during the depression, 161;
    during WWII, 191; and baby boom
    after WWII, 195, 203, 219, 251, 281
Bishop, Bridget, 9
Black, Dora, 134
"Black Cabinet." *See* Federal Council on
    Negro Affairs
Blackmun, Harry A., 292
Black Power movement, 253, 265
Blackstone, William, 4
Blackwell, Alice Stone, 44, 108
Blackwell, Anna, 31
Blackwell, Antoinette. *See* Brown

Blackwell, Antoinette
Blackwell, Elizabeth, 34, 43
Blackwell, Emily, 43
Blackwell, Henry, 31, 42–45, 47, 49, 78–
    79, 108
Blackwell, Samuel, 31, 45
Black Women Oral History Project, 303–6
Black Women Organized for Action, 264
Blair, Karen, 97
Blanchard, Phyllis, 124, 138–39
Blatch, Harriot Stanton, 108–10, 231, 326
    (n. 34)
"Blondie." *See* Comic strips
Blood, Colonel James H., 77
Bloomer, Amelia, 47
Bloomer girl, 121
Bloomers, 48, 121; as relief from corsets,
    41–42
Blow-up, 245
Blubery, Ethelda, 120
Blue Lagoon, 276
Bly, Robert, 285
Bogart, Humphrey, 206
"Bonanza," 217
Boone, Pat, 203
Berkman, Alexander, 81
Boston Female Liberation, 253–54
Bostonians, The, 55
Bowen, Ashley, 6
Bowie, David, 276
Boyce, Neith, 83–86
Boyer, Elizabeth, 250
Boyer, Gene, 249
Boy George, 276
Braden, Anne, 109 (n. 46), 251
Bradstreet, Ann, 7–8
Bradstreet, Simon, 7
Brandt, Lilian, 155
Braude, Ann, 31
Bread and Roses, 353 (n. 35)
Breckinridge, Madeline, 105
Brent, Margeret and Mary, 5
"Bringing Up Father." *See* Comic strips
Britten, Florence, 121, 161

Brock, Bill, 274
Bromley, Dorothy Dunbar, 121, 123, 161
Brooks, Gwendolyn, 356 (n. 102)
Brotherhood of Sleeping Car Porters, 185
*Brought to Bed: Childbearing in America,
1750–1950*, 219–20
Brown Blackwell, Antoinette, 27, 37, 44,
48, 65
Brown, Charles Brockden, 13
Brown, Helen Gurley, 245, 255
Brown, Judith, 254
Brownmiller, Susan, 261
Brown v. Board of Education, 224, 246
Bryan, William Jennings, 119
Bryant, Louise, 86
Buck, John Lossing, 238
Buck, Pearl, 233, 237–38, 241
Bullard, Laura Curtis, 41
Buller-Moore, Ollie, 249
Bumstead, Dagwood, 202, 204
Bunny Hug (dance), 120
Bureau of Labor Statistics, 285
Bureau of Vocational Information, 141
Burgess, Ernest W., 121–22
Burlage, Robb, 251
Burning Questions, 356 (n. 102)
Burn, Harry, 117
Burns, Lucy, 112, 137
Burroughs, Nannie Helen, 107, 110
Business and Professional Women's Club,
231
Butch Cassidy and the Sundance Kid, 245
Butler, Rhett, 147, 157
Byrne, Ethel, 89

Cabot, Ella, 67–69
Cabot, Richard Clark, 67–69
Cagney, James, 147, 283
Caldwell, Erskine, 159
Caldwell, Sarah, 309
Calhoun, Arthur, 55, 129
California Women's Economic Agenda
Project, 293
Calvinists, 6–8; view of women, 18; view of
men's and women's sexuality, 51

Camelot, 245
Campbell, D'Ann, 171
Career versus marriage, 68, 123–24, 138–
43, 192, 287–88
Carr, Lois Green, 3
Cartwright, Ben, 217
Cary, Mary Ann Shadd, 106
Cason, Sandra "Casey." *See* Hayden, Casey
Castration of women, 57
Catt, Carrie Chapman, 108, 114, 135–36,
232; in suffrage movement, 100–102,
105, 117; and Alice Paul, 294
Catt, George, 101
Cavan, Mrs.: cofounder of Working
Women's Protective Union, 31
Cavan, Ruth Shonle, 154–57
CCC. *See* Civilian Conservation Corps
Cell 16, 254–55
Chadwick, Dorothy, 6
Chafe, William, 171
Chandler, Lucinda, 41
Channing, Grace, 62–63
Channing, William Ellery, 24
Chapman, Leo, 101
Charleston (dance), 120
Charlotte Temple: A Tale of Truth, 19–20
Chicago Herald, 92
Child, David Lee, 47–48
Child, Lydia Maria, 47–48
Childbirth, 53, 57; in colonial times, 5–6;
use of drugs in, 128, 220. *See also*
Physicians
Child care: during WWII, 182–84; called
for by President's Commission on the
Status of Women, 248; urged by
National Organization for Women,
250; in the 1980s, 287–90; as a current
issue for feminism, 293, 295
Child custody, 35, 40
Child Development Act, 274
Childrearing, 53–54, 128
Children of the Great Depression, 153
Childs, Lyn, 177
Chinn, May Edward, 304
Chisholm, Shirley, 250, 264

Chodorow, Nancy, 258
Cincinnati, Ohio: site of women's rights convention (1855), 32
CIO. *See* Congress of Industrial Organizations
Civilian Conservation Corps, 162
Civil Rights Act (1964), 232, 249, 274
Civil rights movement, 246, 253, 264; and African-American women, 224; and sexism, 251–52, 267
Civil War: effect on the power of southern women, 94–95
Cixous, Hélène, 235
Claflin, Tennessee, 76, 79
Clark, Evans, 138
Clark, Mae, 147, 283
Clark, Septima, 224
Clayburgh, Jill, 283
Clay sisters (Mary, Anne, Sallie, Laura), 105
Cleveland, Ohio: site of women's rights convention (1853), 32
Clitoridectomy: as treatment for masturbation, 57
Clive, Alan, 171
Coalition of Labor Union Women, 270
Cohn, David, 216
Coitus interruptus, 54, 71
Colbert, Claudette, 151
Cole, Anne, 9
Colonial period: women's experience in, 1–10, 280, 312 (n. 2)
Colorado: and women's suffrage, 99
Colored Women's Progressive Association, 106, 109
Colored Women's YWCA, 107
Color Purple, The, 356 (n. 102)
Comic strips, 98–99, 148, 159, 174–75, 202
Commentaries (William Blackstone), 4
Commerce, Department of, 289
Commissions on the Status of Women, Third Annual Conference of, 249
Committee for National Defense, 165
Communitarian feminism, 101. *See also* Catt, Carrie Chapman

Communitarian movement, 74
Comprehensive Health Manpower Training Act (1971), 274
Comstock Law, 79, 88
Conference to Draft a United Nations Charter, 165
Congress, U.S.: addressed by Victoria Woodhull, 76; and bills of concern to women, 101; fails to pass the ERA, 199; and legislation on women's rights, 275–76
Congressional Union, 108, 112. *See also* National Woman's Party
Congress of Industrial Organizations, 168, 180
Congress of Racial Equality, 254
Congress to Unite Women, 307
Connecticut Committee for the ERA, 350 (n. 8)
Connelly, Marc, 159
Connolly, James, 299, 302
Connor, Bull, 224, 246
Conroy, Catherine, 249
Consciousness-raising, 28, 255, 265. *See also* Feminist consciousness
Constantia. *See* Murray, Judith Sargent
Consumers' League, 164. *See also* National Consumers' League
Contraception, 54, 57, 74, 219; opposed by Elizabeth Cady Stanton, 61; increase of use in during the 1930s, 145, 160–62
Controversy and Coalition, 307
Cookman Institute: merges with Mary McLeod Bethune's school for girls, 165
Cooley, Winnifred Harper, 112
Cooper, Anna Julia, 107, 110
Copley, John Singleton, 5
Cosmopolitan, 55, 245
Cott, Nancy, 16, 51, 313 (n. 1), 315 (n. 2)
Cotton, Ann Lake, 6
Courage to Be Happy, The, 235
Cox, Marcelene, 192
Crawford, Joan, 146, 176, 206
Cressman, Luther, 240
Croly, Herbert, 101

Crosby, Bing, 173
Cross, Laura, 308
Crossing Delancy, 283
"Cult of True Womanhood," 16–25;
    challenged by the "new woman," 98
Cummins, Maria, 20

Daily Democrat, 31
Daily Transcript (Philadelphia), 29
Daly, Mary, 255–56
Dances, 120
Daring to Be Bad, 278
Darling, 245
Darrow, Clarence, 119
D'Arusmont, Phiquepal, 76
Darwell, Jane, 175
Daughters of Bilitis, 254
Davies, Caroline, 249
Davis, Angela, 258, 266, 269
Davis, Bette, 146, 206
Davis, Maxine, 122
Davis, Paulina Wright, 31, 36
Dawson, Dorothy, 251
Dawson, Lillian Cantor, 152
Day, Doris, 206
Day care. *See* Child care
Death of a Salesman, The, 214
De Beauvoir, Simone, 233–36, 241, 261,
    296
*Decade of Women: A Ms. History of the Seventies
    in Words and Pictures*, 307
Declaration of Sentiments: at Seneca Falls
    Convention, 26, 29
Dee, Sandra, 206
DeGarmo, Rhoda, 30
Degler, Carl, 52, 249
Dell, Floyd, 83
Delta Sigma Theta Sorority, 106, 108
D'Emilio, John, 54, 217
Democratic National Committee, 164;
    Women's Division, 164
Demos, John, 9
Dennett, Mary Ware, 89
Densmore, Dana, 255, 353 (n. 35)

Depression of 1929: and empowerment of
    women, 144; and employment of
    women, 149–50; and altered sexual
    roles, 152–57; studies of families in,
    339 (n. 46); and traditional female
    roles, 168–69; ended by WWII, 174;
    as turning point for women's gaining
    domestic power, 199, 281
Devanna, Mary Anne, 288
Dewson, Mary, 164
Dial, 24
Dialectic of Sex, The, 260–61
Dickinson, Austin, 71
Dickinson, Emily, 71
Dietrich, Marlene, 146
Dillinger, John, 159
Dillon, Matt, 217
Dingwall, Eric, 216
Dinnerstein, Dorothy, 258
Dior, Christian, 197
Disney, Walt, 146
Division of Negro Affairs, 165
Divorce, 12, 48, 125, 214; in colonial
    times, 7; reform urged by early
    feminists, 37–40, 44; during the
    depression, 151; and WWII, 191, 193,
    195; current increase in, 286–87
Dodd, Christopher, 290
Dodge, Mabel, 83–87
Doe v. Bolton, 308
Dolan, Terry, 276
Dollinger, Genora Johnson, 167
Dorr, Rheta Childe, 133, 326 (n. 34)
Dorsey, Tommy, 173
Double Indemnity, 176
Douglass, Fredrick, 30
Dreier, Mary, 111
Dubbert, Joe, 55
DuBois, Ellen, 100
Dunbar, Roxanne, 353 (n. 35)
Duniway, Abigail Scott, 328 (n. 17)
Dunn, Nora E., 141
Dunne, Irene, 176
Durr, Virginia, 251

Dwight, Timothy, 55
Dyer, Mary, 8
Dykes, Eva B., 304

Eagle Forum, 277
Earhart, Amelia, 133, 147, 159
Earle, Louisa, 104
East, Catherine, 249
Easterlin, Richard A., 338 (n. 36)
Eastman, Crystal, 84, 112, 139–40, 326
    (n. 34),
Eastman, Max, 87, 139
Eastwood, Clint, 217
Eastwood, Mary, 249
Ebony, 223
Echols, Alice, 278
Economic Research and Action Projects,
    252
Eden, Barbara, 245
Edenton Proclamation, 12
Edmunds-Tucker Act (1887), 99
Educational Amendment Act (1972), 274
Education of women, 9–16 passim, 96–97;
    and professional positions held, 142,
    274–75, 286, 349 (n. 65); and college
    and graduate school enrollment, 198,
    222, 244, 275
EEOC. *See* Equal Employment Opportu-
    nity Commission
Egalitarianism: feminists retreat from, xi,
    115; as issue between the NWP and the
    NAWSA, 133. *See also* Marriage,
    egalitarian; Moral superiority of women
Elder, Glen Jr., 153–54
Ellington, Duke, 168
Ellis, Havelock, 32
Emerson, Ralph Waldo, 24
English Women's Social and Political
    Union, 110
Enlightenment: and free love, 74; extolled
    by Frances Wright, 76
Episcopal church, 268
Equal Credit Opportunity Act, 274

Equal Employment Opportunity Act
    (1972), 308
Equal Employment Opportunity Commis-
    sion, 250, 308
Equal Pay Act (1963), 274
Equal Rights, 135, 231
Equal Rights Amendment, 143, 227–49
    passim, 256, 263, 264, 281, 295, 307–
    9; opposed by southern states, 105;
    introduced (1923), 132; and protective
    laws, 136; supported by Eleanor
    Roosevelt, 165; defeated in the 1940s,
    199; defeated in the 1980s, 270–72,
    276–78, 291
ERA. *See* Equal Rights Amendment
Evangelicals, 52, 105
Evans, Augusta Jane, 20

Fair Employment Practices Commission,
    185
Falk, Candace, 81
Falwell, Jerry, 278
Family Encounters the Depression, The, 153
Family issues. *See* Child care; Child
    custody; Childrearing; Divorce;
    Housekeeping; Marriage; Motherhood
Family Protection Act, 278
Family violence. *See* Abuse of wife
Farm Security Administration, 159, 161
Farnham, Marynia, 228–29
Farrell, James T., 159
Fasteau, Brenda Feigen, 275, 308
Father's Legacy to His Daughter, A, 52
Fearful Freedom, A, 294
Fear of Flying, 356 (n. 102)
Federal Council on Negro Affairs, 165
Federal Emergency Relief Administration,
    162
Federal Home Loan Bank Board, 308
Federally Employed Women, 250
Federation of Women Shareholders, 350 (n. 8)
Female Eunuch, The, 260
Females Opposed to Equality, 277

Feminine Mystique, The, 207, 238, 259, 291
Feminism: defined, viii; varieties of, 243–
    44, 255–59, 278–79, 315 (n. 1), 327
    (n. 2); split after women's suffrage
    gained, 118, 132–33; liberal versus
    radical, 243–44, 263. *See also*
    Antifeminism
Feminist Alliance, 83
Feminist consciousness, 16, 27, 50; defined,
    viii; emergence of, xi, 33, 171, 202;
    from women's experience in families,
    280. *See also* Consciousness–raising
Feminist marriage. *See* Marriage, egalitar-
    ian
Feminists, The, 254
FERA. *See* Federal Emergency Relief
    Administration
Ferree, Myra Marx, 263, 307
"Fibber McGee and Molly," 173
Films: during the depression, 146–47; in
    the 1940s, 175–77; in the 1950s, 206;
    in the 1960s, 245; in the 1980s, 283–
    84
Firestone, Shulamith, 252–55, 260
Fish, Sarah, 30
Fisher, J., 216
Fitzgerald, F. Scott, 72, 140
Fitzgerald, Zelda, 72
Flapper, 83, 87, 96, 123, 142, 179;
    Greenwich Village radicals as, 83;
    replaces Gibson girl, 120–21; eclipsed
    by Ma Joad, 143
Flax, Jane, 258
Fleischman, Doris E., 229
Flexner, Eleanor, 100
Flynn, Elizabeth Gurley, 88, 326 (n. 34)
FOE. *See* Females Opposed to Equality
Fonda, Jane, 283
*For Colored Girls Only Who Have Considered
    Suicide When the Rainbow Is Enuf*, 356
    (n. 102)
Ford, Harrison, 283
Ford, John, 175
Ford, Judith Ann, 243
Fortune, 216

Fortune, Leo, 240
Forum, 142
Foster, Abby Kelley, 47
Foster, Stephen Symonds, 47
Fox, Muriel, 249
Fox Trot (dance), 120
Frances Sylva: daughter of Frances Wright,
    76
Frazier, Brenda, 159
Frazier, E. Franklin, 223
Frederick, Christine, 126
Freedman, Estelle B., 54, 217
Freeman, Jo, 246, 252
Frelinghuysen University: established by
    Anna Julia Cooper, 107
French, Marilyn, 356 (n. 102)
Freud, Sigmund, 128, 232, 234; and
    Greenwich Village radicals, 83
Frick, Henry, 81
Friedan, Betty, 201, 202, 228, 235, 239,
    250, 255, 262–63; and *The Feminine
    Mystique*, 207–14, 219–23 passim, 238,
    259; founds the National Organization
    for Women, 249; and *The Second Stage*,
    290–91
Friedman, Lawrence J., 320 (n. 69)
Fryer, Douglas Henry, 140
Fuller, Margaret, 24
Fuller, Walter, 140
*Functions and Disorders of the Reproductive
    Organs, The*, 51
Fundamentalists, 119, 277, 278
Furies, The (lesbian-feminist group), 256

Gable, Clark, 151, 157, 173
Gage, Matilda Joslyn, 41, 58
Gallico, Paul, 193
"Gangbusters," 173
Garbo, Greta, 146
Garrett, Mary J., 106
Garrison, William Lloyd, 30–31, 39
Garvey, Helen, 252
Gaslight, 176
Gay, Peter, 53

General Federation of Women's Clubs, 97, 350 (n. 8)

General Motors, sit-down strike at, 167

Generation of Vipers, A, 210, 234

Genessee Meeting, 28

Giardiana, Carol, 254

Gibbons, Abby, 39

GI Bill, 189, 198

Gibson, Charles Dana, 98

Gibson girl, 98–99, 120, 178, 282

Giles, Nell, 178, 192

Gilkes, Cheryl, 304–5

Gilman, Charlotte Perkins, 51, 83, 134, 326 (n. 34); "material feminism" of, 62–65

Gilman, Houghton, 62

Gilmore, Rufus H., 138

Gish, Lillian, 276

Glasgow, Ellen, 95

Glaspell, Susan, 84–85, 326 (n. 34)

Gluck, Sherna, 196

Godey's Lady's Book, 16, 19, 26

"Gold Diggers of 1933," 159

Golden Notebook The, 356 (n. 102)

Goldman, Emma, 86, 88, 329 (n. 21); espouses free love, 36; as sex radical, 73, 75, 79–83, 90

Goldman, Olive, 234

Goldmark, Pauline and Josephine, 110

Goldstein, Betty. *See* Friedan, Betty

Gone with the Wind, 147

Good, Sarah, 9

Good Earth, The, 237

Good Housekeeping, 205, 245

Goodman, Benny, 168

Goodman, Ellen, 282

Goodsell, Willystine, 124–25

Gordon, Flash. *See* Comic strips

Gordon, Linda, 353 (n. 35)

Gorman, Margaret, 120

Graham, Dick, 249

Grapes of Wrath, The, 143, 149, 175, 206

Grassroots Group of Second-Class Citizens, 271

Great Depression. *See* Depression of 1929

Greek Slave, 73

Greeley, Horace, 30

Green Pastures, 159

Greenwich Village radicals, 73, 83–87, 90

Greenwood, Grace, 23

Greer, Germaine, 255, 260

Gregg, Kate L., 138

Gregory, John, 52

Grey, Zane, 217

Griffith, Melanie, 283

Griffiths, Martha, 249, 274, 270

Grimké, Angelina, 31, 45, 46, 47, 251. *See also* Weld, Angelina Grimké

Grimké, Sarah, 31, 45, 251

Grizzly Bear (dance), 120

"Gunsmoke," 217

Gyn/Ecology, 256

Hacker, Helen, 216

Hagood, Margaret Jarman, 157

Hahne, Dellie, 170, 186–87

Hale, Ruth, 135

Hale, Sarah Josepha, 16

Hall, G. Stanley, 54

Hallowell, Sarah, 30

Hamer, Fannie Lou, 224

Hames, Marjorie Pitts, 308

Hamilton, G. V., 121

Hammer, Mike, 217

Hanish, Carol, 351 (n. 1)

Hapgood, Hutchins, 83–85

Happiness of Motherhood Eternal, 277

"Happy Days Are Here Again," 159

Harland, Marion, 20

Harlow, Jean, 146

Harper's, 142

Harriman, Florence Jaffray, 162

Harris, Corra, 131

Harris, Lou, 264, 265

Harris, Marvin, 240

Harris v. McRae, 278

Hartmann, Heidi, 288

Harvard Law School: rejects woman applicant, 141, 268

Haskell, Kathryn, 150
Hatch, Orrin, 289
Hawaii: liberalizes abortion laws, 307; first state to ratify ERA, 308
Hawthorne, Sophia, 22–23
Hayden, Casey, 251–52
Hayden, Tom, 251
Hayden rider, 270
Hedger, Gena, 151
Hefner, Hugh, 217–18
Height, Dorothy, 264
Heilbrun, Carolyn, 255
Held, John Jr., 121
Hellman, Lillian, 159
Hemmons, Willa Mae, 267
Hentz, Caroline, 20
Hepburn, Katharine, 146, 176, 206
Hernandez, Aileen, 264, 269
Herring, John Woodbridge, 140
Hersh, Blanche Glassman, 47
Hess, Beth B., 307
Heterodoxy (women's club), 325 (n. 34)
Hewitt, Nancy, 16, 30
Hewlett, Sylvia Ann, 288–89, 291
Heywood, Angela, 61
Hibbens, Ann, 9
Hicks, Elias, 315 (n. 2). See also Quakers
Hicksites. See Quakers
Higginson, Thomas Wentworth, 47
Hillquit, Morris, 84
Hirth, Emma P., 141
Hispanic women, 279, 293
Hitler, Adolf, 160, 168, 235
Hochschild, Arlie, 285
Hocking, Richard, 324 (n. 54)
Holbrook, Stewart, 158
Holliday, Billie, 186
Hollingworth, Leta, 133
Hollis, Florence, 171
HOME. See Happiness of Motherhood Eternal
"Home Life," 40
Homeward Bound: American Families in the Cold War Era, 203

Hooker, Isabella Beecher, 31, 62
Hooks, Bell, 266, 269
Hoover, Herbert, 145
Hoover, J. Edgar, 159
Hopkins, Alison Turnbull, 326 (n. 34)
Horne, Lena, 186
Horse Trot (dance), 120
Housekeeping: and scientific domesticity, 125–27, 146; after WWII, 207–8
Howe, Julia Ward, 65, 77
Howe, Marie Jenny, 325 (n. 34)
Howes, Ethel Puffer, 65, 129
Howland, Marie Stevens, 65
Hubbard, Rev. Winslow, 55
Human Life Amendment, 278
Hunt, Jane, 28
Hurston, Zora Neale, 356 (n. 102)
Hutchinson, Anne, 8
Hyde Amendment, 278

I Am Curious Yellow, 245
"I Dream of Jeannie," 245
I Know Why the Caged Bird Sings, 356 (n. 102)
Illinois Association of Colored Women, 185
"I Love Lucy," 204
"In Der Fuehrer's Face," 173
Industrialization: and effect on women, 15, 48. See also Labor force; Unionism
Industrial Women's League for Equality, 350 (n. 8)
Industrial Workers of the World: Margaret Sanger active in, 88
Indutz, Phineas, 249
Institute for the Coordination of Women's Interests, 129
International Alliance of Women, 229
International Ladies Garment Workers Union, 112, 168
International Planned Parenthood Foundation, 89. See also Sanger, Margaret
Intimate Matters: A History of Sexuality in America, 217

Irigaray, Luce, 235
Iron John, 285
Irving, Amy, 283
Irwin, Inez Haynes, 138, 326 (n. 34)
Irwin, Will, 138
I Saw Hitler, 235
"Is You or Is You Ain't My Baby?" 190
It Ain't Me Babe, 307
It Happened One Night, 151

Jack, Bill, 192
"Jack Benny Show," 173
Jacobi, Paula, 326 (n. 34)
Jacobs, Pattie, 105
Jaffe, Rona, 213
Jagger, Mick, 276
James, Henry, 55
Janeway, Elizabeth, 255
Jazz: and the sexual revolution, 122
Jews, Orthodox, 277
Johnson, Grace Nail, 326 (n. 34)
Johnson, President Lyndon, 352 (n. 14)
Jones, Beverly, 254
Jong, Erica, 356 (n. 102)
Julia, 283
Justice and Gender, 136

Kael, Pauline, 190
Kaiser Shipyards, 183–84
Kaminer, Wendy, 294
Karlsen, Carol, 9
Kearney, Belle, 105
Keaton, Diane, 283
Kelley, Florence, 110, 136, 315 (n. 2),
Kelly, E. Lowell, 299–302
Kemp, Maida Springer, 305
Kennedy, Florynce, 264, 269, 272
Kennedy, President John F., 165, 246, 247,
    252. *See also* President's Commission
    on the Status of Women
Kennedy, Robert, 252
Kenya: holds feminism conference, 295
Kerber, Linda, 12–13
Kershner, Jacob, 81

Kettler, Ernestine Hara, 113
Key, Ellen, 129
Kilgore-Murray Bill, 199
King, Martin Luther, 252
King, Mary, 252
Kinsey, Alfred, 196, 218
Kirchwey, Freda, 138
Kirschbaum, Kathryn, 309
Kiss Me Kate, 173
Kittredge, Charmian. *See* London,
    Charmian
Knight, Elizabeth, 9
Koedt, Anne, 254
Komarovsky, Mirra, 152–53, 351 (n. 26)
Korn/Ferry International, 287
Kraditor, Aileen, 100
Kramer v. Kramer, 276
Kristeva, Julia, 235
Krupa, Gene, 173
Ku Klux Klan, 119, 165–66

Labor, Department of: Office of Contract
    Compliance, 250
Labor force: and women, 15, 18; during
    WWI, 114–15; during WWII, 177–
    82; after WWII, 199, 221–22, 244; in
    the 1960s, 247–48. *See also* Unionism;
    Industrialization
Lacasse, Walter, 139
Laddey, Paula, 141
Ladies Home Journal, 122, 134, 155, 192,
    205, 213, 220; and romantic surrender,
    130–31; Eleanor Roosevelt writes in,
    163; articles by Dorothy Thompson,
    235–36; sit-in at, 243, 307; and the
    typical heroine, 245
Ladies' Wreath, 32
"Lady at Lockheed, The," 178
"Lady Bountiful." *See* Comic strips
Lady's New Year's Gift, 52
Lafferty, Jeanne, 353 (n. 35)
LaFollette, Fola, 326 (n. 34)
LaFollette, Robert, 326 (n. 34)
LaFollette, Suzanne, 129

Landis, Paul, 217
Lanham Act, 183
Lathrop, Julia, 137, 162
Lavender Menace Action, 255, 307
Lawrence, D. H., 87
Lawrence of Arabia, 245
Lazarfeld, Paul, 152
League of Women Voters, 132, 164, 166, 199; originally the National American Woman Suffrage Association, 133; and child welfare standards, 137; denies concern with women's issues, 229
Leavitt, Judith Walzer, 128, 220
Left Hand of Darkness, The, 356 (n. 102)
Leghorn, Lisa, 353 (n. 35)
Le Guin, Ursula, 356 (n. 102)
LeKachman, Robert, 196
Lerner, Gerda, 315 (n. 1)
Lesbianism, 259, 269, 307, 326 (n. 34); and radical feminist groups, 255–57
Lesser Life: The Myth of Women's Liberation in America, A, 288
Lessing, Doris, 356 (n. 102)
Letters on the Equality of the Sexes and the Condition of Women, 45
Let the Record Speak, 235
Levine, Suzanne, 307
Lewis, Mrs. Lawrence, 112
Lewis, Sinclair, 235
Liberator (Max Eastman), 139
Liberator (William Lloyd Garrison), 30
Life, 273
Lily, 47
Lincoln, Mary Todd, 31
Lindsey, Judge Ben B., 129
Listen, Hans! 235
Little Foxes, 159
Little Orphan Annie. *See* Comic strips
Livermore, Daniel, 47
Livermore, Mary A., 31, 47, 65, 77
Loman, Willy, 214
London, Charmian, 71–72
London, Jack, 71–72
London, Joy, 72
Lonely Crowd, The, 209, 216

Loomis, Mabel, 70–71
Lorde, Audre, 269
Lost Generation, The, 122
Love, Anarchy, and Emma Goldman, 81
Lucy Stone League, 350 (n. 8)
Luhan, Mabel. *See* Dodge, Mabel
Lujan, Tony, 87
Luker, Kristin, 273
Lundberg, Ferdinand, 228–29
Lutz, Alma, 135
Lying–In: A History of Childbirth in America, 220
Lyman, Ella. *See* Cabot, Ella
Lynching, 66, 106, 108, 109, 186
Lynd, Robert and Helen, 125, 127, 152

"Ma." *See* Comic strips
McAlmon, Victoria, 138–39
McCable, Jewel Jackson, 264
McCall's, 205, 208, 245
McCarthy, Joe, 200, 203, 232–34
McClintock, Mary Ann, 28, 31
McClintock, Thomas, 31
McCormick, Katherine Dexter, 89
McCormick, Ruth Hanna, 137
McDaniel, Hattie, 175
McFarland, Daniel, 318 (n. 41)
McGinley, Phyllis, 234
McGlen, Nancy E., 230
McMahon, John R., 122
McMillan, Lucille Foster, 162
McNutt, Paul, 191
McQueen, Butterfly, 175
Mademoiselle, 205
Ma Joad, 143, 149, 175, 206
Malcolm X, 252
Manasses, Carlyn, 124
Manchester, William, 174, 196
Man in the Gray Flannel Suit, The, 215
Mann, Horace, 24
Man of La Mancha, The, 245
March, Emily, 130
Marine Corps Women's Reserves, 188
Marjorie, Morningstar, 215
Marot, Helen, 111

Marriage: opposed by Emma Goldman, 79–
83, increases during WWII, 190–91;
opposed by radical feminists, 253–54;
longitudinal study of, 299–302
Marriage, "companionate," 129, 282
Marriage, egalitarian, 123–25; examples of,
42–48, 67–72; in 1920s, 118. *See also*
Egalitarianism
Marriage, hierarchical: criticized by
Spiritualists, 31; criticized by early
feminists, 33–37, 39, 43–44
Martin, John Biddulph, 79
Martindale, Anna, 82
Marxist feminism, 258–59. *See also*
Feminism: varieties of
"Mary Tyler Moore Show," 245
Mason, Priscilla, 13–14
Massachusetts Committee for the ERA, 350
(n. 8)
Masses, 138
Masters and Johnson, 121
"Material feminism." *See* Gilman, Charlotte
Perkins
Matthews, Glenna, 125
Mature Mind, The, 215
May, Elaine Tyler, 125, 203
Mead, Margaret, 187, 207, 233–35, 247;
on couples during WWII, 170, 172,
194; life and career of, 239–41
Medicaid, 278
Memoirs of an Ex-Prom Queen, 356 (n. 102)
Menninger, Karl, 234
Mental and Moral Philosophy, 16
Meriwether, Elizabeth Avery, 105
Merman, Ethel, 173
Merriam, Eve, 233, 238–39, 241
Methodist church. *See* Southern Methodist
church
Methodist Student Movement, 251
Metropolitan Opera, 309
Mexican American Women's Association,
269
Meyerowitz, Joanne, 87
Michigan: and women's suffrage, 99
Michigan, University of: first to incorporate

affirmative action, 308
Middletown in Transition, 152
Midnight Cowboy, 245
Midwives, 56, 58
Mildred Pierce, 176
Miles, Catherine Cox, 299
Mill, John Stuart, 234
Millay, Edna St. Vincent, 85, 133
Miller, Arthur, 214
Miller, Charles Dudley, 47–48
Miller, Daisy, 86
Miller, Elizabeth Smith, 35, 47–48, 41
Miller, Emma Guffy, 137
Miller, Glenn, 168, 173
Millett, Kate, 255, 259, 260, 261
Miss America pageant, 120; feminist
protest at, 242–43
Mitchell, Juliet, 258
Mitchell, Lucy Miller, 165, 304
Mitchell, Margaret, 159
Mitchell, Weir, 62
Mobilizing Women for War, 179
Modern Women: The Lost Sex, 228–29
Mohr, James, 56
Monroe, Marilyn, 206, 216
Montagu, Ashley, 234, 236
Montgomery, Elizabeth, 245
Montgomery, Ellen, 20
Montgomery, Ala.: site of bus boycott, 224
Moore, Audley, 305
Moral purity movement, 65–66
Moral superiority of women, 55, 61, 79; as
viewed in the nineteenth century, 18,
22, 25, 26; and the suffrage movement,
94, 107; and the National Women's
Trade Union League, 111; illustrated by
Eleanor Roosevelt, 162–63
Morgan, Robin, 351 (n. 1)
Morris, Esther, 328 (n. 17)
Morrison, Toni, 356 (n. 102)
Mosher, Clelia, 52
Mosken, Robert, 216
Moskowitz, Belle, 137
Most, Johann, 81
Mother Earth, 82

Motherhood: scientific approach to, 53–54, 125–30; as voluntary, 59–62, 65–68; ambivalence of National Woman's Party toward, 135; views of after WWII, 208–10; and radical feminists, 254–55

Mothers of the South, 157

motive (magazine), 251

Mott, James, 29, 45, 47

Mott, Lucretia, 27–29, 39, 45, 47, 59, 77

Mowrer, Ernest R., 129

Moynihan, Daniel P., 266

Moynihan Report: The Negro Family: The Case for National Action, The, 266

Ms., 275

Muller v. Oregon, 110

Multi-Party Committee of Women, 350 (n. 8)

Munford, Mary, 105

Murray, Judith Sargent, 12

Murray, Pauli, 264, 267–69

Mussolini, Benito, 160

"My Day," 163

NAACP. *See* National Association for the Advancement of Colored People

Nash, Diane, 252

Nashoba, Tenn.: site of communitarian experiment, 75–76

Nation, 137–40

National Abortion Federation, 273

National Abortion Rights Action League, 308

National American Woman Suffrage Association, 40, 64, 77–78, 101–18 passim, 133

National Association for the Advancement of Colored People, 165, 224

National Association of Black Professional Women, 264

National Association of Colored Women, 106, 108, 165, 231–32

National Association of Women Lawyers, 350 (n. 8)

National Black Feminist Organization, 264, 308

National Coalition against Domestic Violence, 309

National Coalition of American Nuns, 257

National Coalition of 100 Black Women, 264

National Conference for New Politics, 252

National Conference of Puerto Rican Women, 269

National Consumers' League, 110, 137

National Council of Negro Women, 165, 185, 264

National Council of Women, 350 (n. 8)

National Federation of Afro–American Women, 106

National Labor Relations Act, 168

National Organization for Women, 249–75 passim, 293, 295

National Soapbox Derby, 308

National Training School for Girls, 107–8

National Woman's Party, 132–40 passim, 193, 247, 272, 326 (n. 34); and the suffrage struggle, 108, 112–14, 117; and the Equal Rights Amendment, 132, 227, 230–32, 248

National Woman Suffrage Association, 78. *See also* National American Woman Suffrage Association

National Woman's Rights Convention, 36, 43

National Women's Political Caucus, 250, 308

National Women's Trade Union League, 110–11, 137, 164, 199

National Youth Administration, 165

Native Americans, 164, 279

NAWSA. *See* National American Woman Suffrage Association

Nebraska: and women's suffrage, 99

Nelson, Gunvar, 351 (n. 1)

Nelson, Harriet, 204, 209

Nelson, Ozzie, 204

Neuman, Charlcia, 196

New Deal, 137, 159; and birth control, 160–61; women serving in, 162, 165
New Harmony, Ind.: site of communitarian experiment, 75
New Jersey: grants women the right to vote, 14
Newman, Edward, 208
New Masses, 139
New Right, 276, 278, 295
New Russia, 235
Newsweek, 284
New York: liberalizes abortion laws, 307
New York City: site of women's rights conventions (1853, 1856, 1860), 32
New Yorker, 159, 236
New Yorkers for Abortion Repeal, 254
New York Herald Tribune, 235
New York League of Women Voters, 134–35
New York Radical Feminists, 254
New York Stock Exchange, 243
New York Times, 112, 275
New York Tribune, 30
New York World Telegram, 146
9–5 (working women's organization), 270
Nixon, President Richard M., 274
North Carolina, University of: rejects black applicant, 267
Northeastern Federation of Colored Women's Clubs, 106
North Star, 30
Norton, Eleanor Holmes, 264, 266, 269
Norton, Mary Beth, 3, 12
Notorious, 176
NOW. *See* National Organization for Women
Nurse, Francis, 9
Nurse, Rebecca, 9
Nurses Training Act (1971), 274
NWP. *See* National Woman's Party

O'Connor, Karen, 230
Odets, Clifford, 159

Office of War Information, 178. *See also* War Manpower Commission
Of Men and Women, 237
Of Woman Born: Motherhood as Experience and Institution, 256,
O'Hanrahan, Inka, 249
O'Hara, Scarlett, 147, 157
O'Keeffe, Georgia, 133
Once upon a Christmas, 235
O'Neill, June, 287
O'Neill, William, 100, 327 (n. 2),
"On the Record," 235
"Open Letter to True Men, An," 262
"Operation Buttonhole," 231
Oregon: and women's suffrage, 99
O'Reilly, Leonora, 111
"Organization man," 214–18
Organization Man (book), 215
Osbourne, Sarah, 9
O'Sullivan, Mary Kenney, 65
Overstreet, H. A., 215
Owen, Robert, 75
Owen, Ruth Bryan, 162
Owen, Sarah, 30–31
Ozick, Cynthia, 255

Page, Patti, 203
Palmer, A. Mitchell, 119
Pamela, 19
Pan African Congress Conference, 107
Pankhurst, Emmeline, 110, 114
Papashvily, Helen, 21
Parker, Dorothy, 178
Parks, Rosa, 109, 224
Parsons, Elsie Clews, 133
Passionlessness of women, 66; as an ideal in the nineteenth century, 50–53, 87; attacked by Elizabeth Cady Stanton, 61; rejected by sex radicals, 73–75
Paterson (N.J.) Strike Pageant, 85
Paul, Alice, 103, 111, 241, 315 (n. 2); leadership in National Woman's Party, 112–14, 230, 232–33, 248; on

protectionism vs. egalitarianism, 136, 294

Payne Elizabeth Anne, 111

Peabody, Elizabeth, 22–24

Peabody, Mary: marries Horace Mann, 24

Peace and freedom movement, 252

Pearl Harbor, 170, 180, 184

Peirce, Melusina Fay, 65

Pemberton, Kate, 166–67

Pepper, William, 252

Perkins, Frances, 110, 162–63

Philadelphia: site of women's rights convention (1854), 32

Philadelphia Public Ledger, 29

Philipse, Margaret Hardenbrook, 5

Phillips, Howard, 276, 278

Phillips, Wendell, 34, 39

"Phyllis." *See* Comic strips

Phyllis Schlafly Report, The, 277

Physicians: changing role in childbirth, 56, 66, 220; battle against abortion, 57–58. *See also* Childbirth

Piercy, Marge, 356 (n. 102)

Pinchot, Cornelia Bryce, 137, 139

Pinchot, Gifford, 139

Pincus, Gregory, 89

Pins and Needles, 168

Pioneers (woman's group), 350 (n. 8)

Planned Parenthood Federation of America, 89, 219

Playboy, 217–18

"Please Give Me Something to Remember You By," 190

Pleck, Elizabeth, 37

Podheretz, Norman, 205

Political Guide, 235

Ponselle, Elsa, 151

Porter, Cole, 173

Portrait of a Lady, The, 55

Post, Amy, 30, 316 (n. 2)

Power of Sexual Surrender, The, 218–19

Powers, Hiram, 73

PPFA. *See* Planned Parenthood Federation of America

Pratt, Carolyn, 188–89

Prentice, Frances Woodward, 161

President's Commission on the Status of Women, 165, 232, 247–48

Presley, Elvis, 203

Pretty Baby, 276

Prince (rock star), 276

Profamily stance: importance of in feminist movement, viii, 169, 280–81

Progressive movement, 96, 102; feminists among, 115

Prostitution, 51, 54, 58–60; opposed by feminists, 134–35, 255

Protectionism: as divisive issue among feminists, 135–36

Proud Shoes, 268

Pruette, Lorine, 116, 123, 140

Public Enemy, 147

Puritans, 2, 9

Putnam, George, 24

Putnam family, 9

Puzzled America, 157

Quakers, 31, 45; view of marriage and childrearing, 7–8, 27, 47–48; and idea of separate spheres, 16; and Hicksite groups, 28, 30, 315 (n. 2); support feminism, 74; focus on suffrage, 79. *See also* Spiritualists; Mott, Lucretia

Racism: in the suffrage movement, 105–6; in the feminist movement, 263–65

Ranck, Katherine Howland, 154–57

Randolph, A. Philip, 185

Rape, 4, 255, 279; as weapon of patriarchy, 261

Rauh, Ida, 326 (n. 34)

Rawalt, Marguerite, 249

Reagan, President Ronald, 278, 289

Redbook, 208–9

Red Cross, 185, 189

Redgrave, Vannessa, 283

Redstockings, 253–54

Reed, Donna, 209

Reed, John, 85–86

Refugees: Anarchy or Organization? 235
Reitman, Ben, 81–82, 86
Revenue Act (1971), 274
Revolution (periodical of Stanton and
    Anthony), 36–37, 41, 64, 48
Revolution. *See* American Revolution
Rhode, Deborah, 136
Rice, John Andrew, 94
Rich, Adrienne, 256
Richards, Donna, 252
Richards, Ellen Swallow, 65, 126
Richardson, Albert, 318 (n. 41)
Richardson, Samuel, 19
Riesman, David, 209
Ripley, George, 24
Ripley, Sarah, 24
Roberts, Kenneth, 159
Roberts, Mrs.: cofounder of Working
    Women's Protective Union, 31
Robins, Margaret Dreier, 111, 136
Robinson, Dorothy R., 304
Robinson, Marie, 218
Robinson, Harriet, 47
Robinson, Ruby Doris Smith, 252
Robinson, William, 47
Roche, Josephine, 162
Rochester, N.Y.: origin of women's rights
    movement, 16; site of women's rights
    convention, 30
Rockefeller, Abby Aldrich, 255, 353 (n. 35)
Rodman, Henrietta, 65, 83, 85, 326 (n. 34)
Roe v. Wade, 273, 279, 291–93, 308
Rogers, Lou, 140
Rogers, Will, 159
Roles of women and men, 55, 152, 209–10,
    266, 284–85. *See also* Spheres of women
    and men
Roman Catholic church, 57, 277, 278
Roosevelt, Eleanor, 137, 233, 241, 268; and
    work for the dispossessed, 162–66, 237;
    on the President's Commission on the
    Status of Women, 247
Roosevelt, Franklin, 149, 159, 164, 185,
    189, 268
Roosevelt, Theodore, 158

"Rosamond." *See* Comic strips
Rose, Ernestine Potowski, 38, 48
Rosenberg, Julius and Ethel, 234
"Rosie's Beau." *See* Comic strips
"Rosie the Riveter," 178, 282, 195
Rossi, Alice, 249, 255
Rousseau, Jean–Jacques, 74
Rowson, Susanna Haswell, 19
Rubin, Gayle, 258
Rudnick, Lois Palken, 86
Ruffin, Josephine St. Pierre, 107, 110
Rupp, Leila, 171, 179, 349 (n. 8)
Rush, Benjamin, 13
Russell, Rosalind, 146
Ryan, Mary P., 321 (n. 8)

Sacco and Vanzetti, 119
Sachs, Sadie, 88
Sage, Abby, 318 (n. 41)
St. Joan Society, 350 (n. 8)
Salem, Mass.: and witchcraft trials, 8–9
"Sallie Snooks, Stenographer." *See* Comic
    strips
Sampson, Deborah, 12
Sanger, Margaret, 73, 83, 87–90, 135, 161,
    219. *See also* International Planned
    Parenthood Federation
Sanger, William, 88
Saturday Evening Post, 148
Saturday Review, 234
Savile, George, 52
Saxon, Elizabeth Lyle, 105
Schlafly, Phyllis, 276–78
Schlesinger Library: conducts Black Women
    Oral History Project, 303
Schmearguntz, 351 (n. 1)
Schneiderman, Rose, 111
Schroeder, Pat, 290
Scopes, John T., 119
Scott, Anne Firor, 95, 97
Scribner's, 142, 161
SDS. *See* Students for a Democratic Society
Seabury, Florence Wooston, 326 (n. 34)
Second Sex, The, 233–235
Second Shift, The, 285

Second Stage, The, 290

Seneca Falls, N.Y.: and the Declaration of Sentiments, 26; home of Elizabeth Cady Stanton, 27; commemorative conference at, 132

Seneca Falls Convention (1848), 29–30, 117

Servanthood, indentured: and women, 3

Sewell, Mary Wright, 31

Sex and the Single Girl, 245

Sex radicals, 73–91

Sexual Behavior in the Human Female, 218

Sexuality, female, 41, 52–53, 61, 65, 121, 217–18

Sexual liberation movement, xii

Sexual Politics, 259

Sexual power: defined, ix

"Shadow, The," 173

Shange, Ntozake, 356 (n. 102)

Shaw, Anna Howard, 103–5, 118

Shepard, Sam, 283

Sheppard-Towner Maternity Act, 135–37

Showalter, Elaine, 137

Shulman, Alix Kates, 351 (n. 1), 356 (n. 102)

Sills, Beverly, 309

Simpson, Georgiana, 304

Sims, J. Marion, 51

Sinatra, Frank, 173

Slee, J. Noah, 89

Slocombe, Lorna, 205

Smeal, Eleanor, 295

Smith, Jane Norman, 134

Smith, Lillian, 251

Smith, Mary Ruffin, 268

Smith-Rosenberg, Carroll, 16, 58

SNCC. *See* Student Non-Violent Coordinating Committee

Snelling, Paula, 251

Socialist feminism, 257–58. *See also* Feminism: varieties of

"Social Progress," 38

Social purity movement, 58–59. *See also* Women's Christian Temperance Union

Social Security Administration, 150

Solomon, Barbara, 96

"Some Day My Prince Will Come," 146

Somerville, Nellie Nugent, 105, 137

Soroptimist (women's movement organization), 350 (n. 8)

Sorry Wrong Number, 176

South Dakota: and women's suffrage, 99

Southern Methodist church, 109

Southworth, Mrs. E. D. E. N., 20

Spade, Sam, 157

Spheres of women and men, 2–20 passim, 32–33, 102. *See also* Roles of women and men

Spillane, Mickey, 217

Spiritualists, 78; advocate marriage reform, 27, 31–32, 48; and women's rights movement, 31; focus on women's suffrage, 79

Spock, Dr. Benjamin, 198, 308

Stanley, Louise, 162

Stansell, Christine, 60, 322 (n. 28)

Stanton, Elizabeth Cady, 16, 48, 64, 80, 110, 231, 257; and Seneca Falls convention, 27–30; as early women's rights leader, 33–42; on abortion, 58; on female sexuality, 61; and Victoria Woodhull, 76–78

Stanton, Henry, 28, 35

Stanton-Anthony Brigade, 254

Stanwyck, Barbara, 176

Starr, Brenda. *See* Comic strips

Stebbins, Catherine Fish, 30

Steinem, Gloria, 213, 250, 255, 262, 272, 307, 308

Stembridge, Jane, 251

Stetson, Walter, 62–63

Stevens, Doris, 134, 326 (n. 34)

Stevenson, Adlai, 164

Stewart, Maria W., 106, 110

Stokes, Rose Pastor, 326 (n. 34)

Stone, Hannah and Abraham, 218

Stone, Lucy, 27, 41–49 passim, 69, 77–78, 230

Story of the Woman's Party, The, 138
Stouffer, Samuel, 152
Stowe, Harriet Beecher, 17, 21, 31, 62
Stricker, Frank, 142
Student Non–Violent Coordinating
    Committee, 251–52
Students for a Democratic Society, 251–54
Studies in General Science, 38
Subjection of Women, The, 234
Suffrage, for women, 92–115; called for by
    early feminist conventions, 29–30; as
    feminist goal, 34; as profamily issue, 93,
    100; and the feminist agenda, 100–101;
    views of radicals in the movement,
    112–15
Sullivan, Ellen, 162
Sunset Boulevard, 206
Suppressed Desire, 85
Surfacing, 356 (n. 102)
Swanson, Gloria, 206
Syracuse, N.Y.: site of women's rights
    convention (1852), 32, 36

Taft, Jessica, 133
Taggard, Genevieve, 139
Talbot, Marion, 133
Tanneyhill, Ann, 305
Tar Baby, 356 (n. 102)
Tax, Meredith, 356 (n. 35)
Taylor, Verta, 349 (n. 8)
Temperance movement, 59
Temple, Shirley, 159
Terman, Lewis M., 121, 299
Terrell, Mary Church, 108–9, 110, 230
Terrell, Robert Heberton, 108
Terry, Peggy, 187
Tess, 276
"That Girl," 245
Theology, feminist, 256, 257
"There Is a Woman Waiting for Me," 61
These Modern Women, 137
This Is the Army, 173
Thomas bill, 183
Thomas, Marlo, 245

Thompson, Dorothy, 233, 235–37, 241
Thompson, Helen, 133
Thompson, Mary, 304
Thoreau, Henry David, 24
Tilton, Benjamin, 78
Tilton, Elizabeth, 78
Time, 158, 309
Tituba (West Indian slave), 9
Todd, David Peck, 70–71
Todd, Millicent, 70
Together Again, 176
Toleration, Act of, 9
Tompkins, Jane, 19
Tootsie, 276
"To the Women on the Left," 252
Tracy, Dick. *See* Comic strips
Treatise on Domestic Economy, A, 17
Truman, President Harry S., 165
Truth, Sojourner, 26, 31, 107, 110, 251
Tucker, Mary Logan, 326 (n. 34)
Tugwell, Rexford, 164
Turner, Banks, 117
Turning Point, The, 276

Uncle Tom's Cabin, 314 (n. 20)
Unionism: after the depression, 166–68;
    and women during WWII, 180. *See
    also* Labor force; Industrialization
Unitarianism, 47
United Auto Workers, 167, 180, 191
United Nations: Human Rights Commis-
    sion, 164
Universalism, 47
Unmarried Woman, An, 276
Unwelcome Child, The, 58
Urban Institute, 287
Utah: and women's suffrage, 99

Vanderbilt, Commodore, 77
Van Pelt, Charles, 60
Van Vechten, Carl, 87
Varela, Mary, 252
"Vic and Sade," 173
Victor-Victoria, 276

Victory girls, 190
Vietnam War, 246, 252, 253, 276
Views of women. *See* "Angel in the House";
   "Cult of True Womanhood"
Viguerie, Richard, 276
Virginia, 95
Vogue, 284
Voice from the South, A, 107
Voluntary associations: women active in, 97
Vought, Lizzie. *See* Ward, Lizzie

Waiting for Lefty, 159
Walker, Alice, 356 (n. 102)
Walker, Clovis, 184
Walker, Seth, 117
Waller, Willard, 128–29
Wallin, Paul, 122
Walsh, Andrea S., 175
Walsh, Lorena, 3
Walsh, Richard, 238
Ward, Lester, 69–70
Ward, Lizzie, 69–70
Ware, Caroline, 268
Ware, Cellestine, 263–64
War Manpower Commission, 178, 191
Warner, Susan. *See* Wetherell, Elizabeth
War Production Board, 174
Warren, Mercy Otis, 12
Warrior, Betsy, 353 (n. 35), 255
Washington, Booker T., 166
Washington (state): and women's suffrage,
   99
Watson, John B., 128
Wayne, John, 215
Webb, Marilyn Salzman, 253
Webster v. Reproductive Health Services, 291–
   92
Weddington, Sarah, 308
Weitzman, Lenore, 286–87
Weixel, Lola, 177, 196
Weld, Angelina Grimké, 31, 45, 46, 47,
   251. *See also* Grimké, Angelina
Weld, Theodore, 45, 46, 47
Wells-Barnett, Ida, 108, 109, 110

Welter, Barbara, 16, 17
"We're the Janes Who Make the Planes,"
   178
Wertz, Richard and Dorothy, 220
West, Mae, 146, 149
West, U.S.: women's experience in, 99–100
Wetherell, Elizabeth [pseud. Susan
   Warner], 20
Weyrich, Paul, 276, 278
White, Margaret, 184
White, Sue Shelton, 105, 137–38
Whitman, Walt, 61
Who's Afraid of Virginia Woolf? 245
Whyte, William, 215
Wide, Wide World, 20
Willard, Frances, 31, 34, 59, 65
Willis, Ellen, 253
Wilson, Woodrow, 112, 113
WITCH (Women's International Terrorist
   Coven from Hell), 243
Witchcraft trials, 8–9
WITCH Resurrectus, 254
Wolf, Anna W. M., 184
Wollstonecraft, Mary, 76
Women as a Force in History, 231
Woman of the Year, 176, 235
Woman on the Edge of Time, 356 (n. 102)
Woman Rebel, 89
Woman Rebels, A, 176
Woman's Bible, 257
Woman's Era, 107
Woman's Home Companion, 179, 191
Woman's Journal, 38, 41, 44, 48
Woman's Room, The, 356 (n. 102)
Woman Suffrage Defended, 47
Women Adrift, 87
Women against the Ratification of the
   ERA, 277
Women and Economics, 63
Women Employed, 270
Women for Economic Justice in Massachu-
   setts, 293
Women in World Affairs, 231 (n. 8)
Women Lawyers–Boston, 254

Women Office Workers, 270
Women's Action Alliance, 275, 308
Women's Agenda in Pennsylvania, 293
Women's Airforce Service Pilots, 188
Women's Anti-Slavery Society, 45
Women's Army Corps, 188
Women's Auxiliary of the National Colored Baptist Convention, 108
Women's Bureau, Department of Labor, 136, 168, 249, 344 (n. 78)
Women's Christian Temperance Union, 59, 97
Women's club movement, 97
Women's Committee on Interracial Cooperation, 251
Women's Emergency Brigade, 167
Women's Equality Action League, 250
Women's Film and Female Experience, 1940–1950, 175
Women's International League for Peace and Freedom, 108, 166
Women's International Terrorist Coven from Hell (WITCH), 243
Women's Joint Congressional Committee, 229
Women's Joint Legislative Committee, 350 (n. 8)
Women's Land Army, 180
Women's Liberation Club–Bronx High School of Science, 254
Women's National Abortion Coalition, 308
Women's Political Union, 110
"Women's ways of knowing," xi. *See also* Egalitarianism
Women Who Want to Be Women, 277
Wonder Woman. *See* Comic strips
Wood, Grant, 159
Woodhull, Byron, 77
Woodhull, Victoria, 36, 65, 73, 76–79, 82, 90
Woodhull, Zula Maud, 77
Woodhull and Claflin's Weekly, 78

Woodward, Charlotte, 32
Woolcott, Alexander, 236
Worcester, Mass.: site of woman's rights convention (1850), 32
Working Girl, 283
Working Women: A National Association of Office Workers, 270
Working Women's Protective Union, 31
Works Progress Administration, 159, 162, 174
World Anti-Slavery, 27
World's Congress of Representative Women, 107
World War I, 114, 115, 142
World War II: and changing roles of women, 171–72, 191; and female power, 174–77; and women in the labor force, 177–84; and women in the military, 188–89; as turning point for women's gaining domestic power, 281
WPA. *See* Works Progress Administration
Wright, Frances, 73, 75–76, 90, 325 (n. 12)
Wright, Frank Lloyd, 159
Wright, Henry C., 58
Wright, Margaret, 188
Wright, Martha Coffin, 28, 48
WTUL. *See* National Women's Trade Union League
WWWW, 277
Wylie, Philip, 210, 234
Wyoming: and women's suffrage, 99

Yankee Doodle Dandy, 173
Yard, Molly, 295
Young Ladies Academy of Philadelphia, 13
Youth and Sex, 161
YWCA, 199

Zonta (women's movement organization), 350 (n. 8)